# HANDCRAFT
### ~ILLUSTRATED~
## ~1995~

Published by
**Boston Common Press Limited Partnership**
17 Station Street
Brookline Village, Massachusetts 02146

ISBN: 0-9640179-4-6
ISSN: 1072-0529

# 1995 HANDCRAFT ILLUSTRATED INDEX

**Antiquing**

| | | |
|---|---|---|
| Antique Brass Frames | Jan/Feb | 18 |

**Bookbinding**

| | | |
|---|---|---|
| Panoramic Photo Album | Jan/Feb | 20 |

**Book Reviews**

| | | |
|---|---|---|
| Decorating with Paper | May/Jun | 28 |
| Paper Magic | May/Jun | 28 |
| Creative Interior Design | May/Jun | 28 |

**Candles/Candlesticks**

| | | |
|---|---|---|
| Crystal Bead Drop Candlestick | Mar/Apr | BC |
| Seashell Candles | May/Jun | 11 |

**Centerpieces**

| | | |
|---|---|---|
| White Silk Centerpiece | Jan/Feb | 28 |

**Decorative Food**

| | | |
|---|---|---|
| Basket-Weave Cake with Pansies | Mar/Apr | 28 |
| Best Pastry for Decorative Pie Edges | Sep/Oct | 12 |
| Candied Violet and Holly Holiday Decorations | Nov/Dec | 33 |
| Frozen Floral Ice Bucket | Jul/Aug | BC |
| Marbled Chocolate Strawberries | May/Jun | 24 |
| Quick Charlotte Royale | Jul/Aug | 11 |

**Decorative Painting**

| | | |
|---|---|---|
| French Tinware Cachepot | Mar/Apr | 6 |
| Peach and Vine Ladder-Back Chair | May/Jun | 6 |

**Decoupage**

| | | |
|---|---|---|
| Decorating with Decoupage | Jan/Feb | 15 |

**Dolls**

| | | |
|---|---|---|
| Heirloom Father Christmas | Nov/Dec | 30 |

**Dried Flowers**

| | | |
|---|---|---|
| Best Way to Dry Roses | May/Jun | 20 |
| Dried Flower Valance | Jul/Aug | 26 |
| Miniature Flower Baskets | Mar/Apr | 9 |
| Quick-Dried Flower Arranging | Jan/Feb | 10 |
| Quick-Dried Hydrangea Wreath | Sep/Oct | 11 |
| Rose Petal Frame | Jul/Aug | 16 |

**Embroidery**

| | | |
|---|---|---|
| Silk Ribbon Embroidery | May/Jun | 22 |

**Faux Finishes**

| | | |
|---|---|---|
| 10-Minute Faux Finishes | Mar/Apr | 14 |
| Bird's-Eye Maple Faux Finish | Jul/Aug | 18 |
| Foolproof Wood Grain Faux Finish | Sep/Oct | 20 |
| Foolproof Sponged Wall Finishes | Jul/Aug | 28 |
| How to Create a Faux Suede Finish | May/Jun | 8 |

**Field Guides**

| | | |
|---|---|---|
| Decorative Tassels and Tiebacks | Sep/Oct | 30 |
| Fresh Greens | Nov/Dec | 45 |
| Home-Grown Dried Flowers | Jul/Aug | 31 |
| Miniature Baskets | Mar/Apr | 30 |
| Paper Lace Doilies | Jan/Feb | 30 |
| Shells | May/Jun | 30 |

**Frames**

| | | |
|---|---|---|
| Adirondack Twig Frame | Sep/Oct | 24 |
| Antique Brass Frames | Jan/Feb | 16 |
| Folk Art Frame | Sep/Oct | 16 |
| Miter-Box Frame | Mar/Apr | 17 |
| Rose Petal Frame | Jul/Aug | 16 |

**Fresh Flowers and Foliage**

| | | |
|---|---|---|
| Bittersweet Topiary | Sep/Oct | 22 |
| Decorative Outdoor Urn | Sep/Oct | BC |
| Demi-Lune Style Tulips | May/Jun | 25 |
| Fabulous Farmstand Bouquets | Jul/Aug | 6 |
| Frozen Floral Ice Bucket | Jul/Aug | BC |
| Natural Floral China | May/Jun | BC |

**Giftwrap/Packaging**

| | | |
|---|---|---|
| Best Way to Tie Multiloop Bows | Nov/Dec | 34 |
| Brown Kraft Paper Giftwrap | Sep/Oct | 25 |
| Folk Art Bandbox | Jan/Feb | BC |
| Quick Projects | May/Jun | 33 |

**Gilding/Leafing**

| | | |
|---|---|---|
| Gilded Cut-Metal Sconce | Jan/Feb | 6 |
| Gold and Silver Leaf Plate Chargers | Jan/Feb | 26 |
| Quick Gilded Autumn Leaves | Sep/Oct | 21 |

**Glass**

| | | |
|---|---|---|
| Gold and Silver Leaf Plate Chargers | Jan/Feb | 26 |
| Star Frost Vase | Jan/Feb | 24 |

**Lamp Shades**

| | | |
|---|---|---|
| Quick Projects | Mar/Apr | 33 |

**Master Projects**

| | | |
|---|---|---|
| 3-Panel Folding Screen | May/Jun | 12 |
| Heirloom Father Christmas | Nov/Dec | 30 |

**Metalworking**

| | | |
|---|---|---|
| Gilded Cut-Metal Sconce | Jan/Feb | 6 |

*BC= Back Cover*

**Notes from Readers**

| | | |
|---|---|---|
| Backgammon Board, Pattern for Fabric | Mar/Apr | 3 |
| Bakelite, What Is | Jul/Aug | 2 |
| Bathroom Woodwork, Painting versus Staining | May/Jun | 3 |
| Berlin Work, Definition of | Mar/Apr | 2 |
| Bobeches, In Search of Unadorned | Nov/Dec | 2 |
| Buckram, Best Use of | May/Jun | 2 |
| Candlemaking Molds, Using Rubber for | Jul/Aug | 2 |
| Candy Thermometer, Testing for Accuracy | Sep/Oct | 3 |
| Christmas Tree Decorations, Unusual | Sep/Oct | 2 |
| Cleaning Floral Containers | Nov/Dec | 3 |
| Cleaning Marble | Jul/Aug | 3 |
| Cleaning an Old Brass Lamp | May/Jun | 3 |
| Color Combinations, Finding New | Sep/Oct | 3 |
| Colored Pencils versus Watercolor Pencils | Jan/Feb | 3 |
| Concrete, Removing Stains from | Jul/Aug | 3 |
| Craft Supplies, Hard to Find | Nov/Dec | 2 |
| Cut Flowers, Storing | Jan/Feb | 3 |
| Damage from Pliers, Preventing | Jul/Aug | 2 |
| Decorating Canvas Sneakers, Selecting Paint for | Mar/Apr | 3 |
| Decorative Paper, Creative Uses for Scraps of | Jan/Feb | 3 |
| Drapes that Stretch, Cure for | May/Jun | 3 |
| Dried Flower Head, Replacing Broken | Sep/Oct | 3 |
| Drying Hydrangeas | Mar/Apr | 2 |
| Earthenware versus Stoneware and Porcelain | May/Jun | 3 |
| Electric Styrofoam Cutter, Locating an | Nov/Dec | 2 |
| Endangered Flowers, Information on | Mar/Apr | 2 |
| Etched-Glass Plates, Storing | Jul/Aug | 3 |
| Fabric, Adhering to a Blank Book | Sep/Oct | 3 |
| Fabric-Covered Cornice Boards | Sep/Oct | 2 |
| Fabric, Safeguarding from Liquids | Sep/Oct | 2 |
| Face Molds for Dolls and Jewelry | Jan/Feb | 2 |
| Faux-Finishing a Tabletop | Sep/Oct | 3 |
| Flammable Rags, Disposing of | Jul/Aug | 3 |
| Flesh-toned Shades of Fabric | Mar/Apr | 3 |
| Florist Foam for Unusually Shaped Vases | May/Jun | 3 |
| Flowers, Freeze-Drying | Sep/Oct | 2 |
| Flowers, Preventing Droopy | Mar/Apr | 3 |
| Flowers, Preserving the Color of Pressed | Mar/Apr | 2 |
| Flowers, Sending Long Distance | Sep/Oct | 2 |
| Fresh Flowers, Adding to a Silk Arrangement | Jan/Feb | 3 |
| Glitter, Working Neatly with | Nov/Dec | 2 |
| Greeting Cards, Ideas for Displaying | Sep/Oct | 2 |
| Gustave Stickley, Learning About | Jul/Aug | 3 |
| Knitting Unique Sweaters and Hats for Children | Sep/Oct | 2 |
| Knotted Wood, Preparing for Painting | Sep/Oct | 3 |
| Hue, Tone, Shade, Defined | Sep/Oct | 3 |
| Laminating Fabric | May/Jun | 3 |
| Lollipop Molds, Mail-Order | May/Jun | 2 |
| Markers for Coloring, Best | Jul/Aug | 2 |
| Metallic Taste from Flatware, Removing | Nov/Dec | 2 |
| Napkins, Best for Folded Designs | May/Jun | 2 |
| Paint Eraser, In Search of | Sep/Oct | 3 |
| Paintbrush Cleaner, All-Purpose | Nov/Dec | 3 |
| Painting Around a Doorknob | Jan/Feb | 3 |
| Painting Cotton Cafe Curtains | Mar/Apr | 3 |
| Pearl Necklaces, Thread for | Mar/Apr | 3 |
| Place Cards, Make Your Own | May/Jun | 2 |
| Pop-Up Cards, Patterns for | May/Jun | 2 |
| Quilt Designs from the 1930s | Jul/Aug | 2 |
| Reproduction Fabric, Mail-Order | May/Jun | 2 |
| Rotary Cutters for Arthritis Sufferers | Jul/Aug | 2 |
| Rubber Cement, Safety of Use | Jan/Feb | 2 |
| Rubber-Stamping with Paint | Jan/Feb | 2 |
| Rubber Stamps, Finding Specialty | Jul/Aug | 2 |
| Sewing Problems, Toll-Free Assistance with | Nov/Dec | 3 |
| Shagreen, Identifying | Nov/Dec | 2 |
| Shaker Furniture, Mail-Order | Nov/Dec | 3 |
| Silhouette, Origin of Word | Mar/Apr | 2 |
| Silver from Tarnishing, Preventing | Nov/Dec | 3 |
| Skin Cleansers, Nonirritating | Nov/Dec | 3 |
| Snapped Stems, Using | Mar/Apr | 3 |
| Snowglobes, Locating Materials for | Nov/Dec | 3 |
| Stain-proof Finish for Fabric Place Mats | Jan/Feb | 2 |
| Terra-Cotta Flowerpots, Priming | Nov/Dec | 3 |
| Textile Markers, Nontoxic | Nov/Dec | 3 |
| Theorem Painting versus Stenciling | Sep/Oct | 3 |
| Wall and Floor Tile, Difference Between | Jul/Aug | 3 |
| Wallpaper Choices for a Tiny Bathroom | Jan/Feb | 3 |
| Wax, Removing from a Tablecloth | Nov/Dec | 2 |
| Woodworking Questions, Answers to Your | Jul/Aug | 2 |
| Woven Reed Baskets, Cleaning | Jul/Aug | 2 |
| Wrapping Paper, Storing Leftover | Nov/Dec | 3 |
| X-Acto Knife, Right Way to Use | Jan/Feb | 3 |
| Yarn, How to Make Colorfast | May/Jun | 2 |

**Ornaments**

| | | |
|---|---|---|
| Trio of Glass Ball Ornaments | Nov/Dec | 6 |
| Tulle-Wrapped Ornament | Nov/Dec | 36 |

**Paper Crafts**

| | | |
|---|---|---|
| Brown Kraft Paper Giftwrap | Sep/Oct | 25 |
| Decorating with Decoupage | Jan/Feb | 15 |
| Edwardian Silk Writing Folio | Mar/Apr | 15 |
| Folk Art Bandbox | Jan/Feb | BC |
| Foolproof Greeting Cards | Nov/Dec | 22 |
| Panoramic Photo Album | Jan/Feb | 20 |

**Place Settings**

| | | |
|---|---|---|
| 10-Minute Tassel Place Mat | Nov/Dec | 37 |
| Gold and Silver Leaf Plate Chargers | Jan/Feb | 26 |
| Lacework Teacloth | Jan/Feb | 17 |
| Napkin Rings (Quick Projects) | Nov/Dec | 49 |
| Natural Floral China | May/Jun | BC |
| Quick Decorating Ideas | May/Jun | 29 |
| Tasseled Napkin Ring | Jan/Feb | 9 |

**Potpourri**

| | | |
|---|---|---|
| Christmas Potpourri Demystified | Nov/Dec | 14 |

*BC= Back Cover*

**Product Testing**

| | | |
|---|---|---|
| Air-Dry and Heat-Set Clays | Sep/Oct | 26 |
| All-Purpose White Glues | May/Jun | 26 |
| Hot-Glue Guns | Jan/Feb | 12 |
| Lightweight Dressmaker's Shears | Jul/Aug | 23 |
| Metallic Paints | Mar/Apr | 10 |
| Sewing Machines | Nov/Dec | 41 |

**Quick Projects**

| | | |
|---|---|---|
| Gift Bags | May/Jun | 33 |
| Globe Topiaries | Sep/Oct | 33 |
| Lamp Shades | Mar/Apr | 33 |
| Napkin Rings | Nov/Dec | 49 |
| Pillowcases | Jul/Aug | 33 |
| Terra-Cotta Pots | Jan/Feb | 33 |

**Ribbon Crafts**

| | | |
|---|---|---|
| Best Way to Tie Multiloop Bows | Nov/Dec | 34 |
| How to Make Antique Velvet Roses | Nov/Dec | 27 |
| How to Make Your Own Wire-Edged Ribbon | Nov/Dec | 12 |

**Quick Tips**

| | | |
|---|---|---|
| Antiquing New Hardware | May/Jun | 5 |
| Bias Welting, No-Sew | May/Jun | 4 |
| Bows, Reviving Limp | Nov/Dec | 4 |
| Bread Eraser | Sep/Oct | 4 |
| Button Basting, Fast | Sep/Oct | 5 |
| Cookie Hole Cutter | Sep/Oct | 4 |
| Custom Borders | Nov/Dec | 5 |
| Cutting a Large Circle of Fabric | May/Jun | 5 |
| Drywall, Repairing Holes in | Jan/Feb | 5 |
| Easy Stripes (Painted "Wallpaper") | Nov/Dec | 5 |
| Encouraging Blooms | May/Jun | 5 |
| Fancy 4-Watt Bulbs | Nov/Dec | 4 |
| Find the Center of | Nov/Dec | 5 |
| Foam Blocks, Joining | May/Jun | 4 |
| Foam Paintbrush, Instant | Sep/Oct | 4 |
| French Seams, Buckle-Free | Jan/Feb | 4 |
| Fringe, Controlling Unruly | Jul/Aug | 5 |
| Glue Drips, Removing | Mar/Apr | 5 |
| Hangers, Nonslip | Sep/Oct | 5 |
| Hot Glue, Removing | Jul/Aug | 5 |
| Instant Ruler | May/Jun | 5 |
| Invisible Connection (for Greens) | Nov/Dec | 4 |
| Marble Mirage | Jul/Aug | 5 |
| Miniclamps | Jul/Aug | 5 |
| Nail Holder | May/Jun | 5 |
| Paintbrush, Preventing from Drying Out | Mar/Apr | 4 |
| Paint Palette, Stay-Moist | Sep/Oct | 5 |
| Paint Touch-Up Kit | Jul/Aug | 5 |
| Painter's Lift | Jul/Aug | 4 |
| Pillow Corners, Square | Jul/Aug | 4 |
| Pinecones, Bleached White | Jul/Aug | 4 |
| Plant-Potting Tip | Sep/Oct | 4 |
| Plaster Walls, Repairing Cracks in | Jan/Feb | 5 |
| Pom-Poms, Make Your Own | Jan/Feb | 4 |
| Pouring Liquid into Small Opening | Mar/Apr | 4 |
| Prints, Perfectly Matched | Mar/Apr | 5 |
| Raffia, Braiding | May/Jun | 5 |
| Roses, Preventing Drooping | Mar/Apr | 5 |
| Sanding, Smooth | Jul/Aug | 5 |
| Silk Flowers, Downsizing | Sep/Oct | 4 |
| Silk Flowers, Perking Up Limp | Nov/Dec | 4 |
| Spattering with an Old Toothbrush | May/Jun | 4 |
| Stand Up Straight (Long-Stemmed Flowers) | Nov/Dec | 4 |
| Steaming Out Dents in Wood | Mar/Apr | 4 |
| Stenciled Icing | Jul/Aug | 4 |
| Stenciling Shortcut | Sep/Oct | 5 |
| Stenciling Through Netting | Mar/Apr | 5 |
| Tulips, Keeping Fresh | Mar/Apr | 4 |
| Wiring a Pinecone Invisibly | Sep/Oct | 5 |
| Woody-Stemmed Flowers, Making Last Longer | May/Jun | 4 |
| Wreath Hanger, No-Hole | Nov/Dec | 5 |
| Wreath, One-Minute | Nov/Dec | 5 |
| Wreath, Weaving Your Own | Nov/Dec | 5 |
| Yarn and Ribbon Organizer | Sep/Oct | 5 |
| Zipper, Shortening a | Jan/Feb | 5 |

**Rubber Stamps**

| | | |
|---|---|---|
| Buyer's Guide to Rubber Stamps | Nov/Dec | 38 |

**Seasonal Projects**

| | | |
|---|---|---|
| Apple Tree Carved Pumpkin | Sep/Oct | 6 |
| Candied Violet and Holly Holiday Decorations | Nov/Dec | 33 |
| Christmas Potpourri Demystified | Nov/Dec | 14 |
| Three Cuffed Decorator Christmas Stockings | Nov/Dec | 16 |
| Trio of Glass Ball Ornaments | Nov/Dec | 6 |
| Tulle-Wrapped Ornament | Nov/Dec | 36 |
| Ukrainian Easter Eggs | Mar/Apr | 20 |

**Sewing**

| | | |
|---|---|---|
| 10-Minute Tassel Place Mat | Nov/Dec | 37 |
| Cedar Chip Sachets | Mar/Apr | 26 |
| Lacework Teacloth | Jan/Feb | 17 |
| Lined Velvet Pouches | Sep/Oct | 14 |
| Low-Sew Slipcover | Jul/Aug | 22 |
| Pillowcases (Quick Projects) | Jul/Aug | 33 |
| Silk Ribbon Embroidery | May/Jun | 22 |
| Three Cuffed Decorator Christmas Stockings | Nov/Dec | 16 |
| Two-Sheet Duvet Cover | Mar/Apr | 23 |
| Victorian Frame Bow | May/Jun | 18 |

**Silk Flowers**

| | | |
|---|---|---|
| Silk Peony Bouquet | Mar/Apr | 13 |
| White Silk Centerpiece | Jan/Feb | 28 |

**Soap**

| | | |
|---|---|---|
| Fastest Way to Make Hand-Molded Soap | Nov/Dec | 20 |

**Soft Furnishings**

| | | |
|---|---|---|
| 10-Minute Tassel Place Mat | Nov/Dec | 37 |
| Two-Sheet Duvet Cover | Mar/Apr | 23 |

*BC= Back Cover*

| | | |
|---|---|---|
| Lacework Teacloth | Jan/Feb | 17 |
| Low-Sew Slipcover | Jul/Aug | 22 |
| Napkin Rings (Quick Projects) | Nov/Dec | 49 |
| Pillowcases (Quick Projects) | Jul/Aug | 33 |
| Quick Transfer Pillows | May/Jun | 16 |
| Tasseled Napkin Ring | Jan/Feb | 9 |

**Stenciling**

| | | |
|---|---|---|
| Bronze Stenciling with Acrylics | Sep/Oct | 8 |
| Color-Blended Stenciling | Jul/Aug | 12 |
| Star Frost Vase | Jan/Feb | 24 |

**Topiary**

| | | |
|---|---|---|
| Bittersweet Topiary | Sep/Oct | 22 |
| Topiary (Quick Projects) | Sep/Oct | 33 |
| Tannebaum Topiary | Nov/Dec | BC |

**Woodworking**

| | | |
|---|---|---|
| 3-Panel Folding Screen | May/Jun | 12 |
| Carved Fish Decoy | Jul/Aug | 8 |
| Miter-Box Frame | Mar/Apr | 17 |

**Wreaths**

| | | |
|---|---|---|
| How to Make an Infinite Variety of Wreaths | Nov/Dec | 8 |
| Quick Dried Hydrangea Wreath | Sep/Oct | 11 |

*BC= Back Cover*

NUMBER FIVE

JANUARY/FEBRUARY 1995

# HANDCRAFT
## ~ ILLUSTRATED ~

## Quick Dried Flower Arrangements

Fast and Easy Designs
Using the 4-Color Method

### SPECIAL INSERT
## Vintage Prints for Decoupage

Use this Issue's Antique
Prints for Classic Decorating

## Rating Hot-Glue Guns

Top Guns in Dual-, Low-,
and High-Temp Categories

## Antique Brass Frames in Minutes

$25 LACEWORK
TABLECLOTH

·

QUICK GILDED
NAPKIN RINGS

·

GLASS ETCHING
MADE EASY

SECRETS OF SILK FLOWER
ARRANGING

$4.00 U.S./$4.95 CANADA

0  71486 02716  4

01

MAKE THE ARRANGEMENT ABOVE IN LESS THAN 30 MINUTES USING JUST 4 TYPES OF DRIED FLOWERS: CASPIA, LARKSPUR, EVERLASTING, AND YARROW. SEE PAGE 10.

# TABLE
## OF CONTENTS

## Notes from Readers .........................2

Stain-proof finishes for place mats; face molds for dolls and jewelry; rubber stamping with paint; and wallpaper choices for a tiny bathroom.

## Quick Tips ...............................4

Buckle-free French seams; make your own pom-poms; shortening a zipper; how to repair cracks in plaster walls; and repairing holes in drywall.

## Gilded Cut-Metal Sconce.................6

Transform copper tubing, rubber chair leg tips, and cut-metal foil into a gilded French sconce.

## Tasseled Napkin Ring.......................9

Make this gilded napkin ring from an ordinary curtain ring and silk-twist thread.

## Quick Dried Flower Arranging.........10

Build a $30 arrangement or a $100 arrangement using a simple three-tier construction principle.

## Testing Hot-Glue Guns.....................12

The Crafty line of guns fares the best overall, while Black & Decker takes the gold in the dual-temp category.

### Special Insert: Decoupage

## Decorating with Decoupage...........15

Transform any wall or flat surface using our antique prints and simple decoupage techniques.

## Lacework Teacloth....................17

Stitch up this elegant teacloth for under $25 using dinner napkins and lace.

## Antique Brass Frames.....................18

Transform an ordinary brass frame into a Victorian antique using stamped metal findings and a simple patina solution.

## Panoramic Photo Album.................20

Learn to take your own panoramic photos and create a hand-bound album for displaying them.

## Star Frost Vase..............................24

Transform an ordinary vase into frosted glassware using etching compound and stencils.

## Gold and Silver Leaf Plate Chargers................................26

Use our foolproof recipe to leaf a set of glass plate chargers.

## White Silk Centerpiece....................28

Use a three-part construction technique to create a variety of silk flower arrangements.

## Field Guide to Lace Doilies.............30

Lace doilies can be used to line a bread basket, or for making fans, cornucopias, or valentines.

## Sources and Resources....................31

Mail-order sources for materials used throughout this issue.

## Quick Projects............................33

Turn your terra-cotta flowerpots into decorative planters using moss, marbling, decoupage, verdi-gris, stripes, shells, or rosebuds.

## Folk Art Bandbox...........Back Cover

Turn a wooden or cardboard bandbox into taste-ful gift packaging using wallpaper border. Illustration by Dan Brown.

**GILDED
CUT-METAL SCONCE**
*page 6*

**TASSELED
NAPKIN RING**
*page 9*

**QUICK DRIED FLOWER
ARRANGING**
*page 10*

**LACEWORK
TEACLOTH**
*page 17*

**STAR FROST
VASE**
*page 24*

**GOLD AND SILVER LE
PLATE CHARGERS**
*page 26*

# HANDCRAFT
## ~ ILLUSTRATED ~

| | |
|---|---|
| **Editor** | CAROL ENDLER STERBENZ |
| **Executive Editor** | BARBARA BOURASSA |
| **Senior Editor** | MICHIO RYAN |
| **Managing Editor** | MAURA LYONS |
| **Assistant Managing Editor** | TRICIA O'BRIEN |
| **Directions Editors** | CANDIE FRANKEL |
| | SUSAN WILSON |
| **Editorial Assistant** | KIM N. RUSSELLO |
| **Copy Editor** | KURT TIDMORE |

| | |
|---|---|
| **Art Director** | MEG BIRNBAUM |
| **Special Projects Designer** | AMY KLEE |
| **Photo Stylist** | SYLVIA LACHTER |

| | |
|---|---|
| **Publisher and Founder** | CHRISTOPHER KIMBALL |
| **Editorial Consultant** | RAYMOND WAITES |

| | |
|---|---|
| **Marketing Director** | ADRIENNE KIMBALL |
| **Circulation Director** | ELAINE REPUCCI |
| **Circulation Assistant** | JENNIFER L. KEENE |
| | JONATHAN VENIER |
| **Production Director** | JAMES MCCORMACK |
| **Production Assistants** | SHEILA DATZ |
| | PAMELA SLATTERY |
| **Publicity Director** | CAROL ROSEN KAGAN |
| **Treasurer** | JANET CARLSON |
| **Accounting Assistant** | MANDY SHITO |
| **Office Manager** | JENNY THORNBURY |
| **Office Assistant** | SARAH CHUNG |

*Handcraft Illustrated* (ISSN 1072-0529) is published bimonthly by Natural Health Limited Partners, 17 Station Street, P.O. Box 509, Brookline, MA 02147-0509. Copyright 1994 Natural Health Limited Partners. Second-class postage paid in Boston, MA, and additional mailing offices. Editorial office: 17 Station Street, P.O. Box 509, Brookline, MA 02147-0509. Editorial contributions should be sent to: Editor, *Handcraft Illustrated*, P.O. Box 509, Brookline, MA 02147-0509. We cannot assume responsibility for manuscripts submitted to us. Submissions will be returned only if accompanied by a large self-addressed stamped envelope. Subscription rates: $24.95 for one year; $45 for two years; $65 for three years. (Canada: add $3 per year; all other foreign add $12 per year.) Postmaster: Send all new orders, subscription inquiries, and change of address notices to *Handcraft Illustrated*, P.O. Box 51383, Boulder, CO 80322-1383. Single copies: $4 in U.S., $4.95 in Canada and foreign. Back issues available for $5 each. PRINTED IN THE U.S.A.

Rather than put ™ in every occurrence of trademarked names, we state that we are using the names only and in an editorial fashion and to the benefit of the trademark owner, with no intention of infringement of the trademark.

**Note to Readers:** Every effort has been made to present the information in this publication in a clear, complete, and accurate manner. It is important that all instructions are followed carefully, as failure to do so could result in injury. Natural Health Limited Partners, the editors, and the authors disclaim any and all liability resulting therefrom.

# EDITORIAL

I've often been asked how I got my start in crafts. Actually, I can't remember a specific instant when I realized that I loved crafts and needlework, but there were countless experiences that clearly guided my steps toward making handcrafts such an important part of my life.

As a child, I always seemed to have some kind of art supply in my hands. When I was six, I received a narrow box filled with pastel sticks swathed in a layer of felt, a

CAROL ENDLER STERBENZ

birthday gift from my father, who always surprised us with something "impractical." At ten I had my own paint box with a lid that opened on a hinge to reveal two trays filled with the most sublime watercolors imaginable. I used to sit at the kitchen table with my sisters, painting greeting cards. Sometimes I even painted decorations on my homework, though I was told by more than one teacher that I wasn't in art class.

It seems the kitchen table was always the center of our craft and needlework activity. When I was about seven, I sat there (often grumpy and impatient) as my mother taught me to embroider. I wasn't happy as I tried to make the needle sew straight lines or form the letters of the alphabet. In the beginning, I could only manage uneven trails of thread in knots and dashes that puckered the fabric into tiny, permanent wrinkles. Somehow, though, I kept at it, and all the while my mother entertained me with fascinating stories of her childhood in Finland, a country with a rich cultural heritage that reveres fine handwork. I still remember her descriptions of an entire room in her house filled with embroidered linen—a room reserved especially for the thickly woven linen sheets, pillowcases, and coverlets made from flax on large handlooms and emblazoned with swirling monograms and floral curlicues.

In Finland, needlework and crafts were taught in school. After the fundamental academics were presented each day, the class was divided into two groups. The boys were taught woodworking, and the girls were taught needlework. As the girls got older, the sophistication of the skills they learned increased. In the first grade girls learned hand sewing and knitting, in the second and third grade they learned embroidery, and by the fourth grade they were expected to master the treadle sewing machine and sew a man's dress shirt!

Little did I know, as my mother told me these stories, that she was passing on not only her personal history, but also her beliefs about the value of tradition, the importance of doing one's best, and the joy of making things by hand. And the joy finally appeared for me, too. At age eleven, I mastered the satin stitch and came to love the sheen of the thread and the sound of the needle piercing linen tightly stretched on an embroidery hoop. I started looking for my own projects to sew. Although I wasn't ready to tackle a man's shirt, I did create a doll's apron from an unworn section of an embroidered pillowcase.

When I look back at those times, I don't remember actually going out to buy needlework or craft materials. Instead, we looked around the house and used what we found. My mother was the most creative innovator of all—once she made a ballerina tutu (in the style of a Degas sculpture) from real parachute silk saved after the war.

It's that kind of resourcefulness and inventiveness that I came to expect from myself, and such an expectation has bred very interesting transformations of ordinary things. Last spring I saw a convex mirror with a gilded frame that I thought I could make in a different style. All I needed was a convex mirror, because I knew I could redesign the frame from my stash of supplies. I discovered, however, that convex mirrors are very expensive. I searched and searched for a substitute with no success. Eventually I forgot about the project and went on to other things. Months later, when our family was driving home from a vacation, we pulled into a truck stop for gas. I wandered into the adjacent convenience store and there in front of me was a display rack with a stack of convex mirrors! Each one was packed in a cardboard sleeve that advertised "the best-reflecting truck mirrors on the road," for only $8.95!

Robert Fulgum once said that the most ordinary things can be sources of pleasure if one invests pleasure in them. I did. On that day, for me, the truck stop was transformed into an art store. What joy! And joy to you and yours in this new year. ◆

*Carol Endler Sterbenz*

## STAIN-PROOF FINISH FOR FABRIC PLACE MATS

*I've been searching for place mats that do not require laundering but can be cleaned with a damp cloth. The "secret" is applying some sort of fabric finish, similar to a lacquer, to the finished place mat. Can you help me?*

PAT KILLINGSWORTH
Seattle, WA

We consulted Pearl Paint, one of the foremost art supply stores in New York, and were told that laminating a fabric or covering it with a varnish such as polyurethane would make it possible to clean the fabric with a sponge, but would also result in a stiff-looking finish. We recommend Clear Coat, a clear, waterproof varnish manufactured by Createx that can be sprayed or airbrushed. One coat produces a clear, protective, flexible, matte finish; you can build up the barrier by applying several coats.

Fabric that has been coated with Clear Coat can be wiped off with a damp sponge, but spraying fabric with Clear Coat doesn't mean you'll never have to launder your place mats again. The product simply reduces the chance of permanent staining.

## RUBBER-STAMPING WITH PAINT

*Is it possible to use rubber stamps with paint? I'm thinking about decorating a raw pine toy chest, and I'd like to use some of the beautiful rubber-stamp designs available nowadays.*

BARBARA ARTALE
Larchmont, NY

Rubber-stamping is possible with acrylic paint, given a few important facts and the proper preparation. (Some oil-based paints contain solvents that may damage the stamp's rubber surface.) First, patch any holes in the chest with wood filler and fine-sand the entire surface, then paint the chest with a sealer (preferably one with stain-killing properties, to mask any knots in the wood). Apply one or two coats of your base coat; acrylic-based enamel paint is a good choice, as it's very durable.

The actual stamping is a little tricky. First, select a stamp with thick, bold lines rather than one with fine detail. Make sure the paint on the surface of the chest is completely dry before you begin, and use the same type of paint that you used for the base coat. Pour a thin layer of the paint onto a paper plate, then lightly touch the stamp to the surface to coat it. Stamp the image a couple of times onto a piece of paper to remove excess paint, as paint is much thicker than ink. Then stamp it onto the chest with an even motion. Rinse off the stamp with water or paint thinner every few images to maintain a clear impression. When the rubber-stamped images are dry, protect the chest with a coat of acrylic (water-based) sealer, such as Mod Podge.

Practice stamping with paint onto wood before you attempt to decorate your toy chest, as the paint can sometimes cause blurry images. Practicing will give you a feel for how much paint is right and where to place your stamp on the surface to create the best image.

## FACE MOLDS FOR DOLLS AND JEWELRY

*I'd like to know where people buy molds for dolls' faces and jewelry. Can you help?*

SUSAN WISE
Boalsbury, PA

You can contact the American Art Clay Company (AMACO) in Indianapolis for a catalog or information on stores in your area that carry their products. AMACO's catalog features a wide array of products, from modeling clays and plastics (including Puppen Fimo, especially designed for modeling dolls) to instructional books and videos. The catalog also features a range of molds for dolls and fashion jewelry.

## IS RUBBER CEMENT SAFE TO USE?

*Your new magazine is attractive, but I have a complaint about the Charter Issue (November/December 1993). In the item on page 3 about reusing gift wrap, the writer recommends using rubber cement. When I was working in the art department at Abbott Laboratories in 1945, the medical director forbade us to use rubber cement, as the solvent in it is benzene, which is carcinogenic. The sensible substitute is nontoxic glue stick.*

*My other complaint is the assertion that you can cut intricate decoupage pictures with manicure scissors. I've found that the best way to cut them is with a small scalpel, which is much more comfortable to use than an X-Acto knife. With care, a so-called disposable scalpel can be sharpened over and over and will do a superb job. Also, if you cut black paper, such as your rose background, and glue it to a black background, the white edge will show unless you go over it with a black felt tip pen. It makes the difference between a professional job and loving-hands-at-home. It looks much better to cut right to the flower and leaf edges, and that is why the interior bits of black should be removed with a scalpel, which is obviously impossible with manicure scissors.*

NANCY MAINVILLE
Santa Fe, NM

By calling the 800 number listed on the jar of Best-Test Paper Cement, we contacted the Union Rubber Company in Trenton, New Jersey, regarding your inquiry. According to the company, not all rubber cement formulas contain benzene, nor are all rubber cement products derived from the same formula. Best-Test, for example, contains natural rubber and heptane instead of benzene, and is certified as safe by the Art & Craft Materials Institute. This is not to say that rubber cement should be used without extreme caution; it's just that not all brands contain benzene, toluene, or xylene, which are more dangerous. Union Rubber was happy to send us information regarding the contents of their product, and you can probably ask the same of other rubber cement manufacturers if you want to evaluate their products for yourself.

We checked with several art supply stores and discovered that rubber cement still sells well because it's repositionable and durable. It's also what the majority of art schools instruct their students to use. Again, that doesn't mean rubber cement should be used with reckless abandon, only that it is unlikely to harm you unless you work with it day in and day out, year after year, in a poorly ventilated space. For most of our projects, however, rubber cement is not necessary. There are many nontoxic permanent glues on the market today, such as Sobo, Mod Podge, and glue sticks.

Your suggestion of using a black felt-tip marker is a good one. Regarding the use of X-Acto knives, mat knives, and scalpels (all sold at art supply stores), yes, you are right: these are more precise cutting tools than manicure scissors. A scalpel is lighter and, for some, more comfortable than an X-Acto knife, and can be resharpened, although it is usually inexpensive to replace.

## CREATIVE USES FOR SCRAPS OF DECORATIVE PAPER

*Do you have any suggestions for using scraps of decorative paper? I have lots of odds and ends that are too small to be used for a large project, but I just can't bear to throw them away.*
TINA HARGESS
Jersey City, NJ

Leftover paper scraps can be made into a variety of practical items, such as gift tags, postcards, or bookmarks. You can make a fancy gift tag by mounting your paper scrap onto thin mat board (make sure the grain of the paper matches the grain of the board, *see* "Determining Paper Grain," Notes from Readers, November/December 1994), cutting the board to the desired shape, and punching a hole through the top center for a ribbon. You can enhance the tag with stickers, glitter, photographs, pictures from magazines, cut-out letters, calligraphy, and so on. Bookmarks and postcards can be made in the same fashion. You may want to laminate the bookmark to make it last longer. (There are plenty of shops where you can get this done for a dollar or two.)

## ADDING FRESH FLOWERS TO A SILK ARRANGEMENT

*I'd like to add fresh flowers to a silk flower arrangement to spruce it up. But what do I do about water?*
LUCINDA REEVES
Rochester, MN

There's no doubt about it—if you want to have complete freedom of design and incorporate real flowers, you will need to place the entire arrangement in water. Don't worry about the silk flowers, though. Yes, the florist tape on the stems will inevitably disintegrate in the water, but the stems can easily be rewrapped with new tape once the real flowers have died. Florist foam can be helpful in these combined arrangements, as it will hold the flowers securely in place and, by absorbing water like a sponge, will nurture the real flowers.

If you can't bear to get water on your silk flowers' stems, you can place real flowers in a small glass or container of water in the center of your arrangement and arrange the silk flowers around it. You should anchor the glass and disguise its presence (particularly if you're using a clear container) by surrounding it with marbles or small stones. You can then use the mar-

bles or stones to secure the silk flowers in position. This method is not particularly flexible design-wise, but it does work.

## COLORED PENCILS VERSUS WATERCOLOR PENCILS

*What's the difference between colored pencils and watercolor pencils?*
PETER ROBBINS
Chicago, IL

Colored pencils are made of non-water-soluble pigment that has been mixed with a binder, usually wax. Because wax is not water-soluble, colored pencils repel water and are primarily used for drawing.

Watercolor pencils contain pigment mixed with a binder, usually a water-soluble gum. The gum allows the color to adhere to paper, but its solubility enables the color to spread once water has been applied to it, thus allowing you to manipulate it. Artist's turpentine (not to be confused with household turpentine) can be used to do the same thing with colored pencils.

## TIPS FOR STORING CUT FLOWERS

*What's the best way to store cut flowers?*
BETH DANIELS
Colorado Springs, CO

Ideally, flowers should be stored in a cool, dark area. If you're not going to arrange them immediately, you can put them in a thirty-three to thirty-five-degree refrigerator. Never store flowers with fruits or vegetables, as these foods release ethylene gas, a ripening agent which can cause the flowers to wane prematurely.

## WALLPAPER CHOICES FOR A TINY BATHROOM

*Do you have any tips on choosing wallpaper for the high ceiling in a tiny bathroom? I'll be painting the walls and molding.*
MELISSA STERNS
Charlotte, NC

Like every other aspect of home decor, choosing wallpaper is a matter of taste. As a general rule of thumb, we suggest that you select a random or a two-way pattern—one that doesn't have a right-side-up. If you use a right-side-up pattern, it will appear to be upside down from the other side of room. (This applies to

rooms of all sizes.)

Because the room is small, consider a paper that matches or is close to the paint color you'll be using. This way the walls and ceiling will work together instead of against each other; that is, unless you're striving for a more offbeat effect. A small, allover pattern with a light background would be a good choice, as dark colors and dense patterns will make the room seem smaller, despite your high ceiling. When applying paper to the ceiling, be sure to paint the walls before you apply the paper. It's easier to remove wallpaper paste from paint than it is to clean paint from wallpaper.

## THE RIGHT WAY TO USE AN X-ACTO KNIFE

*Is there a right way to use an X-Acto knife?*
STUART FISHER
Brooklyn, NY

When using an X-Acto knife, make sure the blade is sharp. Not only is it more difficult to cut with a dull blade, the additional pressure required to make the cut may actually tear the paper rather than cut it. Always hold the knife upright, but tilted in the direction of the cut (a knife tilted sideways produces a beveled edge). Slide the knife alongside a metal T-square, straightedge, or ruler as you cut; this ensures a clean, straight line.

If you follow these basic guidelines, you should be able to cut through most papers in a single stroke. Dense board, such as chipboard, should not be cut in a single stroke, as its thickness may cause you to tilt the knife. Instead, make several even cuts along the metal straightedge.

## PAINTING AROUND A DOORKNOB

*Is it possible to paint a door without removing the doorknob?*
JANE DELROSE
Tempe, AZ

Cover the doorknob with a small plastic sandwich bag, then tape the ends of the bag to the edge of the door plate. A word of warning: For this time-saving method to work, the edge of the door plate must be flat enough to provide a surface that can hold the tape firmly. It should have straight sides or be perfectly round. Otherwise, you're better off removing the doorknob and its hardware. ♦

# Quick Tips

## Buckle-Free French Seams

The straight French seam, a joining technique that conceals a fabric's raw edges, is especially appropriate for sheers, fabrics that ravel easily, and small, delicate items such as lace sachets or doll clothes. When sewing French seams, buckling is a common problem, but this can be prevented by triple-pressing the fabric to define the seam and make it pliable. To make a ¼" French seam, you will need the two fabric pieces that will be joined (each with a ⅝" seam allowance), matching thread, a sewing machine, sharp scissors, and an iron.

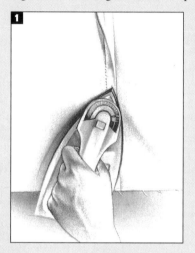

1. Place the fabric pieces *wrong* sides together and stitch a seam ⅜" (not ⅝") from the raw edges. Press the seam open. Next, press both seam allowances to one side and then to the other side.

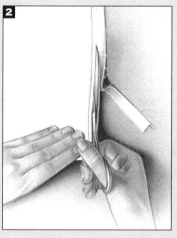

2. Using scissors, trim the seam through both layers a scant ⅛" from the stitching.

3. Fold the pieces right sides together, concealing the stitching and the seam's narrow raw edges. Sew a second seam ¼" from the folded seam line.

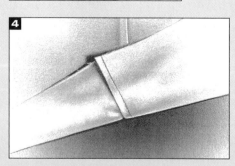

4. Press the finished seam first to one side and then to the other side. Turn the fabric over and press it from the right side.

## Make Your Own Pom-Poms

You can make perfect pom-poms by using six-strand embroidery floss in premeasured skeins. Available in a wide array of colors, the floss fluffs out into full, 1" pom-poms with a soft chenille surface. To make one pom-pom, you'll need an 8.7-yard skein of floss, three unsharpened pencils, scissors, and a ruler.

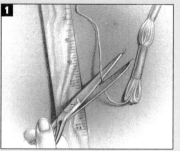

1. Pull the loose thread (do not remove paper wrappers), and measure and cut a 10" length. Set the 10" length aside.

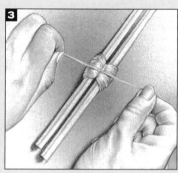

3. Slide out the middle pencil. Wind the 10" reserved strand twice around the middle section of the wound floss between the two pencils. Tie the ends in a simple knot and tighten it so the wound floss assumes a butterfly shape.

4. Slide out the remaining two pencils, pull the knot tighter to curl the wound floss into a circle, and tie again to complete a square knot. Using scissors, clip through the loops on each side of the knot.

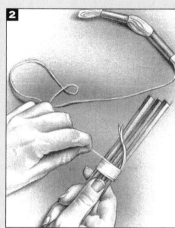

2. Hold three pencils side by side in one hand. With the other hand, pull the skein's loose end and begin winding it firmly around the pencils, securing the loose end with the first few wraps. Set each successive wrap snugly against the previous round. Continue winding until 1" of the pencils is covered, then holding the wound thread with a finger, wind in the opposite direction, making another layer over the previous wraps. Repeat this process until the entire skein is used up.

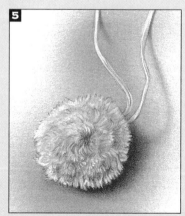

5. Shape the pom-pom and fluff out the strands.

ILLUSTRATIONS BY HARRY DAVIS

# Shortening a Zipper

If you've got a nylon zipper that's too long for your intended project, here's an easy means of shortening it. It will also work in the case of "in-between size" zipper openings (buy the next larger size zipper and trim it down). In addition to the zipper, you'll need matching thread, a zigzag sewing machine, sharp utility scissors, one straight pin, and a tape measure or ruler.

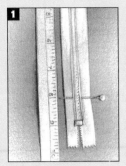

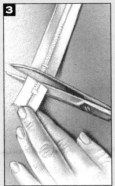

**1.** Zip up the zipper. Measure down from the top of the zipper slide to the desired length, then insert the straight pin to mark the position where you want the new zipper to stop.

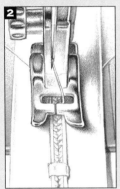

**2.** Set the sewing machine for a very wide zigzag stitch (about ³⁄₁₆"). Set the stitch length at zero. Position the pinned section of the zipper directly under the needle. Remove the pin and lower the presser foot. Zigzag back and forth across the zipper teeth eight to twelve times in the same place.

**3.** Remove the zipper from the machine. Draw the thread ends to the back, tie them in a square knot, and trim off the ends. Using sharp utility scissors, trim off the lower end of the zipper about ¾" below the new zipper stop. Install the shortened zipper as usual.

# Repairing Cracks in Plaster Walls

Repairing minor cracks in a plaster wall before you paint or redecorate is an easy, do-it-yourself job, provided you have the right materials and tools. For a professional-looking job, you'll need premixed spackling compound, a stiff paint scraper, a flexible putty knife, a paper face mask, a soft-bristled brush, and sandpaper in 150-grit and several finer grades. As with all painting projects, lay a dropcloth before you begin, and prime the repaired area before painting.

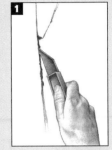

**1.** Using a stiff paint scraper, dig out any loose plaster chips from the crack. Cut in under the surface plaster so that the back of the crack (away from the surface) is wider than the part you can see. (This process, called undercutting, helps the dried spackling compound hold to the wall.) Brush away dust and loose particles using the soft-bristled brush.

**2.** Apply the spackling compound to the wall with a putty knife, spreading it generously over the entire crack so it extends about 1½" beyond each side. Smooth the compound even with the wall surface. Use a fanning motion to feather the edges of the spackled area so they merge and fade into the wall surface.

**3.** Let the spackle dry thoroughly, following manufacturer's recommendations. Put on the paper face mask, and sand the spackled area lightly with a folded piece of 150-grit sandpaper. Repeat steps 2 and 3 as necessary, sanding each layer of spackling compound with a finer grade of sandpaper until the surface is smooth.

# Repairing Holes in Drywall

Repairing holes in drywall board, such as Sheetrock, is a quick do-it-yourself job. You'll need a piece of drywall larger than the damaged area and of the same thickness as your walls, premixed spackling compound, a flexible putty knife, a retractable-blade utility knife, a paper face mask, a pencil, sandpaper in 150-grit and several finer grades, and a drop cloth. Be sure to prime the repaired area before painting.

**1.** Cover the floor area below the hole with the drop cloth. Draw a rectangle around the damaged area of drywall, allowing at least a 1" margin on all sides. Using a utility knife, cut along the drawn line at a 45-degree angle, as if you were cutting out the top of a pumpkin. Insert a finger into the hole and carefully lift out the damaged section.

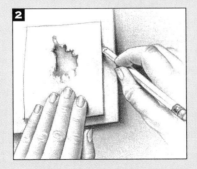

**2.** Lay the damaged section on the scrap piece of drywall and trace around it. Cut out this replacement piece using a 45-degree angle as in step 1.

**3.** Set the replacement piece into the wall. It should sink slightly below the surface. If it bulges, shave the edges with the utility knife, maintaining the 45-degree angle, until the fit is right. Coat the edges of the patch with spackling compound before inserting it into the hole.

**4.** Apply spackling compound to the entire area with a putty knife, then use the putty knife to smooth the surface.

**5.** Let the spackle dry thoroughly, following manufacturer's recommendations. Put on the face mask. Sand the spackled area lightly with a folded piece of 150-grit sandpaper, then repeat steps 4 and 5 as necessary, sanding with progressively finer grades of sandpaper after each spackling application, until the surface is smooth.

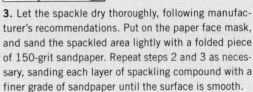

**ATTENTION READERS: RECEIVE A FREE SUBSCRIPTION IF WE PUBLISH YOUR TIP.** Do you have a unique shortcut or technique you'd like to share with other readers? We'll give you a one-year complimentary subscription for each Quick Tip that we publish. Send a description of your special technique to: Quick Tips, *Handcraft Illustrated*, P.O. Box 509, 17 Station Street, Brookline Village, MA 02147-0509. Please include your name, address, and daytime phone number. Unfortunately, we can only acknowledge receipt of tips actually used in the magazine.

# Gilded Cut-Metal Sconce

*Transform copper tubing, rubber chair leg tips, and cut-metal foil into a gilded French sconce.*

Believe it or not, most of the materials used in creating this sconce can be found in any hardware store. The spine of the piece is formed from quarter-inch hollow copper tubing, the candle cups are made from rubber chair leg tips, and the decorative leaves are cut from copper tooling foil. The entire arrangement is wired together with 20-gauge wire, spray-painted, and gilded. From start to finish, the project takes about two days.

We tried several versions of this project before we arrived at the final design. We started out working with three-eighths-inch copper tubing (the dimension of copper tubing always refers to the outside diameter).

We found that tubing this large was quite difficult to bend into smooth, controlled arcs. The loop at the top of the sconce ended up crimping (folding in on itself) instead of retaining a smooth, rounded shape. To resolve this problem, we switched to the quarter-inch copper tubing, which we found much easier to work with. The arcs were more symmetrical, but we still ended up with a crimp in the top loop. To eliminate this, we tested a length of ball chain, inserting it into the tubing in order

*In two days, you can transform hollow copper tubing, rubber chair leg tips, and copper tooling foil into an elegant gilded sconce.*

to control the bending process. (Ball chain, commonly used as pull chain for light fixtures, is sold by the foot in hardware stores. The size refers to the number of balls per inch. For this project, 6-ball chain worked best.) By pressing out against the inner wall of the tubing, the tiny balls prevent the tubing from crimping and collapsing in on itself as it is bending. We found that brass ball chain gave

way under the pressure, and the tubing still crimped, but nickel-plated steel chain, which is harder than brass, worked well.

Our original design also called for using a metal candle cup, but such cups aren't always widely available, so we substituted a rubber furniture leg tip. (Naturally, you're free to use metal candle cups if you find them.) Although rubber doesn't sound as elegant as metal, once the tip is painted and gilded, it looks fine. When you're shopping for chair tips, look for curving, graceful designs as opposed to squarer shapes. Avoid plastic; rubber grips the candle much better.

A few general notes before you get started: Copper tubing, which ranges in price from about 50¢ to $1 a foot, comes in a large coil. Ask the clerk not to unbend the coil as it is measured, since the less it is manipulated beforehand, the

easier it will be to bend. As you shape the framework of the sconce, strive for perfectly matched bends on the first try. Once the tubing has been bent, subsequent bends become more difficult to make. Before bending the tubing, evaluate the sconce's shape and make your adjustments with a sure, even hand rather than with excessive tinkering. If the tubing should crimp at any point during your work, don't worry about it, but don't try to bend it back, or it may crack or break. (If your tubing does crimp, you can cover the crimp with a leaf, or leave it as is to add character to the project.)

The copper tooling foil should be cut and handled with care, as the edges are sharp, and the foil wrinkles easily. To form the leaves' crisp interior notches, cut in from two directions rather than trying to manipulate the scissors around a tight turn.

Attach the copper foil leaves to the sconce using 20-gauge wire, then twist the wires together using linesman's pliers, available in any hardware store. Linesman's pliers have a broader nose and finer teeth than regular pliers, making it easier to grip and twist fine wire.

(If you haven't applied gold or silver leaf before, *see* "How to Gild Almost Any Surface," September/October 1994.)

### GILDED CUT-METAL SCONCE

- 4' ¼"-diameter copper tubing
- 4' nickel-plated steel 6-ball chain
-    Gold metallic spray paint
-    Quick-dry synthetic gold size varnish
- 1½' 16-gauge copper wire
- 5 5½" x 5½" sheets gold composition leaf

## Leaf Pattern Pieces

Using a copy machine, enlarge the leaf patterns at right until the large leaf measures 6⅛" long, the small leaf measures 4½" long, and the candle cup leaf measures 3" long. Trace the enlarged patterns onto tracing paper, brush your cardboard with clear glue, then stick the tracings on the cardboard, smoothing out any wrinkles or bubbles with your fingers. Let the patterns dry one-half hour, and cut each one out to form a template.

**Candle Cup**

**Small Leaf**

**Large Leaf**

PATTERNS BY ROBERTA FRAUWIRTH/PHOTOGRAPH BY STEVEN MAYS

5' 3"-wide copper tooling foil
2 yards 4"-wide metallic gold
   ribbon
3 pairs ½" to 1½" plastic or
   crystal chandelier drops
2 rubber chair leg tips, ¾" to
   1" in diameter, or 2 metal
   candle cups
5 yards 20-gauge brass
   jeweler's wire

2 ⁵⁄₃₂ x 1" steel machine screws
2 washers to match screws
   5-minute epoxy adhesive kit

*You'll also need:* access to a
copy machine with enlarging capabilities; hardwood burnishing
stick with round ball ends or eraser
stick (eraser that looks like a pencil and has a brush at one end);
chair; broomstick; linesman's pliers with built-in wire cutters; utility scissors; screwdriver; awl; two
1"-wide disposable paintbrushes;
computer mouse pad or similar
pliable surface such as scrap of
low pile carpet; index cards or
heavyweight paper plate; lightweight cardboard; red permanent
marker; tracing paper; brown kraft
paper; pencil; tape measure; masking tape; stiff paintbrush; toothpicks; table knife; soft rag; clear
arts-and-crafts glue; paint thinner
or mineral spirits; and two 8"
white or cream tapers.

*Other items, if necessary:* spray
lacquer (to seal sconce after gilding) and Fun-Tak (for adhering
candles in cups). ◆

## CREATING THE FRAMEWORK

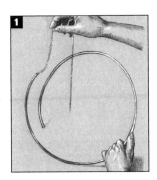

**1.** Using the pliers, snip 3"
off one end of the ball chain.
Insert the remaining chain
into the ¼" copper tubing,
turning the tubing so gravity
draws the chain in. When the
chain is no longer visible, tape
the ends of the tubing to prevent the chain from falling
out.

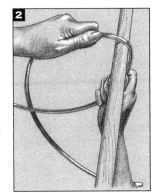

**2.** Measure and mark the midpoint of the tubing with the red
permanent marker. Sit in a chair and prop the broomstick diagonally in front of you, with one end on the floor and the other
end resting on your shoulder. Press the midpoint of the tubing
against the broomstick, bending the free ends down to form an
upside-down U. Remove the broomstick.

**3.** Compress the U with your hand so
the sides touch about 2" below the arc
to form point A. Separate the tubing below point A into two gentle arcs about
1" apart at the widest point. Bend them
back together about 7" below point A to form point B.

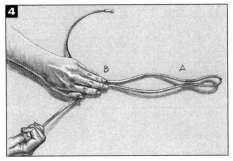

**4.** One piece at a time, bend each end of the
tubing forward, up, and out to the side in a wide
arc to form the candle-supporting arms of the
sconce. Do your best to make the arcs identical.

**5.** Lay the sconce on a flat surface. Bend
the section of tubing, starting at point A and
extending about 2" past point B up off the
surface. Hold the sconce up and examine it
from the sides, front, and back to check the
bends and the overall symmetry. Make sure
the tips on the candle-supporting arms point
straight up, and adjust the sconce as necessary. The tubing should touch the wall in
three places—just beyond point A, and 3" to
4" past point B on both candle-supporting
arms—to form a triangle.

**6.** Using the pliers, cut a 12" length -
of 20-gauge brass wire. Hold the wire
against the tubing at point A, allowing
1½" of wire to extend off to one side.
Wind the other, longer, end of the wire
around both tubes, setting each successive wrap snugly against the previous one, until about 1½" of wire remains. Turn the framework over, then
grip both wire ends with the lineman's
pliers and twist them together in a
tight spiral. Trim the twisted wire if
necessary, then bend it flat against
the tubing. Repeat this process at
point B.

**7.** Cut the 16-gauge copper wire into two 9" lengths.
Hold the two pieces together, and bend them into an arc
that matches the shape of the candle-supporting arms.
Position each wire arc on the backside of a candle-
supporting arm with the end about 2" below point B.
Temporarily tape each wire arc to its arm about 4" below
point B, then wrap the end closest to point B with an 8"
length of 20-gauge brass wire as in step 6. Using a toothpick, mix about 1
teaspoon of epoxy
on an index card or
paper plate, follow-
ing the manufac-
turer's directions.
Spread the epoxy
with a toothpick
over each wire-
wrapped joint,
working it in thor-
oughly between the
wires and onto the
tubing. Let it set
for 15 minutes.

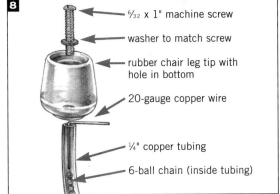

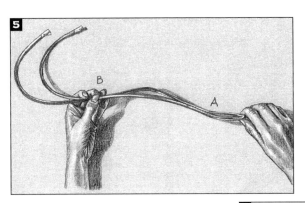

⁵⁄₃₂ x 1" machine screw
washer to match screw
rubber chair leg tip with
hole in bottom
20-gauge copper wire
¼" copper tubing
6-ball chain (inside tubing)

**8.** Using an awl, pierce a hole in the center of one rubber
chair leg tip. Put a washer on one of the screws, then insert
the screw down into the rubber cup and out the hole in the
bottom. Cut a 2" piece of 20-gauge brass wire, bend it into
a 90-degree angle, and insert one end into the copper tubing. Mix about ½ teaspoon of epoxy. Using a toothpick, coat
the threads of the screw with epoxy. Using the screwdriver,
screw the screw securely into the copper tubing. Bend the
exposed 20-gauge wire down against the tubing. Repeat to
make the second candle cup.

## Making and Attaching the Leaves

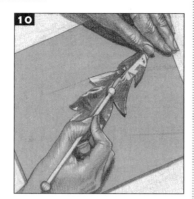

**9.** Using a copy machine, enlarge the leaf pattern pieces on page 6 until the large leaf measures 6⅛" long, the small leaf measures 4½" long, and the candle cup leaf measures 3" long. Trace the three enlarged leaf patterns onto tracing paper. Brush lightweight cardboard with clear glue, and stick the tracings on the cardboard, smoothing out any wrinkles or bubbles with your fingers. Let this dry about ½ hour, then cut out the patterns to form templates. Unroll the copper foil onto a flat surface. Lay the large leaf template diagonally on top of the foil and trace its outline using the red permanent marker. Repeat this process with all three templates, positioning each leaf diagonally, to outline six large leaves, six small leaves, and four candle cup leaves. Using utility scissors, cut out the leaves.

**10.** Lay each leaf on a hard, flat work surface and smooth the edges by pressing them firmly with the ball end of the burnishing stick or eraser stick. To define the leaf's spine and add three-dimensionality, lay each leaf on the computer mouse pad and run the ball or eraser tip down the center of the leaf, pressing hardest near the stem and decreasing the pressure to almost nothing as you approach the tip of the leaf. As you define the spine in this way, the leaf will curl backward. To correct this, bend the leaf tip and serrations forward with your fingers, then turn the leaf wrong-side up on the mouse pad and rub outward from the spine in short, ½" strokes with the burnishing stick or eraser stick.

**11.** Remove the tape from the tubing and wires. Beginning at the top of one 16-gauge wire arm, attach two small leaves, then three large leaves to the arm, starting at the tip and working down towards the joint. To attach the first small leaf, wrap the stem of the leaf around the tip of the wire arm, then secure the leaf with a 4" length of 20-gauge wire. Wrap and twist the wire as in step 6 of "Creating the Framework," page 7. Attach the second small leaf about 1½" down the wire arm so it conceals the joint of the first leaf. Continue down the arm, repeating this process with the three large leaves. Repeat the process on the second wire arm.

Next, position two candle cup leaves around the base of each candle cup, then fasten both stems in place by wrapping them with a 5" length of 20-gauge wire. Attach one remaining small leaf to conceal the wire arm joint. Secure any wobbly leaves temporarily with tape. Mix about 1 tablespoon of epoxy, and work it into all the joints of the leaves and wires. Let it set for 15 minutes. Repeat the process on the other side.

## Finishing the Sconce

**12.** *Note: When spray-painting, always work in a well-ventilated area, following the manufacturer's directions and using a large piece of cardboard as a backdrop to catch the overspray.* Spray-paint the entire sconce with gold paint. Turn the sconce as necessary to paint the inside leaf joints and the undersides of the leaves. To guard against drips, do not hold the can too close to the sconce, and apply several light coats of paint instead of one heavy one. Let the paint dry thoroughly, preferably overnight, but at least 2 hours.

Cover your workspace with a fresh sheet of kraft paper, then lay the sconce flat. Using a 1" paint brush, apply a thin, even coat of size to all surfaces—the leaves, the tubing, the  wire arms, and the candle cups. Let the size dry until it is tacky to the touch, anywhere from ½ hour to 3 hours. Clean the brush with paint thinner or mineral spirits.

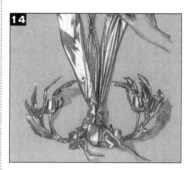

**14.** Lay the sconce on a flat surface. Center the metallic ribbon horizontally across point B. Bring the ends of the ribbon down behind the arms of the sconce, then up between them and underneath the horizontal portion of the ribbon to form a soft knot.

**13.** Using a table knife moistened with your breath, transfer a sheet of gold leaf onto a clean piece of kraft paper. With perfectly dry fingertips, tear the leaf into small, irregularly shaped pieces. Lift a piece of leaf with a damp fingertip, lay it on the tacky sconce surface, and tamp it into place with a dry, stiff paintbrush. Continue applying the gold leaf as desired. Let the sconce dry overnight.

The following day, burnish the gilded surfaces with a soft rag. Give the leaves a final shaping; the small leaves near the arm tips, for instance, can be curled tightly to resemble new growth. If desired, seal the sconce's surface by applying a thin coat of clear lacquer. Let dry following manufacturer's recommendations.

**15.** Bring the ends of the ribbon up the front of the sconce and then through the opening at the top, above the wire joint at point A. Draw the ends of the ribbon 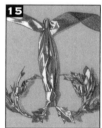 back around to the front, and tie in a soft bow around point A. (If necessary, use the color photograph on page 6 as a reference.)

**16.** Cut six 4" lengths of 20-gauge wire. Slide a chandelier drop to the center of each wire, then bend the wire ends straight up into a hairpin shape. Using the pliers, grip both ends of the wire about ½" above the drop, and twist several times to form a tight spiral. Separate the wires into a V shape above the spiral and curve the ends toward each other to form a pinch-type clasp. Clip each drop onto the sconce with crystals dangling freely, as shown in the photograph on page 6. To mount the sconce on the wall, slip the top loop onto a nail hammered into the wall. Set the candles in the cups, and secure them with Fun-Tak if necessary.

# Tasseled Napkin Ring

*Make this gilded napkin ring from an ordinary curtain ring and silk-twist thread.*

BY GENEVIEVE A. STERBENZ

Although this napkin ring looks sophisticated, its beginnings are actually quite humble. Making a complete set to match your table linens is as easy as gilding several ordinary wooden curtain rings and attaching tassels assembled from skeins of silk and metallic thread.

For this napkin ring, I used a wooden curtain ring (also known as a pole ring) with an inside diameter of one and three-fourths inches. (It was designed to go on a one-and-three-eighths- inch-diameter pole.) The ring features a screw-in eyehook and comes in a package of seven rings. I experimented with plastic shower curtain rings, but found that bending the sides apart to insert the tassel put a strain on the gilded surface and ran the risk of cracking it. The wooden curtain rings, however, are thick and sturdy enough for frequent use.

Because I wanted to create a fancier napkin ring, I opted for leafing versus just painting. (Naturally, you're free to use spray paint alone,

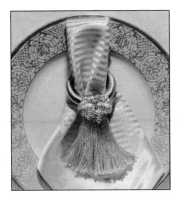

*For a plumper tassel such as this, use one additional skein of gold silk-twist thread.*

but I think gilding gives a more finished look.) Gilding, or applying gold leaf, may sound complicated, but with an item as small as a napkin ring, it's very quick and easy to do. When I applied the size directly to the raw wood, the wood absorbed it almost immediately, as it would any first coat of size or paint. To prevent this, I sealed the wood with gold spray paint, but you can also use the first coat of size as a sealer. (Be sure to work in a well-ventilated area when using spray paint.) Of course, there's no reason you have to use gold paint. Applying the gold leaf randomly over a contrasting base color creates an antique look.

I chose silk-twist thread for this napkin ring because the thickness of the thread creates a nice, plump tassel. I tried embroidery floss, but the thread was rather limp, even when all the strands were collected together in the tassel. For a finishing touch, I added the stamped gold grape cluster. A wide variety of these stamped

metal findings are available at most craft stores.

(If this is your first gilding project, *see* "How to Gild Almost Any Surface" in the September/October 1994 issue.)

### TASSELED NAPKIN RING

- 1 roll or skein (about 15 yards) gold silk-twist or tassel thread
- 1 roll (about 15 yards) metallic gold twine
  Wooden curtain ring
  Stamped grape cluster finding
  Gold Krylon spray paint
  Quick-dry synthetic varnish size
- 1 book composition gold leaf
  Clear lacquer spray

*You'll also need:* ¼"-wide artist's paintbrush; brown kraft paper; 3" x 9" piece of heavy-duty cardboard; white tacky glue; coat hanger; clothesline or other strong cord; table knife; soft cloth or rag; wire cutters; ruler; scissors; and pliers.

*Other items, if necessary:* second skein of gold silk-twist thread (for plumper tassels). ◆

**Genevieve A. Sterbenz** is a freelance writer and designer based in New York.

---

## Making the Napkin Ring

Before starting, cover your workspace with brown kraft paper, then lay the curtain ring on the paper and spray-paint one side. When the ring is dry (about 10 minutes), paint the other side. When the paint is dry, add two additional coats. While the paint is drying, cut an 8" length from the straight portion of the coat hanger using the

wire cutters. Using your pliers, bend it into an S-shaped hook, then set it aside. Hang a clothesline or strong cord to create a drying line. Holding the ring by the eyehook, brush on a thin, even coat of the size, then slip the S-shaped hook through the eyehook and hang the ring on the line. Let the ring dry until tacky (about 60 minutes).

**1.** Moisten the blade of a table knife with your breath, then use the blade to drag a sheet of gold leaf onto a clean sheet of kraft paper. Use perfectly dry fingertips to tear the leaf into small pieces. Holding the ring by the eyehook, remove the S-shaped hook. Pick up a piece of gold leaf with your fingertip and position it on the ring; tap and smooth it into place. Continue the process to cover the entire ring. Hang the ring on the line using the S-shaped hook and let it dry overnight. When dry, use a soft cloth or rag to burnish the gold leaf, then spray on clear lacquer.

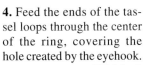

**2.** Cut an 18" length of silk-twist thread and set it aside. Wind the remaining thread lengthwise around the cardboard, then gently slide the thread off the cardboard. (To make a thicker tassel, repeat the process with a second skein of thread.) Repeat the winding process with the gold nylon twine. Lay the twine flat on top of the thread, lining up the loops as closely as possible.

**3.** Wrap the 18" length of thread around the tassel loops approximately 1½" to one side of

their center point, and tie in a square knot.

**4.** Feed the ends of the tassel loops through the center of the ring, covering the hole created by the eyehook.

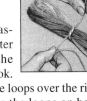

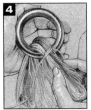

Fold the loops over the ring to make the loops on both sides even. Wrap the remaining loose ends of the 18" thread several times around the tassel at the base of the ring and tie with a square knot. Affix the stamped grape cluster with a dab of glue.

# Quick Dried Flower Arranging

*Build either of these beautiful arrangements using
a simple three-tier construction principle.*

Although these two half-relief dried flower arrangements look very similar, the arrangement on the left costs about $30 to make, while the one on the right, which uses larger quantities of flowers, costs about $100 to make. Both arrangements use the same quick and easy construction technique—building three tiers of flowers, each with a different color (green, blue, or pink). To finish the arrangements, we distributed yellow flowers throughout. Using this model, you can determine the final cost of your dried flower arrangement according to the type of flowers you prefer, the cost of those flowers, and the quantity of flowers used.

We made the $30 arrangement using a total of nine packages of floral material: green caspia, blue larkspur, pink everlasting, and golden yarrow. We split the arrangement horizontally into three sections, then filled the back of the arrangement with green caspia, the middle section with blue larkspur, and the front with pink everlasting (also known as strawflower). The golden yarrow was used to fill in any gaps and to unify the look of the arrangement.

The same construction technique works equally well with greater quantities and varieties of flowers, as shown by the $100 arrangement on the right. For this arrangement, we used the same colors of green caspia, blue larkspur, pink everlasting, and golden yarrow, but supplemented the green section with light green love-lies-bleeding (also known as prince's feather), the blue section with purple larkspur, and the pink section with light and dark pink roses and purple stirlingia. We also added large- and small-head yellow roses and yellow tansy throughout the arrangement.

*You can make this arrangement in about thirty minutes using $30 worth of dried flowers and foliage.*

*The three tiers of color in this $100 arrangement have been supplemented by roses, tansy, and pom-poms.*

Both half-relief arrangements are designed specifically for use on a shelf or against a wall. Depending on the size of your container and the space you need to fill, you can build a modest or a majestic arrangement. Each of the finished arrangements pictured above measures about sixteen inches high and twelve inches wide. For a narrower arrangement, build upward; for a wider arrangement, build sideways.

Before you buy your materials, shop for the rectangular box, as it may affect the quantity of flowers needed. The boxes pictured above measure nine inches long by seven inches wide by five inches high. (Most craft stores carry a range of inexpensive pine boxes, from the simple to the ornate. If you need a specific size, you could also make your own.) We painted the box

using sea-foam green acrylic craft paint. For quickest results, cut a household sponge roughly into thirds and use one piece to apply the paint. The sponge lets you work the paint into the corners of the box, and can be thrown out for quick cleanup. To save time, paint the exterior of the box completely, but paint only the top inch of the box's interior. Once the foam and flowers are in place, the unpainted areas won't show.

Depending on the size of the box, you may need to cut two blocks of green urethane foam to get a snug fit. The foam cuts easily with any serrated kitchen knife. You can also use Oasis if you prefer, or florist foam if you have some sitting around; just be sure it's completely dry.

Once the box is filled with foam, use a pencil or pen to divide

the foam along the length of the box into three equal sections, each of which will correspond to one color. We found it easiest to insert the dried flowers by working from the back of the arrangement forward. Start by filling in the back third of the foam with your green foliage. Use the longest pieces at the center, then cut the pieces as needed to create a soft fan shape. (Depending on the size of your box, the tallest piece should measure nine to twelve inches above the rim of the box.) When you've created a strong green backdrop for the arrangement, fill in the middle third with the blue and/or purple flowers. The height of this second section should fall just under the green foliage, about eight inches at the highest. Angle the flower heads forward toward the front to create depth. Fill the front third of the foam with the pink flowers. These flowers should be the shortest and should be angled down and forward to conceal the top of the box.

Next, blend the strong borders between the color sections by inserting a few of the blue flowers into the pink section, and a few of the pink flowers into the blue section. Soften the side and front borders with small stems of caspia, then finish by dispersing the yellow flowers throughout the arrangement.

A few notes about purchasing dried flowers: The quantities in the materials lists are based on commercially packaged flowers, but both quantities and prices will vary by locale. Each package of caspia, for instance, contained ten to twelve branches, each of which could be broken into multiple stems. One package of larkspur,

on the other hand, contained more than twenty-five stems.

When purchasing pink everlasting, look for those with wire stems, or wire the stems yourself. The stem of the everlasting is rather weak, and without wiring, it often flops over.

### QUICK DRIED FLOWER ARRANGING

**$30 Arrangement**
2  packages golden yarrow
2  packages pink everlasting or strawflower
3  packages blue larkspur
2  packages green caspia

**$100 Arrangement**
12  dark pink roses
12  light pink roses
24  pink everlasting or strawflower
12  small-head yellow roses
12  large-head yellow roses

1  package yellow tansy
1  package golden yarrow
1  package blue larkspur
1  package purple larkspur
1  package purple stirlingia
1  package green caspia
1  package light green love-lies-bleeding

9" x 7" x 5" wooden box
2  blocks 7⅞" x 3⅞" x 2⅞" green urethane foam
Sea-foam green acrylic craft paint

*You'll also need:* new household sponge; scissors; serrated kitchen knife; plastic container or paper plates; pencil or pen; fine-gauge florist wire; wire cutters; ruler; and brown kraft paper.

### Preparing the Box
1. Cover work space with brown kraft paper. Pour a 2" to 3"

puddle of paint into plastic container or onto several paper plates. Cut household sponge into thirds using scissors, then use one piece of sponge to paint outside of box and 1" down into interior. Let dry 10 to 15 minutes.

2. Fill interior of box with foam, trimming pieces with serrated knife to fit snugly and even with rim of box.

3. Divide container lengthwise into thirds by marking top of foam with pencil or pen.

4. To wire pink everlasting, use wire cutters to cut 10" to 12" lengths of wire. Insert end of one wire through base of each flower head, then even out wire on either side of flower head. Bring wire ends together and twist along stem to strengthen it.

5. Complete the design by proceeding to appropriate steps below. ◆

---

## MAKING THE $30 ARRANGEMENT

1. Open the packages and set aside 10 stems of larkspur, 8 to 10 stems of pink everlasting, and several caspia branches for later use. Insert the green caspia branches and stems into the back third of the foam, trimming the stems to 10" to 13" to create a soft fan shape. Arrange the caspia with the heads facing upward and slightly forward for a full backdrop of color. Fill the middle third of the foam with blue larkspur trimmed to about 8" to 9" (insert 1" of stem to leave 7" to 8"); angle any shorter stems forward. Fill in the front third of the foam with pink everlasting trimmed to 5" to 6".

2. Blend the hard borders of color between the sections by inserting the reserved larkspur into the section of pink everlasting, and the reserved pink everlasting into the section of blue larkspur. Fill in the front and side edges with smaller pieces of reserved caspia.

3. Insert 6" to 8" sections of golden yarrow throughout the arrangement.

## MAKING THE $100 ARRANGEMENT

1. Insert the green caspia branches and stems into the back third of the arrangement, trimming the stems to 10" to 13" to create a soft fan shape. Arrange the caspia with the heads facing upward and slightly forward for a full backdrop of color. Fill the middle third of the arrangement with stems of blue larkspur trimmed to about 8" or 9" and purple larkspur trimmed to about 7" or 8"; angle any shorter stems forward. Fill the front third of the arrangement with light and dark pink roses trimmed to about 5", 6", and 8". Angle each rose head forward.

2. Add stems of light green love-lies-bleeding to the green row in a soft spray. Insert stems of the pink everlasting to further blend the border between the blue and pink sections.

3. Trim stems of the large- and small-head yellow roses to about 10" and insert the roses into the green tier. Add the yellow tansy around the roses, pulling up single stems so the tansy heads are higher than the roses. Trim the golden yarrow stems to 8" to 10" and insert them throughout the arrangement. Insert the stirlingia in clusters around the pink roses.

# Testing Hot-Glue Guns

*The Crafty line of guns fares the best overall, while Black & Decker takes the gold in the dual-temp category.*

BY RODNEY T. STERBENZ

Next to the sewing machine, the hot-glue gun has emerged in the last ten years as the must-have tool for handcrafts and home decorating. Able to "instantly" adhere everything from wood and fabric to dried flowers and paper, hot-glue guns have actually been around since the 1950s, when they were used in the shoe industry for quick repairs on loose soles or broken heels. Today more than thirty different models of hot-glue guns are available, ranging from generic guns priced from about $5 to full-featured, brand-name models that cost up to $20 or more.

Modern hot-glue guns can be grouped into three categories: traditional high-temp guns, newer low-temp guns, and dual-temperature guns, which can switch between high-temp (380 degrees) and low-temp (225 to 240 degrees). High-temp guns are best suited for bonding wood, plastic, aluminum, and glass; low-temp guns are best suited for bonding surfaces that might burn, melt, or buckle at higher temperatures, such as Styrofoam or balloons, as well as fabric, paper, ribbon, lace, and dried flowers.

Hot-glue guns fall into two sizes. The more popular standard size measures six or seven inches from end to end, weighs seven to ten ounces, and uses standard-size glue sticks. Miniature guns look about the same but are considerably smaller (about four inches long and three to five ounces) and use smaller glue sticks. The mini guns are best suited for small jobs since their smaller glue sticks require frequent reloading.

For this test, I started with fourteen guns of varying size, but before I even plugged them in I was able to narrow the field to only eleven. I was not interested in any gun unless it was approved by the UL (Underwriter's Laboratory), was of one of the standard sizes that used readily available glue sticks, and was comfortable to hold. The three mini guns that didn't make the cut (ranging in price from $2.97 to $3.99) were simply too small for an adult's hand.

After making this first cut, I categorized the remaining guns according to type (dual-temp, high-temp, or low-temp), since temperature determines how quickly, safely, and effectively each gun works. Then I considered each gun in terms of its overall design (Was it comfortable to hold? Was the trigger easy to pull?), its

## 40 Years of Hot-Glue Gun Development

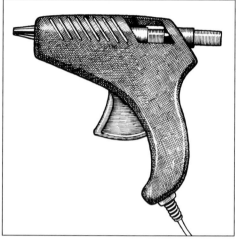

*A glue gun such as the one pictured above might have been used in the 1950s to reattach loose soles or broken heels to shoes. The design and safety of the modern glue gun at right relies on such features as a durable plastic housing and a reinforced electrical cord.*

function (Was the gun stand stable? Was the gun easy to load? Did the glue move smoothly through the gun and come out in a controllable flow? Did the glue bond quickly and effectively?), and its safety (Was the nozzle dependable? Did the gun heat up and cool down in a reasonable time? What was the chance of getting burned? Would the gun break if dropped?). On the dual-temp guns, I also evaluated the placement and effectiveness of the temperature switch.

After spending forty hours working with eleven guns, I've outlined my recommendations on page 13.

### Testing Design Factors

For starters, I evaluated the comfort of each glue gun resting in the hand. For this portion of the test, I asked for the help of two men and two women, as I wanted to see if the full-size guns were too large for a woman's hand or too small for a man's. Each gun was picked up and held normally, and the trigger was pulled.

Although all the Crafty guns were comfortable to hold, all four testers preferred the same two models: the Hot-Melt Duchess and the Magic Melt Magic Pro. The triggers on these two guns were easy to reach and pull. Since the trigger is pulled back parallel to the barrel of the gun, the glue is dispensed in an even, consistent line. Most of the other guns use a trigger design in which a wedge of plastic wide enough to accommodate two fingers

is squeezed into the handle. This kind of trigger is comfortable only when fully depressed, and when released, the trigger can pinch the fingers.

To test the guns for resistance to breakage, I dropped each gun from a four-foot-high countertop onto ceramic tile. All of the guns survived undamaged.

### Testing Features and Functions

Each gun I evaluated came with a gun stand, a small metal bracket designed to provide a safe place to rest the gun once it has been plugged in. Although it may not seem important, the stand is critical, as it keeps the hot nozzle off the work surface. (Without it, you'd have to prop the gun up or purchase a special heat-resistant work surface, like the $5.99, eight-inch square pad Surebonder offers.)

Whether the stand is a detachable wire bracket (like those found on the Westex Glue Gun and Ben Franklin's Glue Gun) or one molded into the gun (like the Crafty Hot Melt Duchess and the Crafty Magic Melt Magic Pro), all the stands worked fine. It was actually the guns' electrical cords that proved troublesome. Any movement of the cord, which typically extends from the bottom of the handle, can easily cause the gun to fall over. This happens more often than you'd expect, since all glue guns, because they weigh so little, tip over easily. It's easy to set a gun back up after it has fallen, but I had to keep a close eye on them to make sure their cords didn't pull them over.

In addition to knocking over your hot-glue gun, the cord can also limit your range of movement. Most cords range in length from fifty-seven to seventy-two inches; if the packaging indicates a length, purchase the longest one possible. (I found one "cordless" glue gun, the Crafty Hot-Melt Cordless. It dispenses hot glue for between five and fifteen minutes before it has to be plugged back into an electrical source.)

Loading the glue stick is pretty straightforward in all these guns: push the glue stick into the hole at the back, then wait several minutes for the tip of the stick to melt. Once this has happened, dispense the glue through the gun's nozzle by pulling the trigger. Each of the guns performed adequately in extruding a thin, even line of melted glue. However, every nozzle, regardless of its manufacturer's claims, dripped glue when the gun was at rest. For the most part, this was not a serious problem, as the drips that formed rarely fell onto the work surface.

**Testing Bonding Properties**

Any of these guns will give you a sturdy bond in less than sixty seconds, which is the primary advantage to hot glue over other forms of adhesive.

I tested the low-temp guns (and the low-temp setting on the dual-temp guns) by gluing the following materials to themselves: typing paper, balloons, Styrofoam packing filler, sec-

## Hot-Glue Guns in Order of Preference

TOP GUNS

The hot-glue guns were evaluated on a number of points, including overall design, function, and safety. For the most part, the guns don't vary much in their ability to bond a variety of materials (notable exceptions are listed below). Given this, the key factor in ranking the guns became design and comfort. The preferred guns, the Black & Decker dual-temp and the two Crafty guns at right, were the most comfortable to hold over an extended period of time, and rested the most natural in the hand.

The guns are grouped into three categories: high-temp (380 degrees), low-temp (225 to 240 degrees), and dual-temp (guns that can switch back and forth between both temperature ranges). Given a choice between the three categories, I'd recommend a low-temp gun, as it will give you the most flexibility across a variety of craft projects.

A note about prices. All of the guns tested in this article where purchased at either Ben Franklin or Fabric Bonanza; the retail prices you find may vary slightly.

**DUAL-TEMP GUN**
Black & Decker
2-Temp Glue Gun

**HIGH-TEMP GUN**
Crafty's Hot Melt
Duchess

**LOW-TEMP GUN**
Crafty's Magic Melt
Magic Pro

### HIGH-TEMP GUNS

(IN ORDER OF PREFERENCE)

**CRAFTY'S HOT MELT DUCHESS**

**Price:** $9.99
**Performance:** Although this gun requires a longer bonding time (20 to 40 seconds, versus 10 to 20 for other guns in its temperature category), it is very comfortable to use and easily and consistently dispenses an even stream of glue. Although the trigger became hot over time, the gun's comfortable design outweighs this disadvantage.

**WESTEX GLUE GUN**

**Price:** $10.99
**Performance:** This was among the fastest of the guns in bonding aluminum, but the gun's body became hot during use. It is not as comfortable to hold over time as other guns.

**FABRIC BONZANA'S TR IGGER HOT MELT GLUE GUN**

**Price:** $9.50
**Performance:** The Tr Igger features a wedgelike trigger that, when released after depression, can pinch the fingers. The gun is not as comfortable to hold over extended periods of time as some others. It is among the fastest in bonding aluminum.

**CRAFTY'S FULL SIZE HOT MELT**

**Price:** $17.99
**Performance:** Although this gun's trigger became hot during use, the gun is comfortable to use over extended periods of time, which outweighs the hot trigger problem. It was among the slowest in bonding glass, however.

**BEN FRANKLIN'S GLUE GUN**

**Price:** $10.99
**Performance:** This gun is not as comfortable to hold over extended periods of time as some others. Its features are virtually identical to those of the Darice gun, but this gun's body stayed cooler. It was among the fastest in bonding aluminum.

**DARICE'S GLUE GUN**

**Price:** $9.99
**Performance:** The gun's body heats up with extended use. The design is not as comfortable as other guns for extended use.

### LOW-TEMP GUNS

(IN ORDER OF PREFERENCE)

**CRAFTY'S MAGIC MELT MAGIC PRO**

**Price:** $12.99
**Performance:** This gun is slightly smaller than the Crafty Magic Melt gun, making it comfortable for smaller hands. The gun's rounded edges and contoured handle make it comfortable for extended use. This gun operates at slightly higher temperature than the Magic Melt gun, but features a switch designed to control the rate at which the gun dispenses glue, which is a real plus. This was the best performer in consistently extruding a thin, even line of melted glue.

**CRAFTY'S MAGIC MELT**

**Price:** $12.99
**Performance:** The gun's body, which is slightly larger than the other guns, stays cooler over time, a distinct advantage. The trigger is harder to pull, but when depressed, it gives good control over the flow of glue.

### DUAL-TEMP GUNS

(IN ORDER OF PREFERENCE)

**BLACK & DECKER 2-TEMP GLUE GUN**

**Price:** $19.99
**Performance:** Although the handle of this gun is a bit awkward to hold, the gun effectively bonded more materials than the Generic dual-temp gun, and formed bonds quicker than the Surebonder dual-temp gun. The switch for changing the gun's temperature is located on the back of the handle, a placement that makes accidental changes in temperature less likely than the other two guns in this category.

**GENERIC DUAL TEMP GLUE GUN**

**Price:** $10.99
**Performance:** The design of this gun makes it somewhat awkward to hold and not as comfortable as the Black & Decker gun. It is not recommended for gluing plastics, as the gun completely dissolved Styrofoam and bubble wrap during testing. It appears to run hotter than other guns. The switch for changing the gun's temperature is located exactly where the thumb rests when using the gun, making it easy to inadvertently change temperatures.

**SUREBONDER DUAL-TEMPERATURE GLUE GUN**

**Price:** $16.99
**Performance:** This gun is not as comfortable to hold as the Black & Decker gun. The switch for changing the gun's temperature is located where the thumb rests when you're using the gun, making it easy to inadvertently change temperatures. This is the slowest of all the guns in bonding aluminum.

tions of an empty two-liter soda bottle, light-weight plastic bubble-wrap, and quarter-inch Plexiglas. In general, bonding time was almost instant, taking anywhere from ten to sixty seconds.

All the guns successfully bonded the paper and the balloons without causing any surface damage. In the case of plastics, however, results were mixed. The Generic Dual Temp Glue Gun completely melted the Styrofoam, while the Crafty Magic Melt Magic Pro caused minimal but still visible damage. I attributed this to the fact that the Crafty Magic Melt Magic Pro and the Generic Dual Temp Glue Gun appear to run hotter than the other low-temp guns.

None of the guns could successfully bond the plastic soda bottle without severely warping or completely melting it, and the Dual Temp and the Magic Pro guns also melted the bubble wrap. Despite manufacturers' claims to the contrary, I don't recommend using any low-temp glue gun for plastic thinner than a quarter-inch. If you do so, you run the risk of warping or melting the plastic.

For the high-temp guns, I bonded the following materials to themselves: unfinished pine, sections of an empty two-liter plastic soda bottle, sections of an aluminum soda can, and a glass beer bottle. In general, the bonding time was dependent on the materials' density, heat conductivity, and porosity. In some cases, such as with glass, it also appeared that some glue sticks bonded and/or hardened quicker than others.

Although each gun was capable of forming a sturdy bond on wood, the results, as expected, were dismal when it came to plastic. Every test ended in severe melting due, of course, to the high temperature (380 degrees versus 225

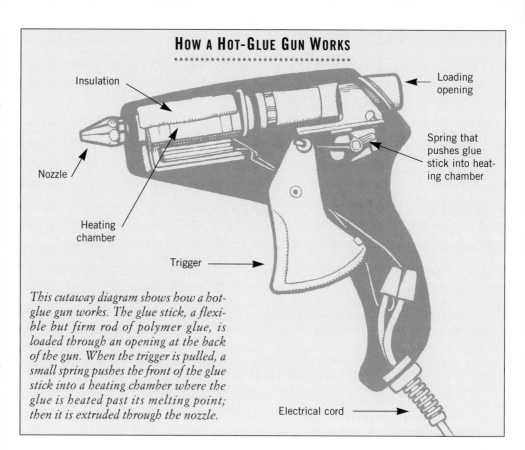

## HOW A HOT-GLUE GUN WORKS

Insulation

Loading opening

Spring that pushes glue stick into heating chamber

Nozzle

Heating chamber

Trigger

Electrical cord

*This cutaway diagram shows how a hot-glue gun works. The glue stick, a flexible but firm rod of polymer glue, is loaded through an opening at the back of the gun. When the trigger is pulled, a small spring pushes the front of the glue stick into a heating chamber where the glue is heated past its melting point; then it is extruded through the nozzle.*

to 240 degrees). The caution against using a hot-glue gun on plastic less than a quarter-inch thick still holds.

### Testing Safety Considerations

Because hot-glue guns require electricity and the glue is heated to at least 225 degrees, I felt safety was an important issue.

Both low- and high-temp guns can—and often do—cause burns. Although low-temp guns were developed, in part, to lower the risk, every experienced hot-glue gun user has probably received at least a slight burn at one time or another. In large part, this is because glue dispensed onto the surface of a project remains hot for eight to twenty-five seconds, and it's within this window of opportunity that the second material or object is pressed into place. Any glue that squeezes out from between the materials can stick to your fingers and cause a burn. While most hot-glue guns come with fairly explicit warnings regarding how to avoid burns (such as advising you never to touch the gun's nozzle) and how to treat accidental burns (telling you to place the burned area in cold water), it doesn't appear as though hot-glue gun manufacturers have developed a foolproof way to eliminate burns. Many manufacturers are working on developing safer guns, however, and current models can be used safely and effectively when a few simple precautions are taken.

To evaluate the safety of the guns, I plugged each one into an outlet and let it sit for two hours, a time chosen because it seemed like

long enough to complete a typical project. After two hours, the plastic housing of the gun itself usually becomes hot. This is not serious as long as the trigger and handle remain cool, but such was not the case with the Crafty Full Size Hot Melt or Hot Melt Duchess. This is of some concern, since it is impossible to operate the guns comfortably when the triggers are hot. It should be noted, however, that the two Crafty guns whose triggers became hot can be used for shorter periods of time if their positive features outweigh this drawback.

In some ways, the time it takes for a gun to cool down is more important than the time it takes for a gun to heat up. Although the guns took various periods of time to heat up, they all took at least an hour to cool down to the point where they could be stored safely. When you're finished using your glue gun, I recommend you keep it unplugged on its stand in an open space until it is cool to the touch. Don't test the coolness by touching the nozzle, or you might burn yourself; instead, feel the body of the gun. If the plastic is warm, wait at least another half an hour. Once the body is cool, touch the nozzle of the gun to a plastic surface, such as an empty two-liter soda bottle; if the nozzle does not leave a mark, the gun is cool enough to store upright on an open shelf. Guns that are completely cool can be stored in a box or drawer, but *be absolutely certain* the gun is cool to avoid the risk of fire. ◆

**Rodney Sterbenz** is a full-time student at New York University.

# Decorating with Decoupage

*Transform any wall or flat surface using simple decoupage techniques and the antique prints on this issue's insert.*

This article will teach you how to decorate a flat surface, such as a wall, a kitchen cupboard, or a closet door, using a series of simple decoupage techniques and the antique botanicals and prints on this issue's insert.

All decoupage projects require three main steps: preparing the surface, attaching the images with some form of adhesive, and sealing the surface. In this project, the surface is prepared with a coat of acrylic urethane or other water-based, clear liquid varnish. The prints on this issue's insert are first photocopied, then attached to the wall with matte medium or Mod Podge. Once the prints are adhered in place, the surface is sealed with several thin coats of the acrylic urethane or other water-based varnish.

The antique botanical and bird prints found on this issue's insert (*see* following pages) can be enlarged and used to decorate a foyer or bathroom, or kept at their original size and used to decorate a smaller space.

This project is essentially a smaller variation of a full-size print room. Print rooms, which were popular in the eighteenth century, were created by gluing engravings directly on the wall, then "framing" the prints with paper borders, "hanging" them with fanciful bows and ornaments, and linking them with swags and garlands. Many print rooms mixed different types of rectangles, ovals, octagons, or circles containing landscapes, sporting scenes, drawings of stately homes or churches, or ancestral portraits.

We do not know for certain what type of glue was used in the eighteenth century, since so few original print rooms still exist for examination, but reasonable guesses include gum arabic, warm varnish, egg whites, or flour-and-water paste (similar to what you may have used as a child). Such paste had to be boiled in a double boiler, stored in a tightly sealed container, and used within a few days before it spoiled. Today's matte media are ready to use without mixing and are nontoxic, fast-drying, and odor-free. Like substances bond better with like substances, so it's important that all the products in your decoupage project be acrylic or water-based for compatibility. In addition, we recommend matte medium versus glossy medium, as it adheres in a tighter bond.

Before gluing the prints in place, it's important to prepare the surface. First and foremost, the wall must be level and smooth and be covered with matte or semigloss paint. The varnishes and glues used for this project will not adhere to glossy paint, so you may need to repaint. The wall (or whatever surface you're using) must also be completely free from dirt, dust, and grease. (Semigloss walls can be washed with a sponge and a bucket of warm water and detergent. Matte walls may need repainting.)

Once the wall is clean and dry, apply a layer of acrylic urethane or other clear varnish using a roller to smooth out

*The decoupage arrangement shown here can be duplicated in a small foyer or bathroom, or expanded to fill a larger space using multiple prints.*

and fill in any small imperfections. The urethane seals the wall surface against water and ensures that the paper lies perfectly smooth against the surface, without any bumps or ridges.

For the final composition shown in the photograph above, we used a photocopier to enlarge the prints by 200 percent onto off-white bond paper. (Bond paper is stronger than standard copy paper, and we like the off-white images against the pale green background.) Be sure to copy the larger bows for use with the largest botanical print. As a precaution against smudging or smearing, we recommend spraying two thin coats of acrylic sealer on the front of each photocopied image.

Choosing a tool for cutting out the images is a matter of personal preference. We find that straight scissors work best on straight lines, while curved scissors work best for curved lines. You may prefer an X-Acto knife or scalpel. If you do, be sure to work on a protective cutting surface, such as a self-healing cutting mat. We recommend trimming the ornamental picture hangers off the smaller prints and handling them separately.

How you arrange the prints on the wall is also a matter of personal taste. The arrangement above could easily be duplicated in a small foyer, or expanded, by making several copies of each print, to fill a larger space. For variation, consider enlarging some prints and reducing others by varying amounts. If you opt to create your own design, keep in mind that the success of a print room composition depends on maintaining careful balance, as well as interesting and varied space, between the images. Play around with various compositions before gluing anything in place.

Arrange the prints to your liking, then affix each one to the surface with dots of putty adhesive, such as Fun-Tak or UHU Holdit. To align the prints, you can use a variety of tools, such as a T-square or a carpenter's level, but we recommend using a plumb line. Such a device, also useful in hanging wallpaper, is easily assembled using a plumb bob (available at most hardware stores) or a large lead sinker (available at sporting goods stores) and an eight- to ten-foot length of string. Have a partner hold the free end of the plumb line against the wall, as close to the ceiling as possible, or tack the line in place with a thumb tack. The weight of the plumb bob will pull the string straight. Square up the print with the plumb line and mark the correct placement by outlining the print with chalk.

Before attaching the prints to the wall, coat them on both sides with matte medium for added strength. When dry, the matte medium encases the paper, giving it an ultrathin, transparent seal that prevents the image from stretching or tearing when you mount it on the wall. (If you are mounting images larger than eleven by seventeen inches, it may be useful to wet-mount the images. Although not required for this project, wet-mounting makes it easier to control large pieces of paper that might otherwise buckle or wrinkle in the gluing process. In addition, the images shrink and lie flat as they dry. To wet-mount prints, sandwich each one between two wet Handiwipes for ten minutes to dampen and stretch the paper. Then coat the back of the wet print or the area within the chalk outline on the wall with matte medium. Lift the print with both hands, and starting at the top edge of the chalked outline, roll the print downwards, pressing it onto the surface with a damp Handiwipe. Cover the print with the Handiwipe and roll it flat with a brayer (a small roller usually used in the graphic arts industry or for applying ink), then clean away any excess glue.

The next coat of matte medium or Mod Podge is used as glue. Don't use white glue, as it dries too quickly, leaving little time for adjustments. When applying medium to the picture, it's better to be generous and wipe off any extra than to be too skimpy. Apply an even coat over the back of the image using a disposable foam brush. The edges will dry first; if they do not have enough glue on them, they will lift as they dry. Once the image is coated, place it within the chalk outline, then roll out any air bubbles or wrinkles and remove any excess medium using any one of several devices: a brayer, a wooden dowel, a smooth glass bottle, or a rolling pin. Start rolling at the center of the print and roll outward. Attach the picture hangers and bows in the same manner.

When the glue is dry, examine all the prints' edges, inch by inch, to make sure they're securely adhered. If any edges pop up, apply a dot of matte medium under them using a toothpick, press the loose edge against the wall, wipe off any excess medium that squeezes out, and roll the print back down with the brayer or dowel.

If an air bubble appears in the middle of a print, it should be eliminated. If possible, find a black line in the image above the bubble, and slice along the line using a single-edge razor blade. Apply glue under the paper on both sides of the cut with a toothpick, then press the cut area down with your finger until it adheres. If the bubble occurs in a solid white area, use a pin or a very thin sewing needle to prick a hole in the paper, then apply a tiny dot of glue into the hole using the pin or needle and press with your fingertip until the glue sets. (Wet-mounting also helps reduce the number of air bubbles, so consider using that method if needed.)

A final coat of acrylic urethane or other clear varnish protects the decoupage surface from dirt, increases its water resistance, fills any imperfections, and smoothes the transition from the edge of the print to the wall. One note about such varnishes: Be wary of varnishes that claim to "dry clear." Many such products actually only dry clear for one coat, but take on a yellowish cast when multiple coats are used. In our experience, acrylic urethane stays clear even after multiple coats.

### DECORATING WITH DECOUPAGE

Botanical and bird images (*see* special insert, following pages)
Off-white bond paper
Matte medium or matte Mod Podge
Acrylic urethane or other water-based, clear liquid varnish
Acrylic spray sealer

*You'll also need:* access to a photocopier with enlarging capabilities; short nap paint roller with extension handle and paint tray; tack cloth; rubber brayer, smooth glass bottle, rolling pin, or 1"-diameter wooden dowel; X-Acto knife, straight scissors, or scalpel; curved manicure scissors or X-Acto knife; 1"- or 2"-wide disposable foam brush; Handiwipes; wax paper; chalk; stepladder or step stool; removable putty adhesive; any size plumb bob or large lead sinker; 8' to 10' length of string; and brown paper or drop cloth.

*Other items, if necessary:* self-healing cutting mat or other protective surface and metal straightedge (if using X-Acto knife or scalpel); thumb tack (for attaching plumb line); single-edge razor blade, toothpicks, straight pin, and/or thin hand-sewing needle (for eliminating air bubbles).

1. Cover floor with drop cloth. Roll coat of acrylic urethane finish over clean, dry wall. Let dry at least 4 hours, but preferably overnight. (Follow manufacturer's recommendations.)
2. Photocopy images onto off-white bond paper, enlarging 200 percent. Trim off (but don't cut out) ornamental picture hangers, and handle separately in steps that follow.

3. Work in a well-ventilated room, and cover the work surface with brown paper or drop cloth. Following manufacturer's directions, spray thin coat of acrylic sealer on front of all photocopies, including picture hangers. Let dry, then apply second coat. Let dry completely.
4. Spread all photocopies face (sealer side) up on wax paper. Using foam brush, evenly coat front of each print with matte medium; let dry 20 minutes. Turn images over and coat backs; let dry 20 minutes. Wash out foam brush with water. (When dry, prints may be stacked with wax paper interleaved between them.)
5. If using X-Acto knife and metal straightedge, work on a self-healing cutting mat or other protective surface. Cut out all prints. Use straight scissors or X-Acto knife and metal straightedge to cut along straight edges; use curved manicure scissors or X-Acto for longer curved edges. Cut out background and interior areas of bows and picture hangers using manicure scissors or X-Acto knife.
6. Arrange prints on wall, using photograph on page 15 as reference if desired. Affix each with small dots of putty adhesive. Step back to check overall effect. Have partner stand on stepladder or step stool and suspend plumb line down wall, holding free end of plumb line against wall, as close to ceiling as possible, or if alone attach plumb line to wall using tack. Plumb line should almost touch floor. Using string as a guide, moving it along wall as necessary, correct any crooked or misaligned images. As each print is aligned, lightly outline cutout with chalk.
7. Take down and glue prints in place one at a time. Start by removing print and putty from wall, then wipe wall with tack cloth to remove any stray particles.

Working atop wax paper, apply matte medium on back of print, spreading it evenly across entire surface and out to edges using foam brush. Position print, wet side against wall, within chalked outline, and press in place using damp Handiwipe. Cover image with new, dampened Handiwipe and roll brayer, dowel, or other device across surface, working from center outwards to press out air bubbles and excess matte medium. (If necessary, use razor blade or other device to remove air bubbles as described in introduction.) Lift cloth and wipe away any remaining medium from edges before it dries, removing chalk marks in process. Repeat with remaining prints, then attach picture hangers and bows using same method. Let dry at least overnight.
8. Seal wall by rolling coat of acrylic urethane or other clear varnish over the entire surface. ◆

Special thanks to **Dee Davis** and **Wendy Brainerd** of the Adventures in Crafts Studio of New York for consulting on this piece.

# Decorating with Decoupage

These antique botanical and bird prints are designed for you to use in decorating a flat surface, such as a wall, a kitchen cupboard, or a closet door, using decoupage techniques. Before proceeding, photocopy the prints onto off-white bond paper, enlarging them by 200 percent. Be sure to copy the larger bows for use with the largest botanical print.

You can also use the enlarged prints to decorate a small foyer or bathroom, or keep the prints at their original size and decorate a smaller space. ◆

# Lacework Teacloth

*Stitch up this elegant teacloth for under $25 using dinner napkins and lace.*

You can sew up this lacework teacloth in under two hours using four sixteen-inch-square polyester-blend napkins and two widths of acetate lace. Napkins, unlike cloth, require no hemming, which significantly shortens the time required to make this project. Measuring just over thirty-six inches square, this teacloth works well on a small tea or coffee table, such as the one shown in the photograph at right, or as an accent over a larger tablecloth of a different color.

The original design for this tablecloth was a four-by-four arrangement of plain cotton napkins joined by crochet lace. The result, however, was less than satisfactory. Even at the stage where

we pinned the design together, the napkins did not line up, since the crochet lace was easily pulled out of shape as its threads stretched. Cotton crochet lace is extremely difficult to sew as it's apt to get caught in the foot of the sewing machine. Opting for an all-cotton design was also prohibitively expensive. Although we purchased four cotton napkins for about $2.00 each, we needed just over ten yards of cotton crochet lace, which cost anywhere from $13.00 to $20.00 a yard!

In our search for lace that was both elegant and inexpensive, and napkins that wouldn't shrink when washed, we ended up with white sixteen-inch-square polyester-blend napkins with a simple woven pattern and two styles of

machine-made acetate lace. The napkins, priced at $1.50 each, kept their shape after washing, and the two styles of lace, which averaged $1.50 per yard, were less expensive and easier to sew than the cotton lace. The total cost was less than $25.00.

The first three steps of this project involve joining the napkins together with one-inch-wide flat lace. (This lace doesn't need hemming, as its raw edges are ultimately sewn under the scalloped lace.) For this process, overlap the lace

*For a coordinated table setting, use the same napkins for sewing the teacloth and setting your table.*

onto the edge of the napkin an eighth to a quarter of an inch, and allow a half inch to extend beyond each end. Pin the lace in place, then sew it using a narrow zigzag stitch. After the lace has been sewn in place, trim off the half-inch ends even with the edges of the napkin.

Once the napkins have been joined together and edged with one-inch-wide flat lace, attach the scalloped lace to all four sides of the teacloth. Overlap the scalloped lace by a quarter inch. Before attaching the last two lengths, you'll need to stitch a quarter-inch hem on both ends.

### ASSEMBLING THE TEACLOTH

**1.** Press the napkins with an iron set to the appropriate heat setting. Arrange the napkins on a flat surface to form a square, leaving about 1" of space between them. Cut two 17" lengths of the flat lace. Place each length

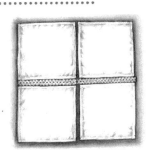

of lace horizontally between two of the napkins, and pin them in place, overlapping the napkin edges by ⅛" to ¼". Stitch the lace to the napkins using a narrow zigzag stitch. Trim the ends of the lace even with the edges of the napkins.

**3.** Cut two 36" lengths of the flat lace. Pin them along the top and bottom edges, overlapping the napkins by ⅛" to ¼" and stitch them in place with a zigzag stitch, then trim the lace ends even with the edges of the napkins.

**2.** Cut three 34" lengths of the flat lace. Pin one length between the two sets of joined napkins, overlapping onto them by ⅛" to ¼". Pin the two remaining lengths along the left and right side, overlapping onto them by ⅛" to ¼". Stitch all three pieces in place using a narrow zigzag stitch, then trim the ends of the lace even with the napkins.

**4.** Cut two 36" and two 40" lengths of the scalloped lace. Pin the 36" lengths in place along the side edges, overlapping the flat lace by ¼", and stitch them in place, then trim the ends of the lace even with the outside of the flat lace. Fold the ends of each 40"-length of scalloped lace ¼" to the wrong side to make a hem, and zigzag this hem in place. Pin these pieces of lace to the top and bottom edges of the teacloth, lining up the hemmed edges with the scalloped lace on the sides, and stitch them in place using a narrow zigzag stitch.

### LACEWORK TEACLOTH

4 16"-square polyester-blend napkins
5⅞ yards 1"-wide flat white acetate lace
4¼ yards 1¾"-wide scalloped white acetate lace
Matching thread

*You'll also need:* zigzag sewing machine; ruler or yardstick; straight pins; iron; and scissors.◆

# Antique Brass Frames

*Transform an ordinary brass frame into a Victorian antique using stamped metal findings and a simple patinating solution.*

### BY MICHIO RYAN

These tarnished brass frames are not the antiques they appear to be. Replicating their oxidized look, however, is a relatively quick process: attach stamped metal findings to an ordinary brass frame, then imitate the effects of age with a bottled patinating formula.

The commercial patinating solution I recommend, Modern Options' Flemish Gray, is designed to replicate in just a few seconds the natural tarnish or corrosion that appears over time when silver is exposed to air. The Flemish Gray solution, one of a few ready-mixed patinating solutions available through retail sources, and by far the easiest to use, creates a nice tarnished finish on solid brass or brass-plated frames and findings. When choosing your frames and findings, avoid "gold-tone" metal frames, which are almost always made from anodized aluminum, or findings made from aluminum or steel, since none of these metals will patinate. The Flemish Gray formula works nicely on solid copper or copper-plated frames and findings if you can find them, but these are less common than brass. If it's not clearly stated on the frames, or you're not sure of the metal, ask before you buy it.

I recommend choosing the stamped metal findings first, and then looking for an appropriate size frame. Most of the findings I found were one- to one-and-three-quarters-inches wide and look best on frames no larger than five by seven inches. I tried a few findings on an eight-by-ten-inch frame, but the proportions were wrong, and the findings looked lost. (Larger findings are more difficult to find, so it's best to keep the entire project to a small scale.)

Although I tested a number of better-made frames, even poorly made ones with gaps at the corners can be rescued with cleverly placed findings. I recommend buying very plain frames or ones with minimal surface decoration as these set off the findings best. Flutings and beads at the edges of the frame are acceptable as long as enough area remains to attach the findings. Flat-faced frames work best because they provide a large flat area on which to glue the findings. Curved frames such as ovals can be used if the points of contact form a triangle to adequately support the finding.

Virtually all new brass frames have a pro-tective transparent lacquer finish (to prevent tarnishing) which needs to be removed before patinating. I tested both lacquer thinner and paint stripper for this process, and I recommend paint stripper. The lacquer thinner was faster, but did not remove all the lacquer at the corner joints or in the nooks and crannies of the frame. When I tried using very fine (#0000) steel wool with the lacquer thinner on the nooks and crannies, the steel wool left tiny scratches which were visible after patinating. When shopping for paint stripper, avoid products that contain methylene chloride, as it is both flammable and toxic. I recommend 3M's Safest Stripper paint remover, a safer, water-based stripper that worked quite consistently.

Note: In the testing process, I found a few frames on which the paint stripper did not work. Instead of going on smoothly like paint, the stripper beaded up on the frame's surface. For these frames, I used acetone, the primary ingredient in nail polish remover. If you must use acetone, it can be purchased most inexpensively in a hardware store. To use it, pour a small amount in a shallow glass or tin container (don't use plastic, as acetone disintegrates some plastics) and use a cotton ball or Q-tip to rub away the lacquer. (As with paint stripper, steel wool is also effective here, but may leave tiny scratches.)

Lacquer can also be removed with either Noxon 7 or denatured alcohol, but you'll have to rub harder and longer with these. *Always work in a well-ventilated area when using chemical solutions such as paint stripper, acetone, or alcohol.* Cover your work space with newspaper, wear gloves and protective eye wear, and keep in mind that such chemicals are extremely flammable.

Don't expect the frame to change color after you've removed the lacquer, since you're removing a clear coating. Any remaining lac-

*You can create antiques from modern brass frames in minutes using a bottled patinating solution.*

quer will be visible as hazy areas.

Once the lacquer has been removed, clean any oil off the frame using denatured alcohol. (If you're using acetone, this is not necessary, as the acetone will have stripped off any oils.) Next, attach the findings. The best method is to solder them on, but this is a difficult process. With care, a strong epoxy adhesive will work nearly as well. I recommend the "five-minute" epoxy rather than the "two-ton" epoxy; although the latter is stronger, it takes much longer to set. Many epoxies, such as Devcon, come in a double tube dispenser, which is easy to use because it simultaneously dispenses the correct amount of each component. Follow the manufacturer's instructions for the best results. Epoxy comes in both a clear and a colored form (gray or black). I recommend the colored form since it's easier to see exactly where you're putting it, but both work equally well for this particular project.

Once the findings are attached to the frame, you can apply the Flemish Gray formula. (Remember to keep all patinating solutions out of the reach of children, wear latex gloves and eye goggles, work in a well-ventilated area, and always follow the manufacturer's instructions.) Within seconds, the frames and findings should turn a beautiful bluish gray-black. If sections of the frame or findings do not turn color, there may be hardened epoxy or residual oil or lacquer on them preventing the chemical reaction. Remove oil or lacquer with a cotton ball and denatured alcohol; remove epoxy with the tip of a sharp knife blade (being careful not to scratch the frame), and clean the frame or finding with denatured alcohol when you're done. This process will also remove most of the patination that has already taken place. When the metal is dry, reapply the Flemish Gray solution.

Before sealing the frames with a coat of clear spray lacquer, you'll want to highlight the relief areas of the findings by buffing with very fine steel wool until the brass begins to show. For a more antiqued look, allow the deep crevices to remain dark. Buff the low areas of relief with a soft cloth. For an overall lighter finish, lightly buff the entire frame with soft cloth until the silver-black finish starts turning a warmer brass color.

The tarnishing techniques described in this article can also be applied to solid brass or brass-plated boxes, hand mirrors, and other decorative objects.

## ANTIQUE BRASS FRAMES

Brass findings and frames as follows:

3½" x 5" rectangular frame
4 corner findings

2" x 3" rectangular frame
3"-wide finding with center motif

2" x 3" oval frame
2½"-wide finding with center motif

Modern Options Flemish Gray patina
   solution
Clear spray lacquer
5-minute epoxy adhesive
Very fine (#0000) steel wool
3M's Safest Stripper paint remover
Denatured alcohol (smallest amount)

*You'll also need:* protective eye wear; emery board; small plastic container; toothpicks or other small wooden sticks; plastic food wrap; old clean toothbrush; at least 2 pairs disposable latex gloves; ¾"-wide masking tape; dishwashing detergent; soft cloth; 1"-wide disposable paintbrush; 1"-wide bristle paintbrush; paper towels; index cards or paper plates; and newspaper.

*Other items, if necessary:* Noxon 7 metal cleaner/polish and a second old, clean toothbrush (for cleaning dirty findings); and acetone, shallow glass or tin container, and cotton balls or Q-tips (to strip lacquer off certain frames).

### Preparing the Frames

Always work in a well-ventilated area when using chemical solutions such as paint stripper or patinating solution. Cover the work space with newspaper, and wear gloves and protective eye wear. (Always read the manufacturer's directions before using paint stripper, as stripping times vary.)

1. Remove backing, stand, and glass from frames and set aside in a safe place. Using dis-

### ATTACHING THE FINDINGS

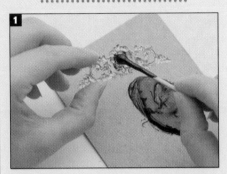

**1.** Fill in any concave areas on the backs of the findings with epoxy, then let them set for about 10 minutes.

**2.** Hold the findings up to the frame to determine their approximate positions, then lightly abrade the contact points with the tip of the emery board to improve adhesion.

### ANTIQUING THE FRAME

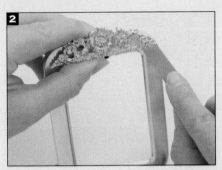

**3.** Apply the patinating solution to the frames and findings with a clean bristle brush, making sure you brush the solution into any crevices.

posable paintbrush, cover frames with paint stripper. Wrap frames with plastic food wrap and set aside for no longer than manufacturer's directions specify. (If necessary, use acetone for stripping as described in introduction.)

2. Unwrap frames from plastic and remove stripper with paper towels. Gently scrub out softened lacquer from crevices. When completely stripped, wash frame with warm water and dishwashing detergent, and dry with paper towels.

3. If using tarnished or dirty findings, apply metal cleaner with clean toothbrush. (Skip this step for shiny, new findings.) Clean *all* findings with denatured alcohol and clean toothbrush to remove oily residues, then dry findings with paper towels.

4. Mix epoxy on index card or paper plate following manufacturer's directions. (Make about a teaspoon, and make more as you run out.) Turn findings to backside; use toothpick or small wooden stick to fill in concave portion with epoxy. Put aside to set following manufacturer's recommendations, about 10 minutes.

5. Hold findings up to frame to determine positioning, then lightly abrade contact points on frame with tip of emery board to improve adhesion. Mix second batch of epoxy and apply small (⅛") dots of epoxy to abraded contact points. (Don't let epoxy flow beyond edge of finding, or it will prevent patinating solution from reacting.) Remove extra epoxy before it hardens with clean toothpick or wooden stick. Tape findings in place with masking tape and set aside to dry, frame facing down, following manufacturer's directions, at least 10 minutes.

### Antiquing the Frames

1. Remove tape from frames and findings. Before proceeding, examine findings to make sure they are securely in place. If not, wait until epoxy is hard. Pour 1 tablespoon patinating solution into small plastic container. Remove any residual oil from frames using paper towel dipped in alcohol. Place frames face up on newspaper. Apply patinating solution to frames and findings with bristle paintbrush, taking care to brush inside crevices. Apply additional solution as necessary until entire frame has changed to an even, bluish gray-black.

2. Rinse frames thoroughly with warm water and pat dry with paper towels. Do not rub frame while rinsing or patinated finish may rub off. Set aside to dry for 5 minutes.

3. Using steel wool, highlight higher relief areas of findings. Use soft cloth to buff low areas of relief. For overall lighter finish, lightly buff entire frame with soft cloth until silver-black begins turning to warmer brass color.

4. Cover workspace with newspaper, then seal frame with coat of clear spray lacquer. Let dry completely. Restore glass, backing, and stand to frame. ◆

# Panoramic Photo Album

*Learn how to take your own panoramic photos and create a hand-bound album for displaying them.*

BY SYLVIA LACHTER

This article will teach you how to take panoramic photos and how to create a photo album for displaying your panoramas. The hand-bound album, made using cardboard, paper, glue, and book cloth, can be assembled in less than three hours.

For some time I have taken my own panoramic photographs using a standard point-and-shoot camera. The process is fairly simple: I break the scene into four to six segments, shoot each segment as a separate four-by-six-inch photo, then line up the photos side by side to create a panoramic view. After creating hundreds of these photographs over the years, I decided to organize and preserve them by putting them in albums. When I found no existing album could accommodate their unusual size, I designed my own hand-bound ten-by-twenty-three-and-one-half-inch album.

If you're not familiar with panoramic photographs, I've included instructions on how to create your own. (*See* "How to Shoot a Panoramic Series of Photos," below.) The album described here can be adjusted to accommodate photos measuring three and one half inches by nine and three fourths inches produced by disposable panoramic cameras, which range in price from about $8 to $19, or those produced by more expensive, non-disposable panoramic cameras. To make this smaller-sized album, follow the main directions, but substitute the measurements provided in "A Smaller Version of the Panoramic Album," page 21.

The first decision I had to make when designing my album was

*These panoramic photos, assembled from four or five standard-size photos, turn an everyday scene into a wide-angle work of art.*

size. The width of my panoramic photos varied a great deal, depending on the number of photos taken and the amount of overlap between them. For some scenes, I combined six photos for a total width of almost thirty inches. Most of my shots, however, measured about twenty inches wide. I settled on twenty-three and one half inches by ten inches, because it would give me a nice frame around the pictures I shot holding my camera horizontally while still accommodating those shot holding the camera vertically. Because of the extreme width of the page, it made sense to have the book open from bottom to top, and to put the binding along the top edge.

I recommend using acid-free paper (or as close to acid-free as possible) when making the album, since paper that contains acid will discolor your photos over time. White acid-free paper can easily be found at most art supply or paper stores ; nearly acid-free paper is generally available in other colors. For my albums I chose black paper because I prefer the way it

## HOW TO SHOOT A PANORAMIC SERIES OF PHOTOS

I've been shooting panoramas for years as a comprehensive and effective way of documenting my travels, parties, or favorite vistas. You don't need to invest in expensive equipment to do this—any point-and-shoot camera will work.

Most point-and-shoot cameras are rangefinder cameras. When you look through the viewfinder of a rangefinder camera, you're not looking directly through the lens, so what you see is not exactly what the camera sees. To ensure that your panorama won't have any breaks in it because of this, shoot the pictures so they overlap slightly.

It's nice to have a tripod to help you keep the image level as you pan across your vista, but I rarely use one. I just take a deep breath, brace my elbows against my body to keep the camera steady, and shoot.

I start by finding my center frame, the point of interest that I want to build my panoramic picture around. After quickly scanning the image right to left or left to right, I start shooting. I usually start on the left side, shoot the first frame, then move right to the next frame, leaving a small overlap between them. I continue this process with the third, fourth, or however many pictures

I choose to shoot. On average I generally shoot four to six pictures per panorama, though at times I've shot as many as seven or eight. Remember, you can hold the camera horizontally or vertically. The ones shot vertically are interesting because they give you a bigger image.

The next step comes when you get the prints back from processing. To assemble the panorama, lay the prints out face up and overlap them to form a continuous image. Once you've composed the panorama, take the first print and run half the width of a piece of transparent tape along the edge, then position the second print on top of it so it's properly aligned and held in place by the tape. (You should always tape the backs together—never put the tape on the front of the photos.) Continue in this manner across the panorama until you have it completely assembled. Some people like to use dabs of glue to put their pictures together, but I prefer Scotch Removable Magic Tape because it allows for easy repositioning. Generally, the top and bottom edges of an assembled panorama will not be perfectly straight, although I see this as a creative element. But if you like, you can trim the edges using a metal straightedge and an X-Acto knife.

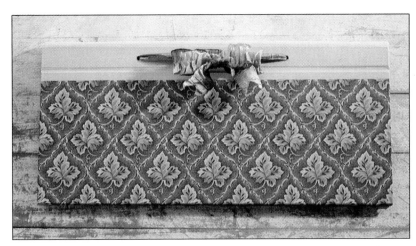

*You can create a library of panoramic photo albums by changing the album's cover paper and ribbon.*

frames color pictures, but white or off-white will work equally well, particularly for a wedding album. You can purchase paper close to the size you want or in larger sheets; both will need to be cut down to an exact size using a long metal straightedge and an X-Acto knife with a sharp blade.

Before you purchase your paper, poke around the store. I recommend feeling several different paper samples. To gauge their texture and weight better, rub the corner of each sample sheet between your forefinger and thumb. In large part, paper selection is a matter of personal taste, but some guidelines are appropriate.

In most countries outside the United States, paper weight is expressed in grams per square meter ($g/m^2$), meaning a square meter of paper weighs so many grams. Airmail paper weighs around 45 $g/m^2$; copy machine paper around 80 $g/m^2$. Above 250 $g/m^2$, paper officially becomes card. Using this method of measurement, you can compare any paper, regardless of sheet size.

Most paper stores describe their papers as either text or cover. Within these two categories they subdivide papers into light-, medium-, or heavyweight, according to their weight. (Some may list actual poundage, but many do not.) Paper is usually arranged in bins with the type of paper, weight, and color clearly marked. For the outside cover of the album, I recommend using medium- or heavyweight cover paper, although any weight cover stock

will work. For the inside front and back covers I recommend using mediumweight text paper, which can also be used for the album pages. Choose the same paper for the divider strips (the small strips separating the pages) as the pages; this way the pages and divider strips will blend nicely. Remember that every book is unique—unless measured precisely, there will always be some variation. If necessary, trim any papers before gluing them in place in order to create smooth, even edges.

The album shell (the outer part, which is later covered) should be made from firm three- or four-ply cardboard stock. When buying book cloth and wire-edged ribbon, find a color that matches or coordinates with your cover paper. (If you prefer unwired ribbon, *see* illustration 14 on page 23 for instructions on how to thread it through the album's holes using a paper clip.)

While making the album, I tested a variety of squeeze-bottle glues. Sobo high-tack glue performs better than Elmer's when working with hard-to-adhere edges and thick paper. Sobo glue becomes tacky almost immediately after application, which makes it easier to glue the paper edges in place. Elmer's, on the other hand, allowed the paper to curl back, which meant I had to weight it down with books in order to have it dry flat.

I chose to spread the glue with a cardboard strip instead of a paintbrush. High-tack glue has a viscous consistency that makes it difficult to spread over a large surface with a brush.

When applying high-tack glue, I recommend covering your work surface with brown kraft paper, because the ink in newspaper can rub off onto the project or your fingers. To apply the high-tack glue, work on the wrong side of the paper. Squeeze a line of glue about one-quarter inch in from the edge of the paper, then immediately squeeze a zigzag line across the remaining paper. Drag the cardboard strip from the center of the paper outward, past the paper's edge and onto the kraft paper to ensure strong adhesion along the edge of the paper. Repeat this procedure on the surface where the paper will be adhered. (If the corners or edges curl back, weight the glued paper with heavy books and let it dry for half an hour more.)

Once the book is assembled, you'll need to drill holes through the covers and pages to bind the book. Any quarter-inch drill bit will work, but I recommend using a brad point drill bit, as it gives a very clean cut. (Brad point drill bits are available in most hardware stores.)

### PANORAMIC PHOTO ALBUM

1 sheet 20" x 26" decorative medium- or heavyweight cover paper for outside front and back covers
1 sheet 16" x 24" decorative mediumweight text paper for inside front and back covers
5 sheets 40" x 26" medium-weight text paper for album pages and divider sheets
1 sheet 22" x 23½" 3- or 4-ply cardboard stock for album shell
1 foot 28"-wide book cloth for album binding
2½ yards 1½"-wide wire-edged or standard ribbon
Sobo high-tack glue

*You'll also need:* hand or electric drill with ¼" drill bit (preferably brad point); 2 pieces scrap wood measuring approximately 23½" x 4" x ¾"; 2 C-clamps with 6" openings; cutting mat or other protective device for work surface; brown kraft paper; 2" x 6" strip of cardboard; scissors; metal 30" (or longer) straightedge; utility knife; X-Acto knife; brayer or other burnishing tool; felt marker; pencil; and any size clean paintbrush.

*Other items, if necessary:* paper clip (for using as hook with non-wire-edged ribbon). ◆

---

## A SMALLER VERSION OF THE PANORAMIC ALBUM

You can make a smaller version of the album (it measures 9" x 13") for the 3½" x 9¾" panoramic photos taken with disposable panoramic cameras. Follow the directions outlined for the larger album, but substitute the following measurements.

**1.** Cut 3 pieces of cardboard: front cover: 7¾" x 13"; hinge: 1" x 13"; back cover: 9" x 13". Cut 2 pieces of book cloth: 6" x 17" and 6" x 11".
**2.** When gluing the cardboard pieces to a 6" x 17" piece of book cloth, let 1" of extra book cloth extend out on each side. The book cloth should overlap the front cover by 1½" and the back cover by 2½". Leave ¼" between the front cover and the hinge; leave ¾" between the hinge and the back cover.
**3.** Cut 2 sheets of cover paper measuring 8¾" x 15". When measuring from the bottom edge of the front cover to the hinge, place your marks at 7¾". Allow 1" of paper to extend beyond the sides of the covers.
**4.** Cut 2 sheets of inside cover paper: 7½" x 12½".
**5.** Cut 17 sheets of album page paper: 8¾" x 12½". Cut 16 divider strips: 1" x 12½".
**6.** Draw a straight line on one piece of the wood ½" in from one long edge. Mark drill points on this line at 3½", 5", 8", and 9½".

# Making the Panoramic Photo Album

For the cutting in steps 1 and 5, work on a large, flat surface, and use a cutting mat or other material heavy enough to protect your work surface. Use a metal straightedge and a utility knife to cut the cardboard. Use an X-Acto knife to cut the paper and the book cloth. For the gluing processes, cover the work surface with kraft paper. The gluing technique is outlined in step 2; repeat as necessary during other steps.

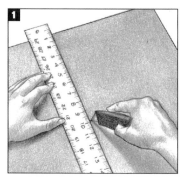

**1.** Lay the cardboard flat and cut three pieces with the following dimensions: front cover, 8¼" x 23½"; hinge, 1½" x 23½"; back cover, 10" x 23½". Cut two pieces of book cloth with the following measurements: 6" x 27½" and 6" x 21½".

**2.** To assemble the album cover shell, lay the front cover, hinge, and back cover pieces on the wrong side of the 6" x 27½" piece of book cloth, using measurements in the illustration for placement. Glue down the pieces by squeezing a line of glue about ¼" from the edge of the cardboard (or paper), then immediately squeeze a zigzag line of glue across the remaining paper. Brush the glue from the center of the paper out to the edges using the cardboard strip; repeat the process on the book cloth. Press the two surfaces firmly together with your fingers, and roll a brayer or burnishing tool firmly across them to ensure adhesion.

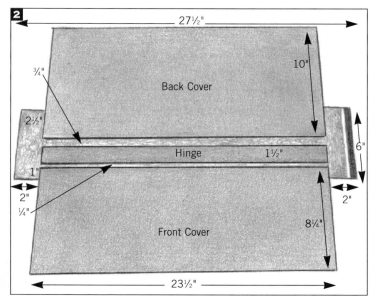

**3.** Apply glue to the 2" book cloth extensions on each side, then fold the book cloth to the inside of the album shell. Press it down with your fingers and burnish it with a brayer or burnishing tool.

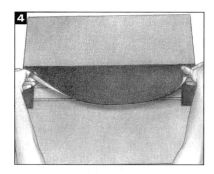

**4.** Apply glue to the 6" x 21½" piece of book cloth, then press it in place as shown, aligning the edges and overlapping the book cloth extensions in step 3 by 1". (From this point on, the side of the shell where you attached this second piece of book cloth is referred to as the *inside* of the album shell; the other side is the *outside* of the album shell.)

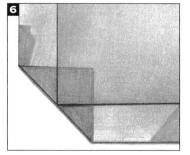

**5.** Cut two pieces of outside cover paper measuring 9¼" x 25½". Set the sheets aside. Lay the album shell flat with the front cover closest to you, the book cloth-covered hinge running horizontally, and the outside of the shell facing up. Measure from the bottom edge of the front cover toward the hinge 8¼" and make a light pencil mark on the right and left sides of the shell. Repeat this process on the back cover. Position the cover paper on the front cover using the pencil marks as guides. Allow 1" of paper to extend beyond the sides and bottom of the front cover. Glue the paper in place and press it down with your fingers, then burnish it with a brayer or burnishing tool. Let it dry at least 15 minutes, then repeat the process on the back cover.

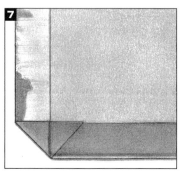

**6.** Turn the album shell over so the inside is facing up. Using the illustration as a reference, apply glue to one corner of the front cover paper and fold it inwards to create a triangle. Press the glued surface down with your fingers and burnish it with a brayer or burnishing tool. Repeat this at the other outside corner.

**7.** Glue and fold the remaining overlaps on all sides of the front cover to the inside of the shell. Press them down with your fingers and burnish them with a brayer or burnishing tool. Let the glue dry for 15 minutes. Repeat steps 6 and 7 on the back cover.

ILLUSTRATIONS BY WENDY WRAY

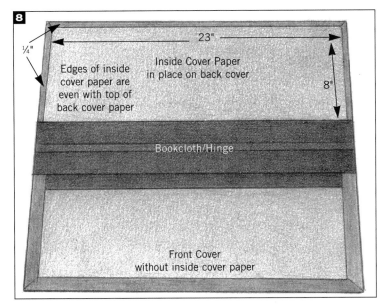

**8.** Cut two pieces of inside cover paper, each measuring 23" x 8". Lay the album shell open with the inside facing up. Position one piece of inside cover paper so the top edge aligns with the back cover overlap formed in step 7, and ¼" of the back cover overlap is visible on three sides. Glue the inside cover paper in place, press down on it with your fingers, and burnish it with a brayer or burnishing tool. Let the glue dry for 15 minutes. Repeat process for front cover.

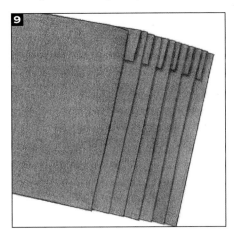

**9.** Cut 17 sheets from the album page paper, each measuring 23" x 9¾". Cut 16 divider strips from the same type of paper, each measuring 1½" x 23". Stack them, alternating the pages and the divider strips, beginning and ending with a page. Neatly lay the pages and divider strips inside the album cover.

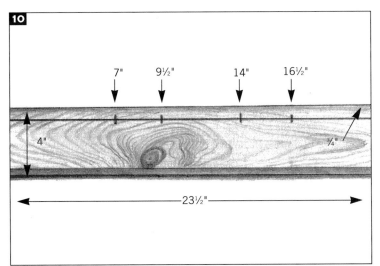

**10.** To make a drill guide, lay one of the 23½" x 4" x ¾" boards down flat and draw a straight line ¾" from one long side. With a felt marker, mark drill points along this line at 7", 9½", 14", and 16½".

**11.** Using the illustration as a guide, sandwich the album between the drill guide and the other piece of wood, lining up the edges of the album with the edges of the wood. Clamp the album and the wood together on the edge of your workspace with the C-clamps. At the four marks on the drill guide, drill down through the wood and the album until the drill goes into the second board.

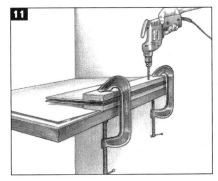

When all the holes are drilled, remove the C-clamps and boards, being careful not to let the pieces of the album shift. Brush away any sawdust or paper dust with a clean paintbrush.

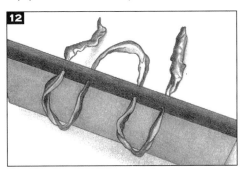

**12.** Twist the ends of the wire-edged ribbon to create a stiff point. Then, starting at the back cover, thread the ends of the ribbon first through the 9½" and 14" holes, and then back through the 7" and 16½" holes.

**13.** Thread the ends of the ribbon back through the 9½" and 14" holes. The ribbon can be tied with a square knot, followed by a single bow, followed by another square knot to keep the bow from untying, or it can be made more elaborate with a series of stacked bows separated by square knots. Be sure to end the series with a square knot to

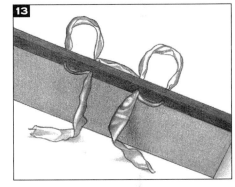

keep it from coming untied. Adjust the bow(s) for shape, and clip the ends of the ribbon as necessary.

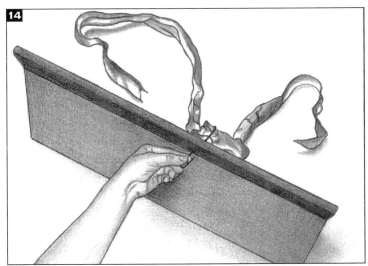

**14.** If you're using ribbon without wired edges, bend a paper clip into a narrow hook. Push the hook through each hole, catch the ribbon on the other side, and pull the ribbon back through. Go through the holes in the order given in steps 12 and 13, and tie the ribbon as instructed in step 13.

# Star Frost Vase

*Transform an ordinary vase into frosted glassware using etching compound and stencils.*

BY MICHIO RYAN

*Using Armour Etch and a variety of stencils, you can create custom glassware; you can also use Armour Etch to highlight relief areas on a bottle or lamp base.*

Traditionally, glass is frosted in one of two ways: either by using physical abrasion, such as grinding or sandblasting, or by applying specialized and often dangerous chemicals, which "eat" into the surface of the glass.

While this project uses the latter method, the chemicals used are found in paste form in a product called Armour Etch, an etching cream that is easy to handle and frosts glass in about one minute. (Although Armour Etch is safe enough to be sold in art supply and craft stores, take care not to get it on your skin or in your eyes.) To further simplify the etching process, I used ready-made star stencils to create the pattern. Using this method, even beginners can transform ordinary glassware into a frosted masterpiece in an afternoon's time.

Just about any glass except Pyrex will work for this project, as will any design available in a ready-made stencil. I used Armour's Rub'n'Etch glass etching stencil kit, which contains a stencil sheet with seventy stars in five sizes, a backing sheet, and a wooden craft stick. I used a total of thirty-seven stars on the vase: sixteen of the largest, six of the smallest, and five each of the three middle sizes, but naturally you can adapt the design to your own taste.

I applied the stars in a graduated pattern, with larger stars applied near the bottom of the vase and smaller stars towards the top. I spaced the stars closer together at the bottom and further apart at the top. I also placed each star with its arms pointing in different directions from those of neighboring stars. Free-form design is very forgiving, however, so don't worry too much about positioning. If you're feeling uncertain, practice on a glass jar using several of the smaller stencils in order to get a feel for

how the stencils and etching cream work.

If you are frosting a serving bowl, frost only the outside, since any oils or moisture from the bowl's contents will temporarily conceal the frosted effect.

A few notes on etching cream: Be sure to clean your glassware thoroughly before starting. Even small traces of oil will prevent the stencils from sticking properly and can interfere with the reaction of the etching cream. Also, I recommend wearing latex gloves. Since Armour Etch reacts with porcelain or metal as easily as with glass, be sure to rinse your sink thoroughly after use. If left in the sink for prolonged periods of time, the cream could damage the surface.

Armour Etch works best when glass, air, and cream temperatures are above seventy degrees. On a warm day, you can use the cream directly from its container; otherwise, place the closed container in a small cup of hot tap water for ten minutes before use. One additional note: Since etching cream works quickly and must be rinsed off right away, plan on stenciling eight to ten stars at a time and repeating the process as necessary with any remaining stars.

### STAR FROST VASE

10" clear glass vase
Armour Etch glass-etching cream
Armour's Rub'n'Etch glass etching
   stencil kit

*You'll also need:* glass jar for practicing; ½"-wide masking tape; ½"-wide disposable paintbrush; latex gloves, scissors; window cleaning solution; rubbing alcohol; kraft paper; felt-tip marker; paper towels; and watch or clock with second hand.

1. Clean jar or vase with window cleaner and paper towel.

2. Using felt-tip marker, mark 37 random dots on interior surface for positioning of stars. To change layout or remove felt-tip marks, rub vase with paper towel moistened with rubbing alcohol.

3. Cut stencil sheet along solid lines to separate into 37 individual squares. Handle sheet and squares by edges and avoid touching the stencil's cloudy (adhesive) surface. Position 8 to 10 stencils on outside of vase, cloudy (adhesive) side down, and fasten each in place

along one edge with small piece of masking tape. To avoid overlapping tapes, choose stars that are far apart.

4. Using flat edge of wooden stick provided in kit, rub shiny surface of each stencil until tone changes from dark to light blue. Rub firmly but not too briskly to avoid marring stencil underneath. When entire image has turned color, lift off clear backing, leaving blue star stencil adhered to surface.

5. To protect surrounding glass from etching cream, mask outside edges of each stencil with small pieces of masking tape. Stick pieces of tape to glass, overlapping blue stencil as much as possible without covering star. (This step is especially critical with small stars, since their points are very close to the edge.) If tape overlaps a neighboring star, trim it to fit before pressing in place. To seal tape tightly, press down tape edges with wooden stick.

6. Hold vase up to light and check each stencil for lifted edges, bubbles, pinholes, tears, or cracks. (Even small cracks will allow etching cream to seep beyond stencil and spoil the effect.) Any of the above problems should be fixed with small pieces of tape.

If the edge of a star is damaged or cracked, remove defective stencil, clean area with window cleaner, dry thoroughly, and apply new stencil. To make sure seal is tight, lay white backing sheet from kit on top of each star and rub firmly but not too briskly with wooden stick.

7. For rest of frosting process, work beside sink and provide ample ventilation. Cover work area with kraft paper and wear latex gloves. Turn vase upside down on kraft paper. Shake Armour Etch container well before opening. Dip brush into cream and dab generous 1/16"-thick coat on each star stencil, staying within taped areas. (It shouldn't take more than 30 seconds to apply cream to 8 to 10 stars.) The coat needn't be even, but dab over thin spots or stars will not be uniformly frosted. Avoid applying cream too thickly, or it may drip. Clean up any spatters or drips immediately with damp paper towel.

8. Allow cream to remain on glass exactly 60 seconds, then rinse off immediately by holding vase under warm running water. Set vase aside and continue running water into sink for 30 to 60 seconds to thoroughly rinse and remove any traces of cream. Peel off stencils and tape from vase and rub off any remaining residue using window cleaner and paper towels. When glass is thoroughly dry, frosted stars will appear.

9. Repeat appropriate parts of steps 3 through 8 with remaining stars, working in groups of 8 to 10 until all 37 stars are etched.

10. When all stars are frosted, remove felt-tip pen marks from inside of vase using paper towels and rubbing alcohol. Clean paintbrush with warm water. ◆

# Frosting the Vase

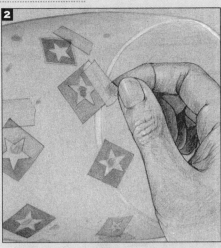

**1.** After positioning the stencils on the outside of the vase, rub the shiny surface of each stencil until the tone changes from dark to light blue.

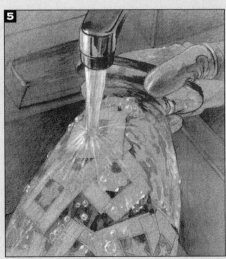

**2.** When the entire image has become light blue, lift off the clear backing.

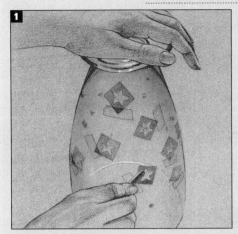

**3.** To protect the surrounding glass from the etching cream, mask all four edges of each stencil with small pieces of masking tape.

**4.** Apply a generous coat of etching cream to each star stencil, taking care to stay within the taped areas. Dab over any thin areas.

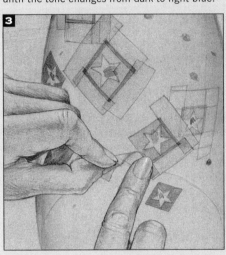

**5.** Allow the cream to remain on the glass exactly 60 seconds, then rinse it off immediately by holding the vase under warm running tap water. Remove any traces of cream.

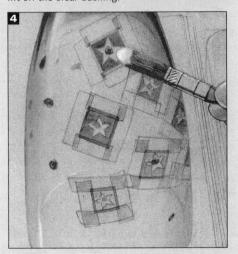

**6.** Peel off the stencils and tape from the vase, and rub off any remaining residue using window cleaner and paper towels.

# Gold and Silver Leaf Plate Chargers

*Use our foolproof recipe to leaf a set of glass plate chargers.*

These beautiful glass chargers, designed to sit beneath an appetizer, salad, or dessert plate, feature metallic leafing on the back of the plate's rim. Leafing glass usually requires precision because any gaps are very noticeable on the smooth surface. We chose this Mikasa plate because the hammered texture on the rim will hide a less-than-perfect application of leaf. In addition, because leaf is applied to the back of the plate's rim rather than the front, the glass layer through which you see the leafing helps conceal any minor mistakes.

Before settling on this particular plate, we tested a number of others. We tried leafing a rimless (coupe) plate, but the dividing line between the leafed and unleafed areas had to be carefully drawn in by hand. This works fine if you've got good freehand drawing skills, but a wobbly line won't look professional. Also, trimming the leaf to match the drawn line requires skill with a sharp blade. The well-defined rim on the Mikasa plate, on the other hand, provides a natural guide for dividing the leafed and unleafed areas. In our effort to resolve the wobbly line problem, we considered leafing the entire backside of a plate, but realized that any leaf in contact with the table would rub off. We contemplated raising the plate off the table with clear plastic stick-on bumpers but decided the finished result would have looked less than elegant.

We also tested a beautiful plate with a heavy grape relief design, but found that the reliefed areas created problems. When you apply leaf to a textured surface, hairline cracks or gaps appear where the leaf doesn't fill the "valleys," or depressions between raised areas on the surface. Filling hairline cracks is as simple as applying a second layer of leaf, but the deep valleys of the grape design created even larger gaps than normal. To fill those gaps, which occurred mainly at the grape stems and edges, we had to painstakingly apply leaf inside each valley individually and tamp it in place with a small brush. The effort was time-consuming, and we weren't satisfied with the overall results. Unless you have a lot of time on your hands and are feeling especially patient (the plate has to dry at least overnight between leaf applications), we don't recommend heavily reliefed designs. (For additional information, *see* "How to Gild Almost Any Surface," September/October 1994.)

Before you get started, keep the following points in mind. The odor of the size may persist for a few days, so be sure to leaf your chargers at least three days before you intend to use them; if the air is particularly humid in your area, you'll need to allow four or five days. Your work area should be clean and well-ventilated, but be sure there is no breeze, as metallic leaf can easily be blown away. We recommend using quick-dry size or your project may take two or three days to dry. Be sure your brushes are very clean or brand new since paint particles can contaminate a sized surface, and the oils in size can contaminate paint.

When applying size, use a light touch to apply an even coat to the back of the plate's rim, stopping before you reach the inner edge of the bottom of the plate. Brush the size up to the outside lip of the rim, but take care not to get any on the front of the plate, or it will stick to your work surface when you lay it face down to dry. When you have come full circle around the plate with the size, blend the seam with a brush to conceal it. Hold the plate up to the light and look for brownish areas, which indicate a heavy buildup of size. If the size is allowed to dry this thick, you'll end up with ugly brown lines in the leaf. Remove any such areas or drips with a swipe of the brush.

To handle the plate without leaving fingerprints on it, drape newsprint over the edge of your work surface. With one hand under the center of the plate, set the plate face down, extending off the edge of the table, with just enough of it on the table to keep it from falling. Then slide the newsprint, which will pull the plate with it, back onto the table with the other hand. Reverse this process when you pick the plate up. (If you're new to leafing, we recommend working on only two plates at a time. More experienced leafers can work on up to eight plates at a time.)

*This eleven-inch gold and silver leafed charger is designed for use with a dessert or appetizer plate.*

Depending on the humidity, the sized surface will be sticky and ready for leafing in one to three hours. Test the surface by touching it with a clean finger; if it feels like transparent tape, it's ready. If you accidentally let the size dry beyond the tacky stage, remove it with paint stripper (we recommend 3M's Safest Stripper paint remover), following the manufacturer's directions. (If you were leafing the surface of an opaque object, this wouldn't be necessary—you could reapply a second coat of size right over the first. Because the leaf on the charger is seen from behind the glass, however, the first coat of size will show up as a brown layer sandwiched between the glass and the leaf, so it must be removed.)

Once the size has dried to the appropriate stickiness, you apply both kinds of leaf, then let the object dry thoroughly before burnishing, which smoothes out and removes any loose pieces of leaf. The longer you let the object dry before burnishing, the better. The glaze continues to harden as long as it's left to dry, and the harder the glaze, the easier the burnishing process will be. We let one of the plates dry twenty-four hours before burnishing, and it worked fine. But when we burnished a plate that had been left to dry for four days, the burnishing was noticeably faster and smoother.

We tested a number of materials for burnishing, including a cosmetic puff, which turned out to be a mistake. Most cosmetic puffs are made from synthetic fibers, which can scratch the leaf. We had much better results with 100 percent cotton balls like those you find in a first-aid kit. We also tried using a clean, lint-free cotton rag for burnishing, and that worked fine too. Don't use a rag with seams as these can scratch the leaf. Once you've burnished the plate, you'll need to create a crisp, clean line of leaf around the rim's edge using a single-edge razor blade. (*See* photograph 5, at right.)

Under normal indoor conditions, composition leaf will retain its bright finish for some time without the benefit of sealing. Spray-sealing with a clear lacquer, however, will delay the eventual tarnishing and minimize any damage from moisture or abrasion. Applying sealer on top of leaf always dulls the brilliance a bit, but in this case the sealant is applied to the backside of the plate, and the luster of the leaf seen through the glass is unaffected.

As with any leafed glass, extensive handling can wear off the thin layer of leaf. However, with a few precautions these glass chargers will wear well. As with decorative plate liners, food is never put directly on the chargers, so they may not need washing after every use. When washing is necessary, hand-wash them with warm water and ordinary dishwashing detergent, then dry them with a towel. (Air drying may result in spotting, especially if the chargers have not been sealed.) They should never be allowed to stand or soak in water, nor should they be washed in a dishwasher. When stacking the chargers, layer paper towels between them to prevent scratching.

### GOLD AND SILVER LEAF CHARGERS

1–8 Bern clear 11" buffet plates from
    Mikasa/Studio Nova
    4-ounce can quick-dry synthetic size
1  book aluminum (silver) leaf
2  books composition (gold) leaf
    Clear lacquer spray

*You'll also need:* new or very clean #10 round sable or sabelline brush; denatured alcohol; sharp single-edge razor blade; table knife; small, perfectly clean can or jar; brown kraft paper; 100 percent cotton balls; mineral spirits; washcloth; and 2-quart juice can or similar-sized container.

*Other items, if necessary:* 3M's Safest Stripper paint remover (for removing dried-on size); paper towels and Magic Goo Gone (for removing price sticker adhesive); and soft rag (for burnishing). ◆

# Leafing a Set of Glass Chargers

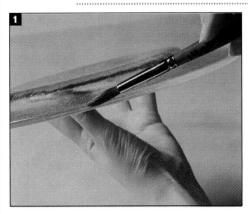

**1.** Work in a well-ventilated, dust-free area; cover the work surface with brown kraft paper. Clean the plate, removing fingerprints and oils with a cotton ball moistened with alcohol. If necessary, scrape off label adhesive with a single-edge razor blade, and dissolve any stubborn adhesive with Magic Goo Gone. Pour a small amount of size into a small jar or can. Hold the plate upside down in one hand, with your fingers spread to support the center of the plate. Using the #10 brush, apply a thin, even coat of size around the entire back of the rim. Stop just short of the bottom of the plate on the inner edge, and brush the size around the lip on the outside edge. Use the brush to blend any gaps in the size or remove any drips. To set the plate down, drape kraft paper over the edge of your table, and set the plate so that just enough of it rests on the table to keep it from falling. Then pull the plate back onto the table by pulling the kraft paper. Repeat this entire process on the remaining plates. When finished, clean the brush with mineral spirits.

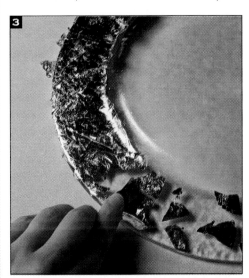

**3.** Repeat step 2 with the composition gold leaf, but overlay the entire rim, including the silver areas. Then rest a sheet of tissue from the leaf book on the plate's rim and gently buff the leaf through the tissue to ensure a good bond. Fill in any unleafed areas with bits of extra leaf. Let the plates dry at least overnight or longer if possible. Repeat this process on the remaining plates.

**2.** Start checking the size for tackiness one-half hour after it was applied. When it feels sticky, like transparent tape, you're ready to continue. If size dries beyond the tacky stage, remove the size with stripper and resize. With clean, dry hands, lift the tissue cover off the aluminum (silver) leaf book. Moisten the blade of a table knife with your breath, then touch the blade to the edge of a sheet of the leaf, and trail the leaf onto a clean sheet of kraft paper. Using dry fingertips, tear the leaf into irregular 1" pieces. Lift pieces of the torn leaf and lay them on the sticky rim of the plate. Tamp in place with a finger tip. Repeat this with the remaining pieces of silver leaf until approximately half of the rim's surface is covered. Repeat this entire process on the remaining plates.

**4.** Burnish the leafed area with cotton balls or a soft rag. To repair any cracks or gaps that appear, apply size to the entire rim, as in step 1, covering the gold and silver leaf. Then re-leaf the entire rim with gold leaf *only*. Let it dry overnight, and burnish it as above. Repeat this process on the remaining plates.

**5.** Place a washcloth on top of a juice can or similar container to prevent scratching, then set the plate upside down on top of the can and hold it down firmly in the middle with one hand. Holding the single-edge razor blade in your other hand, cut against the plate rim at a 45-degree angle to trim off the excess leaf and leave a crisp edge. To seal, spray the entire rim with clear lacquer. Transfer the plate to kraft paper and let dry following manufacturer's directions. Repeat this process until all the plates are trimmed and sealed.

# White Silk Centerpiece

*Use a three-part construction technique to create a variety of silk flower arrangements.*

BY LAURA LUCERO AND KAREN KETTERING

*The gold accents in this centerpiece would work well with the gold and silver leaf plate chargers on page 26. For a wider arrangement, stretch the arms outward.*

This formal silk flower centerpiece uses a quick, simple assembly technique that allows a variety of creative interpretations. The arrangement comprises two identical arms, each made by binding bouquets of foliage and flowers to a long stem, which is then inserted into a moss-covered foam block base.

Using this construction, you can build an endless variety of centerpieces. We chose to bend the arms in an S shape for the arrangement pictured above, but you could stretch the arms out to form one long piece, scrunch the arms toward the center block for a smaller centerpiece, lengthen or shorten the piece by creating longer or shorter arms, or create a rounder arrangement by adding arms of equal or varying length. To update the piece from season to season or year to year, you could substitute different arms, mix and match a variety of arms and bases, add one or two new items, or do a small amount of rearranging.

We estimate the total cost of this piece at between $70 and $80, which is comparable to a fresh floral arrangement of equal size. (Your actual cost may be less, depending on any substitutions you make and where you purchase your supplies. The magnolia, for instance, was priced at $10.39 at Leewards, but you could substitute any large white flower.) Although fresh flowers have a strong appeal, silk arrangements offer several advantages. For starters, a silk floral centerpiece will last indefinitely, can be reused year after year, and can be unpacked and table-ready in just a few minutes. Furthermore, unlike fresh flowers, whose color, texture, and variety are often limited by season or supplier, the full range of silk flowers is typically available year-round.

For this arrangement we chose a monochromatic color theme, which makes the arrangement more formal. The piece, which uses a palette of white (such as cream, pearl, and off-white) is accented by gold fruit and would work well with gilded chargers. (*See* "Gold and Silver Leaf Plate Chargers," page 26.)

To add a few additional gold highlights, we spray-painted the magnolia with a very light dusting of gold. You can add extra hints of gold to the arrangement by spray-painting other flowers or foliage. Before spray-painting, cover your work space with kraft paper. Make sure the room is well ventilated and follow the manufacturer's instructions. For best results, hold the spray paint can nearly upright about fifteen to eighteen inches from the object. If you want more gold in the arrangement, consider spray-painting the birch bud branches gold before arranging them.

To differentiate between various types of roses, we refer to the roses used in this arrangement as either open or closed. Open roses look like they are at the peak of bloom, with petals fully unfurled. Closed roses, on the other hand, look more like buds; the closed petals form almost a teardrop shape.

To make the arm sections, you'll need to bind together several bouquets of foliage and flowers. As you are wiring the bunches together, be sure to cinch the wire very tightly to prevent the bouquets from slipping. In general, longer stems work to your advantage by strengthening the structure, so don't trim the stems before binding. Always use wire cutters when trimming silk flowers, as household scissors will be ruined by cutting wire. We used one long blueberry stem for the spine of each arm, but you can also create a spine by binding together six or more 18-gauge floral stem wires with florist tape. If you choose this technique, be sure to stretch the tape as you wind it tightly around the entire length of the stem wires. Leave about six inches of the stem free of flowers or foliage to insert into the foam base.

For a more permanent arrangement, apply hot glue to the ends of the stems immediately before inserting them into the foam base. The stems will be securely set within minutes. For coordinating decorations, consider making miniature matching garlands to tie onto the backs of chairs or door frames or to use as drapery tiebacks. Twine garlands around your chandelier or other lighting fixtures, or arrange single or small bunches of matching flowers or foliage next to place cards or place settings.

## WHITE SILK CENTERPIECE

1  silk English or Holland ivy bush
2  silk ficus or philodendron bushes
12  birch bud branches (each about 12" long)
6  silk white ranunculus buds

PHOTOGRAPH BY STEVEN MAYS

3 silk white ranunculus flowers
1 silk white magnolia stem (one blossom
  and one bud)
4 large sprigs silk white lilac
4 large (5"-diameter) open white silk roses
7 medium (3"- to 4"-diameter) open white
  parchment paper or dried-look roses
4 small (1½"- to 2"-diameter) closed
  white parchment paper or dried-look
  silk roses
2 small (1½"- to 2"-diameter) closed
  white silk roses
6 gilded hollow textured fruits (such as
  apples, pomegranates, or pears)
4 blueberry branches (with berries), about
  24" long
12 1"-diameter white opalescent ball picks
6 ¼"-diameter white opalescent wired balls
  Brilliant Gold Design Master spray paint
1 block urethane foam, 7⅞" x 3⅞" x 2⅞"
1 package 18", 18-gauge floral stem wires
1 4-ounce bag Spanish moss
  24-gauge green florist wire

*You'll also need:* hot-glue gun and glue sticks; ¾" craft wire pins; green florist tape; wire cutters; scissors; serrated kitchen knife; latex gloves; kraft paper; and safety glasses.

### Creating the Arm Sections

1. Using wire cutters, cut ivy and ficus (or philodendron) bushes into 6" pieces.

2. With small point of scissors, drill small hole in base of gilded fruit. With wire cutters, cut two 18-gauge floral stem wires into thirds to yield six 6" pieces. Bend over ¼" to ½" of wire tip, then apply hot glue to tip of wire, insert wire into hole in fruit, and set aside to dry.

3. Using wire cutters, cut 2 large lilac sprigs into 6 small pieces. Attach each piece to a 6" to 8" length of floral stem wire with green florist tape to form a small lilac sprig.

4. Make 2 each of the following bouquets, one for each arm section. Layer the foliage and flowers in the order noted, then wire together each bunch using 24-gauge green florist wire. (Cut 6 small sprigs of lilac from 2 of the large lilac stems.)

A. First bouquet: ficus (or philodendron) stem, ivy stem, birch bud branch, ranunculus bud, three ¼" opalescent wired balls twisted together, and small lilac sprig.

B. Second bouquet: ficus (or philodendron) stem, ivy stem, birch bud branch, ranunculus bud, small lilac sprig, and medium white parchment paper or dried-look silk rose.

C. Third bouquet: ficus (or philodendron) stem, ivy stem, birch bud branch, ranunculus bud, small lilac sprig, medium white parchment paper or dried-look silk rose, and three 1" opalescent ball picks twisted together.

D. Fourth bouquet: ficus (or philodendron) stem, ivy stem, birch bud branch, ranunculus flower, large lilac sprig, small white parchment paper or dried-look silk rose, and a gilded fruit.

5. Lay one blueberry branch flat on table to form spine of garland. Wire first bouquet (A) to blueberry branch so bouquet head extends 6" to 8" over blueberries. Lay head of second bouquet (B) over stems of first bouquet (A) and wire in place. Attach third and fourth bouquets (C and D) in same manner, leaving a 6" length of blueberry stem uncovered at the end. Repeat process to create second arm section.

### Making the Base of the Arrangement

1. Using kitchen knife, cut foam in half to make block measuring about 4" x 3⅞" x 2⅞". Cover with moss, pinning moss in place with craft wire pins.

2. With wire cutters, trim stems of remaining flowers to within 6" to 8" of flower head.

3. Insert a few ivy and ficus (or philodendron) stems into foam. To create an oval shape, use longest stems at sides, followed by medium-length stems, and then shortest stems in center.

4. Cover work space with kraft paper; put on safety glasses and latex gloves. Position extra piece of foam block nearby. Spray very thin coat of gold spray paint on magnolia blossom. Stick stem into foam block until flower is dry, about 5 to 10 minutes. Spray-paint any other flowers or foliage gold as desired, and stick in foam block or lay on newspaper until dry, about 5 to 10 minutes.

5. When magnolia is dry, place it in center of base arrangement. Arrange 4 large open white silk roses around magnolia, then add 3 medium parchment paper or dried-look silk roses, 2 blueberry branches, and six 1"

opalescent ball picks that have been twisted into sets of 3.

6. Arrange remaining gilded fruit, birch bud branches, and flowers as desired.

7. Bend arm sections into softly curving S shapes, then insert exposed end of arm into sides of centerpiece. Adjust bends of arm section as necessary. ◆

**Laura Lucero** and **Karen Kettering** own and operate Cranberry Lane, an interior accents and silk floral store in Santa Clarita, California.

## MAKING THE CENTERPIECE
··········

**1.** Wire the first bouquet to the blueberry stem, extending the head of the bouquet 6" to 8" over the blueberries. Lay the head of the second bouquet over the stems of the first bouquet and wire the bouquet in place.

**2.** Attach the third and fourth bouquets in the same manner as the first and second. Be sure to leave a 6" length of blueberry stem exposed at one end so you can insert it into the base of the arrangement.

**3.** Cover the foam block with moss, pinning the moss in place with craft wire pins.

**4.** To create an oval shape for the center of the arrangement, use the longest stems at the sides, followed by the medium stems, and then the shortest stems in the center.

# Field Guide to Paper Lace Doilies

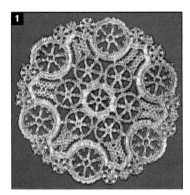

**1.** 4"-diameter gold foil medallion lace doily; Royal Lace

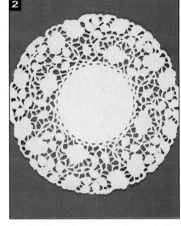

**2.** 8"-diameter white lace doily; Williams-Sonoma

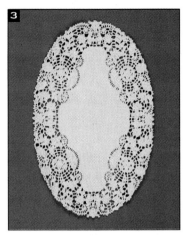

**3.** 5" x 8" white lace oval mat; Artifacts

**4.** 8"-diameter party decor silver doily; Paper Art

**5.** 9½"-square white vogue doyley; Crowndale

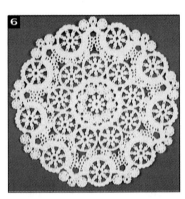

**6.** 8"-diameter white medallion lace doily; Royal Lace

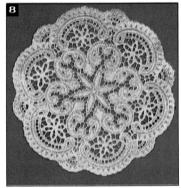

**7.** 6"-diameter white French lace heart-shaped doily; Hallmark

The doily (also spelled doyley) takes its name from the name of a seventeenth-century draper, who popularized the filigree paper lace mat by selling inexpensive versions at his shop on The Strand, London.

Lace doilies can be used in a variety of ways. To dress up your table settings, place large (eight- to ten-inch) round doilies under your dinnerware or between a plate and a charger. Smaller versions can be used as coasters, or beneath cups and saucers. Doilies also make great linings for bread baskets, dessert trays, or small floral arrangements. They can also be used under centerpieces or to wrap small gifts or party favors. Strips of doilies can be used to edge the shelves of kitchen cabinets, closets, and armoires.

Doilies are also useful for a variety of craft projects. You can make fans or cornucopias by curling or folding round doilies, or envelopes, stationary, greeting cards, and miniature sachets by folding square or rectangular doilies. Doilies—alone or accented with small nosegays, cut-out images, ribbons, or stamped metal findings—also make beautiful valentines. ◆

**8.** 8"-diameter round gold foil doily; Dekorativ

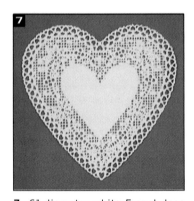

**9.** 7"-square white lace doily; Hallmark

**10.** 8" x 12" white decorative lace mat; Carlton Cards

**11.** 10" x 14½" white Battenburg lace place mat; Artifacts

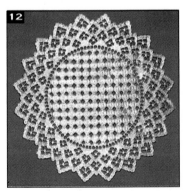

**12.** 9¾"-diameter gold foil doily; Dekorativ

PHOTOGRAPHS BY STEVEN MAYS

# SOURCES
## AND RESOURCES

Most of the materials needed for the projects in this issue are available at your local craft supply, hardware or paint store, florist, fabric shop, or bead and jewelry supply. The following are specific mail-order sources for particular items, arranged by project. The suggested retail prices listed here are current at press time. Contact the suppliers directly to confirm up-to-date prices and availability of poducts.

### Notes from Readers; pages 2–3

*Stain-proof Finish for Fabric Place Mats:* Createx Clear Coat Varnish for $16.80 per 32 ounces from Pearl Paint. *Rubber-Stamping with Paint:* Large selection of rubber stamps ranging from $2 to $11.50 from Stampendous. Wood filler for $4.75 per ½ pint, clear polyurethane sealer for $16.25 per quart, sanding pads for $4.50 per pack of 5, turpentine for $5.75 per quart, and varnish from $8.25 per pint, all from Constantine's Woodworker's Catalog. Selection of oil and acrylic paints from $2 from Pearl Paint. Mod Podge for $1.99 per 4 ounces from Sunshine Discount Crafts. *Is Rubber Cement Safe to Use?:* Best-Test Rubber Paper Cement for $1.75 per 4 ounces, UHU Glue Stick for 71¢ per 0.28 ounces, Sobo glue for $2.47 per 8 ounces, and mat cutters from $8.39, all from Pearl Paint. X-Acto Surgrip utility knife for $4.99, Sharpie black fine-point marker for $1.09, and a selection of cutting tools and blades, all from Co-op Artists' Materials. *Creative Uses for Scraps of Decorative Paper:* Selection of mat boards from 59¢ from Pearl Paint. Calligraphy pens for $3.53 from Ott's Discount Art Supply. Selection of glitter from 99¢ per ¾-ounce tube and glitter paints from 99¢ per ounce from Enterprise Art. Ribbon from 70¢ per 5 yards from Newark Dressmaker Supply. *Adding Fresh Flowers to a Silk Arrangement:* Large selection of silk flowers from $1.50 from May Silk. 8" x 4" x 3" florist foam for 87¢ from Craft King. Florist tape for $1.35 from Newark Dressmaker Supply. *Colored Pencils Versus Watercolor Pencils:* Watercolor pencils for $9.77 per 12 pencils and colored pencils from $4.86 per 12 pencils from Pearl Paint. *Wallpaper Choices for a Tiny Bathroom:* Victorian wallpaper from $39 to $59 per roll from Bradbury and Bradbury. *The Right Way to Use an X-Acto Knife:* X-Acto Surgrip utility knife for $4.99 and X-Acto blades for $1.59 per pack of 5 from Co-op Artist's Materials. *Painting Around a Doorknob:* Reclosable plastic bags for $1.35 per 100 from Craft King.

### Quick Tips; pages 4–5

*Buckle-Free French Seams:* Selection of fabric from $3.40 per yard, thread from $1.70 per 300 yards, and scissors from $10.75, all from Newark Dressmaker Supply. Irons from $12 and sewing machines from $140 from Service Merchandise. *Make Your Own Pom-poms:* DMC Floss for 35¢ for 8.7 yards and Snip Scissors for $4.99 from Mary Maxim. Kimberly Drawing Pencil Set for $1.89 and Laser Scissors for $6.06 from Craft King. *Shortening a Zipper:* Nylon zippers from 45¢, steel dressmaker pins for $1.75 per 350, thread from $1.70 per 300 yards, tape measure for $1.25, and scissors from $10.75, all from Newark Dressmaker Supply. Selection of sewing machines from $140 from Service Merchandise. *Repairing Cracks in Plaster Walls:* Spackling compound for $3 per quart, paint scrapers from $3.90, putty knifes or putty trowels for 75¢, sandpaper from 29¢, drop cloths from 69¢, and soft-bristled paintbrushes from $2, all from Pearl Paint. 3M Non-Toxic Paper Mask for $13.90 per box of 50 from Dick Blick. *Repairing Holes in Drywall:* Spackling compound for $3 per quart, putty knives from 75¢, sandpaper from 29¢, drop cloths from 69¢, all from Pearl Paint. Olfa utility knife for $6.78 from Daniel Smith. 3M Non-Toxic Paper Mask for $13.90 per box of 50 from Dick Blick.

### Gilded Cut-Metal Sconce; pages 6–8

Delta Gloss Varnish for $3.90 for 8 ounces, gold spray paint for $2.89 for 16 ounces, 20-gauge gold wire for $2.16 per 15-yard spool, Laser scissors from $6.06, 4½" long-nose pliers for $5.79, and epoxy coating for $6 per pint kit, all from Craft King. 16-gauge wire for $1.19 from Kirchen Brothers Crafts. ¾" masking tape for $6, Sharpie red permanent marker for $1.09, selection of paintbrushes from 75¢, Beinfang Parchment 100 tracing paper for $5 per 100-sheet pad, and 20" x 30" LextraMax 1000 illustration board for $2.60, all from Co-op Artists' Materials. Drop cloth from 69¢ for 9' x 12' plastic cloth, kraft paper from 89¢ per roll, cardboard from 72¢, burnishers from $1.85, lacquer spray for $4.10 per 12 ounces, pliers from $8, and copper tubing from 28¢ per foot, all from Pearl Paint. Index cards for 65¢ per pack of 100 from Reliable. 1½" crystal chandelier drop for $1.15 and jewel ball chain for $8 per foot from Renovator's. Composition leaf for $5.65 per 25-sheet book, Daniel Smith Odorless Mineral Spirits for $4.72 per pint, and frame hangers for $1.40, all from Daniel Smith. 2½"-long awl for

$2.25, clear tacky glue for $2.10, tape measure for $1.25, and metallic ribbon from $1.60 per 5 yards, all from Newark Dressmaker Supply. Screwdrivers from $3.50 and screws from $2.10 per bag of 100 from Constantine's Woodworker's Catalog. Ivory beeswax tapers for $8 per set of 3 from Pottery Barn.

### Tasseled Napkin Ring; page 9

Wood curtain rings for $8 per 7 from Pottery Barn. Gold leaf for $5.95 per 25 sheets, gold sizing for $5.23 per 4 ounces, Cut-Rite Scissors for $3.50, and selection of paintbrushes from 75¢, all from Co-op Artists' Materials. Rubber gloves for $1.23 for 5 pairs, gold metallic skein for $2.08 per 27 yards, and Plaid's white tacky glue for 89¢ per 4 ounces, all from Craft King. Cardboard from 72¢, clear lacquer spray for $3.49 per 11 ounces, gold Krylon spray paint for $3.85 per 16 ounces, wire cutters from $6, and pliers from $8, all from Pearl Paint. Gold nylon beading thread for $1.50 per 100-yard spool and sturdy rat-tail cord for 25¢ per yard from Earth Guild. Grape cluster embellishment for 70¢ from Creative Beginnings.

### Quick Dried Flower Arranging; pages 10–11

Caspia for $6.25 per 4 ounces, pink strawflowers for $4.15 per bunch, larkspur for $4.75 per bunch, yellow yarrow for $4.40 per bunch, pink roses for $14.35 per bunch, yellow roses for $11.50 per bunch, and tansy for $3.95 per bunch, all from Mills Floral. 8" x 4" x 3" florist foam for 87¢ and Ceramcoat green acrylic paint for $1.19 per 2 ounces from Craft King. Love-lies-bleeding (amaranthus) for $2.55 per bunch and stirlingia for $6.35 per bunch from Floral Express.

### Testing Hot-Glue Guns; pages 12–14

Crafty's Magic Melt Glue Gun for $13.29, Crafty's Full Size Hot Melt for $13.29, and Black & Decker 2-Temp Glue Gun for $25.89, all from Pearl Paint. Dual Temper Cordless Glue Gun for $22.99 from Craft King. Low Temp and High Temp Glue Guns for $10.50 each from Newark Dressmaker Supply. Low-Temp Trigger Fed Glue Gun for $15.80, Dual-Temp Glue Gun for $22.90, and Cordless Dual-Temp Glue Gun for $25.90, all from Dick Blick.

### Decorating with Decoupage; pages 15–16

Large selection of decoupage prints from $1 each, Mod Podge for $4.50, sealer for $6.50, and decoupage finish for $5.95, all from Adventures in Crafts.

Soft rubber Speedball brayers from $7.10, Olfa utility knife for $6.78 and blades for $4.23 per 6, X-Acto Self-sealing Reversible Cutting Bases from $9.85, Daniel Smith acrylic medium for $4.82 per 8 ounces, Chinese Butcher Painting Tray for $5.96, and Superfine Cover Paper for 92¢ per sheet, all from Daniel Smith. Steel dressmaker pins for $1.75 per 350 from Newark Dressmaker Supply. Short nap paint roller for $3.19, 9" handle for $2.79, and 4' extension for $2.70, dowels from 20¢, drop cloths from 69¢, paint scrapers from $2, chalk for 60¢ per 12 pieces, epoxy putty for $3.78 per 2 ounces, and foam paint rollers from $2.41, all from Pearl Paint.

### Lacework Teacloth; page 17

Selection of threads from 40¢ per 200 yards, variety of white lace from $1 per 10 yards, Lightweight Bent Trimmer dressmaker shears for $4.40, straight pins for $1.75 per 250, and 14 in 1 Sewing Measurement Gauge for $1.05, all from Home-Sew. Selection of sewing machines from $140 and irons from $12 from Service Merchandise. Top stitch and zipper guide set for $4.75 per 2 guides from G Street Fabrics. Hotel napkins from $15 per 12 from Williams-Sonoma.

### Antique Brass Frames; pages 18–19

Large selection of frames in a variety of shapes and sizes from Exposures. Clear lacquer spray for $3.49 per 11 ounces, 3M's Safest Stripper Paint Remover for $9.67 per quart, patina solution from $15, denatured alcohol for $2.40 per pint, and steel wool from $1.60, all from Pearl Paint. Rubber gloves from $1.23 per 5 pairs, wooden craft sticks for $3.55 per 1000, epoxy coating for $6 per pint kit, and a large selection of findings in various shapes and sizes, all from Craft King. ¾"-wide masking tape for $2.56 per 60 yards, plastic containers from 60¢, metal palette cups from 73¢, and selection of paint brushes from 75¢, all from Co-op Artists' Materials. Safety goggles for $4.67 and acetone for $2.28 per pint from Pearl Paint. Simichrome Polish for $7 per 1¾-ounce tube from Renovator's.

### Panoramic Photo Album; pages 20–23

Large selection of exotic and decorative papers from 75¢ per sheet, Olfa utility knife for $6.78, selection of colored framing boards from $1.09 per board, Matline measuring tool for $6.65, X-Acto Self-sealing Reversible Cutting Bases from $9.85, all from Daniel Smith. 6"-opening adjustable C-clamp for $9.95,

X-Acto knife for $2.80, Swivel Head Drill Tool for $14.95, and ¼" brad point bits for $5.95, all from The Woodworker's Store. Cardboard from 72¢, markers from $2, and burnishers from $1.84, all from Pearl Paint. Wire-edged ribbon from $1.75 per yard, large squeeze bottle Sobo glue for $1.85, and scissors from $10.75, all from Newark Dressmaker Supply. Variety of book cloth from $4.60 per yard from The Bookbinder's Warehouse.

### Star Frost Vase; page 24
10" clear glass vase for $19 from Pottery Barn (Cornelia #564286, not available through catalog). Rubber gloves for $1.23 for 5 pairs and Laser scissors from $7.41 from Craft King. ½"-wide masking tape for $4.89 for 60-yard roll, Sharpie black fine-point marker for $1.09, and ½" nylon easel paintbrush for $1.55, all from Co-op Artists' Materials. Armour Etch glass etching cream for $3.80 for 3 ounces, Armour Etch glass etching stencil kit for $10.36, and kraft paper from 89¢ per roll, all from Pearl Paint. Windex for $5.12 for 32 ounces from Reliable. Weck canning jars for $13 for set of 8 from Williams-Sonoma.

### Gold and Silver Leaf Plate Chargers; pages 26–27
Bern clear 11" buffet plates for $5.99 each from Mikasa Factory Store. Aluminum leaf for $5.65 per 25-sheet book, composition leaf for $5.65 per 25-sheet book, Olfa utility knife for $4.23, odorless mineral spirits for $4.50 for 1 pint, natural sponges from $2.10, and #10 Daniel Smith Kolinsky sable round brush for $11.13, all from Daniel Smith. Clear lacquer spray for $3.49 per 11 ounces, 3M's Safest Stripper Paint Remover for $9.67 per quart, gold size for $5.37 per 6-ounce can, Neatness jars for $1.10, kraft paper from 89¢ per roll, and denatured alcohol for $2.40 per pint, all from Pearl Paint.

### White Silk Centerpiece; pages 28–29
Large selection of silk plants and flowers from May Silk. English ivy plants from $4.90, Holland ivy plants from $4.90, rose and bud deluxe stems from $2.25 per stem, rose spray for $1.90, half-open rose stem for $5.90 per stem, fully open rose stem for $6.90, magnolia stems for $3.90, ranunculus spray for $2, ficus spray for $1.90, birch spray for $1.90, philo plant for $4.90, lilac stem for $3.40, berry spray for $4.90, and assortment of soft plastic fruit for $4.90 per bag, all from May Silk. Spanish moss for $2.35 per 8-ounce bag, florist tape for $1.61, rubber gloves for $1.23 per 5 pairs, Village Classic bright gold spray

paint for $3.10 per 6 ounces, Mini Magic Melt Lo-Temp Glue Gun for $6.15 and glue sticks for $2.75 per 60, green florist wire for $1.09, 8" x 4" x 3" florist foam for 87¢, Laser Multi Purpose Shears for $13.48, all from Craft King. Safety goggles for $4.67 and kraft paper for 89¢ per roll from Pearl Paint. 18-gauge 18" stem wire for 69¢ from Sunshine Discount Crafts.

### Field Guide to Paper Lace Doilies; page 30
6" paper lace heart-shaped doily for $3.45 per 100, 4" white paper lace round doily for $3.95 per 100, 4" gold or silver paper lace round doily for $3.95 per 24, 8" white paper lace round doily for $4.95 per 100, and 8" gold or silver paper lace round doily for $6.25 per 24, all from Newark Dressmaker Supply. Heart-shaped doilies for $9.50 per set of 2 from Pottery Barn.

### Quick Projects; page 33
Terra-cotta pots for $9.99 per set of 3 from Pottery Barn. Selection of PlasTerra pots from $1.49 from Akro-Mils Specialty Products. *Moss-covered Pot:* Sheet moss for $22.25 per 5 pounds from Mills Floral Supply. Rubber cement with brush for $1.96 per 4 ounces and Sobo glue for $1.45 per 4 ounces from Ott's Discount Art Supply. Wire-edged ribbon for $2.70 per 3 yards and scissors from $4.40 from Home-Sew. *Marbled Pot:* Selection of acrylic paints from $1.99 per 2 ounces, #1 and #2 artist's paintbrushes from 50¢, and sponges from 69¢ from Ott's Discount Art Supply. *Rose Decoupage:* Decoupage papers for $3.69, Mod Podge for $1.99 per 4 ounces, Treasure Crystal Cote high gloss finish coating for $1.80, and black acrylic gloss enamel for $1.99 per 2-ounce squeeze bottle from Sunshine Discount Crafts. *Verdigris Pot with Brass Accents:* 1"-wide foam brush for 35¢ from Dick Blick. Ceramcoat acrylic paints from Delta for $1.19 per 2 ounces, Plaid's white tacky glue for 89¢ per 4 ounces, and decorative brass filigrees for 95¢ each, all from Craft King. *Festive Striped Pot:* Selection of acrylic paints from $1.99 per 2 ounces and acrylic gloss medium for $5.96 per 8 ounces from Ott's Discount Art Supply. *Rope Swag with Shells:* White 6mm twist for $4.75 per 100 yards, Plaid's white tacky glue for 89¢ per 4 ounces, Mini Magic Melt Lo-Temp Glue Gun for $6.15 and glue sticks for $2.75 per 60, Village Classic bright gold spray paint for $3.10 per 6 ounces, all from Craft King. Selection of shell-shaped brass charms and filigrees from 40¢ each from Creative Beginnings. *Rose Bud Collar:* Miniature rose buds for $1 per 6 buds,

mini glue gun for $4.50 and mini glue sticks for $1.50 per 20, all from Newark Dressmaker Supply.

### Folk Art Bandbox; back cover
Mod Podge for $1.96 per 4 ounces, 1"-wide sponge applicator for 33¢, and Delta acrylic paints for $1.19 per 2 ounces, all from Craft King. X-Acto knife for 99¢ and 12" aluminum ruler for $2.27 from Ott's Discount Art Supply. Sample packets of historic wallpapers for $5 from Charles Rupert. Bandboxes in an assortment of sizes for $10.50 per 7 boxes and selection of ribbon from $1.25 per 10 yards from Home-Sew. Hotel napkins from $15 per 12 from Williams-Sonoma.

---

T he following companies are mentioned in the listings above. Contact each individually for a price list or catalog.

**Adventures in Crafts,** P.O. Box 6058, Yorkville Station, New York, NY 10128; 212-410-9793
**Akro-Mils Specialty Products,** 1293 South Main Street, Akron, OH 44301; 216-253-5592
**American Art Clay Company,** 4714 West Sixteenth Street, Indianapolis, IN 46222; 800-374-1600
**Artifacts Inc.,** RCD, P.O. Box 3399, Palestine, TX 75802
**Bookbinder's Warehouse,** 31 Division Street, Keyport, NJ 07735; 908-264-0306
**Bradbury and Bradbury,** P.O. Box 155, Benicia, CA 94510; 707-746-1900
**Charles Rupert,** 2004 Oak Bay Avenue, Victoria, B.C., Canada V8R 1E4; 604-592-4916
**Carlton Cards,** One American Road, Cleveland, OH 44144; 800-321-3040
**Constantine's Woodworker's Catalog,** 2050 Eastchester Road, Bronx, NY 10461-2297; 800-223-8087
**Co-op Artists' Materials,** P.O. Box 53097, Atlanta, GA 30355; 800-877-3242
**Craft King Discount Craft Supply,** P.O. Box 53097, Lakeland, FL 33804; 800-769-9494
**Creative Beginnings,** 475 Morro Bay Boulevard, Morro Bay, CA 93442; 800-992-0276
**Creative Craft House,** P.O. Box 2567, Bullhead City, AZ 86430; 602-754-3300
**Daniel Smith,** P.O. Box 84268, Seattle, WA 98124-5568; 800-426-6740
**Dick Blick,** P.O. Box 1267, Galesburg, IL 61402-1267; 800-447-8192
**Earth Guild,** 33 Haywood Street, Asheville, NC 28801; 800-327-8448

**Enterprise Art,** P.O. Box 2918, Largo, FL 34648; 800-366-2218
**Exposures,** One Memory Lane, P.O. Box 3615, Oshkosh, WI 54903-3615; 800-222-4947
**Floral Express,** 11 Armco Avenue, Caribou, ME 04736; 800-392-7417
**G Street Fabrics,** 12240 Wilkins Avenue, Rockville, MD 20852; 800-333-9191
**Hallmark Cards, Inc.,** P.O. Box 419580-MD 216, Kansas City, MO 64108; 800-425-5627
**Home-Sew,** P.O. Box 4099, Bethlehem, PA 18018-0099; 610-867-3833
**Kirchen Bros. Crafts,** P.O. Box 1016, Skokie, IL 60076; 708-647-6747
**Mary Maxim Needlework and Crafts,** 2001 Holland Avenue, P.O. Box 5019, Port Huron, MI 48061-5019; 800-962-9504
**May Silk,** 13262 Moore Street, Cerritos, CA 90703; 800-282-7455
**Mikasa Factory Store,** 25 Enterprise Avenue, Secaucus, NJ 07096; 201-867-3517
**Mills Floral Supply,** 4550 Peachtree Lakes Drive, Duluth, GA 30136; 800-762-7939
**Newark Dressmaker Supply,** 6473 Ruch Road, P.O. Box 20730, Lehigh Valley, PA 18002-0730; 800-736-6783
**Ott's Discount Art Supply,** 102 Hungate Drive, Greenville, NC 27858; 800-356-3289
**Paper Art Company,** 7240 Shadeland Station, Suite 300, Indianapolis, IN 46256; 800-428-5017
**Pearl Paint,** 308 Canal Street, New York, NY 10013; 800-221-6845
**Pottery Barn,** 100 North Point Street, San Francisco, CA 94133; 800-922-9934
**Reliable,** 101 W. Van Buren, Chicago, IL 60607; 800-735-4000
**Renovator's,** P.O. Box 2515, Conway, NH 03818-2515; 800-659-2211
**Royal Lace,** 93 North Avenue, Garwood, NJ 07027; 800-526-4280
**Service Merchandise,** P.O. Box 25130, Nashville, TN 37202-5130; 800-251-1212
**Stampendous,** 1357 South Lewis Street, Anaheim, CA 92805; 800-869-0474
**Sunshine Discount Crafts,** P.O. Box 301, Largo, FL 34649-0301; 813-538-2878
**Village Flowers,** 297 Main Street, Huntington, NY 11743; 516-427-0996
**Williams-Sonoma,** P.O. Box 7456, San Francisco, CA 94120-7456; 800-541-2233
**The Woodworker's Store,** 21801 Industrial Boulevard, Rogers, MN 55374-9514; 800-279-4441 ◆

# Quick Projects

**Unfinished Terra-Cotta Pot**

**Verdigris Pot with Brass Accents**

Although a naturally aged, unfinished terra-cotta pot has an appeal all its own, you can also decorate these pots to match a dried floral arrangement or add color to a windowsill. You can find terra-cotta pots in a variety of sizes; diameters range from two inches to twenty-four inches. (The terra-cotta pots used here measure three inches in diameter.) Look for them in garden centers and even grocery stores; prices range from 39¢ to $15 or more, depending on their size and the amount of surface decoration. One note of caution: water will damage any decoration applied to the surface of a terra-cotta pot. If you want to use these pots for planting, be sure to line them with a plastic liner or pot the plant in a smaller plastic container that fits inside the terra-cotta pot.

**Moss-Covered Pot**—To cover the outside of the pot with a lush layer of green moss, cut a twelve-by-four-and-one-half-inch rectangle from a large sheet of moss (the kind that looks like sod) using a pair of scissors. Pull away some of the soil or root system under the moss to create an even, lightweight covering. (Take care not to tear the moss). Apply one coat of rubber cement to the exterior of the pot to seal the porous terra-cotta surface. Don't coat the bottom, but add a ring of glue to the inside rim at the top of the pot. When the rubber cement has dried completely, apply a second coat, then wrap the moss around the pot and over the top edge, holding it in place with firm pressure until it adheres. Using scissors, trim the moss even with the bottom of the pot, and tie a length of wire-edged ribbon into a bow just under the rim.

**Marbled Pot**—Tear a clean, damp kitchen sponge to form irregular edges, then sponge-paint the outside of the pot using mauve acrylic paint. Let the pot dry completely. Use a second piece of clean, damp sponge dipped in cream-colored acrylic paint to add mottling and texture. Dip a #1 or #2 artist's paintbrush into the cream-colored paint and paint several uneven lines to simulate the veins in marble. Smudge the lines with your finger for a more authentic look.

**Rose Decoupage**—Paint the pot black using semigloss acrylic paint; let the pot dry completely. Cut out small images (for example, the rose inserts in the Charter Issue, November/December 1993) and glue them to the pot using a decoupage medium such as Mod Podge. Smooth all the cut edges of the roses and leaves flat, then apply a coat of semigloss acrylic medium to seal and protect the pot.

**Verdigris Pot with Brass Accents**—Using a foam brush, paint the pot with moss green acrylic paint; let the pot dry completely. Dip the tip of a clean foam brush into hunter green acrylic paint. Dab irregular, dime-sized dots by touching, then twisting the foam brush against the painted surface. When the paint is dry, attach the stamped brass medallions to the pot's rim using white tacky glue.

**Festive Striped Pot**—Paint the exterior and top inside rim of the pot yellow using acrylic paint; let the pot dry completely. Using low-tack masking tape, mark off vertical strips, then paint every other strip red. Let pot dry completely, then repeat process to fill in blue stripes. Seal pot with semigloss acrylic medium.

**Rope Swag with Shells**—Drape white cotton string into three swags of graduated sizes, and secure them in place with white tacky glue. When the glue is dry, spray-paint the entire pot gold and let the paint dry completely. Repeat for second coat. Hot-glue shell-shaped buttons or earrings to each side of the swag.

**Rosebud Collar**—Using a hot-glue gun, secure rows of miniature dried rosebuds along the top rim of the pot. Make a ring of rosebuds at the bottom of the rim, then work around the pot and up to the rim. Hot-glue each rosebud separately at its stem. ◆

**Festive Striped Pot**

**Marbled Pot**

**Rope Swag with Shells**

**Rose Decoupage**

**Rosebud Collar**

# Folk Art Bandbox

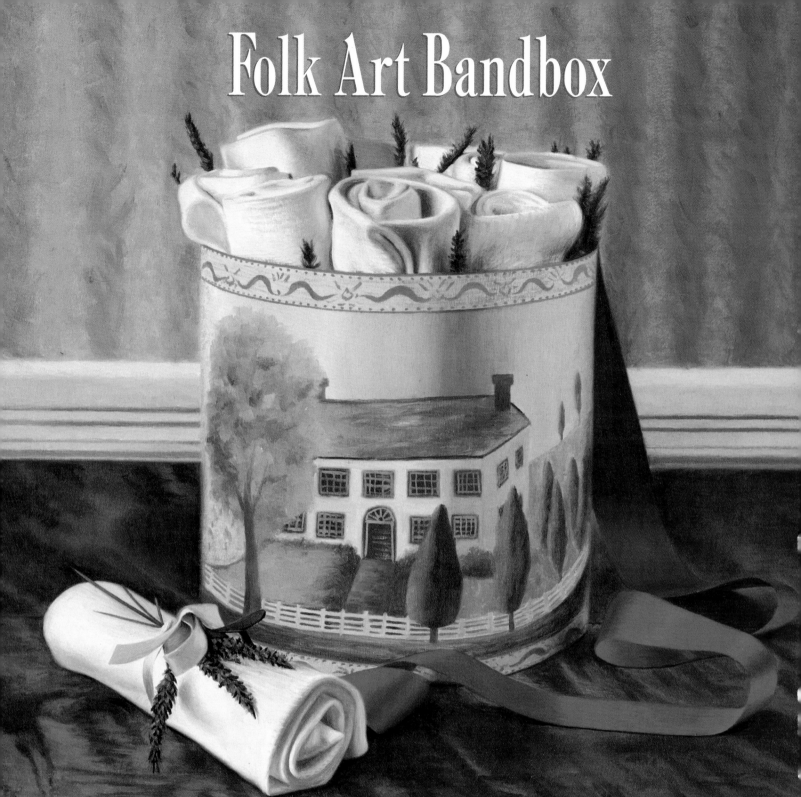

Y ou can create reusable and beautiful gift packaging using a cardboard or wooden bandbox measuring 8" across and 7½" high. You'll also need a strip of prepasted wallpaper border measuring at least 26" long and 9" wide. Using a straightedge and an X-Acto knife, trim the strip to 8" wide, then set aside the remainder for use on the lid. Wrap the border around the box to check the fit; trim to leave a ¼" overlap at the ends. Dampen the back of the border. (Apply Mod Podge with a sponge to borders that are not prepasted.) Line up the bottom edge of the border with the bottom edge of the bandbox. Wrap the border around the box, and press it in place. Fold over the extra ½" of the border to the inside of the box at the top edge. (If you're using borders that are not prepasted, recoat the ½" extra with Mod Podge using a sponge before pressing it to the inside of the box.) With a piece of sponge, paint the lid barn red using acrylic paint, then let dry at least ½ hour. Trim the remaining border to fit the lid, then attach it to the lid as directed above. If desired, fill the box with rolled napkins tied with ribbon and accented with lavender.

# HANDCRAFT
## ~ ILLUSTRATED ~

**SPECIAL INSERT**

## Edwardian Stationery Folio

Make a Quick Writing Folio
Using Our Antique Images

## Testing Metallic Paints

21 Paints Compared for Color,
Finish, and Ease of Use

## Secrets of Mitering Frames

How to Build Professional
Frames with a $6 Miter Box

## 10-Minute Faux Finishes

Rejuvenate Any Object with a
Sponge and Acrylic Paint

## Quick Duvet Cover from Flat Sheets

$2 CEDAR SACHETS

FAST BASKET-WEAVE CAKE

$4.00 U.S./$4.95 CANADA

0 71486 02716 4

04

**MINIATURE SPRINGTIME BASKETS:** TURN LEFTOVER DRIED FLOWERS INTO
MINI-BASKETS FOR QUICK HOME DECORATING.

Notes from Readers .........................2

Origin of the word silhouette; preserving the color of pressed flowers; and painting cotton curtains.

Quick Tips ...................................4

Preventing a paintbrush from drying out; steaming out dents in wood; keeping tulips fresh; pouring liquid into a small opening; perfectly matched prints; stenciling through netting; removing glue drips; and preventing drooping roses.

French Tinware Cachepot..................6

Create the look of lacquered French tinware using paint and our oval cartouche.

Miniature Flower Baskets....................9

Use your leftover dried flowers to make this trio of springtime baskets.

Testing Metallic Paints...................10

We put twenty-one metallic paints through their paces to determine the best performers in color, sheen, and ease of use.

Silk Peony Bouquet......................13

You can make this simple bouquet in less than an hour using silk flowers, foliage, and a two-foot dowel.

10-Minute Faux Finishes................14

Use a household sponge and acrylic paint to transform any wooden object.

### Special Insert

Edwardian Silk Writing Folio..........15

Use the three-panel apple blossom insert in this issue and less than half a yard of fabric to make an elegant stationery folio.

Miter-Box Frame............................17

Build a custom frame for about $40 using ordinary molding and a wooden miter box.

Ukrainian Easter Eggs..................20

Make your own heirloom Easter eggs using traditional wax-resist and dye techniques.

Two-Sheet Duvet Cover .....................23

Update a bedroom decorating scheme with a duvet cover sewn from a pair of sheets.

Cedar Chip Sachets..…....................26

Make these dainty lace sachets for less than $2 each using cedar shavings from a pet supply store.

Basket-Weave Cake with Pansies......28

Create a basket-weave effect in 20 minutes using Quaker Oat Squares.

Field Guide to
Miniature Baskets........................30

Stock up on these tiny containers for making dried flower arrangements or displaying Easter eggs.

Sources and Resources.....................31

Mail-order sources for materials used throughout this issue.

Quick Projects...............................33

Change the look and feel of any room by updating your lampshades.

Crystal Bead
Drop Candlestick............Back Cover

Re-create the look of an expensive glass-prism chandelier in a candlestick. Illustration by Dan Brown.

**FRENCH TINWARE CACHEPOT**
*page 6*

**MINIATURE FLOWER BASKETS**
*page 9*

**SILK PEONY BOUQUET**
*page 13*

**MITER-BOX FRAME**
*page 17*

**UKRAINIAN EASTER EGGS**
*page 20*

**TWO-SHEET DUVET COVER**
*page 23*

**CEDAR CHIP SACHETS**
*page 26*

# HANDCRAFT
### ~ILLUSTRATED~

*Editor* CAROL ENDLER STERBENZ

*Executive Editor* BARBARA BOURASSA

*Senior Editor* MICHIO RYAN

*Managing Editor* MAURA LYONS

*Assistant Managing Editor* TRICIA O'BRIEN

*Directions Editors* CANDIE FRANKEL
SUSAN WILSON

*Editorial Assistant* KIM N. RUSSELLO

*Copy Editor* KURT TIDMORE

---

*Art Director* MEG BIRNBAUM

*Special Projects Designer* AMY KLEE

*Photo Stylist* SYLVIA LACHTER

---

*Publisher and Founder* CHRISTOPHER KIMBALL

*Editorial Consultant* RAYMOND WAITES

---

*Marketing Director* ADRIENNE KIMBALL

*Circulation Director* ELAINE REPUCCI

*Circulation Assistant* JENNIFER L. KEENE

*Customer Service* JONATHAN VENIER

*Production Director* JAMES MCCORMACK

*Production Assistants* SHEILA DATZ
PAMELA SLATTERY

*Publicity Director* CAROL ROSEN KAGAN

*Treasurer* JANET CARLSON

*Accounting Assistant* MANDY SHITO

*Office Manager* JENNY THORNBURY

*Office Assistant* SARAH CHUNG

*Handcraft Illustrated* (ISSN 1072-0529) is published bimonthly by Boston Common Press Limited Partners, 17 Station Street, P.O. Box 509, Brookline, MA 02147-0509. Copyright 1995 Boston Common Press Limited Partners. Second-class postage paid in Boston, MA, and additional mailing offices. Editorial office: 17 Station Street, P.O. Box 509, Brookline, MA 02147-0509; (617) 232-1000, FAX (617) 232-1572. Editorial contributions should be sent to: Editor, *Handcraft Illustrated*, P.O. Box 509, Brookline, MA 02147-0509. We cannot assume responsibility for manuscripts submitted to us. Submissions will be returned only if accompanied by a large, self-addressed stamped envelope. Subscription rates: $24.95 for one year; $45 for two years; $65 for three years. (Canada: add $3 per year; all other foreign add $12 per year.) Postmaster: Send all new orders, subscription inquiries, and change of address notices to *Handcraft Illustrated*, P.O. Box 51383, Boulder, CO 80322-1383. Single copies $4 in U.S., $4.95 in Canada and foreign. Back issues available for $5 each. PRINTED IN THE U.S.A.

Rather than put ™ in every occurrence of trademarked names, we state that we are using the names only and in an editorial fashion and to the benefit of the trademark owner, with no intention of infringement of the trademark.

**Note to Readers:** Every effort has been made to present the information in this publication in a clear, complete, and accurate manner. It is important that all instructions are followed carefully, as failure to do so could result in injury. Boston Common Press Limited Partners, the editors, and the authors disclaim any and all liability resulting therefrom.

# EDITORIAL

CAROL ENDLER STERBENZ

The other day I started thinking about a characteristic that I thought only I and a small minority of craftspeople might share: staying up all night to work on a project. I'm referring, of course, to the proverbial "all-nighter," that type of behavior usually associated with college students trying to write term papers in a single night, usually the night before the papers are due. Craftspeople rarely discuss this practice, so it's difficult to know if all-nighters are simply too common to talk about or too rare to be mentioned at all.

I would never have thought to contemplate this practice were it not for a recent string of coincidences that suggested I wasn't alone in my willingness to spend all night painting designs on a dresser, faux-finishing a wall, or arranging dried flowers. It's not that these tasks intrinsically require all night to accomplish, but there's something peaceful about settling down to work on a project after the house is quiet. That's not to say that night owls don't witness some pretty amazing things. If I hadn't stayed up all night doing my crafts, I would have missed the night my niece came by late after a date because she knew I would be up and said, "He told me he loved me tonight." Nighttime in my studio has always felt like Christmas—gifts just waiting to appear. It's as if some quiet imaginary machinery is at work there, humming along, urging and inviting me back after the day is over.

What first started me thinking about my nocturnal work habits was a call from one of my editors, who noticed my pattern of leaving late-night messages on our shared e-mail system. She phoned to offer support, believing I must be under an extraordinarily heavy workload if I had to send messages at such bizarre hours . . . 1:00 A.M., 2:41 A.M., 4:00 A.M. I wondered how in the world she knew. Having just become computer literate, I was unaware that each message was accompanied by a log-in time.

Several weeks later, the wife of a craftsman complained to me about their midnight run to the hospital emergency room, and my curiosity was piqued. It seems he was cutting wood for a set of chairs, and he accidentally cut himself. *At midnight?!* It looked suspiciously like an all-nighter to me!

But it wasn't until recently that I realized how staying up past the normal point of human endurance to paint a wall, sew a seam, or saw wood was as common to the community of crafters as say, having a pile of unfinished projects, going on vacations that involve more stops at craft stores than gas stations, converting a member of the family to a particular craft while at the same time turning off another family member, or putting more time into a craft project than into dinner.

A few weeks ago I traveled to upstate New York, where I visited a group of decorative painters. We had never met before, but I immediately felt a strong sense of belonging. One afternoon we took a drive out into the country where we visited a barn that had been converted into a quilt store. Bolts of fabric were stacked in columns that rose from the wide plank floors to the rafters overhead. I wanted to buy a quarter yard of each fabric I saw, but I reluctantly narrowed the "must-haves" to a half-dozen choices. As I waited in line to pay, I noticed a stack of newsletters marked "free." I took one and opened it up to a calendar of upcoming events. On one line I read, "Join our quilting club." I moved my eyes down a few lines and saw: "ALL-NIGHTER: Friendship Star. If you've never come to one of our all-night adventures, now is the time. Fee includes midnight snack!"

*Carol Endler Sterbenz*

P.S. I'm writing this letter to you in the halo of a single light; it's 2:00 A.M. Perhaps you are also reading it in the early morning hours. Isn't it great to know that we're comrades in this peaceful, underground, nocturnal world—craftspeople flourishing in the quiet of the night? Yes, I think so too.

# NOTES FROM READERS

## ORIGIN OF THE WORD SILHOUETTE

*Do you happen to know the origin of the term silhouette?*

PAIGE WESTMAN
Bedford, NY

Silhouettes, generally thought of as likenesses of individuals in profile and usually cut from dark paper and mounted on a light background, were a popular craft in the nineteenth century. They were as common in Victorian households as photographic portraits are in our homes today.

The silhouette is named for Etienne de Silhouette, a French Minister of Finance who held the post for a brief time in 1759. According to *Textile Designs*, a book on the history of textiles by Susan Meller and Joost Elffers, de Silhouette was influential in having a ban on printed textiles lifted, which did not endear him to the textile weavers of that era, who, for obvious reasons, were opposed to the development of the cloth-printing industry. To protest de Silhouette's action, the textile weavers circulated flyers that exhibited an exaggerated likeness of him cut from black paper. As Meller and Elffers point out, it is thought that either because of the flyers or because of the "penny-pinching economies [de Silhouette] imposed, silhouettes—which are far easier, quicker, and therefore cheaper to produce than painted portraits—have been called by his name ever since."

## TIPS ON DRYING HYDRANGEAS

*For some reason I have been unable to find the secret to drying hydrangeas successfully. I've tried setting them in an inch or two of water, allowing them to dry slowly, and I've tried air-drying them in an upside-down position. Using either method, they tend to shrivel. Please let me know what I am doing wrong.*

MARY HERTSLET
Bethesda, MD

We consulted Seaport Flowers in Brooklyn, New York, who told us that drying hydrangeas successfully requires picking the flower when it is dry on the bush. This is when the florets feel dry but are not yet brittle, and when the color is at its most vibrant (usually when the flower is in full bloom). Unfortunately, if you're attempting to air-dry store-bought flowers, your odds of being successful are not good, since the flowers were probably picked from the bush before their prime.

Hydrangeas are generally best picked in mid-to late September, but because the flowers begin to bloom in June, the September date is approximate. Keep a close watch to find the right time. Seaport Flowers also recommends air-drying hydrangeas in a place out of the sunlight, where the air is crisp, dry, and well-circulated.

## PRESERVING THE COLOR OF PRESSED FLOWERS

*Is there a way to preserve the color of pressed flowers?*

MRS. GERDON FAHLAND
Oswego, OR

We consulted Rob Wood, author of *The Art of Dried Flowers* and owner of Spoutwood Farm in Glen Park, Pennsylvania, where he teaches classes in dried-flower arranging. He told us there is no fail-safe way of preserving the color of pressed flowers. Some flowers simply retain their color better than others, and once a flower has been picked, it is subject to natural deterioration. A pressed flower may fare a bit better than a dried flower, as it is typically dried within the dark confines of the pages of a book or press.

Wood's advice is similar to that of Seaport Flowers regarding drying hydrangeas (*see* above). To get the most color from your flowers, pick them just before they reach their peak of color, which is usually at the height of bloom (the flower will continue to ripen once it has been removed from the plant). Then immediately press or dry the flowers in a place that is as dark and dry as possible.

It's also possible to "enhance" the color of dried flowers by artificial means. Ground chalk, cosmetic blush, and powdered eye shadows can be brushed on the petals, although the effect is not wholly natural and will be more effective with some plants than others. Artificial floral sprays are another possibility, although they produce more natural effects with leaves than with flowers. To get the best results, we suggest you try using flowers that naturally retain their color well. Statice, yarrow, bottle brush, craspedia, sunflowers, strawflowers, cornflowers, bright pink or magenta roses (the lighter yellow and orange varieties tend to turn yellow, while the reds tend to turn purple-black), love-lies-bleeding, and lemon leaves are some flowers that hold their color well but do not all press flat. You'll need to experiment.

## THE DEFINITION OF BERLIN WORK

*What is Berlin work?*

MELANIE KEEFER
Milton, MA

Needlepoint was perhaps the most widely practiced of the needlework crafts of the Victorian era. During that time, German printers began producing a vast array of stitching charts in grid format, which were hand-colored by women factory artisans. The popularity of the new color charts inspired Victorian women to refer to their needlepoint work—an endeavor they pursued with great seriousness, ambition, and pride—as "Berlin work."

## FINDING INFORMATION ON ENDANGERED FLOWERS

*I'd like to pick my own flowers for drying, but I'm concerned about picking an endangered species. How do I obtain a list of endangered plants in my area?*

LISA BAILEY
Hamilton, OH

We consulted botanists at The Nature Conservancy in Arlington, Virginia, who suggest that you begin at your local library, which may have books on rare plants in your area or resources for getting information on endangered plant species where you live. The Nature Conservancy also suggests contacting a native plant society in your area, The Nature Conservancy field office in your state, or your state government to find out about its Natural Heritage program. (Natural Heritage programs are state-run organizations that focus on protecting endangered animals and plants.) Another option: your local county extension office.

## THREAD FOR PEARL NECKLACES

*I'd like to make a cultured pearl necklace. Is there a special thread I should use? I'd like the finished piece to sit just below the collarbone.*

FRANNY PERKINS
Santa Barbara, CA

Silk thread, available in a wide range of colors and weights, is probably your best option. Unlike a stiffer thread such as tigertail (nylon fused on wire), which might kink, such thread will allow the finished necklace to drape softly at the length you describe. Silk thread also knots well and does not stretch as much as other threads, thus lengthening the life of your finished piece. Generally, sizes #A and #D are good choices for small pearls, while #E and #F can be used for larger ones.

## PREVENTING DROOPY FLOWERS

*I recently used Oasis for the first time to arrange a vase of beautiful, fresh roses for a dinner party. Thankfully I bought the flowers the same day as the party—the arrangement looked withered by the next morning. Have you any idea what went wrong?*

PENNY CRAWFORD
Grosse Pointe, MI

Since you mentioned that your flowers were fresh, it leads us to believe that you may not have prepared the Oasis properly. Oasis must be soaked to the core before any flowers are inserted. Simply submerge it in water for about ten minutes, or until there are no more bubbles. Preparing the Oasis this way enables it to hold enough water to sustain the flowers.

Another trick is to cut flower stems at an angle (*see* Quick Tips, page 4). Not only will the stems be easier to place into the Oasis, but they will also absorb water more efficiently.

## TIPS ON USING SNAPPED STEMS

*Do you have any suggestions for integrating a flower with a snapped stem into an arrangement? I'd hate to tell you the number of flowers I've placed in a small juice glass or thrown away.*

ROSEMARY HALLORAN
Morristown, NJ

An interesting vase might not be a bad item to have on hand in such cases, as flowers can often look dramatic when their stems are cut down and the flowers are placed in a small, low vase (picture, for example, a centerpiece of large pale pink roses in a low cobalt glass bowl).

Another option is to use floral picks. These are available in various lengths, usually from three to six inches long, and are designed to elongate stems. The pointed end fits easily into Oasis foam, making it simple to incorporate the "repaired" flower into your arrangement. Wrap florist tape once or twice around the stem just above the bottom, hold the pick perpendicular to the stem, and twist the tape around the pick and stem to join them together. Bear in mind that floral picks are not water-carrying devices; they merely allow you greater design flexibility by extending the length—not the life—of flowers.

## FINDING A PATTERN FOR A FABRIC BACKGAMMON BOARD

*Do you know where I can get a pattern for a fabric backgammon board?*

JODIE CAVANAUGH
New Britain, CT

Keepsake Quilting, of Centre Harbor, New Hampshire, stocks a range of game board patterns, from backgammon to checkers, chess and Chinese checkers. Fabric games are nice for a summer house gift, or for children to take to the beach or to camp. The board patterns come with instructions, diagrams, and full-size templates.

## FINDING FLESH-TONED SHADES OF FABRIC

*I found a simple pattern for a pancake doll, but I'm having a hard time finding fabric in a flesh-toned shade. Everything seems to be too yellow or too pink. Can you help?*

ANNETTE LECHAUX
New Orleans, LA

We took your question to Jodie Davis, author of *Easy-to-Make Dolls and All the Trimmings* and the forthcoming *Teach Yourself Cloth Dollmaking.* Davis recommends that you buy off-white, unbleached, 100 percent cotton fabric—available at any fabric or quilting store—and dye it to the exact tone you need.

Household dyes such as RIT can be used to achieve believable skin tones, but finding the right shade may require some experimentation. Davis suggests testing several swatches of fabric before committing yourself to a whole piece. She begins by using less color rather than more, then increases the color as she needs it. The amount of dye used affects the final color of the cloth more strongly than the length of time the cloth soaks in the dye. Remember, wet fabric looks darker than dry, so let the fabric dry before adding more dye.

To simulate Caucasian skin tones, Davis combines rose and peach dye in an approximate ratio of 1:2. To simulate African-American skin tones, she recommends experimenting with a deep brown or cocoa color. Asian skin tones require a combination of beige and a pale pink or rose, while Native American skin tones can be achieved with a combination of cocoa with a siennalike tone.

## PAINTING COTTON CAFÉ CURTAINS

*I'd like to paint a design on some cotton café curtains I'm about to make for my kitchen. Do I need to prepare them in any way first? Is there a special brush I should use?*

LINDA ELLIS
Brownsburg, IN

Wash, dry, and iron any fabric to preshrink it and to remove any sizing before you begin to paint on it. You can find stenciling brushes (which have bristles that are short, even, and stiff) for textile painting at your local art supply store, where you'll also find a wide range of textile paints and protective sprays that will not only preserve your finished project, but also allow you to launder it safely.

## SELECTING PAINT FOR DECORATING CANVAS SNEAKERS

*What type of paints should I use to decorate canvas sneakers?*

LEE BACHMAN
Keene, NH

Any acrylic paint will do, although an acrylic fabric paint (also available in marker form) is a better choice, as it provides a more flexible finish. Fabric paints typically need to be heat set, and this is usually done by ironing the fabric on the unmarked side. Because it's not possible to iron sneakers, instead place the fully dried shoes in a clothes dryer for about five minutes. Always read the instructions on the product package before beginning a project like this. Once you've painted your sneakers, you may wish to apply a colorless fabric paint as a top coat to protect your design. (Depending on the paint you select, the top coat may also need to be heat-set.) ◆

# Quick Tips

## Preventing a Paintbrush from Drying Out

To save time during a craft project that involves painting, don't clean the brush every time you take a break or stop for a meal. A plastic bag can keep acrylic or oil craft paints from drying out and the brush bristles pliable for an hour or even overnight. (Note: This method won't work with latex house paint, which tends to form a skin on the bristles, even inside the plastic bag.)

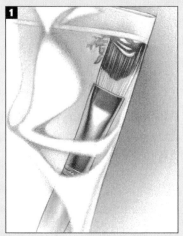

**1.** Slip the brush, bristles first, into a sandwich-sized plastic bag so the wet bristles lodge in a corner.

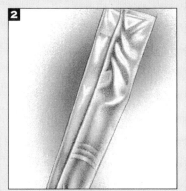

**2.** Wrap the loose section of the bag around the entire brush, then secure the bag to the handle using a twist tie. By sealing off the air, the bag prolongs the paint's usual drying time.

## Steaming Out Dents in Wood

A dent in a *soft* wood such as pine can often be removed with steam. The steam penetrates the compressed fibers and causes them to swell back into place. (Note: This method should work for polyurethaned surfaces, woods that have been stained with oil-based stains, or solid woods. Don't use this method on veneered, varnished, or shellacked surfaces, or those with rubbed oil finishes or wax polish.)

**1.** Moisten a terry washcloth, and squeeze out as much of the moisture as you can. Fold the washcloth into quarters and place it over the dent.

**2.** Hold a dry iron set at medium heat over the damp washcloth for up to 1 minute, or until the steam subsides. Remove the iron and washcloth and examine the dent. Wipe away any condensation with a dry cloth. Repeat as necessary.

## Keeping Tulips Fresh

To keep tulips fresh and prevent their top-heavy stems from drooping over, follow these simple techniques: Be sure to cut (or buy) the blooms early in the day and store them in a cool, moist environment until you are ready to arrange them. To keep the flowers looking their best, you'll need a sharp knife, a 3-gallon galvanized steel bucket filled with cool water, and some newspaper.

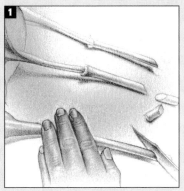

**1.** Using the knife, cut off the ends of the stems at a 45-degree angle. (Don't cut them with scissors or pruning shears, as these can pinch the stems and prevent them from absorbing water.) Trim off any leaves that will be immersed in water.

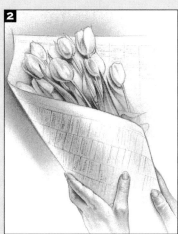

**2.** Lay all the tulips on a layer of newspaper and roll the newspaper into a cone around them.

**3.** Set the cone with the flowers in it into a bucket of cool water, then place the bucket in a garage, basement, or some other cool spot. The metal will stay cool, and in about an hour's time, the water will seep up the sides of the newspaper, creating a moist enclosure for the blooms. Standing in water will also allow the tulip heads to straighten up naturally.

## Pouring Liquid into a Small Opening

When you don't have a funnel to pour a solvent, oil, glaze, or other liquid into a container with a small opening, try this method instead: Hold a flat-tipped (not Phillips) screwdriver almost vertically, with the tip just above the opening of the container. Place the lip of the cup or bowl containing the liquid against the tool's metal shaft and pour slowly. Surface tension will cause the liquid to flow down the shaft directly into the opening.

ILLUSTRATIONS BY HARRY DAVIS

# Perfectly Matched Prints

Draperies, valances, and tablecloths sewn from floral-, landscape-, and medallion-print fabrics look more professional when the prints are perfectly matched at the seam lines. Fusible tape, typically used for hemming and appliqué, can help ensure an even match by preventing large fabric panels from shifting while you sew them. In addition to your fabric, you'll need fusible tape with peel-off paper backing (such as Heat'N Bond), matching thread, a sewing machine, an iron, scissors or a rotary cutter, and a ruler.

**1.** Trim each fabric panel so that a 1" to 3" section of the print is repeated on each of the edges to be joined.

**2.** Press one of the edges 1" to the wrong side, then affix the fusible tape to the flap, just touching the fold, following the manufacturer's directions.

**3.** Peel off the paper tape, leaving the fusible material adhered to the fabric.

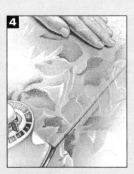

**4.** Lay the panel with the fusible material on top of the other panel, line up the patterns along the folded edge, and press to fuse.

**5.** When the fusible material is cool, open the fabric wrong side up and stitch along the fold crease. Trim the seam ½" from the stitching.

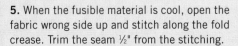
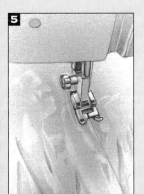

**6.** Press the joined fabrics thoroughly from the wrong and right sides.

# Stenciling through Netting

For a variation on stenciling, try using spray paint and lace netting. Depending on how closely the netting hugs the surface during spraying, the resulting pattern can range from fairly sharp and clear to undulating and subtle. Test different effects on scrap paper before you stencil the actual project. You'll need spray paint, lace netting, scrap paper, and newspaper.

**1.** Use newspaper to protect any areas you don't want painted. Then lay, drape, or hang the netting across the surface to be painted, manipulating it into loose, gentle ripples for an undulating effect, or pulling it tight for a crisper effect. Spray-paint the entire surface, following the paint manufacturer's recommendations.

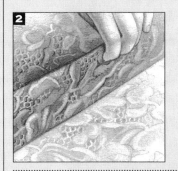

**2.** Immediately lift the netting off the surface. If the surface is large or three-dimensional and there are more areas you wish to paint this way, you can use the same piece of netting to repeat the process.

# Removing Glue Drips

When glue drips in an inopportune spot, a single-edged razor blade makes a handy miniature scraper to neatly lift and remove the unwanted droplets. Simply slide the blade along the length of the bead of glue. This technique works equally well with white craft glue, clear glue gel, or yellow carpenter's glue.

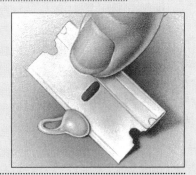

# Preventing Drooping Roses

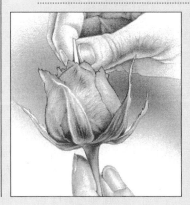

When a rose in a cut-flower arrangement starts to droop prematurely, you can keep it upright for an extra day or two with a round-cut toothpick. Stick the toothpick directly through the center of the rose down into the stem, then snip off any of the toothpick that still shows with pruning shears. This technique also works for top-heavy zinnias.

**ATTENTION READERS: RECEIVE A FREE SUBSCRIPTION IF WE PUBLISH YOUR TIP.** Do you have a unique shortcut or technique you'd like to share with other readers? We'll give you a one-year complimentary subscription for each Quick Tip that we publish. Send a description of your special technique to: Quick Tips, *Handcraft Illustrated*, P.O. Box 509, 17 Station Street, Brookline Village, MA 02147-0509. Please include your name, address, and daytime phone number. Unfortunately, we can only acknowledge receipt of tips actually used in the magazine.

# French Tinware Cachepot

*Create the look of lacquered French tinware using paint and our oval cartouche.*

BY MICHIO RYAN

*Although the finish on this tinware planter may look antique, it was created using a glaze made from burnt umber paint and polyurethane varnish.*

This lacquered cachepot resembles an antique French planter, but it is created using modern materials and techniques. The finish on the tinware is achieved with a combination of paint and varnish; the lacquered look on the oval cartouche is created using transfer medium. Using our techniques, you can create a variety of painted objects limited only by the tinware or brass

pieces and cutout images you find.

A wide variety of tinware is available at craft stores such as Michael's and home accessory stores such as Pottery Barn and Pier One Imports. The tinware used for this project, priced at $25, is available by mail. This particular item has solid brass feet, which I protected with masking tape during painting. Although just about any tinware can be decorated with the techniques outlined in this article, I don't recommend trays, because images applied with transfer medium will not hold up to the abrasion of objects placed on the tray. The edges of a tray could be decorated, however, as the decals are waterproof after they dry thoroughly. (Transfer medium, as the name implies, transfers a color or black-and-white image to a clear backing, which can then be applied to any painted surface. Transfer medium can be found in art supply or craft stores; one well-known brand is Transfer-it.)

If your tinware is already painted or is made from galvanized metal, it will not need priming. If you cannot find galvanized tinware, you can substitute any tinware, but you will need to apply two coats of spray-on primer. If you're not sure whether your container is ready to paint without priming, it's well worth the extra effort to apply the primer. You can also use brass containers. Don't remove the lacquer on the brass—this will serve as the first primer coat. Simply apply one additional coat of spray-on primer.

Before applying the base coat of chrome yellow, remove any oil or grease from your galvanized tin pot using a mixture of water and white distilled vinegar. Don't dunk the metalware item in the water-vinegar mixture, or the rolled rims and other details will hold water and create defects in the succeeding paint steps. (Use denatured alcohol to clean brass planters

or painted metalware.)

Once you've cleaned and, if necessary, primed your pot, it's time to apply the chrome yellow spray-on enamel. When applying the base coat, don't paint the pot's rim; you'll paint it bright gold in the last step. When spray-painting, use even strokes across the surface, and shake the can between strokes. Don't try to get complete coverage with the first coat; you're better off building up several thin coats than trying to cover the cachepot with one heavy coat, which may sag or run. The chrome yellow will seem very bright at first, but the second color will tone down the color considerably.

The soft, rag finish on the cachepot is created with a glaze made of burnt umber artist's oil paint and clear polyurethane varnish. This mixture is wiped on with a paper towel, then dabbed off to create a textured finish. For even more texture, use a second paper towel moistened with paint thinner to remove more of the mixture. (Take care not to use too much thinner, however, as it could cause the varnish to run.) You can create a darker finish by changing the ratio of burnt umber oil paint to varnish, or by loading more of the mixture onto the first paper towel and dabbing it on lightly, then dabbing with a thinner-moistened paper towel to blend the spots.

Note: If you use the cachepot as a planter, be sure to place a plastic liner or container inside, as water can damage the painted finish.

### FRENCH TINWARE CACHEPOT

2 photocopies of cartouche
 (*see* image, page 7)
 Galvanized or painted tinware
 or brass container
 Krylon chrome yellow #1801
 (or equivalent) glossy enamel
 spray paint
 Black semigloss, quick-drying
 enamel paint
 Forest green semigloss, quick-drying
 enamel paint (same brand as
 black paint)
 Ivory gloss finish, quick-drying
 spray paint
 Transfer medium
2 tablespoons satin finish, quick-drying
 polyurethane varnish
 2-ounce tube burnt umber artist's oil paint

1-ounce jar or tube pale gold oil paint
Paint thinner
White distilled vinegar

*You'll also need:* flat, waterproof work surface such as laminated countertop or smooth, plastic cutting board; 1"-wide disposable paintbrush; #10 round brush; ¼"-round, stiff-bristled brush; scissors; rubber cement; small bowl; 2 disposable plastic containers; 1"-wide, low-tack painter's tape; kitchen sponge; paper towels; 1"-wide masking tape; newspaper; tablespoon; protective eyewear for spray-painting steps; and plastic disposable gloves.

*Other items, if necessary:* spray-on metal primer (such as Krylon) and four small pieces of scrap wood (for priming ungalvanized tinware or brass); Q-tips (for removing paint smudges); and denatured alcohol (for cleaning brass).

**Preparing the Metalware Surface**

1. If using brass planters, clean with denatured alcohol. If using galvanized tinware, mix ½ cup vinegar and ½ cup water in small bowl. Using kitchen sponge and vinegar-water solution, wash to remove grease. Rinse with sponge and fresh water, let dry thoroughly, and proceed to step 3.

2. *To prime brass or ungalvanized tinware,* cover workspace with newspaper, keep area well ventilated, and put on protective eyewear. Cover pot's feet (or other decorations) with masking tape. Tip pot at an angle, mouth facing you, and spray-paint interior with primer. Hold paint can nearly upright, about 10" away from pot, and be careful of back spray. Let paint dry following manufacturer's recommendations, then apply second coat. To prevent rim of pot from sticking to newspaper, turn pot upside down and rest each corner on a piece of scrap wood. Apply one coat of primer to outside and bottom of pot. Let dry following manufacturer's recommendations, then apply second coat. Let dry thoroughly.

3. Spray-paint outside and bottom of pot with chrome yellow enamel paint. Let dry following manufacturer's recommendations, then apply second coat. If necessary, apply third coat to cover thin spots. Stand pot upright on feet and dry for at least 2 hours or as recommended by manufacturer.

4. While outside of pot is drying, paint interior finish. In disposable plastic container, mix one part green enamel paint with four parts black enamel paint. (Use stiff-bristled round brush to mix paints and to remove paint from spoon between measurements.) Stand pot upright. Using 1"-wide disposable brush, apply even, thin coat of paint to pot's interior. Check seams and corners for excess or pooling paint; remove with paintbrush. Set pot aside to dry between 4 and 8 hours or as recommended by manufacturer. Clean tablespoon, brushes, and surfaces with paint thinner. Proceed to illustrated directions, below and on following page. ◆

## MAKING THE CARTOUCHE DECAL

For the following two steps, work on a flat, waterproof surface, such as a laminated kitchen counter, or a smooth, plastic cutting board.

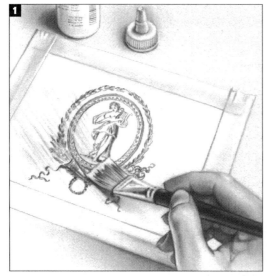

**1.** Attach a photocopy of the cartouche to a flat, waterproof surface by taping it around the edges with masking tape. Apply six successive coats of transfer medium with a soft #10 brush, brushing on each coat perpendicular to the preceding one to minimize brush marks. Paint over the whole cartouche as well as ½" beyond the outline. Let each coat dry 15 minutes before applying the next coat. Wash out the brush thoroughly between coats. Allow the cartouche to dry for 24 hours. (When first applied, the transfer medium looks milky, but it will dry clear.)

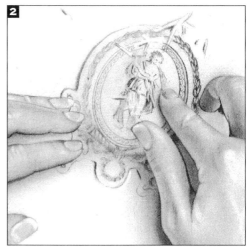

**2.** After 24 hours, peel the cartouche off the waterproof surface and remove the tape from the edges. Clean with a damp sponge and dry the surface. Soak the cartouche in a bowl of warm water for 1 hour, then lay the cartouche face down on the dry, clean surface. Rub the back of the cartouche gently with a fingertip to roll off the paper in small pieces. Continue rubbing gently until all the paper is removed and the copied image is visible. (The cartouche may have reabsorbed some water from soaking so it might be slightly milky again.) Let the cartouche dry on the countertop for 1 hour, or until it is almost transparent. If the cartouche is not transparent, repeat the soaking, rubbing, and drying processes.

## CREATING THE STENCIL MASK AND PAINTING THE IVORY OVAL

**1.** Using the scissors, carefully cut out the oval center of the second pho-

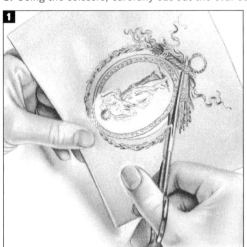

tocopied cartouche and discard the cut-out center. Trim the edges of the oval shape so they are neat and clear. Lay the remaining image face down on a clean piece of newspaper and apply a thin coat of rubber cement to a 1"-wide swath around the inside edges of the cutout area. Let it dry 5 minutes, then apply a second coat. Let it dry 15 minutes.

**2.** Center the stencil mask on one side of the pot (it can be easily peeled off and repositioned). Once in place, press it down firmly with your fingertips to form a good seal.

**3.** Cover the remainder of the pot (leaving the oval area exposed) by taping on newspaper. Lay the pot on its side with the exposed area facing up, then spray-paint the oval with one even coat of ivory spray paint. (Work in a well-ventilated area when using spray paint and wear protective eyewear.) Carefully pull the stencil mask away immediately to prevent the ivory paint from bleeding under it. If the paint bleeds, immediately remove any smudges using a Q-tip dipped in paint thinner. Let the pot dry at least 2 hours. When the ivory paint is dry, remove any remaining rubber cement by rubbing it off with your fingers.

## MIXING AND APPLYING THE RAG GLAZE

**1.** To mix the ragging glaze, combine 2 tablespoons polyurethane varnish and a pea-sized dab of burnt umber oil paint in a disposable plastic container. Mix them thoroughly using a stiff-bristled round brush. (The glaze should be the color of dark molasses, but it will be thinner in consistency.) Pull on the plastic disposable gloves. Put one hand inside the pot to hold it while you paint. Crumple a paper towel into a loose ball and dip one side into the glaze. Apply a thin, even coat of glaze on one side of the pot by smearing on the paint with a light, circular motion of the crumpled paper towel. To create a rag finish, dab and blot the painted surface with a clean paper towel to remove some of the glaze. Rescrunch the paper towel after several dabs to prevent repetitive marks. Repeat the ragging effect on each side of the pot, then let the pot dry 2 hours. For the side with the ivory oval, finish by wiping the glaze away from the oval with a paper towel dipped in paint thinner. Use paint thinner to clean up the brushes and surfaces.

## FINISHING THE POT

**1.** Pick up the transparent cartouche and neatly and carefully trim off extra edging to within ⅛" of the image. Lay the cartouche face down, then use the #10 round brush to apply a thin, even coat of transfer medium to the back of the image and to the area of the pot where the cartouche will be attached. Position the cartouche on the pot, matching the rounded edges with the ivory oval. Smooth the cartouche into place with your fingers, working from the center out to the edges to force out any trapped bubbles, and press the edges down firmly. Take care not to stretch the cartouche out of shape by excessive tugging or pressing. Remove any excess transfer medium with a moistened sponge, then apply a final glazing coat of medium to the entire side of the pot, level the edges of the decal, and even out the finish. Let it dry for 30 minutes.

**2.** Apply low-tack painter's tape under the pot's outside rolled rim, lining up the edge of the tape with the underside of the rolled rim. Apply tape to the interior of the pot approximately ⅛" from the rim. Using the ¼" round brush, paint the exposed pinstripe area with gold oil paint. (If you want, you can also paint other details gold, such as the pot's ring handles, knobs, or feet.) Let the paint dry overnight. Remove the tape from the top edges, then remove the tape from the planter's feet.

ILLUSTRATIONS BY MICHELLE AMATRULA

# Miniature Flower Baskets

*Use your leftover dried flowers to make this trio of springtime baskets.*

*For springtime entertaining, use several of these baskets together as a centerpiece, or make one for each guest's place at the table.*

If you've been wondering what to do with those leftover dried or silk flowers, these miniature baskets are the answer. Each of the baskets pictured here measures between three and four inches wide; you can fill them with a minimum amount of leftover flowers and foliage, or purchase one or two packages of flowers for each.

The construction technique is simple: Fill the container with dry foam, trim the plant stems to two inches, and insert them into the foam. If the stems have broken off, simply hot-glue each flower-head directly to the surface of the dry foam or between the other flowers.

Using this technique, you can fill just about any miniature container with leftover flower heads or foliage, including a tea cup, a china bowl, a sugar bowl and creamer set, a large seashell, miniature wooden or painted tin boxes, or tiny terra-cotta pots. These miniature arrangements will add a dash of color to any room or table setting. Collect several to create a centerpiece, or hang one from a doorknob. (For additional ideas on selecting miniature baskets, see the "Field Guide to Miniature Baskets," page 30.)

## MINIATURE FLOWER BASKETS

*Yields one basket in each shape.*

    Round basket about 4" in diameter
6  yellow tea roses
20  sprigs purple statice
    Dry foam to fill basket
    Plaid FolkArt acrylic paint, Basil Green (#645)

    Round basket about 4" in diameter
15  pink tea roses

    Light-blue mop-headed hydrangeas
    Dry foam to fill basket
    Plaid FolkArt acrylic paint, Taffy (#902)

    Rectangular basket about 3" x 4"
8  pink tea roses
8  sprigs white statice
4  bunches pink cockscomb heads
    Dry foam to fill basket
    Plaid FolkArt acrylic paint, Heartland Blue (#608)

*You'll also need:* Stiff-bristled paintbrush or small piece of household sponge; scissors; newspaper; and table knife.

*Other items, if necessary:* Hot-glue gun and glue sticks (for gluing flowers or foliage without stems).

### Preparing the Basket

1. Cover work space with newspaper. Paint outside and 1" of inner rim of basket using paintbrush or sponge and appropriate color paint. Let dry at least 10 minutes.

2. Using table knife, cut dry foam to fit inside basket. Place foam inside basket and trim foam even with basket rim.

### Preparing the Dried Flowers

1. Lay all flower heads and sprigs on work surface. Sort as in photograph or according to your own design.

2. With scissors, trim stems to approximately 2".

3. Fill each basket as follows, using photograph as reference. For flowers or foliage without stems, hot-glue in place.

*Green round basket:* Insert or hot-glue a straight line of six yellow roses across center of basket, then fill sides with purple statice.

*Taffy-colored round basket:* Insert or hot-glue pink tea roses around rim of basket. Fill center of basket with mop-headed hydrangeas.

*Blue rectangular basket:* Insert or hot-glue a line of four pink roses at each short end of basket. Add one narrow line of white statice adjacent to each line of roses, then fill center with bunches of pink cockscomb. ◆

## AN ALTERNATE DESIGN

For the oval basket on the left, insert or hot-glue a line of seven red roses across the center of the basket, position four yellow rose heads on each end of the line as shown, and fill the rest of the basket with blue Billy Buttons. For the round basket in the middle, use assorted flowers, including roses, everlasting, and statice. To make the rectangular basket on the right, insert blue Billy Buttons around the rim, followed by two parallel rows of white sea lavender. Then fill the center of the basket with purple stirlingia.

# Testing Metallic Paints

*We put twenty-one metallic paints through their paces to determine the best performers in color, sheen, and ease of use.*

### BY MICHIO RYAN

When I began researching the various metallizing methods available on the market for this article, I found a bewildering array of materials. Among others, I found spray paints, brush-on paints, hobby/craft acrylic paints, paste waxes, felt-tip pens, artist's tube paints, high-quality artist's pigment powders you have to mix yourself, washable fabric paints, nonfire ceramist's glazes, specialized high-temp paints, metallic inks, and bookbinder's embossing foil. Many are made for specialized applications, which limits their usefulness. Spray paints and brush-on paints, including the conveniently sized and packaged craft/hobby paints, had the advantages of wide availability, ease of use, applicability on a variety of materials, and durability, so I decided to test them as a group and see how they performed.

Spray paints are almost always solvent-based, with real metal flakes serving as the colorant. Brush-on paints typically have the same combination, but some craft paints are acrylic-based and use mica flakes instead of real metal flakes. I specifically chose paints that are widely available; most spray and brush-on paints can be found in hardware or paint stores; acrylic craft paints are more commonly found in craft and art supply stores.

After testing twenty-one different paints, I outlined the specific characteristics that might make one a better choice for a given project than another. Because there are so many factors to consider, there is no one "best" paint, but the chart on page 12 and the paint samples found throughout this article should help you make your selection.

## Categorizing Metallic Paints

There are three common colors of metallic paints: gold (which includes brass), silver, and copper. Gold is by far the most widely available, the most popular, and the most varied in hue. Several standard shades exist, including pale gold, bright gold, and brass. Less commonly found are such shades as Florentine gold (which has a gray cast) or antique gold (which has a burnt umber cast).

Silver metallic paint varies little in hue from brand to brand, as most are made with pure aluminum flakes. Naturally, none of them accurately reproduce the look of real silver; next to the real thing, they look too bright and bluish-gray. Real silver is not used as a pigment because it would tarnish; the resulting paint would also be very expensive.

Copper is found less frequently as a paint color. It tends to be very orange-red in hue, more like a newly minted penny than an old tarnished one. The paints made with mica flakes are especially reddish. One notable exception is Plaid FolkArt Antique Copper, which is an attractive, dark red-brown.

Some metallic paints appear granular, as if the flakes of metal are embedded under the paint; others seem lustrously smooth, like polished metal. There is also a category of high-shine, spray-on paints that closely resemble electroplating. The sprays and solvent-based, brush-on paints all produce a sheen near gloss, with the exception of Kemp Permagild, which produces a moderately matte surface with a very granular appearance. Acrylics generally yield a semigloss surface with a fairly granular metallic effect.

## Drying Time, Durability, and Coverage

The spray-on, solvent-based paints dried relatively quickly; some even dried to the touch within fifteen minutes. Objects covered with such paints should not be handled for several hours, however, because fingerprints and dents will show up on the shiny surface. This is particularly true with the super-shiny spray paints. Most spray paints look better with two coats, and the recommended drying time between coats varies. In all cases, I recommend following the manufacturer's recommendations.

Water-based acrylics generally cure and dry within an hour or so, but the time is more sensitive to humidity. If the air is particularly damp, allow for additional drying time. Most of the solvent-based brush-on paints are also sensitive to humidity, since they use slower-drying solvents than sprays.

In terms of durability, there isn't a great deal of variation among the paints except by type of paint. Objects with areas of sharp relief naturally show wear quicker, especially in the case of sprayed paints that go on in a thinner film. This is less of a problem if you use the acrylics, which form a thicker and more flexible film. The high-shine sprays are particularly sensitive to abrasion, since the metal flakes lie at the surface. Even after a week of drying, a stroke of a clean finger against the paint can affect the luster. In general, proper preparation and the quality of the object being painted are the most important factors in determining success.

Among the solvent-based paints, all the sprays covered completely in one coat. Most spray-paint manufacturers recommend two

*This pale gold, ultra-shiny apple was covered with **Nybco 18 Kt\* Gold Plate** spray paint.*

*The brass-gold color on this apple is the result of **Krylon Brass Metallic Enamel** spray paint.*

***Krylon Bright Gold Metallic Enamel** spray paint produced the bright gold color of this apple.*

*The silver color of this apple was achieved with **Krylon Chrome-Aluminum** spray paint, which contains flakes of aluminum.*

***Testors Copper** spray-on enamel gives this apple a very red hue.*

thin coats rather than one thick coat to avoid drips, and while the coverage was good after one coat, you'll get smoother results by applying paint in two coats. This applies to all spray paints, but it's particularly true with metallic paints, whose surfaces show even the slightest imperfections because of their high shine. The same rule applies to solvent-based, brush-on paints, with two exceptions (which all produced an even, shiny film after the first coat): Kemp LustRgild enamel and Testors paints.

Acrylics required more paint to completely cover the background color of my test objects, even though they generally lay on in a thicker coat. Some acrylics required several coats to achieve complete color coverage.

### How Metallic Paints Work

Objects painted with metallic paint look different from those that are gilded with metal leaf or plating. Plating and leafing both apply (by different methods) a continuous layer of metal over the surface, whereas paint relies on small particles of metallic pigment suspended in a binder medium and a carrier, which then dries as one layer.

Solvent-based metallic paints contain flakes of real metals such as brass, zinc, aluminum, copper, or some combination of those metals. The palette of metallic paints is thus very true to life but is limited to actual metal colors. "Silver" paint is made of aluminum particles; "gold" paints are made from a combination of metals such as copper and zinc, and the color varies widely by brand, depending on the formulation. "Brass" paints may contain real brass flakes, and are suitable as touch-up paint because they are identical to the object being touched up.

Any paint that contains real metal flakes is susceptible to tarnishing, although the aluminum-pigmented "silver" paints are less tarnish-prone than the "gold" paints containing copper or brass. You can use sealer to retard tarnishing and enhance resistance to abrasion, but all paints will be affected in some way by its use, as the sealer dissolves the binder in the paint, causing the metallic flakes to realign, thereby reducing the sheen. For best results,

use a satin-finish varnish, which simulates the original luster better than a gloss-finish varnish.

Most acrylic paints rely on mica flakes that have been tinted to resemble metal, because real metal particles would oxidize in the water that forms the carrier for acrylic paints. Since the resulting paints are not made of real metal, however, their colors may not match real metal surfaces.

Metallic paints containing metal flakes vary in their degree of shine, depending on several factors. Ordinary metallic paints simply disperse metal pigment in a clear vehicle such as varnish. When dry, the varnish binds the flakes to the surface, producing a granular effect. Ultra-shiny metallic spray paints, on the other hand, contain flat metal flakes that float to the surface while the paint is still wet. The flakes settle in a flat layer so they all reflect light the same way, like a piece of polished metal. In ordinary metallic paints, the flakes settle randomly, so they scatter light in many directions, which produces a metallic but not necessarily a brilliant shine.

### Tips on Using Metallic Paints

Before applying any metallic paint, consider the suitability of the surface for painting. As with gold leafing, any imperfections will be magnified by metallic paints because of the high reflectivity. A cast piece, for instance, may show its mold marks worse with metallic paint than if a solid color or matte paint were used. In addition, some of the solvents used in certain paints will not be compatible with certain materials, especially plastic. Check the label before proceeding.

In virtually all cases, priming is recommended for consistent results. Sealers also provide a barrier between the paint and the surface of the object, which is particularly important with solvent-based paints that contain metal flakes. If such a paint is applied to a bare metal surface (such as brass on alumi-

num), the paint can react with the metal and corrode it over time. Porous materials, such as plaster, will also benefit from sealing, since they may contain moisture and accelerate oxidation, possibly ruining the paint's color.

Acrylics made with mica flakes are not subject to these kinds of degradation, but priming is still recommended. (Spray-on primer is the easiest to use; I've had good results with Nankee Flat Gray Primer.) A coat of primer, however, will not necessarily hide the flaws on an object's surface. Serious flaws should be removed with sandpaper or fine steel wool.

Spraying is probably the easiest method for applying metallic paints. The same kinds of safety and ventilation rules apply as for other spray paints, but metallic paints are apt to contain more solvents such as xylene or toluene, as well as small metal particles that can remain airborne, so you should follow a few additional precautions. Don't work in a kitchen or other room where there is an open flame, such as a pilot light, or a source of sparks. Always follow the manufacturer's recommendations.

I experimented with different kinds of brushes and found that natural bristles worked best for solvent-based paints. If you prefer synthetic bristles, look for nylon paint brushes with feathered ends rather than blunt-cut ones.

Acrylic paints do not contain strong solvents, but proper ventilation is recommended. Acrylics are better applied with a very soft sable or sabeline brush to minimize brush marks. ◆

*The pewter color on this apple was achieved with **Plaid Liquid Leaf** solvent-based craft paint.*

*This apple displays the effects of applying **Krylon Brass** spray paint to unsealed papier-mâché.*

*The matte finish on this apple is a result of applying **Krylon Brass** spray paint to an unsealed, smooth, porous surface.*

*In this sample, **Krylon Brass** spray paint was applied to a textured surface and then buffed with **Plaid Treasure Gold** paste.*

*When spray paint is applied in one thick coat instead of two thin coats, as it was on this apple, the paint is more likely to drip.*

# Testing Metallic Paints

| Manufacturer and Paint Name | Colors Available | Recommended Uses | Not Recommended for Use On | Important Notes |
|---|---|---|---|---|
| **SPRAY PAINTS** | | | | |
| **Krylon Metallic Enamel** (Can features low-shine cap.) | Bright Gold*, Brass*, Chrome-Aluminum, and Copper | Most surfaces. | Extremely porous surfaces, such as unpainted wood, plaster, and bisque. | Overall granular appearance. Bright Gold has an orangy hue; Brass has a greenish hue. |
| **Krylon Metallic Spray Paint** (Can features high-shine cap.) | Gold* (#1706) and Chrome-Aluminum* | Same as above. | Same as above. | Priming greatly increases luster. Less brilliant shine than Super Gold and Nybco 18Kt*. Chrome Aluminum features less lustrous shine than Gold. Gold has a very orangy hue. |
| **New York Bronze Company Nybco 18Kt* Gold Plate** | Gold* (#795) | Same as above. | Same as above. | Priming recommended for most surfaces. |
| **Testors Spray Enamel Colors** | Copper* (#1251), Gold* (#1244), and Silver | Most surfaces, even absorbent ones. | Certain plastics such as polyethylene or vinyl. | Cover unprimed surfaces fairly well. Sheen approximates high-sheen red paints. Copper has a very red hue; Gold is pale blonde. No lead in formula. Available in 3-ounce spray size for small projects. |
| **Zynolite Super Gold Epoxy Gold Finish** | Gold* (#0170) and Silver | Nonporous surfaces, such as metal, glass, ceramic, etc. Also good on flat or high-relief surfaces. | Porous materials, such as unpainted plaster, raw wood, etc., as surface will reduce paint's sheen. | Gold features a bright, honey-gold color. Good coverage with one coat. Super Gold Epoxy Finish produced the best mirrorlike finish. |
| **BRUSH-ON PAINTS** | | | | |
| **Kemp LustRgild Enamel, Leaf-like Finish** | Gold* | Most surfaces. | Some plastics, such as styrenes. | LustRgild Enamel delivered the best high-luster finish among canned paints. Also available as Permagild Exterior Non-Tarnishing Gold Enamel, but finish is more matte and sheen more granular. |
| **Modern Options Gilded Gold** | Gilded Gold*, Copper Topper*, and Silver Plate | Most surfaces. | Extremely smooth nonabsorbent surfaces, such as unprimed metal, plastic, and glass, or surfaces with high relief. | Unusual metal-flake, water-based formula. Very watery consistency and very granular appearance. Requires frequent stirring to keep pigment in suspension. Gilded Gold required several coats for good coverage. Silver Plate has bright aluminum color. |
| **Plasti-kote Odds 'n' Ends** | Brass* (B-33), Pale Gold, Antique Gold, Gold Leaf, Silver, Copper, and Chrome | Most surfaces. | | Very viscous consistency. Lays on in thick coating. Relatively long drying time among brush-on paints. |
| **Sheffield Gold Leaf Finish** | Gold Leaf* | Most surfaces. | Some plastics, such as styrenes. | Paint has bright gold color. Must clean up with acetone. Fast-drying. |
| **HOBBY AND CRAFT PAINTS** | | | | |
| **AMACO Brush 'n Leaf Hobby Exterior Enamel** | Antique Gold* (IL-2) and Old Gold. (Also Gold Leaf, Antique Gold, and Silver Leaf in interior version.) | Most surfaces, including unpainted wood, metal, most plastics, and glass. | Previously painted surfaces and certain plastics, such as styrenes. | Will withstand exposure outdoors. Requires lacquer thinner or acetone for cleanup. Very granular appearance. |
| **Deka Gloss Waterbased Enamel** | Gold* (#341) | Most surfaces, including textiles. | Smooth, glossy surfaces (paint will not cover evenly). | Produces high-gloss finish with rather granular metallic appearance, even when applied to absorbent or rough surfaces. Gold has very greenish hue. Can be heat-hardened onto fabrics. |
| **Plaid FolkArt Acrylic Metallic Colors** | Pure Gold* (#660), Antique Copper* (#666), Inca Gold, Antique Gold, Solid Bronze, Silver Sterling, Copper, and nineteen other jewel tints | Most surfaces, including fabrics (if used with a proprietary additive). | Smooth, glossy surfaces (paint will not cover evenly). | Wide range of very good colors. Copper tested was darker and better than most. More granular effect than other brands. Entire line had excellent coverage. |
| **Plaid Liquid Leaf** | White Fire* (#6140), Renaissance Gold, Florentine Gold, Classic Gold, Brass, Silver, Pewter*, and Copper | Most surfaces, including wood, metal, glass, ceramic, wax, leather, paper, papier-mâché, cardboard, plaster, and bisque. | Not for use on textiles. | Not as high luster as Testors Enamel Hobby Paint and slightly more granular. Very sophisticated colors. Priming will enhance surface finish. |
| **Testors Enamel Hobby Paint** | Gold* (#1144) and Brass* (#1182). (Also five other metal colors and six metallic tints in "Metal Flakes" line.) | Most surfaces, but better on matte surfaces. | Do not use on extremely absorbent surfaces. | Designed for model makers; comes in tiny jars convenient for small jobs. Excellent luster and coverage. Gold is very pale and high-sheen. Gives good finish, even on unprimed, porous surfaces. |

* Indicates color tested

# Silk Peony Bouquet

*You can make this simple bouquet in less than an hour using silk flowers, foliage, and a two-foot dowel.*

*This peony bouquet is made by binding silk flowers onto a dowel. Using this principle, you can create an endless variety of vertical or horizontal arrangements.*

This quick and easy silk peony bouquet looks perfect hanging vertically next to a window or accenting a dull area that needs a hint of color. To make it, all you need is two feet of artificial grapevine; a bouquet of pink silk peonies, light-green rose leaves, and hops; and a wooden dowel two feet long and one inch in diameter.

The dowel, which creates a strong base, gives you flexibility in terms of where you place the bouquet. You can lay it on a mantel, for instance, or hang it vertically next to a door. This same basic design can also be used to make a dried flower bouquet, but keep in mind that dried plants are much more fragile than artificial foliage and flowers, so the binding process may be more difficult, and the finished bouquet will be quite delicate.

If you're short on supplies, you can use the grapevine's wire tendrils to bind the flowers in place. Alternatively, if you use medium-gauge florist wire to bind the foliage in place, the leafy tendrils can be left free as part of the decorative design.

### SILK PEONY BOUQUET

2 stems pink silk peonies (2 blooms and 1 bud each)
8 stems light green silk rose leaves
1 stem hops (three 2-pod clusters)
2 feet artificial grapevine *or* three 30" stems grape leaves, medium to dark green
Wooden dowel, 1" x 2'
Screw eye(s), ¼" to ½" size

*You will also need:* Pliers with built-in wire cutter; pencil; hammer; and any size nail.
*Other items, if necessary:* Spool of medium-gauge florist wire (for binding flowers in place instead of using grapevine tendrils). ◆

## Making the Bouquet

**1.** To make a vertical version of the bouquet, start by marking a point in the middle of one end of the dowel. Using a hammer and nail, make a small starter hole in the end of the dowel at this point, and screw the screw eye into it using the pliers. To make a horizontal version, mark

two points about 4" apart in the middle of the dowel and insert the screw eyes as above. Lay the dowel on a flat work surface, and put the grapevine or the stems of grape leaves on top of it. Bind them to the dowel using either the vine's tendrils or several 5" lengths of florist wire spaced at 4" intervals.

**2.** Separate the hops stem into three 2-pod clusters. Gather four rose leaf stems, one peony stem, and one 2-pod hops cluster into a bouquet. Adjust the stem heights so that each item is well displayed. Lay the bouquet on the grape leaves, with the stems parallel to the dowel and the blooms pointing toward the screw eye, and bind it in place near the middle of the dowel using either the vine's tendrils or the florist wire.

**3.** Gather a second bouquet using the remaining blooms and clusters; position this bouquet to cover the lower stems of the first bouquet. Bind it in place as in step 2.

**4.** Bend the stems that extend beyond the dowel down around the end of the dowel, then up behind it. Bind them in place near the middle of the dowel. Hang the finished bouquet by the screw eye(s). Bend the leaves to create a full look and to fill any empty spaces in the arrangement.

# 10-Minute Faux Finishes

*Use a household sponge and acrylic paint to give any wooden object a verdigris, woodgrain, or tone-on-tone finish.*

### BY CHRIS ALTSCHULER

## VERDIGRIS FINISH

1. Use black paint for the base coat.
2. Apply the green paint using a twisting motion. During some twists, use the sponge to lift up some of the green paint so the black base coat shows through.

## WOODGRAIN FINISH

1. Use orange paint for the base coat.
2. Streak on dark brown paint to simulate the grain of wood. Add more streaks when the first coat of brown is dry.

## TONE-ON-TONE

1. Use a lighter color as a base coat.
2. Sponge on the darker color using any of the three gestures mentioned in the main part of the text. As you work, turn the sponge in your hand and rotate your wrist each time you touch the sponge to the surface.

This article will teach you three fast and easy faux finishes for any wooden object, including frames, furniture, boxes, or molding. To create the verdigris, woodgrain, or tone-on-tone finishes shown at left, you'll need a household cellulose sponge and two colors of acrylic paint.

The sponge is one of the most versatile tools for painted finishes, as it can be used to spread and smear paint like a brush, or to leave a printed, dabbed-on impression. A sponge is also faster than a brush for applying paint, and it adds texture. For any of these faux finishes, a household sponge will work fine. Any size is acceptable, but keep this rule of thumb in mind: The smaller the object, the smaller your sponge should be. Before getting started, cut or tear the sponge into several smaller pieces with rounded or softer edges to give your faux finish a more natural look.

The three finishes in this article all use the same basic techniques: Cover the object with a background color, work the second color into an area with the sponge, then wipe away a little of the paint with the same sponge. There are three basic gestures used when applying sponged finishes: printing, twisting, and streaking.

Printing is the simplest sponged effect of all. For best results, dip the sponge in the paint, dab off the excess, and lightly press the sponge to the surface repeatedly in random patterns. You should be able to get about five impressions with each load of paint. Twisting, on the other hand, will create a softer look without the more distinct impressions achieved by printing. Follow the procedure for printing, but give a little twist as you touch the surface. Streaking is a very strong texture with a lot of energy. To streak, lay on six- to twelve-inch strokes across the surface.

The verdigris finish is created by twisting a sponge loaded with sea-foam green paint over a black background. The woodgrain finish is created by streaking the sponge with dark brown paint in one direction across an orange background. The tone-on-tone effect uses two tones of paint (in this case, light and dark blue) and a combination of all three hand and wrist movements.

When sponge-painting, keep a small pail or bowl of water nearby to occasionally wet your sponge. Dip the sponge in the water to saturate it, then squeeze out the excess water. A properly wrung-out sponge should not drip when you pick it up or press it against the surface you're painting; there should only be enough wetness to render the sponge soft and pliable. You will also need one or more disposable aluminum trays, paper plates, or plastic lids to hold the paint. Keep a small amount of paint on one side of the pan, plate, or lid, and each time you pick up paint with the sponge, dab off the excess on a clean area.

One other important note: When you're creating a sponged finish, be sure to use the same type of paint for the base coat and the second coat to ensure a strong bond between them.

### 10-MINUTE FAUX FINISHES

Wooden object for painting
2-ounce bottle acrylic craft paint in each color (*see* color samples, at left)

*You'll also need:* household sponge; small pail or medium-size bowl; scissors; and disposable aluminum pans, paper plates, or plastic lids.

*Other items, if necessary:* sandpaper (for smoothing surface); tack cloth or soft rag (to remove dust).

1. Prepare surface to be painted by sanding or dusting as appropriate. Fill small pail or bowl with water. Cut or tear at least two pieces of sponge to size.
2. Squeeze small amount of base coat color onto aluminum pan, paper plate, or plastic lid. Dip sponge into pail or bowl and squeeze out excess moisture. Dip moist sponge into paint, and dab off excess on side of pan. Sponge paint evenly onto surface and into crevices. Let dry following manufacturer's directions. Apply second layer of base color. Let dry thoroughly.
3. Squeeze small amount of second color into clean pan, plate, or lid. Dip second sponge into pail or bowl and squeeze out excess moisture. Dip moist sponge into paint and dab off excess. Dab paint onto surface, using sponge to print, twist, or streak color, depending on effect desired (*see* left). ◆

**Chris Altschuler** is a decorative painter and wallpaper maker in Chicago.

PHOTOGRAPHS BY RICHARD FELBER

# Edwardian Silk Writing Folio

*Use the apple blossom insert in this issue and less than half a yard of fabric to make an elegant stationery folio.*

With a minimal amount of time and material, you can make an elegant and beautiful stationery folio to give as a gift or to keep for yourself. In addition to this issue's insert, the writing folio uses three-eighths yard of fabric for its lining, a small amount of bookcloth for the hinges, a sheet of brown paper for its back cover, and chipboard and two-ply bristol board for creating the book's stiffness and for making the folio's stationery pockets.

This folio, which measures eight and three-fourths inches wide by nine and one-half inches high, is designed for personal letter size paper and envelopes. It will also hold smaller thank-you notes and envelopes or greeting cards.

Creating the stationery folio involves three main steps: gluing the bookcloth to the chipboard backing to create the hinges; gluing the panels and brown paper to the chipboard to decorate the folio's front cover, back cover, and overleaf; and making the fabric-lined stationery pockets to finish the inside of the folio.

Each of these steps involves a fair amount of gluing, creasing, and bonding. We recommend high-tack glues such as Sobo over ordinary white glues such as Elmer's for this project because of their relatively low water content, which produces a faster bond with less warping of the chipboard. When working with the chipboard, do not apply the glue to the chipboard first, as it will absorb the moisture from the glue almost immediately. Instead, apply a thin bead of glue near the edge of the paper, and then a zigzag pattern across the rest of the paper. To spread the glue in a thin, even coat, we recommend cutting a one-inch-by-six-inch scrap of chipboard to use as a spatula. Work quickly so the glue doesn't dry too much or get absorbed into the paper. Avoid applying too much glue, or the excess may bleed out onto a surface (such as on the bookcloth) and be impossible to remove.

Once the materials have been glued, crease any edges with the bone folder or a second one-inch-by-six-inch scrap of chipboard, and secure the bond by rolling the surface with a brayer, a wallpaper seam roller, or a six-inch-to eight-inch-long wooden dowel with a one-inch diameter.

Although some stationery folios are lined with paper, lining made from fabric will wear

*This eight-and-three-fourths-inch-by-nine-and-one-half-inch folio, assembled using this issue's special insert, can hold a variety of different sizes of stationery or informals.*

much better over time. You may be able to find a stiff paper already covered with a suitable fabric, but it's also very easy to make the lining yourself. While silk moiré feels wonderful compared to synthetic acetate, we found moiré difficult to laminate successfully for use as the lining and pockets. Less stiff and thinner than acetate, the silk moiré was harder to position, and the glue bled through it and left stains. We found that acetate bonds easily without shifting or bleeding. Although it is somewhat glossier than many silks, it is less expensive and much easier to handle.

### EDWARDIAN SILK WRITING FOLIO

2-panel insert (*see* following pages)
⅜  yard 45"-wide rose acetate

1  piece 12" x 12" taupe bookcloth
1  sheet 22" x 28" double-thick (⅛") chipboard
1  sheet 20" x 30" white two-ply bristol board, plate finish
1  sheet 8½" x 11", 70 lb coated or glossy brown paper to match brown color on insert panel for back cover

*You'll also need:* Sobo high-tack glue; pencil; metal straightedge; X-Acto knife; self-healing cutting mat; brown kraft paper; bone folder or 1" x 6" piece of chipboard cut from leftover chipboard; brayer, wallpaper seam roller, or 1"-diameter wooden dowel; 1" x 6" chipboard "spatula" for spreading glue, cut from leftover chipboard; iron; and several books, any size, for weighting. ◆

# Making the Folio

For all the cutting steps, work on a self-healing mat or other protective cutting surface and use an X-Acto knife and a metal straightedge.

**1.** Remove the special insert from the magazine and trim off the extra paper along the outside borders as marked. Flex the chipboard horizontally and vertically to determine the grain; the grain runs in the direction of the axis of least resistance. Measure and cut three 8¼" x 9½" panels from the chipboard, with the 9½" edge running parallel to the grain. Cover the work surface with brown kraft paper. Measure and cut two 2¾" x 11½" strips from the bookcloth. On the paper-backed side of each strip, draw a line 1" in

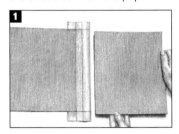

from and parallel to all four edges using a pencil. Position the bookcloth strips on your work surface, cloth side down. Lay the three chipboard panels side by side on top of the bookcloth, with the edges of the chipboard panel overlapping the strips by 1" and with 1" of the strips extending out from the tops and bottoms of the panels.

**2.** Glue the bookcloth strips in position, one at a time, to form the folio hinges. To glue each strip, lay it cloth side down on a clean area of kraft paper and apply glue to the 1" border. Using the chipboard spatula, spread the glue smoothly to cover the area between the pencil lines and the edges; to be sure the edges get enough glue, spread the glue right out onto the kraft paper. Leave the middle area free of glue. Position the two chipboard

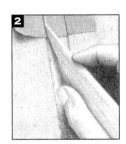

panels on the strip, and press down firmly to adhere. Fold the strip of bookcloth at the top and bottom to the inside and press in place from the center out with the bone folder. Burnish the bookcloth with the bone folder or chipboard, then roll it down with the brayer (or substitute).

**3.** Measure and cut two 2¾" x 9 ¼" strips from the bookcloth. Apply glue to the wrong side of each strip using the spatula, then affix them to the inside of the hinges, ⅛" from the top and bottom of the folio. Burnish each from the center out, making a sharp crease with the bone folder at the edge of each panel. When

the center area is securely affixed, burnish the flaps at each side.

**4.** Trim the sides of the 8½" x 11" piece of brown paper so the back cover measures 6¾" x 11". Turn the folio over. Lay the two insert panels and the brown back cover on top of the folio to check the fit. The brown back cover should extend ¾" at the top and bottom, while each outside panel (the front cover and the overleaf) should overlap its hinge by ¼" and extend ¾" beyond the top, bottom, and side edges. Working on one panel at a time, lay it wrong side up on a clean area of the kraft paper. Apply glue generously over the entire panel, then spread it with the chipboard spatula, scraping any excess beyond the edge of the paper. Let the glue set for 20 seconds, then lift the insert panel by one corner and position it on its coordinating folio panel. Remove any rings and/or dangling jewelry from your right hand (reverse if left-handed). Starting at the center of the panel and working out toward the edges, gently press down on the insert with the open palm of your hand, then roll the panel with the brayer to eliminate any bubbles. Repeat for the remaining two panels; let each of them dry ½ hour.

**5.** Turn the folio over. Work on one panel at a time. Apply glue to the wrong side of the brown edges of the panel overhanging the chipboard's edge. Fold the corner (if the panel has them) first, bringing the point of the paper over the corner of the chipboard at a 45-degree angle. Press it in place for a few seconds, then repeat this on the remaining corner. Dab glue on any unglued areas which have been folded over from the front. Fold the long side flap between the corners up and onto the chipboard panel and

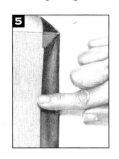

crease it with the bone folder. Fold and crease the top and bottom flaps in the same way. Burnish them with the bone folder, then roll them smooth with the brayer. Repeat for the remaining two panels; let each dry ½ hour.

**6.** Iron your fabric to remove the wrinkles. Cut five rectangles from the bristol board using the measurements and grain direction shown on the diagram. Using the bristol rectangles as templates and allowing a 1" border around each template, cut five rec-

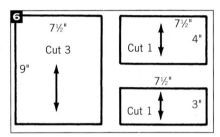

tangles from the fabric. Refer to the diagram above for grain direction. Apply glue to one bristol board rectangle at a time, spreading it out beyond the edges with the chipboard spatula. Lay the corresponding piece of fabric on top, and roll it with the brayer, proceeding gently so the glue does not bleed through the fabric. Sandwich each fabric-covered rectangle between two clean sheets of kraft paper and weight it lightly with several books for 15 minutes. Repeat this process for the remaining pieces of bristol board and fabric.

**7.** Using the tip of a warm iron (do not use steam), press the fabric flaps onto the wrong side of the bristol board. Glue down the corners and the flaps of the three 7½" x 9" panels, using the methods outlined in step 5. Then glue down one long edge of the two smaller rectangles and position each on top of one of the

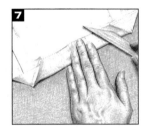

7½" x 9" panels. Turn both pieces over and fold and glue the remaining flaps on the small pieces to the wrong side of each 7½" x 9" panel to make the stationery pockets.

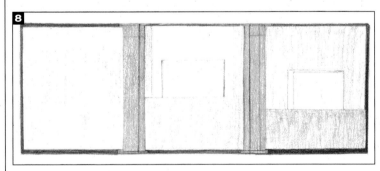

**8.** Coat the backs of each fabric panel with glue, spreading it evenly with the chipboard spatula. Position each panel on the inside of the open folio, placing the panel with the large pocket in the middle, the panel with the small pocket on the right, and the plain panel on the left. The edges of the folio should extend ¼" beyond the fabric panel edges. Weight each panel with books and let it dry several hours.

ILLUSTRATIONS BY DAN BROWN, DIAGRAM #6 BY ROBERTA FRAUWIRTH

TRIM HERE

SEE DIRECTIONS ON PAGES 15 AND 16

FRONT COVER

# Miter-Box Frame

*Build a custom frame for about $40 using ordinary molding and a wooden miter box.*

BY ELLEN RIXFORD

*You can make this custom pickled frame with a miter box and about $40 worth of materials.*

Having pictures professionally framed can be an expensive proposition, especially if you want a specific color to match your decorating scheme or a design other than the standard frame moldings. The custom-made frame shown at the right, which I estimate would cost between $200 and $300 in a frame shop, cost me about $40 to put together. There are two keys to the savings: The frame is built by combining several standard wooden moldings for the final shape, and you assemble the frame yourself using a miter box to cut the corners.

Miter boxes are available in any hardware store or lumberyard. Look for a wooden miter box with at least three cutting slots: a 90-degree angle and right and left 45-degree angles. To make this frame, I tested a wooden miter box priced around $6.50, and a plastic miter box that cost around $20. I preferred the wooden box because it shifted around less.

Once you've purchased or borrowed a miter box, you'll need to select molding. To build this frame, I purchased four wooden moldings—a 1¾" base molding, a 2¼" chair rail molding, a 1⅜" picture molding, and ¼" quarter-round molding—plus an equal quantity of 1⁹⁄₁₆" lattice and ¾" x 2½" pine board without knots or serious flaws. The pine board (which I will refer to as backing board) serves as the base of the frame; it supports the molding and helps to form a lip on the inside edge of the frame which holds the picture and any mat and/or protective glass in place. The lattice is sandwiched between the molding and the backing board to lift the molding into a more pleasing position. Neither the backing board nor the lattice can be seen in the finished frame, but you can see them in a diagram representing a side view of the frame on page 18.

Partly as a result of the way lumber is cut and partly because of tradition, the nominal dimension of lumber, meaning what it is called, is always larger than the actual dimension of the wood. In addition, since lumber is cut in huge quantities, it is available only in relatively standard sizes. While the pine backing board I used actually measured ¾" x 2½", it is called a 1 x 3 to indicate the approximate size of the board before it was "dressed down" to its final shape. This system holds true only with boards, however. Millwork—wood that has been milled to a special shape, including molding, half-round, and lattice—is referred to by its actual dimensions.

The pine backing board only needs to be wide enough to hold the moldings, and thick enough to provide an adequate lip to hold whatever item you intend to frame. (It doesn't need to be as wide as the frame you intend to build.) If you're framing something thin, like a photograph, the backing board should be thick enough to provide space for the glass, the mat, the photo, and its backing material (plus a little space for the brads that will hold the picture in place). If, on the other hand, you're framing a painting on a stretched canvas, you'll need a deeper lip, so you'll have to use a thicker backing board. As for the lattice, if the moldings you choose work well as they are, you may not need any lattice at all. However, if the molding toward the outside of the frame needs to be lifted up, use lattice to do it.

Before you buy any wood, I recommend taking a preliminary trip to a lumberyard or a home supply warehouse to look at moldings. Moldings come in a wide variety of widths and shapes; some ornate, some simple. Look for pine molding priced from about 50¢ to $1 a foot. Pricier, more decorative moldings, such as crown molding (averaging about $2.59 a foot), will also work for this project, but they will dramatically increase the cost of the finished frame. Some lumberyards have charts and/or samples of the moldings on display. Although these can be helpful, the moldings may be glued in place, so you won't be able to hold them next to each other to see how they look together, which is key to assembling an attractive frame. If that is the case, you'll have to use your imagination to figure out which moldings will work best together.

Once you've decided what moldings you like, you'll need to determine the approximate size of the finished frame. Start with the dimensions of the picture you intend to frame. In my case, the picture was 12" high and 16" across. (Note: The actual frame opening is ¼" to ⅜" smaller all around to allow for the lip that extends over the picture and holds it in place.)

The width of the frame depends on the moldings you select. While you cannot know the exact molding width at this stage, you need to decide on an approximate width in order to determine how many feet of molding to buy. Let's say you want the molding on your finished frame to equal that of our frame: 4¼" wide. The approximate length of each side of the finished frame will equal the length of that side of the picture, plus twice the width of the molding. In my example, the finished frame will be approximately 20½" (12" + 4¼" + 4¼") high and 24½" (16" + 4¼" + 4¼") across.

To determine how many feet of molding to buy, add up the lengths of all four sides of the frame, add an extra 12" to allow for the miter cuts, and round the total up to the nearest foot. In my example, the total equals 90" (20½" + 20½" + 24½" + 24½" + 12" = 102" or 8½', which I rounded up to 9'). Remember, you must purchase this quantity of *each* molding.

To build the frame, you'll have to assemble the four sides of the frame from the moldings, then miter the ends at the correct 45-degree angle. Once the mitered sides are glued and nailed together, they will form a rectangle with four 90-degree corners. (If you have difficulty visualizing how the mitered corners are going to fit together, cut some sample miters out of scrap molding and see how they fit.) Rather than mitering each piece of molding separately and then trying to glue them together, it's much easier to glue them first and then miter them all at once. Before you cut them, however, you'll need to measure across the width of the assembled moldings to determine whether it will all fit in the miter box together, or if the sides must be mitered in two sections.

If your mitered corners don't match up perfectly, minor flaws can be camouflaged with spackling compound which can be applied with your fingertip into the cracks between the moldings, into the countersunk nail holes, and across the miters. The compound will be dry enough to sand in about half an hour. Hold the sandpaper in your hand rather than using a sanding block. After filling the cracks and sanding the spackling compound, I opted to leave the frame as it was for a pickled effect, but you can paint it with primer followed by paint. For other finishing ideas, see "10-Minute Faux Finishes," page 14. However you finish the frame, be sure to protect it with a coat or two of clear satin-finish polyurethane.

*Note: It is extremely important that you operate any sharp tools with care and knowledge of their operating procedures. Misuse can cause serious injury.*

### MITER-BOX FRAME

2–4   assorted wooden moldings (*see* step 1 to determine quantity)
⅜"- to ½"-thick pine board (*see* steps 1 and 2 to determine width and quantity)
Brads (long enough to attach molding to backing board)
8   6d ("six-penny") finishing nails
Yellow carpenter's glue
Spackling compound
Clear, satin-finish polyurethane

*You'll also need:* miter box; backsaw; hammer; countersink or nail set; interior trim paintbrush with angled bristles; right-angle triangle; retractable steel tape measure; transparent grid ruler; pencil; clean cloth; toothpicks; paper face mask; sandpaper (100-grit or finer); two C-clamps with 5"-wide jaws and wood scraps; calculator; and scrap paper.

*Other items, if necessary:* lattice (for supporting moldings; *see* steps 1 and 2 to determine length); scrap wood (for lining floor of miter box); white latex paint and rags (for pickled effect); pliers (for removing brads); and glass pane (if framing prints).

### Purchasing the Molding

1. Measure and write down dimensions of picture to be framed. Estimate maximum pos-sible width of finished molding, then add twice this measurement to each picture dimension to determine approximate size of finished frame. Add together the lengths of all four sides of finished frame, add another 12" for mitering allowance, and round up total to nearest foot. (*See* example on page 17 in main portion of story.)

2. Select two to four moldings to compose surface of frame, making sure total width of frame does not exceed estimate from step 1. Select pine backing board ⅜" to ½" thick and 1" to 2" narrower than width of frame, but no wider than can be cut in miter box. Select any additional trims, such as half- or quarter-round, to fill out front surface of frame, and/or lattice to support and lift moldings from underneath. Purchase each piece of wood using final measurement from step 1, above.

### Assembling the Molding

1. Using miter box and backsaw, straight-cut each length of molding and backing board into four pieces, two equal to measurement of shorter frame sides plus 3" and two equal to longer frame sides plus 3". (If necessary, use one or more pieces of scrap wood under the molding to raise it to the saw level.) Organize pieces into one group for each side of frame.

2. Hold pieces for each side of frame together, backing board on bottom, moldings on top, and lattice, if used, sandwiched in between. Adjust position so molding that forms inside edge of frame extends ¼" to ⅜" beyond backing board to form a lip on which picture and/or glass will rest.

Measure across width of assembled molding, starting at inside edge, to determine how many pieces will fit in miter box. If width of assembled molding is less than width of miter box, moldings that make up each side can be glued together and mitered all at once. Otherwise, you'll need to glue moldings in two sections, cut the miters of each section individually, then glue the sections together to make each side of frame. If this latter example is the case, you'll be working with a total of eight pieces: four sections which make up the inside edges of the frame (and which are glued to the backing board), and four sections which make up the outside edges of the frame. The miters on the inside sections are cut first and determine the starting point for the miters on the outside sections.

3. Hold pieces for one frame section together and turn them over. Working one section at a time, use transparent grid ruler to confirm and even up width of lip on inside edge. Write down width for use in step 2 of "Cutting the Miters," below. Remove ruler and mark overlap by drawing a line on wrong side of molding using edge of backing board as guide. Turn frame section over and draw line(s) on backing board to mark edge of each molding, removing and re-

## A SIDE VIEW OF THE FRAME

The photograph at left identifies the various moldings and wood before assembly; the side-view diagram shows the position of the various moldings and wood on the finished frame. **1.** Picture hanging molding. **2.** Quarter round. **3.** Chair rail molding. **4.** Base molding. **5.** Lattice. **6.** 1 x 3 pine backing board.

placing moldings as necessary to make marks.

4. *In this step, glue together pieces in sections that fit in the miter box, as determined in step 2, at left.* For the pieces of molding that rest on the backing board, spread glue evenly over first penciled section of backing board and evenly across underside of inside molding, stopping at pencil line that marks start of overlap. Press two glue-covered surfaces together, aligning edges against pencil lines. Using damp cloth and tip of toothpick, immediately wipe away any glue that oozes out between pieces. Repeat process to glue additional moldings to backing board. Using two 5" C-clamps, clamp assembly to edge of table or workbench with backing board facing down. Insert small pieces of scrap wood between clamp and frame to avoid marring frame.

5. While glue is still partially wet, hammer brads into molding every 4" to 5" and down into backing board, but leave nail head sticking slightly above surface of molding. Use countersink or nail set to drive brad heads slightly below surface of molding. Repeat steps 3 through 5 to glue remaining frame sections to backing board or to each other if applicable. Let glue dry overnight.

### Cutting the Miters

1. *In this step, miter four inside sections of frame only. (If working with eight pieces, the outside sections of the frame will be mitered in step 4.)* Position miter box so lip hangs over edge of table or workbench. Place one inside section in miter box with backing board resting flat on floor of box and inner edge (with lip) flush against back wall of box. Using illustration 5 as reference, place saw blade into the two

    PHOTOGRAPH BY RICHARD FELBER, DIAGRAM BY KEVIN MOELLER

slots that slant away from you to the left, so frame section extends 1" to the right of saw blade at point closest to you. Hold side of section firmly against back wall of box, and saw smoothly to make miter cut. Be careful not to splinter wood as you reach end of cut. Repeat this step to miter one end of each inside section.

2. Subtract width of lip on inner edge of frame (*see* "Assembling the Molding," step 3) from picture's dimensions to determine frame's inner dimensions, and write down result. Using these dimensions, measure inner edge of each inside section of frame, starting at mitered cut; mark where new mitered cut should begin using pencil. To check measurements, line up sections from opposite sides of frame with inner edges together. Remeasure and re-mark if necessary.

3. Place one inside section in miter box as directed in step 1, with inner edge (with lip) flush against back wall. Adjust section so mark on inner edge lines up with back wall's right-slanting miter slot. Place saw blade in this slot and its mate on front wall, and saw through assembled molding. Repeat for remaining three inside sections of frame. *If your frame consists of inside and outside sections, proceed to step 4. If each side of your frame consists of only one section, go directly to Assembling and Finishing the Frame.*

4. Place one outside section in miter box with inner edge (edge that will be glued to inside section) flush against back wall of miter box and right end extending 1" beyond saw blade as in step 1. (Be sure to place molding in miter box in the same position as it will be placed on the finished frame so that miters line up properly.) Saw through molding to make miter cut as above. Repeat for each outside section of frame. Fit one outside section against matching inside section, and line up miters at right edge. Make a small mark on outside section to show where miter on left edge should begin. Line up outside section in miter box as in step 3 and make cut. Repeat with remaining three outside sections.

**Assembling and Finishing the Frame**

1. If each side of frame was built and mitered in two sections, glue and nail each pair of sections together using techniques in step 4 and 5 of "Assembling the Molding," page 18, to form complete frame sides. Let dry overnight.

2. Lay all frame sides face up on flat work surface; butt corners together to check miters. Apply glue to all butting surfaces of mitered cuts and press frame sides together, matching inside and outside edges of frame. Use damp cloth and point of toothpick to remove any glue that oozes out of joints. Hold triangle inside each corner and square up corner as necessary.

3. When glue begins to set, tap two brads into each corner, stopping with heads just short

of molding surface. Brads should be inserted approximately ½" from point of corner. Recheck inside corners with triangle and adjust as necessary. (If frame is noticeably skewed, remove brads with pliers, realign frame, and reposition brads.) Let glue set one hour, then drive down heads of brads just below surface of wood with countersink or nail set. Turn frame over, and drive two finishing nails into each corner of pine backing board to further secure frame. Finishing nails should be inserted approximately 1" from point of corner.

4. Using fingertip, apply spackling compound to nail holes, mitered joints, and cracks if

needed. When dry, put on face mask and lightly sand all spackled areas. Wipe off dust with damp cloth. Respackle and resand if necessary.

5. With damp cloth, wipe off dust from entire frame. Wipe on white paint with clean rag for pickled effect, or prime and paint. Let frame dry overnight, then apply coat of polyurethane. If framing prints, drop in glass pane before hanging. ◆

**Ellen Rixford**, a professional sculptor, puppet maker, and photographer based in New York, is the author of *3 Dimensional Illustration* (Watson-Guptill, 1993).

# Making the Miter-Box Frame

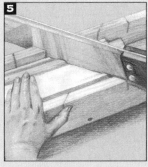

**1.** Place the molding that will form the inner edge of the frame against the pine backing board, then use the grid ruler to measure the frame's lip.

**2.** To glue together the pine backing board and the piece of molding that will form the frame's lip, apply glue to both marked-off sections.

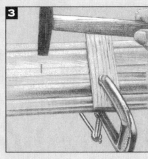

**3.** When clamping the molding, use small pieces of scrap wood to protect the frame's surface.

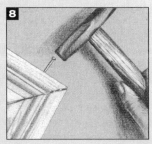

**4.** A nail set (also called a countersink) is used to drive the heads of the brads below the surface of the molding. The holes will later be filled with spackling compound.

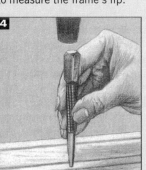

**5.** When making the miter cuts, position the assembled molding in the miter box with the inner edge (with lip) resting snugly against the back wall of the box.

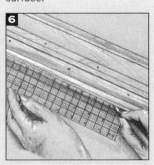

**6.** After the first miters have been cut, measure the inner edge in order to mark the location of the second miter cut.

**7.** Once the mark for the second miter cut has been made, line up that mark with the correct slot on the miter box.

**8.** Once you've glued the mitered corners together, tap a brad into each side of the molding to strengthen the corner joint.

**9.** Less-than-perfect mitered corners can be concealed with spackling compound. Use the compound to fill in all nail holes and any cracks between the moldings.

# Ukrainian Easter Eggs

*Make your own heirloom Easter eggs using traditional wax-resist and dye techniques.*

BY CHRISTINE YOUNG WITH SUZANNE GUZZO

*The tulip design on this Ukrainian egg, like most plant designs used in decorating eggs, symbolizes the celebration of life.*

This article will teach you the traditional Ukrainian art of making *pysanky*, intricately decorated Easter eggs. Although our egg's design may look complicated, its wax-resist and dye techniques are actually quite simple and straightforward.

It is important not to confuse this particular type of egg decoration with the edible, hard-boiled Easter eggs that you may remember from your childhood. For this project, you'll be decorating raw eggs using simple designs and chemical aniline dyes, meaning the resulting eggs are *not edible*. (Over time, the egg yolk dries into a lump and the egg white turns to dust.) Given their intricate designs, pysanky require a certain amount of time and patience to decorate. Using the wax-resist method outlined here, each egg will take between two and three hours to complete. To offset this, consider gathering a group of friends together for an egg-decorating session (something like an old-fashioned quilting bee) so you can share wax and dyes, or decorate one or two pysanky each year and build your collection slowly. (You can reduce the amount of time involved in this project by using a simpler design. Use just half the designs shown, or design your own egg using the miniature illustrations on page 21.)

To get started, you'll need to purchase about $10 to $15 of egg-decorating supplies, including a *kistka* (a special stylus for drawing the designs on the egg) and several packets of aniline dye. The kistka (the plural is *kistky*) has a hollow brass cone at the tip to hold the wax; the cone is held in the flame of a candle for a few seconds until it is hot, then scooped into a cake of solid wax, which softens on contact with the hot cone. When the cone is reheated, the wax melts and flows out the tiny hole at the end of the cone. The kistka is held like a pencil and is used to draw designs on the egg.

Because the dye cannot penetrate the wax, any areas covered with wax will remain the color of the surface to which they were applied. The first wax designs drawn on the egg, for instance, will remain white, as they are drawn on the bare shell. When the first designs are complete, the egg is dipped in yellow dye, thereby coloring any unwaxed areas yellow. Areas that are to remain yellow are then covered with wax, and the egg is dipped in orange dye. This process is repeated with red dye, and finally dark blue dye, the last color used. (Because green tends to dull succeeding colors, it is applied differently. Once the egg has been dyed yellow, you'll hand-color the green areas using a permanent marker or a wet watercolor pencil, then cover the green areas with wax.) When all the designs have been drawn and the egg dipped in successive dyes, the wax is melted off to reveal an intricate, beautifully colored design. The last step is to seal the egg with varnish, which further protects the intricate designs.

A standard kistka is priced at around $2, but we recommend purchasing a deluxe version, which costs about $5. The deluxe kistka features a heat-resistant plastic handle and a solid brass tip, which retains heat and helps keep the wax hot and flowing longer.

Kistky come in three styles: fine-, medium-, and heavy-point. The fine-point is best for detailed designs, such as the one featured in this article. When we tried making the egg with a medium-point kistka, we had trouble fitting in all the designs, and the resulting decorations looked cramped. The medium- and heavy-point kistky are useful, however, if you need to fill in a large area with wax.

Packets of dye cost about 75¢ each. There

## Color Sequence for Decorating the Egg

These two diagrams outline the color sequence for drawing the designs in wax. The black areas represent the designs that should be drawn first in order to remain white. The white areas represent those designs that should be drawn last; they will become dark blue after the egg is dipped in the last dye. In between these starting and ending steps, draw in all the yellow designs before dipping the egg in yellow dye, all the orange designs before dipping the egg in orange dye, and all the red designs before dipping the egg in red dye. (The green tulip leaves should be hand-colored with a green permanent marker or watercolor pencil after dipping the egg in yellow dye.)

This egg is a little more difficult than most because the tulip is free-form rather than geometric. We recommend using a pencil to draw the geometric border and interior designs first, then draw pencil guidelines for the three tulips and seven stems inside each oval, taking care to leave room between the stems for the tulip leaves. Finally, use the pencil to add the pussy willow ovals, using the stem as a guideline.

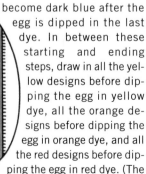

   ILLUSTRATIONS BY ROBERTA FRAUWIRTH, PHOTOGRAPH BY STEPHEN MAYS

## WHAT DO THE DESIGNS MEAN?

Ukrainian egg designs generally fall into three broad categories—geometric, plant, or animal—each with its own set of meanings.

Geometric patterns, which can help divide the egg into logical areas, include dots, ribbons, ladders, combs, nets, and basket weaves. Ribbons symbolize a never-ending line representing everlasting life; the ribbons of waves represent water. Circle designs include the sun, which stands for good fortune, or nobility when it is surrounded by dots.

Plant patterns generally symbolize the celebration of life. The eight-petal rose stands for love and beauty; the evergreen tree stands for youth and health. Sunflowers indicate the warmth of the sun's rays; roses symbolize love and caring.

The animal category is rarer, as it is usually too difficult to detail a whole animal. Shapes are stylized and generally fall into two categories: animal parts, such as feet or horns,

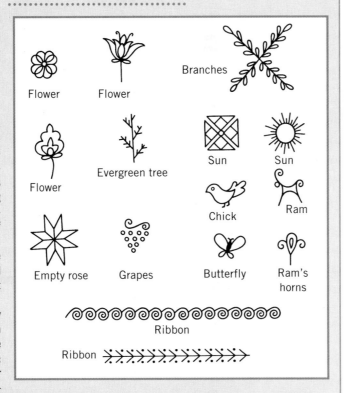

Flower · Flower · Branches · Flower · Evergreen tree · Sun · Sun · Empty rose · Grapes · Chick · Ram · Butterfly · Ram's horns · Ribbon · Ribbon

and abstract whole animals, such as deer or horses, both of which stand for good health, wealth, and prosperity. The butterfly symbolizes hope; storks, hens, and chicks represent fertility and wish fulfillment; and the fish stands for Christianity.

across the color wheel from each other (e.g., yellow and purple or orange and blue) will result in muddy tones, as the dyes will counteract each other's intensity. When you dye an egg, be sure to proceed from the lightest color to the darkest. Choose a well-lit spot to work so that you can see the details of your design. To protect your work table from the dyes, I recommend covering it with plastic first, followed by several layers of newspaper.

When selecting eggs, look for flawless shells. Many eggs have small deposits on the outside of the shell, or translucent areas, which may indicate weak spots. Before getting started, clean the eggs. Don't use soap and water because soap can prevent the dye from adhering to the shell. Instead, clean them and at the same time test them for tiny holes by putting them in a pot or bowl of water along with a teaspoon of baking soda. If you see any bubbles, don't use the egg. (There's no need to blow out the insides of the egg for this project, although it can be done with an egg blower after the egg is dyed.)

After you wash and test the eggs, dry them with a towel and let them come to room temperature. If the egg is too cold, the wax will not flow smoothly. Always handle eggs with clean hands, since oils on your hands can adhere to the shell and prevent the wax or dyes from sticking.

Once the eggs have dried, you can varnish them with polyurethane, which will protect them for years to come. (*See* "Varnishing the Eggs," page 22.)

### UKRAINIAN EASTER EGGS

Aniline egg dyes, 1 packet each of the following colors: yellow, orange, red, and dark blue
1 teaspoon baking soda
¼ teaspoon setting powder *or* white vinegar
White eggs

*You'll also need:* Green permanent marker or watercolor pencil; fine-point kistka; pure beeswax patty; 4 clean, low, wide-mouthed jars; 4 expendable metal soupspoons or tablespoons; masking tape; black permanent marker; 8" to 10" candle in stand; matches; teakettle; Pyrex measuring cup; lint-free cloths or paper towels; plastic drop cloth; newspaper; pencil; 2 clean dish or hand towels; measuring spoons; old dishwashing gloves; and medium-size bowl or pot.

*Other items, if necessary:* 4" piece of 32-gauge steel wire (for unplugging tip of kistka).

*See* instructions on page 22. ◆

**Christine Young** has been decorating eggs for more than ten years. **Suzanne Guzzo** is a freelance writer living in Huntington, New York.

are two types of dye used in egg decorating: chemical aniline (which is not edible and which we used for this project) and organic vegetable (which is edible). We tested both types, and the aniline dyes produced richer, more intense colors on the eggs. The organic dyes produce more pastel tones (the black is actually a dark green, not a true black) but can be used by children or on hard-boiled eggs that are going to be eaten. It is *very important* not to confuse the dyes, because aniline dye will penetrate the shell and make the egg poisonous. As a precaution when using aniline dyes, keep a pair of disposable plastic gloves handy and slip them on when moving the eggs in or out of the dyes. If dye accidentally gets on your hands and you can't wash it off, use a pumice stone to remove it.

Always follow a few other basic precautions when working with aniline dyes. When mixing the dyes, add the dye powder to the hot water (*not* the hot water to the dye powder). If you add powder to the jar first, it will hit the bottom and create a small cloud of dust, which should not be inhaled. When the powder hits the water, on the other hand, the particles dissolve almost instantly and do not become air-

borne. Take care not to eat when working with the dyes; if you get dye on your fingers, you might accidentally get it into your mouth.

In addition to the dyes, you'll need a low, widemouthed glass jar with a cover (such as an empty salsa or peanut butter jar) for each dye color. The wide mouth (at least three inches in diameter) is essential for easy insertion and removal of the egg. You'll also need an old metal soupspoon or tablespoon for each dye jar. The spoons, jars, and gloves should remain a part of your dye kit and should not be reused—*ever*—for food preparation or cleanup.

Although it sounds elementary, it's important to label all the jars with their color names before you start mixing dyes in order to avoid confusion. The dye baths are quite dark, and once the colors are mixed it is hard to tell them apart. After the dye is dissolved, add a small amount of setting powder or white distilled vinegar to help the dye adhere to the egg.

Aniline dyes come in many colors—pink, black, dark red, bright red, yellow, orange, green, blue, violet, brown, aquamarine—and can be mixed together to create new colors. Take note, however: Mixing colors that are

# Decorating the Eggs

To clean the eggs and test them for tiny holes, place the eggs in a bowl or pot of water and add 1 teaspoon of baking soda. Watch for air bubbles coming from the eggs; only use those without air bubbles. Dry the eggs on a dish or hand towel and let them come to room temperature. Fill the teakettle with water and bring it to a boil, then set it aside. Set up your work space by spreading out a plastic drop cloth topped with several layers of newspaper. With a black permanent marker, write the color of the dye on a piece of masking tape and affix it to the outside of each jar. Following the instructions on the dye packets, measure the hot water from the teakettle in a Pyrex measuring cup, pour it into the jars, and add the dyes. Mix each color with a separate metal spoon until the dye is dissolved, then add ¼ teaspoon setting powder or vinegar to each color. Let the dyes cool to room temperature. Arrange the jars sequentially, from the lightest color to the darkest.

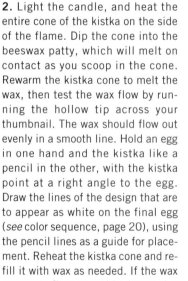

**1.** Mark a dot lightly with a pencil at the top and bottom of the egg. Draw a light line around the entire egg, going through both dots. Draw a second line around the egg, passing through the dots at a right angle to the first line and dividing the egg into fourths. Draw a horizontal line around the middle of the egg to divide it into eighths. Sketch the entire design lightly with pencil on the egg.

**2.** Light the candle, and heat the entire cone of the kistka on the side of the flame. Dip the cone into the beeswax patty, which will melt on contact as you scoop in the cone. Rewarm the kistka cone to melt the wax, then test the wax flow by running the hollow tip across your thumbnail. The wax should flow out evenly in a smooth line. Hold an egg in one hand and the kistka like a pencil in the other, with the kistka point at a right angle to the egg. Draw the lines of the design that are to appear as white on the final egg (*see* color sequence, page 20), using the pencil lines as a guide for placement. Reheat the kistka cone and refill it with wax as needed. If the wax

ceases to flow smoothly, insert the steel wire into the hole at the end of the kistka tip to unblock it.

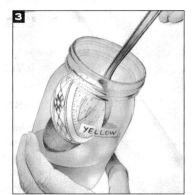

**3.** When all the areas to remain white are covered with wax, lower the egg on a metal spoon into the yellow dye. Let the egg sit for 5 minutes or until the color reaches the desired intensity. Slip on the plastic gloves, lift the egg from the dye with the spoon, and gently blot the egg dry with a paper towel or lint-free cloth.

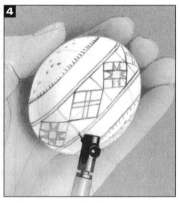

**4.** Repeat step 2, putting wax over the areas you want to remain yellow. Any green areas, such as the tulip leaves, should also be colored now. Fill in the leaves by hand with a permanent marker or a wet watercolor pencil, then cover these hand-colored areas with wax. With another spoon, lower the egg into the next darkest color in the series (orange), and proceed as in step 3.

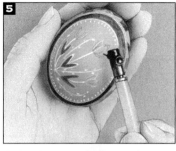

**5.** Repeat steps 2 through 4 as appropriate for the remaining two colors (red and then dark blue), applying wax to preserve the color of the previously dyed section and dipping the egg into successively darker-colored dyes. (As you work, the egg will become increasingly wax-coated, obscuring the design and colors.) After you've dyed it in the darkest color (dark blue), remove the egg from the dye and blot it dry with paper towels or lint-free cloth.

**6.** To remove the wax and reveal the design, hold the egg up to the side of the candle flame until the wax liquifies. (Don't hold the egg in the flame, or it will scorch.) Remove the egg from the flame and gently wipe off the liquid wax with a paper towel or lint-free cloth. Continue heating and wiping off the liquid wax, rotating the egg so it doesn't get uncomfortably warm to handle. (The pencil lines will come off with the wax, but a thin layer of clear wax will remain on the egg, giving it a slight sheen.)

---

Once the egg has dried, you can varnish it with clear marine varnish or polyurethane. Marine varnish is a little more expensive, but it covers in one coat. Polyurethane usually requires two or more coats.

Marine varnish or polyurethane

*You'll also need:* one sheet graph paper; any size wooden board; hammer; 1¼" brads; disposable plastic gloves (*not* latex); and plastic spoon.

## VARNISHING THE EGGS

**1.** Before varnishing the egg, make a drying rack by laying a sheet of graph paper on top of any size board. Using the graph paper as a guide, hammer in 1¼" brads every inch in rows spaced 1" apart. Stagger every other row by ½" so that adjacent nail heads form triangles instead of squares.

**2.** To varnish the egg, slip on the plastic gloves and ladle a dime-sized blob of varnish into the palm of your hand. Roll the egg around in your hand until it is coated, and then set the egg on the drying rack. To clean up, remove and discard the gloves.

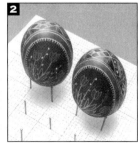

ILLUSTRATIONS BY NENAD JAKESEVIC

# Two-Sheet Duvet Cover

*Update a bedroom decorating scheme with a duvet cover sewn from a pair of sheets.*

BY MARY FRAZIER

*To further coordinate this bedroom's decor, we attached matching tabs to the bed's pillows.*

In an afternoon's time, you can sew this beautiful duvet cover from two color-coordinated flat sheets. The duvet cover shown in the photograph, which measures 66" x 84", was sewn from one full-size flat sheet and one queen-size flat sheet. The full-size sheet was used to make the duvet's lining and flap, while the queen-sized sheet was used for the duvet's front, welting, and ties.

To determine what size sheets to buy, measure the duvet to be covered and add 1" for seam allowances to both the width and length. The sheet for making the duvet lining must be at least as wide and 4" longer. (Most flat sheets have the following standard measurements: twin = 70" x 105"; full-size = 80" x 105"; queen-size = 90" x 110"; and king-size = 110" x 110".) To make the duvet cover, welting, and ties, choose the next larger size sheet than the one you chose for the duvet lining. For instance, if your duvet measures 75" x 100", you'll need a full-size flat sheet for the lining and a queen-size flat sheet for the front, welting, and ties. (Although the cutting diagrams on page 25 are for a 66" x 84" duvet cover, you can follow the same basic cutting layout regardless of the size of the duvet. The pieces will be arranged the same way, and only the specific measurements will vary.)

You also have a second option: using store-bought welting instead of sewing your own. If you choose to follow this route, purchase two sheets of the same size, as you won't need the extra fabric for the welting. For example, to cover the 75" x 100" duvet above, you'd need two full-size flat sheets.

Whether you're making your own welting or using store-bought welting, the duvet measurements determined earlier will also be used to calculate the total yardage of welting needed. Add the duvet's width and length together, double the total, and add three inches. Round the resulting number up to the nearest quarter yard. This final yardage is the quantity of welting you'll need. If you're using store-bought welting, use this number when purchasing it; if you're making your own, use this number to purchase the welting cord.

To make your own welting, you'll cut several strips of fabric from the larger sheet, sew them together to create one long strip, then encase the welting cord inside the strip of fabric (*see* illustrations 1 through 6, page 24). It's important to cut the strips of welting fabric on the bias in order to give the welting the extra stretch it needs to round the corners of the duvet cover. (The bias is the direction in which the fabric gives or stretches the most.) To ensure your fabric is cut correctly, use the diagram on page 25.

The duvet cover must have an opening for inserting the duvet. Although I considered a number of different closures for this opening, I ended up using tabs, which are repeated on the pillowcases for a coordinated look. (If you decide to make matching tabs for your pillowcases, you'll need to cut one or more additional tab strips from the larger sheet. I used six tabs per pillowcase; each additional tab strip yields approximately ten tabs.)

The duvet front, lining, ties, and welting can all be cut out with scissors, but for faster, more accurate cuts, I recommend using a rotary cutter and accessories. A rotary cutter is a round, razorlike blade attached to a plastic handle. To use it, hold it like a pizza cutter and roll the blade across the fabric. A self-healing cutting mat placed under the fabric provides resistance and protects the work surface. Perfect straight cuts are made by rolling the blade

along the edge of a clear acrylic cutting guide called a rotary cutting ruler.

If you're tempted to use "irregular" sheets for this project, take note: Many sheets are labeled irregular because they are not perfect rectangles. This doesn't mean they can't be used, but it may mean that the pattern isn't printed straight, or that the sheet doesn't square up. If you've fallen in love with the design on an irregular sheet, before you begin, measure the sheet along both diagonals to determine if it's a true rectangle. Then, if necessary, trim the sheet to either make a perfect rectangle or to make the pattern run straight.

### TWO-SHEET DUVET COVER

The directions below are written for a full-size duvet measuring 66" x 84". The queen-size flat sheet includes enough fabric to make co-ordinating welting. If your duvet is a different size, or you chose to use store-bought welting, refer to the introductory text to determine what size sheets to purchase. If using other sheets, make the appropriate substitution when following the directions.

- 1 full-size flat sheet
- 1 queen-size flat sheet
  Thread to match
- 8½ yards ½" cotton welting cord *or* store-bought piping

*You'll also need:* sewing machine with zipper foot; scissors and yardstick or rotary cutter (with accessories) and rotary cutting ruler; seam ripper; tape measure; fabric-marking pencil; chopstick or pencil; scrap paper; iron; straight pins; and calculator.

#### Cutting the Sheets

1. Using tape measure, measure width and length of duvet to be covered. Add 1" seam allowance to each dimension and jot down results. Press both flat sheets to remove wrinkles.

2. To cut front of duvet cover, lay larger (queen-size) sheet on large, flat work surface. Using scissors or rotary cutter and accessories, cut straight across sheet to remove double-stitched hem at bottom of sheet. Using the Queen-Size Flat Sheet diagram on page 25 as reference, use fabric-marking pencil and yardstick or rotary cutting ruler to transfer measurements from step 1 to sheet. Cut out duvet

## ASSEMBLING THE WELTING

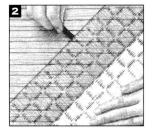

**1.** Lay the largest remaining piece from the queen-size sheet on the work surface, and trim off extra fabric (if any) to yield a rectangle with a length equal to the length of the duvet and a width of about 23". Fold this rectangle diagonally from one corner by matching one short edge to one long edge. Cut along the fold with your scissors or rotary cutter, then discard the leftover triangle of material. Repeat the process at the opposite short edge to create a large parallelogram. The short sides of this parallelogram will run along the bias.

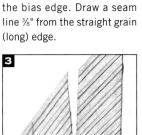

**2.** Using a rotary cutting ruler or a clear plastic grid ruler and a fabric pencil or chalk, mark lines every 3" parallel to the bias edge. Draw a seam line ⅜" from the straight grain (long) edge.

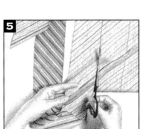

**3.** Cut along the first marked line for 5" or 6".

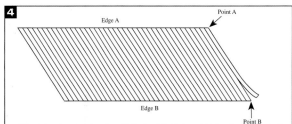

**4.** Holding the cut section aside, pin the straight grain edges (edges A and B) together, right sides facing, so that point A almost matches point B. In order to pin the two edges together, form the fabric into a spiral as you adjust the seamline.

Edge A          Point A
Edge B          Point B

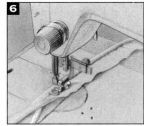

**5.** Cut along the marked lines to make one long, continuous bias strip.

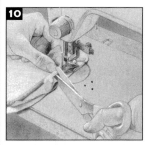

**6.** Wrap the bias strip around the welting cord, right sides out and edges matching. Using the zipper foot, machine-baste approximately ½" from the edges, or as close as possible to the cord without stitching over it.

## MAKING AND ATTACHING THE TABS

**7.** After pressing the seam open, stitch across the strips, perpendicular to the seam, every 6½" to 8". Cut across the strip to make individual tabs.

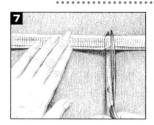

**8.** After marking off the locations for the tabs with pins, position the tabs, then topstitch them in place from the right side using an hourglass shape.

**9.** Pin the flap and the lining together, right sides up and hemmed edges overlapping by 4". Fold the tabs on the flap up and back off the lining (like tab on right). Position a new tab on the lining, overlapping and matching the tab on the flap (like tab on left). The end of the tab on the lining should fall 1½" below the edge of the flap. Pin the new tab to the lining, then pin the remaining tabs in place using the same technique. Topstitch the new tabs to the lining using an hourglass shape.

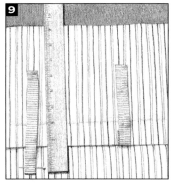

## ATTACHING THE WELTING TO THE DUVET COVER

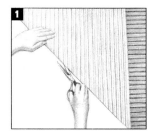

**10.** Machine-baste the welting to the duvet cover front, right sides together. To finish the ends of the welting in a continuous seam, sew around the edge of the duvet cover, but stop with the needle in the down position 2" from where you started. Trim off the excess welting 1" beyond the beginning, then peel the fabric back from both ends and hold the ends together. Cut them with the scissors so the ends butt neatly.

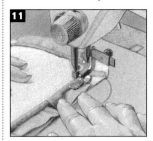

**11.** Fold one end of the fabric strip ½" to the inside, then position the other end of the fabric strip between this fold and the cord. Wrap both ends around the cord, concealing the raw edge, and complete the last few inches of stitching.

---

cover front along marked lines, then set front piece aside.

3. Using the Queen-Size Flat Sheet diagram as reference, mark and cut two 1½" tab strips from top hem of sheet. If making matching tabs for pillowcases, cut additional tab strips from unused top portion of sheet. (One strip yields approximately ten tabs.) Set aside largest remaining piece of sheet for cutting bias strips in step 2 of "Assembling the Welting," at right.

4. To make duvet cover lining, lay smaller (full-size) sheet on large, flat work surface. Using Full-Size Flat Sheet diagram on page 25 as reference, measure and mark a rectangle as wide as duvet and as long as duvet *minus* 4", using top hemmed edge of sheet as top edge of

duvet lining. Then measure and mark flap at bottom of sheet; flap should measure 8" across and be the same width as duvet lining. Use sheet's double-stitched bottom hem as flap's bottom edge. Cut out both pieces using scissors or rotary cutter, then set pieces aside.

**Assembling the Welting**

1. If using store-bought welting, proceed to step 1, "Making the Tabs," page 25. If making your own welting, use Queen-Size Flat Sheet diagram on page 25 as reference and lay largest remaining piece from larger (queen-size) sheet on work surface, and trim off extra fabric (if any) to yield a rectangle with length equal to duvet and width of about 23". Using illustration 1

above as reference, fold rectangle diagonally from one corner by matching one short edge to one long edge. Cut along fold with scissors or rotary cutter, then discard leftover triangle of material. Repeat process at opposite short edge to create large parallelogram as shown in Queen-Size Flat Sheet diagram. (Short sides of parallelogram now run along fabric's bias.)

2. Work on wrong side of parallelogram fabric. Using rotary cutting ruler or clear plastic grid ruler and fabric pencil or chalk, mark lines every 3" parallel to bias edge (*see* illustration 2). When finished, draw a seam line ⅜" from the straight grain (long) edge (This seam line is not visible in illustration 2, as we used a striped sheet for illustration purposes). Using illustra-

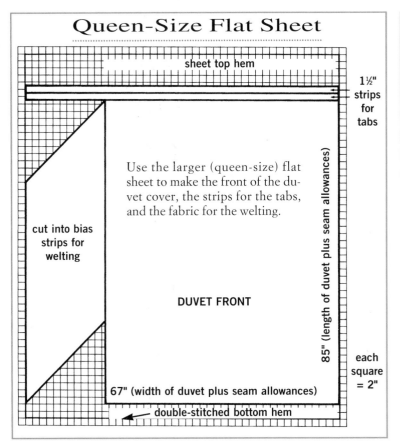

## Queen-Size Flat Sheet

sheet top hem

1½" strips for tabs

Use the larger (queen-size) flat sheet to make the front of the duvet cover, the strips for the tabs, and the fabric for the welting.

cut into bias strips for welting

85" (length of duvet plus seam allowances)

DUVET FRONT

each square = 2"

67" (width of duvet plus seam allowances)

double-stitched bottom hem

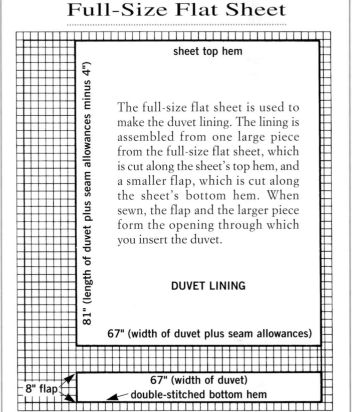

## Full-Size Flat Sheet

sheet top hem

The full-size flat sheet is used to make the duvet lining. The lining is assembled from one large piece from the full-size flat sheet, which is cut along the sheet's top hem, and a smaller flap, which is cut along the sheet's bottom hem. When sewn, the flap and the larger piece form the opening through which you insert the duvet.

81" (length of duvet plus seam allowances minus 4")

DUVET LINING

67" (width of duvet plus seam allowances)

8" flap

67" (width of duvet)
double-stitched bottom hem

tion 3 on page 24 as reference, cut along first marked line for 5" or 6".

3. Using diagram 4 on page 24 as reference, pin straight grain edges (edge A and edge B) together, right sides facing, so that point A almost matches point B. A small triangle of point B about the size of the seam allowance will extend out beyond point A. In order to pin edge A and edge B together, you will have to form the fabric into a spiral as you adjust the seamline, a somewhat awkward maneuver. Note: The points at other end of the strip will not meet.

4. Cut along marked lines to make one continuous bias strip as shown in illustration 5, page 24. (Cutting proceeds as it would for shorter strips, except ends of strips are already sewn together.) Periodically stop and measure yardage; cut yardage determined in step 1 plus 6". Trim ends straight across.

5. Wrap bias strip around welting cord, right side out and edges matching. Using zipper foot, machine-baste approximately ½" from edges, or as close as possible to cord without stitching over it (illustration 6, page 24). Set covered cord aside.

### Making the Tabs

1. Fold 1½"-wide strips cut in step 3 of "Cutting the Sheets" in half lengthwise, right sides together and edges matching. Stitch ¼" from edges along entire length of each strip. Lightly press seam open.

2. Stitch across each strip, perpendicular to

seam, every 6½". Using illustration 7 on page 24 as reference, cut across each strip just to right of stitching to make individual tabs. Clip corners diagonally. Using chopstick or eraser end of pencil, turn tabs right side out through open end. Press from right side, then tuck raw edges ⅜" to inside and press again. To make tabs for pillowcases (if needed), repeat steps 1 and 2.

### Assembling the Duvet Cover

1. Place flap right side up on flat surface. Using yardstick, find center of hemmed edge; insert pin at center. Measure 3" out to each side from center pin and insert pins as markers. Continue inserting pins every 6" to ends of flap. Remove center pin.

2. Place one tab on flap at each pin marker; tucked end of each tab should overlap edge of flap by ¾" (illustration 8, page 24). Topstitch an hourglass shape from right side to secure tab to flap. Repeat with remaining tabs.

3. Position flap and lining, right sides up with hemmed edges of both pieces overlapping by 4". (Once in place, overall length of lining created by both pieces should equal length of duvet cover determined in step 1 of "Cutting the Sheets.") Pin flap to lining at edges to secure in position. Fold tabs on flap back off of lining (illustration 9, tab on right). Position new tab on lining, overlapping and matching tab on flap (illustration 9, tab at left); end of tab should fall 1½" below edge of flap. Pin tab to lining, then pin remaining tabs in place using

same technique. Stitch all these tabs in place by topstitching in an hourglass shape.

4. Pin welting around edge of duvet cover front, right sides together and edges matching. Using zipper foot, machine-baste through all layers ½" from edges, gently rounding welting at corners. To finish ends in a continuous seam, continue sewing around edge, but stop with needle down, 2" from where you began. Trim off excess welting 1" beyond original starting point. Using illustration 10 as reference, peel fabric back from both ends of welting cord, hold ends of welting cord together, and cut both at once with scissors so ends butt neatly. Fold one end of welting fabric ½" to inside; position other end of welting fabric between this fold and welting cord. Rewrap both ends around welting cord, concealing raw edge, and complete last few inches of stitching (see illustration 11).

5. Lay cover lining on top of cover front, right sides together and edges matching, with welting sandwiched in between. Set machine to 10 to 12 stitches per inch. Using zipper foot, stitch all around cover, staying as close to welting cord as possible. Turn cover right side out through flap opening. Examine welting edge and pick out any visible basting stitches with seam ripper.

6. Insert duvet into cover; tie each pair of tabs closed. Do not pull knots tight. ◆

**Mary Frazier** is a professional seamstress based in New York.

# Cedar Chip Sachets

*Make two different dainty lace sachets for less than $2 each
using cedar shavings from a pet supply store.*

BY LISA SHERRY

*Either of the two styles of sachets shown here (capelet sachet, top, and
flounce hem sachet, bottom) can be made with 6"- to 9"-wide tulle lace.*

These lace sachets may look expensive, but each one costs under $2 to make. The key: using cedar shavings sold as hamster bedding in pet supply stores instead of cedar chips marketed as potpourri or closet freshener. A thirty-two-ounce bag of cedar hamster bedding, typically priced around $3.49, can fill thirty sachets at a cost of only 12¢ each; individually packaged, one-ounce bags of cedar chips cost around $1.79 and will fill only one sachet each. Both products contain 100 percent cedar chips. The difference in price—the main difference I could find between the two—is probably a result of the grade of cedar used in making the chips. Cedar is a natural moth repellent and a good substitute for mothballs. Once the cedar scent begins to fade, refill the sachet with fresh chips.

For best results, choose a lace with a tulle foundation, which will contain the cedar shavings without inhibiting their scent. Any tulle-type lace trim ranging from six to nine inches wide and bought by the yard will work fine. Some laces are designed with one scalloped edge while others have two scalloped edges. You can use either type of lace for both the designs shown.

For sewing lace, I recommend using a narrow French seam to enclose the raw edges. (*See* "How to Make a French Seam," below.) French seams are stronger and more durable than a single row of stitching and help to compensate for the delicacy of the fabric.

I also recommend using your sewing machine's single-hole needle plate instead of the zigzag plate when sewing the seams. The zigzag plate has a wide opening that allows the needle to move from side to side during sewing, and sometimes the rapid down-ward thrust of the needle causes thin, delicate fabrics to get bunched up inside this hole and jam the stitching. The single hole plate gives delicate fabrics more support underneath and has less of an opening to swallow them up.

Another tip when sewing lace: To avoid the thread bulk buildup at seams that is caused by backtacking and knotting ends, set the machine for very tiny stitches, just a bit above zero stitches per inch, and stitch forward for four or five stitches to anchor the thread. Then switch to a normal stitch length (ten to twelve stitches per inch) and stitch until you reach the last quarter inch of the seam. Finish off with tiny stitches, and clip off the loose thread ends. The tight, tiny stitches at the beginning and the end of the seam will keep the threads from pulling out without adding extra bulk.

## CEDAR CHIP SACHETS

$\frac{3}{8}$ yard tulle-type white or ecru lace trim, 6" to 9" wide

3" rayon tassel to match lace

$\frac{3}{4}$ yard $\frac{5}{16}$"-wide double-sided satin ribbon in coordinating color

1 ounce hamster cedar shavings

## HOW TO MAKE A FRENCH SEAM

The straight French seam, a joining technique that conceals a fabric's raw edges, is especially appropriate for sheers or unlined curtains, draperies, table toppers, dust ruffles, fabrics that ravel easily, and small, delicate items such as these lace sachets. A French seam looks like a plain seam from the right side of the fabric and like a narrow tuck from the wrong side of the fabric. French seams are difficult to sew on curves, so they're best used on straight seams.

When sewing French seams, buckling is a common problem, but this can be prevented by triple-pressing the fabric to define the seam and make it pliable. To make a one-fourth-inch French seam, allow a five-eighths-inch seam allowance on each of the pieces of fabric to be joined.

For illustrations of this process, *see* "Buckle-Free French Seams," in the Quick Tips section of the January/February 1995 issue.

**1.** Place the fabric pieces wrong sides together and stitch a seam ⅜" (not ⅝") from the raw edges. Press the seam open, then to one side, then finish by pressing the seam to the other side.

**2.** Using scissors, trim the seam through both layers a scant ⅛" from the stitching.

**3.** Fold the fabric pieces right sides together, concealing the stitching and the seam's narrow raw edges. Sew a second seam ¼" from the folded seam line.

**4.** Press the finished French seam first to one side and then to the other. Turn the fabric over and press it from the right side.

*You'll also need:* thread; sewing machine with single-hole needle plate; scissors; and iron.

*Other items, if necessary:* tapestry needle (for capelet sachet).

**Flounce Hem Sachet**

1. Lay lace on flat surface with raw edges at right and left. Fold lace in half, wrong sides together with raw edges and scalloped edges matching. Using matching thread, stitch raw edges together ³⁄₈" from edge. Press seam open, then to each side. Trim seam a scant ¹⁄₈" from stitching.

2. Turn sachet wrong side out and fold along seamline, concealing stitching and seam's narrow raw edges. Stitch a second seam ¼" from folded seam to complete French seam. Press seam first to one side and then the other. Turn fabric over and press from right side.

3. Turn tube right side out and lay flat with seam at one side. Straight-stitch about 1½" in from bottom scalloped edge to create flounce hem.

4. Fill sachet about two-thirds full with hamster shavings. Pinch top (do not twist), wrap ribbon around twice, and tie in snug, single knot. Slip tassel loop onto ribbon, then complete tying bow. Snip ribbon ends diagonally.

**Capelet Sachet**

1. Lay lace on flat surface with raw edges at right and left. Fold down top third of lace to create capelet with scalloped edge. Using matching thread, stitch ½" from folded edge to make a casing.

2. Fold lace rectangle in half crosswise, capelet facing out and short raw edges matching. Stitch ³⁄₈" from raw edges through all layers. Press seam open, then to each side. Trim seam a scant ¹⁄₈" from stitching.

3. Turn lace tube wrong side out and fold along seamline. Stitch a second seam ¼" from folded seam to complete French seam, concealing stitching and seam's narrow raw edges. Press seam first to one side and then the other. Turn fabric over and press from right side.

4. Turn tube right side out and lay flat with seam centered at back. Straight-stitch about 1" from the edge without capelet. Trim seam a scant ¹⁄₈" from stitching.

## MAKING THE FLOUNCE HEM SACHET

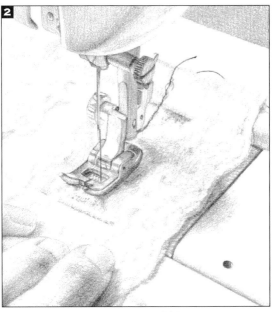

**1.** After stitching the raw edges together ³⁄₈" from the edge, press the seam open. Trim the seam approximately ¹⁄₈" from the stitching, then turn the lace tube wrong side out and fold it along the seamline. Stitch a scant ¼" from the fold to complete the French seam.

**2.** To create a flounce hem, turn the sachet right side out and lay it flat with the seam at one side. Straight-stitch about 1½" in from the scalloped edge.

## MAKING THE CAPELET SACHET

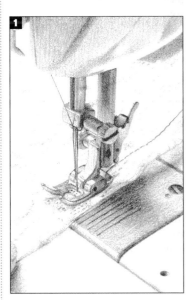

**2.** Once you've sewn the sachet's edges together with a French seam, turn the lace tube right side out and lay it flat with the seam centered at the back. Straight-stitch about 1" from the edge without the capelet, then finish this edge with a French seam.

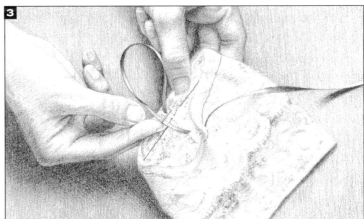

**1.** Fold down the top third of the lace to create the capelet, then stitch ½" from the folded edge to make a casing.

**3.** To thread the ribbon through the casing, insert the tapestry needle into the casing at the center front of the bag, but reemerge at the inside back to cross over the French seam.

Turn wrong side out and finger-press seam. Stitch a scant ¼" from fold to complete French seam. Turn pouch right side out.

5. Thread ribbon through tapestry needle eye. Insert needle into casing at center front of pouch, pushing it through any existing opening in tulle. Draw needle through casing, emerging and reentering at back of pouch to cross over French seam. Continue threading through casing, emerging at center front of pouch. Even up ends of ribbon.

6. Fill sachet with shavings un-til firm and plump. Pull ribbon drawstring closed, tie in a single knot, slip on tassel, and tie bow. Snip ribbon ends diagonally. ◆

**Lisa Sherry** is a freelance craftsperson and writer living in Sag Harbor, New York.

# Basket-Weave Cake with Pansies

*Create a basket-weave effect in 20 minutes using Quaker Oat Squares.*

## BY ROSEMARY CHERIS LITTMAN

*This cake, made to resemble a springtime basket of pansies, makes an elegant centerpiece as well as a delicious dessert.*

Although at a glance this may look like a basket of fresh-picked pansies, it's really a delicious chocolate cake.

As any professional cake decorator will tell you, creating an icing basket-weave effect is an extremely time-consuming process. You can make this basket weave, however, in about twenty minutes using cinnamon-flavored Quaker Oat Squares. I topped this cake with crystallized pansies, one of several edible species of flowers. Pansies have a very mild wintergreen flavor. You can purchase crystallized edible flowers through mail order or in gourmet grocery shops, or you can make your own using the simple recipes on the next page. For a variation, use the crystallizing recipes to sugarcoat other edible flowers such as nasturtiums, rose petals, or violets.

A few things to keep in mind: If you decide to crystallize your own pansies, make sure you use flowers that were not grown with pesti-cides. People who are prone to allergies can have an allergic reaction to flowers, as with any food. (Note: Not all flowers are edible, and some are even poisonous. Always proceed with extreme caution and never eat unfamiliar flowers. If in doubt, order your edible flowers from a reliable source.) For best results, always use flowers at their peak; avoid unopened buds and faded or wilted flowers.

The recipes for Old-Fashioned Chocolate Cake and Coffee Buttercream Icing, developed by Steven Schmidt, are taken from the July/August 1994 issue of *Cook's Illustrated*.

### BASKET-WEAVE CAKE WITH PANSIES

#### Old-Fashioned Chocolate Cake

    Shortening to grease baking pans and lining paper
18  tablespoons (2¼ sticks) unsalted butter, softened

1¾  cups plus 2 tablespoons sugar
3  large eggs, at room temperature
1¾  cups plus 2 tablespoons all-purpose flour plus enough to flour baking pans
¾  teaspoons baking soda
¾  teaspoons salt
¾  cups nonalkalized cocoa (such as Hershey's)
1  tablespoon instant espresso or instant coffee
1  tablespoon pure vanilla extract
1½  cups plus 3 tablespoons milk, at room temperature

#### Coffee Buttercream Icing

2  tablespoons instant espresso or instant coffee
2  tablespoons coffee liqueur
2  tablespoons pure vanilla extract
1  pound (4 sticks) unsalted butter, softened
4  cups confectioners sugar
¼  cup beaten egg, pasteurized cream, *or* 2 beaten egg yolks

#### Basket-Weave and Pansy Decorations

    Cinnamon-flavored Quaker Oat Squares breakfast cereal
2–3  dozen pansies (purchase by mail order *or* crystallize your own; *see* "How to Make Your Own Crystallized Pansies," page 29)

### Making the Cake

1. Adjust oven rack to center position and heat oven to 350 degrees. Grease three 8"-round baking pans with shortening. Line pan bottoms with waxed or parchment paper, and grease paper as well. Dust pan with flour; tap out excess.

2. Beat butter in bowl of electric mixer set at medium-high speed until smooth and shiny, about 30 seconds. Gradually sprinkle in sugar and beat until mixture is fluffy and almost white, 3 to 5 minutes. Add eggs one at a time, beating 1 full minute after each addition.

3. Whisk flour, baking soda, salt, cocoa, and espresso in medium-size bowl until no lumps of cocoa remain. Add vanilla to milk. With mixer on lowest speed, add about one-third of dry ingredients to butter-sugar mixture and mix well. Follow with about one-third of milk-vanilla mixture; mix until ingredients are almost incorporated. Repeat process to in-

corporate all of mixtures. When batter is blended, stop mixer and scrape sides of bowl with rubber spatula. Return mixer to low speed, and beat until batter looks satiny, about 15 seconds longer.

4. Divide batter evenly between pans. With rubber spatula, spread batter to sides of pan and smooth the top. Bake cakes until skewer inserted in center comes out clean or with just a crumb or two adhering; 23 to 30 minutes. Transfer pans to wire racks; cool for 10 minutes. Run knife around side of each pan, invert cakes onto racks, and peel off paper liners. Reinvert cakes onto additional racks; cool completely before frosting.

### Making the Icing

1. Mix espresso, coffee liqueur, and vanilla in small cup until coffee dissolves; set aside. Beat butter in bowl of electric mixer at medium-high speed until fluffy, about 1 minute. Add sugar and beat 3 minutes longer. Add coffee mixture and egg or cream to frosting; beat until frosting mounds around beaters in fluffy mass, 3 to 5 minutes longer.

2. Place first layer of cake on cake plate or platter; use long, metal spatula to spread with a portion of frosting. Put second layer of cake on top of first layer; frost top of second layer. Then put third layer of cake on top of second, and frost top of third layer. Then frost sides of all three layers. When cake is covered, use spatula to mound up extra icing toward center of cake top. When flowers are placed on this mound, they will give the effect of a "full" basket. Use damp paper towels to wipe away any frosting from cake plate.

### Making the Basket Weave

1. To create basket weave, press one Oat Square into icing on side of cake, very close to platter, then press a second Oat Square next to it with lines perpendicular to the first Oat Square. Continue pressing Oat Squares onto cake, alternating direction of lines, until you have made one row encircling cake. As you near the end, adjust spacing, if necessary, so last square is perpendicular to first one. (Because icing is a similar color to cereal, it won't matter if a small amount of icing shows through spaces.)

2. Repeat step 1 to cover sides of cake with rows of Oat Squares, making squares in second and higher rows perpendicular to squares in row below. (Don't cover top of cake.) If crystallizing your own pansies, follow directions below. Refrigerate cake until flowers are ready. When pansies are ready (or if using mail-order pansies), arrange as shown in photograph, covering entire top of cake. If desired, flowers can extend down onto cake plate; glue them onto the cereal with dabs of icing. ◆

**Rosemary Cheris Littman** is an artist based in Teaneck, New Jersey, who paints and sculpts custom-designed cakes.

## HOW TO MAKE YOUR OWN CRYSTALLIZED PANSIES

To decorate the basket-weave cake, I used about three dozen crystallized pansies. You can crystallize your own pansies (provided you use organic pansies or those that have been grown without the use of pesticides) for significantly less money than buying them. Mail-order crystallized pansies cost anywhere from $1.50 to $3.00 each, depending on where you buy them.

There are two primary ways to crystallize edible flowers: One method uses egg whites; the other uses gum arabic. Both methods require superfine sugar for the final coating, which can be purchased where bar supplies are sold. The advantage of gum arabic, which is available in art supply stores, is that it preserves the flowers for up to several months if they are kept in a lidded jar. On the other hand, gum arabic takes longer to dry and can leave the flower with a thicker coating and a slightly distorted shape. The egg white and sugar combination is just as effective for crystallizing flowers, and in fact preserves the rich color and shape of the flower better than gum arabic, although the results will only last a day or two.

Note: The eggs used in the egg white method are raw, so this method should not be used if the crystallized flowers might be eaten by pregnant women, infants and young children, the elderly, or anyone else whose health might be compromised by such ingredients. It is safest to use powdered egg whites.

If using the egg white method, make the flowers the day before or the same day as making the cake; if using gum arabic, make them at least a week ahead of time.

### EGG WHITE METHOD

Organic pansies
2 egg whites
Superfine sugar

*You'll also need:* scissors; small bowl; electric or hand mixer; small, new paintbrush; teaspoon; and 1 to 3 narrow-grid cake racks.

1. With scissors, snip off any discolored petals or stems from flowers. Beat egg whites in small bowl until foamy and smooth; do not overbeat.

2. Holding pansy in one hand over bowl, use paintbrush to coat top and bottom of petals with light, even coating of egg white. (Do not oversaturate or sugar coating may form into globs.) Fill teaspoon with sugar. Hold pansy upside down by stem and sprinkle sugar evenly on underside of flower; turn flower upright and sprinkle sugar to cover all petals evenly.

3. Lay flower on wire rack. Repeat step 2 with remaining flowers. Flowers can be placed directly on cake, or allowed to dry for half a day.

### GUM ARABIC METHOD

3  teaspoons gum arabic
¼  cup granulated sugar
Superfine sugar
Organic pansies

*You'll also need:* measuring cup; double boiler; medium saucepan; scissors; new, clean paintbrush; teaspoon; and 1 to 3 narrow-grid cake racks.

1. In the top of double boiler, over simmering water, dissolve gum arabic in ¼ cup of water. When gum arabic has dissolved, remove mixture from heat and allow to cool.

2. Add granulated sugar to ¼ cup water in medium saucepan, and bring mixture to boil. Remove from heat and stir until sugar dissolves and mixture becomes syrupy. Allow to cool.

3. With scissors, snip off any discolored petals or stems from flowers. Holding pansy in one hand, use paintbrush to coat top and bottom of petals with light, even coating of gum arabic mixture. (The gum arabic may bead up on the pansy petal; if this happens, rub the petal with paintbrush to break up the beads.) Repeat painting process with sugar-water mixture, then fill teaspoon with sugar. Hold pansy upside down by stem and sprinkle sugar evenly on underside of flower; turn flower upright and sprinkle sugar to cover all petals evenly.

4. Lay flower on wire rack. Repeat step 3 with remaining flowers. After flowers have dried at least half a day, turn each flower over and let dry 2 to 5 more days.

*The pansies on the left have been crystallized using the egg white method, while those on the right were done using gum arabic.*

# Field Guide to Miniature Baskets

**Manufacturer, description, and suggested retail price**

**1.** Palecek, 3" x 4" oval pewter scallop basket, $10

**2.** MCK & Co., rectangular woven bamboo blue drummer basket (set of three), $22

**3.** Desti Imports Inc., round bamboo basket (set of twelve), $36

**4.** MCK & Co., miniature bark and twig wall basket, $7.50

**5.** MCK & Co., Shaker plain woven basket (set of three), $22

**6.** MCK & Co., miniature rectangular whitewash basket with two side handles, $4

**7.** MCK & Co., klee 4" flower pots (set of six), $21

**8.** MCK & Co., green pirot painted rectangular bamboo basket with ears (set of two), $20

**9.** Desti Imports Inc., rectangular rattan buri box (set of twelve), $48

**10.** Desti Imports Inc., miniature bamboo basket (set of twelve), $36

**11.** MCK & Co., willow twig square flower basket (set of two), $9

**12.** Desti Imports Inc., rectangular ban ban and bamboo tray (set of twelve), $30

**13.** MCK & Co., woven bamboo klee bowls with ears (assortment of four), $24

**14.** MCK & Co., miniature bustle basket with vine handle, $5

**15.** MCK & Co., woven bamboo miniature klee pot assortment (set of six), $20

**16.** Palecek, pewter wicker loop soap holder, $9

**17.** MCK & Co., birch bark bouquet basket (set of two), $15

PHOTOGRAPH BY STEPHEN MAYS

# SOURCES
## AND RESOURCES

Most of the materials needed for the projects in this issue are available at your local craft supply, hardware or paint store, florist, fabric shop, or bead and jewelry supply. The following are specific mail-order sources for particular items, arranged by project. The suggested retail prices listed are current at press time. Contact the suppliers directly to confirm up-to-date prices and availability of products.

### Notes from Readers; pages 2–3
*Tips on Drying Hydrangeas:* Climbing hydrangeas, pot-grown plants for $19.95 each or $53.85 per 3 from White Flower Farm. *Preserving the Color of Pressed Flowers:* Petal Porcelain for $2.45 per 8 ounces from Sunshine Discount Crafts. *How to Store a Quilt:* Large selection of acid-free paper for $1 per sheet from Pearl Paint. *Thread for Pearl Necklaces:* Silk thread for $4.10 per 100 yards from Newark Dressmaker Supply. Silk buttonhold twist (size F) for $9.40 per 185 yard spool from Atlantic Thread and Supply. *Preventing Drooping Flowers:* Oasis floral brick for $1.79 from Creative Craft House. *Tips on Using Snapped Stems:* Oasis floral brick for $1.79 from Creative Craft House. Wooden floral picks for 89¢ and floral tape for $1.61 per 60 yards from Craft King. *Finding a Pattern for a Fabric Backgammon Board:* Selection of game board patterns for $5.50 from Keepsake Quilting. *Finding Flesh-Toned Shades of Fabric:* 100-percent cotton, unbleached, ivory fabric for $15 per 3 yards from Quilts and Other Comforts. Large selection of dyes from $2.39 per 1 ounce from Earth Guild. *Painting Cotton Café Curtains:* Textile paints from $1.79 per 1 ounce and stenciling brushes from $1.69 per 1 from Pearl Paint. Irons from $10 from Service Merchandise. Selection of fabrics from $3.40 per yard from Newark Dressmaker Supply. *Selecting the Right Paint for Decorating Canvas Sneakers:* Acrylic fabric paint from 99¢ per 2 ounces from Sunshine Discount Crafts.

### Quick Tips; pages 4–5
*Preventing a Paintbrush from Drying Out:* Large selection of acrylic and oil paints from $2.11 per 40 ml tube from Pearl Paint. Plastic bags from $1.55 per 100 from Craft King. *Keeping Tulips Fresh:* Tulips for $18 per dozen from Village Flowers. *Steaming Out Dents in Wood:* Irons from $10 from Service Merchandise. *Pouring Liquid into a Small Opening:* Selection of screwdrivers from $5.50 from Frog Tool Company. *Perfectly Matched Prints:* Selection of print fabrics from $4.50

per yard, thread from $1.70 per 350 yards, Olfa rotary cutter for $8.45, scissors from $10.75, and C-Thru plastic ruler for $4, all from Newark Dressmaker Supply. HeatnBond Lite for $1.84 per 17" x 36" piece from Clotilde. Selection of sewing machines from $55 and irons from $10 from Service Merchand*ise*. *Stenciling Through Netting:* Large selection of lace from $1 per yard from The Smocking Bonnet. Laces also available from 60¢ per 10 yards from Home-Sew and Newark Dressmaker Supply. Spray paint from $2.95 per 13 ounces from Dick Blick. *Removing Glue Drips:* Single-edged razor blade for $9.56 per 100 and heavy-duty utility blade for $1.76 per 5 from Co-op Artist's Materials. Plaid's Tacky Glue for 88¢ from Sunshine Discount Crafts. Sobo glue for $1.70 per 4 ounces from Jerry's Artarama. Titebond yellow glue for $2.95 per 8 ounces from Woodcraft. Selection of washcloths from $6 per 2 from Coming Home. *Preventing Drooping Roses:* Roses from $35 per half dozen from Village Flowers. Felco pruning shears for $39 from White Flower Farm.

### French Tinware Cachepot; pages 6–8
Tinware square tapered planter (6 5/8" square x 7 1/4" high) for $25 from Tinker Bob's Tinware. Krylon spray paint for $4.30 per 12-ounce can, and a selection of other spray enamels from $2.95 per 13-ounce can, Winsor & Newton burnt umber oil paint and a selection of other oil colors from $2.90 per 1.25 ounces, 1-Shot 4-ounce enamel paint for $36.60 per set of 12, polyurethane varnish for $5.50 per pint, Quality paint thinner for $3.30 per quart, 1-Shot acrylic bonding primer for $9.40 per quart, scissors from $1.25, Best-Test rubber cement for $2.10 per 4 ounces, Cubby Ware containers for $2.30 per package of 10, 1"-wide masking tape for $1.25 per 60-yard roll, 1" Economy artist's tape for $3.70 per 60-yard roll, rectangular poly sponge for $1.20, large selection of paint brushes from 70¢, safety goggles for $1.95, denatured alcohol from $5.90 per pint, and disposable polyethylene gloves for $1.90 per 100, all from Dick Blick. Aleene's Transfer-it for $1.88 per 2-ounce squeeze bottle and Delta transfer medium for $4.12 per 12 ounces from Pearl Paint.

### Miniature Flower Baskets; page 9
Miniature baskets for $4.99 each from Ben Franklin. Statice in a variety of colors for $3.90 per 4-ounce bunch, tea

rose heads from $4.50 per ounce and rose stems from $10 per 20 stems, all from Mills Floral Supply. Folk Art acrylic paint for $1.09 per 2 ounces, Folk Art paint brushes from $2.19, foam block for 89¢, scissors from $1.99, mini low-temp trigger-fed glue gun for $3.50 and glue sticks for $1.39 per 50, all from Sunshine Discount Crafts. Cockscomb for $5.80 per bunch, hydrangeas from $2.50 per bunch, plus a variety of other dried flowers from 10¢ per bunch, all from Floral Express.

### Testing Metallic Paints; pages 10–12
Variety of metallic paints available from Pearl Paint, Dick Blick, Craft King, and Daniel Smith. Prices start at approximately $1.30.

### Silk Peony Bouquet; page 13
Grape leaves with grape spray for $5.90, rose and bud deluxe stems from $2.25 per stem, and peony spray for $2.90, all from May Silk. Florist wire for $1.15 per 10-yard spool and Fiskar's Craft Snip for $11 from Newark Dressmaker Supply. Dowels from 20¢ from Pearl Paint. Hammers from $15.50 and screws from $2.75 per box of 100 from Woodcraft.

### 10-Minute Faux Finishes; page 14
Selection of unpainted wood items from 55¢, Laser scissors for $6.49, sponge brush for 25¢, and Americana acrylic paint for 99¢ per 2-ounce squeeze bottle, all from Sunshine Discount Crafts. Sandpaper from 29¢, metal palette cups from 34¢, and storage containers with screw-on lids from 30¢, all from Pearl Paint.

### Edwardian Silk Writing Folio; pages 15–16
Selection of bookcloth from $4.60 per yard, self-healing mats from $21, bone folders from $2.90, metal triangular gauge for $5, Soupercoup mat knife for $8.60, and glue brushes from $5.35, all from Bookbinder's Warehouse. Acetate from 88¢ per sheet or $3.89 per roll, 2-ply bristol board from $7.10, chipboard from 84¢, Sobo glue for $2.47 per 8 ounces, kraft paper from 89¢ per roll, and dowels from 20¢, all from Pearl Paint. Irons from $10 from Service Merchandise.

### Miter Box Frame; pages 17–19
Selection of hardwood moldings from $1.55 each, precision miter box for $29.95, 14" backsaw for $14.95, brad

setter for $10.25, 6d nails for $3.95 per 50 and other decorative steel cut nails from $2.95 per 100, all from Constantine's Woodworker's Catalog. Spackling compound for $3 per quart, sandpaper from 29¢, and 1"-wide interior trim brush for $8.21, all from Pearl Paint. 4" adjustable C-Clamp for $7.95, satin polyurethane for $10.95 per quart, and retractable tape measure for $6.95, all from The Woodworkers' Store. Straight backsaw for $6.50, Japanese combination square for $12.95, Titebond glue for $2.95 per 8 ounces, hammers from $8.50, finishing rags for $4.95 per pound, and a large selection of wood, all from Woodcraft. Finishing brads for $12.99 per 5,000 and selection of pliers from $7.99 from Northern. Latex paint from $5 per quart from Pearl Paint.

### Ukrainian Easter Eggs; pages 20–22
Aniline egg dye for 75¢ per packet; setting powder for 75¢; pure beeswax patties for 50¢; kistka from $1.75; and set of dipper, guide band, and 2 candles for 60¢; all from Surma. Drop cloths from 69¢, permanent markers from $2, watercolor pencils from 81¢, and masking tape from 42¢ per 60 yards from Pearl Paint. Tea kettles from $40, Weck 6-ounce canning jars for $13 per set of 8, stainless-steel measuring spoons for $9, and Pyrex measuring cup for $7, all from Williams-Sonoma. 32-gauge wire for $1.69 per 10-yard spool from Kirchen Brother's Crafts. PVC-coated gloves for $1.79 per pair, finishing brads for $12.99 per 5,000, and hammers from $4.99, all from Northern. Wood boards in a variety of sizes from $1.55 and polyurethane satin for $13.75 per pint from Woodcraft.

### Two-Sheet Duvet Cover; pages 23–25
Large selection of sheets from $21 for queen size and $14 for double from Coming Home. Selection of thread from $1.70 per 350 yards, cotton piping cord from 70¢ per 10 yards, scissors from $10.75, rotary cutter for $8.45 and guide for $3.70, seam ripper for 85¢, tape measure for $1.25, fabric-marking pencil for 95¢, and straight pins from $1.75 per 400, all from Newark Dressmaker Supply. Sewing machines from $55 and irons from $10 from Service Merchandise.

### Cedar Chip Sachets; pages 26–27
6"-wide white tulle for $6.25 per 25-yard roll, satin ribbon from 70¢ per 5 yards, thread from $1.70 per 350 yards, scissors from $10.75, tassel fringe

for $3.95 per 4 yards, and tapestry needle for 80¢, all from Newark Dressmaker Supply. Irons from $10 and selection of sewing machines from $55 from Service Merchandise. Cedar chips for $1.24 per 4 ounces from The Ginger Tree.

### Basket-Weave Cake with Pansies; pages 28–29

Crystallized pansies for $30 per 12 (plus $8.25 for shipping and handling outside of California) from Grapevine Trading Company. Organic pansies for $2.25 per packet from Shepherd's Garden Seeds. Tiered cooling rack set for $9.95 per set of 3, egg-white powder for $3.95 per 4 ounces, gum paste mix for $4.50 per 1-pound bag, hobby brushes for $1.95 per pack of 10, and double-boiler maker for $3.95, all from Kitchen Krafts. Pyrex 4-ounce measuring cup for $7, stainless-steel double-boiler for $39, Henckles kitchen shears for $23, and Cuisinart hand blender for $50, all from Williams-Sonoma.

### Field Guide to Miniature Baskets; page 30

Selection of miniature baskets for $4.99 each from Ben Franklin. A variety of baskets from 30¢ from Creative Craft House. Market baskets for $6.35 per set of 3 from Craft King. Hanging twig bird's nest basket for 49¢ from Kirchen Brother's Crafts.

### Quick Projects; page 33

*Woven Band with Scallop Fringe:* Selection of fringes and trims from $3.75 per yard, metallic trims from $1, tacky glue for $2.10, Fray Check for $2.60, or weighted tape for $2.80 per 4 yards, all from Newark Dressmaker Supply. *Beaded Fringe:* Pearl strands from 69¢, 8mm plastic beads from 59¢, and low-temp mini glue gun for $3.19 and glue sticks for $1.20 per 25 pieces, all from Craft King. *Pleated Marbled Paper:* Selection of marbled papers and other exotic and decorative papers from $3.75 per sheet from Daniel Smith. Mini clothespins for $2.29 per 50 and Plaid's white tacky glue for 89¢ from Craft King. *Love Note:* Fabric brush markers for $2.19 and Bond fabric glue for $1.59 from Craft King. 1/4" satin ribbon for 80¢ per 5 yards from Newark Dressmaker Supply. *Plain and Embroidered Ribbon Trim:* 1" satin ribbon for $1.75 per 5 yards, a selection of other ribbons from 95¢ per 5 yards, and tacky glue for $2.10 per 4 ounces from Newark Dressmaker Supply.

### Crystal Bead Drop Candlestick; back cover

Bud vase for $2.49 (SKU #1008 Hancock), glass candlestick for $2.99, glass coaster for $2.50, and 8mm round faceted beads for $1.50, all from Ben Franklin. Plastic bobeche from 50¢, bobeche with crystal prisms for $24.95 per set of 2, and 8" white taper candles for $2.65 per set of 2, all from The Candle Shop. 8mm clear round beads from 99¢ per package, rattail stringing cord for 49¢ per 60 inches, 4 1/2" round tip cutters for $6.75, and craft wire from $1.99 per 40 yards, all from Sunshine Discount Crafts. Pro-quality art blades from 99¢ per 5 from Jerry's Artarama. Silicone gel from $2 per 2-ounce squeeze bottle from Pearl Paint.

---

The following companies are mentioned in the listings above. Contact each individually for a price list or catalog.

**Atlantic Thread and Supply,** 695 Red Oak Road, Stockbridge, GA 30281; 800-847-1001

**Ben Franklin Retail Stores, Inc.,** 500 East North Avenue, Carol Stream, IL 60188; 708-462-6100

**Bookbinder's Warehouse,** 31 Division Street, Keyport, NJ 07735; 908-264-0306

**The Candle Shop,** 29 Main Street, Cold Spring Harbor, NY 11724; 516-692-5788

**Clotilde,** 2 Sew Smart Way B8031, Stevens Point, WI 54481-8031; 800-772-2891

**Constantine's Woodworker's Catalog,** 2050 Eastchester Road, Bronx, NY 10461-2297; 800-223-8087

**Co-op Artists' Materials,** P.O. Box 53097, Atlanta, GA 30355; 800-877-3242

**Coming Home,** 1 Land's End Lane, Dodgeville, WI 53595; 800-345-3696

**Craft King Discount Craft Supply,** P.O. Box 53097, Lakeland, FL 33804; 800-769-9494

**Creative Craft House,** P.O. Box 2567, Bullhead City, AZ 86430; 602-754-3300

**Daniel Smith,** P.O. Box 84268, Seattle, WA 98124-5568; 800-426-6740

**Dick Blick,** P.O. Box 1267, Galesburg, IL 61402-1267; 800-447-8192

**Earth Guild,** 33 Haywood Street, Asheville, NC 28801; 800-327-8448

**Floral Express,** 11 Armco Avenue, Caribou, ME 04736; 800-392-7417

**The Ginger Tree,** 245 Lee Road 122, Opelika, AL 36801; 205-745-4864

**Grapevine Trading Company,** 59 Maxwell Court, Santa Rosa, CA 95401; 707-576-3950

**Home-Sew,** P.O. Box 4099, Bethlehem, PA 18018-0099; 610-867-3833

**Jerry's Artarama,** P.O. Box 1105, New Hyde Park, New York, NY 11040; 800-U-ARTIST

**Keepsake Quilting,** Box 1618, Centre Harbor, NH 03226-1618; 603-253-8731

**Kirchen Brother's Crafts,** Box 1016, Skokie, IL 60076; 708-647-6747

**Kitchen Krafts,** P.O. Box 805, Mt. Laurel, NJ 08054-0805; 800-776-0575

**May Silk,** 16202 Distribution Way, Cerritos, CA 90703; 800-282-7455

**Mills Floral Supply,** 4550 Peachtree Lakes Drive, Duluth, GA 30136; 800-762-7939

**The Nature Conservancy,** 1815 North Lynn Street, Arlington, VA 22209; 800-628-6860

**Newark Dressmaker Supply,** 6473 Ruch Road, P.O. Box 20730, Lehigh Valley, PA 18002-0730; 800-736-6783

**Northern,** P.O. Box 1499, Burnsville, MN 55337-0499; 800-533-5545

**Pearl Paint,** 308 Canal Street, New York, NY 10013; 800-221-6845

**Quilts and Other Comforts,** P.O. Box 4101, Golden, CO 80402-4101; 303-420-4272 ext. 100

**Seaport Flowers,** 214 Hicks Street, Brooklyn, NY 11201; 718-858-6443

**Service Merchandise,** P.O. Box 25130, Nashville, TN 37202-5130; 800-251-1212

**Shepherd's Garden Seeds,** 30 Irene Street, Torrington, CT 06790; 203-482-3638

**The Smocking Bonnet;** P.O. Box 555, Cooksville, MD 21723; 800-524-1678

**Sunshine Discount Crafts,** P.O. Box 301, Largo, FL 34649-0301; 813-538-2878

**Surma,** 11 East 7th Street, New York, NY 10003; 212-477-0729

**Tinker Bob's Tinware,** 209 Summit Street, Norwich, CT 06360; 203-886-7365

**Village Flowers,** 297 Main Street, Huntington, NY 11743; 516-427-0996

**Williams-Sonoma,** P.O. Box 7456, San Francisco, CA 94120-7456; 800-541-2233

**White Flower Farm,** P.O. Box 50, Litchfield, CT 06759-0050; 203-496-9600

**Woodcraft,** 210 Wood County Industrial Park, P.O. Box 1686, Parkersburg, WV 26102-1686; 800-225-1153

**The Woodworkers' Store,** 21801 Industrial Boulevard, Rogers, MN 55374-9514; 800-279-4441 ◆

---

The Dried Rose Bouquet featured on the back cover of the July/August 1994 issue of *Handcraft Illustrated* is available as a kit including all the necessary materials. The cost is $19.95 plus $1.50 shipping and handling. To order the kit, send a check or money order for $21.45, or send your credit card number (we accept American Express, VISA, and Mastercard), the expiration date, and an authorized signature to: Rose Kit, *Handcraft Illustrated*, P.O. Box 509, Brookline Village, MA 02147-0509.

# Quick Projects

Decorating a lampshade to reflect your own personal style and taste is quick and easy to do. For the designs shown here, we decorated three different shades: two plain shades (each priced around $7), and a pleated fabric shade (which cost about $14). All three shades measure approximately 4" in diameter at the bottom rim and 4" from the bottom rim to the top rim. They're appropriate for small lamps, wall sconces, or chandeliers.

**Pleated Marble Paper**

**Woven Band with Scallop Fringe**—Use a plain black shade. Purchase a length of 1½"-wide scallop fringe equal to the bottom circumference of the shade plus 1" to 2" for overlap (approximately 15" total). Before cutting the fringe, wrap a piece of tape around each end to prevent the ends from raveling. Wrap the fringe around the bottom rim of the shade, securing it in place with a thin line of quick-drying white glue as you wrap. Fold over one end of the fringe, then overlap the folded fringe over the raw end of the fringe at the back of the shade and secure it with glue. Add a length of ¼"-wide flat gold trim (approximately 11") around the top of the shade, gluing it in place and overlapping it at the back.

**Beaded Fringe**—Use an off-white pleated fabric shade. Wrap a strand of clear 8mm plastic beads one and one-half times around the bottom of the shade (approximately 21"). (Purchase beads attached to a strand, not strung loose on the strand.) Secure the ends of the strand at the back of the shade with a dab of hot glue and rest the shade on a tall drinking glass. Cut twenty 1"-long strands of the beads from a 20"-length and hot-glue them around the bottom of the shade at even intervals to form a fringe. Hot-glue one end of a 20" strand of seed pearls to the back of the shade approximately 1" above the bead fringe. Allow the strand to drape down into a 1"-long scallop, and hot-glue the top pearl of the scallop to the shade. Continue draping and hot-gluing the scallops around the shade at 1" intervals. (If necessary, put a rubber band around the shade to mark where the top of the scallops go.) Use an 11" length of seed pearls to encircle the top of the shade.

**Woven Band with Scallop Fringe**

**Love Note**

**Pleated Marbled Paper**—Use any color plain shade. Trim a sheet of printed marbled paper so it measures twice the circumference of the bottom of the shade (approximately 24") in one direction and the height of the shade plus ½" (approximately 4½") in the other direction. Lay the strip of marbled paper face up on a flat work surface with a short side toward you. Fold sharp, even, ½"-wide pleats across the full length of the paper, taking care to make the pleats neat. Wrap the pleated paper around the shade, trimming off any extra length to achieve the right amount of pleating. Overlap the ends at the back of the shade, and secure them with quick-drying white glue. Squeeze a bead of glue around the outside top of the shade, and gently push the pleats into the glue to secure them to the shade. Clamp in place temporarily using a clothespin every 3".

**Love Note**—You can use a permanent fabric marker to write your favorite poem or sayings on a plain white shade. Stuff the inside of the shade with soft tissue paper to provide a sturdier writing surface, and lean the shade on your knee as you write. Don't let the point of the marker rest on the fabric or the ink may bleed. Cut and glue a length of ¼"-wide black satin ribbon around the top and bottom of the shade.

**Beaded Fringe**

**Plain and Embroidered Ribbon Trim**—Wind a 4-yard length of blue, 1"-wide satin ribbon around a plain shade. Secure the end of the ribbon behind the front top center of the shade with quick-drying white glue, then start wrapping the ribbon around the shade. Overlap each wrap by at least ¼". Glue the end of the ribbon to the inside of the shade. Cut a band of embroidered ribbon the height of the shade plus 2" (approximately 6 ¼"). Glue one end of it inside the top of the shade, drape it down the outside, and glue the other end of it to the inside of the shade. ◆

**Plain and Embroidered Ribbon Trim**

# Crystal Bead Drop Candlestick

In a candle flame, heat the end of an opened paper clip for 10 to 15 seconds, then use it to puncture ten evenly spaced holes close to the perimeter of a 3"-wide plastic bobeche (a small device designed to catch candle drips). Heat the paper clip again and puncture five evenly spaced holes around the perimeter of a second 3"-wide bobeche, then set both bobeches aside. Attach the base of a 10"-high bud vase to an overturned 3½"-diameter glass coaster using clear silicone gel; then attach the ten-hole bobeche, concave side up, to the top rim of the bud vase using the gel. Attach the base of a 2½"-high glass candlestick atop the ten-hole bobeche. Set aside for 24 hours. With wire cutters, cut ten 4" pieces of rose wire. String a 1"-long plastic chandelier drop and four 8mm clear plastic beads onto five of the pieces of wire, then string a 1"-long chandelier drop and six 8mm clear plastic beads onto the remaining five pieces of wire. Attach the four- and six-bead pieces alternately around the ten-hole bobeche, twisting the wire up against the bottom of the bobeche to secure them. Trim off any extra wire. String seventy-five 8mm clear plastic beads on a long length of white heavy-duty thread. Using five 1" pieces of wire, secure this string of beads to the five-hole bobeche to form hanging loops. Trim off any extra wire. Insert an 8" white taper candle into the candlestick, then slip the five-hole bobeche over the candle. Clean up any drops of silicone gel with a single-edge razor blade.

# HANDCRAFT
## ~ ILLUSTRATED ~

## 5-Step Folding Screen

### Build Your Own for a Fraction of What Showrooms Charge

## Foolproof Faux Finishes for Walls

### Transform Any Room with Just Two Shades of Paint

## Testing All-Purpose White Glues

### Many Bonding Claims Simply Aren't True

## The Best Way to Dry Roses

### Silica Gel Tops the List of Dessicants

**SECRETS OF SILK RIBBON EMBROIDERY**

**30-MINUTE SEASHELL CANDLES**

**QUICK CLASSIC PILLOWS**

$4.00 U.S./$4.95 CANADA

**PEACH AND VINE LADDER-BACK CHAIR:** TURN A JUNKYARD FIND INTO A WORK OF ART WITH OUR ORIGINAL PATTERNS.

**PEACH AND VINE
LADDER-BACK CHAIR**
*page 6*

**HOW TO CREATE A FAUX
SUEDE FINISH**
*page 8*

**SEASHELL CANDLES**
*page 11*

## Notes from Readers .........................2

Pattern for pop-up cards; mail-order lollipop molds; making yarn colorfast; tips on laminating fabric; and cleaning an old brass lamp.

## Quick Tips ................................4

No-sew bias welting; joining foam blocks; antiquing new hardware; cutting a large circle of fabric; encouraging blooms; and using a dollar bill as an instant ruler.

## Peach and Vine Ladder-Back Chair......6

Transform an ordinary wooden chair into a hand-painted heirloom using acrylic paint.

## How to Create a Faux Suede Finish........8

Give any room a soft ambience using two tones of paint and a wad of cheesecloth.

## Seashell Candles............................11

Make these simple candles in under an hour from old candle stubs and homemade wicks.

## Master Project:
## Three-Panel Folding Screen.............12

Make your own decorator-quality screen with two double rolls of wallpaper and three hollow-core doors.

## Quick Transfer Pillows....................16

Bring a classic decor to any room with these fast and easy pillows.

## Victorian Frame Bow.....................18

Make an elegant picture frame bow in under three hours using a variety of time-saving techniques.

## The Best Way to Dry Roses ...........20

Learn three foolproof techniques for turning your live roses into timeless beauties.

## Silk Ribbon Embroidery...............22

Using silk ribbon and six basic stitches, you can create textured, three-dimensional stitchwork.

## Marbled Chocolate Strawberries......24

This simple and delicious dessert will dress up any table, from a picnic to a formal dinner.

## Demi-Lune Style Tulips.....................25

Create the look of a full arrangement with just half the flowers.

## Testing All-Purpose White Glues......26

After we put eight general-purpose glues through their paces, Delta's Velverette topped the list.

## Book Reviews.............................28

Explore the possibilities for decorating in *Decorating with Paper* and *Paper Magic*. Learn the fundamentals of design with *Creative Interior Design*.

## Quick Decorating Ideas.................29

Create an intimate setting for dinner in minutes using everyday household items in new ways.

## Field Guide to Shells.................30

Use these shells to make seashell candles, or to start a collection.

## Sources and Resources..................32

Mail-order sources for materials used in this issue.

## Quick Projects..............................33

Using a minimum of materials, you can create custom closures for gift bags.

## Natural Floral China.........Back Cover

Design your own floral china by arranging sprigs of ivy and flowers between two glass plates. Illustration by Dan Brown.

**THREE-PANEL FOLDING
SCREEN**
*page 12*

**MARBLED CHOCOLATE
STRAWBERRIES**
*page 24*

**DEMI-LUNE STYLE TULIPS**
*page 25*

**QUICK PROJECTS**
*page 33*

# HANDCRAFT
## ~ ILLUSTRATED ~

| | |
|---|---|
| Editor | CAROL ENDLER STERBENZ |
| Executive Editor | BARBARA BOURASSA |
| Senior Editor | MICHIO RYAN |
| Managing Editor | MAURA LYONS |
| Assistant Managing Editor | TRICIA O'BRIEN |
| Directions Editors | CANDIE FRANKEL |
| | LISA CLARK |
| Editorial Assistant | KIM N. RUSSELLO |
| Copy Editor | GARY PFITZER |

| | |
|---|---|
| Art Director | MEG BIRNBAUM |
| Special Projects Designer | AMY KLEE |
| Photo Stylist | SYLVIA LACHTER |

| | |
|---|---|
| Publisher and Founder | CHRISTOPHER KIMBALL |
| Editorial Consultant | RAYMOND WAITES |

| | |
|---|---|
| Marketing Director | ADRIENNE KIMBALL |
| Circulation Director | ELAINE REPUCCI |
| Ass't Circulation Manager | JENNIFER L. KEENE |
| Customer Service | JONATHAN VENIER |
| Production Director | JAMES MCCORMACK |
| Production Assistants | SHEILA DATZ |
| | PAMELA SLATTERY |
| Ass't Computer Admin. | MATT FRIGO |
| Production Artist | KEVIN MOELLER |

| | |
|---|---|
| V.P./Business Manager | JEFFREY FEINGOLD |
| Controller | LISA A. CARULLO |
| Accounting Assistant | MANDY SHITO |
| Office Manager | JENNY THORNBURY |
| Office Assistant | SARAH CHUNG |

*Handcraft Illustrated* (ISSN 1072-0529) is published bimonthly by Boston Common Press Limited Partners, 17 Station Street, P.O. Box 509, Brookline, MA 02147-0509. Copyright 1995 Boston Common Press Limited Partners. Second-class postage paid in Boston, MA, and additional mailing offices. Editorial office: 17 Station Street, P.O. Box 509, Brookline, MA 02147-0509; (617) 232-1000, FAX (617) 232-1572. Editorial contributions should be sent to: Editor, *Handcraft Illustrated*, P.O. Box 509, Brookline, MA 02147-0509. We cannot assume responsibility for manuscripts submitted to us. Submissions will be returned only if accompanied by a large, self-addressed stamped envelope. Subscription rates: $24.95 for one year; $45 for two years; $65 for three years. (Canada: add $3 per year; all other foreign add $12 per year.) Postmaster: Send all new orders, subscription inquiries, and change of address notices to *Handcraft Illustrated*, P.O. Box 51383, Boulder, CO 80322-1383. Single copies $4 in U.S., $4.95 in Canada and foreign. Back issues available for $5 each. PRINTED IN THE U.S.A.

Rather than put ™ in every occurrence of trademarked names, we state that we are using the names only and in an editorial fashion and to the benefit of the trademark owner, with no intention of infringment of the trademark.

**Note to Readers:** Every effort has been made to present the information in this publication in a clear, complete, and accurate manner. It is important that all instructions are followed carefully, as failure to do so could result in injury. Boston Common Press Limited Partners, the editors, and the authors disclaim any and all liability resulting therefrom.

# EDITORIAL

I recently discovered two cigar boxes I had forgotten about on the top shelf of my coat closet. Pasted across each lid was what looked like a dollar bill with the words "Republica de Cuba Julio 16/1912" engraved across it. Inscribed nearby, in large black letters written in a bold hand, were the words "Negatives, '37–'48." I raised the lid of one of the boxes, and looked inside. . . . Stacked neatly were countless amber envelopes, each carefully marked in the same bold hand—"Koben Haven," "NY '33," "Big Snow '48," "Family Xmas '49," "Long Island." I knew immediately I was holding the collection of negatives my father had given me twenty years ago depicting his journey from Denmark to America.

CAROL ENDLER STERBENZ

I felt a rush of tender expectation as I began slipping the glass negatives out of their envelopes and holding up each one to a bare light bulb to carefully scrutinize the reverse images. A horse-drawn hay wagon in front of a thatched-roof farmhouse bathed in eerie light as if from a solar eclipse; a church spire piercing a stormy sky; a huge, wedge-shaped hull of a ship rising up from a foreign pier; the Statue of Liberty rising ghostlike over icy water. I continued looking through the negatives, moving quickly through a series of pictures depicting New York street scenes full of old cars and uncrowded sidewalks, recalling with sharp clarity the stories that each told.

My rhythm changed suddenly, however, when I found myself staring at the familiar face of my father. Looking about twenty-five years old, he wore a fashionable suit and rested one foot on the running board of a '39 Ford coupe. A rush of memories flooded over me.

They say one father is more than a hundred schoolmasters, and this was certainly true of my dad. He used to talk a lot about the value of hard work. It was only through commitment to hard work that one learned and developed skills, he used to tell me, skills that could be developed to a point where they could be forgotten and you could become absorbed in the joy of work. It was this joy that moved you forward when the original excitement of an activity dwindled. I remember his words so clearly: Hard work brings with it gifts like inspiration and creation and the exhilaration of seeing something new emerge from diligent effort. To my father, creation was not only an act of the will, it was an act of the heart. To him, it was the love of fabric, the joy in the smell of paint, the ecstasy of sculpting rock that motivated one to search for the undiscovered possibilities in cloth, canvas, or stone. "The sculptor's hand can only break the spell to free the figures slumbering in the stone," I.M. Lerner wrote in 1968 in *Heredity, Evolution and Society*. My father would agree. The spell was the hard work, the love of the medium, and the commitment to finding the figures slumbering therein; that would bring the greatest joy of all, the creation of something new.

With these words in mind, I look at restitching a quilt square, searching out every book on decoupage, or even discarding a craft project to begin again from scratch as promising its own rewards. Each is a necessary step to help me reach that point where creative truth reveals itself. Like the poet, who waits for that one line, the one around which he will pen the others that will surely follow, we await the moment when the craft we're working on takes off on its own, with us rushing after it, exhilarated by the creation we see emerging in our hands. When we finish, our creations contain all the rich experiences of the time spent working and the permanent gifts that come from having done so. We are changed; we are new.

When I look at my crafts, especially the ones I give my children or the ones I bring out around the holidays, I see steps in my own life's journey, each embodying the accumulated experiences and feelings I had to that point. To me, crafts stand like photographic negatives, holding an album of my life in the "photography" of my own choosing, whether it be wood, paper, cloth, or paint. If I should be lucky enough to fit all my crafts in a cigar box and you should happen upon it one day, you would be able to decipher a very happy life (as well as what would have to be the most enormous cigar box ever made). ◆

*Carol Endler Sterbenz*

## PATTERNS FOR POP-UP CARDS

*Do you know where I can get patterns for making pop-up cards?*

JAMIE EHRLICH
Fairfax, VA

We found a terrific paperback book that not only teaches you how to make pop-up cards but also includes examples of different types of pop-up greetings. *Perfect Pop-Up: Designing Greeting Cards the Easy Way* by Tom Nelson also includes additional techniques, information on designing your own cards, and actual templates. Your local craft store or bookstore may be able to order the book for you, or you can write directly to the author, as the book is self-published (*see* Sources and Resources, page 31).

## MAKE YOUR OWN PLACE CARDS

*I'd like to make place cards for a bridal luncheon I'm having for my daughter. I want something simple—but not boring. Do you have any suggestions?*

SUZANNE YOUNG
Oakland Park, FL

How about making a simple die-cut card? To make the card, all you need is card stock, an X-Acto knife, a small graphic image, (*see* ideas below) a glue stick, a ruler, and a pencil. Cut the card stock to a rectangle twice the size of the place card you want to make, then glue the image to the center of the paper. Using a pencil and a ruler, draw a very light line across the center of the card, stopping at either side of the image. Then, with the X-Acto knife, score where the image meets the line, and cut out the portion of the image that sits above the line. Fold the card on the line so that the top of the image stands up. (For an entire set of place cards made in this way, *see* "Victorian Place Cards," page 16 in the November/December 1994 issue.)

Some images you might want to use are a single rose or a tiny photograph of your daughter as a child or of your daughter and her fiancé. You can also use stickers, a photograph that has been reduced and cut down to the main image, a hand-colored photocopy of a photograph, or a colorful image made with a rubber stamp. Be sure to choose an image that will pop up sufficiently once the card has been folded; a heart, for example, would work well, as its rounded top edges would stand away from the fold nicely.

## THE BEST USE OF BUCKRAM

*I have an old fabric-covered family photo album that I'd like to have re-covered. A friend mentioned using buckram. What sort of fabric is this, and is it the best choice?*

KATHY HUNT
Fairmont, WV

First made in Bokhara, a city in southern Russia, buckram is standard book cloth. It is a coarse, stiffly finished, heavily sized cotton that is used in bookbinding and in millinery to stiffen cloth. Buckram's heavy weight makes it a very durable book cover, but there are fine book cloths available in lighter weights and in a wider range of colors that may better suit your purposes. A supple leather, such as calfskin or goatskin, is another option.

We suggest that you consult a bookbinder or bookbinding supply store to review appropriate choices for your album. The Center for Book Arts, in New York, New York, may be able to help you locate a reputable bookbinder or bookbinding supplier in your area.

## THE BEST NAPKINS FOR FOLDED DESIGNS

*Is there a certain size napkin that should be used when making a napkin-fold design? Does it matter what the napkin is made of?*

PAULINE GRANGER
Campbell, MO

The majority of napkin-fold designs work best when made from twenty-inch-square napkins. More complicated folds may require even larger napkins, while simple folds can be made with smaller ones. In the end, it's a matter of experimentation and personal preference, although many napkin design books will tell you exactly what size napkin to use.

A starched, 100 percent cotton or linen napkin will hold creases better than a napkin made from a synthetic blend. (Blends do work well, however, for designs that need to spread out, such as fans.) Paper napkins can also be used, although they should be three-ply or thicker to hold a crease.

## A MAIL-ORDER SOURCE FOR LOLLIPOP MOLDS

*Do you have a good source for lollipop molds that feature motifs?*

WENDY SEGAL
Bronxville, NY

Try Sweet Celebrations in Burnsville, Minnesota (*see* Sources and Resources, page 31). They manufacture an extensive line of cake-decorating and candy-making tools and related products. Catalogs are free.

## HOW TO MAKE YARN COLORFAST

*I have some great yarn that I would like to use in a needlepoint project. The problem is the yarn is not colorfast. I'm afraid I'll ruin my project when I block it. Can you help?*

ALISON GORDY
Sonoma, CA

Colorfast yarns are a better choice for precisely the reason you state—they do not run. Rinse out any dye residues from a non-colorfast, washable yarn by soaking the full skeins in lukewarm water until there is no longer any runoff. Open up the skeins and be sure to let the yarn air-dry completely before you use it.

## A MAIL-ORDER SOURCE FOR REPRODUCTION FABRIC

*Can you recommend a good source for quilting-weight reproductions of early cotton fabrics?*

JOYCE REID
Hope Valley, RI

The Patchworks, in Amsterdam, Montana, carries an extensive line of quilting-weight cotton fabrics that are reproductions of original printed and dyed textiles produced between 1810 and 1940. Their 750 fabrics range from early prints to more complex patterns favored in the Victorian era to flour-sack prints of the thirties. A catalog is available for $1; sample sets range from $3 to $12.50, depending on the number of samples in the set.

## FLORIST FOAM FOR UNUSUALLY SHAPED VASES

*I have a vase that I'd love to use for a special silk flower arrangement. Is there something more permanent than floral foam available on the market?*

ANDREA GRIFFITHS
Spokane, WA

Try an expanding florist adhesive, such as Arrange-It Expanding Floral Adhesive. This product is quite easy to use: simply fill the container of your choice with dirt, rocks, or loose foam, then spray the adhesive into the container. The foam will expand to fit the contours of the pot and will be dry in thirty minutes. The foam has two distinct disadvantages, however: the flowers cannot be rearranged once they are set in the adhesive, and the adhesive is not removable, so we don't advise using it with valuable china or crockery. Arrange-It Expanding Floral Adhesive is manufactured by Convenience Products of Fenton, Missouri.

## PAINTING VERSUS STAINING BATHROOM WOODWORK

*Which is better to use in a bathroom—paint or clear stain? I'd like to put a clear finish on a wooden linen closet in our master bathroom, but my wife wants to paint it.*

BEN CURTIS
Portland, ME

Alkyd or latex paints are not invulnerable to bathroom humidity, but they are generally more durable than varnish or shellac. Over time, light will cause such clear finishes to crack and become dull, water will cause them to peel, and the acids in the natural oils in your hands will cause them to soften. On the other hand, polyurethane, another type of clear finish, forms a plastic coating that is certainly on par with alkyd paint, and typically better than latex paint.

If you opt for paint, alkyd paint will hold up better in the long run than latex paint, as oil-based paint is more resistant to mildew and moisture and dries to a harder, more scratch-resistant finish. Alkyd paint has a few drawbacks, though: it is messier to work with and clean up, it often smells unpleasant while drying, and it takes longer to dry than water-based (acrylic or latex) paint.

If you opt for a clear finish, select one that dries flexible, so it will move with the wood as it expands and contracts with changes in the room's humidity. Polyurethane is a good choice, as are water-based finishes. Because water-based finishes are relatively new to the market (they have been available just a little over five years), however, it's too early in the game to say how well they will hold up in the long run—although they definitely are not as flexible as polyurethane.

## TIPS ON LAMINATING FABRIC

*Is it possible to laminate ordinary fabric as opposed to buying laminated fabric off the bolt? I'd like to make a soil-resistant kitchen apron for my granddaughter.*

PATTI COLLINS
Moore, OK

You might want to try HeatnBond Iron-On Flexible Vinyl. HeatnBond is a repositionable, lightweight vinyl that is appropriate for clothing, tablecloths, napkins, place mats, and other accessory items. HeatnBond comes in both matte and glossy finish, and is available either twenty-four inches wide by the yard, or seventeen inches wide in two-yard pre-packs.

HeatnBond is easy to use. Peel away the protective backing, then place the vinyl on the fabric face. Once the vinyl is positioned, the paper backing is laid on top as a press cloth, and the vinyl is fused permanently to the fabric by ironing it with an iron set on low. Fabrics coated with HeatnBond are washable but should not be dry cleaned.

## TIPS ON CLEANING AN OLD BRASS LAMP

*I would like to clean an old brass lamp that is quite tarnished and seems to be coated with some grease as well as gummy bits of adhesive. Do you have any ideas?*

LUCY SLAYBAUGH
Coeur d'Alene, ID

We recommend starting with WD-40, as it's effective at removing grease and adhesives. Work in a well-ventilated area and wear protective gloves. Place the lamp on an ample spread of newspaper or brown kraft paper, then clean one small section at a time by spraying it, allowing the WD-40 to sit on the surface for a few minutes, then gently rubbing the saturated area with a clean cloth or paper towel to remove the dirt. Repeat this process until you have worked your way around the lamp. If the lamp is extremely dirty, you may have to repeat the cleaning process two or even three times.

Once the lamp is clean, we recommend using Never Dull, a polish for cleaning and polishing virtually any metal. Never Dull will remove further rust and corrosion and restore the luster of the brass. Unlike liquid metal cleaners, Never Dull is easy and fairly clean to use; best of all, it does not leave unsightly deposits in crevices and detail work.

## A CURE FOR DRAPES THAT STRETCH

*I recently made some floor-length drapes with double hems that I hung from hardwood rods and rings. The drapes looked great at first, but after a week, they were too long. What did I do wrong?*

JANINE FARWELL
Galesburg, IL

When hemming newly made drapes, it is always a wise idea to pin the hem to the desired length, and then allow the drapery to hang for several days. Then check the hems, adjust them if necessary, and take the drapes down to sew them. This way, you can alter the hem length should the curtain panels stretch, which is possible with weightier fabrics. To ensure that the drapes hang evenly, you can sew small, flat weights into the lower corners after hemming.

## EARTHENWARE VERSUS STONEWARE AND PORCELAIN

*What's the difference between earthenware, stoneware, and porcelain?*

LAURA VOGEL
Dallas, TX

Earthenware, stoneware, and porcelain represent the three basic categories into which ceramic ware is classified. This classification is based upon the ceramic's particular constitution. Earthenware, a moderately to very porous clay fired at low heat, is the most resistant to thermal shock, but is soft and chips easily. Stoneware is a stronger, nonporous, opaque clay fired at a higher temperature than earthenware; it is also heavier and more durable than earthenware. Porcelain is the most durable of the three; it is translucent, very hard, fine-grained, and fired at very high temperatures. ◆

# Quick Tips

## No-Sew Bias Welting

Here's a method of making welting without a sewing machine. You'll need enough continuous bias strip and piping cord for your project, the same amount of ⅞"-wide iron-on tape adhesive, and an iron.

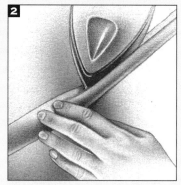

1. Following the instructions that come with the tape adhesive, affix the tape to the wrong side of the bias strip ⅛" from the edge. Peel off and discard the paper tape.

2. Place the piping cord on the bias strip. Starting at one end, fold the strip over the cord, with the long edges matching, and fuse the edges together with the tip of the iron, securing the cord inside.

## Making Woody-Stemmed Flowers Last Longer

Woody-stemmed flowers, such as football mums, and flowering branches, such as lilacs, typically have difficulty taking in the large amounts of water they need to stay fresh in cut flower arrangements. Some floral experts recommend the following tips. You'll need a mallet or hammer, a sharp knife or florist scissors, a source of boiling or very hot water, as well as cool water, a Pyrex container, and a bucket.

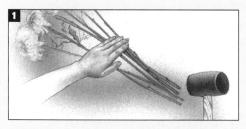

1. Remove the lower leaves from the stems using a sharp knife or florist scissors, then crush the bottom 2" of the stem with a mallet or hammer to break up the tough tissue and expose more of the surfaces that absorb water.

2. Plunge the crushed stems in 2" to 3" of boiling or very hot water for 60 seconds, then transfer them immediately to a bucket of fresh, cool water and let them stand upright in it until you are ready to arrange them. The extremely hot water helps clear air bubbles from the stem tissue and opens up the cells.

## Joining Foam Blocks

When a large floral arrangement calls for two or more foam blocks to be positioned side by side, jumbo paper clips can help the blocks stay together without shifting.

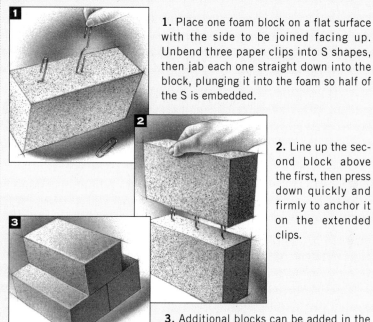

1. Place one foam block on a flat surface with the side to be joined facing up. Unbend three paper clips into S shapes, then jab each one straight down into the block, plunging it into the foam so half of the S is embedded.

2. Line up the second block above the first, then press down quickly and firmly to anchor it on the extended clips.

3. Additional blocks can be added in the same way.

## Spattering with an Old Toothbrush

Spattering, a painting technique that randomly distributes pinpoint-size flecks of paint across a surface, can be used to intensify a color by introducing its complement, or to simulate a natural surface, such as lichen on stone. Spattering is easily done with an ordinary, worn-out toothbrush. Be sure to wear old clothes and safety glasses and use a drop cloth when you try this, since stray droplets can travel surprisingly far.

Thin the paint for spattering with water (for acrylic and latex paints) or a solvent (for oil-based and alkyd paints) until it reaches a milky consistency. Dip the toothbrush bristles into the thinned paint and shake off the excess. Hold the toothbrush 4" to 12" from the surface to be spattered, then run your thumb firmly along the ends of the bristles to spatter the paint. Repeat this over the entire surface until the specks reach the desired density. Different looks can be achieved by spattering onto wet paint (which will cause the droplets to bleed and blur slightly) or by spattering with two or three different colors in succession.

ILLUSTRATIONS BY HARRY DAVIS

# Antiquing New Hardware

To look authentic and antique, the hardware on old or distressed furniture should be subdued, not shiny or brassy. This brush-on, wipe-off glaze recipe is a quick way to make new hardware look antique. You'll need burnt umber artist's oil paint, an oil glaze, a disposable paper plate, a small paintbrush, and a lint-free cloth.

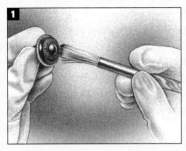

**1.** Place small amounts of the burnt umber paint and oil glaze on separate areas of a disposable plate. Dip the brush first into the paint, then into the glaze, then brush this mixture onto the hardware, allowing it to pool in the crevices to bring out the design.

**2.** With a soft, lint-free rag, gently wipe the excess mixture off the hardware, leaving behind a light layer of color to tone down the shiny finish. Let the hardware dry completely before reattaching it to the furniture.

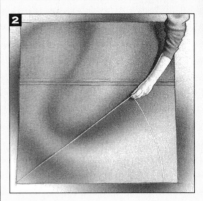

# Braiding Raffia

To make a flexible and durable base for wreaths, swags, or vertically oriented dried flower arrangements, try braided raffia.

**1.** Start with a fistful of raffia strands. Fasten them together at one end with a rubber band, and comb out the strands with your fingers. Divide the free ends into three equal sections, and braid the sections just as you would long hair, by crossing the outside sections alternately over the center section.

**2.** When you reach the end of the braid, secure it with another rubber band. Conceal both of the rubber bands by wrapping each with a single strand of raffia and tying the ends securely. Dried, preserved, or silk flowers can be inserted into the braid or hot-glued onto it as desired.

# Nail Holder

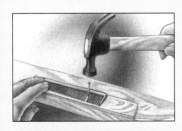

Here's a tip that will help you start small nails and brads by keeping them upright during those first few taps of the hammer. Simply hold the nail or brad between the teeth of an old comb. If you should miss with the hammer, it will hit the comb, not your fingers.

# Cutting a Large Circle of Fabric

It's easy to mark and cut large circles of fabric for round tablecloths, pillows, cushions, fabric wreaths, or tree skirts using a compass created from string, a safety pin, and a fabric-marking pencil.

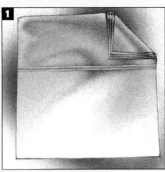

**1.** Start with a square of fabric 2" larger than the diameter of the circle you want. Fold the fabric into quarters to make a smaller square.

**2.** Cut a length of string about 5" longer than the radius of the circle you want. Tie one end of it in a slipknot around the fabric-marking pencil and fasten the other end to the safety pin ring so that the distance from the pin to the pencil equals the radius of the circle. Attach the safety pin through all four layers of fabric at the folded corner at the center of the fabric. Hold the pin steady with one hand (or have a partner help), pull the string taut, and mark a quarter circle on the fabric. Cut through all four layers along the marked line, then unfold the fabric to reveal your circle.

# Encouraging Blooms

To encourage the closed blooms on a gladiolus or freesia stem to open, snip off the topmost buds (which are not mature enough to flower) with a sharp knife or florist scissors. This enables the more mature buds lower down on the stem to drink in the water they need to blossom.

# Instant Ruler

For an approximate measure of large or small objects on those occasions when you don't have a tape measure handy—perhaps on a spur-of-the-moment shopping jaunt—just whip out a U.S. dollar bill. Measuring about 6" long and 2½" wide, it can help you gauge the approximate dimensions of furniture, picture frames, or other objects.

---

# Peach and Vine Ladder-Back Chair

*Transform an ordinary wooden chair into a hand-painted heirloom using acrylic paint.*

## BY BETH PALMER

*This hand-painted ladder-back chair might sell for hundreds of dollars, but you can make your own for a quarter of that price using acrylic paint and our original patterns.*

In painting this ladder-back chair, I employed a classic peach-and-vine design using bold tones of quick-dry acrylic paint. The pattern is versatile and adaptable to both large and small areas; the vines could grace a tabletop as easily as they decorate this chair's slats. By turning the pattern upside down and using only half of it on some parts of the chair, I've given the appearance of several patterns. By painting several different chairs with the same design and color, you could turn a series of mismatched chairs into a single set. For this project, I chose a five-slat chair from Pottery Barn, but you could apply this design just as easily to a yard-sale find or a wooden stool.

The project's major steps involve sanding the chair, applying primer to the chair, tracing the peach and vine patterns onto the primed surface, painting the background, then filling in the fruit and leaf designs with acrylic paint. When you transfer the design to the chair, you can follow my example exactly, or you can customize your piece and change the placement to suit your personal taste. For a more elaborate look, duplicate the pattern to add fruit or leaves; for a sparser look (and a quicker project), paint only the chair's top slat. If your chair will sit against a table with its back showing prominently in the room, consider painting the pattern on the back of the top slat as well.

If you use Liquitex paint, as I did, you'll be able to match the colors with a minimum of mixing. Should you decide to use another brand of paint, you will probably need to blend colors to match the ones shown. As you work, remember that acrylic paints dry quickly. Blend and use the colors one at a time, using shiny, glazed paper plates or plastic food tub lids as mixing palettes. When mixing colors, use small amounts. I used single drops of paint and circles about the size of a nickel.

For the painting steps, the size of the area to be covered and the required detail will determine which paintbrush you use. For priming, I used a two-inch-wide paintbrush. For painting the chair blue, I started with a one-inch-wide brush, then used #4 and #1 round artist's brushes as needed to paint around the traced patterns. I recommend a #00 brush for painting the leaves and stems, the #1 brush for painting the peaches, and the #00 brush for outlining the fruit and leaves in white.

Rinse your brush thoroughly in water between colors, then roll the brush tip on a rag to remove any excess water before painting again. Let the paint dry thoroughly (about an hour) before adding the next coat. If you want to speed this process, blow-dry the paint with a hand-held dryer set to the "warm" (not hot) setting. For the final drying, let the chair stand for at least eight hours before varnishing.

### PEACH AND VINE LADDER-BACK CHAIR

Ladder-back chair
White interior latex primer
Water-based varnish, satin finish
2 2-ounce bottles Liquitex acrylic paint, light blue violet
2-ounce bottles Liquitex acrylic paint, one each in the following colors: naphthol crimson, titanium white, brilliant yellow, and hooker's green

*You'll also need:* access to a photocopier; drop cloth; 10 sheets 120-grit sandpaper; 2 sheets blue, nonwax, dressmaker's tracing paper; sharp pencil; 1"- and 2"-wide paintbrushes; round artist's paintbrushes, 1 each, sizes #00, #1, and #4; Phillips-head screw-

## Preparing the Chair

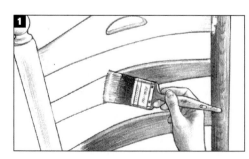

**1.** Sand the entire chair lightly with 120-grit sandpaper, wipe with a damp cloth, then use a 2"-wide brush to cover the chair with latex primer.

**2.** To transfer the patterns to the chair, place the dressmaker's tracing paper against the chair, with the transfer surface against the wood. Then lay the pattern on top of the transfer paper and trace over the lines with a sharp pencil.

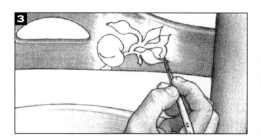

**3.** Paint the chair frame with the light blue violet acrylic paint, first using the 1"-wide brush, followed by the #4 and #1 round brushes to fill in around the traced patterns.

ILLUSTRATIONS BY WENDY WRAY/PHOTOGRAPH BY STEVEN MAYS

# Peach and Vine Diagrams

These patterns can be used as they are, or split along the cut line and used in two pieces on separate parts of the chair. If your chair's top slat features an opening, as ours does, the peach design will have to be split into two parts. Start by enlarging each pattern until it is 6¾" long.

To transfer the pattern to the chair, place the dressmaker's tracing paper against the chair, with the transfer surface toward the chair. Then lay the pattern on top of the transfer paper and trace over the pattern lines with a sharp pencil.

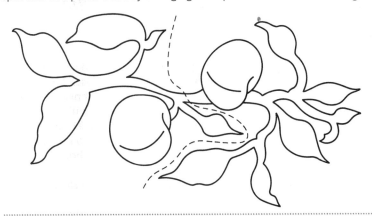 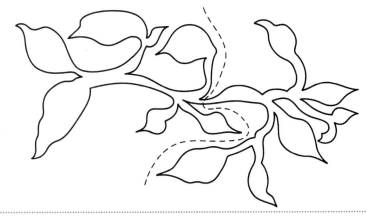

driver; clean rags; shiny, glazed paper plates or plastic food tub lids; soap; and ruler.

*Other items, if necessary:* blow dryer (to speed drying); masking tape and brown kraft paper (if using rush-bottom chair without removable seat).

1. Using photocopier, enlarge peach and vine patterns above until each measures 6¾" long, or other desired size. Turn chair upside down. With screwdriver, remove screws that hold on rush seat. Set seat and screws aside. If using rush-bottom chair without removable seat, mask seat completely with masking tape and kraft paper. If using chair with wooden seat, prime and paint seat as outlined below.

2. Working in a well-lit and well-ventilated area for painting, cover work surface with drop cloth. Lightly sand chair frame, then wipe off dust with damp rag. Paint entire chair frame with primer, using 2"-wide paintbrush. Clean paintbrush in warm, soapy water. Allow primer to dry completely (at least 2 hours).

3. Working with one piece of pattern at a time, place dressmaker's tracing paper against a slat or chair rail, with transfer surface facing chair. Lay pattern on top of transfer paper, then trace over pattern lines with pencil to transfer pattern to chair. Continue to transfer patterns to slats and chair rails as desired.

4. Paint chair frame with light blue violet paint, starting with 1"-wide brush. (If decorating chair with wooden seat, paint seat light blue violet using 1"-wide brush.) Use #4 and #1 brushes as needed to paint around traced patterns. Rinse brushes with water and dry them. Allow chair to dry for 2 hours (or blow-dry on warm setting), then add second coat of light blue violet paint. Rinse brushes in water and dry them. Let chair dry at least 2 more hours.

5. Using #00 brush, mix two nickle-size spots of hooker's green paint with one nickle-size spot of titanium white paint on paper plate. Paint all leaves and stems with #00 brush. Rinse brush in water and dry. Let chair dry at least 1 hour. Using #1 brush, paint peaches brilliant yellow. Rinse brush in water and dry. Let chair dry 1 hour, then apply second coat of yellow to peaches. Let dry 1 hour before proceeding.

6. Make light orange paint by squeezing one drop naphthol crimson paint into three nickle-sized spots of brilliant yellow paint. Blend thoroughly, then add two drops titanium white

and blend again. Painting over brilliant yellow base color, paint the right side, the top indentation, and the center line of each peach with #1 brush. Let dry at least 1 hour.

7. Working on clean area of paper plate, mix one nickle-sized spot of titanium white with two drops water. Test paint's thickness by evenly painting a few 6" lines on paper plate using #00 brush. Hold plate vertically for a moment. If paint is too thick, it will not spread properly; if too thin, it will run. If necessary, add more paint or more water to reach correct consistency. Then use #00 brush to outline leaves, vines, and peaches with white paint. Wash brush. Let chair dry overnight.

8. With 2"-wide brush, apply varnish to entire painted surface. Do not allow varnish to pool at wood joints, and check covered areas to prevent drips from forming. (Drips can be removed with a swipe of the brush.) Let chair dry overnight, then add second coat and let dry overnight again. When varnish is completely dry, replace chair seat or remove masking tape and kraft paper. ◆

**Beth Palmer** is a visual artist whose work has been featured in several books and magazines.

## Painting the Peach Design

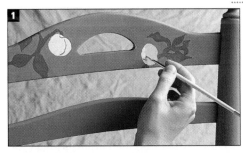 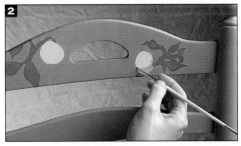 

**1.** To paint the peaches, start by using the #1 paintbrush to fill in the entire peach forms with brilliant yellow paint. Apply two coats.

**2.** Using the light orange paint and the #1 brush, paint each peach's right side, top indentation, and center line.

**3.** For the final step before varnishing, outline the leaves, vines, and peaches with white paint using the #00 brush.

# How to Create a Faux Suede Finish

*Give any room a soft ambience using two tones of paint and a wad of cheesecloth.*

### BY STU AND VI CUTBILL

*A faux suede finish, which mimics the look of real suede, is ideal for rooms where you want a peaceful, soothing atmosphere.*

This article will teach you a simple painting technique that yields a rich, sophisticated, suedelike finish for your walls.

The key to sueding's lush look is the use of related colors, such as teal green glaze over a pale green ground color. The colors create a tone-on-tone effect that mimics the look of suede. This technique is well suited to rooms where you want to create a peaceful, soothing atmosphere.

Before explaining the technique, we'll define a few key terms. Ground color refers to the base coat of paint, the color that goes on the wall first and which will show through the glaze. A glaze, a translucent, varnishlike medium to which you add color, is applied over the ground color, then partially removed with cheesecloth. The cheesecloth is "pounced" (bounced lightly) against the wet glaze to create a finely textured, billowy pattern. Glaze can be mixed in one of three viscosities: thick, medium, or thin. This project requires a medium-viscosity glaze about the consistency of whole milk.

To achieve the finish shown in the photograph above, we used Benjamin Moore #677 (oil-based, eggshell finish) paint as the ground color and a glaze made from Benjamin Moore #679 oil-based paint, Benjamin Moore glazing liquid, and paint thinner. (*See* paint chips, page 9. For an alternative color combination, *see* sample, page 9.) If you want to create your own color combinations, keep the following points in mind: The ground color should differ enough from the glaze color so that there is some contrast between them. This is what creates the apparent texture of sueding. The ground color and glaze color can be from the same color family or they can be quite different in both color and shade. When the color of the glaze is lighter than the ground color, the effect may look chalky or milky (which you might find desirable). However, the best suede effects are usually created with a lighter ground color and a darker glaze from the same family of colors (*see* "How To Mix Your Own Glaze for Faux Suede Finishes," page 10).

We recommend you use an alkyd (oil-based), eggshell finish ground color so that the glaze will glide onto it smoothly and can be easily manipulated with the cheesecloth. Avoid flat or matte finishes; they will absorb the glaze. You can also use latex (water-based) paint for your ground color, as long as it has an eggshell finish.

When working with oil-based paint, be sure you have good ventilation and wear rubber gloves. Always read the manufacturer's labels and follow the directions carefully.

### Practice the Sueding Technique

Once you've decided on three or four possible ground colors, select several paint chips from your local paint store. Mix up several batches of glaze (see "How to Mix Your Own Glaze for Faux Suede Finishes," page 10) and apply the glaze right over the paint chips to see what the effect will be. Once you have determined the proper glaze formula, jot down the recipe and keep it in a safe place.

Then, before painting your walls, you can practice the technique on a piece of drywall or a large illustration board. Start by painting this test surface with the ground color. Let the paint dry fully—usually overnight. Next, mix a batch of the glaze and prepare the cheesecloth.

Cheesecloth, priced at about 75¢ per yard, is sold in hardware, houseware, and art supply stores. To suede an average-size room with about four hundred square feet of wall space, you will need twelve pieces of cheesecloth, each four feet long (sixteen yards total). To prepare the cheesecloth, cut it into four-foot lengths, soak them in warm water, wring them out, and place them in a dryer until they are "curly dry." This way, the frayed cut edges will come loose in the dryer and not on your walls. The drying also gives the cheesecloth more body.

## 3 STEPS TO A SUEDED FINISH

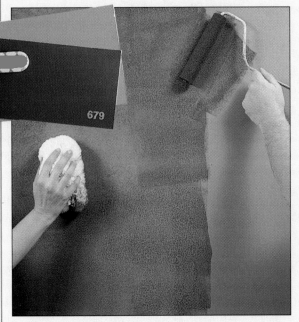

1. Select a base paint and glaze color such as those shown above. 2. Paint the wall with the base color and let it dry overnight. 3. Mix up a batch of glaze. Working with a partner, have one person roll on the glaze while the second "lifts" it off with a cheesecloth pad.

Once the cheesecloth is dry, lay it out flat, then fold it into a pad that will fit into the palm of your hand by folding it in half, and in half again to make a square. Tuck the edges under so that a smooth, rounded surface faces out toward the wall.

To begin applying the glaze, pour one to two cups into a paint tray. Using a paint roller, apply the glaze in even strokes to about a third of your test surface. As soon as the glaze is applied, working from left to right, take the cheesecloth pad and "pounce" it on the glazed surface. Lift the pad off the wall, then rotate the cheesecloth slightly in your hand and change the direction and position of your movement to create contrasting light and dark areas and avoid making a repetitive pattern. The light and dark areas can be as large or small as you like, but try to be fairly consistent. If any roller marks are visible, use the cheesecloth to blend them in.

Leave a three-inch strip of wet, untouched glaze at the right edge. As you roll the glaze over the next section, overlap this edge slightly to make a seamless joint, but avoid putting too much glaze on the overlapped area. Continue rolling on the glaze and pouncing the cheesecloth until the whole test area has been sueded, then stand back and look at your work. Is the texture consistent? If the glaze is still wet, you can go back and dab areas where the glaze is too heavy. If the glaze has started to get tacky,

don't go back over it, as this will make the glaze blotchy. As long as the overall look is consistent, don't worry about minor irregularities.

### Getting Ready to Suede Your Walls

In order to suede large unbroken surfaces, it's easiest to work with a partner. One person, the "applier," rolls the glaze on a section three to four feet wide and the full height of the wall. Then the applier moves to the next section to allow the "sueder" to go over the glaze with the cheesecloth. (*See* photograph, at left.) Because the sueder bears the major responsibility for how the finish looks, he or she should have the right of way, meaning the applier should take charge of repositioning the step ladder and supplies. Periodically one partner should step back to check for consistency and overall effect.

Your sueding will not look like anyone else's because your hand and arm motions are distinctly your own, and your work will never be exactly the same twice. For this reason, if you work with a partner, don't switch roles during the process or the sections may not match.

Prepare the room by moving as much of the furniture as possible out and moving whatever remains away from the walls. Spread tarps or drop cloths to protect the floor and any furniture still in the room.

In rooms where all four walls will be sueded, it might seem logical to start on one wall and go right around the room. However, we don't recommend this because when you reach a corner, you will have difficulty applying the glaze on one wall without disturbing the adjoining one. To get perfect corners, tape around a wall with painter's tape—a wide paper tape with a low-tack adhesive on one edge—and paint that wall, then move to the opposite wall and repeat this process. When these two walls are dry, do the other two walls, first taping off the newly sueded walls to protect them. Even though you're using tape to protect the surfaces you don't want painted, work as neatly as you can and don't count on the tape too much to protect the unpainted areas. In our testing, when we deliberately brushed glaze right over the tape, we found that the paint sometimes seeped under it.

Never stop work halfway along a wall. If the glaze edge dries, it will form a darker layer when more glaze is rolled over it. Once all your walls are sueded, remove all the tape and clean up stray drops of glaze from the woodwork or floors with paper towels moistened in paint thinner.

### SUEDED FINISH

*Covers one average-size room (about 400 square feet of wall space)*

4 quarts oil-based glaze (*see* "How to Mix Your Own Glaze for Faux Suede Finishes," page 10)
1–2 gallons Benjamin Moore alkyd paint, eggshell finish (ground color)

*You'll also need:* 16 yards 36"-wide cheese-

## AN ALTERNATIVE COLOR CHOICE

For this sueded finish, use Benjamin Moore #054 oil-based, eggshell-finish paint for the base color (lighter paint chip), and a medium-viscosity glaze made by mixing Benjamin Moore #056 (darker paint chip) oil-based paint, Benjamin Moore glazing liquid, and paint thinner.

cloth; drywall or illustration board for testing; 9" lambswool paint roller; 2"-wide paintbrush; paint roller tray or 5-gallon bucket with paint screen; paint roller extension handle; paint thinner; wide painter's tape; drop cloth; stepladder; rubber gloves; measuring tape; scissors; access to clothes dryer; and large bowl or basin.

### Preparing the Cheesecloth

Cut cheesecloth into 4'-long pieces. Plunge pieces into warm water, wring them out, and dry in dryer for 20 minutes, or until bone dry. Lay pieces on flat surface and smooth "curly" edges. Fold in half, then in half again to form a square. Tuck edges under to make puffy pad 3" to 4" square.

### Practicing the Sueding Technique

1. *When working with oil-based paint, work in well-ventilated area, protect floor and work space with drop cloths, and wear rubber gloves.* Pour 1 to 2 cups ground-color alkyd paint into tray or bucket. Using roller, paint test surface. Let dry overnight. Clean tools with paint thinner.

2. Pour 1 to 2 cups glaze into tray or bucket. Using roller, apply glaze to one-third of test surface. Work from left to right. Hold cheesecloth pad in palm of hand, and "pounce" it against surface to lift off glaze and reveal ground color. Rotate pad slightly each time to vary impression, and vary strength of pounces for lighter or darker effect. Leave 3" strip of glaze at right edge undisturbed.

3. Repeat step 2 on second and third sections of test surface, in each case back-rolling onto edge of previously applied glaze to eliminate seam. When finished, step back and review work. Light and dark areas should appear in a random (not jarring) pattern. If necessary, touch up wet glaze, but avoid touching glaze that has become tacky. Let test surface dry thoroughly. When dry, move test surface into the room you plan to suede and view it over the course of a day to make sure color is appropriate.

### Sueding Your Walls

1. *When working with oil-based paint, work in well-ventilated area, protect floor and work space with drop cloths, and wear rubber gloves.* Remove furniture or move it to center of room and cover with drop cloth, take down pictures and window treatments, and remove outlet and switch plate covers and wall-mounted light fixtures. Protect trim, doors, and ceiling with painter's tape.

2. Fill tray or bucket with paint for ground color. Using paintbrush, paint edges of walls. Using roller with extension handle, paint rest of walls. Let dry overnight. Clean tools with paint thinner.

3. *For remaining steps, work with a part-*ner. Use painter's tape to protect ceiling, baseboard, and walls adjacent to wall you plan to suede. Fill tray or bucket with glaze. Starting at the left edge, have partner roll glaze onto wall from floor to ceiling for 3' or 4'. Roll glaze as close as possible to ceiling, adjoining walls, and baseboards. With dry brush, stipple glaze in these areas so ground color is completely covered. As soon as glaze has been applied, begin pouncing it with cheesecloth pad to create suede effect. Work from edge of wall to edge of rolled area. As edge of rolled area is neared, have partner roll glaze onto next section of wall. Partner should step back occasionally to review work. Correct flaws only if glaze is not yet tacky.

4. When end of wall is reached, remove tape immediately. Repeat step 3 to suede opposite wall on same day. Let paint dry overnight. Suede two remaining walls after first two walls are completely dry. ◆

**Stu** and **Vi Cutbill** are one of Canada's leading teams of faux-finishing artists and the inventors of the Cutbill system of block printing.

---

### THE WRONG WAY TO SUEDE A WALL

Instead of twisting, sliding, or wiping the cheesecloth across the surface, as shown here, concentrate on "pouncing" the cheesecloth softly on the wall. Change the direction and the motion of the pad only when the pad is not in contact with the wall.

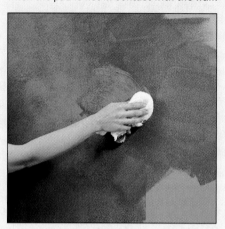

---

# How to Mix Your Own Glaze for Faux Suede Finishes

Mixing glaze is not a science; it's more like cooking without a recipe. How the glaze behaves depends partly on the surface to which it's applied, partly on the air's temperature and humidity, and partly on the brand of glazing liquid used. To get glaze that performs well for you, you may need to experiment with various formulas before you begin work on your project.

Glaze dries fairly quickly, but you can keep it workable a little longer by adding a few tablespoons of double-boiled linseed oil per quart of glaze. Using kerosene instead of paint thinner will also make the glaze stay workable longer. Another method is to wipe down the wall with paint thinner, and while it is wet, apply the glaze over it.

The amount of glaze you'll need depends on how large an area you're covering. Make sure you mix enough because mixing a new batch that matches exactly is difficult. Three to four quarts of glaze will cover about four hundred square feet of wall, enough for an average room.

#### GLAZE FOR SUEDING

1 or more quarts Benjamin Moore alkyd paint #679 in flat or eggshell finish
2 or more quarts Benjamin Moore glazing liquid
1 or more quarts odorless paint thinner

*You'll also need:* 2-gallon plastic bucket; empty 1-gallon container(s) with lid(s); illustration board or drywall painted with ground color; paint-stirring sticks; ice cream sticks or other small mixing devices; measuring spoons; plastic cups or pie plates; and disposable paintbrush.

*Other items, if necessary:* 1 or more quarts kerosene or double-boiled linseed oil (for adjusting viscosity of glaze).

1. In plastic cup or pie plate, measure 1 tablespoon paint, 2 tablespoons glazing liquid, and 1 tablespoon paint thinner. Mix well with ice cream stick. Mixture should have consistency of whole milk and should coat ice cream stick yet still run freely. If mixture is too thick, add more paint thinner in ¼-teaspoon increments, keeping track of amount used so you can calculate overall proportions.

2. Brush glaze onto illustration board or drywall. If glaze cannot be worked after 15 minutes, retest with a new mixture in which you have substituted kerosene for paint thinner or to which you have added a few drops of linseed oil.

3. Following the proportions arrived at in steps 1 and 2, in bucket mix 4 quarts of glaze for each 400 square feet of wall surface. Seal mixed glaze in gallon container(s) until ready to use.

PHOTOGRAPH BY BILL MILNE

# Seashell Candles

*Make these simple candles in under an hour from old candle stubs and homemade wicks.*

BY SYLVIA LACHTER

If you can boil water, you can make these beautiful seashell candles. Arrange three or four of them on a windowsill, or use them as outdoor lighting on a porch or deck. Package a few candles together in a box and you've got a quick and simple hostess gift.

The materials list for this project is short: You'll need some pretty seashells, some wax, some kind of wicking, and a double boiler made from a measuring cup or an empty tin can and a saucepan.

If the beach near you doesn't have any interesting seashells, try your local pet store, the bath department of a store like Pier 1, or a large craft store. Be sure to check them carefully for tiny cracks or holes, which can be patched with white craft glue.

You can get the wax for your candles by buying wax blocks or new candles, but I used the half-burned stubs of candles that I already had lying around. On average, it took one or two small candle stubs to fill one shell. If you like, you can add color to the wax by melting a crayon with the candle stubs. You can add scent by using scented oil, which is also available in craft shops. The strength of scented oil varies depending on the manufacturer, but usually just a few drops of it are enough for these small shell candles.

In addition to wax, you'll need wicks. You have three options: purchase them in a candle or craft supply store, use an unburned wick from an old candle, or make your own. I tested all three options, and they all worked well. If you chose to purchase wicks, look for wire-core or braided wicks, which come square (for large pillar candles) and flat (for small candles). Wire-core wick is made by braiding prepared cotton around a very thin wire core, which melts as the wick burns down. The main advantage to this type of wick is that the wire stiffens it, so it will stand by itself as you pour the wax around it. Braided wick, on the other hand, has no core; it is braided from three strands of unbleached cotton. Both types of wick come in three thicknesses. For candles under two inches in diameter, look for W-1 (wire core) and B-1 (braided) wicks.

You can also use an unburned wick from an old candle, or make your own wick from

*Use these romantic seashell candles to decorate a screened porch or as outdoor lighting on a garden deck.*

butcher twine, but the latter must be treated with a mixture of salt, borax, and water in order to ensure that it burns evenly and without smoke.

## SEASHELL CANDLES

Seashells, each 2"–4" across
Wax, new candles, or candle stubs
Wire-core wick, braided wick, wicks
   removed from existing candles,
   or homemade wick, about 3"
   per seashell

*You'll also need:* paring knife; cutting board; stove; old saucepan; old metal measuring cup with spout *or* empty tin can to fit inside saucepan; oven mitt and/or tongs; scissors; dish towel; and newspaper or brown kraft paper.

*Other items, if necessary:* butcher twine, salt, borax, measuring spoon, and bowl (for making wick from twine); white craft glue (for filling cracks or holes in shells); needle-nose pliers (for bending spout in tin can); tweezers (for positioning certain wicks); concentrated oil scent (for scenting candles); crayons (for tinting candles); and artificial pearls (for decorating candles).

1. If using purchased or recycled wick, go directly to step 2. *If making wick from butcher twine,* dissolve 2 tablespoons salt and 4 tablespoons borax in 2 cups water. Soak twine in solution for 8 hours, then drip-dry overnight.

2. Test shells for small holes by filling each shell with water and watching for leaks. To plug small holes, dry shell with dish towel, then apply small amount of white craft glue to hole or crack on outside of shell. Let glue dry completely.

3. Lay newspaper or brown kraft paper on kitchen counter convenient to stove but not too close to burner. Set shells on work surface, making sure each is stable with cavity facing up. In saucepan bring 1" of water to boil.

4. If using tin can, use pliers to bend rim into V-shaped spout. Working on cutting board with paring knife, slice wax into chunks no larger than ½" across. As you slice wax candle stubs off, set aside those wicks long enough for use in candles. Place wax chunks in metal measuring cup or tin can. If tinting candles, add crayons to wax. Using tongs and/or oven mitt, lower cup or can into boiling water. Reduce to simmer until wax melts.

5. If using homemade wicks, dip twine quickly in and out of wax. When cool, run twine between fingers to remove excess wax. Use tongs and/or mitt to lift cup or can, and carefully pour a few drops of hot wax into cavity of one shell. Replace cup or can into simmering saucepan. If using wire-core wick, twist end into a circle and press it into hot wax, adjusting wick so it stands upright. If using another kind of wick, hold one end of wick with tweezers and press other end into hot wax until wax sets. Repeat to attach wicks to remaining shells.

6. Using tongs and/or oven mitt, pour melted wax into each shell cavity. If wick bends over, hold it upright with tweezers or prop it against shell until wax sets. To scent candle, add two or more drops of concentrated scent oil to wax before wax hardens. To add pearl to candle, wait until wax begins to set, then press pearl into surface far from wick. When candles have cooled completely, use scissors to snip off excess wick within ½" of wax surface. ◆

# 3-Panel Folding Screen

*Transform two double rolls of wallpaper and three hollow-core doors into a decorator-quality folding screen.*

### BY MICHIO RYAN

Purchased in a furniture store or a decorator showroom, this folding three-panel screen might cost anywhere from $750 to $1,000. You can make your own for about a quarter of the cost, however, using two double rolls of wallpaper, three hollow-core doors, and welting and lattice to finish the edges.

Screens can be used as a quick coverup for radiators or storage boxes, to reshape an awkward room layout by softening a corner, or as a temporary or stationary room divider. A screen is also a great decorative device. I've designed this one with a different wallpaper and coordinating trim on each side, so you can transform a room's atmosphere just by turning it around.

This screen is relatively lightweight because it's made with hollow-core doors, so you can readily move it, use it, and store it. The doors' smooth, flat surfaces are perfect for wallpapering. Since the doors will be covered with wallpaper, it's not important what wood they're made of. The doors measure twenty inches wide and eighty inches high, so they reach well above eye level for privacy. The standard thickness for hollow-core doors is one and three-eighths inches.

Once the doors are wallpapered, they are edged with "dressed" clear pine lattice, pine strips that have been planed and sanded to a smooth finish. Your lattice should measure exactly one and three-eighths inches wide to match the doors, and it should be about three-sixteenths of an inch thick. (If you buy doors with a thickness of other than one-and-three-eighths inches, adjust the width of the lattice accordingly.)

*A three-panel screen like this one can be used as a temporary room divider or to hide radiators or storage boxes.*

The lattice is cut straight across to form butt joints at the corners of the doors. Don't cut the lattice to fit the doors until the doors have been wallpapered and trimmed with welting. These decorations add a fraction of an inch to the doors' widths and heights, and the lattice's joints will not fit tightly if measurements are taken before the thickness of the decorations has been taken into account.

The doors (and lattice) should be primed with a light-colored, matte-finish latex paint, preferably white. This will seal the doors so they won't warp from the wet wallpaper glue, improve the glue's adhesion, and prevent the darker wood from showing through the wallpaper. For best results, apply the paint to each door using a small roller, such as Shur-Line's Trim & Touch-Up Roller Kit.

### Selecting the Wallpaper

Before we go any further, let's define a few wallpaper terms. Wallpaper is actually a generic term that includes all the types of decorative paper for walls. To keep things clear, I use the trade industry term "sidewall" to refer to the paper that is applied vertically. Sidewalls do not include borders, corner pieces, or bottom trims, which are identified separately. When referring to wallpaper in this article, I've listed the pattern name, the colorway (or color scheme), and the wallpaper's catalog number, which is specific to each col-

orway, as well as to the pattern.

In designing this screen, I chose Schumacher wallpapers (which must be purchased through a decorator) because I love the way they look, but you can use any pattern that suits your needs. The rich pastel arabesque pattern ("Leaf Arabesque," aqua colorway, #516210) on one side of this screen can create an intimate setting for a bedroom, or serve as a dramatic backdrop in a dining room. The monochromatic grille pattern on the other side suits a more formal and public setting such as a living room. (I used the following papers to create the grille pattern: top border, center motif—"Ramee's Gilded Wreath," tan colorway, #516682; top border, side motif—"Ramee's Palmette," tan colorway, #516692; bottom border—"Ramee's Rosette," tan colorway, #516842; and sidewall—"Ramee's Gilded Ironwork," tan colorway, #516662.) For examples of other wallpaper combinations, *see* the photographs on page 13.

Papers that have a matte finish are more suitable for this project than glossy vinyl-covered papers, which may throw off an unattractive glare. Flat papers will fare better than heavily embossed or figured papers, which may be damaged when the screen is folded flat.

Wallpapers are manufactured in two widths: American wallpapers typically measure about twenty and one-half inches wide, which will conveniently fit across a twenty-inch door panel. Designer and European papers are often twenty-seven inches wide. When you shop for wallpaper, you're likely to encounter the terms "single," "double," and "triple" roll. As a rule of thumb, a single roll is about five yards long, a double roll is ten yards long, and a triple roll is fifteen yards long, although variations do occur. For this project, you will need about thirty linear feet of wallpaper; that will allow twenty feet for covering the doors and an extra ten feet for matching the patterns. One double roll for each side of your screen should be adequate.

To ensure accurate placement, the papers for the doors should be trimmed to size before pasting. Just as when you're papering a wall, you must adjust for the vertical repeat so the pattern will be continuous across the three panels. Since each door is separated from the one next to it by two strips of lattice, two pieces of welting, and a hinge, approximately three-quarters of an inch has to be trimmed out of the horizontal repeat or the pattern will appear disjointed at the folds of the screen. A standard twenty-and-one-half-inch-wide roll will give you enough paper to fold the extra one-quarter to one-half inch of paper over the edges of each twenty-inch-wide door, which eliminates the need for trimming and is per-

fect for creating the illusion of a continuous pattern. For twenty-seven-inch-wide rolls, however, the width must be trimmed down to twenty and three-quarters inches, leaving a three-eighths-inch foldover at each edge. If you're using twenty-seven-inch-wide paper, two of the doors can be covered this way, but the third door must be papered in two sections for the horizontal repeat to work properly. The diagram on page 14 shows three possible layouts if you opt for twenty-seven-inch wallpaper.

For best results, first lay out and rough-cut three wallpaper sections to cover the doors, then trim each section so it fits its door properly. I recommend laying the three doors side by side on the floor or across a tabletop. First find a pleasing placement for the center section pattern. If the print is large, decide where to interrupt the design at the top and bottom edges. Once you've determined the approximate placement of the center section, rough-cut the paper a few inches below the bottom edge of the door. To match the pattern at the sides, before you cut the second sheet of wallpaper, slide it

along the first sheet until they match. (There may be a lot of waste at the top of the second sheet.) Once again, rough-cut the paper a few inches below the door. Locate and cut the third sheet the same way.

Once you've rough-cut all three sheets, line up the edges of the patterns and mark lines straight across the tops and bottoms so that each sheet measures exactly eighty-one inches long. (This allows a one-half-inch overlap at the top and bottom of each door when the paper is pasted in place.) Once the three pieces of paper are the proper length, twenty-seven-inch wallpapers will need to be trimmed to fit, as shown in the diagram on page 14. Note that the door with the seam can be on the right or the left; make your decision on the basis of how the pattern of your wallpaper fits on the screen.

Even in a seemingly random pattern there is an "up" direction, which may not be immediately apparent but which will be noticeable when the wallpaper is hung. Some wallpaper manufacturers include a leaflet or print an arrow on the wrong-side margins to help you out. Be sure that the pattern runs

in the correct direction and in the same direction for all three doors.

Cord welting, although a small element in the overall design, gives the screen the professionally finished look of better upholstery, so select the best quality you can afford. The one-eighth-inch-diameter welting comes with its own attached tape, which is sandwiched between the edge of each door and the lattice. Resist the temptation to cut costs by using plain welting without the taped edge (usually less than $1 per yard). I tried gluing untaped welting onto the door's edge, but it was difficult to keep straight, it turned corners less tidily, and in the end it looked less professional.

The three doors used in the screen are connected with one-and-one-eighth-inch folding screen hinges, which let the doors fold either way. Although the hinge width is one-quarter inch shy of the one-and-three-eighths-inch lattice width, our test screen still folded flat as long as the welting did not exceed one-eighth inch in diameter. You will also need to buy one-and-one-quarter-inch screws, since the screws that are provided with the hinges are too short to reach through the lattice

*When selecting wallpaper for your screen, keep in mind that patterns that might be too dramatic for use on walls will work fine on a screen.*

## Alternative Wallpaper Choices

### JASMINE STAR

For this Moorish effect, paint the lattice red and use gold welting. The top border and sidewall, all by Schumacher, are "Fringed Festoon," cinnamon and plum colorway, #516751 and "Jasmine Star," apple colorway, #516821.

### EKHINOS PATTERN

To create this mocha and gold screen, we painted the lattice gold and selected a tan and white rope welting. The screen's top border is Schumacher's "Ekhinos," mocha colorway, #502617, while the sidewall is "Jasmine Star," metallic and ivory colorway, #516827.

into the door frame.

The screen can stand on small ball feet or furniture glides, or it need not have feet at all. However, if it does, the feet should be only as wide as the doors are thick, or else they will bump into each other and prevent the screen from folding completely.

### THREE-PANEL FOLDING SCREEN

........................................

Double roll (30 yards) 20" or 27"-wide wallpaper, 1 each, patterns A and B

34½ yards ⅛"-diameter cord welting in color(s) to coordinate with wallpaper

3 20" x 80" x 1⅜" hollow-core, flush-panel doors

6 9' lengths ¼" x 1⅜" dressed, clear, pine lattice

4 1⅛" folding screen hinges

3d ("three-penny") finishing nails

4 ounces metallic gold or brass paint

1 quart matte finish white latex paint

Wallpaper activator (for prepasted wallpapers) or ready-mixed, nonstaining vinyl wallpaper paste (for unpasted wallpapers)

Spackling compound

16 1¼" #6 countersunk Phillips wood screws (for folding screen hinges only)

*You'll also need:* 3" roller and tray kit; two or three 1"-wide disposable bristle or foam paintbrushes; wallpaper smoothing brush; wooden brayer; fine-tooth backsaw *or* fine-tooth coping saw; miter box; hammer; nail set; staple gun with ⁵⁄₁₆" staples; T-square or triangle; Phillips screwdriver; mat knife; tack cloth; brown kraft paper or newsprint; 180-grit sandpaper; sanding block; cellulose sponge; pencil; scissors; clean rags; and yardstick or ruler.

*Other items, if necessary:* six 1 ¼"-diameter ball feet *or* six 1"-diameter metal carpet glides (for finishing bottom of screen); fray preventer (if using wide welting).

**Painting the Doors and Lattice**

1. Hold lattice together on edge in miter box and cut with backsaw or coping saw to get six 81" and six 21" lengths. Discard excess lattice. Using sanding block, lightly sand all lattice and doors, then wipe with tack cloth. If using wooden ball feet, sand smooth and wipe with tack cloth.

2. Using roller, prime large flat surfaces of doors and lattice with white paint. (If necessary, let dry and apply second coat.) Using disposable brush, prime edges of doors and all surfaces of ball feet (if using), wiping up any drips as you go with clean rags. Clean up painting equipment with warm water. Let all pieces dry at least 1 hour, then sand lightly and wipe with tack cloth.

3. Using disposable brush, paint lattice and ball feet (if using) with gold paint. Leave one side of lat-

tice unpainted, as it will be positioned face down against door. Clean up painting equipment following manufacturer's directions.

**Cutting the Wallpaper**

1. Lay doors side by side on floor. Unroll wallpaper A on center door, adjusting position so design looks good and paper extends at least 2" beyond top of door. Using mat knife, cut 2" below bottom of door. Unroll additional paper on adjacent door, sliding paper carefully so that patterns match at edges. New piece should extend at least 2" beyond top and bottom edges of door. (If it extends more than 2" beyond, trim off excess.) Cut wallpaper. Repeat process to cut wallpaper for third door.

2. Lay center section of wallpaper face up on large, flat surface. Using yardstick or ruler and pencil, draw a line ½" beyond where top and bottom edges of door will come. Use triangle to ensure 90-degree cuts. Using scissors, cut on these lines to create one

## Possible Layouts for 27-Inch-Wide Wallpaper

........................................

If using twenty-seven-inch-wide wallpaper, refer to the diagrams below to determine the best layout. Once you decide on one, draw a long vertical cutting line on each wallpaper section, then use scissors to cut along the marked line. (You should have four sections for layouts A or B, or three sections for layout C.) To avoid confusion, number each panel 1, 2, or 3 on the top edge; then number the corresponding wallpaper sections on the top of the paper's wrong side.

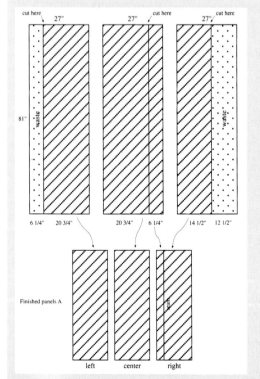

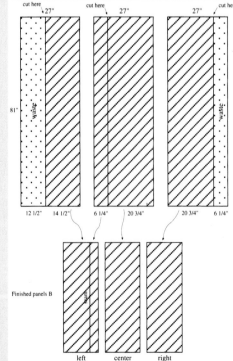

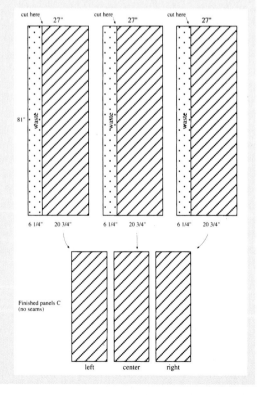

DIAGRAM BY KEVIN MOELLER

81"-long section. Use this section of wallpaper as a guide to mark and cut the two remaining wallpaper sections, matching the patterns at the sides first.

3. If using 20"-wide wallpaper, number each door 1, 2, or 3 on top edge; number corresponding wallpaper sections on top of wrong side. Proceed to step 4. If using 27"-wide wallpaper, refer to diagram on page 14 to determine whether wallpaper pattern will look better following layout A, B, or C. Once you decide, draw a long vertical cutting line on each wallpaper section, then use scissors to cut along marked line. (You should have four sections for layouts A or B, or three sections for layout C.) Number each door 1, 2, or 3 on top edge; then number corresponding wallpaper sections on top of wrong side to prevent confusion during pasting.

4. Repeat appropriate parts of steps 1 through 3 to cut wallpaper B for other side of screen.

**Pasting the Wallpaper**

1. Cover work surface with several layers of newsprint or kraft paper. Lay wallpaper A center section (for use on middle door) wrong side up. Using roller, apply activator or wallpaper adhesive, as appropriate, directly from container to back of wallpaper, spreading it evenly and rolling off edges onto newsprint to make sure edges are fully moistened. To "book" wallpaper, fold ends of wallpaper back, wet sides touching, as shown above, and let sit for 5 to 10 minutes or as directed by paper manufacturer, until paper is limp and edges are relaxed, not curled.

2. To position paper on door, lift two top corners and touch them to top corners of door, with paper's edge extending ½" beyond door edge. Make sure side overhangs are even, then carefully unfurl paper onto door. Using smoothing brush, smooth paper from center out. Roll paper with wooden brayer to remove air bubbles, then roll edges. Fold overhangs onto edges of door. If edges have dried out and won't stay

## How to "Book" Wallpaper

A fter coating your wallpaper with adhesive or activator, fold each end in on itself as shown. Let the paper sit for five to ten minutes before pasting it in place.

stuck down, rewet these with activator or adhesive and fold them over again. Wipe papers with damp cellulose sponge to remove paste residue.

3. Repeat steps 1 and 2 to cover remaining two doors with wallpaper A. If applying two wallpaper sections to one surface, affix one section at a time and butt edges with patterns matching. Roll seam with brayer after adhesive has begun to dry (up to 10 minutes after paper is applied).

4. Let doors dry 30 minutes. Turn them over, taking care to keep them in order, and repeat steps 1 to 3 with wallpaper B on backs of doors. When finished, prop doors up so air can circulate on both sides; let dry overnight.

**Attaching the Welting and Lattice**

1. To attach welting, set door on edge and stand astride it, holding it upright with your legs. Starting near one corner of long edge and leaving an 11" tail of welting free, place welting tape against edge of door so welting cord sits on wallpapered surface. Using staple gun, staple welting tape to edge of door every 1" to 2" for entire length of door, pulling tape taut but not stretching it. (*See* illustration 1.) Proceed around corner and down short edge of door. Lay door on opposite edge to continue. After rounding third corner, stop and staple 11" tail into place around fourth corner.

2. Continue stapling two free ends of welting. If welting cord is narrow, simply overlap ends at center and fold away from edge, trimming off excess for a neat finish. If welting cord is thick and

## Finishing the Screen's Edges

**1.** Staple the welting tape along the edges of each door, through the folded-over wallpaper. The welting cord itself should lie on the face of the door, but the welting tape lies on the edge of the door.

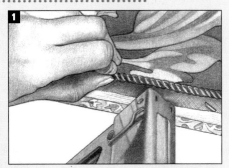

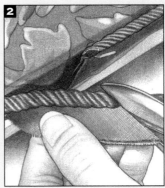

**2.** To finish thicker taped welting like this, cut each end diagonally so ends butt together.

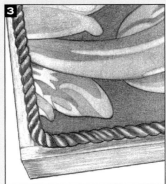

**3.** On the finished corner, the lattice covers the welting tape and the staples.

overlap will be too bulky under lattice, cut each end diagonally so that cut ends will butt; immediately apply a dot of fray preventer to each end, then staple down welting (illustration 2). Repeat steps 1 and 2 to trim *both* sides of all three doors.

3. Position a short lattice on short edge of one door so one end of lattice lines up with exposed side of welting tape on adjoining edge of door. Make a pencil mark for opposite end of lattice. Check this measurement by holding the marked lattice against short edge of other two doors. If it matches, straight-cut all short lattice to this length together in miter box, as in Painting the Doors and Lattice, step 1. If there are variations from door to door, mark and trim each lattice separately. After trimming six lattice, nail each in place with 3d nails spaced 4" apart. (For easier nailing, lay lattice flat on floor and drive nails partway through, then position lattice on door and complete nailing process.)

4. After nailing six short lattice in position, measure and mark long lattice in same way, so each

one forms butt joints with short lattice. Nail lattice in place (illustration 3). To secure joints, drive two nails side by side into edge of door rather than into butt joint itself.

5. Countersink all nails with nail set and fill holes with spackle applied with your fingertip. Also fill cracks at butt joints with spackle. Let dry. Paint spackled areas with white paint, let dry, then repaint with gold paint.

**Assembling and Finishing the Screen**

1. To attach hinges, set two doors together on edge, with edges to be joined facing up. Draw light pencil lines 18" from top and bottom of door. Lay hinges against lines, mark screw holes on door using hammer and nail set, then screw hinges in place at marked holes. Repeat to join remaining doors, making sure wallpapers face the same direction.

2. To attach ball feet or carpet glides to screen, mark crosshairs 4" from sides of doors and centered in lattice. Screw in ball feet or hammer in glides. ◆

# Quick Transfer Pillows

*Bring a classic decor to any room with these fast and easy pillows.*

*Using transfer medium, you can make black-and-white pillows like these, or transfer color images for a different look.*

Introducing a touch of classic styling to your home's interior needn't require major renovations—one easy place to start is with these pillows. Although they resemble pillows you might find in a decorator showroom, making them at home is a snap using transfer medium and the black-and-white images on the next page.

Transfer medium, as its name implies, transfers images from ordinary paper to another surface. For this project we used Picture This transfer medium, which is especially designed for fabric. The resulting pillow can be washed, dried, and ironed, and the number and kind of pillows you create are limited only by the images you choose. When shopping for pillows, be certain to select those made of at least 50 percent cotton; if you have a choice, 100 percent cotton is preferable. The transfer medium will not work with nylon or polyester fabrics.

There are a few key points to keep in mind before proceeding. When making a copy of the image you intend to use, be sure to use a dry toner photocopier like those found in most offices, and make the copy onto plain paper, as shiny or coated paper will not work. Before copying, measure the dimensions of the pillow; then (if necessary) enlarge the image to leave a minimum two-inch border all around the design. This may seem like a wide border when the pillow is laid flat, but when it is stuffed,

these areas curve down toward the seams and will look much smaller. For a fourteen-inch-square pillow, for example, your image should not exceed ten inches square. If you choose images other than those provided on the next page, avoid designs with letters or numbers because the images will be reversed when they are transferred.

Before transferring the design, wash the pillow cover to preshrink it and remove any sizing. This project is easier if the pillow cover zips off, but if it doesn't, simply open a seam along one edge and remove the pillow's stuffing. After the transfer is complete, restuff the pillow and slip-stitch the opening closed.

## QUICK TRANSFER PILLOWS

Black-and-white image (*see* page 17)
14"- to 20"-square off-white or cream-
    colored cotton throw pillow
Picture This transfer medium for fabric
4   gold tassels
Gold sewing thread

*You'll also need:* access to dry toner photocopier; uncoated, white paper; access to washer and dryer; wax paper; plastic grocery bag without printing or printed logo; stiff, smooth piece of cardboard 2" smaller than pillow; iron; tape measure, ruler, or yardstick; scissors; hand sewing needle; 1"-wide foam brush; sponge; washcloth; paper towels; 1"-diameter or larger dowel, brayer, or rolling pin; and low-tack tape.

*Other items, if necessary:* seam ripper, clean plastic bag, and cream thread (if using pillow without zipper); and press cloth or towel (for ironing finished pillows).

1. Unzip pillow cover and remove pillow form. If cover has no zipper, use seam ripper to pick out stitches along one edge, then remove stuffing and store it in clean plastic bag. Machine-wash pillow cover, then tumble dry. Press smooth

with iron. Measure pillow horizontally and vertically, and jot down dimensions.

2. Use dry toner photocopier and uncoated paper to enlarge black-and-white image; area of enlarged image should be 4" less than the dimensions recorded in step 1.

3. Lay pillow cover right side up on flat work surface. Slip cardboard into plastic bag without writing or logo, then slide protected cardboard inside pillow cover through opening. With your hands, smooth plastic and pillow fabric until cover lies smooth.

4. Using scissors, trim excess paper from enlarged image, leaving clean, even ⅛" border all around image. Center image face down on pillow cover and mark position of top, bottom, and sides with small pieces of low-tack tape.

5. Remove image from pillow and place printed side up on work surface protected with wax paper. Using foam brush, apply coat (approximately ¹⁄₁₆" thick) of Picture This transfer medium onto printed side of image; coat should be heavy enough to cloud image but not so heavy as to obscure lines completely. Place image, coated side down, on pillow cover between tape markers. Lay one paper towel on top, then roll dowel (or substitute) lightly over surface, working from center out, using consistent pressure to adhere image to fabric. Remove paper towel and tape. With fingertips, press down all around outside edge of image to ensure strong bond. Using another paper towel, blot any excess medium oozing beyond edges. Let dry 24 hours.

6. Place wet washcloth on image and let sit 5 minutes to soften paper. Remove washcloth. Using damp sponge, rub over image in a circular motion to remove softened paper. Let dry 30 minutes. Repeat rubbing procedure until all paper is removed and image is clean. Let image cure 72 hours, then turn pillow cover inside out, machine wash in cool water, and tumble dry on permanent press or low heat setting. If ironing is required, set iron on lowest steam setting, and use press cloth or towel between iron and pillow.

7. Turn washed cover right side out. Using gold thread and hand sewing needle, tack a gold tassel to each corner. Reinsert pillow form through opening and zip closed, or reinsert stuffing and slip-stitch pillow opening. ◆

   PILLOW PHOTOGRAPH BY STEVEN MAYS/TASSEL PHOTOGRAPH BY DAVID HENDERSON

These black-and-white images are designed for use in the "Quick Transfer Pillows" project on page 16, but they could also be used for decoupage projects, framed and used as art, or hand-colored, copied, and/or reduced to make bookplates, gift tags, or note cards.

# Victorian Frame Bow

### *Make an elegant picture frame bow in under 3 hours using a variety of time-saving techniques.*

#### BY MARY FRAZIER

Looking for a quick way to dress up a wall or highlight a special framed picture? Consider making a picture frame bow. Using the quick, simple methods outlined here, in just an evening you can make a bow to match your decor.

Traditionally, assembling a bow like this would require several trips between the sewing machine and the ironing board. But by grouping like tasks together, I finished the entire bow in approximately two-and-a-half hours. The bow's design also helps speed up the process. For instance, several edges are turned under and concealed, rather than finished, and the bow is made by sewing and pinching, instead of by trying to tie a perfect bow. To speed up the cutting time, I recommend using a rotary cutter and its accessories (cutting guide and self-healing cutting mat) instead of scissors to cut the fabric. Although scissors will work fine, the pieces of the bow all have straight edges, and a rotary cutter is much faster on these.

From a one-and-one-quarter-yard piece of fifty-four-inch-wide fabric, you can make the bow shown here; its tails are thirty-two inches long and the bow itself is ten inches wide. This size bow is suitable for a picture frame about fifteen to twenty inches long, but you can adjust the proportions of the bow and its tails to fit just about any size frame.

For best results, use fabric with body (such as chintz or moiré) so your bow will look crisp. I tested two fabrics: a pale yellow chintz and a green plaid quilting cotton. Both bows turned out well, but the chintz was easier to work with because of its heavier weight. The chintz bow also looked more formal, making it a better choice for a living room. The cotton bow might be appropriate for a child's room.

Choose a fabric that will coordinate with other small details in your room, such as curtain tiebacks, a valance, or upholstery trim, either by matching the fabric or by duplicating the color. If you select a fabric that exactly matches large expanses of other fabrics in the room such as curtains or upholstery, you may create an overbearing effect.

*Want to highlight a special picture? You can sew your own picture frame bow in under three hours using one and one-quarter yards of fabric. This sea-foam green chintz bow works well in a formal setting.*

## PICTURE FRAME BOW

1¼ yards 54"-wide moiré, chintz, or other firmly woven fabric
Matching thread
⅝" diameter plastic curtain ring

*You'll also need:* sewing machine; iron; ironing board; rotary cutter, cutting guide, and self-healing mat; scissors; pins; hand sewing needle; ruler; fabric-marking pencil; 2 picture-hanging hooks; and hammer.

### Making the Picture Frame Bow

Steam-press fabric to remove any wrinkles. Following "Cutting Out the Picture Frame Bow," page 19, use rotary cutter or scissors to cut one tie, two streamers, and one bow from fabric. The longer edges of all four pieces should be cut parallel to the fabric's selvage. Fold bow and streamers in half lengthwise, right sides together, and stitch longer edges of each, making ½" seams. Take all four pieces to ironing board, and press seams of bow and streamers open, centering them as you go. Turn bow right side out and press it so seam is centered on one side.

For the following instructions, refer to the illustrations on page 19.

1. In order shown in illustration 1, press raw edges of tie to wrong side to form one 1¼" x 10" strip, then cut tie in half to form two parts.

2. Return to sewing machine. Fold bow in half with seam facing out and raw edges matching. Stitch raw edges together, making a ½" seam.

3. Refold bow so raw edges are inside, and lay it flat with newer seam at left. Pin all layers together to prevent shifting. Using ruler and fabric-marking pencil, measure and mark a line 10" from and parallel to left edge. Stitch through all layers along this line, dividing bow into two sections.

4. To create four bow loops, hold two layers of fabric at left open with your fingers, align stitching done in step 3 on seam, and put smaller, center section on top. Then turn bow over and stitch in seamline "ditch" through all layers to anchor loops. (*See* illustration 8.)

5. To form points at one end of each streamer, measure and mark a dot on seamline 2½" from end. Mark dots on each folded edge ½" from end. Draw lines connecting three points.

6. Stitch through both layers on marked lines, pivoting at center dot to form a V. Trim fabric ½" from stitching, clip corners, and clip

into seam allowance at V, stopping just before pivot dot. Turn streamer right side out, and pick out points with pin to make them sharp and crisp. Carry streamers to ironing board and press them both on side with seam.

7. Return to sewing machine. Stack streamers seam side down, and stitch raw edges together. Fold stitched edge down 4" to seam side, and stitch over previous stitching through all layers.

8. To assemble bow, pinch center of bow at stitching in the seamline "ditch."

9. Wrap one tie around pinched section, lapping pressed end over raw end at back to form loop. Adjust bow so loop is snug but not tight, and hand stitch overlapped ends securely. Slip remaining tie through loop at back of bow. Pinch streamers at seam line and lay pinched section against this tie. Then wrap tie around streamers and hand stitch pressed end as you did for first loop.

10. Hand stitch curtain ring to top of second tie to form hanger. Determine position of bow and picture on wall, and hammer in picture-hanging hook for each. Hang bow first, then slip streamers down between back of framed picture and its hanging wire to mount picture on wall. Fluff bow with your fingertips for fullness. ◆

**Mary Frazier** is a professional seamstress based in Lloyd Harbor, New York.

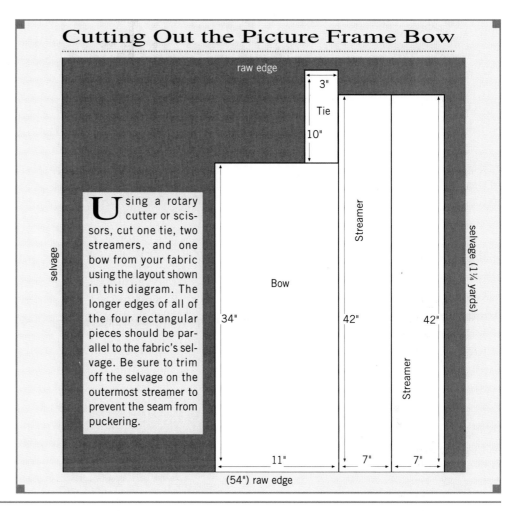

## Cutting Out the Picture Frame Bow

raw edge

3"

Tie

10"

Bow

34"

11"

Streamer

42"

7"

Streamer

42"

7"

selvage

selvage (1¼ yards)

(54") raw edge

Using a rotary cutter or scissors, cut one tie, two streamers, and one bow from your fabric using the layout shown in this diagram. The longer edges of all of the four rectangular pieces should be parallel to the fabric's selvage. Be sure to trim off the selvage on the outermost streamer to prevent the seam from puckering.

### MAKING THE TIES

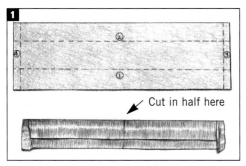

**1**

Cut in half here

### SEWING THE BOW

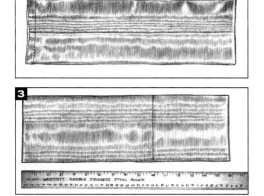

**2**

**3**

### MAKING THE STREAMERS

**5**

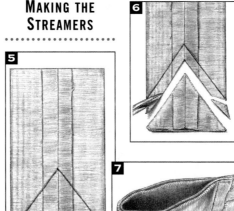

**6**

**7**

### PINCHING THE BOW

**8**

**9**

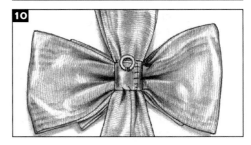

**10**

**4**

# The Best Way to Dry Roses

*Learn three foolproof techniques for turning your live
roses into timeless beauties.*

**W**e set out to research this article with one goal in mind: to create the perfect dried rose. After several failed experiments, including a few roses that literally fell apart, we've determined the three best ways to dry a rose blossom: using silica gel, using silica gel and a microwave oven to speed up the process, and air-drying.

In order for a rose to dry in a lifelike and beautiful shape, rather than becoming a moldy or crumpled mass, some element—be it air, sand, or something else—must absorb the moisture from the rose. One easy way to remove such moisture is to "bury" the rose in a desiccant, or drying agent. Some easily found desiccants include sand, borax, cornmeal, and silica gel. To determine the best desiccant, we tested all four of these substances alone and in combination. Silica gel, a nontoxic compound widely available in craft and florist shops, far and away produced the best results for small quantities of roses. (The silica gel approach is best for that one exceptional rose or two; for large quantities of roses, air-drying spares you from having to buy a large quantity of silica gel or investing as much of your time.)

Originally developed to absorb moisture in such packaged products as potato chips and electronic equipment, silica gel is actually not a "gel" at all, but a saltlike substance that can hold up to 40 percent of its weight in water.

While easy to use, silica gel has two minor drawbacks. For starters, the rose must stand upright in the gel so the silica grains can be dropped in between the petals. This means clip-

## Air-Drying

Blemish-free, partially opened
roses or buds on stems

*You'll also need:* area for drying that is warm, dry, dark, and draft-free, such as basement furnace room or hall closet; wide rubber band; pruning shears; and hammer and nail or hanging hook.

**1.** Using pruning shears, clip stems of six to eight roses so they are equal in length, at least 6" long. Bunch stems together and secure ends with wide rubber band.

**2.** Install hook or hammer a nail into support beam for hanging roses. Turn bouquet upside down and slip section of rubber band around hook or nail so roses hang down and air circulates around them.

**3.** Allow 3 to 6 days for drying. Beginning on day 3, check roses periodically by lightly squeezing a flower head to see if it is dry. Roses are ready for use when flower head, calyx, and stem are dry and brittle.

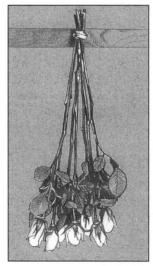

### TIPS ON SELECTING ROSES
No one rose in our testing dried better than any other. Garden varieties may be hand-picked for shape and color, but store-bought roses dry beautifully as well. Roses should be picked when petals are dry and beginning to open.

## Silica Gel

Blemish-free, partially opened
roses or buds
Prewired green florist picks
Green florist tape

*You'll also need:* silica gel; tin containers with tight-fitting lids; plastic tape; ruler; pruning shears; fine sabeline paintbrush; goggles; particle mask; soupspoon; and large bowl.

*Other items, if necessary:* disposable latex gloves (to prevent dryness of hands); and vase (to set stems in if roses are dewy or wet).

**1.** When using silica gel, work outdoors or in well-ventilated area, wear gloves if your hands are prone to dryness, and wear a particle mask and goggles, as the fine dust that comes off the gel can irritate mucous membranes.

**2.** If roses are dewy or wet, set stems in water for a few hours to give moisture on petals a chance to evaporate. When surface moisture is gone, use pruning shears to clip off each stem 1" below calyx. Pour silica gel into tin container to a level of 1". Insert rose blossom stem first into gel, so petals are at least 1" from interior wall of container. If drying several roses in a large container, allow at least 1" between them.

**3.** Using soupspoon, gently spoon gel crystals around each rose. To

PHOTOGRAPHS BY RICHARD FELBER

ping off the stem one inch from the blossom and attaching a false stem later. (If you were to lay a rose and its stem down and then cover them with silica gel, it would end up drying in a very distorted shape.) The best means of keeping a single rose upright is to use a small tin. If you have a number of roses to dry, you can use a larger container as long as the roses are at least one inch from the sides and bottom of the container, one inch from each other, and two inches from the lid, so the gel can surround them. With repeated use, the gel will absorb the maximum amount of water, and its tiny blue indicator crystals will turn pink.

Silica can be reused, however. To dry silica gel for reuse, simply spread it out on a large pan and place in a 300-degree oven for about one half hour. Once the gel has cooled, it may be used again. When storing silica gel, be sure to seal the container tightly, as it will also absorb water from the atmosphere.

The second drawback to silica gel is the time required to dry the roses: anywhere from three to seven days. In trying to shorten drying times, however, we discovered our second-best

method for drying roses: accelerate the action of the silica gel with a microwave oven. This reduced the drying time to a few hours at most. (Note: Other desiccants we tested did not work with the microwave oven method.)

When using the silica gel microwave oven method, you will have to experiment with your particular oven in order to determine the time and temperature settings that produce the best results. We recommend starting at the highest setting (often power level 10) for thirty seconds and adjusting the time and/or power level from there. Keep in mind that a microwaved rose will continue to lose moisture after it is removed from the silica gel. Within several days, as individual petals shrink up, you will be able to brush out any trapped crystals.

The third method of drying roses—ordinary air-drying—works well on a fairly consistent basis, though it takes at least several days. The air-drying method produces roses that look dry, unlike silica gel roses, which just might pass for fresh. This difference is, in fact, one of the prime deciding factors when selecting a method for drying your roses: how the end

product will look.

A rose dried with silica gel more closely resembles a live rose in color and shape, although its texture is somewhat like paper. Roses dried using the silica gel microwave oven method appear a little bit paler than those dried in silica gel alone. The outer petals develop a curl, and the veins in the outer petals become visible, but on the whole they are equally as beautiful. An air-dried rose, on the other hand, shrinks and darkens considerably, and ends up with slightly shriveled edges. Air-dried roses do, however, have their stems (with leaves) attached, an important consideration if you prefer real stems to ones created with florist picks and tape.

A few other tips before you get started: Don't dry roses right after a rain, as the desiccant will stick to the petals, making removal more difficult. In addition, the desiccant will have to drink in so much extra water that its absorptive ability will be diminished. Furthermore, if you are using the silica gel and microwave oven technique, excess water on the petals may cause the rose to burn. ◆

---

avoid crushing outer petals, let crystals slide from spoon down along inner wall of tin toward rose. Once gel has begun to support rose by gently piling up around it, lightly sprinkle crystals over top of rose to fill in spaces between petals. Take care not to crush any petals, especially inner petals, by pouring on gel too heavily. Continue adding gel on top of roses to a level of ½" to 1". Remove goggles, mask, and gloves.

**4.** Place lid firmly on container, and seal edge with plastic tape. Let container rest undisturbed for 3 days. On day 3, open container and carefully pour off topmost layer of silica gel into bowl until petals are showing. Touch petals and center of rose with your fingertip. If petals are pliable or center of rose gives, replace gel on top and reseal container. Check again on day 4 and each succeeding day until petals are dry and rose is stiff.

**5.** To remove rose, put on goggles, particle mask, and gloves, and carefully pour off topmost layer of gel or mixture into bowl until you can see top of rose. Continue pouring gel away from rose until you can lift it out by its stem. Turn rose upside down over bowl, and shake gently to slough off crystals. Run bristles of paintbrush between petals to remove remaining loose crystals. Follow directions below to create false stem.

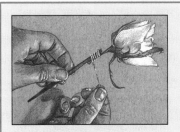

## CREATING A FALSE STEM

**1.** To attach the dried rose to a prewired florist pick, hold the stem of the rose against the top ½" of the prewired pick and wind the wire firmly around both the stem and the pick.

**2.** Starting at the calyx, wind the florist tape down the rose stem and around the wired section, stretching the tape slightly as you go. Continue wrapping the tape partway down the pick, tear the tape from the roll, and press the torn end firmly around the pick.

## Microwave

Blemish-free, partially opened roses or buds
Prewired green florist picks
Green florist tape

*You'll also need:* silica gel; microwave oven; microwavable containers with lids; pruning shears; ruler; fine sabeline paintbrush; goggles; particle mask; soupspoon; and large bowl.

*Other items, if necessary:* disposable latex gloves (to prevent dryness of hands); oven mitts (for removing microwave containers); and vase (to set stems in if roses are dewy or wet).

**1.** Follow steps 1 through 3 of "Silica Gel," page 20, using microwavable container instead of tin.

**2.** Set cover on container but do not create a tight seal. Place container in microwave oven. Microwave for 30 seconds at highest setting.

**3.** Using oven mitts if necessary, remove container from microwave oven. Press cover firmly to seal it, and let sit 30 minutes. Open container, carefully brush back top layer of gel, and examine topmost petals. If petals are pliable, replace gel carefully and repeat steps 2 and 3 until petals are dry and stiff.

**4.** Follow step 5 of "Silica Gel" at left. If rose appears overdry or discolored, retry with new roses, setting microwave oven for less time or lower power level.

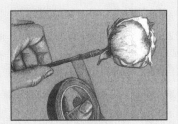

# Silk Ribbon Embroidery

*Using silk ribbon and six basic stitches, you can create textured, three-dimensional stitchwork in just a few hours.*

BY MARIE BROWNING

*The bouquet above uses the Japanese ribbon stitch for the pink flowers and dark-green leaves, an extended fly stitch at the base of each flower or leaf, and a stem stitch to create the light-green stems. The design at right features the same elements as the bouquet as well as a web rose and one pink flower created with the padded Japanese ribbon stitch. (The white, machine-made stitches in the upper right corner were already present, and I worked the silk ribbon stitches around it.)*

**W**hether you're a first-time stitcher or a seasoned needleworker looking for a new technique, silk ribbon embroidery is quick and easy to master. Many of the stitches are the same as those used in traditional floss embroidery, but silk ribbon gives them a textured, three-dimensional quality that would take much longer to achieve using embroidery floss. In addition, silk ribbon covers more surface area with fewer stitches than embroidery floss, because you're using a band of ribbon instead of a double thread. Unlike floss embroidery projects, which may require several weeks to complete, a variety of items may be decoratively embroidered with silk ribbon in just a few hours.

This article features six basic floral stitches. You can apply them to white cotton pillow covers, for instance, or use them to embellish any number of other items, including small upholstered jewelry boxes, fabric napkin rings, pillowcases, bedspreads, eyeglass cases, fabric picture frames, or curtain tiebacks. Consider adorning the corner of a pillowcase, hankie, or vest with a single rosebud, or adding white silk ribbon embroidery to a white christening gown. If you opt for white pillow covers, look for those that already feature some machine-stitched embroidery, and work the stitches around those designs, as shown at left. You can also work the embroidery on a plain white cotton pillow cover, or use different-colored silk ribbon and perle cotton on a darker background color.

To get started, you'll need a few basic supplies: silk ribbon, perle cotton, needles, and an embroidery hoop. Silk ribbon is very soft and pliable and has an appealing luster that nothing else can match. Most of the silk ribbon available today is produced in Japan and comes in a wide array of colors; standard widths include 2mm, 4mm, and 7mm. I've chosen a 4mm ribbon, since it is the most widely available and the most versatile. Depending on where you live, you may have difficulty finding silk ribbon in retail stores, as this form of embroidery has only recently become popular in North America. If finer needlework stores in your area do not yet stock it, you can purchase it by mail; ribbon usually costs between 50¢ and 65¢ per yard. (*See* Sources and Resources, page 31.)

In addition to silk ribbon, you'll need several skeins of size 12 perle cotton thread to create the accent and anchor stitches. The size 12 thread is delicate and may be difficult to find, but it can also be ordered through the mail. You can substitute a single strand of embroidery floss, but it will lack the luster of perle cotton. A ball of size 12 perle cotton contains about 140 yards of thread and costs about $1.50.

To make the basic stitches, you'll need two needles. A size 22 chenille needle, which has a sharp point and a large eye, works best for 4mm silk ribbon. The size 12 perle cotton will work with a medium-size (3, 5, or 7) embroidery needle. To give the stitches loft, I recommend using an embroidery hoop, which holds the fabric taut and helps you control the tension of the ribbon. To use an embroidery

hoop, place the inner ring of the hoop on the underside of the project and center it under the area where you'll be stitching. From the outside, place the outer ring of the hoop on top of the inner ring, trapping the cloth in between the two hoops, and tighten the screw on the outer hoop. To prevent the hoop from permanently creasing the fabric, remove it whenever you take a break from stitching. If your project doesn't fit in an embroidery hoop, work the stitches carefully to avoid distorting the fabric.

For best results, follow these tips and techniques. Use twelve- to fourteen-inch lengths of silk ribbon; longer lengths are difficult to control and overhandling may cause them to fray. Before embroidering any silk ribbon stitches, "lock" the ribbon onto the needle as shown in the illustrations on the next page to prevent the ribbon from slipping. To anchor your first stitch, leave a half-inch tail of ribbon on the wrong side of your work, hold the tail flat against the fabric so that the needle pierces straight through the tail as you complete the stitch, then trim off the excess tail.

While embroidering, manipulate the ribbon carefully. To prevent the ribbon from twisting, hold it flat with your left thumb (reverse if left-handed) as you work. To end, weave the ribbon under several previous stitches on the wrong side, and trim off the loose end to prevent accidental snags.

If you're an experienced needleworker, you may want to experiment using silk ribbon with other simple embroidery stitches such as French knots, lazy daisy, chain stitch, featherstitch, and couching. For even more variation, mix in buttons, beads, and charms with your stitching. To prevent the edges from fraying and to keep the silk ribbon lustrous, I recommend dry cleaning your silk ribbon embroidery projects. ◆

**Marie Browning,** a fine arts specialist and craft instructor, is co-owner of Kindred Spirits in Victoria, British Columbia, Canada.

# Silk Ribbon Embroidery Stitch Guide

## THREADING YOUR NEEDLE

To prevent your silk ribbon from slipping out of the needle, you'll need to lock it onto the needle. Cut the ribbon at an angle, and thread the needle. Pull about 2" of the ribbon through the needle's eye, then use the point of the needle to pierce through the ribbon, about ¼" from the end. Gently pull on the long, loose end of the ribbon until it draws the pierced end up the needle shaft, locking it around the eye.

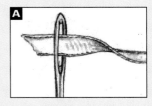

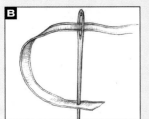

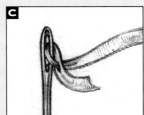

## 1. STRAIGHT STITCH

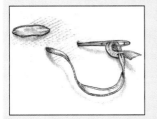

The straight stitch, which uses silk ribbon, is simple yet beautiful. You can vary the length of this stitch to create a variety of effects. This stitch forms the foundation for the padded Japanese ribbon stitch.

## 2. STEM STITCH

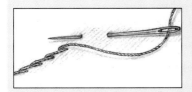

The perle-cotton stem stitch can be used anywhere a single line is needed. The line can be straight or curved to suggest long stems or vines. To keep the stitches consistent, always bring the needle up on the same side of the thread.

## 3. JAPANESE RIBBON STITCH

Similar to the straight stitch, this silk ribbon stitch has a decorative curled effect at one end that suggests a leaf or flower petal. Start as you would for a straight stitch, making sure the ribbon lies flat on the fabric. To complete the stitch, pierce through the center of the ribbon and gently draw the needle through to the wrong side until the ribbon curls at the tip. Do not pull too tightly or the effect will be lost. This stitch can be varied by changing its length or the tension of the ribbon.

## 4. EXTENDED FLY STITCH

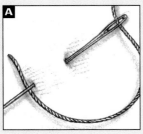

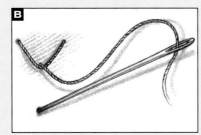

Use this perle cotton stitch to start the anchor for the web rose and to accent the rosebud. (*See* stiches 5 and 6 below.)

## 5. WEB ROSE

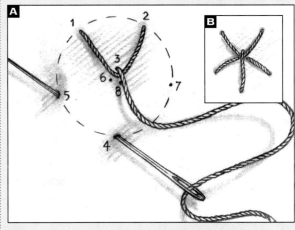

To form the perle cotton anchor stitches, make an extended fly stitch, then add two more straight stitches to form five spokes. Knot it off at the back. To weave the rose around this web, bring a chenille needle threaded with silk ribbon up at the center, then run ribbon over and under the spokes, filling the area from the center out. For best results, allow the ribbon to twist and keep it loose.

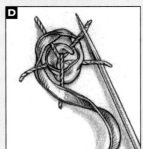

## 6. PADDED JAPANESE RIBBON STITCH

For this layered silk ribbon stitch, start with a straight stitch, then work a Japanese ribbon stitch on top. To make a rosebud, add an extended fly stitch and a straight stitch with perle cotton at the base.

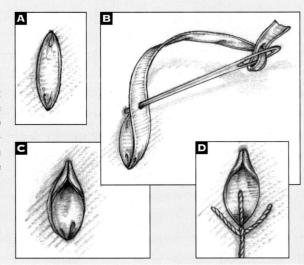

# Marbled Chocolate Strawberries

*This simple and delicious dessert will dress up any table,
from a picnic to a formal dinner.*

Fresh strawberries are delicious by themselves, but dipped in chocolate they become an especially elegant and delectable treat. A beautifully marbled variation is easily created using melted white and dark chocolates, a feast for the eyes as well as for the palate.

We started by dipping the berries in melted white chocolate. To accentuate the marbled effect, we chose semisweet chocolate for its rich, dark brown color. If you don't like the taste of semisweet chocolate, you can use lighter brown milk chocolate, but the marbling will be more subtle.

To eliminate a lengthy and potentially fattening search on your part, we tested a wide variety of chocolates (from chips to bars) and flavors (white, dark, semisweet, and milk chocolate).

For white chocolate, we recommend Hershey's Vanilla Milk chips or the Ghirardelli Classic White Confection bar. We had trouble with the Ghirardelli Classic White chips; they didn't melt evenly.

The best complement to the flavor of the strawberry is a chocolate with a delicate flavor and a smooth texture for easier dipping.

As far as melting dark and semisweet chocolate is concerned, all the chips are basically the same: It takes approximately three minutes to melt four ounces of each. There were significant differences, however, in taste and texture. Those with the smoothest texture were Ghirardelli semisweet chips and Saco semisweet chocolate chips. The Saco chips had a more subtle flavor; they didn't "sting" as very, very sweet chocolate can do. We found Nestle's Toll House chips too strong tasting and a little rough in texture.

We also tested two kinds of dark chocolate bars: Hershey's Special Dark and Ghirardelli's Sweet Dark. While the Ghirardelli is a better quality chocolate, we would recommend either one for taste.

If you like milk chocolate, there's a large selection from which to choose. Nestle's Toll House milk chocolate chips work fine, but it's much cheaper to buy a candy bar. Our first choice among the milk chocolate bars is the Hershey bar. It has the darkest color and tastes great. If you can't find Hershey's milk chocolate, we recommend Cadbury or Dove brands. Although they are both fairly light in color, they're smoother than the Hershey bar. We also tested Hershey's Kisses, and while they're suitable for this project, it takes a fair amount of time to remove all the paper strips and foil wrappers.

*Marbled chocolate strawberries not only taste great, they double as a beautiful decorative dessert.*

## MARBLED CHOCOLATE STRAWBERRIES

1 pint ripe strawberries (about 12 strawberries)
6 ounces white chocolate
1 tablespoon heavy cream
2 ounces dark or semisweet chocolate
1 teaspoon butter

*You'll also need:* fork with narrow tines; wooden skewer; wax paper; double boiler; small saucepan; glass measuring cup; pot holders; 2 miniature whisks or ordinary forks; paper towels; and cookie sheet.

1. Wash strawberries in cool water and pat dry with paper towels. Leave hulls on. If strawberries have stems, leave them on as well. Set aside. Cover cookie sheet with wax paper.

2. Fill bottom half of double boiler half full with water and bring to simmer. Put white chocolate and cream in top of double boiler. At same time, fill bottom of saucepan with 1" of water, place dark or semisweet chocolate and butter in glass measuring cup inside saucepan, and bring water to a simmer. As chocolates melt, combine with cream or butter using a separate miniature whisk or fork for each chocolate.

3. When both chocolates are fully melted, remove top boiler from heat and place on pot holder, propping one side of pan up with additional pot holders so white chocolate collects in pool on lower side of pot. Place saucepan with melted dark chocolate on another pot holder alongside white chocolate.

4. Hold one strawberry by top third or stem and dip bottom half or two-thirds of berry into white chocolate. Dip tines of narrow-tined fork in dark chocolate, then blot on sides of pot until tines are just lightly coated. Gently draw tips of fork tines across surface of white chocolate to leave parallel lines of dark chocolate. Vary pattern by moving fork up and down or across fruit, creating wavy lines. Drag pointed tip of skewer perpendicular to dark-chocolate lines to create marbled pattern. (If chocolate in pots begins to harden or looks grainy, reheat over water to restore creamy consistency.)

5. Set each marbled berry on wax paper–covered cookie sheet. Repeat until cookie sheet is full. Place strawberries in refrigerator until ready to serve. The chocolate will be set in about 10 minutes.◆

MARBLED STRAWBERRY PHOTOGRAPH BY STEVEN MAYS/ SMALL STRAWBERRY PHOTOGRAPH BY DAVID HENDERSON

# Demi-Lune Style Tulips

*Create a full arrangement using half the usual number of flowers.*

Spring gardens may be filled with all kinds of flowering bulbs, but none is more elegant and sensuous than the tulip. Available in a myriad of sizes, textures, and colors, the tulip is a hardy perennial that makes a good transition to indoor displays.

One place that can always benefit from the addition of flowers is a narrow foyer or a side table in a hallway. Here, space is usually limited, and flowers arranged in the traditional bravura centerpiece style are often in the way. Arranging tulips in the demi-lune style is one solution. This arrangement acquires its name from the half-moon shape formed by its cascading flower heads. It appears full and sumptuous, even though the flowers are arranged in a half-moon configuration across the front of the arrangement, with only a relatively shallow cascade of flowers coming forward.

Our demi-lune bouquet uses forty yellow tulips, with stems measuring fourteen inches long. The silver vase was chosen to highlight the soft, curving lines of the tulips, and to provide a stable base; it is ten inches high with a six inch flared opening, which allows the stems to bend naturally in a soft arc as they mature. We also used an everyday drinking glass inside the silver vase to hold the central flowers in place. When selecting a glass for this purpose, look for one about two inches shorter than your vase and narrow enough to fit in the bottom of the vase with room for the stems around it.

If you choose a shorter-stemmed tulip, use a vase that visually balances the height of the flowers while at the same time providing enough support. One good rule of thumb regarding the proportions of the flowers to the vase is that the flowers and their

*This demi-lune arrangement will work with a variety of long-stemmed flowers, including daffodils, dahlias, or roses.*

stems can be twice as long as the vase is high, as long as the vase is stable. Visual appeal and stability of the arrangement should always determine your choice.

### DEMI-LUNE STYLE TULIPS

40 yellow French tulips
    10"-high opaque vase with
      6" flared opening
    Drinking glass,
      approximately 2" shorter
      than vase
    Oasis florist foam

*You'll also need*: florist shears or scissors; sharp knife; and large, deep container or bucket.

1. Remove any leaves that will fall below vase's water line, then make a clean, diagonal cut at bottom of each stem to provide a larger area for water absorption.

While making arrangement, store tulips in container or bucket of fresh, cool water, and remove them one at a time, as needed.

2. Using sharp knife, sculpt a block of Oasis to fit in bottom of vase. Trim height of Oasis so drinking glass rests 2" below top of vase. Insert Oasis in vase. Fill drinking glass with cool water and place inside vase, resting on Oasis.

3. From the right, insert one tulip stem into space between drinking glass and back wall of vase so end of stem rests against left side of vase. Insert second stem from left side, allowing it to cross first stem at bottom of vase so end rests against right side of vase.

4. Insert 23 more stems in same way across back of arrangement, alternating left and right sides, until a soft half-moon shape forms.

5. Trim 1" to 2" off 10 of remaining tulips; insert them one at a time into space in front of drinking glass. Allow flower heads to fall gently forward.

6. Trim stems of remaining 5 tulips by 2" to 4" and arrange inside drinking glass, letting them cascade forward as shown in photograph. Adjust tulips as necessary until half-moon effect is achieved. Fill vase three-quarters full of fresh water. ◆

## CREATING THE DEMI-LUNE ARRANGEMENT

**1.** Start by inserting one tulip stem in the space between the glass and the inside of the vase so that the stem rests against the left side of the vase. Repeat this on the opposite side, then insert 23 more stems in the same way.

**2.** Trim 1" to 2" off of 10 of the remaining tulips, and insert them in the space in front of the glass. Finish by trimming another 2" to 4" off the remaining 5 tulips and arranging those inside the drinking glass.

# Testing All-Purpose White Glues

*After we put eight general-purpose glues through their paces,
Delta's Velverette topped the list.*

We started the research for this article at two large chain stores: Pearl Paint, an art supply and paint store, and Ben Franklin's, a craft store. Between the two stores, we found more than thirty types of glue, including epoxy, hot-melt glue, rubber cement, wood glue, and white craft glue.

For testing purposes, we narrowed our search to white craft glue, because it is water-soluble for quick cleanup and relatively inexpensive. Within that category, two major types of glue exist: all-purpose glues, designed for adhering a wide range of craft materials, and material-specific glues, designed for use on one type of material (for example, fabric or paper). For this article we zeroed in on all-purpose white craft glues, because they bond a wide variety of craft materials, which makes them more versatile as part of a crafter's tool kit. We ended up with eight brands of glue.

Each of the nine brands claims it is smooth, strong, quick-drying, and dries both transparent and flexible. Each glue also claims that it is nontoxic (we didn't test this) and that it can be used successfully on most porous and nonporous materials. After several days of testing, however, we discovered that some of these claims simply aren't true. (*See* results, page 27.) We also evaluated the glue's bottle and dispenser, and tested each brand for ease of use and for controllability of the glue flow.

On the basis of our findings, we ranked Delta's Velverette as the best performer. The glue is easy to dispense, glues most materials quickly, creates a strong bond, can be used with a wide range of craft projects (especially those mixing porous and nonporous materials), doesn't run, and dries the most transparent of all the glues we tested. Velverette's only shortcoming is that it must be spread with a brush when applied to larger areas because its nib dispenses only a straight and narrow stream of glue. (There is always a trade-off in dispensers that allow such fine control.)

Our second choice is Bond's Instant Grrrip.

It has most of the same qualities as Velverette with the exception of a thinner consistency. It was also the only glue to permanently bond wood to plastic, although it didn't dry as transparent as Velverette.

Our third choice is Bond's 484: Tacky Extra Thick White Cement, with one major drawback—the dispenser. The glue comes in a syringe-style dispenser with a long tip, a cylindrical body, and a plunger. The syringe dispenses glue when the plunger is pushed down or forward toward the cylinder, moving against the column of glue and forcing it through the hole in the tip. This design makes it difficult to regulate the flow of glue. In one test we pushed down the plunger using minimal pressure; a stream of glue continued to flow for forty seconds until we stopped it by pulling back on the plunger. On the other hand, the syringe works well for its intended purpose—injecting a stream of glue into small, narrow spaces. If you're covering larger areas, you'll need to smear the glue with your finger, a cardboard spatula, or a stiff brush. (*Note:* At press time the company was considering eliminating the syringe packaging and offering the glue only in jar form.)

## Application and Bonding Properties

Most white, all-purpose craft glue comes in a conveniently small four-ounce bottle, although some are also packaged in larger sizes for bigger projects. Prices range from 71¢ for a bottle of Elmer's School Glue to $3.62 for Bond's Instant Grrrip. In all cases, we bought the smallest available quantity.

To test the consistency of each glue, we placed pea-size blobs of glue in a straight row on a piece of glossy paper. We then placed a metallic bead on each blob of glue, and turned the paper upright. As one would expect, we found that the thicker the glue's consistency, the more successfully it held the bead in place when the test materials were lifted upright. The thickest glues, Delta's Velverette and Plaid's Tacky Glue (in that order), held the bead firmly and shrunk around the bead as they dried. None of the other glues tested held the bead for more than four seconds; the glue blobs turned into narrow streams of glue, and the beads dropped off almost immediately when the paper was placed upright. Elmer's School Glue and

Elmer's Glue-All ran the quickest and had the thinnest consistencies of all the glues tested.

We also tested the glues for drying times, but found there wasn't much variation between them. Most white glues, when applied to porous materials, dry to the touch within an hour, and dry thoroughly in about a day, depending on the density of the materials being joined. In projects that use paper, fabric, or absorbent woods such as soft pine, the drying time is between two and four hours.

For denser, less absorbent woods and nonporous materials such as plastic, the white glues took at least one day to dry completely, and sometimes never dried at all. Naturally, if very quick drying time is a necessity, other types of adhesive, such as hot glue, spray adhesive, or rubber cement, are preferable. Keep in mind, however, that a quick-drying glue doesn't guarantee the strongest bond.

In general, all-purpose white glues are well-suited for porous materials or for small, nonporous items such as beads. They are not suited for situations where the bond might be exposed to water, since the glue is water soluble, or for bonds that will experience severe strain. Specialized adhesives such as silicone gel, epoxy, or wood glue are better choices for large, nonporous items where severe stresses may be encountered.

## Evaluating the Dispenser

Dispenser tops vary by bottle. Some, such as Bond's Instant Grrrip, are opened by cutting off a section of the top with scissors; others, such as Bond's 484: Tacky Extra Thick White Cement, have a precut top. Both these glues have separate plastic caps for sealing the tip, a small item that could easily be lost. More common is the standard twist cap (such as that found on Elmer's Glue-All and Delta's Sobo), which unscrews along a threaded stem and both opens the dispenser tip and regulates the flow of glue.

In general, the latter is most versatile. For starters, the top stays on the bottle. As it is unscrewed, the cap releases a progressively larger bead of glue through its top. When it is consistently squeezed, the tip will dispense a smooth bead of glue. However, twist cap dispensers do have one drawback: the tip easily clogs if glue is allowed to dry inside a slightly un-

PHOTOGRAPH BY DAVID HENDERSON

screwed cap. It is well worth the trouble to screw the cap tight and wipe its tip with a damp sponge after each use. If you don't, the glue dries inside the twist cap, jamming the threads and making it difficult to close.

The plastic bottles for all-purpose white glues are designed to be held easily in one hand (even the syringe style) and are soft enough to respond to gentle squeezing. However, because of their thick consistency, some glues require more pressure. Plaid's Tacky Glue, for instance, is so thick that care must be taken not to squeeze the bottle too hard, or the pressure builds up and too much glue comes out at once. On the other hand, Elmer's School Glue is relatively thin and comes out quickly, as does Bond's Instant Grrrip; a relatively gentle squeeze can shoot out more glue than you need.

To some extent, the flow of the glue can be controlled by the size of the opening. If a glue is very thick, you can cut more of the tapered tip off of a cutaway nozzle so that a wider stream of glue comes out, or the tip of a twist cap can be opened farther; the larger hole will allow the glue to be extruded with less pressure, and it will be easier to control. If a glue is very runny, on the other hand, cut only a small portion of the tip away or open a twist cap less; the smaller hole will increase the pressure needed to release a consistent stream of glue. Be sure to test the consistency of your glue on scrap paper before using it on your intended project. ◆

---

# Testing All-Purpose Glues

We tested each of the eight glues shown below to determine which were most effective in bonding four types of craft materials: paper (stationery weight), fabric (muslin), wood (pine molding), and plastic (strips cut from a plastic soda bottle). Half the tests involved gluing the material to itself (e.g., paper to paper), and half the tests involved gluing one material to each of the others (e.g., paper to wood, plastic, and fabric.) All the glues performed comparably in gluing fabric to fabric, wood to wood, paper to wood, fabric to paper, and fabric to wood. The real differences showed up when bonding plastic, where results were decidedly mixed. The results below are not ranked in order of preference but presented in alphabetical order by glue name. (The top three glues are shown at right.) All glues were purchased at Pearl Paint and Ben Franklin's; retail prices may vary slightly by store or region.

### TOP GLUES

 **Velverette**

 **Instant Grrrip**

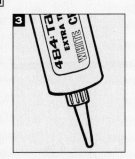 **484: Tacky Extra Thick Cement**

---

### 484: TACKY EXTRA THICK WHITE CEMENT (BOND)

**Price:** $1.78, 0.8 ounce
**Performance:** One of only two glues that didn't buckle the paper when gluing paper to paper. Formed partial bond between plastics, but took approximately 40 hours to dry thoroughly. Unable to bond plastic to wood. Dries transparent.

### ELMER'S GLUE-ALL (BORDEN)

**Price:** $1.49, 4 ounces
**Performance:** Not recommended for use on plastics. In testing, this glue was unable to form a bond between plastics, or between plastics and other materials. Does not dry transparent.

### ELMER'S SCHOOL GLUE (BORDEN)

**Price:** 71¢, 1¼ ounces
**Performance:** Not recommended for use on plastics. In testing, this glue was unable to form a bond between plastics, or between plastics and other materials. Does not dry transparent.

### INSTANT GRRRIP (BOND)

**Price:** $3.62, 4 ounces
**Performance:** Unable to form bond between plastics; glue between test strips of plastic never dried. Was able to glue plastic to other materials, however, including paper, fabric, and wood. Dries transparent.

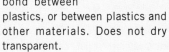

### TACKY GLUE (PLAID)

**Price:** $1.49, 4 ounces
**Performance:** Formed partial bond between plastic and plastic; dried thoroughly after about 40 hours. Unable to form bond between paper and plastic, fabric and plastic, and wood and plastic. Does not dry transparent.

### SOBO (DELTA)

**Price:** $1.04, 2 ounces
**Performance:** The only glue that didn't buckle the paper both when bonding paper to paper and paper to plastic. Formed partial bond between plastic and plastic. Worked well when gluing paper or fabric to plastic, but unable to bond wood and plastic. Dries transparent.

### STIK CRAFT CEMENT (BOND)

**Price:** $2.58, 4 ounces
**Performance:** Unable to form bond between plastic and plastic; glue never dried between test strips. When bonding paper and plastic, one of two glues that didn't buckle the paper. Formed bond between fabric and plastic, but unable to form bond between wood and plastic. Dries transparent.

### VELVERETTE (DELTA)

**Price:** $1.72, 4 ounces
**Performance:** Unable to form bond between plastic and plastic. More successful at bonding paper to plastic and fabric to plastic, but formed only a partial bond between wood and plastic. Dried the most transparent of all nine glues.

# Book Reviews

### Decorating with Paper
Donna Lang and Lucretia Robertson
Clarkson Potter, $24.95

### Paper Magic
Jane Gordon-Clark
Pantheon Books, $24

"**B**e bold! Be fearless!" say design firm partners Donna Lang and Lucretia Robertson in their introduction to *Decorating with Paper.* "Above all, don't be afraid to let your imagination fly." And theirs do as they explore every possibility for decorating with paper. In 224 pages, most in full color, the authors share simple and elaborate paper projects—many from the residential and commercial spaces they have designed. Here you'll find not only lavish floral papered rooms, traditional print rooms, and a monumental Greco-Roman sunroom complete with wallpaper pillars, but a leopard-print foyer and a "stone" wall covered with specially treated paper bags.

Beyond their innovative wall and ceiling treatments, the authors offer several unique paper-enhanced accessories. Forgoing the traditional decoupage technique, Lang and Robertson create unexpected accents—a wastepaper basket embellished with a Napoleon portrait, a faux marble tabletop fashioned from wallpaper scraps—with paper cutouts and, often, just a few coats of latex urethane. By the authors' own admission, some of their decoupage work, such as a frame decorated with reproduction monkey prints, borders on the "whimsical" and "amusing."

For those with tamer tastes, Jane Gordon-Clark's *Paper Magic* offers a more traditional approach to decorating with wallpaper. Elegant and practical, it's a complete guide to the history and how-to of wallpaper.

*Paper Magic* traces the origins of paper wall decoration from the painstaking craft of block-printing to exquisite hand-painted Chinese papers to the charming print rooms of the eigh-

teenth century. Gordon-Clark studies each wallpaper effect in detail: trompe l'oeil papers that imitate damask and moiré, pillars and plasterwork, marble and granite; pictorial effects; repeat patterns; plus borders, dadoes, and friezes. The accompanying full-color photographs (almost two hundred of them) illustrate the author's point: "Wallpaper in this book is far from a byword for some mindless utilitarian patterned cover-up."

Throughout *Paper Magic* Gordon-Clark offers practical applications for each element of wall decoration, such as using borders to alter the proportions of a room and adding formality and balance to a room with panels. But the room projects provide this book's real magic: a breezy tent-room created with striped paper and rope-and-swag borders on the walls and ceiling; a warm update on the print room featuring colored botanical prints framed with wallpaper borders; and a "Pompeian" hallway papered in earth tones, classical prints, and bold Greek key pattern borders.

More than showcases for beautiful wallpapers, both *Paper Magic* and *Decorating with Paper* promote a hands-on approach to interior design. Donna Lang and the late Lucretia Robertson (who died shortly after their book's completion) supply directions for a variety of techniques and projects, such as customizing borders and imitating inlay with cut paper. (I had excellent results with their shortcut decoupage method and found the latex urethane easy to use. Their paper fan fire screen directions also produced an elegant room accent.) Each book devotes a full chapter to technique—estimating wallpaper quantities, papering ceilings, hanging cutout decoration, and decoupage—although only *Paper Magic* includes how-to illustrations.

Both books will inspire and inform the ambitious and artistic paperhanger. They will also, as Lang and Robertson assert, forever change the way you think about wallpaper.

—*Kathleen Berlew*

### Creative Interior Design
Ward Lock, $19.95

**I**n the introduction to *Creative Interior Design,* a full-color, 384-page decorating handbook, the authors promise that you can have the home of your dreams without a team of professional designers to guide you. And they deliver.

In an exhaustive study on the use of color, the first chapters explore a variety of decorating palettes and demonstrate how the right color can "raise" a ceiling or make a room feel larger. Photographs, illustrations, and "swatches" help you choose a decorating style. A refreshing note: This book does not call for the purchase of period pieces, but encourages the reader to "take from the style as much or as little as you like." For Art Deco accessories, for instance, the authors suggest bric-a-brac, clocks, pottery, and glass that can be found "inexpensively in market stalls and in junk shops."

And what about curtains, pillows, and furniture covers? You can sew your own in Chapter 4, which is called *"Curtains and Soft Furnishings."* Well-illustrated and clearly written, the directions have one drawback—measurements are given only in metric units. When making a cushion and a café curtain, I eventually stopped trying to convert to inches and worked in centimeters. Depending on your math skills or on whether or not you own a metric tape measure, this may or may not pose a problem. (Another note about the book's British origin: some of the design schemes may look a bit dated to an American audience, but the decorating advice is still sound on this side of the Atlantic.) Brief sidebars scattered throughout the book offer simple projects, such as a dried-flower topiary, which I found easy and inexpensive to construct.

And that's the beauty of *Creative Interior Design.* It explains everything from grouping pictures to re-creating a Georgian room. Best of all, it makes a Georgian-look room, or any other style, accessible and affordable. ◆

—*Kathleen Berlew*

# Quick Decorating Ideas

You can create an intimate setting for dinner in a matter of moments by using a variety of everyday items in new and interesting ways.

**1.** Rule of thumb: When in doubt, use white. Oversized white linen napkins work well as place mats, especially when positioned diagonally. If you don't have white napkins on hand, white dish towels work equally well. Just run a hot iron over them and put them on the table.

**2.** For your napkins, stick to white as well. For an elegant touch, tie them in wire-edged ribbon with a sprig of fresh flowers or greens.

**3.** White china always works—even if it's chipped and mismatched. When in doubt, use one color to unify the scheme, such as the cobalt blue wine glasses and matching salad plates shown here.

**4.** To avoid a large bouquet in the middle of the table, opt for a small bouquet at each place setting. Cobalt blue Tŷ Nant water bottles make perfect vases, as do miniature bud vases or clean baby-food jars.

**5.** To create more unique lighting, look around for items that can double as candle holders. Old wooden textile factory spools work well, although they may need extra slender candles.

**6.** To dress up the chairs, pull a fancy white pillow sham or case over the back of each one.

**7.** The finishing touch, a five-minute center-piece with a rustic, natural appeal: Fill your three-tiered wire basket from the kitchen with fresh white eggs. ◆

**Linda Sims** is an interior designer and high school teacher.

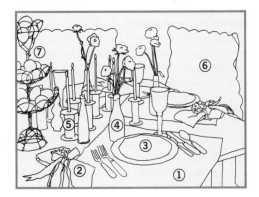

# Field Guide to Shells

**Type of shell (Latin name), regions where found, retail price:**

Source: *American Seashells, Second Edition.* R. Tucker Abbott, © 1974, Litton Educational Publishing, Inc.

1.  Green Abalone *(Haliotis fulgens)*, southern California, $7.95
2.  Junonia *(Scaphella junonia)*, southeastern United States, $9
3.  Lion's Paw *(Lyropecten nodosus)*, Florida, $30
4.  Knobbed Whelk *(Busycon carica)*, Massachusetts to northeastern Florida, $6.50
5.  Pink-Mouth Murex *(Murex erythrostomus)*, Gulf of California, $3
6.  Rooster Tail Conch *(Strombus gallus)*, southeastern Florida, $9
7.  Banded Tulip *(Fasciolaria lilium)*, North Carolina to Texas, $3
8.  Ventricose Colus *(Colus ventricosus)*, Maine, $15
9.  West Indian Fighting Conch *(Strombus pugilis)*, southeastern Florida, $9
10. Rooster Tail Conch *(Strombus gallus)*, southeastern Florida, $9
11. Northern Radix (Nigrite) Murex *(Murex nigritus)*, Gulf of California, $20
12. New England Neptune *(Neptunea lyrata decemcostata)*, Cape Cod to Nova Scotia, $15
13. Channeled Whelk *(Busycon canaliculatum)*, Cape Cod to northeastern Florida, $10.50
14. Apple Murex *(Murex pomum)*, southeastern United States, $6
15. (Common) Fig Shell *(Ficus communis)*, North Carolina to Gulf of Mexico, $1.50
16. (Western) Three-winged Murex *(Pteropurpura trialata)*, California, $6.50
17. Atlantic Bay Scallop *(Argopecten irradians)*, Maryland to Louisiana, $1
18. Pacific Thorny Oyster *(Spondylus priceps)*, Gulf of California, $30

PHOTOGRAPH BY STEVEN MAYS

# SOURCES
## AND RESOURCES

Most of the materials needed for the projects in this issue are available at your local craft supply, hardware, or paint store, florist, fabric shop, or bead and jewelry supply. The following are specific mail-order sources for particular items, arranged by project. The suggested retail prices listed here are current at press time. Contact the suppliers directly to confirm up-to-date prices and availability of products.

### Notes from Readers; pages 2–3
*Patterns for Pop-Up Cards:* To order *Perfect Pop-Up: Designing Greeting Cards the Easy Way,* you may write directly to Tom Nelson, 800 Washington Avenue N., Minneapolis, MN 55401-1129. *Make Your Own Place Cards:* Ross glue stick for 50¢, X-Acto knife for $2.65, rulers from 50¢, and selection of paper and boards from $1.20, all from Dick Blick. Large selection of rubber stamps ranging from $2 to $11.50 from Stampendous. *The Best Use of Buckram:* Selection of book cloth from $2 per yard and selection of leathers ranging from $3.75 to $19.50 per square foot from The Bookbinder's Warehouse. *The Best Napkins for Folded Designs:* 20"-square dinner napkins for $45 per set of 12 and 12¼"-square cocktail napkins for $24 per set of 12 from Williams-Sonoma. 20"-square linen napkins for $11 per set of 4 from Coming Home. *How to Make Yarn Colorfast:* Large selection of yarn from Annie's Attic and Mary Maxim. Prices start at $1.29 per skein. *Florist Foam for Unusually Shaped Vases:* Arrange-It Expanding Floral Adhesive for $7.99 per 8 ounces from Ben Franklin. *Tips on Laminating Fabric:* HeatNBond for $1.99 per yard from Ben Franklin. *Painting versus Staining Bathroom Woodwork:* Latex paint from $5 per quart, alkyd paint from $4.87 per 40-ml tube, and polyurethane from $3 per ½ pint, all from Pearl Paint. *Tips on Cleaning an Old Brass Lamp:* WD-40 for $2.69 per 9-ounce can, kraft paper from 89¢, and cotton gloves for $3.51, all from Pearl Paint. Never Dull metal polish for $3.49 per can from The Antique Hardware Store. *Earthenware versus Stoneware and Porcelain:* Variety of ceramic ware available from Pottery Barn. Prices vary.

### Quick Tips; pages 4–5
*No-Sew Bias Welting:* Bias tape from 75¢ per 5 yards, corded piping for $1.35 per 2½ yards, and Iron-on mending tape for $2.65, all from Newark Dressmaker Supply. Irons from $10 from Service Merchandise. *Joining Foam Blocks:*

8" x 4" x 3" floral foam for 87¢ from Craft King. *Helping Woody-Stemmed Flowers Last Longer:* Large selection of mum plants from $5.95 each, lilac plants from $19.95 each, and florist needle-nose scissors for $19, all from White Flower Farm. Mallets from $16.45 from Constantine's Woodworker's Catalog. Pyrex Storage-Plus Set for $29 per set of three from Williams-Sonoma. *Spattering with an Old Toothbrush:* Safety goggles for $4.67, drop cloths from 69¢, oil paint from $2.58 per 37ml tube, alkyd paint from $4.87 per 60ml tube, acrylic paint from $2.11 per 40ml tube, and latex paint from $5 per quart, all from Pearl Paint. *Antiquing New Hardware:* Winsor & Newton burnt umber oil paint for $2.90 per 37ml tube, oil glazing medium for $3.90 per 2½-ounce bottle, and selection of paintbrushes from 30¢, all from Dick Blick. *Cutting a Large Circle of Fabric:* Selection of fabric from $3.40 per yard, safety pins for $1.55 per 50 pins, fabric-marking pencil for 95¢, and thread from $1.70, all from Newark Dressmaker Supply. *Braiding Raffia:* Raffia for $1.49 per 2 ounces from Sunshine Discount Crafts. Raffia hank for $5.50 per 12 ounces and raffia ribbon for $4.65 per roll from Mills Floral Supply. *Encouraging Blooms:* Gladiolus plants from $9.95 and florist needle-nose scissors for $19 from White Flower Farm. *Nail Holder:* Decorative steel cut nails from $2.95 per 100, decorative steel brads for $3.95 per 200 from Constantine's Woodworker's Catalog. Selection of hammers from $12.20 from Frog Tool Company.

### Peach and Vine Ladder-Back Chair; pages 6–7
Ladder-back chair for $149 from Pottery Barn (catalog item #18-835-199). Liquitex acrylic paint for $3.49 per 4-ounce tube, latex paint from $5 per quart, kraft paper from 89¢, drop cloths from 69¢, sandpaper from 29¢, selection of paintbrushes from 90¢, and masking tape from $1.96 per 60 yards, all from Pearl Paint. Dressmaker's tracing paper for $1.75 per 6 sheets from Newark Dressmaker Supply. Screwdrivers from $3.50 from Constantine's Woodworker's Catalog.

### How to Create a Faux Suede Finish; pages 8–10
Benjamin Moore alkyd paint for approximately $21 per gallon and Benjamin Moore glaze for approximately $6.50 per quart (contact your local retailer to confirm prices and availability). Odorless paint thinner for $3.30 per quart, linseed oil for $12.50 per quart, Cubby Ware plastic containers for $2.30 per

package of 10, paintbrushes from 30¢, 36"-wide cheesecloth for $2.90 per 5 yards, and Economy artist's tape from $2.40 per 60 yards, all from Dick Blick. Drop cloths from 69¢, 9" paint roller from $1.10, paint roller extensions from $3, and paint roller trays from $1.89, all from Pearl Paint. Rubber gloves for $1.23 per 5 pairs, wood craft sticks for $3.55 per 1,000 pieces, and Laser scissors from $6.06, all from Craft King. Tape measure for $1.25 from Newark Dressmaker Supply.

### Seashell Candles; page 11
Large selection of shells from $1 from Shell Cellar. Pourette wax for $1.01 per pound, square braided wick for 50¢ per 3 yards, lead core wick from 65¢ per 2 yards, Pourette scent for $2.10 per ½ ounce, and a variety of other candle-making supplies from Pourette Candle Making Supplies. Beeswax for $8 per pound, selection of candle scents for $2 per bottle, candlewicks from 12¢ per yard, wick bases for 20¢ per dozen, needle-nose pliers for $8.50, tweezers for $5.85, and Bond glue for $1.80 per 1 ounce, all from Earth Guild. Scissors from $6.06, selection of pearls from 36¢ per package, and jute twine from $1.29 per 6 ounces, all from Craft King. Kraft paper from 89¢ per roll from Pearl Paint. Stainless steel measuring spoons for $9, Pyrex Counter Savers for $28 per set of 2, and mitt and pot holder set for $4.99, all from Williams-Sonoma.

### Three-Panel Folding Screen; pages 12–15
Schumacher wallpaper, prices vary by retailer. (Use 800 number to locate nearest retailer.) Victorian wallpaper from $39 to $59 per roll from Bradbury and Bradbury. Welting cord from $17.50 per 500 yards, fray check for $2.05 per ⅗-ounce bottle, scissors from $6.85, and 36" yardstick for $2.50, all from Atlantic Thread and Supply. 3" nonmortise door hinges for $2.10 per pair, screwdrivers from $3.50, precision miter box for $29.95, 14" backsaw for $14.95, finishing nails from $2.95 per 100, wood screws from $3.50 per 100, 180-grit sandpaper for $3.95 per pack of 10 sheets, sanding block for $4.45, Lustregild bright gold enamel for $5.95 per ½ pint, and selection of ball feet and carpet glides from $1.45, all from Constantine's Woodworker's Catalog. Latex paint from $5 per quart, spackling compound for $3 per quart, kraft paper from 89¢ per roll, Bond's 484 tacky glue for $2.05 per 4 ounces, light-duty staple gun for $12.21 and 5⁵⁄₁₆" staples for $1.86, 3" paint rollers for $1.69, paint trays from $1.29, wallpaper paste

for $3 per quart, and brayers from $4, all from Pearl Paint. Surgrip Utility metal retractable knife for $4.95, foam brushes from 45¢, sponges from $2.75, and 1"-wide gesso brush for $1.95, all from Co-op Artist's Materials.

### Quick Transfer Pillows; pages 16–17
Sulky gold thread for $2.90, selection of other thread from $1.70 per 350 yards, scissors from $10.75, hand sewing needles from 75¢, tape measure for $1.25, C-thru plastic ruler for $4, tassel fringe for $3.95 per 4 yards, and seam ripper for 85¢, all from Newark Dressmaker Supply. Selection of pillow cases from $19 from Coming Home. Delta transfer medium for $4.12 per 12 ounces and dowels from 20¢ from Pearl Paint. Foam brushes from 45¢, sponges from $2.75, 9" x 12" bright white sulphite paper for $6.33 per 500 sheets, and artist's tape from $5.88 per 60 yards, all from Co-op Artist's Materials.

### Victorian Frame Bow; pages 18–19
Selection of woven fabrics from $3.23 per yard from Fiber Naturals. Thread from $1.70 per 350 yards, upholstery plastic rings for 85¢ per 24, Olfa rotary cutter for $8.45 and guide for $3.70, Olfa cutting mat for $18.95, scissors from $10.75, hand sewing needles from 75¢, steel dressmaker pins for $1.75 per 350, fabric-marking pencil for 95¢, and C-thru plastic ruler for $4, all from Newark Dressmaker Supply. Selection of hammers from $12.20 from Frog Tool Company. Selection of sewing machines from $55 and irons from $10 from Service Merchandise.

### The Best Way to Dry Roses; pages 20–21
Silica gel for $3.91 per quart, Floratape for $1.61 per 60 yards, wood floral picks for 89¢ per 60 pieces, cubbyware for $1.75 per 12 pieces, and rubber gloves for $1.23 per 5 pairs, all from Craft King. Roses for $35 per half dozen from Village Flowers. Felco pruning shears for $39.95 from White Flower Farm. Safety goggles for $1.95, 3M nontoxic particle mask for $13.90 per box of 50, Scotch tape from $2.15, and paintbrushes from 40¢, all from Dick Blick.

### Silk Ribbon Embroidery; pages 22–23
Size 12 Pearl cotton balls for $1.59 per 141 yards and embroidery needles for 75¢ per package of 15 from DMC (Herrschners Inc.). 2mm and 4mm silk ribbon floss for $1.60 per 5 yards, 7mm silk ribbon floss for $3.15 per 5 yards, and embroidery needles for $2.49 per

package of 25, all from YLI. One hundred percent polyester, 4 mm Silk-Ease embroidery ribbon for $1.69 per 5 yards from C.M. Offray & Son, Inc.

### Marbled Chocolate Strawberries; page 24
Chromed steel, 8½"-long magic whisk for $5.50, half-sheet baking pan for $14, 13" x 34" reversible super parchment for $10, Rosti 1-2-3 bowl for $12.50, Pyrex measuring cup set for $16 per set of 3, matching mitt and potholder for $4.99, All-Clad double boiler insert for $36, cook's fork for $6, and 11½"-long bamboo skewers for $5 per set of 2, all from Williams-Sonoma.

### Demi-Lune Style Tulips; page 25
Tulips for $18 per dozen and 3" x 7" x 3" Oasis floral foam for $2.50 from Village Flowers. Selection of vases in a variety of shapes and sizes from Pottery Barn. Florist buckets from $29, florist shears for $27, and selection of vases from $14, all from Gardeners Eden.

### Testing All-Purpose White Glues; pages 26–27
All glues purchased at Pearl Paint and Ben Franklin's. Selection of glues also available from Craft King, Dick Blick, and Ott's Discount Art Supply. Prices range from 71¢ to $2.58.

### Book Reviews; page 28
*Paper Magic* and *Decorating with Paper* available through Random House. *Creative Interior Design* available at Barnes and Noble stores.

### Quick Decorating Ideas; page 29
White linen napkins for $11 per set of 4, white linen tablecloths from $21, and selection of pillow cases from $19, all from Coming Home. White porcelain oval plates for $36 per set of 6 from Williams-Sonoma. Irons from $10 from Service Merchandise. Turn-of-the-century wooden spool candleholders from $3 from Artifacts. Selection of wire-edged ribbon from $1.20 per yard from Newark Dressmaker Supply. Blue Delft bud vase for $9.95, cobalt wine glasses for $9.95 each, cobalt dinner plates for $59.95 per set of 4, cobalt dessert plates for $44.95, two-tiered wire basket rack for $31.95, and 10" white taper candles for $7.50 per set of 6, all from Crate and Barrel.

### Field Guide to Shells; page 30
All shells purchased from Shell Cellar. Contact the store directly to confirm up-to-date prices and availability of shells.

### Quick Projects; page 33
*Leaf and Tassel:* Silver elastic cord for 88¢ per 90", 4½" embroidery scissors for $6.06, and fancy sequin leaves for 45¢ per 60, all from Craft King. Tassel fringe for $2.65 per 4 yards from Home-Sew. *"Gucci" Stripe with Coat of Arms:* Large selection of stamped brass embellishments from 20¢ from Creative Beginnings. Low temper mini glue gun for $3.19 and mini glue sticks for $1.65 per 25 from Craft King. *Dried Orange Slice and Cinnamon Stick with Raffia Tie:* 4½" embroidery scissors for $6.06, white elastic cord for 88¢ per 90", 3" cinnamon sticks for $1.75 per ¼ pound, and raffia straw satin for 96¢ per 24-yard skein, all from Craft King. Natural dried orange slices for $5.95 per 10 from Newark Dressmaker Supply. *Gold Sun Ornament with Sheer Ribbon:* 4½" embroidery scissors for $6.06, gold elastic cord for 88¢ per 90", and black satin ribbon for $1.75 per 30 yards, all from Craft King. Large selection of stamped brass embellishments from 20¢ from Creative Beginnings. *Golden Ribbon:* Excel knife for $1.65 and 18" stainless steel ruler for $6.99 from Jerry's Artarama. Multipurpose scissors for $7.41, low temper mini glue gun for $3.19 and mini glue sticks for $1.65 per 25, all from Craft King. Large selection of stamped brass embellishments from 20¢ from Creative Beginnings. Gold metallic ribbon from $1.60 per 5 yards from Newark Dressmaker Supply. *Gold Cord and Tassels:* Gold metallic elastic cord for $1.80 per 5 yards, embroidery scissors for $13.85, and cotton tassel fringe for $3.95 per 4 yards, all from Newark Dressmaker Supply.

### Natural Floral China; back cover
Bern clear 11" buffet plates for $5.99 each from Mikasa Factory Store. Sprigs of ivy from 50¢ each, nigella stems from $1.50 each, plox stems from $3.50 each, and white hydrangea stems from $5 each from Village Flowers.

---

The following companies are mentioned in the listings above. Contact each individually for a price list or catalog.

**Annie's Attic,** 1 Annie Lane, Box 212B, Big Sandy, TX 75755; 800-582-6643
**The Antique Hardware and Home Store,** 1-C Matthews Court, Hilton Head Island, SC 29926; 800-422-9982
**Artifacts,** 1006 N. Mallard, Palestine, TX 75801; 800-678-4178
**Atlanta Thread and Supply,** 695 Red Oak Road, Stockbridge, GA 30281; 800- 847-1001
**Barnes and Noble,** 105 5th Avenue, New York, NY 10003; 212-633-3300
**Ben Franklin Retail Stores, Inc.,**

500 East N. Avenue, Carol Stream, IL 60188; 708-462-6100
**Benjamin Moore,** 51 Chestnut Ridge Road, Montvale, NJ 07645; 800-826-2623
**The Bookbinder's Warehouse,** 31 Division Street, Keyport, NJ 07735; 908-264-0306
**Bradbury and Bradbury,** P.O. Box 155, Benicia, CA 94510; 707-746-1900
**The Center for Book Arts,** 626 Broadway, 5th Floor, New York, NY 10012; 212-460-9768
**C.M. Offray & Son, Inc.,** Route 24, Box 601, Chester, NJ 07930-0601; 908-879-4700
**Coming Home,** 1 Land's End Lane, Dodgeville, WI 53595; 800-345-3696
**Constantine's Woodworker's Catalog,** 2050 Eastchester Road, Bronx, NY 10461-2297; 800-223-8087
**Co-op Artists' Materials,** P.O. Box 53097, Atlanta, GA 30355; 800-877-3242
**Convenience Products,** 866 Horan Drive, Fenton, MO 63026-2416; 800-325-6180
**Craft King Discount Craft Supply,** P.O. Box 53097, Lakeland, FL 33804; 800-769-9494
**Crate and Barrel,** P.O. Box 9059, Wheeling, IL 60090-9059; 800-323-5461
**Creative Craft House,** P.O. Box 2567, Bullhead City, AZ 86430; 602-754-3300
**Dick Blick,** P.O. Box 1267, Galesburg, IL 61402-1267; 800-447-8192
**Earth Guild,** 33 Haywood Street, Asheville, NC 28801; 800-327-8448
**Fiber Naturals,** 710 Daniel Shays Highway, New Salem, MA 01355; 800-342-3707.
**Frog Tool Company,** P.O. Box 8325, Chicago, IL 60680-8325; 800-648-1270
**Gardeners Eden,** P.O. Box 7303, San Francisco, CA 94120-7307; 800-822-9600
**Herrschners Inc.,** 2800 Hoover Road, Stevens Point, WI 54492-0001; 800-441-0838
**Home-Sew,** P.O. Box 4099, Bethlehem, PA 18018-0099; 610-867-3833
**Jerry's Artarama,** P.O. Box 1105, New Hyde Park, New York, NY 11040; 800-U-ARTIST
**Mary Maxim,** 2001 Holland Avenue, P.O. Box 5019, Port Huron, MI 48061-5019; 800-962-9504
**Mikasa Factory Store,** 25 Enterprise Avenue, Secaucus, NJ 07094; 201-867-3517
**Mills Floral Supply,** 4550 Peachtree Lakes Drive, Duluth, GA 30136; 800-762-7939
**Newark Dressmaker Supply,** 6473 Ruch Road, P.O. Box 20730, Lehigh Valley,

PA 18002-0730; 800-736-6783
**Ott's Discount Art Supply,** 102 Hungate Drive, Grenville, NC 27858; 800-356-3289
**The Patchworks,** 6676 Amsterdam Road, Amsterdam, MT 59741-8315; 406-282-7218
**Pearl Paint,** 308 Canal Street, New York, NY 10013; 800-221-6845
**Random House,** Order Department, 400 Hahn Road, Westminster, MD 21157; 800-733-3000, ext. 3000
**Schumacher,** 79 Madison Avenue, New York, NY 10016; 800-332-3384
**Service Merchandise,** P.O. Box 25130, Nashville, TN 37202-5130; 800-251-1212
**Shell Cellar,** South Street Seaport, 89 South Street, New York, NY 10038; 212-962-1076
**Stampendous,** 1357 South Lewis Street, Anaheim, CA 92805; 800-869-0474
**Sunshine Discount Crafts,** P.O. Box 301, Largo, FL 34649-0301; 813-538-2878
**Sweet Celebrations,** 7009 Washington Avenue S., Edina, MN 55439; 800-480-2505
**Village Flowers,** 297 Main Street, Huntington, NY 11743; 516-427-0996
**White Flower Farm,** P.O. Box 50, Litchfield, CT 06759-0050; 203-496-9600
**Williams-Sonoma,** P.O. Box 7456, San Francisco, CA 94120-7456; 800-541-2233
**YLI,** P.O. Box 109, Provo, UT 84603-0109; 800-854-1932 ◆

---

The Dried Rose Bouquet featured on the back cover of the July/August 1994 issue of *Handcraft Illustrated* is available as a kit including all the necessary materials. The cost is $19.95 plus $1.50 shipping and handling. To order the kit, send a check or money order for $21.45, or send your credit card number (we accept American Express, VISA, and Mastercard), the expiration date, and an authorized signature to: Rose Kit, *Handcraft Illustrated,* P.O. Box 509, Brookline Village, MA 02147-0529.

# Quick Projects

**Leaf and Tassel**

**Gold Sun Ornament with Sheer Ribbon**

G ift bags, which are available in a wide range of colors, sizes, and prices, are perfect wraps for small hostess, brunch, or wedding gifts. To make yours unique, consider adding your own simple gift bag closures using a minimum of materials.

**Leaf and Tassel**—Remove cord handles from bag. If bag does not have handles, use point of manicure scissors to make two ⅛"-diameter holes through bag from front to back. Place gift in bag. Fold ½ yard of silver string elastic in half to form loop, and push folded end of loop through holes on right, across back of bag, and return through holes on left. Pull bag shut by pulling loose ends of elastic through looped end. Tie beaded leaf and gold tassel to ends of elastic.

**"Gucci" Stripe with Coat of Arms**—Select striped bag with knotted cord handles. Place gift in bag. Through mouth of bag, pull ends of cords into bag so handles are tight on outside. Tie ends that are diagonal from each other together in double knots. Hot-glue a stamped brass coat of arms to top center of bag.

**Dried Orange Slice with Raffia Tie**—Use point of manicure scissors to make ⅛"-diameter hole through front and back of bag as well as hole in center of dried orange slice. Place gift in bag. Tie ends of 9" white elastic string together to form loop. Pull end of elastic loop farthest from knot through hole in orange slice, then stick 3" cinnamon stick through loop to prevent it from pulling back through orange slice. Pull knotted end of elastic loop through holes, ending with knot at back of bag and pulling orange slice flat against front of bag. Stretch elastic from back of bag up and over orange slice at front of bag. Tie bow made of three or four 20" strands of raffia around cinnamon stick.

**Gold Sun Ornament with Sheer Ribbon**—Use point of manicure scissors to make ⅛"-diameter hole through front and back of bag. Tie ends of 4" string of gold elastic together to make loop. Place gift in bag. Pull elastic loop through both sets of holes, securing knotted end at back of bag. Cut length of sheer, black ribbon three and one-half times height of bag. Thread ribbon down through elastic loop on front of bag, around bottom of bag, and up through knotted end of elastic at back. Tie ends of ribbon together in knot on top of bag and cut ends into V shape. Loop elastic at front of bag over rays of stamped sun ornament.

**Golden Ribbon**—Remove handles from tall, narrow bag. Open bag and flatten bottom. Make 3" cuts down left and right sides of bag, cutting along front folds. Cut straight across front of bag and across folds on sides, leaving a flap at the back. Flatten bag, and trim flap with scissors into U shape. Fold flap over front of bag. Use metal straightedge and X-Acto knife to cut ½"-wide slit centered 1" from bottom of flap, cutting through all layers of bag. Fold ½ yard of ½"-wide gold ribbon in half and hot glue ends just below flap on front of bag. Hot glue brass stamping over ends of ribbon. Place gift in bag, then pull loop of ribbon through slit and over top of bag to front.

**Gold Cord and Tassels**—Remove handles from tall, narrow bag. Open bag and flatten bottom. Make 3" cuts down left and right sides of bag, cutting along front folds. Cut straight across front of bag and across folds on sides, leaving a 3" to 4" back flap. If bag does not have holes for handles, use point of manicure scissors to make two ⅛"-diameter holes through bag, ¼" from cut edge of flap. Cut two lengths of twisted gold string, each about two and one-quarter times the height of bag. Thread one length through each hole and knot end at back of flap to secure. Attach tassel to other end of each string. Place gift in bag, then secure closed by pulling strings under bottom of bag, crisscrossing in front, and tucking tassels around front string. ◆

**"Gucci" Stripe with Coat of Arms**

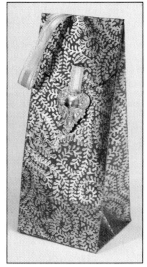

**Golden Ribbon**

**Dried Orange Slice with Raffia Tie**

**Gold Cord and Tassels**

# Natural Floral China

**T**o create your own floral china patterns, arrange twelve ivy leaves in a circular, clock-face pattern on an 11"-diameter clear glass plate. Place a blue nigella flower at the twelve-, four-, and eight-o'clock positions, then fill in the open spaces on the rim with pink phlox blossoms and single petals from florets of white hydrangeas. To make the flowers and leaves lie flat, press them down with a fingernail, breaking the stems or veins if necessary, then stack a second clear glass plate on the decorated plate to hold the flowers in place. *Note: These flowers are for decoration only, and are not meant to be eaten.*

NUMBER EIGHT

AUGUST 1995

# Handcraft
## ILLUSTRATED

### Secrets of Color-Blended Stenciling
*Create a Hand-Painted Look in 3 Easy Steps*

### Fabulous Cosmos Bouquets
*Expert Tips for Growing This Classic Annual*

### Cottage Slipcover
*Five Cotton Dishtowels Serve as Fabric*

### Foolproof Sponged Wall Finishes
*Build Texture in Minutes Using a Sponge and Paint*

#### ALSO

Dried Flower Window Valance

The Best Lightweight Shears for Home Decorating

*Transform a $5 Frame into a Beautiful Heirloom Using Roses from Your Garden*

$4.00 U.S./$4.95 CANADA

# Contents

## 2
### NOTES FROM READERS
Quilt designs from the '30s; finding specialty rubber stamps; rotary cutters for arthritis sufferers.

## 4
### QUICK TIPS
Bleaching pinecones; using household items as clamps; removing hot glue.

## 6
### FABULOUS FARMSTAND BOUQUETS
Learn to grow your own cosmos, then choose from one of three quick and easy arrangements.

## 8
### CARVED FISH DECOY
Carve a folk-art fish using a few basic woodworking tools.

## 11
### QUICK CHARLOTTE ROYALE
Make this easy dessert with two loaves of white bread and a jar of preserves.

## 12
### COLOR-BLENDED STENCILING
Learn the secret of creating a hand-painted look using stencils.

## 16
### ROSE PETAL FRAME
Make this delicate frame in two easy steps.

## 18
### BIRD'S-EYE MAPLE FAUX FINISH
Create the look of this rare and beautiful wood in six stages.

## 22
### LOW-SEW SLIPCOVER
Stitch up this slip-on chair cover in under an hour using dishtowels.

## 23
### TESTING LIGHTWEIGHT DRESSMAKER'S SHEARS
A pair of KAI's eight-inch models take the gold in comfort, performance, and precision.

## 26
### DRIED FLOWER VALANCE
Assemble this unique window treatment in minutes using dried flowers and an ordinary curtain rod.

## 28
### FOOLPROOF SPONGED WALL FINISHES
Give your walls exciting visual texture with a household or sea sponge and two shades of latex paint.

## 31
### FIELD GUIDE TO HOME-GROWN DRIED FLOWERS
With one or two seed packets and a small plot of land, you can easily grow and dry any of these flowers yourself.

## 32
### SOURCES AND RESOURCES
Mail-order sources for materials used throughout this issue.

## 33
### QUICK PROJECTS
Perk up your pillowcases in a matter of minutes using lace, ribbon, or cord.

*Back Cover*
**FROZEN FLORAL ICE BUCKET**
Make a beautiful frozen bucket that will last for hours using fresh flowers. Illustration by Dan Brown.

*Cover Photograph by Steven Mays*

**Learn the secrets of color-blended stenciling, page 12**

**Bird's-eye maple chest, page 18**

**Carve your own decoy, page 8**

# Handcraft
### ILLUSTRATED

EDITOR
**Carol Endler Sterbenz**

EXECUTIVE EDITOR
**Barbara Bourassa**

SENIOR EDITOR
**Michio Ryan**

MANAGING EDITOR
**Maura Lyons**

ASSISTANT MANAGING EDITOR
**Tricia O'Brien**

DIRECTIONS EDITOR
**Candie Frankel**

EDITORIAL ASSISTANT
**Kim N. Russello**

COPY EDITOR
**Gary Pfitzer**

DESIGNER
**Lisa Puccio**

SPECIAL PROJECTS DESIGNER
**Amy Klee**

PHOTO STYLIST
**Sylvia Lachter**

❧

PUBLISHER AND FOUNDER
**Christopher Kimball**

EDITORIAL CONSULTANT
**Raymond Waites**

MARKETING DIRECTOR
**Adrienne Kimball**

CIRCULATION DIRECTOR
**Elaine Repucci**

ASS'T CIRCULATION MANAGER
**Jennifer L. Keene**

CIRCULATION COORDINATOR
**Jonathan Venier**

CIRCULATION ASSISTANT
**C. Maria Pannozzo**

PRODUCTION DIRECTOR
**James McCormack**

PRODUCTION ASSISTANTS
**Sheila Datz**
**Pamela Slattery**

ASSISTANT COMPUTER ADMINISTRATOR
**Matt Frigo**

PRODUCTION ARTIST
**Kevin Moeller**

❧

V.P./GENERAL MANAGER
**Jeffrey Feingold**

CONTROLLER
**Lisa A. Carullo**

ACCOUNTING ASSISTANT
**Mandy Shito**

OFFICE MANAGER
**Jenny Thornbury**

OFFICE ASSISTANT
**Sarah Chung**

*Handcraft Illustrated* (ISSN 1072-0529) is published bi-monthly by Boston Common Press Limited Partners, 17 Station Street, P.O. Box 509, Brookline, MA 02147-0509. Copyright 1995 Boston Common Press Limited Partners. Second-class postage paid in Boston, MA, and additional mailing offices, USPS #012487. For list rental information, please contact Direct Media, 200 Pemberwick Rd., Greenwich, CT 06830; 203-532-1000. Editorial office: 17 Station Street, P.O. Box 509, Brookline, MA 02147-0509; (617) 232-1000, FAX (617) 232-1572. Editorial contributions should be sent to: Editor, *Handcraft Illustrated*, P.O. Box 509, Brookline, MA 02147-0509. We cannot assume responsibility for manuscripts submitted to us. Submissions will be returned only if accompanied by a large, self-addressed stamped envelope. Subscription rates: $24.95 for one year; $45 for two years; $65 for three years. (Canada: add $3 per year; all other foreign add $12 per year.) Postmaster: Send all new orders, subscription inquiries, and change of address notices to *Handcraft Illustrated*, P.O. Box 51383, Boulder, CO 80322-1383. Single copies: $4 in U.S., $4.95 in Canada and foreign. Back issues available for $5 each. PRINTED IN THE U.S.A.

Rather than put ™ in every occurrence of trademarked names, we state that we are using the names only and in an editorial fashion and to the benefit of the trademark owner, with no intention of infringment of the trademark.

**Note to Readers:** Every effort has been made to present the information in this publication in a clear, complete, and accurate manner. It is important that all instructions are followed carefully, as failure to do so could result in injury. Boston Common Press Limited Partners, the editors, and the authors disclaim any and all liability resulting therefrom.

## FROM THE EDITOR

I HAVE A ROOM OF MY OWN NOW—A PRIVATE space filled with all my favorite stuff, and one in which I can work and think and be inspired. This hasn't always been the case, however. When I was a child, I not only shared a bedroom with my two sisters, I also shared a work space in a converted nursery that we unimaginatively called "the little room."

The little room had long been emptied of cribs and beds when my parents moved in a long pine table, three chairs, three lamps, and an old wooden radio with a glowing amber dial, four knobs, and a top lid that opened up to reveal a flocked turntable for 78 rpm records.

The radio was pretty important to me back then because it identified that strategic third of work space on the long table—the section reserved for my oldest sister, Joan. Nancy sat at the far right end of the table, I sat in the middle, and Joan sat, well, next to the radio. By virtue of this arrangement, Joan got to control which radio stations we listened to.

Her power, however, was of a provisional sort based on a couple simple house rules: #1—No singing at the table; and #2—No radio on during homework. Since my sisters and I spent a good deal of time in the little room, Joan seemed pretty powerful, or as powerful as circumstances allowed.

As careful as we were to follow the house rules, however, we sometimes found our way around them, especially on Saturdays when my parents were outside working in the garden or doing errands and we were inside trying to do our homework. When the coast was deemed clear, we played the radio and sang, all the time one of us keeping an ear tuned for any strange sound that might alert us to our parents' return. When warned, Joan would turn off the radio, camouflaging the "snap" of the knob with a short cough for insurance.

As time went along, we got more daring, requiring only that our parents be out of earshot before turning on the radio. With the deftness of a safecracker, Joan could, in one coordinated motion, turn on the radio (no coughing by this time), sweep the plastic arrow across the channel dial with one knob, and modulate the volume of the music with another knob. Soon faint but discernible strains of Elvis Presley or Brenda Lee would hang in the room like gossamer veils, and we found ourselves quietly singing the tunes.

From time to time, we left all caution behind, and our humming turned to singing with abandon, complete with three-part harmony. Lost in the melody and having a fine time, we wouldn't hear my father's steps until it was too late and he was standing right behind us. He would simply lean over, unplug the radio, and carry it out of the room. We were left staring at each other, silently accusing the other of singing too loud.

Despite the seemingly serious nature of that little room, we enjoyed the camaraderie it fostered, while at the same time we each carried forward a wish for a room of our own. And, not unpredictably, each of us got one. My first "workroom" was only a kitchen table placed in the midst of the cacophony of family life, but that was followed by a drafting table and shelf space tucked into the eave of an old beach house near the bay. Eventually, as an adult I ended up with an entire room of my own in a hundred-year-old Victorian house with a wraparound porch. My room was exactly as I had hoped it would be.

> I set about filling my room both with items that I needed and ones that compelled and inspired me.

I set about filling my room both with items that I needed and ones that compelled and inspired me: stacks of fabric piled neatly on shelves, vine baskets holding practically every magazine I had ever read, and boxes and boxes of supplies. Photos of the kids and friends and pets blotched the bulletin board, while sketches and pictures torn hastily from magazines littered almost every other unused space on the wall. And, of course, the one thing saved from my first workroom—the old wooden radio with the amber dial.

The amber dial has been dark a very long time, as the radio stopped working long ago, but I keep the radio anyway. Nowadays, in an even newer workroom, it sits next to a sleek, molded plastic player with a stack of CDs leaning precariously to one side. I still work in silence during the incubation stage of designing, but then things change. I press a few buttons and smile as I hear the strains of Brenda Lee and Elvis Presley, and the work seems to flow so easily. In my own room, I sing out loud every time I hear them.

# Notes
## FROM READERS

### Preventing Damage from Pliers

Is there a way to prevent damage to items when using pliers?

WENDY ARMSTRONG
AMHERST, MA

Electrical shrink-fit tubing, available at most electrical supply stores, can be fitted to the jaws of pliers and tweezers to prevent such damage. Just buy tubing that is slightly larger than the jaws of the tool in question. To affix the tubing to the tool, cut off a three-quarter-inch piece, slide it over the jaws, then secure it by heating it gently for a few seconds with a blow dryer. The tubing can be cut off should removal become necessary.

### Quilt Designs from the 1930s

I've been looking for a specific quilting book on designs from the thirties entitled *My Mother's Quilts*, but I can't find it. The book has some really unusual patterns from that time. Can you help?

ELAINE STERLING
MOUNT PLEASANT, NY

*My Mother's Quilts* has been reprinted by Dover Publications of Mineola, New York, as *Quilt Designs from the Thirties* (author Sara Nephew). Your local sewing shop may stock it or be able to order it for you. You can also order it directly from Dover Publications by writing or calling the company at 31 East 2nd Street, Mineola, NY 11501; 516-294-7000.

### What Is Bakelite?

What is Bakelite, and when was it first made?

NICOLE KUNZ
PASADENA, CA

Bakelite, developed in 1907 by chemist Leo Baekeland in Yonkers, New York, was the first synthetic plastic that didn't melt or catch fire. It was used to fashion a wide variety of objects, from napkin rings and flatware to jewelry. When Bakelite was first manufactured, it was made to resemble expen-sive natural materials, such as ivory, bone, and tortoiseshell, but the Art Deco era influenced designers to create more offbeat designs in unique shapes and vibrant colors, including red, orange, ochre, black, and green.

Heat- and corrosion-resistant, Bakelite was thought to be tough but attractive—a perfect partner for another early-twen-tieth-century invention, stainless steel. But this excitement was short-lived: Bakelite's popular-ity for cutlery handles began to slip away with the advent of the dishwasher, as the material lost its vibrance under the machine's extreme hot water and drying temperatures. Today, Bakelite is quite collectible, although it is not yet antique.

### Finding Specialty Rubber Stamps

I'd like to find a rubber stamp company that offers a good selec-tion of fairy and fairylike images. All I seem able to find in stores is the odd image here and there.

GRACE SCHROEDER
WAYZATA, MN

You're in luck. Maine Street Stamps in Kingfield, Maine, offers a wonderful selection of fairy images as well as period fashion images and antiques, including Victorian, Edwardian, and Art Deco. Call or write for a catalog: Maine Street Stamps, P.O. Box 14, Kingfield, ME 04947; 207-265-2500.

Another option is to have your own stamp made, although the cost is $15 to $20 versus $2 to $5 for a stamp purchased in a store. Look through the many clip art books available at your local art supply store to find appealing images (graphic designers use these sources all the time), then contact a sta-tioner, offset printer, or rubber stamp store in your area to reproduce the image on a stamp for you. This is within legal bounds as long as you use the stamps for personal, not com-mercial, purposes. (If the stamps are used for commercial purpos-es, you may violate a copyright.)

### Answers to Your Woodworking Questions

Do have any recommended sources for answering wood-working-related questions?

PAUL VOLLMER
PALATINE, IL

Shopsmith, Inc., of Dayton, Ohio, is an organization dedi-cated to answering questions about woodworking—and what queries they cannot answer immediately, they will research for you. Questions may be sub-mitted by mail or phone to Shopsmith, Inc., 6640 Poe Avenue, Dayton, OH 45414; 800-543-7586.

### Using Rubber for Candlemaking Molds

What special precautions do I have to take if I use rubber molds for candlemaking?

JUSTINE PEARL
GREENSBORO, NC

Virtually any material that can withstand the heat of melted wax can be used as a candle mold. Wax poured into card-board or rubber should be between 150 and 165 degrees, while wax poured into metal can be between 190 and 200 degrees.

Before filling any mold with wax, coat the inside of the mold with a light layer of silicone spray to allow easy removal of the candle. Molds that are wider at the top than at the base also facilitate candle removal. If you opt for a rubber mold, never use stearine in the candle's wax, as this substance rots rubber. Because stearine (which acts to bind wax and dye) should not be used with rubber, you'll need to melt the wax and the dye together in these instances, as opposed to the usual sequence of melting the wax, dissolving the stearine, and then adding the dye. Smearing the outside of the mold with dishwashing liq-uid will make it more pliable and help you peel it away from the set candle.

### The Best Markers for Coloring

Can you recommend a marker with a good-quality tip for col-oring invitations and the like?

SANDY MYERS
BILLINGS, MT

Marvy, Tombo, and Staedtler all produce fine-quality markers. For coloring we recommend the Marvy LePlume II, the Tombo ABT, and the Staedtler Mars Graphic 3000. All three are dou-ble-pointed pens: One end of the pen contains a very fine tip for detail work, while the other end contains a brushlike tip, which is perfect for filling in large areas or creating a watercolor-like effect. The pens, available in a wide range of colors, can be found at most art supply stores.

### Rotary Cutters for Arthritis Sufferers

I am a quilter who suffers from mild arthritis. Could you recom-mend a rotary cutter that might help take some of the cutting pressure off my hand?

MYLENE LEONARD
AURORA, CO

Try the Fiskars Rotary Cutter, which won a 1994 GOLD Industrial Design Excellence Award (IDEA) from the Industrial Designers Society of America. The first ergonomi-cally designed cutter on the market, the product features contoured handles that make cutting more comfortable and reduce fatigue by distributing cutting pressure over the larger area of your hand. The rounded handle also enables you to apply downward pressure without any sharp point of contact on your hand. Your local sewing or quilting shop should carry the cutter, but if you find it difficult to locate, contact Fiskars Inc. at 7811 West Stewart Avenue, P.O. Box 8027, Wausau, WI 54402-8027; 715-842-2091.

## Storing Etched-Glass Plates

I recently acquired a beautiful set of antique etched-glass dinner plates. What's the best way to store them? I'm afraid of scratching them.

ANNA DE BETHUNE
ST. LOUIS, MO

Many housewares stores sell ready-made felt or quilted disks designed to be sandwiched between plates. If you can't find disks of this sort, it is simple enough to buy sturdy felt and cut circles of the appropriate size yourself.

## Disposing of Flammable Rags

What is the proper way to dispose of rags that have been used with mineral spirits?

LESLIE ARTIN
CHATTANOOGA, TN

Never put used oil-based-paint- or solvent-saturated rags into a sealed plastic bag, as they have been known to spontaneously combust. Any rag that has been soaked in a solvent (i.e., mineral spirits, denatured alcohol, or paint thinner), linseed oil, or water-based, furniture-finish stripper should be spread out flat or hung from a clothesline. The drying process should take place in a well-ventilated area and out of reach of children, pets, and any heat source so the solvent can evaporate safely and completely. Once the rag is dry, you can dispose of it with your household garbage. In the case of lead-based solvents (or any questionable substance, for that matter), contact your local sanitation

department for detailed instructions regarding disposal.

## The Difference between Wall and Floor Tile

What is the difference between ceramic wall and floor tile?

JACK POLLARD
WICHITA, KS

Ceramic floor tiles are harder and typically have less glaze than wall tiles. That means you can use floor tiles to cover a wall surface, but not always vice versa. Wall tiles are too slippery to be used safely as flooring and too fragile to withstand everyday wear and tear.

One way to check whether tiles are suitable for floor use is to look at the back side of the tile or the manufacturer's specification sheet for the tile's wear rating. A tile rated "3" or greater is acceptable for floors.

## Learning about Gustave Stickley

I've developed an interest in the American Arts & Crafts Movement, particularly the work of Gustave Stickley. Can you tell me anything about him? I'm particularly interested in the significance of the stamp Als Ik Kan on his furniture.

CAMERON PORTER
MYSTIC, CT

Gustave Stickley (1857–1942) was one of the four most influential figures in the American Arts & Crafts Movement. The other three were Frank Lloyd Wright, Charles Greene, and Henry Greene. The movement was characterized by a belief in the simplicity of construction of an object, quality of personal craftsmanship (as opposed to industrialization), honesty of design, and truth of materials, principles that were similar in

many respects to the ideals of the Shakers and artisan guilds of the Middle Ages. In addition to being one of the most influential designers of his time, Stickley was also the editor of *Craftsman Magazine* from 1901 to 1916.

Stickley began his career as a furniture maker at his uncle's chair factory in Brandt, Pennsylvania. In 1884, he started his own furniture business with his brothers, Charles and Albert, in Binghamton, New York. In 1899, he moved the business, then called United Crafts, to Syracuse, New York. In 1904, he changed the name of his company to Craftsman Workshop, as he felt this name was more humble and thus more in keeping with the simplicity of his furniture—known for its handsome proportions and straightforward design—most of which was made of oak.

Stickley used a joiner's compass as his company's trademark, accompanied by the motto, Als Ik Kan, a Flemish version of William Morris's (the leader of the English Arts & Crafts Movement) motto, *Si Je Puis*, which means "To the Best of My Abilities." The motto most likely refers to Stickley's belief in high-quality but simple construction. Stickley's signature was stamped below the trademark, which signified his personal (although unlikely) inspection of the piece. Not all of his pieces bear this stamp, however.

## Tips on Cleaning Marble

I just moved into an apartment with a terrific marble fireplace, but the mantle appears to be stained from potted plants.

What's the best way to remove the stains and to clean the marble?

GWEN CATES
BROOKLYN HEIGHTS, NY

Marble is very porous, so objects such as planters and/or drinking glasses will wreak havoc upon its surface. To remove the stains, use a stain remover specifically made for marble, carefully following the manufacturer's instructions. Never use a colored polish or cloth, as the dye will seep into the stone. To polish marble, use a white hard polish and a soft white cloth. Rub the polish hard into the marble to make it shine. If you prefer a more matte look, use a soft polish.

## Removing Stains from Concrete

Is it possible to remove ground-in stains from concrete? I'd like to clean up an old walkway and small patio area.

DALE KING
PROVO, UT

Try this solution for removing ground-in stains and dirt from concrete surfaces: Pour household bleach over the stained areas, let it soak in for ten minutes, then rinse thoroughly with water.

## Cleaning Woven Reed Baskets

What is the best way to clean a dirty woven reed basket? Is there a way to restore the luster of the fibers?

MICHELLE BAUMITTER
MAPLE HEIGHTS, OH

Start by washing the basket with a soft brush and mild liquid soap such as Ivory, then dry it as quickly as possible outdoors in the shade. Once the basket is dry, restore the moisture to the fibers by applying a mixture of linseed oil and pure turpentine in a 3:1 ratio with a soft cloth. Wetting baskets once a year (again, drying them quickly outdoors in the shade) will help keep them clean and supple. ◆

# Quick TIPS

*Unique and original tips and techniques designed to save you time and effort*

### Bleached White Pinecones

Instead of painting pinecones white for holiday craft projects, reader Beverly DeMartino, of Glendale, Arizona, suggests bleaching them. Simply soak the cones overnight in a solution of one part chlorine bleach to one part water, then set them in a sunny area to dry.

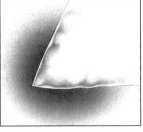

**Flared-out pillow**

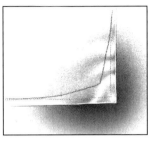

**Sew in toward the dot**

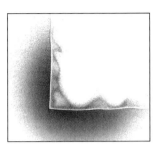

**Squared-up pillow**

### Square Corners

For pillow corners that "square up" instead of flare out when stuffed, try this easy sewing tip. At each corner of the pillow, mark a dot ½" to 1" in from the usual pivot point. As you sew the side seams, sew in toward this dot. Once you've sewn all four sides of the pillow, use your scissors to clip the corners diagonally before turning the pillow cover back to the right side.

### Stenciled Icing

Stencils designed for home decor can make a quick finish to home-baked chocolate cakes and brownies when you're pressed for time. Lay the stencil on top of the cake while it is still warm (but not hot) from the oven and sprinkle confectioners' sugar over the surface using a wire mesh strainer.

### A Painter's Lift

To raise a chair or lightweight table up off the drop cloth so you can paint the legs more smoothly, insert a pushpin into the underside of each leg before you begin. Use this same technique to raise picture frames, stools, small bookcases, or molding off the work surface so you can achieve a clean, drip-free finish along the edges.

ILLUSTRATIONS BY HARRY DAVIS

## Smooth Sanding

To detect a "missed" spot when sanding wood, slip a nylon pantyhose leg or nylon knee-high over your hand, then run your hand lightly over the wood surface. Any rough areas will snag the nylon fibers.

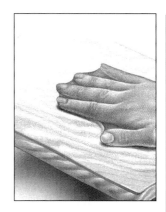

**1. Set the hair dryer to medium and hold it a few inches from the glued area.**

**2. After 10 to 15 seconds, carefully peel off the softened glue.**

## Removing Hot Glue

To remove hardened hot glue from delicate trims, Annie Thiels of Baton

Rouge, Louisiana, uses her hair dryer. *Note:* Don't set the dryer too hot or hold it too close to the glue.

## Paint Touch-Up Kit

To keep custom-mixed interior paint handy for touch-ups, Judith Bartlett of Deerfield, Illinois, uses an empty nail polish bottle. The little brush is just the right size for tackling nicks and scratches.

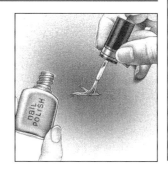

## Marble Mirage

Marbles in the base of a clear glass fishbowl vase, while attractive, can pinch the stems of cut flowers and make arranging difficult. For this remedy, you'll need florist foam, plastic wrap, a knife, and about half the number of marbles you would ordinarily need to fill your glass vase. Cut a block of foam small enough to fit into the base of the vase without touching its inside walls. Wrap a piece of plastic wrap around the block to cover the four sides, leaving the top and bottom uncovered. (The plastic wrap helps soften the foam's green color, lending a watery quality to the arrangement.) Set the block into the vase and distribute the marbles around it. Flower stems can be inserted directly into the foam.

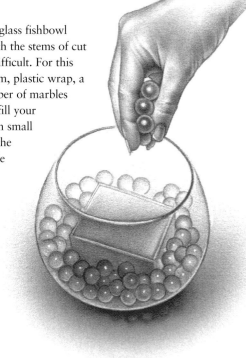

## Controlling Unruly Fringe

To prevent the long fringe or tassels on an upholstery trim from getting tangled or caught in a seam as you attach the trim, lay a strip of low-tack painter's tape across the bottom edge before you begin.

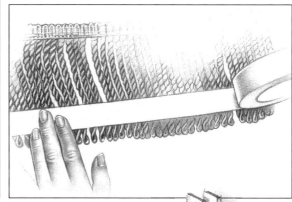

## Miniclamps

To hold project parts in position while the glue dries, Laurel Schmalz of Elk Grove Village, Illinois, turns to familiar household items. Among the objects she has used are drawers that are partly closed, pants hangers, spring-clip clothespins, and clip-on earrings.

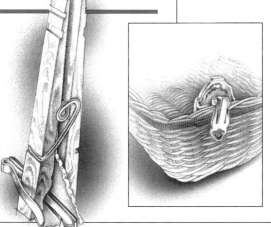

# Fabulous Farmstand Bouquets

*Learn to grow your own cosmos, then choose from one of three quick and easy arrangements.*

ಈ BY NELLIE CALL

This bouquet works well in a window, where the white cosmos and blue pitcher can catch the sunlight.

## When to Cut Your Cosmos

The best time to cut blooms is just after the buds have opened and before the pollen sheds. Cut flowers either in the cool of early morning, when the plants' water reserves are high, or in the evening, when their sugar reserves are high. Cut stems about sixteen inches long, then strip the leaves off the lower half of the stem. Fill a bucket with water to within a few inches of the flowers, and set it in a cool, dark place for at least two hours.

COSMOS, A CHEERFUL, DAISY-like flower that blooms from July to September, is one of the easiest annuals to grow, cut, and arrange. While its light, airy form works well with other flowers in a bouquet, these plants also make beautiful arrangements on their own. Following are three of my favorite quick arrangements, each of which requires about forty stems of cosmos. You can purchase your flowers at a farmstand, or grow your own, a simple and very satisfying task.

Like other annuals, cosmos grows, flowers, and produces seed in the year in which the seeds are sown. Whether used in mass plantings or as a background plant in a sunny border, cosmos blooms early and continuously throughout the season.

Cosmos seed is easily found in hardware stores and nurseries. Locally, you are apt to find only the most common type, *Cosmos bipinnatus* 'Sensation Mix'—a mixture of pink, dark pink, and white blooms—but a wide variety of flowers are available through seed catalogs such as Park Seed. For the bouquets pictured here, we used *Cosmos bipinnatus* 'Sensation Mix,' although the other varieties of cosmos are just as easy to grow and cut.

Cosmos seed is large and easy to handle. You can get a jump on spring by sowing the seeds indoors five to seven weeks before the last frost, but in my experience cosmos germinates and

## Cobalt Pitcher of Cosmos

**1** Fill the pitcher with water. Select several large stems for the center of the arrangement. Build the bouquet with one hand, turning and adding the cosmos in tiers from the high point in the center to the lower tiers around the edges.

**2** Trim off any leaves that will be below the water level and trim the length to a little shorter than twice the height of the pitcher. Place the bouquet in the pitcher; arrange the flowers evenly for a finished look.

### COBALT PITCHER OF COSMOS
■ Cobalt pitcher, 9" tall with a 3½" opening
■ 40 stems white cosmos, cut and conditioned

*You'll also need:* florist or other sharp scissors.

grows so quickly and reliably that it is easier to sow seeds outdoors wherever you want them, once all danger of frost is past. (This date will vary, depending on what region of the country you're in. Use a zone map, found in most gardening books or on the back of the seed packet, to determine the best planting time for your area of the country.) Seeds should be sown a quarter inch deep and twelve to fifteen inches apart; the plants will germinate in five to ten days. When the plants are three to four inches tall, thin the seedlings to eight to twelve

inches apart. The plants will flower eight to ten weeks after sowing and continue blooming until frost.

Cosmos thrives, with limited moisture and in just about any soil, with no added fertilizer. Native to Mexico, cosmos likes heat and requires a spot that receives sun most of the day. Plants are large and branched, reaching three to four feet, with delicate fernlike foliage. ◆

*Nellie Call owns and operates Flower Fields, a fresh-flower farm in Batavia, New York.*

## Cosmos Basket

**1** Place the container into the basket so it comes to about ½" below the top edge of the basket; cut the top of the container if necessary. Cut a 2" slice of Oasis with a sharp knife. Trim the Oasis to fit snugly in the bottom half of the container.

This basket makes a nice centerpiece for a picnic.

**2** Place a pinch of clay or tape on the bottom of the container to anchor it to the bottom of the basket. Fill the container with water to within ¼" of the top. Cut the flowers to equal the longest side of the basket.

**3** Using the Oasis as an anchor, insert approximately half the stems around the inside perimeter of the container, making certain that the flower heads radiate outward. Trim the remaining stems for the center about 1" shorter than the perimeter stems; insert gently in the center of the container and in any open spaces. Balance the arrangement as you go, keeping the sides even and the colors randomly mixed. Add more water to the container daily.

**COSMOS BASKET**

- 40 stems cosmos, cut and conditioned
- Small basket, 3" to 4" tall, 6" to 8" wide, tapering to 5" to 6" opening
- Empty 8-ounce yogurt or similar size plastic container
- Oasis or water-absorbing floral foam
- Small pinch of florist clay or tape

*You'll also need:* sharp knife and florist or other sharp scissors.

## Cosmos Topiary

**COSMOS TOPIARY**

- Clay pot, 5½" in diameter and 5" tall
- Jar or glass to fit inside clay pot
- 40 stems mixed-color cosmos, cut and conditioned
- Sphagnum or other dried moss
- Several small pieces Oasis or other water-absorbing floral foam
- 4 to 6 strands raffia

*You'll also need:* small, square, wooden box; ruler; and florist or other sharp scissors.

**1** Place the jar inside the pot; fill jar with water to within 1" of the top. Place small blocks of Oasis around the jar to center and secure it inside the pot. Gather strands of raffia and knot them at both ends. Collect the stems together, keeping the flower heads level and compact. Add flowers until the stem bunch is slightly smaller in diameter than the jar. Trim the stems even to about 17", including the blossoms. Strip the leaves from the lower stems as necessary to streamline the "trunk" of the topiary.

**2** Wrap the raffia twice around the bouquet just below the flower heads. Lay the bouquet over a box to protect the blossoms, then tie the raffia into a bow.

**3** Squeeze the ends of the stems together and fit the bouquet into the jar, standing it up straight. Cover the top of the pot around the topiary trunk with moss. Water daily by lifting the moss slightly and pouring the water directly into the jar as necessary.

Watered daily, this live topiary should last for at least a week.

## Carving the Fish

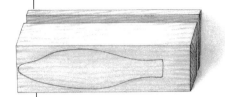

**1** Saw off a ½"-thick section from one 3" x 12" face of the bass-wood block. Lay the fish pattern on the block and trace around the pattern using a pencil.

**2** Use a band-saw or coping saw to cut out the fish along all the marked lines. Use the coping saw to cut a tail slit to a depth of about ⅜".

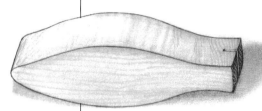

**3** Using a bench knife, carve off all the right-angle edges of the fish to suggest a gently rounded oval. Always direct the knife blade away from you.

**4** With the tip of the knife blade, scribe the jaw and gill marks to a depth of 1/16", then bring each one into relief. Cut all seven fin slits ¼" deep.

# Carved Fish Decoy

*Carve and decorate your own folk-art fish using a few basic woodworking tools and acrylic craft paint.*

BY MIKE DENARO

TRADITIONALLY, FISHERMEN used realistic decoys such as this one to coax a larger fish within spearing distance of an ice-fishing hole. Those fishermen spent long winter nights making their decoys, first carving the body of the fish from wood and then imitating the authentic markings using brushes and paints.

You can carve and decorate this fish decoy in one or two days, however, using a few basic woodworking tools, a block of basswood, four shades of acrylic craft paint, and a thin sheet of copper or brass for the fins and tail. The folk-art style and country colors of your finished decoy will make a welcome display on a tabletop, mantel, sideboard, or shelf in a country cupboard.

I recommend basswood for this project because it's relatively strong, yet still easy to carve. Basswood is widely available in hobby shops and by mail order; the two-by-three-by-twelve-inch block you'll need for this project sells for $4 to $8. If you cannot find basswood, you can substitute tupelo, another form of wood that is easy to carve. Tupelo and basswood are priced similarly.

The carving knife I use, commonly called a "bench knife,"

has a large comfortable handle and a small blade, which gives even first-time carvers a great deal of control. Before starting any carving project, make sure your knife blade is as sharp as possible. Working with a dull blade can be dangerous, since the more pressure you have to apply, the less control you will have.

The fish shown below is a walleye, named for its large bulging eyes, which help it see in low light conditions. While the painting steps I've outlined are the correct color sequence for the walleye species, you can create a trout, a perch, or even an imaginary fish with colors to suit your decorating scheme.

*Mike DeNaro is the manager of Main Street Nursery in Huntington, New York, and enjoys woodworking and carving in his spare time.*

### INSTRUCTIONS
## Cutting the Fish Blank

**1.** Using photocopier and heavy-weight paper, enlarge fish and six fin patterns on page 10 at same percentage so that fish measures 9¼" long. Cut out patterns along marked lines. Set aside fin patterns.

**2.** Referring to illustration 1, page 8, use table saw or have lumberyard use table saw to cut ½"-thick section from one 3" x 12" face of basswood block. Discard ½"-thick section of wood.

**3.** Lay fish pattern on basswood block so tip of jaw (mouth) almost touches one end and about 3" of block extends beyond fish's tail. Trace around pattern using pencil, then remove pattern from block.

**4.** Use bandsaw (wear safety goggles) or coping saw to cut out fish along marked lines. To use coping saw, stand basswood block vertically, fish jaw pointing up,

and secure bottom, unmarked section in workbench vise. Saw along unobscured outline from jaw to tail on each side of fish, then reposition block horizontally to cut edge of tail. Remove fish from vise and discard wood scraps.

**5.** Referring to illustration 2, page 8, and using ruler and pencil, draft guideline for tail slit along center of tail end of fish blank. Secure fish in vise. Using coping saw, cut along marked line to depth of ⅜".

## Carving the Fish

**1.** Using bench knife, carve off all right-angle edges of fish to suggest gently rounded oval as in illustration 3, page 8. Work over entire fish blank, removing small chips of wood and moving regularly from one area to next, until entire block takes shape. Take care not to overwork any one area, always direct knife blade away from you, and keep fingers out of blade's path. Taper front end of emerging fish to shape jaw. Taper opposite end and gently round edges near tail slit. Chip off extra wood along sides of body near top of fish so belly is slightly fuller than top of fish.

**2.** Referring to enlarged fish pattern and using pencil, lightly sketch in lines for gills, jaw (mouth), eyes, and fin slits 1 through 5 on fish body. Be sure to sketch in fin slits 4 and 5 on each side of fish. Examine fish from top, underside, and head-on to make sure gills, jaw, eyes, and slits 4 and 5 line up from side to side.

**3.** Using tip of knife blade, scribe jaw and gill marks to depth of ¹⁄₁₆". To bring jaw into relief, place tip of knife blade at 45-degree angle ⅛" beyond scribed line, and cut inwards to form V-shaped groove. Use same technique to bring gills into relief. *(See* illustration 4, page 8.) If curves prove difficult, take small chips until you

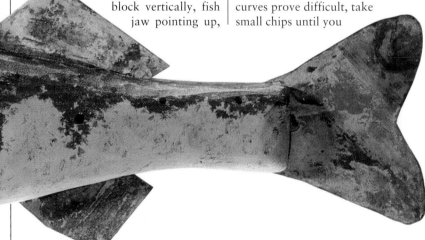

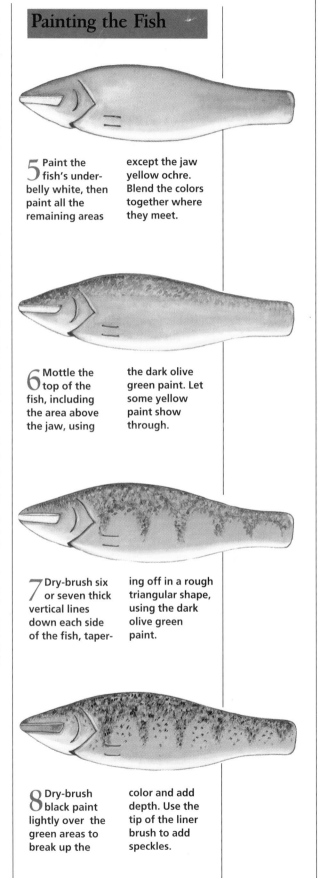

## Painting the Fish

**5** Paint the fish's underbelly white, then paint all the remaining areas except the jaw yellow ochre. Blend the colors together where they meet.

**6** Mottle the top of the fish, including the area above the jaw, using the dark olive green paint. Let some yellow paint show through.

**7** Dry-brush six or seven thick vertical lines down each side of the fish, tapering off in a rough triangular shape, using the dark olive green paint.

**8** Dry-brush black paint lightly over the green areas to break up the color and add depth. Use the tip of the liner brush to add speckles.

# Fish and Fin Patterns

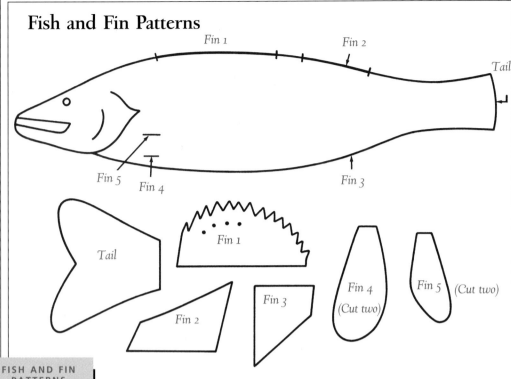

**FISH AND FIN
PATTERNS**

Using a photo-
copier and heavy-
weight paper,
enlarge and copy
all seven pattern
pieces at the same
percentage until
the fish measures
9¼" long. Cut out
the pattern pieces
along the marked
lines. The fish
body will be
traced onto the
basswood block,
while the fin and
tail patterns will
be traced onto
copper or brass
sheeting.

get a nice smooth line. Cut all seven fin slits ¼" deep.

4. Using sandpaper, sand entire fish lightly to smooth rough areas yet still leave evidence of hand-whittling. Slide tip of knife blade through fin slits to dislodge particles from sanding.

## Cutting and Oxidizing the Fins

1. Using sharp pencil, trace fin and tail patterns on brass or copper sheeting; make two tracings of fins 4 and 5. Using tin snips or aviation shears, cut out seven fins and tail. To make sharp inner angles on fin 1, cut into each angle from two directions. *Note:* Handle cutout fins carefully, as edges are sharp.

2. Lay fin 1 on block of scrap wood. Put on safety goggles. Referring to pattern and using drill with 3/32" bit, drill four small holes near top of fin.

3. Lay each fin, in turn, on scrap wood. Pound edges and drilled holes with hammer until fin lies flat. Put on particle mask. Roughen both sides of each fin by rubbing with steel wool, and smooth edges with metal file. Remove particle mask, but continue wearing goggles.

4. Put on rubber gloves. Pour Patina Green solution into shallow, wide-mouthed glass jar to level of ½". Drop fins and two brass upholstery tacks into

solution, one piece at a time, then remove each with tweezers. Prop coated pieces against piece of scrap wood for maximum air circulation, and let dry. Green patina will emerge in about 20 minutes and continue to intensify over a few days. When pieces are perfectly dry (once the patina has emerged), they may be redipped, if desired, to intensify patina finish.

## Painting and Finishing the Fish

1. Insert fin 1 into its slit, deepening or extending slit as necessary with bench knife to get a good fit. (You can now use the fin as a handle while painting the fish. If you get paint on the fin, it can easily be scraped off when the paint is dry. Each time you need a new color of paint, squeeze a few drops onto a paper plate.)

2. Using flat ¼" to ½" brush, paint fish underbelly antique white, as in illustration 5, page 9. Extend white area slightly up sides of fish, but no further than fin slits 5. Rinse brush in water and pat dry on paper towel to remove excess moisture and keep dried paint from ruining brush. Using second flat ¼" to ½" brush, paint all remaining areas except jaw yellow ochre. Rinse brush in water and pat dry on paper towel. Before yellow ochre paint dries, apply

additional white paint along edge where yellow and white paints meet. Rinse and pat dry brush. Blend both colors together with the third flat brush (make sure it is clean and dry) for subtle transition from underbelly to upper body. If necessary, use fingertip to finish blending colors as paints dry.

3. Dip ¼" stencil brush into dark olive green paint, then wipe brush across clean area of paper plate to shed excess paint. When brush is almost dry, paint top of fish, including area above jaw, dark olive green, as in illustration 6, page 9. Extend green color about ⅜" down each side of fish, reloading and preparing dry brush as necessary. Green coloring should appear mottled, with some yellow ochre paint showing through.

4. Continue using dry brush and dark olive green paint. Paint six or seven thick vertical lines from top of fish down each side and tapering off in rough triangular shape ⅜" to ⅝" above white underbelly, as in illustration 7, page 9. To keep lines even on both sides, look at fish from above every few minutes. Dab dark olive green paint over entire yellow ochre surface using very dry brush to mottle paint. Rinse brush in water and pat dry on paper towel. Using liner brush, paint jaw dark olive green. Rinse and pat brush dry.

5. Load second dry stencil brush with black paint, following dry brush technique in step 3. Brush black paint lightly over green areas to break up color and add depth, as in illustration 8, page 9. Load liner brush with black paint. Touch tip of liner brush to green areas at random to speckle fish. Let paint dry 1 hour. After paint has dried, rub fish with steel wool to get rid of fuzziness that covers fish.

6. Test-fit each fin in its slit, and deepen or extend slits with bench knife as necessary. If desired, rub liquid wax onto fish body using clean, lint-free cloth. Mix small amount of epoxy on disposable card following manufacturer's directions. Working one fin at a time, dip edge that attaches to fish into epoxy, then wipe off excess epoxy with clean toothpick. Insert fin into corresponding slit (be sure to use epoxy sparingly so it doesn't ooze out of slit onto body). Dip shaft of each brass upholstery tack into epoxy, then hammer tack into head, sinking edges into surface, to form fish's eyes. ◆

PATTERN BY ROBERTA FRAUWIRTH

# Quick Charlotte Royale

*Make this easy dessert with two loaves of white bread and a jar of preserves.*

THOUGH THIS DESSERT MAY look difficult and time-consuming, it's actually very easy to make, and there's no baking involved. (*See* the January/February 1994 issue of *Cook's Illustrated* for other variations on this recipe.)

### Jelly Rolls
2   freshly baked 1-pound loaves unsliced white bread
    Confectioners' sugar
1–1⅓ cups raspberry preserves

### Raspberry Mousse
1   tablespoon unflavored gelatin
1½  tablespoons juice from ½ lemon
¼   cup granulated sugar
    Pinch of salt
1   pint fresh raspberries pureed and strained, or 12 ounces frozen, unsweetened raspberries, thawed, pureed, and strained (1 cup)
3   tablespoons fruit liqueur (optional for flavoring mousse)
¾   cup chilled heavy cream

### Raspberry Sauce
    (*See* box at right for raspberry sauce recipe.)

*You'll also need:* long serrated knife; cutting board; flour sifter; table knife; waxed paper; plastic wrap; 1½-quart bowl; sponge; large serving spoon; small saucepan; measuring spoons; wooden spoon; measuring cup; whisk; electric mixer; small mixing bowl; small bowl with cover; cake server; and cake plate.

#### INSTRUCTIONS
**1.** Using serrated knife, slice off crust from all six sides of loaf so that remainder measures approximately 3½" x 3½" x 6½". Slice brick into five to seven 6½"-long pieces, each approximately ½" thick. Repeat for second loaf. Select eight most even slices.

**2.** Sift sugar over cutting-board surface. Lay one bread slice on sugar. Using table knife, spread slice with thin layer

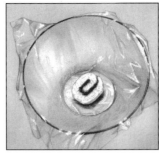

**1** Place one bread circle in the bottom of a bowl lined with plastic wrap.

**2** Surround the first jelly circle with six more circles, then line the sides of the bowl.

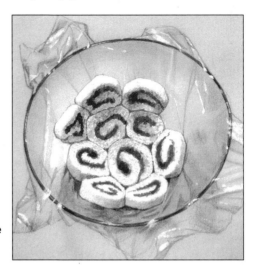

of preserves. Roll slice from short end, jelly roll fashion. Tear off 9" piece of waxed paper from roll, wrap around rolled bread, and twist ends securely. Repeat with remaining slices to make eight rolls. Refrigerate rolls 1 hour.

**3.** Line 1½-quart bowl with 18" piece of plastic wrap, allowing excess to drape over rim. Remove rolls from refrigerator. Unwrap one roll and set on cutting board. Using serrated knife, slice roll into ½"-thick circles, wiping knife on damp sponge after each slice. Slice remaining rolls to yield fifty circles.

**4.** Place one bread circle in bottom of bowl, then surround it with additional circles. Continue adding circles to line sides of bowl. If circles are too large to

fill areas near rim, cut some in half and position cut edge against rim.

**5.** *For the mousse:* Combine gelatin and ¼ cup cold water in small saucepan; let stand about 2 minutes. Stir in ½ cup hot water, lemon juice, sugar, and salt; cook over low heat, stirring constantly, until sugar and gelatin dissolve. Stir in berry puree and liqueur (if using); refrigerate, whisking occasionally, until mixture thickens to consistency of raw egg whites.

**6.** In mixing bowl using electric mixer, whip chilled cream to soft peaks; fold into mousse. Spoon filling into circle-lined bowl to within ½" of rim. Fill in top of bowl with remaining circles and scraps, level to bowl's rim. Bring draped plastic wrap over circles, then cover with another piece of wrap. Refrigerate at least 3 hours.

**7.** To unmold charlotte royale, remove plastic wrap and fold back flaps of inner wrapping. Place cake plate on top of royale and invert royale onto plate. Peel off plastic. Cut royale into wedges and serve with sauce (*see* box, above). ◆

**There's no baking involved with this dessert.**

---

**RECIPE**

### Raspberry Sauce
■ 1 pint fresh raspberries, pureed and strained, or 12 ounces frozen unsweetened raspberries, thawed, pureed, and strained (1 cup)
■ 3 tablespoons sugar
■ 1 tablespoon juice from ½ lemon
■ 2 tablespoons fruit liqueur

Mix together all ingredients above in small bowl; refrigerate until ready to serve.

**This project, which features a simple strawberry motif on one corner of an off-white napkin, is well suited for beginning stencilers.**

# Color-Blended Stenciling

*Learn the secret of creating a hand-painted look using stencils.*

❧ BY DEBORAH MILLER GABLER

**Blueberry and strawberry stencils**

THIS ARTICLE WILL TEACH you the basics of color-blended stenciling, a decorative stenciling technique that is much easier than its lush colors and painterly application would have you believe.

In traditional stenciling, paint is applied to a surface through a cutout template, or stencil. The color is typically opaque and uniform, without shading or variation, and second and third colors can only be introduced through the use of additional stencils, which are placed alongside or overlapping the initial design. Color-blended stenciling begins where these techniques leave off. Instead of using a single color per stencil, it involves overlaying and blending multiple colors within the same cutout. While it is certainly not the fastest method of stenciling, it is nevertheless simple to master, letting even first-timers render beautiful, subtly highlighted images that rival those created using freehand decorative painting

techniques. Color-blended stenciling also results in a sense of dimension, shading, and realism not generally associated with stenciling.

## Selecting a Project

Color-blended stencil designs can be applied to a variety of surfaces in the home, from walls and wood to paper and fabric. Possible projects include wooden boxes, planters, furniture, and kitchen cupboards; paper goods, such as stationery and notecards (you could even stencil a "print" for framing); and fabric-oriented projects, such as

curtains, pillows, and tablecloths.

To illustrate projects of varying size and complexity, I stenciled three different 100 percent cotton fabric surfaces— a napkin, a place mat, and a three-by-five-foot cotton floor rug—using a pear and strawberry stencil design. (*See* "Cutting Your Own Stencil," page 14, to cut this stencil for your projects.) This versatile design can be used on its own, as shown on the place mat, or side by side in a running border, as shown on the rug. You can also break out single elements, such as the strawberry cluster shown on the napkin. Should you choose a different stencil than the one offered here for your project, you are bound to find that it contains similar options for using more or less decoration.

If this is your first stenciling effort, I suggest working on a small area—a pillow or a chair slat—so that you can concentrate on becoming acquainted with the color-blending technique. If you already have some stenciling experience, you can advance to a larger piece of furniture, a table runner, or a set of place mats. To make a strong decorating statement, try a running border on an area rug, floor, or wall. A free-form leafy vine, like the one bordering my rug (*see* next page ), can also appear solo, trailing along a random course to decorate a tight or awkward space that might not accommodate a symmetrical design. A few leaves and tendrils climb-

## Cutting Your Own Stencil

To cut your own stencil from any of the designs shown on these pages, follow these guidelines. If using the three-pear design, you will need to photocopy and cut two versions of the stencil: In one, cut away all the unshaded areas, and in the other, cut away all the shaded areas. You can use the

blueberries or strawberries individually or to create a border. Elements from the larger pear stencil can also be isolated for individual use by laying masking tape over any adjacent open areas that you don't want to include. (For additional directions, *see* "Cutting Your Own Stencil," page 14.)

## Materials

- Item to be stenciled
- ½-ounce containers Delta Stencil Magic Paint Creme in desired colors. (For color choices, *see* "Fundamentals of Color-Blended Stenciling," page 14.)

*You'll also need:*
at least two 9" x 12" sheets heavyweight layout or stenciling vellum, X-Acto knife with new blade, self-healing cutting mat, permanent black marker, and access to photocopier with single-sheet feed and enlarging capabilities *or* stencil of your choice; stiff-bristled tradi-tional and/or fabric stencil brushes, ⅛" to ½" wide, at least one per stencil cream color; palette pad or clean scrap paper; masking tape; and paper towels.

*Other items, if necessary:* Scotchguard (for sealing stenciled fabrics); Krylon spray varnish (for sealing paper or surfaces exposed to water); 600-grit sandpaper (for roughing up surfaces with satin finishes); transparent tape (for repairing vellum stencils); odorless turpentine (for cleanup); and liner brush (for adding seeds to strawberries).

ing over a windowsill or along a base-board, for instance, is one way to develop the vine motif.

### Selecting Your Materials
Although a range of paints, from acrylic craft paint to tube oils, can be used for color-blended stenciling, I recommend Delta nontoxic, oil-based stencil cream paints for the best results. As the name implies, stencil cream paints were developed specifically for stenciling. The dense, ultrasmooth cream blends and feathers beautifully, meaning any mixing of colors can be done right on your project instead of on a separate palette.

For fine line work with a brush, mix in a few drops of turpentine until the cream reaches an inklike consistency. After a few weeks' drying or "curing" time, the cream paints are washable. Delta creams do not need to be heat-set, nor do they become brittle, retaining their intensity of color and durability even when used underfoot, as in the rug project. (*Note:* Brands of stencil cream other than Delta may require heat-setting on fabric.)

You can apply stencil cream paints with traditional, natural-bristle stencil brushes or synthetic, fabric stencil brushes. Both types feature a round ferrule; the traditional brush bristles are clipped straight across while the fabric brush bristles are tapered. The bristles are slightly stiff in order to effectively manipulate the cream, which is denser than most acrylic paints. You'll need a minimum of one brush for each color, and you may prefer several: a larger brush for broad areas (such as the pears) and smaller brushes for detail.

Once you decide on a project, spend some time preparing the surface for stenciling. Fabrics should be 100 per-cent cotton, prewashed and dried to allow for shrinkage when the item is cleaned later on. Walls should be spack-led, sanded, and painted with a ground coat. Delta stencil creams adhere well to flat paint, either latex or oil-based, as well as an eggshell finish, but you'll need to lightly sand satin finishes to give them some "tooth." Paper requires no special preparation but should be heavyweight and sturdy.

### Understanding the Technique
The challenge of color-blended stenciling is deciding which color sequences to use. The color samples on pages 14 and 15 showing how one color is worked alongside another, and the accompanying text, will guide you as you embark on your own projects. Oddly enough, beginners sometimes have an easier time catching on to the color-blended approach; more experienced stencilers who are used to applying one color per cutout may find they have to "reprogram" themselves about stenciling.

Before you apply paint to your actual project, you should practice two brush-work techniques on paper. One is to "pull" the color in from the outside edges of the stencil in a sweeping motion. This brush technique lets you enhance curved shapes such as the pears. The other is to work the brush in a circular motion, concentrating color along the edges of the stencil for crisp definition, then letting it fade toward the center to suggest a highlight.

For the best results, follow these tips. To load your brush, rub the bristles gently in the paint cream, then sweep them across a clean section of paper. To prevent dark spots on the stenciled sur-face, always touch the brush bristles to the stencil, not the surface, as you begin each stroke.

This cotton rug features the pear motif stenciled in a continuous border approximately twelve inches from the rug's edge, accented with a sweeping brown vine of leaves and strawberries.

This place mat uses one pear of each color, but the design would work equally well with three yellow or red pears.

## Finishing Your Project

When stenciling is completed, let your project cure for at least two weeks (four weeks for satin finishes) to give the paints time to penetrate the surface and set. Cream paints applied to wood surfaces or walls can be damp-sponged after curing. Areas apt to be splashed by water—such as a kitchen or bathroom wall—can be protected with a light coat of matte or satin-finish Krylon spray varnish. (You may even want to initially protect such heavily splashed areas with a light misting of Krylon spray varnish during the curing phase.) I don't recommend using polyurethane on stenciled walls, as it can yellow.

Rugs, pillows, and other fabric furnishings that will be tread on or handled can be sprayed with Scotchguard after curing to protect from stains and spills. Stenciled images that will be framed under glass need no sealing, but paper images exposed to air, such as those on a lampshade or stationery, can be sealed with a very light coat of Krylon spray varnish.

*Deborah Miller Gabler, owner of Shady Lane Designs in Hamburg, New York, is a freelance designer and teacher specializing in custom lampshades and stenciling.*

## INSTRUCTIONS

### Cutting Your Own Stencil

To cut your own stencil from any of the designs on pages 12 and 13, follow these guidelines. If using the three-pear design, you will actually create two separate stencils: one for all the unshaded areas and the second for all the shaded areas. You can also cut away the remaining freestanding design elements for individual use. In addition, elements from the larger pear stencil can be isolated for individual use by laying masking tape over any adjacent open areas that you don't want to include.

**1.** Using copier, enlarge stencil design(s) of choice to desired size, then copy twice on separate sheets of vellum.

**2.** Using X-Acto knife and cutting mat, cut all unshaded areas from one vellum stencil. Cut smallest areas first, then proceed to larger areas. To cut smooth curves, keep knife blade stationary and rotate vellum sheet away from you. To cut pointed leaf tips, cut into tip from each side. To prevent vellum from tearing when cutting tendrils, cut inner edge of each curve first, then outer edge. To repair a mistake or strengthen a weak spot, place transparent tape over problem area on both sides of sheet, then recut. Using black marker, label completed stencil as "A."

**3.** Repeat step 2 on second vellum stencil, but cut away all shaded areas. Label completed stencil as "B."

### Stenciling the Design

**1.** If working on fabric, prewash and dry it. If working on surface with satin finish, lightly rough up area to be stenciled with sandpaper.

**2.** Open each paint container and rub

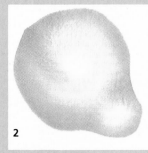

1

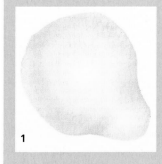

2

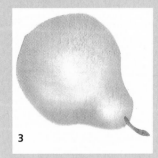

3

## Fundamentals of Color-Blended Stenciling

Use the techniques and color recommendations outlined here to create a color-blended pear and strawberry design. To stencil another design of your choosing, you'll need to adjust the colors. For more natural-looking results, use colors that are related (e.g., yellow and orange, green and blue, purple and red) rather than opposite (e.g., red and green, yellow and purple, orange and blue). Keep notes on various color combinations in case you want to repeat any as you proceed or in future projects.

**Green pear:**
**1) Yellow Citron base**
**2) Jungle Green over Yellow Citron 3) Christmas Green over Jungle Green to accentuate curves and shadows; touch of Garnet Red to add glow.**

Pears: Apply the color to the pears in two circular shapes—a smaller circle atop a larger one—by concentrating the color at the pear's edges and fading to a white highlight near the pear's center.

For green pears, start with a base coat of Yellow Citron; apply the paint in circular strokes around the top and bottom circles that form the pear shape, working from the outside edges in towards the center. Then brush on a little Christmas Green around the outside edges; last, shade the bottom of the pear with a bit of Jungle Green. Shade a bit on either side of the pear's neck where the circles curve away from one another.

On another pear, create a darker look by base-coating

COLOR SAMPLES BY DEBORAH MILLER GABLER/PHOTOGRAPH BY STEVEN MAYS

waxy coating off surface of paint with paper towel.

**3.** Position stencil A (or stencil of choice) on project surface, and secure corners with masking tape. Load brush with paint (*see* "Fundamentals of Color-Blended Stenciling" below for color choices), then dab brush on clean section of palette to shed any excess paint. Hold down stencil as close to surface as possible using free hand. Again referring to "Fundamentals of Color-Blended Stenciling," brush paint onto surface through cutout openings of stencil A, either by touching brush to vellum and drawing color in toward center of cutout area, following natural contours, or by moving brush in circular motion around cutout edges. Softly color following cutout areas: pears; leaves and strawberry caps; blueberries; flower centers and small green leaves

surrounding flowers; and stems and tendrils. Use separate brush for each color. When finished, remove stencil A.

**4.** Align stencil B perfectly with partially completed design and tape at corners. Apply paint through all cutout openings as in step 3 above, coloring following items: remaining pear; remaining leaves; remaining blueberries; flowers; strawberries; and remaining stems and tendrils. When done, remove stencil B.

**5.** If stenciling a border: Align stencil A in appropriate orientation to stencil design just made (depending on whether you're right- or left-handed, work in a direction to avoid smearing freshly painted work) and repeat step 3, varying colors for a more painterly look. Align stencil B in new position and repeat step 4. Continue in this manner until border is complete.

## Sealing the Design

**1.** Let paint cure four weeks if applied to surface with satin finish, two weeks for fabrics and surfaces with flat or eggshell finish.

**2.** To protect stenciled fabrics from stains and soil, treat them with Scotchguard spray. Seal surfaces that will be exposed to water or damp with two light coats Krylon spray varnish. Seal exposed paper with very light coat of varnish.

3. To clean brushes, use turpentine or soap and water. Let bristles dry thoroughly before reuse, as wet bristles can dilute paint and cause it to bleed and/or streak. To clean stencil, lay on flat surface and wipe away paint using paper towel moistened with turpentine. (Do this periodically during large projects to prevent accumulated paint from marring stenciled surface.) ◆

the fruit with Yellow Ochre, then adding Jungle Green and finally a touch of Garnet Red to the area near a strawberry. Red pears may be toned down a bit by applying a base coat of Yellow Ochre or Sunflower Yellow, then applying Barn Red or Garnet Red. A touch of green or brown can darken any areas that should be shaded. Red paint applied over green will give you a different look from green paint applied over red, so try both color schemes to obtain some variation.

If working on a large area such as a wall or rug, I recommend creating three different colored pears in each print, then changing their positions as you move on to the next repeat. This gives a more colorful and less repetitive design.

Strawberries: For an orange berry, apply a light base coat of Sunflower Yellow. Then load a second brush with Barn Red and pull it in from the edges of the berry, fading towards the center.

For variation, leave the tip of one or two berries yellow to create a few unripe berries, or brush a bit of Christmas Green onto the tip or sides. If you want a brilliant red berry, use Garnet Red, building up the color to its darkest value at the rounded edges or under the cap of the berry. If deeper shading is needed,

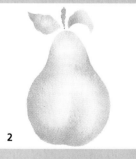

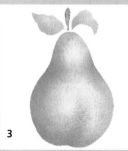

add some Barn Red. Use a liner brush loaded with Chocolate Brown or Jungle Green or brown marker to add a few seeds to your strawberries.

Blueberries: Using Royal Blue loaded lightly on a small brush, make a circular motion around each blueberry with the brush resting mostly on the vellum. This will automatically darken and round out the edges while leaving a highlight in the berry's center.

Make sure the berries that are behind others are the darkest by applying the paint a little more liberally.

**Red pear:**
**1)** Yellow Ochre base to define shape **2)** Jungle Green and Christmas Green leaves; Barn Red over Yellow Ochre **3)** Garnet Red over Yellow Ochre and Barn Red; a touch of Garnet Red on leaves; Chocolate Brown stem.

**Strawberry cluster:**
**1)** Sunflower Yellow base on left side of each berry and on tip of one leaf; Christmas Green base on remaining leaves and caps; Royal Blue around blueberries **2)** Garnet Red on right side of strawberries to define shape; Jungle Green to darken leaves **3)** Intensify Garnet Red and add Barn Red under caps; accent leaves with Barn Red; Chocolate stems.

The frame on the left was made with the petals of Sweetheart Minuette roses; the frame on the right was made using Sweetheart Porcelina roses.

# Rose Petal Frame

*Turn an ordinary picture frame into a unique treasure using dried rose petals.*

THIS BEAUTIFUL, DELICATE frame is decorated with rose petals dried in silica gel. The petals sit in silica gel crystals for several days, after which you can finish the frame in an afternoon's time.

Silica gel, a compound widely available in craft and florist shops, was originally developed to absorb moisture in such packaged products as potato chips. The "gel," actually not a gel at all, but a saltlike substance that contains tiny blue indicator crystals, can absorb up to forty percent of its weight in water. When the gel has absorbed the maximum amount of water from the rose petals, the crystals will turn pink.

The silica gel crystals will dry the rose petals without curling them or noticeably altering their natural color. While the crystals are nontoxic, they do release a very fine powder during pouring that is potentially irritating to mucous membranes. To minimize the dust, be sure to work in a well-ventilated area and pour the silica gel crystals slowly.

The "glue" for this technique is acrylic matte medium. A gummy, white liquid, matte medium softens the petals so they are more pliable, and binds them permanently to the frame. We tested several brands and found that Liquitex Acrylic Matte Medium performed the best. Several other brands gave the petals a yellowish tint or left them otherwise discolored.

When you shop for a frame, look for one with a wide border to provide the most surface area to show off the petals. The frame we chose, measuring six inches square with a three-inch-square opening, required about ninety-five petals. Of course, you can adjust the petal amount to decorate any size frame you wish. Always dry more petals than you'll actually need, since not all will be perfect.

For one of our frames, we bought one dozen Sweetheart Minuette roses, which yield ten to twelve petals per rose.

Ranging from just one-half to one inch wide, these diminutive petals suit the frame proportions perfectly. To mimic the flower's natural growth pattern, we placed small petals along the inner part of the frame border, medium-sized petals in the middle, and large ones at the outer edge. Petals from solid-color roses, such as the peachy orange Sweetheart Porcelinas used for the second frame pictured above, offer a completely different look.

When selecting your roses, be sure to use only those roses with dry petals. If you apply silica gel to wet petals (such as those picked after a rainstorm or while the dew is still wet), the gel will stick to the petals, making removal more difficult. In addition, the desiccant will have to absorb so much extra moisture that its overall drying ability will be diminished.

## INSTRUCTIONS
### Drying and Sorting the Petals

1. For each rose, peel back sepals (green "prongs" at base of rose), and gently pull off petals one by one. Select best petals and discard bruised or discolored ones. Set petals aside. Put on goggles, mask, and gloves. Pour thin, even layer of silica gel crystals into bottom of Tupperware container or box. Lay petals in rows on crystals—close

but not overlapping. Using soupspoon, sprinkle crystals over petals until all petals are completely covered. Place another layer of petals in box, and sprinkle crystals to cover. Repeat until all petals are covered. Close container tightly; if lid does not form airtight seal, seal edge with tape. Let container rest undisturbed for 3 days.

2. On day 3, open container, and gently brush aside crystals so you can touch one petal with fingertip. If petal is still pliable, replace crystals on top and reseal container. Check again in same way on day 4 and each succeeding day until petal is dry and stiff when touched. Put on goggles, mask, and gloves. Using slotted spoon or spatula, lift petals from crystals, transfer them to sieve or strainer, then gently shake to shed lingering crystals. Place preserved petals on cookie sheet. Sort through petals to select best-looking ones, and arrange petals by size in four groups: large, medium, small, and smallest.

## Covering the Sides of the Frame

1. Cover work surface with kraft paper. Sand frame lightly to roughen surface for gluing.

2. Pour 2"- to 3"-wide puddle of matte medium onto paper plate. Select six to eight of the smallest petals and place them in medium, using round brush to coat them lightly on both sides. Let petals sit in medium 4 to 5 minutes, until soft and pliable. (Those that are

especially tough or dense may require slightly longer soaking time.) Check petals often, as oversoftening will make them difficult to handle. Continue softening petals in batches of six to eight as you need them for the following steps.

3. Using tweezers, transfer softened

### MATERIALS
- **6" x 6" light-colored wooden picture frame**
- **1 dozen miniature roses**
- **3 pounds silica gel crystals**
- **8-ounce bottle Liquitex Acrylic Matte Medium**

*You'll also need:*
150-grit sandpaper; large, oblong Tupperware container or airtight box with lid; soupspoon; slotted spoon or spatula; wire

sieve or strainer; cookie sheet; round-edge burnisher, wooden dowel or stainless steel knife; 4"-wide acrylic brayer; brown kraft paper; blunt tweezers; soft, small round brush; paper plates; paper towels; waxed paper; goggles; particle mask; and disposable gloves.

*Other items, if necessary:*
electrician's tape (for sealing container).

petals to clean area of plate. Wipe off excess medium with brush. Pick up each petal individually with tweezers and position it with inner side of petal face up on frame. Start at inner corner and work your way around inner opening of frame, laying top one-third of petal on front inner edge and wrapping other two-thirds around to back of frame. Repeat to cover entire inner edge; as petals begin to dry, smooth them down with burnisher (or substitute). Dab off excess medium with fingertip or paper towel. Lay waxed paper on glued frame and roll with brayer to eliminate air

bubbles.

4. Repeat step 3, affixing smallest petals to outer edge of frame. Start at one corner, laying top one-quarter of each petal on front of frame, then wrapping petal around edge and onto back of frame (*see* illustration 1 below). Burnish as before. Repeat until entire outer edge is covered, then roll with brayer as before.

## Covering the Front of the Frame

For the front of the frame, you'll be affixing petals in three rows, working from the outside edge inwards.

1. Soak large petals in medium as above. Starting at any corner and working your way around frame, lay six or seven softened petals on frame side along outer edge of frame front using tweezers as above. With petals slightly touching each other and slightly overlapping the smallest petals already affixed, burnish frame, then roll with brayer as above.

2. Repeat previous step using medium-sized petals, positioning them to slightly overlap large petals (illustration 2).

3. Repeat step 1 using small petals, positioning them to overlap medium-sized petals and pressing excess onto edge of picture opening (illustration 3).

4. When medium is fully dry (about 1 hour), place clean piece of waxed paper over frame front, and weight with flat, heavy object; let dry overnight. The following day, coat entire frame lightly with acrylic matte medium to seal petals completely. ◆

### FOR FURTHER READING
In our May/June 1995 issue, we tested several ways to dry roses, including using desiccants such as silica gel, borax, or sand. Silica gel, far and above, produced the best results. For a full discussion of this subject, *see* "The Best Way to Dry Roses" on page 20 of the May/June 1995 issue.

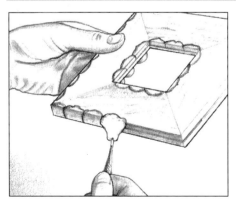

**1** Start by applying the very smallest of the rose petals to the frame's inner and outer edges.

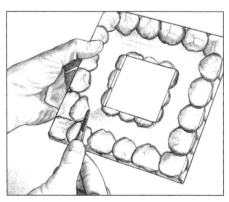

**2** Cover the outermost portion of the frame's front with the large petals, then fill in the second row with medium petals.

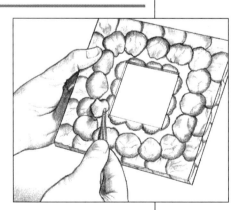

**3** Fill in the innermost row with the small rose petals.

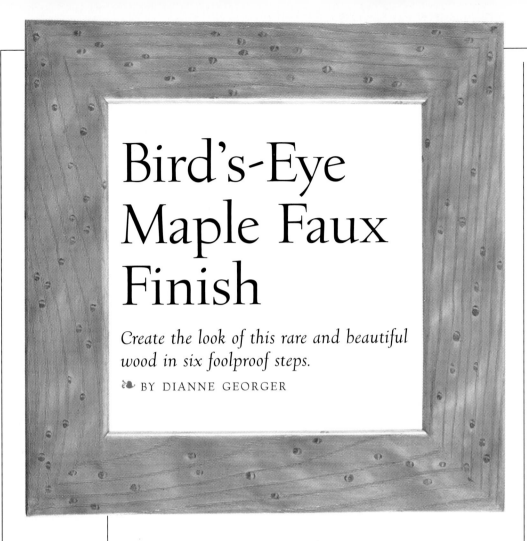

# Bird's-Eye Maple Faux Finish

*Create the look of this rare and beautiful wood in six foolproof steps.*

BY DIANNE GEORGER

**B**IRD'S-EYE MAPLE, NAMED FOR an unusual pattern of markings that resembles bird's eyes, is a relatively rare wood found in the trunk of the sugar maple tree. The scarcity of this beautiful wood makes it an excellent choice for a faux finish; given the number of stages involved in creating this finish, however, it is best suited for small pieces such as the frame and wooden chest shown above and on page 20. Other small projects to consider include a serving tray, cigar box, or Shaker-style bandbox, the top of an occasional table, or mirror frame.

A bird's-eye maple faux finish is best created with an acrylic (water-based) paint, as this gives a cleaner and finer finish. In addition, water-based products dry quickly, are nontoxic and low-odor, and can be cleaned up with soap and water. Water-based acrylic matte varnish, the final coat on the bird's-eye maple effect, dries transparently, producing a beautiful satin finish that won't contribute any color to the finished piece. When working with water-based mediums, I don't recommend removing sanding dust with a tack cloth, as it can leave residue, which may affect the adhesion of the paint and other media. Instead, remove dust by blowing with a hair dryer, then wipe the surface with a damp, lint-free rag.

The process of creating a bird's-eye maple finish breaks out into six stages: base-coating, laying a foundation for the bird's-eyes, coloring the bird's-eyes, painting the grain lines, applying the stain glaze, and finishing with matte varnish. Before starting on the item of your choice, I suggest practicing all six steps on a practice board or piece of scrap wood (of the same wood type as your project) both to try out the techniques and develop a look that pleases you. You may also want to keep a practice board at your side while working on your actual project.

A few notes of importance. Before you apply the base coat, you'll need to cover the surface with a coat of sealer applied with a foam brush. As this will raise the grain of the wood, start by sanding lightly with 220-grit sandpaper, and sand again with 220-grit sandpaper after the sealer has dried.

In an acrylic faux finish project, base-coating is probably the most important step. The base coat must be as smooth

## Creating the Bird's-Eye Maple Faux Finish

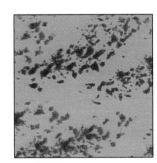

**1** Using a sea sponge loaded with the Molasses paint and retarder mixture, lay down a crossfire pattern of wood.

**2** Use a blending or mop brush to blend the mottled areas along the diagonal.

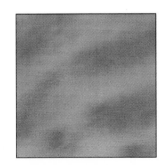

**3** Then blend the mottled areas vertically and horizontally, keeping the pressure very light.

**4** With a damp Q-Tip, wipe out oval areas the size of the Q-Tip head. These ovals form the foundation for the bird's-eyes.

as possible, with no brush marks or ridges, to make your project believable. To prevent these ridges or brush marks, I recommend applying three or four coats of thinned paint with a flat-wash brush versus one coat of full-strength paint.

When laying down color over the base coat, I use a retarder to extend the working time of acrylic paint. In the stages that require a retarder, or a paint and retarder mixture, however, you'll need to force-dry your object using a blow dryer. (Letting the object air-dry can take up to five days.) Set the dryer to warm, hold it eight to twelve inches away from the surface to prevent the paint from blistering, and dry for at least ten minutes. Then let the project cool down for approximately one hour, and repeat the drying process for another ten minutes. When the project is dry, let it cool down for at least a half hour before proceeding to the next painting step.

In the materials list above, I've made specific brand recommendations based on my own experience in creating faux finishes. You're free to substitute other brands, but be aware that they may not perform as these directions indicate. Specifically, if you substitute another brand of paint for the Delta Maple Sugar Tan paint used for the base coat, be sure to select an opaque type of

## MATERIALS

- **Wood item or project**
- **Delta Ceramcoat Water-based Sealer**
- **Jo Sonja's Retarder and Antiquing Medium**
- **Jo Sonja's Clear Glazing Medium**
- **2-ounce bottle Delta Ceramcoat Artist's Acrylic Paint #2062 (Maple Sugar Tan)**
- **2-ounce bottle Folk Art Acrylic Color #943 (Molasses)**
- **Right Step Matte Varnish**

*You'll also need:* lint-free rags; small bowl or dish; hard palette or jar lid; plastic dishes; plastic wrap or zip-lock bags; brown paper bag; Q-Tips; cheesecloth; paper towels; hair dryer; 220-grit sandpaper; 1½" foam brush; two ½" to ¾" synthetic flat-wash brushes (use 1" to 1½" brushes for larger projects); ½" to ¾" blending or mop brush (use 1" to 1½" brushes for larger projects); #0 script liner; #1 liner; 1¼" flat brush; large-holed sea sponge; palette knife; tweezers; scrap wood or practice boards of same wood type as project; and soap.

*Other items, if necessary:* wood putty and craft stick (for filling dents or uneven areas).

paint. (If you substitute another brand name for the second color of paint, Folk Art Molasses, your substitute paint can be transparent.)

### Instructions

### Preparing the Wood Surface

1. If your project has existing hardware, or you plan to add hardware, refer to the materials and directions in "How to Handle Hardware," page 20. Check wood surface for dents, nail holes, or uneven areas. If necessary, fill dents with wood putty using craft stick, then smooth off excess with straight edge of craft stick. Let dry completely, then sand filled areas along grain of wood with 220-grit sandpaper. Repeat if necessary.

2. Sand complete wood surface to be finished with 220-grit sandpaper, always sanding with grain of wood. When finished, blow dust away with hair dryer, then wipe with damp, lint-free rag. Seal wood using sealer and 1½" foam brush, making sure coverage is smooth and even. Let sealer dry at least 1 hour, then sand lightly with 220-grit sandpaper until smooth. Blow dust off and wipe with lint-free rag.

### Stage One

### Base-Coating

1. Fill small bowl or dish with water; place dish and folded paper towel next to work surface. Mix equal quantities Maple Sugar Tan paint and water in plastic dish using palette knife. (The resulting mixture should have the consistency of light cream. If you can see brush marks when you apply the mixture, it is too thick and must be thinned with additional water. You should be able to see the grain of your wood through the first coat of paint.) Wet flat-wash brush, then blot on paper towel; load brush by placing hairs of brush on edge of paint puddle, pressing down and drawing brush toward you. Load brush about three-quarters of the way up the bristles, taking care not to let paint get into ferrule (metal housing for brush hairs). Flip brush over and repeat.

**DESIGNER'S TIP**
## Creating End Grain
If your project has an area that needs end grain, such as the sides and the top of the chest, you'll need to purchase a 10F Loew Cornell flat fabric brush. To create the look of end grain, load the brush with the paint and retarder mixture as in stage 4, steps 1 and 2, and pull down the length of the surface to create long striations. Do not make ovals, as end grain does not contain bird's-eyes.

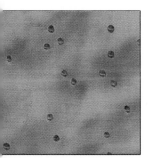

**5** Use a damp #1 liner brush to wipe out a "C" shape in the bottom third of each painted oval.

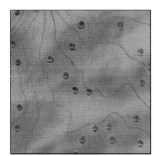

**6** To paint the long, fine grain lines, hold the #0 liner as you would a pencil, but straight up and down.

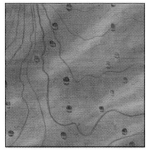

**7** After applying the stain glaze, wipe the glaze off in a jagged motion along the top portion of any mottled areas with a dry Q-Tip.

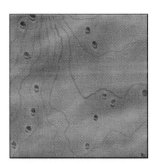

**8** Last, use a blending or mop brush to blend vertically, then horizontally, and finally diagonally.

**When applying a faux finish to a chest such as this one, be sure to follow the instructions for creating end grain and handling the object's hardware (*see* sidebars, page 19 and below).**

2. Apply paint to entire surface of project. Check adjoining surfaces for paint ridges; pass brush lightly over any areas that need smoothing. To paint larger surfaces, use a slip-slap motion, working in a 3"-square area and applying paint in an "x" pattern, then immediately smoothing over in one direction only. Avoid reworking areas, as this may cause acrylic paint to lift. Let first coat dry thoroughly (at least 30 minutes). To speed drying, use hair dryer on warm setting, keeping dryer 8" to 12" away from surface to avoid blistering. (If paint blisters, sand surface and start over.) Allow surface to cool thoroughly before applying second coat. Clean brush with water, and keep dish of paint covered with plastic or store in zip-lock bag between coats.

3. Apply second coat of thinned paint and dry as in step 2. Tear off seamed edges or bottom of brown paper bag, fold edges under, crumple up bag, and use to sand painted surface to smooth paint without removing color. Apply third coat of paint and let dry as in step

2. Surface should now have opaque covering of paint. If you can still see through it, apply one additional coat and dry as in step 2. When final coat of paint is completely dry, apply one coat clear glazing medium with second flat-wash brush to seal base coat and add depth to surface. Clean brushes and other materials with soap and water.

### Stage Two
## Laying a Foundation for the Bird's-Eyes

1. Place within reach two plastic dishes, palette knife, retarder, Molasses paint, flat-wash brush, sea sponge, blending or mop brush, cheesecloth, paper towels, and tweezers. Place a small amount of retarder in one dish, replenishing as needed. In second dish, use palette knife to mix equal quantities of retarder and Molasses paint.

2. Apply scant coat of plain retarder with flat-wash brush, working retarder well into pores of wood. Blot brush on dry paper towel as you go to remove excess retarder. Strive for an even sheen, with no puddling. Pat off any excess retarder with cheesecloth.

3. Wet sea sponge with water, then wring out thor-

oughly. Using sea sponge, lay down a "crossfire" pattern of wood. To do this, quickly dip sponge in paint and retarder mixture, pounce (lightly bounce) off excess on clean, dry paper towel, then pounce onto wood surface in diagonal rows (*see* color tile 1, page 18). Pounced areas should be thin and raggedy, interlacing to give a mottled, rippled effect. Pounce off excess paint/retarder mixture from wood using clean cheesecloth.

4. Using blending or mop brush, blend mottled areas along diagonal (color tile 2) Wipe brush on clean, dry paper towel as you go to remove paint. Take care not to blend paint out completely, but work to eliminate hard lines. Next, blend vertically and then horizontally, using color tile 3 as reference and keeping pressure very light. Check surface for brush hairs, and remove using tweezers.

5. Using damp Q-Tip, lay foundation for bird's-eyes by wiping out oval areas about size of Q-Tip head (color tile 4). Wet and wring out Q-Tip head as necessary. Concentrate ovals in mottled areas, running vertically in clumps of two, three, and four, with occasional singles. Bird's-eyes should run vertically in linear clusters through dark and light areas. Blend lightly vertically using blending or mop brush to elongate ovals; then blend horizontally to even surface out and remove any remaining brush marks. Final blending should be

### DESIGNER'S TIP
## How to Handle Hardware

If you opt for a project such as the chest, or any other project that requires adding or removing hardware, you'll need to deal with that hardware before starting any of the painting steps.

If your project already has hardware, be sure to remove it using the appropriate tools and set it aside in a safe place. Once the faux finish is complete, you can reattach the hardware.

If your project does not have hardware, but you'd like to add it, as I did with the chest, you'll need to determine the placement of the hardware and create any necessary holes before painting the object. If this is the case, start by placing the hinges on the back of the chest. (I positioned mine one and one-half inches in from each outer edge.) While holding the hinge in place, use an awl to make starter holes for the screws. Use a screwdriver to turn the screws in, but don't tighten them down completely at this point.

light enough to eliminate any lines made by brush. Dry with blow dryer (on warm setting) for at least 10 minutes, holding dryer 8" to 12" above surface and moving dryer constantly to avoid blistering. When finish is fully dried and no longer shiny, allow to cool for 1 hour. Repeat drying process for 10 minutes and let cool for at least a half hour. Apply coat of glazing medium using flat-wash brush; let dry overnight. Clean brushes and other painting materials with soap and water.

### Stage Three
## Coloring the Bird's-Eyes

**1.** Place within reach: Molasses paint, glazing medium, #1 liner, 1¼" flat brush, small dish or bowl half-filled with water, hard palette or jar lid, damp folded paper towel, Q-Tips, and cheesecloth. Mix two drops Molasses paint and two drops glazing medium on palette or lid. Pull cotton off one end of Q-Tip so stick is bare. Dip bare end into paint mixture and dab excess off to side. Apply paint inside all oval areas wiped out in stage 2, step 5, by touching Q-Tip stick on surface and dragging down slightly to create oval. Color no more than three ovals at a time. Touch with cheesecloth to remove excess paint and lighten color.

**2.** Use damp #1 liner brush to wipe out a "C" shape in bottom third of each painted oval (*see* color tile 5, page 19). Dip liner in water, blot on damp paper

towel, and repeat. If necessary, use flat brush or dampened Q-Tip to clean up edges of ovals.

### Stage Four
## Painting the Grain Lines

**1.** Have within reach: #0 script liner, Molasses paint, glazing medium, blending or mop brush, hard palette or jar lid, paper towel, and bowl or dish of water. Mix two drops paint with two drops glazing medium on palette or lid. Add drops of water until mixture is very thin, about the consistency of India ink.

**2.** Wet #0 liner and touch to paper towel. Load entire liner (not just tip) with paint mixture. Pull liner away from paint puddle while rolling liner tip to fine point. (You should have lines coming out of your paint puddle when you do this.) Hold liner as you would a pencil, but straight up and down. Using light pressure, paint long, fine grain lines along surface (color tile 6). Some grain lines should be closely spaced and run vertically, following the bird's-eyes; others should trail around the knotlike areas, while still others should run horizontally and be wide and wavy. If you can see any grain ridges of the original wood surface through the layers of paint, follow them with your liner for a realistic look. After painting each grain line, lightly brush along direction of grain with blending or mop brush to slightly blur each line. Wipe brush on paper towel as necessary to remove paint. When finished, let dry for 1 hour or more, then apply one coat glazing medium using flat-wash brush. Wait 8 hours before proceeding to next step. Clean brushes and other painting materials with soap and water.

### Stage Five
## Applying the Stain Glaze

**1.** Have within reach: retarder, Molasses paint, clear glazing medium, plastic dish, flat-wash brush, blending or mop brush, cheesecloth, paper towel, and Q-Tips. Mix two parts

retarder to one part Molasses paint in plastic dish, and sample on practice board. If necessary, thin mixture with additional retarder. (Mixture should not be so dark that it obscures the underlying surface, or so quick to dry that you don't have enough time to blend it.) Once mixture looks right, apply to surface of project with flat-wash brush. Remove excess glaze, especially at edges, by dabbing with cheesecloth.

**2.** Using color tile 7 on page 19 as a reference, wipe glaze off in jagged motion along top portion of dark mottled areas using dry Q-Tip. Next, use blending or mop brush to blend vertically, then horizontally, and last diagonally (color tile 8). Wipe brush on folded paper towel between blendings to remove excess paint.

**3.** To create surrounding halo, touch each bird's-eye using clean Q-Tip, as when wiping out oval areas in stage 2, step 5. Repeat blending process as in step 2 above by working blending or mop brush across surface vertically, horizontally, and then diagonally, taking care not to obliterate halos. Final blending should be light enough to eliminate all brush marks. Force-dry surface using blow dryer as in stage 2, step 5. When dry, surface should appear flat, without sheen. When completely dry, apply coat of glazing medium using flat-wash brush. Let dry 8 hours before next stage. Clean brushes and other painting materials with soap and water.

### Stage Six
## Finishing with Matte Varnish

Apply coat of matte varnish using 1¼" flat brush. If project is large enough, use slip-slap method described in stage 1, step 2. Work quickly and avoid reworking areas you've already done, as this dulls the finish. Let varnish dry at least 8 hours, then repeat process to add two additional coats, letting second coat dry for 8 hours before applying third coat. Clean brush with soap and water. ◆

---

*Dianne Georger teaches painting at the Park Shoppe in Hamburg, New York, and is currently studying faux finish painting.*

---

## The Origin of Graining

**Graining may have originated in ancient Egypt, where a shortage of wood stimulated the development of techniques to imitate wood grain. The use of grained softwoods, such as bird's-eye maple, gained momentum in Europe around the time of the French Revolution, when the military was given first choice of harder wood. Locally grown varieties of wood such as beech and pine were available, but interest turned to more exotic wood in the desire for new effects.**

---

emove the hinges and set ide. Place the lid of the est on the box and align, en repeat above steps.
If you have handles for e side of the chest, you'll ed to follow the same ocedure. I placed mine ne and three-quarters ches down from the top of e box. To find the center acement, measure the dth of the box and divide at number in half. Use a ncil to mark this point ne and three-quarters ches down from the top. hen measure from the cen- r of one screw hole to the nter of the other on the

back of the handle. Divide this number in half and use it to make marks to the left and right of the center point on the chest. Decide if the handle screws will be on the inside or outside of the chest, then use an awl, a nail and hammer, or a drill to make starter holes for the screws. Use a screwdriver to turn the screws in, but, again, don't tighten them down completely at this point. Remove handles and screws and set aside in a safe place. If you opt for a closer, lock, hasp, or pull on the front of the chest, follow the same procedures.

# Low-Sew Slipcover

*Stitch up this slip-on chair cover in under an hour using five cotton dishtowels.*

JUST A FEW EASY SEAMS ARE ALL IT takes to sew this light and summery slipcover. The "fabric" is actually a collection of ordinary cotton dishtowels, which can be mixed and matched any way you wish. Using towels eliminates the need for the measuring and hemming that such a sewing project would normally require.

The total cost of this slipcover depends on the towels you choose. If you select $2 towels, for instance, as we did, your total cost is about $10. We used five different towels to create a casual, cottagey look for our slipcover, but you could sew this chair cover from five of the same solid-color towels for a monochromatic look. For a "dressier" version, try linen or damask towels.

This finished slipcover is designed for a ladder-back-style chair, given the narrow width of the towels. (See "Peach and Vine Ladder-Back Chair," May/June 1995, page 6.) Our chair has a tall, straight back measuring forty-three inches high, with an eighteen-inch-high seat and a seat width of nineteen and one-fourth inches, but the finished slipcover will fit any tall-backed chair of similar dimensions.

### INSTRUCTIONS

**1.** Referring to diagrams above, select towel for each position (1 through 5). Lay towel 1 on flat surface, and using ruler and pencil, measure and mark two lines 1½" and 3½" from one short edge. Cut along marked lines to make two ties, as shown in "back" diagram. Narrow-hem raw edges on both ties and raw edge on towel 1.

**2.** Place towel 1 on top of towel 2, right sides together, and sew around two long sides and one short side ¼" from edges. Sew towel 3 to remaining short edge of towel 2, right sides together. Using iron, press seam open.

**3.** With right sides together, stitch short edge of towel 4 to long edge of towel 3 from A to B, then pivot to stitch from B to C. Backtack at C. Stitch towel 5 to opposite edge of towel 3 in same way. Press seams and turn slipcover right side out.

**4.** Lap free edge of towel 1 over nearest edge of towel 4, and topstitch from C to D. Machine-stitch end of one tie to towel 4 directly below C. Machine-stitch end of second tie to corner of towel 5 at E. Place slipcover on chair and tie closed. ◆

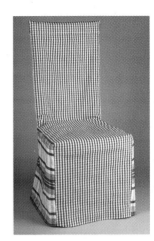

**FRONT**
If the fit on your chair is tight, open up the seams in the front skirt to allow some give.

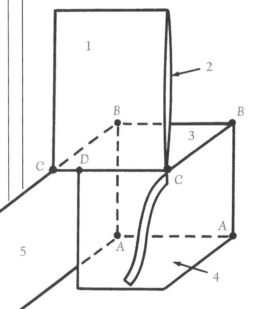

**BACK**
Two narrow ties attached in the back add a finishing touch to the slipcover.

# Testing Lightweight Dressmaker's Shears

*A pair of KAI's eight-inch models take the gold in comfort, performance, and precision.*

BY LISA SHERRY

ALTHOUGH THE WORDS "scissors" and "shears" are used interchangeably by many people, they are really two different types of cutting tools. Scissors are generally less than six inches in length, feature two finger bows of equal size, and are designed for small-scale, more intricate jobs. Shears, on the other hand, are usually eight inches or more in length, feature bows of different sizes (one for the thumb, and the other for two or more fingers), and are designed for cutting longer lengths, larger amounts, or more layers of fabric.

For this article, I tested eleven pairs of lightweight, right-handed or ambidextrous bent dressmaker's shears (aka "trimmers"). Like most lightweight scissors or shears, all the pairs featured plastic handles and weighed about four ounces or less.

I evaluated the shears on several levels—appearance, comfort, performance, and precision—before dropping each pair twice from a height of twenty-nine inches onto a linoleum floor. After dropping each pair, I reevaluated them to see what sort of damage had occurred and whether or not the damage affected their cutting ability. (For additional details, *see* "The Testing Criteria," page 25.)

Overall, the KAI models 5210 and 5220 outperformed all the other models. The KAI shears cut incredibly smoothly through all types of fabric and displayed excellent precision at the tips as well. The only difference between the two is minor: The 5210 has a hard plastic handle and is available in both right- and left-handed versions, while the 5220 has a non-slip, soft plastic handle and is only available in a right-handed version. It also has a slightly larger bottom bow to accommodate a larger hand or additional fingers. The 5210 survived the "drop test" without any damage. Although the 5220 suffered a small nick in its cutting edge after the test, it cut as if the nick wasn't there.

If you're looking for ambidextrous shears, I recommend one of three pairs that I tested: the J. A. Henckels Superfection S. These shears cut the smoothest on all the materials—even though they didn't cut through as many layers as the Mundial Cushion Soft 1860 or the Fiskars Multi-layer 9453—and had the most precision at the tips. I noticed a small nick in the blade of the Superfection S after it was dropped, but it didn't affect the cutting ability or smoothness of the cut at all.

The Mundial Cushion Soft has a nonslip handle with a cushion insert as well as a serrated edge, which proved an advantage when cutting layers of fabric because it prevented slipping. When cutting single layers of lightweight or delicate fabric like voile,

## Before You Buy

I would strongly advise trying out any pair of shears before purchasing them, preferably on the type of fabric(s) you expect to use them for, since comfort is largely a matter of personal preference.

Some sewing stores will let you try out products, while others won't. (Be sure to ask before you assume they won't.) In some stores, the staff may also be using the products they sell, and may let you try them out.

If ordering shears by mail, be sure to check on the return policy before purchasing in case the shears are not comfortable and need to be returned.

A good pair of shears should give an even, clean cut for the full length of the blade without hesitation or roughness. In the industry, this is referred to as a good "run." In addition to what feels comfortable to you and performs effectively, I recom-

mend purchasing only those shears that feature an adjustable screw (versus a rivet-type pivot), as this is the only means of adjusting the shears should the blades become misaligned.

Be sure to note the shears' blade tension as well. Loose blades are easy to open and close but may not cut well. Tight blades are hard to open and close; they may cut cleaner but your hand may tire more easily.

### TESTER'S TIP
If purchasing shears by mail order, consider buying three or four pairs in order to try them out, then keep the most comfortable pair and return the others.

# Lightweight Dressmaker's Shears

| PRODUCT NAME AND MODEL NUMBER | SUGGESTED RETAIL PRICE | RIGHT/LEFT/ AMBIDEXTROUS | WEIGHT | COMFORT OF BOW AND HANDLE |
|---|---|---|---|---|
| Clauss Zephyr Model 208 | $11.64 | Right-handed; left (Model LH 208) available | 2.88 ounces | Good, but shank is sharp |
| Clauss Zephyr Model 308 | $13.49 | Right-handed | 3.68 ounces | Good, but shank is sharp |
| Fiskars Model 9451 | $14.40 | Right-handed; left (Model 9450) available | 2.88 ounces | Loose, but very good long periods of use |
| Fiskars Multi-Layer Model 9453 | $18.50 | Ambidextrous | 2.88 ounces | Good |
| Fiskars Razor Edged Model 9454 | $22.95 | Right-handed | 2.88 ounces | Good, even after long periods of use |
| J. A. Henckels Superfection S Model 41800-211 | $23.00 | Ambidextrous | 3.04 ounces | Very good |
| J. A. Henckels Twin L Model 41300-221 | $20.00 | Right-handed | 3.04 ounces | Good, but felt "seam" on interior of bow |
| KAI Model 5210 | $17.00 | Right-handed; left (Model 5210L) available | 4.00 ounces | Very good |
| KAI Model 5220 | $23.50 | Right-handed; left not available yet | 4.16 ounces | Very good; nonslip feature adds comfort |
| Mundial Cushion Soft Model 1860 | $15.50 | Ambidextrous | 2.88 ounces | Very good; nonslip feature adds comfort |
| Mundial Knife Edged Model 660 | $13.95 | Right-handed; left (Model 661) available | 2.56 ounces | Loose, but very good long periods of use |

however, the serrated edge snagged the fabric. Furthermore, when trying to clip stitches open, the serrations on the bottom edge grabbed the thread, making it difficult to clip the stitch properly.

If you've had trouble finding shears that still prove comfortable over longer periods of cutting time (i.e., five hours or more) and need something more versatile than the Mundial Cushion Soft, I recommend the Fiskars 9451 or the Mundial 660. Of the two plastic-handled shears, the Mundial 660 cut more layers of fabric and cut more smoothly; however, both pairs featured a wide-bottom cutting edge, which made it difficult to open up stitches.

The Clauss Zephyr 208 and 308—among the lightest of the lightweights—were able to hold their own when cutting layers and scored fairly high on point precision, but the shank (the upper part of the bow toward the blade) of both pairs was sharp and ended up irritating my index finger when cutting for long periods of time.

The 308 also sustained significant damage when dropped (a broken and cracked lower handle as well as numerous nicks) and chewed even single layers of all fabrics after the drop test. The 208 suffered no damage to the handles after the drop test, but a nick in the lower blade made it impossible to cut even a single layer of fabric. One other note: All the shears feature an adjustable pivot, and most of the shears had good alignment of the pivot and point, with one exception: the Clauss Zephyr 208.

*Editor's note:* All the shears tested for this article were generously donated by each of the manufacturers represented in the chart above. Gingher, Inc., chose not to participate. ◆

*Lisa Sherry, who spent several years working in a fabric store, writes articles and designs craft projects from her home in Sag Harbor, New York.*

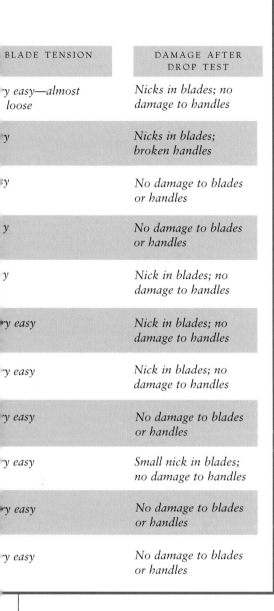

| BLADE TENSION | DAMAGE AFTER DROP TEST |
|---|---|
| ...ry easy—almost ...loose | *Nicks in blades; no damage to handles* |
| ...y | *Nicks in blades; broken handles* |
| ...sy | *No damage to blades or handles* |
| ...y | *No damage to blades or handles* |
| ...y | *Nick in blades; no damage to handles* |
| ...ry easy | *Nick in blades; no damage to handles* |
| ...ry easy | *Nick in blades; no damage to handles* |
| ...y easy | *No damage to blades or handles* |
| ...ry easy | *Small nick in blades; no damage to handles* |
| ...ry easy | *No damage to blades or handles* |
| ...ry easy | *No damage to blades or handles* |

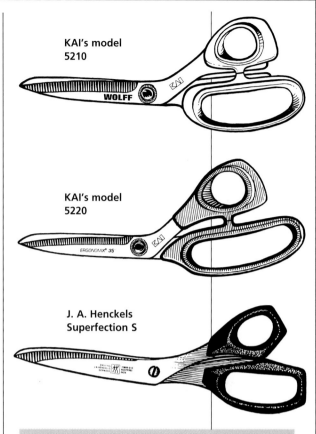

KAI's model 5210

KAI's model 5220

J. A. Henckels Superfection S

## The Testing Criteria

■ **Appearance:** Do the shears have an adjustable pivot? Are the blades properly aligned (i.e., touching at the pivot and at the tips when closed)? Do the blades have smooth, sharp, or rough edges? Are there any nicks or imperfections on the blade's cutting edges?

■ **Comfort:** What is the size of the bow and the material it's made from? What is the contour of the bow? What is the blade tension?

■ **Performance:** Do the blades cut smoothly and cleanly (meaning the cut material falls away from the blades) from the base of the blade to the tip without experiencing any of the following problems: "chewing," in which the blades are unable to cut through the material, and the material ends up getting stuck between the blades; "holding," in which the material is cut through to the tips but remains stuck at the blade tips, caught by a few threads or fibers; or "crossing," in which the fabric is chewed as a result of the handles actually crossing over each other.

■ As part of performance, cutting tests were conducted on the following:

—one layer of: polyester voile, cotton broadcloth, cotton chenille, and eight-ounce cotton duck;

—the maximum number of layers of cotton broadcloth, cotton chenille, and eight-ounce cotton duck that could be cut clean to the tip with one hand.

■ **Precision:** Special tests designed to highlight the performance of the tips included clipping notches in one layer of tissue paper, voile, broadcloth, and duck and clipping stitches (six, eight, twelve, and fifteen per inch) in broadcloth seams with seams pressed open and closed.

■ **Drop test:** Shears were dropped twice from a height of twenty-nine inches onto a linoleum floor, examined for damage to the handles, misalignment of the blades, and nicks, then reevaluated in two cutting tests. In the first, the shears cut one layer of voile, broadcloth, duck cloth, and chenille to determine if they could cut clean to the tips. In the second, they were tested to determine if they could still cut the same maximum number of layers of chenille that they had cut before the drop test.

## After You Buy

Proper care of your shears is essential for ensuring long-term product lifespan and satisfaction. Shears should be stored in a safe, dry place when not in use to prevent damage to the blades. Blades should be wiped clean after use to prevent lint, dust, or grit from getting into the pivot and impairing its action.

Take care not to drop your shears, as we purposely did during testing, since even a good pair of shears can easily be damaged. One easy solution is to string your shears on a ribbon and wear them around your neck, although care should always be taken around sharp edges and tips. Once or twice a year (more often if you do a lot of cutting), apply a drop of oil at the pivot, then thoroughly wipe away any excess to avoid soiling the fabric.

Dressmaker's shears should only be used for cutting fabrics, and never relegated to cutting paper, plastic, cardboard, or tape. If your blades ever need sharpening, I recommend turning the job over to a professional, as home-sharpening gadgets have been known to ruin the cutting edge on a high-quality pair of shears. One other note: Some manufacturers will accept their own shears back for sharpening for a nominal fee.

If you like dried roses, try making this window valance, which features a bouquet of dried roses at its center. It's a great substitute for curtains.

# Dried Flower Valance

*Assemble this unique window treatment in minutes using dried flowers and an ordinary curtain rod.*

### BY SYLVIA LACHTER

WHETHER YOU'RE LOOK-ing for a light and summerlike window treatment, or are just interested in a fresh approach to dressing up a bare window, a valance of dried flowers can be the perfect solution. This valance is quite simple to make: The dried flowers are bundled into small bouquets, then attached to an adjustable curtain rod using florist wire and tape.

I assembled this valance using some of my favorite dried flowers—roses, hydrangea, globe amaranth, statice, daisies, and larkspur—but this design would work well with other flowers. Dried flowers are very fragile, so work carefully to avoid crushing them. I recommend covering your work surface with brown kraft paper or newspaper

for quick and easy cleanup.

This window decoration works wonderfully with sheer curtains, as shown above. Sheers complement the light and airy feel of the dried flowers and can be hung on a tension rod that is recessed into the window frame. If the dried

flower valance is designed to replace existing curtains, permanently or temporarily, remove and set aside the curtains and their hardware.

## INSTRUCTIONS
### Preparing the Bouquets
Cover your work surface with brown kraft paper or newspaper. For each of the steps below, gather the required flowers into a bouquet, then wind the specified length of wire around the stems. Using needle-nose pliers, twist the wire ends together in a tight spiral, snip off the excess wire ½" from the stems, and bend the spiraled section down against the stems. Using pruning shears, cut off any excess stem about ½" below the twisted wire, then wind green florist tape around the wired areas to cover the wire's sharp edges.

**1.** Using pliers, cut two 10" lengths of wire. Gather roses into two bouquets of six to seven roses each. Wind wire around stems to bind each bouquet at a point about 2½" below calyxes, and finish as directed above.

**2.** Divide purple globe amaranth into four groups of twelve to sixteen heads each. Divide pink globe amaranth into four groups of six to eight heads each. Gather one purple globe amaranth group into bouquet, then arrange heads from one pink globe amaranth group around it. Bind stems with 8" length of wire and finish. Repeat to make four bouquets.

**3.** Break off 5"- to 6"-long sprigs from statice and divide into six equal groups. Divide white globe amaranth

## MATERIALS

- 12 to 14 large-petaled, deep pink roses on stems
- 4 reddish green and/or bluish green hydrangea heads, each 3" to 4" across
- 2 large bunches (48 to 64 stems) purple globe amaranth
- 1 large bunch (24 to 32 stems) pink globe amaranth
- 1 medium bunch (16 to 20 stems) white globe amaranth

- 4 bunches lavender statice, each bunch 4" to 6" across
- 2 large bunches (48 to 64 stems) white miniature daisies
- 1 large bunch (24 to 32 stems) pink daisies
- 6 sprigs purple larkspur
- 1 bunch curly wild grass
- 5 yards 1" pink novelty ribbon
- Adjustable curtain rod, to fit window frame 32" to 36" across, with surface-mounting brackets

- Spool of 36-gauge green florist wire
- Green florist tape
- Masking tape

*You'll also need:* tape measure; brown kraft paper or newspaper; needle-nose pliers with built-in wire cutter; pruning shears; four heavy books or bricks; screwdriver and/or hammer; scissors; and pencil.

PHOTOGRAPH BY STEVEN MAYS

into four groups of four to five heads each. Gather sprigs from one statice group into bouquet, then intersperse heads from one white globe amaranth group. Bind stems with 8" length of wire and finish. Repeat to make three more statice/white globe amaranth bouquets and two plain statice bouquets. Using shears, snip off any protruding statice sprigs to keep bouquets round and symmetrical.

**4.** Divide pink daisies into two bouquets of twelve to sixteen heads each. Divide white miniature daisies into four bouquets of twelve to sixteen heads each. Bind stems of each bouquet with 6" length of wire and finish.

**5.** Divide curly wild grass into two bunches about ½" in diameter at stem end. Bind each bunch together 1" from end with 8" length of wire and finish. Use shears to clip and even up ends.

## Assembling the Garland

**1.** Following curtain rod package instructions and using screwdriver or hammer as directed, attach mounting brackets to window frame so rod will extend 32" to 36" across. Mount rod on brackets, then wrap masking tape around rod at joint near center to prevent movement.

**2.** Remove rod from brackets and set it up on its ends on flat work surface, propping each end between two heavy books or bricks. Using tape measure and pencil, measure and mark midpoint of rod. Hold two rose bouquets so they straddle rod at midpoint, close enough to appear to form one bouquet; wrapped stems should extend down along either side of rod toward work surface, and rose heads should rise about 2" above rod (rather than rest directly on rod).

**3.** Unwinding wire directly from spool and leaving 3" free at end, wrap wire six to eight times around stems of both bouquets directly below rod, then six to eight times directly above rod, then diagonally around rod from both directions to form an X. (You'll need to pick up or lift the rod to complete the diagonal). To end off, use pliers to clip wire from spool; twist wire ends together in tight spiral, snip off excess wire ½" from rod and stems, and bend spiraled section down against stems. Wind florist tape around stems and rod to reinforce joint and cover sharp wire edges.

**4.** Following wire and tape method described in previous step, attach two hydrangea heads to rod at each side of roses so each pair covers rod and appears as one bouquet. Using same wire and tape method, attach remaining bouquets in pairs, building valance from center out to sides as follows: two purple and pink globe amaranth bouquets; two statice/white globe amaranth bouquets; one pink daisy bouquet in "top" position and one statice bouquet below it; and two white daisy bouquets. (*See* illustrations 1 through 4.) Evaluate overall spacing of bouquets and make minor adjustments, if necessary, by carefully sliding bouquets along rod.

**5.** Use wire and florist tape to attach bunch of wild grass to each end of rod, and stick sprigs of larkspur into bouquets to add extra color and interest. Mount rod on brackets. Cut ribbon according to number of bows and length desired. Tie bows, then use wire and florist tape to attach them along top of valance, allowing streamers to fall behind flowers. ◆

**1** Cover the center of the valance with two bouquets of deep pink roses, followed by hydrangea heads on either side.

**2** Building outwards from the center, position two purple and pink globe amaranth bouquets on either side of the hydrangea bouquets.

**3** Next, position two statice and white globe amaranth bouquets, followed by one pink daisy bouquet and one lavender statice bouquet below it.

**4** To finish the valance, position two white daisy bouquets at the ends of the curtain rod, and attach a bunch of curly grass to each end of the rod.

# Secrets of Foolproof Sponged Wall Finishes

*Give your walls exciting visual texture with a household or sea sponge and two shades of latex paint.*

❧ BY CHRIS ALTSCHULER

**Print with the ring side of a sea sponge for an open, airy look.**

Of the numerous techniques professional decorators use to give interior walls visual texture and interest, sponging is one of the easiest for the home crafter to master. Sponging involves more than one shade of paint, letting you create tonal effects not possible with a single flat color. If your walls are in less-than-perfect condition, sponging is the made-to-order camouflage, able to obscure ripples, bumps, and other surface blemishes that flat paint only accentuates. Any room in your home, from the kitchen and bathroom to a hallway or bedroom, is a good candidate for a sponging makeover.

As a painting tool, a sponge offers versatility not found in a standard paintbrush. A sponge can be touched against the wall to leave a dappled, printed impression, or streaked along the surface, spreading and smearing paint like a brush. A third method, which borrows elements from both of these techniques, involves first touching the sponge to the surface and then twisting it. Each of these three simple techniques—printing, twisting, and streaking—produces its own distinct texture.

### Choosing a Sponge

Over the years, I've tried all three techniques with various types of sponges, but I recommend just two types: the sea sponge or the cellulose household sponge.

If you can afford one, I recommend a sea sponge for wall-sponging projects. Sold in better paint, art supply, and automotive supply stores, they cost between $6.50 and $30. The price reflects size as well as availability; good and bad years for harvesting these sea creatures cause prices to fluctuate. A sea sponge has two distinct sides: the prickly side, or the side that grows out toward the ocean, and the rock-clinging side, which has a ringed texture. Both can be used for printing, twisting, or streaking to produce a range of effects. (*See* color samples below.)

Cellulose household sponges, in contrast, start at around 50¢ and are widely available at discount stores, hardware stores, and supermarkets. Cellulose is a natural plant fiber that is reconstituted during manufacturing, and it has notable water-absorbing ability. Make sure you don't inadvertently buy a sponge that is made of less absorbent plastic; unfortunately, both cellulose and plastic sponges are sometimes labeled "synthetic," so read the package information carefully.

A sponge made of cellulose lacks the sea sponge's exotic allure, and its uniformly patterned surfaces and sharp, recti-linear edges can work against creating random, varied texture unless you alter the sponge slightly from its original shape and form. To give a rectangular sponge more personality, cut or tear it into several irregular pieces, or bevel the rectangular edges with a craft knife and then rip out small pieces of sponge at random using needle-nose pliers.

For best results, choose a sponge a little larger than your hand. Sea sponges are sold in six-, eight-, ten-, twelve-, and fourteen-inch "cuts," based on the diameter of the sponge when wet. The eight-inch cut (the most common) is the easiest to handle and maneuver into tight corners. A three-by-six-by-one-and-one-half-inch cellulose sponge is

## A Variety of Sea Sponge Effects

### Printing with the Ring Side

**1** For best results, press the sponge against the wall, lift the sponge off the wall, move it to the next area, rotate the wrist slightly, and press again.

### Twisting with the Ring Side

**2** This technique is very similar to printing, but you should twist the wrist before lifting the sponge off the surface.

## Troubleshooting

comparable in size, though a bit heavier. In general, choose a sponge that's a convenient size to grip but not so big that you can't control it. If a sponge is too big and unwieldy, it may tend to "jump" from your hand during particularly vigorous streaking activity.

### Printing, Twisting, and Streaking

The three basic sponging gestures and the finishes they produce are easily recognized (*see* color samples below and on page 30). Printing, the simplest of the three, produces a crisp, clean, understated look that works well in a bedroom, study, or small, intimate space. To print, dip either the prickly or the ring side of the sponge into the paint, dab off the excess, then lightly press the sponge to the wall repeatedly in a random pattern. Don't rush, and be careful not to move or shift the sponge on the wall; instead, simply touch it to the surface. After each press, lift the sponge from the wall and rotate it slightly in your hand. This rotation—particularly important if you are using a household sponge—prevents any repetition of the sponge's texture from becoming notice-

### Dripping Paint
**If your paint drips, your sponge is probably too wet. A properly moistened sponge shouldn't drip when you pick it up or press it lightly against the wall.**

able in the overall pattern. Keep in mind that the harder you press, the darker the print, and the lighter you press, the more delicate the print. You should be able to make between five and ten prints with each load of paint.

Twisting is similar to printing in technique, but quite different in final appearance. Since the resulting look has a bit more energy to it, consider using it in a hallway or dining room in order to create an upbeat mood. Follow the same procedure as for printing except twist your wrist as the sponge hits or lifts off the wall. Instead of sharp, clear prints, aim to create soft, swirly impressions with a hint of motion. Try moving around a small two-square-foot area without breaking contact from the wall as you rotate your wrist back and forth.

Streaking is the most energetic of the three techniques. To streak a wall, draw the sponge vigorously but lightly against the surface in one- to two-foot-long strokes, varying the direction on each pass. Put your arm, not just your wrist, into the motion. The resulting finish will be bold, energetic, and dramatic, best appreciated from across a

spacious room or looking up into an open architectural space, particularly if strong colors are used.

### Tips and Techniques

No matter which sponging gesture you use, your goal is to achieve a texture that has a sort of random evenness. The patterns formed should be loose, undulating, and unpredictable, yet give an overall impression of coherence and stability, without any gaping holes or overworked areas to mar the effect.

To achieve the best results, put a small amount of paint in the bottom of a bucket and load the sponge as evenly as possible, dabbing off the excess on the inside wall of the bucket. If necessary, work the sponging pattern on a piece of scrap paper to eliminate any excess paint. Apply the paint to the wall very lightly at first, then step back and examine your work overall, looking for areas that are noticeably spare or void of color. As you fill in these areas, continue to step back occasionally and view the results. Plan

**To give a household sponge more texture, tear it into several small pieces.**

### Streaking with the Ring Side
**3** Contrary to what you might think, the harder you press, the more the sponge detail is compressed and lost. For maximum texture, press lightly.

### Painting with the Prickly Side
**4** The technique for printing with the prickly side is the same as with the ring side, but the impressions are smaller and denser.

### Twisting with the Prickly Side
**5** As in sample 4, twisting with the prickly side of the sea sponge creates a similar but denser effect.

### Streaking with the Prickly Side
**6** This streaking effect, smoother than the effect created with the ring side of the sponge, resembles a dry-brush technique.

## Household Sponge Effects

### Printing with Household Sponge

**1** Printing is done the same way as with a sea sponge, but cut or rip the sponge into odd shapes for the best results.

### Streaking with Household Sponge

**2** Streaking is similar to the effect created with a sea sponge, but notice that the stroke is fatter.

on at least two passes.

If you find you've applied the paint too heavily in one area and the paint is still wet, you can wipe off the "mistake" with a fresh damp sponge. Make several passes with the sponge, rinsing it thoroughly between wipes, until the area is clean. To prevent smearing, let the wall dry thoroughly before you repaint the area. If the paint has already begun to dry on the wall, you can either darken the overall sponged-on coat to match the problem area or repaint the base coat and start again.

A sponge that is soft, pliable, and in good condition is key to a professional job. Keep a bucket of fresh water at hand, and before you begin painting or if your sponge seems to be drying out as you work, dip it in the water until saturated. Squeeze out the excess water, then give the sponge one final gentle squeeze to remove any lingering drops. A properly moistened sponge should not drip when you pick it up or press it lightly against the wall.

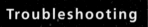

### Dark Spots
If darker areas such as these emerge on your wall, you've probably picked up too much paint on the sponge. Work it through to distribute the paint, and try for less paint on the sponge.

Take care not to let paint dry and harden on your sponge, as you'll need to cut off the painted area. While on a household sponge this is not a problem, on a sea sponge such action may eliminate the interesting outer surface and expose the interior, where the holes are closer together and less pronounced. This may or may not be desirable, depending on the look you're trying to achieve.

### Choosing Your Paint Colors
Sponged wall finishes require two shades of paint: a latex base coat in an eggshell or satin finish, which can be applied with a roller, and one or more latex sponge coats in the same finish. Alkyd (oil-based) paint, with its higher viscosity, won't show off the sponged texture to advantage and is not recommended for sponging.

It's not necessarily a rule that colors in a room must match. If you play the matching game, you're often limited by the choices available in fabrics or carpets. My advice is this: Simply choose the colors you like. Everyone has an intuitive preference for a particular palette. If you go with what feels right, all the colors will likely work together, although they may not match.

While many color combinations are possible, the most fail-safe formula is two different shades (light and dark) of the same hue (color). Typically, the lighter color is sponged over the darker base color, but you can also try the reverse. Light and dark shades can be chosen directly from a paint chip, but a less expensive way is to buy paint in the chosen hue, then mix some of it with white paint for the same hue a few shades lighter. If you must mix hues, keep them very close to each other.

If you're a beginner, I advise toning down your color choices. If you like bright colors, for instance, choose a shade that is a less intense, more earthy version of the color you thought you wanted. Similarly, choose the color in a slightly lighter shade than the color you thought you wanted. The reason is this: Most people react to color on a small scale, where more intense colors work fine. Those same colors played out on a large scale, such as a wall, however, have a much more drastic effect.

Although I generally don't like rules, one important decorating rule I live by is this: A wall should serve as a backdrop for the objects and fabrics in a room, rather than the other way around.

If you're uncertain how a color duo will look on your walls, or if you're trying to narrow your choices, paint and sponge a sample of each combination on a two-foot-square piece of cardboard or foam core. When the sample is dry, tape it to the wall and examine it at different times of the day, by natural and artificial light, to determine if the effect satisfies your expectations.

The samples shown on these two pages used two colors: an off-white base coat, and sponged effects with Benjamin Moore #1418. ◆

*Chris Altschuler is a decorative painter and wallpaper maker living in Chicago.*

### Troubleshooting

**Light Areas**
In this example, too little paint was applied, giving the wall an unfinished look. Spend more time working on such a spot, and try picking up more paint on the sponge.

# Home-Grown Dried Flowers

*With one or two seed packets and a small plot of land,
you can easily grow and dry any of these flowers yourself.*

Common name of flower;
planting conditions; best
method for drying:

**1.** *Cockscomb;* any soil,
sunny position; air-dry
hanging.

**2.** *Yellow everlasting or
strawflower;* any soil, sunny
position; air-dry hanging.

**3.** *Pink everlasting or
strawflower;* any soil, sunny
position; air-dry hanging.

**4.** *Mop-headed hydrangea;*
moist, well-drained soil,
semishady position; air-dry
hanging or standing.

**5.** *Safflower;* any soil, sunny
position; air-dry hanging.

**6.** *Cerise-tinged tea rose;*
well-drained soil, sunny
position; air-dry hanging
or desiccant.

**7.** *Golden-headed yarrow;*
any soil, partial sunlight; air-
dry hanging or standing.

**8.** *Peonies;* any well-drained
soil, sunny position; air-dry
hanging or desiccant.

**9.** *Pink tea rose;* well-
drained soil, sunny position;
air-dry hanging or desiccant.

**10.** *Larkspur;* well-drained
soil, sunny position; air-dry
hanging or standing.

**11.** *Globe amaranth;* any
soil, sunny position; air-dry
hanging.

**12.** *Globe thistle;* any soil,
sunny position; air-dry
hanging.

**13.** *Small-headed yarrow;*

any soil, partial sunlight; air-
dry hanging.

**14.** *Love-in-a-mist;* any soil,
sunny position; air-dry
hanging.

**15.** *Large-flowered sunray;*
any soil, sunny position;
air-dry hanging.

**16.** *Lavender;* any soil,
sunny position; air-dry

hanging.

**17.** *Russian statice;* any soil,
sunny position; air-dry
hanging.

Most of the materials needed for the projects in this issue are available at your local craft supply, hardware, or paint store, florist's, fabric shop, or bead and jewelry supply. Generic craft supplies, such as scissors, all-purpose white glue, paint, ribbon, and thread, can be ordered from such catalogs as Craft King Discount Craft Supply, Dick Blick, Newark Dressmaker Supply, Pearl Paint, or Sunshine Discount Crafts. The following are specific mail-order sources for particular items, arranged by project. The suggested retail prices listed here were current at press time. Contact the suppliers directly to confirm prices and availability of products.

# Sources
## AND RESOURCES

❧

**Quick Tips**; *page 4*
*Bleached White Pinecones:* Pinecones for $2.49 per pound from Craft King. *Controlling Unruly Fringe:* Scotch white artist's tape from $5.88 per 60 yards from Co-op Artists' Materials. *Marble Mirage:* Multicolored marbles for $1.19 from Ben Franklin. *Stenciled Icing:* Selection of precut stencils from $3 from Stencil World.

❧

**Fabulous Farmstand Bouquets**; *page 6*
Cosmos seeds from $1.40 per packet from Thompson and Morgan, Burpee Gardens, Park Seed, and Shepherd's Garden Seeds. Florist clay for $1.28 per 5 ounces, natural raffia for $3.45 per 8 ounces, and Spanish moss for $2.35 per 8 ounces, all from Craft King. Miniature baskets for $8.99 per dozen from Best Buy Floral Supply. Selection of PlasTerra clay pots from $1.49 from Akro-Mils Specialty Products. Cobalt pitcher for $21.95 from Crate and Barrel.

❧

**Carved Fish Decoy**
*page 8*
Super bench knife for $9.95, 2" x 3" x 12" block basswood for $7.95, and file sets from $13.95, all from Wood Carvers Supply. Copper or brass sheeting for $4 per 4" x 10" piece from K&S Engineering Company. Patina Green patinating solution for $18 per 10 ounces from Flax Art and

Design. Butcher's liquid wax for $14.50 per gallon, 5-minute epoxy for $3.56 per 2.5 ounces, and Shiva acrylic paint from $2.52 per 2 ounces, all from Pearl Paint.

❧

**Color-Blended Stenciling**
*page 12*
Delta Stencil Magic Paint Creme for $2.25 per ½ ounce, variety of precut stencil designs from 70¢, and stencil brushes from 95¢, all from Craft King. Krylon spray varnish for $4.20 per 11-ounce can, 9" x 12" Canson vellum for $7.45, and odorless paint thinner for $3.30 per quart, all from Dick Blick. 13" x 20" cotton place mats for $4.99 per set of four, 12"-square cocktail napkins for $15 per set of twelve, and 19½"-square dinner napkins for $24 per set of twelve, all from Williams-Sonoma. Selection of rugs from $29 from Pottery Barn.

❧

**Rose Petal Frame**; *page 16*
Silica gel crystals for $5.21 per 1½ pounds, selection of wooden frames from $5, and Liquitex acrylic matte medium for $5.64 per 8 ounces, all from Pearl Paint. Miniature roses from $3.50 per stem or $42 per dozen from Village Flowers.

❧

**Bird's-Eye Maple Faux Finish**; *page 18*
Large selection of unfinished wood items ranging from 7¢ to $189, Delta Ceramcoat wood sealer for $1.59 per 2 ounces, Jo Sonja's Retarder and Antiquing Medium for $6 per 8 ounces, Jo Sonja's Clear Glazing Medium for $6.99 per 8 ounces, Delta Ceramcoat acrylic paint for $1.79 per 2 ounces, Folk Art acrylic paint for $1.49 per 2 ounces, and Right Step Matte Varnish for $6.55 per 8 ounces, all from The Park Shoppe. Sea sponge for $6.40 from Pearl Paint.

❧

**Low-Sew Slipcover**
*page 22*
Cotton dishtowels in a variety of patterns from $4.99 per set of four from Williams-Sonoma.

❧

**Testing Shears**; *page 23*
Contact shears manufacturers directly to locate the nearest retailer in your area. KAI models are manufactured by Wolff Industries.

❧

**Dried Flower Valance**
*page 26*
Amaranth in a variety of colors from $2.55 per bunch, larkspur (delphinium) for $4.10 per bunch, hydrangea for $2.50 per bunch, statice from $3.65 per bunch, pink roses from $7.55 per bunch, daisies from $2.16 per bunch, selection of wild grasses from $2.50, all from Floral Express. Adjustable café rods for $10 for sizes 29" to 48" from More Window Ways.

❧

**Foolproof Sponged Wall Finishes**; *page 28*
Sea sponge for $6.50 and latex paint from $5 per quart from Pearl Paint. Latex paint in an eggshell finish approximately $22.95 per gallon and latex paint in a satin finish approximately $25.75 per gallon from Benjamin Moore. (Contact your local retailer to confirm prices and availability.)

❧

**Field Guide to Home-Grown Dried Flowers**
*page 31*
Large selection of flower seed packets available from Shepherd's Garden Seeds, Burpee Gardens, Thompson and Morgan, and Park Seed. Prices start at $1.30 per packet.

❧

**Quick Projects**
*page 33*
Selection of pillowcases from

Coming Home, The Company Store, and Domestications. Prices start at $9.99. Lace trims from 95¢ per 5 yards and fringe from $1.85 per 5 yards from Home-Sew.

❧

**Frozen Floral Ice Bucket**
*back cover*
Pink or yellow roses for $5 per stem from Village Flowers. Multicolored marbles for $1.19 from Ben Franklin.

The following companies are mentioned in the listings provided above. Contact each individually for a price list or catalog.

**Akro-Mils Specialty Products,** P.O. Box 989, Akron, OH 44309; 800-253-2467
**Ben Franklin Retail Stores, Inc.,** 500 East N. Avenue, Carol Stream, IL 60188; 708-462-6100
**Benjamin Moore,** 51 Chestnut Ridge Road, Montvale, NJ 07645; 800-826-2623
**Best Buy Floral Supply,** P.O. Box 1982, Cedar Rapids, IA 52406; 800-553-8497
**Burpee Gardens,** 300 Park Avenue, Warminster, PA 18991-0001; 800-888-1447
**Clauss, Inc.,** 223 North Prospect Street, Fremont, OH 43420; 800-225-2877
**Coming Home,** 1 Land's End Lane, Dodgeville, WI 53595; 800-345-3696
**The Company Store,** 500 Company Store Road, La Crosse, WI 54601-4477; 800-289-8508
**Co-op Artists' Materials,** P.O. Box 53097, Atlanta, GA 30355; 800-877-3242
**Craft King Discount Craft Supply,** P.O. Box 90637, Lakeland, FL 33804; 800-769-9494
**Crate and Barrel,** P.O. Box 9059, Wheeling, IL 60090-9059; 800-323-5461
**Dick Blick,** P.O. Box 1267, Galesburg, IL 61402-1267; 800-447-8192
**Domestications,** P.O. Box 40,

Hanover, PA 17333-0040; 800-746-2555
**Fiskars Inc.,** P.O. Box 8027, Wausau, WI 54402-8027; 715-842-2091
**Flax Art and Design,** P.O. Box 7216, San Francisco, CA 94120-7216; 800-343-3529
**Floral Express,** 11 Armco Avenue, Caribou, ME 04736; 800-392-7417
**Home-Sew,** P.O. Box 4099, Bethlehem, PA 18018-0099; 610-867-3833
**J. A. Henckels,** 9 Skyline Drive, Hawthorne, NY 10532; 914-592-7370
**K&S Engineering Company,** 6917 West 59th Street, Chicago, IL 60638; 312-586-8503
**More Window Ways,** A Country Curtains Company, Main Street, Stockbridge, MA 01262-0965; 800-785-9215
**Mundial,** 50 Kerry Place, Norwood, MA 02062; 800-487-2224
**Newark Dressmaker Supply,** 6473 Ruch Road, P.O. Box 20730, Lehigh Valley, PA 18002-0730; 800-736-6783
**Park Seed,** Cokesbury Road, Greenswood, SC 29647-0001; 803-223-7333
**The Park Shoppe,** 54 Lake Street, Hamburg, NY 14075; 716-648-2577
**Pearl Paint,** 308 Canal Street, New York, NY 10013; 800-221-6845
**Pottery Barn,** P.O. Box 7044, San Francisco, CA 94120-7044; 800-922-5507
**Shepherd's Garden Seeds,** 30 Irene Street, Torrington, CT 06790; 203-482-3638
**Stencil World,** P.O. Box 1112, Newport, RI 02840; 800-274-7997
**Sunshine Discount Crafts,** P.O. Box 301, Largo, FL 34649-0301; 813-538-2878
**Thompson and Morgan,** P.O. Box 1308, Jackson, NJ 08527-0308; 800-274-7333
**Village Flowers,** 297 Main Street, Huntington, NY 11743; 516-427-0996
**Williams-Sonoma,** P.O. Box 7456, San Francisco, CA 94120-7456; 800-541-2233
**Wolff Industries, Inc.,** 1250 Southport Road, Spartanburg, SC 29306; 800-888-3832
**Wood Carvers Supply,** P.O. Box 7500, Englewood, FL 34295; 800-284-6229 ◆

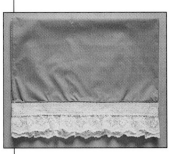

**Sage Green
with Two-Tiered Lace**

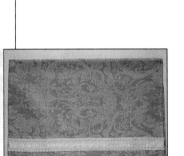

**Blue Damask
with Embroidered Ribbon**

**White-on-White Stripe
with Picket Lace**

**White-on-White Stripe
with Bridal Lace**

# Quick
## PROJECTS

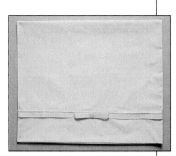

**Peppermint Pink
with Grosgrain Bow**

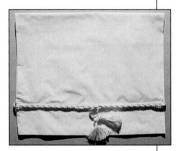

**Gold Embroidered Trim**

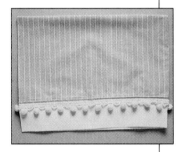

**Linen-Look Stripe
with Ball Fringe**

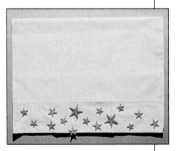

**Gold Stars**

Do your pillowcases need perking up? You can rejuvenate them in just a few minutes by adding lace, ribbon, cord, or ball fringe, among other things. The measurements listed below are for standard 20"-wide pillowcases; to calculate the length of your trim for nonstandard-size pillowcases, double the pillowcase width and add a 1" allowance.

### Sage Green
### with Two-Tiered Lace

Stitch a 41" length of 2½"-wide pre-gathered lace trim 2" from edge of pillowcase; tuck raw ends under for neat finish. Repeat process with second length of lace, but stitch ½" from previous stitching to create tiered effect. Pin and stitch 41" length of 1⅝"-wide ecru trim to remaining exposed section of hem.

### Blue Damask
### with Embroidered Ribbon

Pin and stitch a 41" length of 1⅝"-wide white trim with pink shell embroidery around hem, tucking raw ends under for neat finish.

### White-on-White Stripe
### with Picket Lace

Pin a 41" length of 3"-wide white lace trim with one scalloped edge and one pointed edge around hem so scalloped edge overhangs pillowcase edge by ⅛". Tuck raw ends under for neat finish, then stitch trim ¼" from scalloped edge.

### White-on-White
### Stripe with Bridal Lace

Pin a 41" length of 3"-wide bridal lace 1" above edge of pillowcase. Tuck raw ends under for neat finish, then zigzag along both edges of trim.

### Peppermint Pink
### with Grosgrain Bow

Start with a pink pillowcase with self-piped hem. Stitch a 41" length of ⅝"-wide pink grosgrain ribbon around hem of pillowcase, butting piping. To create bow, cut 10" length of ribbon, overlap ends by ½" to form loop, and secure using water-soluble fabric glue. (Glue will rinse out during first wash.) Flatten loop so glued section is centered at back. Wrap 1½" length of pink ribbon around center of loop to make mock bow, then overlap and glue ends at back. Center bow on pillowcase ribbon and hand-sew in place with pink thread.

### Gold Embroidered Trim

Pin a 41" length of 1"-wide gold metallic embroidered trim around hem of pillowcase. Tuck raw ends under for neat finish, then stitch along both edges of trim.

### Linen-Look Stripe
### with Ball Fringe

Start with a linen-look striped pillowcase with solid ecru hem joined by fagoting. Pin a 41" length of ecru cotton ball fringe around hem of pillowcase just below fagoting. Stitch both edges of fringe tape to hem using zipper foot.

### Gold Stars

Start with a pillowcase with 3¾" hem piped with white satin. Slip a 6" x 19" piece of heavy cardboard covered with plastic wrap inside pillowcase underneath hemmed section. Glue two 1¼", six 1¼", and seven ⅞" gold star appliqués at random on hem using washable fabric glue. Let set undisturbed one to two days until completely dry. ◆

# Frozen Floral Ice Bucket

## MATERIALS
- 5-quart plastic bucket
- 2-liter soda bottle
- Marbles or gravel
- 6 pink and yellow roses
- 1 yellow daisy
- Several leafy green stems

FILL A 5-QUART PLASTIC BUCKET HALFWAY WITH TAP WATER AND LET STAND overnight to disperse air bubbles. Cut off and discard the top third of an empty 2-liter soda bottle. Weight remainder of bottle with marbles or gravel and set into water-filled bucket. Submerge six pink and yellow roses, one yellow daisy (all with stems attached), and several leafy stems in water, positioning them as desired. Place bucket in freezer. During the next three hours, check flowers several times and poke down any that have floated above the surface. Freeze overnight until solid. To unmold ice, run hot tap water around outside of bucket and inside soda bottle. Lift out soda bottle first, then release ice bucket onto clean dishtowel. Place ice bucket onto metal plate or tray and return it to freezer until ready to use. During use, keep plate underneath ice bucket to collect drippings. Ice bucket should last two to three hours out of freezer.

NUMBER NINE

OCTOBER 1995

# Handcraft
## ILLUSTRATED

You Can Assemble
Sumptuous Gift
Pouches Such As These
Using Remnants of
Satin and Velvet.

## Velvet Holiday Gift Pouches
*5 Satin-Lined Bags from
a Yard of Remnant Fabric*

❧

## The Best Pastry for Decorative Pie Edges
*12 Professional-Quality Designs*

## Custom Giftwrap in Minutes
*Transform Kraft Paper Using
Gold Paint or Leaf*

## Rating Heat-Set and Air-Dry Clays
*Fimo or Celluclay? How to Choose*

## Secrets of Quick Bronze Stenciling
*Replicate the Hitchcock Style
Using Acrylic Paint*

### ALSO
Special Insert: Original Folk
Art Paintings

Quick-Gilded Autumn
Leaves

The Art of Pumpkin
Carving

$4.00 U.S./$4.95 CANADA

0 71486 02716 4    10>

# Contents

**Gilded leaves, page 21**

## 2

**NOTES FROM READERS**
Unusual Christmas tree decorations; theorem painting versus stenciling; defining hue, tone, and shade; tips on faux-finishing a tabletop; and adhering fabric to a blank book.

## 4

**QUICK TIPS**
Instant foam paintbrush; downsizing silk flowers; stay-moist paint palette; fast button basting; stenciling shortcut; yarn and ribbon organizer; wiring a pine cone invisibly.

## 6

**APPLE TREE CARVED PUMPKIN**
Carve this classic autumn centerpiece using three bent pastry tube nozzles.

**Bronze stenciled tray, page 8**

## 8

**BRONZE STENCILING WITH ACRYLICS**
Acrylic paint transforms an exacting decorative art into a simple stenciling technique.

## 11

**QUICK DRIED HYDRANGEA WREATH**
Testing shows that the best way of attaching fragile dried hydrangea heads to a wreath is to use floral pins.

## 12

**THE BEST PASTRY FOR DECORATIVE PIE EDGES**
Dress up an ordinary single-crust pie using any one of these twelve simple yet elegant edging techniques.

## 14

**LINED VELVET POUCHES**
Using a streamlined assembly process, you can make five pouches at a time versus creating each one individually.

SPECIAL INSERT

## 16

**FOLK ART FRAME**
Use the original art on this issue's insert, a simple frame design, and a wood-grain faux finish to build this two-panel framed mirror.

## 20

**FOOLPROOF WOOD GRAIN FAUX FINISH**
Create a convincing wood grain faux finish using your index finger and glaze.

## 21

**QUICK GILDED AUTUMN LEAVES**
Forget about traditional gilding methods. "Press" gilding with enamel paint works best.

## 22

**BITTERSWEET TOPIARY**
For topiaries made from vinelike branches, a wire hanger serves as the base of choice.

**Bittersweet topiary, page 22**

**Twig frame, page 24**

## 24

**ADIRONDACK TWIG FRAME**
Give an ordinary picture frame a log cabin look without the use of nails.

## 25

**BROWN KRAFT PAPER GIFTWRAP**
For versatility, availability, and low cost, brown kraft paper proves the giftwrap of choice.

## 26

**TESTING AIR-DRY AND HEAT-SET CLAYS**
Not sure whether to use a heat-set clay such as Fimo or an air-dry clay like Celluclay? We tell you how to choose.

## 30

**FIELD GUIDE TO DECORATIVE TASSELS**
Use them on curtain tiebacks, as key fobs, to dress up the corners of a tablecloth, or as Christmas ornaments.

## 32

**SOURCES AND RESOURCES**
Mail-order sources for materials and supplies used throughout this issue.

## 33

**QUICK PROJECTS**
Turn an ordinary topiary into a decorating accent using a variety of dried or preserved flowers and foliage.

BACK COVER
**DECORATIVE AUTUMN URN**
Create a doorstop arrangement using ornamental cabbage, white roses, and fresh hydrangea.

*Cover photograph by Steven Mays*

# Handcraft
### ILLUSTRATED

EDITOR
**Carol Endler Sterbenz**

EXECUTIVE EDITOR
**Barbara Bourassa**

ART DIRECTOR
**Amy Klee**

SENIOR EDITOR
**Michio Ryan**

MANAGING EDITOR
**Maura Lyons**

ASSISTANT MANAGING EDITOR
**Tricia O'Brien**

DIRECTIONS EDITOR
**Candie Frankel**

EDITORIAL ASSISTANT
**Kim N. Russello**

COPY EDITOR
**Gary Pfitzer**

PHOTO STYLIST
**Sylvia Lachter**

❧

PUBLISHER AND FOUNDER
**Christopher Kimball**

EDITORIAL CONSULTANT
**Raymond Waites**

MARKETING DIRECTOR
**Adrienne Kimball**

CIRCULATION DIRECTOR
**Elaine Repucci**

ASS'T CIRCULATION MANAGER
**Jennifer L. Keene**

CIRCULATION COORDINATOR
**Jonathan Venier**

CIRCULATION ASSISTANT
**C. Maria Pannozzo**

PRODUCTION DIRECTOR
**James McCormack**

PRODUCTION ASSISTANTS
**Sheila Datz**
**Pamela Slattery**

ASSISTANT COMPUTER ADMINISTRATOR
**Matt Frigo**

PRODUCTION ARTIST
**Kevin Moeller**

❧

VICE PRESIDENT
**Jeffrey Feingold**

CONTROLLER
**Lisa A. Carullo**

ACCOUNTING ASSISTANT
**Mandy Shito**

OFFICE MANAGER
**Tonya Estey**

OFFICE ASSISTANT
**Sarah Chung**

*Handcraft Illustrated* (ISSN 1072-0529) is published bi-monthly by Boston Common Press Limited Partners, 17 Station Street, P.O. Box 509, Brookline, MA 02147-0509. Copyright 1995 Boston Common Press Limited Partners. Second-class postage paid in Boston, MA, and additional mailing offices, USPS #012487. For list rental information, please contact Direct Media, 200 Pemberwick Rd., Greenwich, CT 06830; 203-532-1000. Editorial office: 17 Station Street, P.O. Box 509, Brookline, MA 02147-0509; (617) 232-1000, FAX (617) 232-1572. Editorial contributions should be sent to: Editor, *Handcraft Illustrated*, P.O. Box 509, Brookline, MA 02147-0509. We cannot assume responsibility for manuscripts submitted to us. Submissions will be returned only if accompanied by a large, self-addressed stamped envelope. Subscription rates: $24.95 for one year; $45 for two years; $65 for three years. (Canada: add $3 per year; all other foreign add $12 per year.) Postmaster: Send all new orders, subscription inquiries, and change of address notices to *Handcraft Illustrated*, P.O. Box 51383, Boulder, CO 80322-1383. Single copies: $4 in U.S., $4.95 in Canada and foreign. Back issues available for $5 each. PRINTED IN THE U.S.A.

## FROM THE EDITOR

**Friday:** I am standing barefoot in the back of a friend's summer house, a little Cape with shingles bleached white and a screen door that bangs shut on its rusted hinges. I have been watching the last sliver of sun fall below the dunes, which lie like slumbering figures along the water's edge. The air smells like salt and rain, and there's a chill of autumn in the air. For the first time in years, I have taken up a friend's offer to use her beach house. She has good-naturedly attached one condition—that I come out here to play, not to work. This is my first day. As I drift off to sleep, I wonder if it is a promise I can keep.

**Saturday:** I wake up early as usual (as if it's a work day), then remember where I am. The day stretches before me gray and overcast, and I'm not sure what I'm going to do. I start leafing through a stack of decorating magazines and find myself tearing out pictures and circling good design sources. When I'm done, I move to the local newspaper dated two weeks ago and skim the directory at the back. Soon, I am standing in a cluttered shop in the village fingering old ribbons and linen. I decide to buy two snowy white pillowcases with monogrammed initials (not mine) but whose power of recollection is so strong I seem to be back at my grandmother's, a child sleeping between stiff linen sheets that smell like raw flax. I am aware of the pleasure I take in handmade things, and I am reminded of how inextricably linked needlework is to my heritage and my sense of self. I leave the shop with my pillowcases wrapped in brown paper and continue walking along the sidewalk, which the weather has heaved up to resemble an ice floe. I stop in one shop after another, fascinated, as always, by the amazing amount of junk that can be crowded onto floors and shelves and into corners, and even more by the fact that I can still ferret out the good items. In the last shop, I distractedly return a vase to its place when another browser immediately reaches for it and studies it with interest. Suddenly I worry that I have overlooked something inordinately valuable. I leave the shop before I find out, walking back to the house as thunder growls in the distance.

**Sunday:** My eyes open to the syncopated notes of nearby wind chimes. I pull the bed quilt around

> I arrive at my friend's beach house promising to play, not work. I wonder if it's a promise I can keep.

my shoulders and sit on the back porch watching the waves hit the shoreline. The quilt, a paisley design, is made of whole cloth, with one pattern on the front and one pattern on the back. It's slightly lumpy but a dependable shelter. I wonder how many people have taken cover under this quilt, a kind of transgenerational symbol of warmth and protection, passed from hand to hand, from family member to family member, and finally to a stranger. I recognize the universality of quilts and take comfort in them. The light shifts suddenly to dark gray. A sea gull screeches as it flies against the wind, and white clouds shoulder their way across a steely sky. It starts to rain, and I pad back into the house, where I turn on a light in the living-room. The windows turn translucent as the rain washes over them. The house smells like varnish and must. I sit down and look at the slender bouquet of flowers that someone has balanced over an old picture. I wait for the rain to stop.

**Monday:** The sound of my own voice wakes me up. The answering machine is divulging my plan, that I am out "playing." (Is this true, I wonder?) I grab the receiver. A nearby church is sponsoring a fall bazaar, and apparently my friend has volunteered to make pies. A short conversation later, I agree to go in her place. Large bowls hold apple wedges covered with fragrant spices. I join four other women who are rolling out dough along a metal counter. My assignment is to simply seal each two-crust pie by pinching the edges closed. I begin with that intention but amuse myself by shaping leaves and tendrils from the scraps and laying them carefully around the pie edges. I return to the house by four o'clock, warm pie in hand, just in time for the last ferry. A round sun is shining on the horizon. As I look back on the long weekend, I feel particularly lucky to have spent some time immersing myself in what I love. It is clear to me that crafts are linked to my life, both at work and at play. It is what I choose to do. I guess I kept my promise after all.

# Notes
## FROM READERS

### Unusual Christmas Tree Decorations

Recently I saw a beautiful Christmas tree decorated with Styrofoam balls covered with different tapestry fabrics. The hostess had inherited the ornaments from her mother, who had made them. Is there a pattern or instruction book for such ornaments?

A. MAROTTY
NEW YORK, NY

We were unable to find a pattern that would allow you to manipulate something as stiff as actual tapestry around a circular shape, so we assumed that you were using the word "tapestry" to suggest a fabric with a rich, densely patterned design. If so, we have an answer: McCall's Pattern Company of Manhattan, Kansas, makes a Christmas craft kit (pattern #5013) that provides patterns for an array of projects, among them two that show you how to cover Styrofoam balls.

One pattern is for covering the ball with lace, while the other is for covering the ball with fabric ranging from cotton to brocade. Each $6.50 pattern provides templates for covering the ball, and can be obtained directly from McCall's (615 McCall Road, Manhattan, KS 66502; 800-255-2762) or at any fabric store that carries the McCall's patterns.

### Ideas for Displaying Greeting Cards

Our fiftieth anniversary cards were so meaningful and beautiful that I'd like to have them on display to share. I'm searching for ideas other than albums.

MARCY PODAS
EDEN PRAIRIE, MN

There are a number of ways to display a collection of greeting cards, but if you wish to preserve these special messages and protect them from becoming soiled and worn, we suggest putting them in an album, framing them, or storing each card in its own archival sleeve, a special, clear plastic envelope designed to protect paper ephemera.

That said, one interesting idea for a unique album might be to mount the cards and have each matted piece bound into an album. You could also store the cards in an attractive organizer—a pretty hatbox, an old wooden card catalog, even a vintage postcard carousel or rack—and use archival sleeves to prevent the cards from coming in contact with the holder and/or each other.

You may also want to consider consulting your local art supply store or frame shop, as these retailers may be able to suggest other alternatives.

### Freeze-Drying Flowers

Can you tell me how to freeze-dry flowers? The arrangements I've seen are truly exceptional, but very expensive.

KAY HEINEMAN
BALTIMORE, MD

Unfortunately, freeze-drying flowers requires special and very costly machinery, the least expensive of which begins at about $50,000. Furthermore, a wholesaler with the proper equipment would probably not freeze-dry flowers for you unless the order was quite large by commercial standards. Your best option is to obtain freeze-dried flowers in the floral district of a large city near you or to ask your local florist if he can order them for you.

### Safeguarding Fabric from Liquids

In our January/February issue, Pat Killingsworth of Seattle, Washington, asked us to locate a fabric finish that, once sprayed on a fabric, enables one to wipe spills with a damp cloth. We reported on a spray finish that helps protect fabric from absorbing liquid and staining, but it has recently come to our attention through Vee Brueske of Taft, California, that there is a new product on the market, called Craftguard, that completely prevents liquids from penetrating fabric.

Unlike Scotchguard, a protective covering that washes or wears off fabric, Craftguard actually bonds with fabric fibers and does not wash or wear off. This means that liquid that drips on fabric treated with Craftguard will bead up and sit on the fabric until it is wiped away with a damp cloth.

Craftguard is effective on virtually any fabric, and its presence is nondetectable: There is neither an odor, nor a sticky or shiny film. The product is available in eight-ounce and twenty-two-ounce bottles, priced at $9.95 and $19.95 (plus shipping and handling) respectively. For a free brochure with a test card that enables you to try the product at home before you actually order it, write: Craftguard, P.O. Box 472, Tustin, CA 92681, or call 714-730-3856.

### Knitting Unique Sweaters and Hats for Children

Can you recommend any sources for interesting, fun-to-knit sweaters and hats for babies and young children that are somewhat like child-sized versions of what an adult might wear—not too pink, too blue, or too cute?

ELIZABETH MILLMAN
EUGENE, OR

We like the work of Debbie Bliss, who has written *Baby Knits* (St. Martin's Press, 1988), *New Baby Knits* (St. Martin's Press), *1991*), and *Classic Knits for Kids: 30 Traditional Aran and Guernsey Designs for 0–6 Years* (Trafalgar Square, 1994). Bliss's books contain whimsical yet sophisticated patterns that range from simple to complex, from straightforward knit and purl motifs to intricate colorways and cable patterns. Whether you want to make a Chanel-style jacket or a deep-ribbed pullover with raglan sleeves, you'll find that Bliss's work is varied and colorful. Your local knitting shop or bookshop should be able to obtain copies of her books for you.

### Fabric-Covered Cornice Boards

Would you consider running an article on making your own fabric-covered cornice boards for window treatments? My friends and I would love to have these, but they're very expensive to acquire through interior decorators or other custom-made sources.

ELIZABETH DOBBINS
WINDHAM, NH

Instructions for fabric-board cornices can be found in *The Ultimate Curtain Book* by Isabella Forbes, published by Reader's Digest, of Pleasantville, New York, and priced at $19.95. For more information on the subject, check the crafts and/or home design section of a large bookstore or back issues of sewing magazines at your local library.

### Sending Flowers Long-Distance

Do you know of a floral service that enables one to send a personalized arrangement long-distance?

HEATHER FITZGERALD
CAMBRIDGE, MA

We recommend Flowers Direct, of Boca Raton, Florida. Founded three years ago, Flowers Direct is a network of a carefully selected group of some six hundred florists throughout the United States (international services will be offered soon). By calling the service (800-678-7878) and entering the zip code of the area to which you would like to send the flowers, you will be put in direct contact with a florist in that locale. If there is no member florist in that zip code, Flowers Direct will put you in touch with a reputable florist in the area. The company has a 100 percent unconditional satisfaction guarantee: If there are any problems with your order, you can contact customer service at 800-944-5611.

## Replacing a Broken Dried Flower Head

Can you tell me how to properly replace a flower head that's broken off a dried flower topiary?

LEE HAMADA
SAN MATEO, CA

This solution works well for us. Using a pair of tweezers, gently grasp the stem where the flower has broken off. Place a dab of hot glue on the blunt end of the stem, then carefully set the flower head back on top. Hold everything in place until the glue sets up, which should take just a few seconds.

## In Search of a Paint Eraser

Is there such a thing as a paint eraser? I've looked all over for one but can't seem to find it.

CARRIE DRAPER
SAN ANTONIO, TX

Once paint has dried, it is not erasable. One product we found, however, can be of help when paint is still wet. Manufactured by Loew-Cornell, Inc., the "Paint Eraser" is designed to reshape or delete wet paint strokes, or even remove areas of color. Shaped like a pencil, the $4.99 tool has two rubber-edged tips (one has a chisel-like edge, the other is pointed) and can be used to manipulate acrylics, oils, glazes, china paints, and "wet-on-wet" watercolors. The tool can also be used for ceramics and sculpting, as its soft rubber edges can be used on wet clay and greenware. Contact Loew-Cornell at 563 Chestnut Avenue, Teaneck, NJ 07666-2490; 201-836-7070.

## Theorem Painting versus Stenciling

What is the difference between theorem painting and stenciling?

DANIELLE LOWRY
WINNETKA, MN

Technically, there is no difference between stenciling and theorem painting. A "theorem painting" is a picture (usually of a floral or fruit arrangement) produced by stenciling techniques. The only difference is that a theorem painting is usually created on a fabric background, such as a low-pile velvet.

## Defining Hue, Tone, and Shade

What is meant precisely by the terms "hue," "tone," and "shade"?

STEPHANIE MORANIS
ESTES PARK, CO

"Hue" refers to the color family to which a color belongs; an item is referred to as being "blue," "yellow," or "orangish red" in hue. "Tone," or "intensity," describes whether a color is dull or bright. "Shade," or "value," describes a degree of variation in color. For example, the hue of an object may be green, but when you indicate whether it's a light or dark green, you're also referring to its shade.

## Testing a Candy Thermometer for Accuracy

I'd like to make preserves for Christmas, but the thought of using a candy thermometer makes me nervous. Is there a way to test a candy thermometer for accuracy?

DEBORAH BARRY
ATHENS, GA

Try this solution. Bring some water to a boil in a saucepan, then place the thermometer in the water for a few minutes. The temperature should read 212 degrees Fahrenheit (the boiling point of water). If the thermometer registers above or below that temperature, simply add or subtract the same difference from the temperature called for in the recipe.

## Preparing Knotted Wood for Painting

What's the best way to prepare knotted wood for painting and staining?

PETER FEININGER
TIMONIUM, MD

Wood knots must be treated properly before painting, for the resin in the wood can bleed through the paint and stain the finish, or it can clump up and harden beneath the paint surface, ultimately causing it to crack.

To prepare the surface, scrape off any visible resin with a razor. Clean the area with mineral spirits, then seal the knots with a colorless shellac or a primer-sealer product for wood.

## Finding New Color Combinations

I seem to gravitate toward the same color combinations in all of my projects. I'd like some sources for new ideas. Any suggestions?

JULIA SEDRESKY
BURLINGTON, CO

Interior design, art, and textile magazines are always a good source for inspiration, so you might want to keep a file or a clip book of color combinations that appeal to you.

You also might want to try looking at reference books for graphic designers at your local art supply store or bookstore. Although the books are geared for those referring to the Pantone colors used in the printing process, they often display hundreds of color combinations that should spark your imagination.

## Tips on Faux-Finishing a Tabletop

I recently tried to decorate the top of a small wood table by combing a glaze over the top. I used a compatible base coat and glaze (both water-based), and I let the base coat dry completely before I applied the glaze. For some reason, however, the paint didn't go on evenly in some places and tended to get a little gloppy in others. What did I do wrong?

DAVID FRIEDMAN
NEW YORK, NY

You may not have dragged the comb with even pressure. But since combing is rather forgiving in that it is a bit imperfect by nature, it's more likely that you weren't wiping excess glaze off the comb—or weren't doing so often enough.

When using a comb, it is important to wipe off excess glaze on a regular basis. By doing so, you will avoid clogging the comb in such a way that it deposits drops of glaze and uneven ridges of color on your decorative surface. Mutton cloth (also referred to as "stockinet") is a gauzelike material that works effectively to keep a comb clear of excess paint. If you should experience problems like these again, don't be afraid to start over. You can always wipe off a wet surface with a cotton rag, reapply the glaze, and begin to comb again.

## Adhering Fabric to a Blank Book

I'd like to cover some blank books with fabric. Is there a special tool I can buy to make sure the fabric adheres tightly and smoothly to the book? I've tried using a wooden ruler—the results were okay, but not perfect.

ALICE MILLER
HENDERSONVILLE, NC

Professional bookbinders use a tool called a "bone folder." A bone folder, shaped somewhat like a letter opener, but with softly rounded edges, fits more easily in the hand than a ruler, allowing for more precise control. In addition, the tool has a tip, which allows you to push the fabric into the gutter (the fold alongside the spine of the book) and onto the contoured spine. Bone folders are available at bookbinding supply and art supply stores. ◆

# Quick TIPS

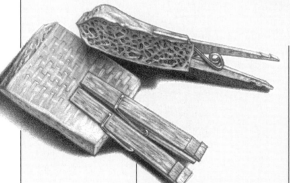

## Instant Foam Paintbrush

You can make an instant foam paintbrush by cutting a sponge into a 1" x 3" piece, beveling the tip with scissors, and clipping a clothespin "handle" to the other end. For a wider sponge, use two clothespins for more support.

## Bread Eraser

If you collect old postcards, calendars, prints, or other ephemera that are marred by surface dirt, you'll appreciate this cleaning tip from Caren Shiloh of Novelty, Ohio.

**1** Break off and discard the crust from a slice of white bread, and mold the remainder into a soft, doughy mass.

**2** Rub the dough ball gently across the paper, as you would an eraser. If the paper is extremely fragile, rub lightly in one direction only.

## Cookie Hole Cutter

Donna Wolff, of Oro Valley, Arizona, offers this tip for making a hanging hole in rolled gingerbread cookies. Instead of boring a hole with a chopstick or wooden spoon before baking—which spreads the dough and sometimes distorts it—Donna uses a plastic drinking straw as a miniature cookie cutter. Simply press one end of the straw down into the dough and lift the straw straight up. The small plug of dough you remove will be lodged in the base of the straw.

## Plant-Potting Tip

If you don't have a bit of window screening or even a pebble handy to cover the drainage hole in a flower pot, use two or three unbleached, basket-style coffee filters. The strong porous fibers will hold back the soil while letting water drain through, with no chlorine residue to harm the plant's roots. Nest the filters in the bottom of the pot, add soil, and then pot your plants as usual.

## Downsizing Silk Flowers

When the search for a particular silk flower yields the perfect color but the flower is too large, here's an easy fix for flowers with concentric rings of petals. You may need some high-tack glue for repairs once the surgery is complete.

**1** Slide the calyx down the stem to gain access to the petals. Remove the outer rings of petals by snipping into the petals. With a straight, leafless stem, you can simply slide the calyx and excess petals right off.

**2** Once the flower is the desired size, replace the calyx, securing it with a dot of high-tack glue if it doesn't snap back into place on its own.

## Stay-Moist Paint Palette

To prevent acrylic paints from forming a skin and drying out during a long painting session, try using a few layers of moist paper towel instead of your usual plastic or paper palette.

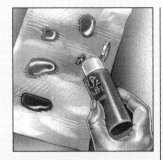

## Fast Button Basting

To better evaluate the size, color, or position of buttons you are considering for a home furnishing, you can baste them in place temporarily with 30-gauge wire. You can also substitute a twist-tie wire stripped of its paper coating.

 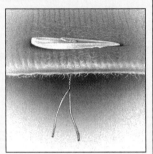

**1** Bend a 2" length of wire into a hairpin shape and thread it through the buttonholes or shank.

**2** Draw the wire through the fabric and then twist the ends together on the wrong side.

## Yarn and Ribbon Organizer

To keep balls of yarn, ribbon, or twine tangle-free, store them in a string grocery tote. Pass the free strands through the holes so you can draw from your supply as needed.

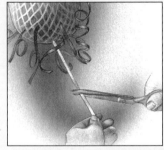

## Stenciling Shortcut

Mary Piwko, a decorative artist in Chicago, Illinois, shares this tip for faster stenciling. Instead of applying acrylic paints with a stencil brush, she uses 1½" cubes cut from high-density upholstery foam. A large piece of foam can be easily cut into a quantity of cubes with an electric carving knife or a long, serrated knife. The fine, dense texture of these foam applicators produces a stipple-like effect that mimics brushwork with far less effort.

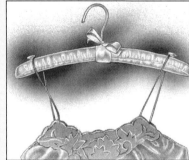 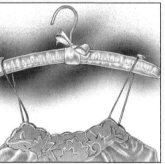 

## Nonslip Hangers

To prevent silky lingerie or sleeveless tops and dresses from slipping off a padded hanger, sew a shank-style button to the top of the hanger at each end.

## Wiring a Pine Cone Invisibly

This easy wiring technique makes a pine cone ready to attach to a wreath or floral arrangement.

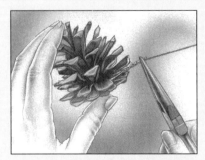 

**1** Cut an 18", 22-gauge florist stem in half. Take one of the halves and lay an end of it against the cone, pressing it between the cone scales, as close to the base as possible, and leaving 2" extending on one side.

**2** Wrap the longer stem end once around the cone, carefully concealing it between the scales, until it meets the shorter stem. Using needle-nose pliers, twist the stems together for ½", then cut any excess.

**3** Bend the remaining long stem down, adjusting its position so that it extends below the cone base and is ready for attachment.

# Apple Tree Carved Pumpkin

*Carve this classic autumn centerpiece using bent pastry tube nozzles.*

🍂 BY CANDIE FRANKEL

**This classic apple tree design can be adjusted for use on pumpkins of varying size or for other large autumn vegetables, such as spaghetti squash.**

THERE'S A SIMPLE TRICK TO creating this intricately carved pumpkin: Instead of using a knife to cut the leaves of the apple tree individually, a time-consuming process that yields inconsistent results, I have discovered you can cut identical leaf shapes using pastry tube nozzles that have been bent to shape.

In my search for tools that I could bend into a leaf shape, I also tested round biscuit cutters. Made of tin, they were easy to bend, but they were only strong enough to pierce the top skin of the pumpkin. Pastry nozzles, made of heftier, nickel-plated brass, were better able to withstand the pressure needed to cut through the thick pumpkin flesh. You can purchase pastry tube nozzles individually for under $2 each, unlike small biscuit cutters, which are more likely to be sold as part of a more expensive set—another reason they are less appealing.

The apple tree design is made in two stages: The first involves tracing, piercing, and cutting the tree trunk pattern on page 7. After you've transferred this portion of the design to the pumpkin and cut out the shapes, you can add as many remaining leaves as you like using the nozzles.

Since pumpkin flesh is thick, you'll need to apply a bit of pressure, using a rocking motion, to the bent nozzle cutters. For crisp, clean cuts, jab the leaf point of the cutter into the skin, then rock it down onto the flesh until the opposite point cuts into the skin.

### INSTRUCTIONS

**1.** Enlarge apple tree trunk pattern on page 7 to measure 9" across. Tear off 6" to 7" piece of plastic wrap and lay on top of pattern. Using marker, trace solid lines

## MATERIALS
- **Large pumpkin, approximately 15 to 18 pounds**
- **Votive candle(s)**

*You'll also need:* apple tree trunk pattern (on page 7); access to photocopier with enlargement feature; two or three metal pastry tube nozzles in graduated sizes, each with opening not exceeding 1¾" diameter; pliers; large chef's knife; serrated kitchen knife; large wooden spoon; noncling plastic wrap; permanent black felt-tip marker; cutting board; and long straight pin with ball head.

1 Position the plastic wrap with the traced pattern on the front of the pumpkin. Using a pin, pierce along the pattern lines every ¼" or so to mark the pumpkin skin.

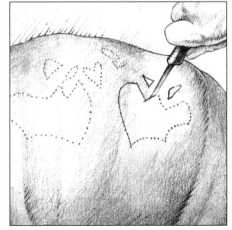

2 Insert the knife along the pierced lines to a depth of 1" to 2", then saw up and down, moving the blade forward in small increments to cut the pattern pieces.

ILLUSTRATIONS BY NENAD JAKESEVIC/PHOTOGRAPH BY STEVEN MAYS

of pattern onto plastic wrap. (Do not trace dashed lines.)

**2.** Turn pumpkin on side on cutting board. Using chef's knife, cut sliver off bottom of pumpkin so it will stand upright without leaning or wobbling. Stand pumpkin upright and choose its "front." Position plastic wrap with traced pattern on front so tree trunk sits above cut edge, then smooth pattern in place. Using pin, pierce along pattern lines every ¼" or so to mark pumpkin skin (*see* illustration 1). Remove pattern.

**3.** To cut pumpkin, insert serrated knife perpendicular to pumpkin surface along pierced line to depth of 1" to 2", then saw up and down, moving blade forward in small increments along line (illustration 2). For sharp corners, cut into each corner from both angles. Repeat process to cut entire pierced pattern.

**4.** To form leaf cutter from pastry nozzle, flatten wider end of nozzle partially with fingers, then use pliers to draw edges toward each other so opening is sausage-shaped. Continuing to use pliers, pinch ends of sausage to make pointed leaf tips (illustration 3). Repeat with remaining pastry nozzle(s).

**5.** To use leaf cutter, jab one pointed tip down into pumpkin skin and flesh below, then rock cutter down until opposite tip penetrates skin and flesh (illustration 4). Press cutter into pumpkin as deep as possible, then rock cutter gently to dislodge. Cut largest leaves first, then fill in blank areas with smaller leaves, using smaller cutters made in step 4. Cut leaves at random on pumpkin above trunk and lower branches, varying spacing and direction in free-form arrangement.

**6.** Turn pumpkin on side. Using serrated knife, trim away excess flesh at bottom of pumpkin blocking entrance to pumpkin cavity, then use large spoon to scoop out pulp and seeds. Discard excess flesh, pulp, and seeds.

**7.** Stand pumpkin upright. Using serrated knife, extend each cut clear through rind. Poke cutout sections into pumpkin cavity using handle of spoon (illustration 5) and discard.

**8.** To illumine apple tree design, set carved pumpkin over one or two votive candles. *Note:* Never leave candles unattended or near flammable materials. ◆

## The History of Carving Pumpkins

The tradition of carving pumpkins probably originated with an assortment of Celtic myths, somewhere around the year 1400 B.C. The Celtic New Year, called Samhain, took place on November 1, which marks the end of the harvest season and the beginning of winter. No night was more foreboding than the eve of Samhain, for just as on this night time belonged to neither the old year nor the new year, the boundary between man and the spirit world seemed to blur as well. According to Celtic legend, October 31 was marked by supernatural beings swarming through the countryside, and the year's dead visiting their homes.

Add to these beliefs a second custom associated with battle. Ancient warriors, the Celts among them, severed the heads of their defeated enemies, mounted them on poles, and displayed them in their ceremonies not only as trophies of victory, but also as charms against the forces of evil.

What better protection, then, against the evil spirits wandering the night of Samhain eve, than to carve a sinister face on a turnip or potato and give it life by placing a lit candle inside? It doesn't take a great leap to transfer that tradition to larger vegetables such as pumpkins, and place them on your doorstep on Halloween night to ward against the spirits of the night.

### Apple Tree Trunk Pattern
To adjust the pattern to the size of your pumpkin, or other chosen fruit or vegetable, measure the area where the design will fit, then enlarge or reduce the pattern shown above to match.

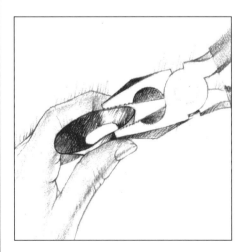

**3** To construct a leaf cutter from a pastry nozzle, flatten the wider end of the nozzle partially with your fingers, then use the pliers to create a leaf-shaped opening.

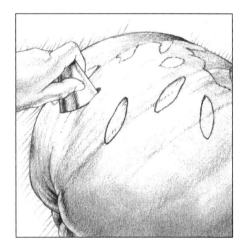

**4** To use the leaf cutter, jab one pointed tip down into the pumpkin skin, then rock the cutter down until the opposite tip penetrates the skin. Rock the cutter gently to dislodge it.

**5** When you've finished with the leaf cutter, poke all cutout sections of the skin into the pumpkin cavity using the handle of a wooden spoon.

# Bronze Stenciling with Acrylics

*Acrylic paint transforms an exacting decorative art into a simple stenciling technique.*

### ❧ BY DEBORAH MILLER GABLER

The base coat on this 12"-high metal bucket is Pittsburgh Paint #7181 Chili Sauce enamel, chosen for its similarity to cinnabar, a color frequently used in Asia and Europe as a background for decorative bronzing.

BRONZE POWDER STENCILING, a centuries-old decorative painting technique, originated in the Far East and spread to Europe and colonial America, where it enjoyed a period of popularity from 1815 to 1850. The style is most recognizable in the Hitchcock chair, which is painted black and stenciled with metallic fruit, flowers, and leaves.

Traditional bronze stenciling techniques involve finely ground metallic powders, which are applied through stencil cutouts using a small scrap of velvet wrapped around a fingertip. Timing is critical, since the powder must adhere to a coat of varnish before it dries completely. By varying the amount of powder and the fingertip pressure, the stenciler can produce the illusion of shaded and overlapping motifs.

While bronze powders are still available at art supply stores, I've discovered that you can achieve a similar effect in a fraction of the time using a stencil brush and metallic acrylic paints. In addition, acrylic paint is more forgiving, as excess paint can be wiped away, while loose bronze powder cannot.

Metallic acrylic paint is manufactured in a full range of traditional bronze powder colors, from pale and rich gold to aluminum (silver) and copper. The bronze stenciling techniques that I've outlined here are suitable for wood (*see* the tray, page 9, and the picture frame, page 10), metal (*see* the flower bucket, left and below), and paper (*see* the picture mat on the "Folk Art Frame," page 17). Just about any new or old object can be stenciled, and by combining the traditional medallion, tulip, fern, and leaf stencils shown below and on page 10, I've decorated objects in a variety of ways.

## Choosing a Base Coat

I think that the base coat, or background color, plays one of the most important roles in giving bronze-stenciled motifs a sense of depth and dimension. The leaves on the tray, for example, appear to tuck behind one another largely because of the subtle way I let the green background color show through. Black, green, and cinnabar base coats, shown on my sample projects, are the traditional background colors for bronze stenciling. Although a black background provides the most contrast, I've also tested medium and pale colors and found them just as effective.

I've used acrylic, latex, or alkyd paint for base coats, depending on the surface to be painted, and all work equally well. (For the best results, follow the paint manufacturer's recommendations.) Many latex formulations are suitable for metal, although I've found that alkyd is a better choice for metal that will have regular contact with water. If you use alkyd paint as a base coat, sand the base coat lightly to give the surface some "tooth" before stenciling. (This will prevent the acrylic metallic paint from "sliding" on the alkyd base coat.) If an object has a large surface area, I recommend interior house paint, as it will give better coverage per dollar than two-ounce

**DESIGNER'S TIP**
As you base-coat your object, paint scraps of posterboard as well. You can use them to try out stencil combinations or to practice your technique.

*Smaller Medallion*

*Corner Motif*

*Floral Medallion*

## Bronze Powder Stencils

**If you plan to use the corner motif or the smaller medallion stencils together on a project, be sure to enlarge them at the** same percentage. For additional tips, *see* "Using and Combining the Stencils," page 10.

STENCIL PATTERNS BY ROBERTA FRAUWIRTH/PHOTOGRAPHS BY STEVEN MAYS

containers of craft acrylic paint. Depending on the size of your object, select a one-inch-, two-inch-, or three-inch-wide natural bristle brush for painting the base coat.

You'll also need a water-based clear gloss or semigloss polyurethane or varnish for finishing the object. Even if you've used a solvent-based basecoat, I recommend a water-based finish to prevent the acrylic stencils from lifting.

*Deborah Miller Gabler, owner of Shady Lane Designs in Hamburg, New York, is a freelance designer and teacher specializing in custom lampshades and stenciling.*

## INSTRUCTIONS
### Preparing the Surface
*Note: Wear safety goggles and particle mask when using sandpaper, steel wool, or wire brush.*

1. *To prepare new wood surface:* Sand surface lightly with 80- and 120-grit sandpaper, wiping away dust between rounds. Apply wood sealer and let dry following manufacturer's directions. Resand with 120-, then 220-grit sandpaper, removing dust between and after sanding.

The base coat on this 20½" by 12" wooden serving tray is Pittsburgh Paint #7002 Green Hedge enamel, chosen to suggest *vert anglaise*, a green frequently used on French lacquered furnishings and decorative objects.

### MATERIALS
- Wooden, metal, or paper object to be stenciled
- Acrylic, latex, or alkyd paint in desired base coat color
- 2-ounce container gold, silver, or copper acrylic paint (such as DecoArt Dazzling Metallic Glorious Gold #DA71)
- Water- or solvent-based clear gloss or semigloss polyurethane or varnish

*You'll also need:*
8 ½" x 11" sheet(s) stencil vellum or Mylar; access to photocopier with single-sheet feed and enlarger; stencil designs of choice from pages 8 and 10; ¼"-diameter round natural bristle stencil brush; 1"-, 2"-, or 3"-wide natural bristle brush; sharp X-Acto knife; self-healing cutting mat; scissors; masking tape; transparent tape; brown kraft paper; newspapers or drop cloth; small wood blocks; and ruler.

*Other items, if necessary:*
brown paper bag (for sanding alkyd oil paint); rust remover such as Naval Jelly or rust inhibitor such as Rustoleum Rust Reformer, spray- or brush-on metal primer such as Rustoleum, dishwashing soap, white vinegar, cotton balls, towels, denatured alcohol, and steel wool or metal file or wire brush (for preparing and/or priming metal surfaces); wood sealer, wood stripper such as 3M Safest Stripper, 80-, 120-, and 220-grit sandpaper, and tack cloth (for preparing and/or sealing wood surfaces); safety goggles and particle mask (if using sandpaper, steel wool, or wire brush); #6 Loew Cornell Liner Brush Series 7350 (for painting narrow accent stripes or fern stems); small oval foam brush or cosmetic applicator (for painting scalloped edge); and odor-free turpentine or mineral spirits (if using alkyd paint and varnish).

2. *To prepare older wood surface:* If finish is smooth and well-adhered, stripping is not necessary. To give surface tooth, sand with 80- or 120-grit sandpaper, and remove dust. To strip blistered or peeling paint, varnish, or lacquer, follow manufacturer's directions. Sand surface, apply wood sealer, and resand as for new wood surface, above.

3. *To prepare new metal surface:* To remove dirt and/or oil, wash galvanized metal objects in warm, soapy water, rinse in 1:1 mixture of water and white vinegar, and dry thoroughly. Swab other metal surfaces using cotton balls and denatured alcohol. Smooth rough spots with steel wool or metal file and clean object again. Galvanized metals do not require priming. To prime other new surfaces, select primer appropriate to surface and follow manufacturer's recommendations.

4. *To prepare older metal surface:* Rub off rust using steel wool or wire brush. Treat stubborn spots with rust remover or rust inhibitor. Clean object using cotton balls and denatured alcohol. Apply appropriate metal primer as for new metal, above.

### Painting the Base Coat
1. Protect work surface. Apply light coat of paint. If object is concave, paint rim and interior first and let dry, then turn object upside down, rest rim on small wood blocks, and paint outside. If object has flat surfaces, paint back or underside first, let dry, elevate painted side on wood blocks, and paint remaining areas. Let dry following manufacturer's recommendations.

2. Repeat to apply second coat as above. Let dry overnight. Clean brushes using water or solvent as appropriate. If using alkyd paint for base coat, "rough" up surface by rubbing lightly with torn section of paper bag.

### Cutting the Stencils
1. Using single-sheet feed, photocopy and enlarge stencil designs on pages 8 and/or 10 onto 8½" x 11" sheet(s) of vellum or Mylar to desired size.

2. Using X-Acto knife and cutting mat, carefully cut stencils along all solid lines; do not cut dashed lines or shaded areas. Cut smallest areas first, then larger areas, to avoid weakening stencil. To cut smooth curves, keep knife blade stationary and rotate Vellum or Mylar sheet away from you. To cut pointed leaf tips, cut into tip from each side. To repair mistakes or strengthen weak spots, apply transparent tape over problem area on both sides, then recut carefully through tape.

3. Trim rough edges of stencil with X-Acto knife. For easier handling, cut sheet into individual stencils.

### Stenciling the Designs
1. Position stencil, using dashed lines as guidelines where available; if surface is curved, secure stencil with masking tape. Squeeze two drops paint onto palette. Touch tip of stenciling brush to paint, then work back and forth and in

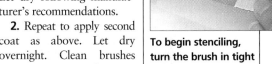

Copy the stencil design onto vellum or Mylar, then cut along the solid lines using an X-Acto knife and a cutting mat.

To begin stenciling, turn the brush in tight circles along the edge of the stencil near the cutout opening.

Continue stenciling, concentrating the bright color near the edges and the tips of the tulip.

To replicate the design found on the black frame on page 10, stencil two tulips back to back, followed by ferns on either side.

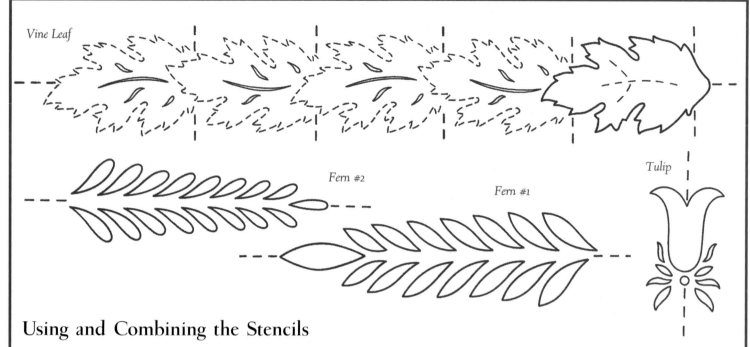

*Vine Leaf*

*Fern #2*

*Fern #1*

*Tulip*

# Using and Combining the Stencils

**• Smaller Medallion (page 8) and Tulip**
Use these designs individually or together. To stencil either design alone, use the horizontal and vertical dashed lines to center the stencil on the object.

**• Fern #1 & Fern #2**
Position these fern stencils symmetrically to extend outward from the medallion and/or the tulip.

**• Floral Medallion (page 8)**
Use this motif on objects with large surface areas, such as the tray, a box, or a cabinet door. Center the stencil on the object and stencil all the cutout areas, concentrating the color in the large central flower. Let the paint dry, then turn the stencil over and add any remaining flowers and leaves (shaded sections on stencil) in the mirror image.

**• Vine Leaf**
This continuous vine motif can be stenciled to follow straight or curved edges. For the straight ver-sion, hold the stencil vertically with the leaf at the bottom and the leaf tip veering toward the left. Stencil the leaf edges, then stencil the veins. Let the paint dry. To fill in the leaves around the veins (indicated by dotted lines on the stencil pattern), turn the stencil over so the leaf tip veers to the right. Center the leaf stencil on the first vein, directly above the left-swaying leaf. Apply the paint, fading toward the vein. Let the paint dry. Turn the stencil back over so the leaf tip veers toward the left again; position it on the next vein, and stencil a third leaf. Continue alternating the leaf direction to establish the pattern; add new veins as needed.

**• Corner Motif (page 8)**
Use this motif to decorate any object with corners or rounded edges, such as a frame, mat, box, drawer front, or cabinet door. (The curved dash line indicates the position of the 7½" x 9½" oval cutout on the picture mat [see "Folk Art Frame," page 16].)

This black frame was base coated with DecoArt Ebony Black Acrylic Paint #DA67.

circular motion to coat bristles and shed excess paint. Brush should seem almost dry.

2. Hold stencil down near cutout edge to prevent accidental shifting. On edge of stencil near cutout opening, begin turning brush in tight circles, crossing into cutout area. Concentrate bright color near edges and at tips of leaves. Use less pressure and apply less paint toward center of motif.

3. Remove tape and lift stencil imme-diately. Let dry 5 minutes.

4. Repeat steps 1 through 3 as desired to extend design. To stencil designs that appear to overlap, stencil foreground, or brightest, motifs first, then move to background motifs. Fade color in back-ground motif as you near foreground edge to create illusion of shadow.

5. To paint narrow metallic accent stripe, as on rim of bucket, or to add stems to ferns, as on top of bucket, load liner brush, wipe on palette to shed excess paint from outside bristles, then draw brush along in straight line. To paint scalloped edge, as on inside rim of bucket, dip foam brush or appli-cator in paint, dab off excess, and touch rounded tip to edge.

6. Clean brushes and other materials in water. Let object dry overnight.

7. Use dry, clean brush to whisk off residue. Apply one or two coats poly-urethane or varnish and let dry following manufacturer's rec-ommendations. Apply one extra coat polyurethane or var-nish to metal that will be exposed to water. Clean brush using water. ◆

# Quick Dried Hydrangea Wreath

*Testing shows that the best way of attaching fragile dried hydrangea heads to a wreath is to use floral pins.*

### BY CAROL ENDLER STERBENZ

WREATH MAKING CAN be a complex and time-consuming process. The complexity of making a wreath is typically determined by two factors: the characteristics of the decorative material and the ease with which it can be attached to the wreath base.

I wanted to make a wreath of dried hydrangea because I had harvested so many blooms. Given their voluminous heads, I assumed that hydrangea would cover a wreath base quicker than other dried materials. At the same time, however, because of their fragility, I wasn't sure the hydrangea would hold up to the process of cutting and attaching to a wreath base.

My first decision involved choosing a wreath base. I opted for a straw base because its broad surface would support the flowers and because I figured it would take well to hot-glue, which was my first choice for attaching the hydrangea. I tested hot-glue with mixed results. Although it dispensed easily and secured the stem to the wreath, streams of glue had to be crisscrossed along the stem, which created globs and "hairs" of cooled glue. Hot-glue was fast, yes, but messy.

Floral picks were a slight improvement. A floral pick includes a fine-gauge wire, which is wrapped around the stem of the hydrangea, and a two-and-one-half-inch wooden spike that is inserted into the straw to anchor the flower. I discovered, however, that wrapping the wire around the stems caused many of them to break.

I finally tested floral pins, which turned out to be the safest, cleanest, and fastest method of securing hydrangea heads to a wreath. Shaped like horseshoes and made of galvanized aluminum, floral pins straddled the stems and could be pushed deep into the straw base, safely trapping the stems in place. In less than an hour, I could pin enough hydrangeas in place to fully decorate a wreath.

In making the design shown here, a sixteen-inch wreath, I used about thirty hydrangea heads. Straw wreath bases are also available in a variety of smaller sizes, including eight-, ten-, and twelve-inch, so it's possible to use fewer hydrangeas and still get the same effect on a smaller scale. During the testing I decorated several sizes of wreaths and discovered that a ten-inch wreath required about fifteen hydrangea heads, while a twelve-inch wreath required about twenty heads. For an eight-inch wreath, I broke the hydrangea heads into smaller florets, as the larger heads looked out of proportion on the smaller wreath base.

### MATERIALS

- 16" straw wreath base
- 30 heads dried hydrangea
- 2 packages floral pins
- 8"-length medium-gauge wire

*You'll also need:* newspaper or brown kraft paper; and florist scissors.

### INSTRUCTIONS

**1.** Cover work space. Thread wire through top center back of wreath base and twist ends together to form hanging loop. Prepare hydrangea by snipping off thicker main stem about 1" below flower head. Hold wreath base up off work surface. Place one head (or floret) at twelve o'clock position, with stem to right side, and attach to outside rim of base using floral pins. Position second head with flowers covering stem of first head, then pin in place. Continue pinning heads in clockwise manner until entire outer circumference of base is covered, leaning wreath away from pinned heads to prevent crushing them.

**2.** Position and pin more heads as in step 1 along inside circumference of base. Fill in gaps with heads or sprigs, holding wreath above work space to prevent crushing attached heads. ◆

This dried hydrangea wreath can be made in a smaller scale by reducing the diameter of the straw wreath base and the attendant number of hydrangea heads.

**1** Start by positioning the hydrangea head's stem facing to the right side (versus pointing in toward the center of the wreath).

**2** Once the outer circumference of the wreath is covered, fill in the inner half with additional heads.

# The Best Pastry for Decorative Pie Edges

*Two tablespoons of butter make the difference between edges that look great after baking and those that don't.*

❧ BY CAROL ENDLER STERBENZ

MY MISSION SEEMED SO SIMple at first: to develop a collection of decorative edges for a single-crust pie. But after some initial designs failed to hold up after baking—becoming misshapen or overinflated—I realized that my real goal was to find a pastry recipe that could stand up to the extra handling required for forming the edges, yet still taste great and maintain the structure of the edges after cooking.

My results in large part depended on the essential ingredients in my recipe and the resulting character of the dough after blending. I based my tests on my basic understanding about pastry: The same ingredients that enhance structure (flour, water, and sugar) might also be the ones to compromise its tenderness; conversely, the ingredient that ensures a tender, flaky crust (fat, in the form of butter and/or vegetable shortening) might also be the same one to undermine whether the crust will hold its shape after baking. To find the perfect pastry, I needed to find the right balance of all those ingredients.

## Testing the Recipes

I based all of my tests on a pastry recipe from the September/October 1994 issue of *Cook's Illustrated* (see "Perfect Pie Crust," page 6), as it had already been declared the perfect combination of flaky texture and great flavor. I prepared the original recipe and formed three designs: the fork-fluted edge, the pinched edge, and the leaves (*see* illustrations). While the *Cook's* dough was easy to manipulate, the designs lost their definition after baking.

By changing the ratio between the pastry's two basic ingredients—fat and flour—I thought I might be able to boost the muscularity of the dough by encouraging more gluten formation, a process whereby the gluten proteins in the flour bond together when exposed to water forming a network that provides shape and texture to the baked pie edge. Since I knew that fat coats the flour and retards this process, I reasoned that if I reduced the fat, more flour would be free for gluten formation.

The original recipe called for ten tablespoons of solid fat: six tablespoons of unsalted butter and four tablespoons of vegetable shortening. I reduced the solid fat content to eight tablespoons: six tablespoons of butter and two tablespoons of vegetable shortening—with all other ingredients kept the same. The resulting dough was easy to handle, the test decorations could be formed quickly, the baked edges were well defined, the texture was tender, and the taste was buttery. By reducing the fat, the pastry had gained more structure.

To confirm that I had just the right balance between fat and flour, I pushed the test further by increasing the amount of flour by one-quarter cup in

## Rope

**Gently squeeze the dough between the thumb and forefinger of your right hand. To make the rope spiral the other way, use your left hand.**

## Reverse Bead

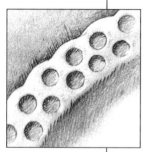

**Press the rounded end of a chopstick into the rim in two staggered rows.**

## Fork-Fluted

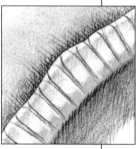

**Press the tines of a table fork into the edge, keeping the spacing uniform all around the pie crust.**

## Leaves

**Draft a leaf pattern on cardboard, then cut out the pattern. Cut the rolled dough around the pattern and score the veins using the tip of a knife. The finished leaves drape and overlap the rim.**

## Rose

**Mold a grape-sized piece of dough into a narrow cone about ¾" long. Flatten a nickel-sized piece of dough into a triangular shape resembling a guitar pick, then make the edges irregular. Press one point of the triangle against the base of the cone and let the broader part curl up and around and off the tip of the cone to form the first petal. Continue adding ever smaller petals in this way.**

## RECIPE

### Flaky Pastry Shell
*Makes a 9" pie shell*

- 1¼ cups all-purpose flour, plus more for surfaces
- ½ teaspoon salt
- 1 tablespoon sugar
- 6 tablespoons (¾ stick) chilled unsalted butter, cut into ¼" pats
- 2 tablespoons chilled vegetable shortening
- 3–3½ tablespoons ice water

three separate trials. With this addition, each pie dough now became difficult to form, making more water a necessity to help blend the ingredients. The baked pie edges held their shapes well, but the crust tasted tough and bland. I concluded that the *Cook's* recipe, minus two tablespoons of shortening, produced a pastry that was tender yet strong enough to produce shapely *and* tasty decorations.

## Making the Decorative Edges

Once I had the recipe finalized, I tested a variety of designs and came up with two categories: decorations made using the existing dough on the pie's edge (dough manipulation) and those that you add on (dough appliqué).

Dough manipulation is the quickest technique because you're working with the existing dough. The appliqué method requires more working time since you must shape separate pieces of dough before attaching them to the rim. Once your shapes are molded or cut, arrange them around the rim and press down gently to assure adhesion.

## Mixing the Dough

**1.** Combine flour, salt, and sugar in medium-sized bowl. Scatter butter pats and shortening over mixture and cut it with fingertips or pastry blender until mixture resembles coarse meal.

**2.** Drizzle 3 tablespoons of the water over mixture. Using blade of rubber spatula, cut mixture into little pieces.

Press down with broad side of spatula so pieces stick together in large clumps. If dough resists gathering, sprinkle remaining water over dry, crumbly patches and press a few more times. Form dough into ball. Wrap in plastic, flatten into 4" disk, and refrigerate at least 30 minutes.

## Lining the Pie Plate

**1.** Unwrap dough and place on floured surface. Dust top with flour. Roll dough in all directions, from center to edges. When disk is 9" in diameter, flip over and continue rolling in all directions until 13" to 14" in diameter and ⅛" to 3/16" thick.

**2.** Fold dough in quarters. Lay in 9" Pyrex pie plate with folded corner at center. Gently unfold, draping excess over plate lip. Trim excess to an even ½" to ¾" all around. If making appliqué-type decorations, retain excess dough for this use.

**3.** Tuck overhanging dough back under itself so folded edge overhangs plate edge by ⅛"; press lightly to seal. Select decorative edge and follow accompanying instructions (*see* illustrations).

## Baking the Crust

**1.** To firm shell, refrigerate 20 minutes. Prick bottom and sides at ½" intervals. Flatten 12" square of aluminum foil inside shell, pressing it flush against sides and over rim. Cover any exposed sections of rim with strips of foil. Prick foil bottom in ten to twelve places. Chill at least 30 minutes (preferably 1 hour or more).

**2.** Heat oven to 400 degrees. Bake shell 15 minutes, pressing down gently on foil with mitt-protected hands to flatten puffs. Start preparing filling of your choice while shell is baking. Remove foil and bake shell for 8 to 10 minutes longer. Pour warm filling into hot pie shell and bake as directed. ◆

## Reverse Scallop

Use the tip of a vegetable peeler to leave scalloped impressions. Hold either side of the peeler up, or alternate the up and down positions for a more ruffly effect.

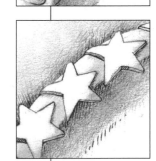

## Stars

Use a small cookie or canapé cutter to cut motifs such as stars from the rolled pastry dough.

## Pinched Edge

To create a pinched edge, push the dough with your thumb against the side of the thumb and forefinger of your other hand. This will create a high ridge with a subtle zigzag.

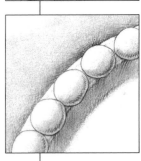

## Button

Roll marble-sized balls of dough between your palms, then flatten them slightly as you position them around the rim.

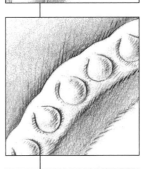

## Teardrop

Use the metal hanging loop at the end of a wire whisk handle to make these teardrop impressions.

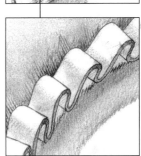

## Crisscross

Place narrow 2"-long strips cut from rolled dough around the rim, slanting in one direction. Add a second tier slanting in the opposite direction to create the crisscross pattern. Tuck the ends under the outside edge. The pie filling will conceal the inside ends.

## Ribbon

Arrange ½"-wide dough strips in an undulating wave pattern. Use the longest strips your dough allows without breaking, and tuck under the loose ends in order to keep the pattern even.

**These lined velvet pouches are perfect for holding gifts, jewelry, lingerie, or small collectibles.**

# Lined Velvet Pouches

*Using a streamlined assembly process, you can make five pouches at a time versus creating each one individually.*

BY NANCY K. JOHNSON

## MATERIALS
*Yields five*
*8" x 7" pouches*
- ½ yard 45"-wide velvet
- ½ yard 45"-wide acetate lining
- 5 27" drapery tiebacks with tasseled ends
- 1 yard soutache or similar narrow cord to match velvet
- Thread to match velvet and lining

*You'll also need:*
contrasting thread for basting; sewing machine; scissors; yardstick and fabric marking pencil or rotary cutter, cutting guide, and self-healing mat; needle; pins; iron; and ironing board.

*Other items, if necessary:*
velvet board or scrap of velvet (for pressing velvet).

TRADITIONALLY, ANY OBJECT designed with a lining—be it a gift bag, a set of drapes, or a jacket—suggests a certain level of complexity. To counter that assumption, I set out to develop a fast and simple technique for making a set of lined gift bags.

On my first try, I cut out individual fabric pieces for each pouch and its lining and sewed them together. As I worked, it occurred to me that I could streamline the process by sewing larger pieces of fabric together first and then cutting them into the smaller pouch pieces. This method helped me achieve a more even seam where the lining joined the pouch and gave my pouches a more professional look. The basic configuration resembles a sock. The bag and lining are sewn together, the bag is turned right side out, and the lining is sewn closed and slipped inside.

For these pouches, I chose velvet for its deep, plush texture and "backbone"—I envisioned a pouch that would stand up on its own without col-

lapsing—but other full-bodied fabrics, such as textured damask, heavyweight satin, and even dress-weight woolens, also worked well with this design and construction method. Rather than buying off the bolt, I first visited the remnant bin, as half a yard each of fabric and lining is all it takes to make five pouches.

To add visual appeal to the pouches, I chose a lining that contrasts in both color and texture. As a general rule, I found that an opaque lining (versus translucent) with slightly less body than the pouch fabric worked best because it reduced the bulk that could discourage flat, clean points and seams. I used an inexpensive acetate lining to give these velvet pouches a traditional look, but for more sheen, you could also use blouse-weight silk or satin.

To keep its contents secure, each pouch uses a simple tie closure. Just about any heavy cord, ribbon, or flat braid, at least twenty-seven inches long, can be used; I discovered that drapery tiebacks with tassels already

attached are an elegant choice.

Assembling the pouches is fairly straightforward. The only difficulty I encountered was at the start, when trying to sew velvet to acetate: The acetate kept slipping. I tried pins, the machine's walking foot, and a fabric glue stick, all without success. I finally resorted to hand-basting the fabrics together using one-half-inch stitches, which only took a few minutes.

Your pouches will have a more professional finish if you press the fabric and seams as you go. I've learned that velvet fares best if pressed from the wrong side with a velvet board placed underneath. A velvet board contains short, closely spaced vertical wires that prevent the velvet's pile from crushing in on itself when the weight of the iron is applied. If you don't have a velvet board, two additional techniques that I tested will also work. In the first, I placed a remnant of velvet right side up on the ironing board and then laid the velvet to be pressed right side down on top of it. The velvet remnant works like a "soft" velvet board to help hold the fibers on both velvet pieces upright. With care, velvet can also be steamed from the right side. Set your iron to the lowest steam setting, then hold the iron so it hovers above the surface of the velvet and let the steam penetrate the fibers. Don't let the full weight of the iron rest on the fabric; this technique requires vigilance as well as coordination and is best reserved for small areas or stubborn wrinkles.

*Nancy K. Johnson is a full-time artist specializing in painting, pottery, and silversmithing.*

## INSTRUCTIONS
### Cutting the Fabric
**1.** Place velvet face side down on ironing or velvet board and press from wrong side, or use one of alternative methods outlined in main text, above.

**2.** *To cut fabric using scissors:* Measure and mark 18" x 40" rectangle on wrong side of velvet. Then mark 40" line down center of rectangle to create two 9"-wide sections. Pin velvet to lining, right sides together. Cut along marked lines, through both layers, to create two 9" x 40" rectangles from each fabric. Remove pins.

**3.** *To cut fabric using rotary cutter:* Lay velvet and lining on cutting mat,

PHOTOGRAPH BY STEVEN MAYS

right sides together. Measure and cut two 9" x 40" rectangles.

## Sewing the Pouches

**1.** Pin each velvet rectangle to lining rectangle, right sides together, ⅜" from one 40" edge (choose the same edge on each piece of velvet so the fabric's nap runs in the same direction). Hand-baste two rectangles together using contrasting color thread. Load machine with thread to match velvet and machine-stitch ½" from basted edge, removing pins as you go (*see* illustration 1, right.) Remove basting.

**2.** Place rectangle lining-side up on ironing board. Fold back lining so both lining and velvet face right side up. With iron on lowest steam setting, and holding iron above fabric, steam lining away from velvet along seam.

**3.** Refold each rectangle wrong sides together so right side of lining faces up and velvet faces ironing board. Make fold in velvet ¼" from seam, as in illustration 2, and finger-press to form top edge. Steam lightly to set crease as in step 2.

**4.** Open each velvet/lining rectangle and lay it flat on work surface. From each rectangle, measure, mark, and cut five 8"-wide x 17"-long rectangles (illustration 3).

**5.** Cut soutache (or substitute) into ten 3½" lengths. Fold each length in half, then tie ends in knot 1" from fold to form loop. Using thread to match velvet, machine-baste one loop to each edge of rectangle's velvet sides 2½" from seam on right side of fabric (illustration 4). Repeat to attach all loops.

**6.** Lay two rectangles, one with loops and one without, right sides together, edges and seams matching. Machine-baste ½" from raw edges across seam for 1". Pin edges together on all four sides. Starting at point A (illustration 5), stitch through both layers ½" from edge around three sides, ending at point B. Repeat to stitch four additional pouches.

**7.** Clip velvet corners diagonally and clip away excess velvet at seams. Turn pouch right side out, and pick out corners with pin. Fold raw edges of lining ¾" to inside, and press with dry iron at lowest setting. Slip-stitch pressed lining edges together using matching thread (illustration 6). Poke lining down into pouch. Resteam folded edge at top of pouch as in step 2. Slip tasseled cord through loops, insert gift in pouch, and tie cord in bow. ◆

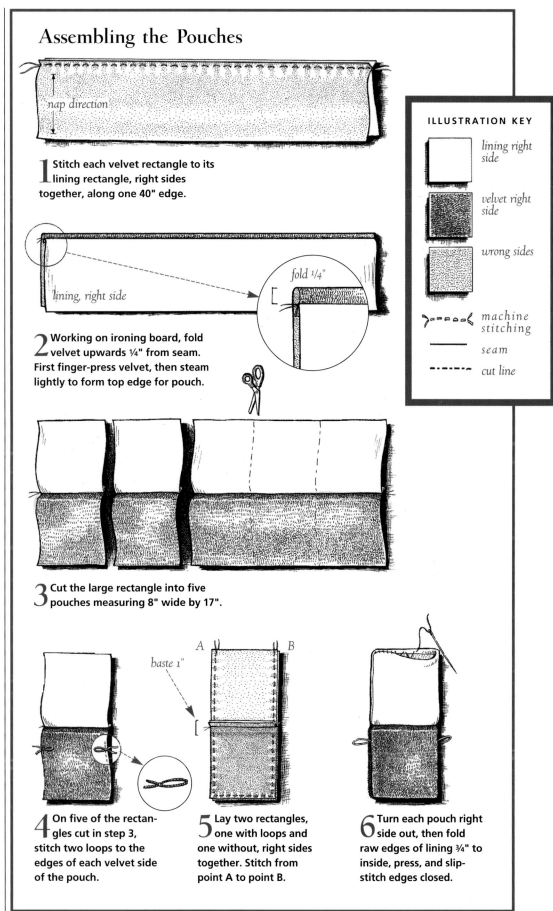

## Assembling the Pouches

*nap direction*

**1** Stitch each velvet rectangle to its lining rectangle, right sides together, along one 40" edge.

*lining, right side*

*fold ¼"*

**2** Working on ironing board, fold velvet upwards ¼" from seam. First finger-press velvet, then steam lightly to form top edge for pouch.

**3** Cut the large rectangle into five pouches measuring 8" wide by 17".

*baste 1"*

A    B

**4** On five of the rectangles cut in step 3, stitch two loops to the edges of each velvet side of the pouch.

**5** Lay two rectangles, one with loops and one without, right sides together. Stitch from point A to point B.

**6** Turn each pouch right side out, then fold raw edges of lining ¾" to inside, press, and slip-stitch edges closed.

**ILLUSTRATION KEY**

lining right side

velvet right side

wrong sides

machine stitching

seam

cut line

# Folk Art Frame

*Use the original art in this issue's insert, a simple frame design, and a wood grain faux finish to build this two-panel framed mirror.*

🐦 BY LARRY PALMER

ALTHOUGH THIS lapped corner frame, along with its decorative wood grain faux finish, folk art image, and stenciled corner pieces, may look complex, as woodworking projects go, it was designed with simplicity in mind. Compared to a mitered corner frame, which requires precise forty-five-degree angled cuts, my lapped corner frame has a relatively forgiving construction approach. For sections of wood that need to be cut to the same length, for instance, I taped them together using masking tape and cut them simultaneously to guarantee precision. In addition, after the corners of the frame were glued, I sawed off the excess wood even with the frame sides, which eliminated the need for any tedious measuring beforehand.

This article will teach you how to build the lapped corner frame, while companion articles in this issue will give you ideas and instructions for finishing your frame (see "Fast and Easy Wood Grain Finish," page 20) and

stenciling the corner of the frame's picture mat (see "Bronze Stenciling with Acrylics," page 8). The folk art painting used in the frame is reproduced in this issue's insert, along with a second original piece of art suitable for framing. I sized the two-panel frame to hold a nine-by-eleven-inch picture mat (which I obtained by trimming down an eleven-by-fourteen-inch picture mat) and an eleven-by-fourteen-inch mirror purchased at a discount store.

First, let me define a few important woodworking terms. I assembled the frame using three types of wood: lattice, baluster, and pine board. Lattice is about one-quarter inch thick and is milled in the following widths: $\frac{3}{4}$", $\frac{7}{8}$", $1\frac{1}{8}$", $1\frac{3}{8}$", $1\frac{5}{8}$", $2\frac{5}{8}$", $3\frac{5}{8}$", and $5\frac{1}{4}$". Baluster, sometimes used for stair railings, is a piece of wood with the same measurements on all four sides, like a cube extended into a board.

Both lattice and baluster are pur-

## MATERIALS

- 9' 1⅝" lattice
- 1' 1⅜" lattice
- 8' 1" x 2" pine board, rip-cut to 1⅜" wide
- 1' ¾" baluster
- 11" x 14" single-pane glass mirror
- 11" x 14" mat, with 7½" x 9½" oval cutout
- 4 antique finish decorative upholstery nails
- 8 ⅝" brads
- Glazier's push points
- Yellow carpenter's glue
- Black acrylic paint

*You'll also need:*
backsaw with small, closely

spaced teeth; carpenter's square; 80-, 120-, and 220-grit sandpaper; sanding block; tack cloth; hammer; stiff, 1"-wide flat paintbrush; utility knife; metal straightedge; several layers newspaper; transparent grid ruler; sponge; ¾"-wide masking tape; pencil; and ½"-wide flat paintbrush.

*Other items, if necessary:*
two pieces heavyweight cardboard, at least 11" x 14" (for mirrors and mats without backing); and pliers or old screwdriver (for removing staples or clips from mirrors with backing).

chased using the actual measurements of the wood. Some varieties of wood, however, such as pine board, are handled differently. Partly as a result of the way lumber is cut and partly because of tradition, the nominal dimension of lumber, meaning what it is called, is always larger than the actual dimension of the wood. In addition, since lumber is cut in huge quantities, it is available only in relatively standard sizes. While the pine board I chose actually measures three-quarters by one and one-half inches, it is called "one by two inches" to indicate the approximate size of the board before it was "dressed down" to its final size.

For my design, however, the "one-by-two" board must be further modified. Every frame features a rabbet, or lipped groove, on the back to hold the mirror and/or artwork in place. The rabbet is formed by gluing one-and-five-eighths-inches-wide lattice to a slightly narrower (one-and-three-eighths-inches-wide) but thicker pine board to form a quarter-inch-wide

## Sawing Clean-Cut Edges

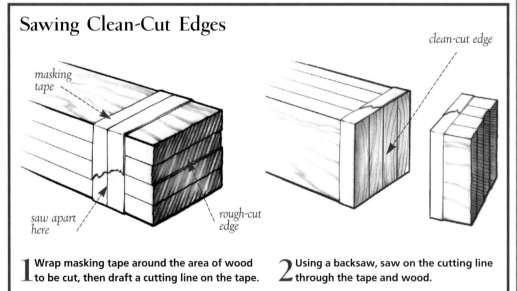

masking tape

saw apart here

rough-cut edge

clean-cut edge

**1** Wrap masking tape around the area of wood to be cut, then draft a cutting line on the tape.

**2** Using a backsaw, saw on the cutting line through the tape and wood.

ILLUSTRATIONS BY MICHAEL GELLATLY/PHOTOGRAPHS BY STEVEN MAYS

## Making the Frame

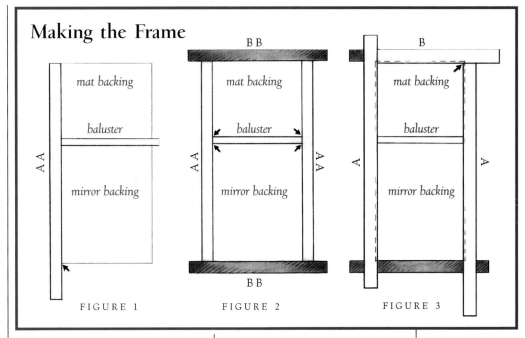

FIGURE 1

FIGURE 2

FIGURE 3

overhang. To get a one-and-three-eighths-inches-wide pine board, I had to make a rip cut (a cut that runs along the wood grain) in the one-by-two board. I made my rip cut using a table saw, but many lumberyards are equipped to make rip cuts for a modest charge—and you can have the wood cut when you buy it. (A crosscut saw, which is typically used for cross-grain cuts, can also be used to make lengthwise cuts.) Examine the lattice and one-by-two critically, and reject any pieces with cracks, prominent knots, or damage to the edges.

I've also used the term "rough cut" throughout this piece. Quite simply, a rough cut is a cut made at the approximate point of measure. It's not the final cut, but a cut designed to make the piece of wood easier to handle.

Careless operation of power tools is the most frequent cause of woodworking accidents, but even hand tools, when improperly used or left in the wrong place, can cause injury. For safety's sake, whenever working with woodworking tools, follow these precautions: Never work in the shop if you are tired. Concentrate on the task at hand. Keep the floor and bench top swept clean of all sawdust and debris. Never wear loose clothing or jewelry—be sure to roll up your sleeves or button them snugly around your wrists. Be certain to tie back long or loose strands of hair. If there is danger of flying chips or particles, be sure to wear safety glasses—eyeglasses are not an adequate substitute.

*Larry Palmer, an X-ray equipment service engineer living in Buffalo, New York, enjoys crafts and woodworking in his spare time. Wood grain faux finish on frame by Michio Ryan. Bronze-stenciled corner accents on picture mat by Deborah Miller Gabler.*

### INSTRUCTIONS
### Preparing the Mirror and Mat

**1.** Lay mirror face down. If mirror has backing, pry staples or clips loose and separate mirror and backing from frame using pliers or old screwdriver. Set aside backing. If no backing is included, lay mirror on cardboard and trace outline. Cover cutting surface with newspaper. Cut cardboard on marked lines in order to make 11" x 14" backing.

**2.** Using grid ruler, draw parallel line

1½" from each 11" edge and 1" from each 14" edge on picture mat. Cut along marked lines to make new 9" x 11" mat. Cut mat backing to match; if no backing is included, cut from cardboard as in step 1.

### Sizing and Cutting the Frame Pieces

**1.** Using backsaw, rough-cut 1⅝" lattice into two 30", two 15", and four 4" strips. Discard excess. Label 30" strips "A" and 15" strips "B." Rough-cut pine board into two 28" and two 17" strips. Discard excess. Label 28" strips "AA" and 17" strips "BB." Label 1⅜"-wide lattice strip "C."

**2.** Clean-cut one end of A, B, C, and AA by stacking and taping several pieces together. Make cut about ½ to 1 inch from end, as shown in illustration 1, page 16. Draft cutting line on tape on all four sides using carpenter's square. Saw on line through tape and wood (illustration 2). Sand clean-cut ends lightly using 80-grit sandpaper in sanding block. Remove tape from all pieces except AA.

**3.** To make 1⅝" x 1⅝" squares, tape four 4"

strips together with tape ½" and 2" from one end. Draft two parallel cutting lines on tape 1⅝" apart. Clean-cut shorter end first, then other end, and sand both cut ends lightly as above.

### Making the Frame

**1.** Lay cardboard backings flat with baluster between them as a spacer; allow a scant ¹⁄₁₆" between them for ease. Lay taped AA strips along one side, aligning clean-cut end with mat

# Final Assembly of the Frame

**HISTORICAL TIDBIT**
The simple design for this two-panel folk art mirror derives from the Federal style of furniture, which prevailed in American interiors from the Revolutionary War into the early nineteenth century. Made of commonly available woods such as pine, the furniture was often stained, combed, or given some other decorative painted finish to imitate more exotic, expensive woods.

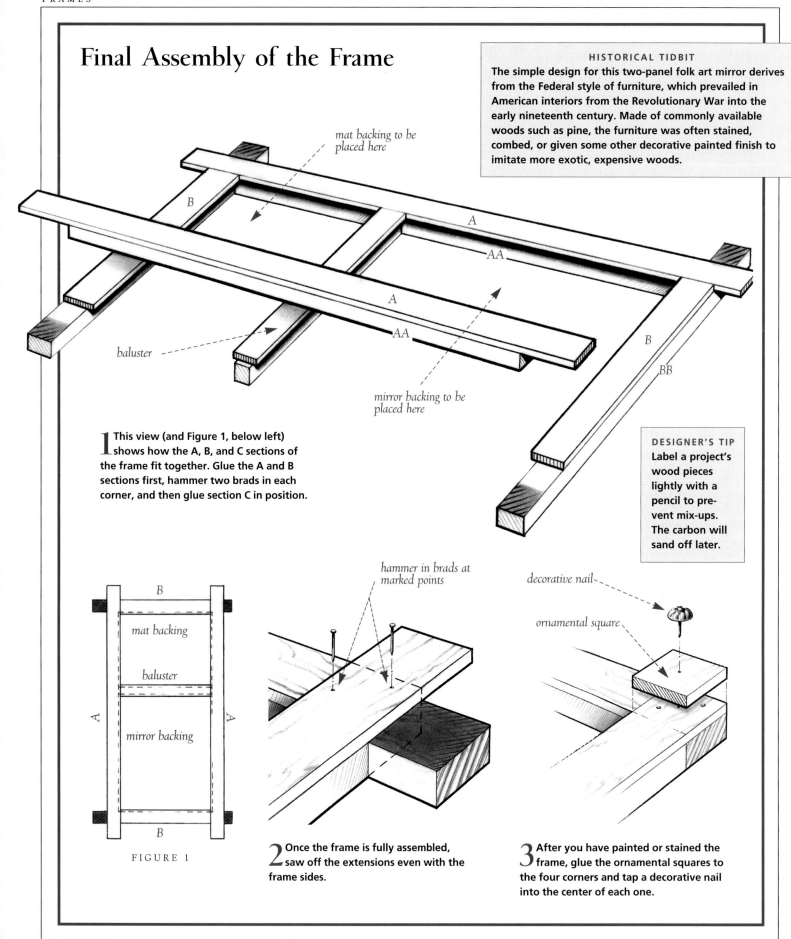

mat backing to be placed here

B

A

AA

baluster

A

AA

mirror backing to be placed here

B

BB

**1** This view (and Figure 1, below left) shows how the A, B, and C sections of the frame fit together. Glue the A and B sections first, hammer two brads in each corner, and then glue section C in position.

**DESIGNER'S TIP**
Label a project's wood pieces lightly with a pencil to prevent mix-ups. The carbon will sand off later.

hammer in brads at marked points

decorative nail

ornamental square

B

mat backing

baluster

A

A

mirror backing

B

FIGURE 1

**2** Once the frame is fully assembled, saw off the extensions even with the frame sides.

**3** After you have painted or stained the frame, glue the ornamental squares to the four corners and tap a decorative nail into the center of each one.

backing. Mark point on AA even with mirror backing (*see* arrow on figure 1, page 17), then clean-cut end and remove tape.

**2.** Remove baluster. Lay AA strips alongside mat and mirror backings, allowing 1/16" ease at edge where board meets backing. Mark baluster position (see arrows on figure 2, page 17) on inside edges of AA. Center BB strips across top and bottom edges of frame. (The extensions will be sawed off after frame is assembled.)

**3.** Arrange two A strips and one B strip on top of AA and BB as shown in figure 3 so outer edges (except extensions) are flush. To ensure accuracy, where possible, butt clean-cut ends. (The inner edge of each A and B strip should overhang the board underneath by 1/4" to create the rabbet.) Mark B at point where A and B meet (arrow on figure 3). Remove B, then stack two B strips and one C strip, with marked B on top. Align and tape clean-cut ends, then clean-cut other end of strips at mark on B. Remove tape.

**4.** Sand full length of A, B, and C strips with 120-grit sandpaper in sanding block. Wipe off dust. Set A and B strips in position on top of AA and BB strips (figure 1 and illustration 1, page 18) so smoothest, clearest side of each piece faces out. Dry-fit (test-fit without gluing) corners to assure alignment. Resand if necessary.

### Final Assembly of the Frame

**1.** Using illustration 1 on page 18 for reference, and working one section at a time, hold each A and B strip against AA or BB, outer edges flush and ends extending evenly. Mark outlines that each piece makes on other. Separate pieces. Using 1"-wide brush, spread glue within penciled areas. Press together, matching edges to pencil outlines. Wipe glue oozing from joints. Secure at each end by wrapping masking tape tightly around glued sections at 4" to 5" intervals, reversing direction every other wrap in order to minimize slippage. Wipe oozing glue. Let dry 1 hour.

> **DESIGNER'S TIP**
> It is far easier to sand small pieces of wood by moving them over a large piece of sandpaper held down on a flat surface than trying to move a sanding block over a tiny piece of wood. You can use this technique to sand the four small wood blocks before you paint them, as in "Finishing the Frame," step 2.

**2.** To assemble C section (illustration 1) from C strip and baluster, center C on baluster so that it extends evenly (about 1/2") beyond C at each end and C hangs 5/16" beyond baluster on each long edge; confirm spacing. Mark outlines, then glue and tape as above. Let dry 1 hour. Mark baluster 1/4" beyond ends of C, then clean-cut at marks.

**3.** Dry-fit two A and two B sections in position, butting ends snugly until corners "lock" (illustration 1). Mark overhang. Remove A sections, and brush glue within pencil guidelines on A and B surfaces. Reset sections into position. To close gaps at corners, tap both sections from opposite ends alternately. Confirm that corners are square, then tap 5/8" brads at inside and outside corners on all four corners (illustration 2). Wipe off oozing glue. Let dry 1 hour.

**4.** Test-fit C section in frame from wrong side, then examine from right side. If hairline crack shows at either end, sand same end of baluster with 120-grit sandpaper in sanding block and retest. Glue C in position from wrong side between marks made in "Making the Frame," step 2. Tape frame to hold sides tightly against C. Let dry overnight.

**5.** Using backsaw, cut off extensions even with four corners (illustration 2), making sure blade rides flush against frame side. After removing all eight extensions, sand each outside corner with 120-grit sandpaper in sanding block until smooth.

### Finishing the Frame

**1.** Sand entire frame very lightly with 220-grit sandpaper and wipe off dust. Stain, paint, or give frame a decorative faux finish. (*See* "Fast and Easy Wood Grain Finish," page 20, for materials and instructions.)

**2.** Sand four corner squares very lightly with 220-grit sandpaper and paint them using 1/2"-wide paintbrush. Glue squares into position and hammer nail into centers (see illustration 3, page 18).

**3.** If desired, decorate corners of mat with bronze stenciling. (*See* "Bronze Stenciling with Acrylics," page 8, for materials and instructions.) *Note:* Be sure to allow for rabbet overlap when positioning stencil.

**4.** Hold mirror, picture and mat, and backings in position from behind with push points. ◆

# Changing the Frame Size

I customized the lapped corner frame to fit an existing piece of artwork and found it's really quite easy. If you're framing just one item, the frame should not go much beyond 18" square in order to remain stable. Keep in mind that the more elongated the frame rectangle, the greater the torque, which can warp the frame and weaken the joints. The strut (C section) helps stabilize the

frame and reduces this tendency to twist.

To determine how much lumber to buy for a custom-sized frame, lay the cardboard backing from the item you plan to frame on a flat work surface. If you are framing two pieces, lay both backings in their "framed" position, leaving a 3/4" space between them. Measure and jot down, rounding up to the nearest inch, the

length (L) and width (W) of the overall unit, then purchase the following amounts of lumber, rounding up to the nearest foot:

- 1 5/8" lattice: 2L + 2W + 22"
- 1 3/8" lattice: 1W
- 1" x 2" pine board, rip-cut to 1 3/8" wide: 2L + 2W + 6"
- 3/4" baluster: 1W

To begin your frame, rough-cut the 1 5/8" lattice into two

pieces L + 3" long and label them "A," two pieces W" long and label them "B," and four pieces 4" long. Rough-cut the rip-cut 1" x 2" pine board into two pieces L" long, labeling them "AA," and two pieces W + 3" long, labeling them "BB." Label 1 3/8" lattice "C." Proceed to "Sizing and Cutting the Frame Pieces," step 2, page 17, to continue making your frame.

# Foolproof Wood Grain Faux Finish

*Create a convincing curly maple faux finish using your index finger and glaze.*

❧ BY MICHIO RYAN

## MATERIALS

- **Bare wood surface, such as Folk Art Frame (see page 16)**
- **½ pint satin finish stain-polyurethane product**

*You'll also need:*
plastic glove; ¼"- to 2"-wide flat brush (choose width appropriate to object); painter's tape; paint stick; paint thinner; drop cloth, newspaper, or large sheet of plastic; 220-grit sandpaper; and tack cloth.

*Other items, if necessary:*
2-ounce container acrylic paint, additional ¼"- to 2"-wide flat brush (choose width appropriate to object), 600-grit silicon carbide wet-dry paper, and damp sponge (all necessary if painting base coat).

A FOLK ART FRAME SUCH AS the one featured on page 16 could be finished in a variety of ways, so I set out to find the simplest technique that would yield the most aesthetically pleasing and historically compatible finish. The curly maple finish I developed is probably among the simplest and most foolproof of all faux finishes: All you need is glaze, a plastic glove, and your index finger to re-create a wood grain finish evocative of early American folk art.

Glaze is a creamy, slow-drying medium that sits on the surface of the wood rather than being absorbed into it. To that end, it can be manipulated while still wet. To create the wood grain effect shown below, I donned a plastic glove, set my index finger on the frame's surface, and rolled it. After rolling, I lifted my finger up, which removed and displaced some of the glaze, then I set it down on the surface approximately one-half inch away from the first impression and repeated the rolling motion to make a second parallel impression.

To save the time of mixing glazes to a specific color, I recommend using a new category of wood finishing products that combine stain with polyurethane. Minwax Polyshades and Defts Step Saver, for example, are both available in a wide palette of wood tones. *Note:* For ordinary staining and finishing, I don't believe these products are reliably consistent—the slightest variation in the top coat thickness makes the stain color uneven—but for folk art wood graining, this varied tonal effect is ideal.

The Minwax glaze can be applied to either bare or painted wood. To be convincing, your faux finish should reflect how real wood panels and veneers are assembled in a piece of furniture. Given the length of the tool (your finger), finger-rolled effects are suitable for projects with narrow spans of wood, such as a picture or mirror frame. In these cases, the glaze is applied perpendicularly to the long edges.

One other important note. Although this finish is extremely simple, finishing a frame such as our Folk Art Frame will take at least five days. You can start by finishing all the flat surfaces on the front of the frame, but for each successive edge, the frame must be propped so the surface is flat

and the glaze is prevented from running. Thereafter the glaze must dry at least eight hours.

## INSTRUCTIONS

*If possible, set up two different work areas—one for sanding and the other for painting/glazing. This separation will prevent the particles released during sanding from settling on any wet surfaces. Protect the painting/glazing work surface with a drop cloth, newspaper, or plastic sheet.*

**1.** Sand all wooden surfaces. Remove dust with tack cloth.

**2.** *If painting base coat:* Apply light coat of paint, and let dry 15 minutes. Apply second coat if necessary. Let dry 30 minutes. Sand lightly with moistened wet-dry paper, and remove dust with sponge.

**3.** Position object with surface to be glazed facing up. Mask all edges adjacent to this surface with painter's tape. Stir stain-polyurethane "glaze" thoroughly. Brush on light coat. Let sit 3 to 5 minutes.

### HISTORICAL TIDBIT
**Faux wood grain finishes originated in Europe, where artisans devoted years to master sophisticated painting, combing, and graining techniques designed to imitate expensive veneer inlays. In eighteenth- and early-nineteenth-century North America, attempts to keep up with European high style gave birth to folk art wood graining. Often perfunctorily rendered, this country cousin displayed vigor, color, and spontaneity—the precise qualities that make folk art finishes so endearing and collectible today.**

**4.** Pull on plastic glove. Set finger on glazed surface, roll it, then lift up, removing and displacing glaze. Set finger down on surface ½" or so away from first impression and repeat rolling motion to make second parallel impression. Continue rolling along entire surface.

**5.** For next 30 minutes, periodically check glaze impressions. A small amount of running is normal and will soften harsh lines, but if pattern should lose too much definition, smooth surface with brush and repeat finger-rolling technique. When pattern has held for 30 minutes, let it dry at least 8 hours.

**6.** Repeat steps 3 to 5 to glaze each remaining surface in turn. Clean up all materials with thinner. ◆

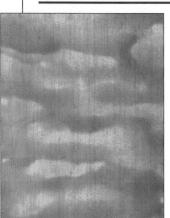

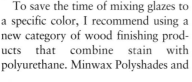

To save the time of mixing glazes for a specific color, this curly maple finish uses Minwax's Polyshades "Pecan" stain in a satin finish. The stain was applied to bare wood.

For the best results, apply the glaze perpendicularly to the frame's long edges. To create ripples suggesting maple grain, "vibrate" your finger as you roll.

PHOTOGRAPHS BY RICHARD FELBER

**1** Brush paint on front of leaves. Begin testing immediately for tapelike tackiness.

**2** Press leaf tacky side down onto metal leaf and rub back of leaf gently.

**3** Gently tear gilded leaf away from sheet of metal leaf.

**4** Run dry brush over leaf edges to remove flakes of metal leaf. Let dry overnight, then gently burnish with dry brush. Clean brush using turpentine.

# Quick Gilded Autumn Leaves

*Forget about traditional gilding methods. "Press" gilding with enamel paint works best.*

❧ BY CANDIE FRANKEL

THE FLEETING BEAUTY OF autumn leaves inspired me to explore a way to preserve them for use as decorative accents on tables, packages and wreaths.

I liked the look of gilded surfaces and knew from previous experience that gold leaf was deceivingly easy to work with. I also knew that the process would require only three simple stages: applying size, a substance with adhesive properties, applying gold leaf to the treated surface, and burnishing. If I could get gold leaf to adhere to a leaf, it would not only add a decorative accent, but it might also preserve the leaf by slowing down or eliminating the normal curling that takes place as a leaf dries. I was surprised by my findings. While discovering that leaves could be gilded, I also developed the fastest and most effective way to gild them. I call it the press method of gilding.

I began by testing a variety of leaves with different shapes, sizes, and colors, all gathered on a dry day. By far the easiest leaves to gild were oak and beech, which have strong cellular structures, making them easy to handle while applying gold leaf. Their pliable, smooth, leatherlike surfaces were hospitable to the application of the adhesive and the gold leaf. As sugar maple leaves are more brilliantly colored than oak or beech, I selectively gilded them to allow the blaze of color to show through. After one week, however, their colors faded. I also tested fresh greenery, namely holly and ivy leaves, and discovered their surfaces took well to gilding. I concluded that most leaves could be gilded as long as the leaf was not brittle to begin with.

There was another aspect that had a significant impact on the gilding process: the thickness of the plant material. Thin leaves like Chinese maple were difficult to handle, as they are small and delicate; the dried leaves curled into a little fist shape after one day and broke easily during the simple brush strokes in the adhesive stage. Navigating this problem turned out to be quite simple, however: I pressed the leaves between the pages of a heavy book so they dried flat.

Since traditional gold leaf size can take an hour or more to reach the correct tack for gilding (*see* "How to Gild Almost Any Surface," September/October 1994 for a full discussion), I decided to test several adhesive alternatives to size that are faster-drying—and discovered an unconventional method of applying the gold leaf in the process. I found rubber cement was easy to apply, and it reached the correct tack in about fifteen minutes. The best performing adhesive, however, was metallic enamel paint: It reached the correct tack in less than five minutes, burnished to a smooth finish (after overnight drying), and added a soft underglow in areas where the metal leaf flaked off.

Traditional gilding techniques require you to break the metallic leaf into small pieces using perfectly dry fingertips, then lift and position the pieces using your fingertip. I found, however, that pressing a leaf tacky side down directly onto the sheet of gold leaf worked just as well and took a fraction of the time. *Note:* Don't try this pressing technique with especially dry or brittle leaves, as they may crack or crumble. In this case, you'll need to apply the metallic leaf in the traditional manner. ◆

---

**MATERIALS**

- 2–4 dozen autumn or green leaves in various sizes
- 1 book metal leaf
- 2-ounce container metallic enamel paint

*You'll also need:*
two ½"-wide paintbrushes; newspaper or brown kraft paper; and mineral spirits or turpentine.

---

# Bittersweet Topiary

*For topiaries made from vinelike branches, a wire hanger serves as the base of choice.*

❧ BY CAROL ENDLER STERBENZ

**For seasonal variations of this topiary, attach stems of artificial flowers, and paint the pot to match.**

I HAVE DESIGNED MANY TOPIARIES and have generally gravitated toward the traditional globe topiary with its classical shape: spherical head and conical pot, separated by a straight stem (*see* Quick Projects, page 33). With this particular configuration in mind, I have then set out to find suitable decorative material. Because the head of the globe topiary is made of dry foam, for instance, the foliage or vegetation has had to be lightweight and voluminous.

The hoop topiary shown here was developed in the reverse manner, as the characteristics of the decorative shrubbery that I wanted to use, bittersweet, dictated the shape and construction of the topiary head. I had to adapt the globe design to the bittersweet's slender, flexible, vinelike branches, which are accented with clusters of burnt orange berries.

The usual method of preparing material and applying it to the globe topiary's foam head is to cut short stems and insert them into the sphere. Quite simply, this did not work with bittersweet. The short lengths were thick and relatively heavy, and they caused the foam to crumble when multiple stems were inserted close to each other. The solution, as it turned out, was to work with the natural shape of the bittersweet's arching branches, which can be easily bent into a hoop shape.

To support the hoop of bittersweet, I needed an armature that was sturdy and thin enough to hold the weight of and be concealed by the interlacing branches of bittersweet. Although a welded wreath frame offered me a hoop shape, it lacked a stem. I tried wiring a separate length of wire cut from a wire hanger onto the bottom of the wreath frame, but when the hoop was decorated, it ended up falling forward at the joint from the weight of the material. The wire hanger, though, had possibilities: It was sturdy, yet flexible enough to shape into a hoop shape with my hands, and it already had a hook, which I could bend into a straight stem. Here was my solution: Bend the wire hanger into a hoop, and lace the bittersweet branches around the wire to form the topiary head.

I tested two types of berry branches: twenty-seven-inch-long artificial branches, which have a generous number of berry sprigs on the top half of each branch, and fresh bittersweet, which can be found in floral shops. The finished artificial topiary, which required just eight branches, was less full than the fresh version, but just as attractive. The fresh topiary, which required three twenty-eight-inch-long branches and fifteen twenty-inch-long branches of fresh bittersweet, will last indefinitely since the berries won't fall off when dry. Both finished topiaries measured eight inches to ten inches wide and fourteen inches to sixteen inches tall.

To highlight the blazing orange color of the berries, I wanted to paint the topiary's pot with a strong, contrasting (but not garish) color. The light mint green and copper colors of a faux verdigris finish, when placed next to the berries, created the color sensation I was looking for and brought to mind an aged copper urn. I studied the verdigris finish and noticed four basic colors: black, forest green, medium gray, and metallic copper. Applying them in sequence using a sponge and random overall dabs, I was able to reproduce the patina of the verdigris finish in just a few minutes.

**INSTRUCTIONS**
## Preparing the Pot

**1.** Cover work surface with newspaper. Cut three 1" to 2" squares from damp sponge. Squeeze small amount of black paint onto paper plate. Dip cut sponge square into paint, then wipe paint on outside surface and inside rim. Repeat until surface is evenly coated. Let pot dry 5 minutes.

**2.** Squeeze small amount of forest green paint onto unused portion of paper plate or clean plate. Dab end of second cut sponge into green paint, blot excess on edge of plate, then touch sponge to pot and immediately lift off, without twisting or rubbing, to create subtle texture. Continue until entire outside surface is textured. Dry 5 minutes. Repeat process using third cut sponge and medium gray paint. Squeeze a few drops metallic copper paint onto plate. Dip finger into paint, blot on edge of plate, then touch finger to pot at random to introduce highlights. Dry 10 minutes. Clean up using warm water and soap.

**3.** Stand foam brick vertically. Using knife, cut ½"-thick slice from largest face of brick (*see* illustration 1, page 23, lower left). To create wedge-shaped pieces, lay ½"-thick slice flat and make alternating slanted cuts about 1" apart (illustration 2).

**4.** Seal drainage hole on inside of pot with tape. Line inside wall of pot with foam wedges, butting edges for snug fit and cutting additional pieces to fill any extra gaps that exist along wall (illustration 3). Line floor of pot with additional scraps of foam.

**5.** Put on particle mask and disposable gloves. In bucket, measure 1 cup cold water and 2 cups plaster, then stir with paint stick until smooth. Pour liquid plaster into center of pot, stopping when pot is half full. If additional plaster is needed to fill pot halfway, mix smaller amount in same 1:2 ratio and add to pot immediately. Discard any remaining plaster in leak-proof container, then clean bucket, measuring cup, and paint stick in cold water. Let plaster cure 1 hour.

## Making the Topiary

**1.** Using pliers, straighten bends in triangular sections of wire hanger, then reshape entire hanger into 11"- to 12"-diameter circle. Unbend and straighten hook section of hanger (*see* illustrations 1 and 2, lower right).

**2.** Wind one 28" bittersweet branch or one 27" artificial branch clockwise in a spiraling manner as far as it goes around wire circle (illustration 3). If necessary, secure stems and/or ends to hanger with short lengths of wire. Set aside bittersweet sprigs that break off. Wrap remainder of wire circle with

additional two 28" bittersweet branches or two 27" artificial branches, moving in a clockwise direction.

**3.** Wind fifteen 20" bittersweet branches or five 27" artificial branches around hanger, anchoring these new branches among those already in place and repeating the spiraling process, building up topiary until it is full and even. Tuck bittersweet sprigs set aside in step 2 into topiary to fill in sparse areas, wiring in place if necessary.

**4.** Using nail, pierce hole in center of plastic lid. Slip lid onto topiary stem, then place topiary in pot so end of stem rests on hardened plaster and lid rests on foam; topiary should stand upright without any further support and lowest berries should just skim top rim of pot. If topiary is too high, use wire cutters to cut excess wire from bottom of stem. If topiary is too low, stack small squares of cardboard between stem and plaster to elevate it to desired height, then tape cardboard in place. Remove both topiary and plastic lid from pot.

**5.** Put on particle mask and disposable gloves. In bucket, measure 2 cups cold water and 4 cups plaster and stir with paint stick until smooth. Pour liquid plaster into center of pot, stopping when plaster is level with top of foam wedges. Insert topiary stem with plastic lid into wet plaster, resting lid on foam

as in previous step. Pour additional plaster into pot to within ¾" of top, covering foam and lid completely. Clean bucket, measuring cup, and paint stick in cold water. Let plaster cure 1 hour or until hard and cool. Conceal plaster by pressing moss into top of pot. ◆

### MATERIALS

- 3 28"-long branches fresh bittersweet
**and**
- 15 20"-long branches fresh bittersweet
*or*
- 8 27"-long branches artificial red berries

- Terra-cotta flower pot, 6" in diameter and 6" high
- 4 ounces sheet or Spanish moss
- Wire coat hanger
- 2-ounce bottles acrylic paint in following colors: black, forest green, medium gray, and metallic copper
- Brick of florist foam
- 4 ½"-diameter sturdy disposable plastic lid

- 4-ounce container plaster of Paris
- Electrical tape

*You'll also need:*
new household sponge; disposable paper plates; bucket; paint stick; measuring cup; particle mask; disposable gloves; newspaper; pliers with built-in wire cutters; long, straight kitchen knife; scissors; ruler; nail; and soap.

*Other items, if necessary:*
fine-gauge wire (for wiring stems or branch ends in place); scraps of cardboard (for elevating topiary to proper height); leak-proof disposable container (for disposing of extra plaster).

---

## Lining the Pot with Foam

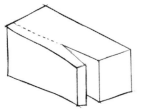

**1** Cut a ½"-thick slice from the largest face of the foam brick.

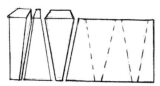

**2** To create wedge-shaped pieces, lay the slice flat and make alternating slanted cuts about 1" apart.

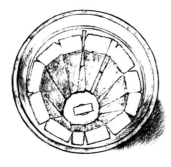

**3** After sealing the drainage hole, line the inside wall of the pot with the foam wedges, butting the edges and cutting extra pieces for a snug fit.

## Shaping and Wrapping the Wire Hanger

**1** Using pliers, straighten the bends in the triangular sections of a wire hanger.

**2** Then reshape the entire hanger into an 11"- to 12"-diameter circle.

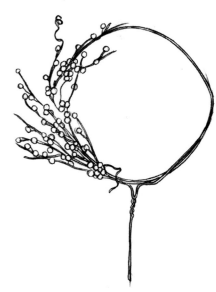

**3** Wind the branches around the topiary form in a clockwise direction.

**1** To start the frame, cut four twigs and glue them in position around the picture opening.

**2** To neatly fill in a section of the frame's front, select, cut, and glue each twig one by one.

**3** To finish, fill in the remaining three front sections with twigs in the same way.

---

**HISTORICAL TIDBIT**

The rustic simplicity of this frame was inspired by late-nineteenth-century Adirondack furniture. This intriguing back-to-nature style incorporated tree branches and bark in the construction of chairs, settees, tables, chests, and even beds.

---

# Adirondack Twig Frame

*Give an ordinary picture frame a log cabin look without the use of nails.*

### BY BRENT PALLAS

IN DESIGNING THIS TWIG FRAME, I looked for a quick and simple process for attaching twigs that would avoid nails or hammering. After testing a number of different glues, I discovered that white tacky glue is the perfect adhesive for attaching a series of narrow twigs, such as birch or apple sapling, to a flat wood picture frame.

You can purchase twigs in season at florist shops, garden centers, and home decor stores; I found a bundle of twelve sixty-inch-long birch branches at Pier One Imports for $3.99. (I discarded about twenty-four inches from each branch, as the twigs near the end were too thin for this project. These twigs can be turned into fire starters, however. Bind fifteen to twenty stems together using cotton string, melt a few candle stubs in a double boiler, and coat each twig bundle with wax.) If you have a yard or access to nearby trees, you may be able to clip low-hanging branches and twigs or retrieve newly fallen twigs instead. To re-create the Adirondack look, the twigs should be as straight, of fairly uniform diameter, and with clean cuts at each end (I clipped mine using handheld pruning shears).

To ensure that the twigs lie as flush to the frame as possible, I recommend a "design-as-you-go" approach. When I first tried making the frame, my idea was to cut all the twigs and then glue them down. The problem with this approach, however, was that no matter how much I fussed, I couldn't prevent gaps between the twigs or get the ends to line up. Then I discovered a simple remedy: Take turns between gluing and cutting. This approach allowed me to slide the length of twig up and down against the adjacent twig until it was snug. Then I cut new twigs to size according to how snugly they rested against those twigs already glued in position. Be sure to use high-tack glue for the instant "grip" this method requires; twigs fastened with ordinary white glue or even yellow carpenter's glue slipped out of position.

*Brent Pallas is a designer and craftsperson based in Manhattan.*

---

**MATERIALS**
- 12 60" branches up to ⅜" diameter *or* 35 to 40 linear feet straight branches and twigs, ¼" to ⅜" diameter
- 5" x 7" wooden picture frame with 1"-wide plane borders
- White high-tack craft glue

*You'll also need:* pruning shears; white lead pencil; ruler; and masking tape.

*Other items, if necessary:* matte finish alkyd spray paint in green, brown, black, or gray, and newspaper (if using light-colored or unfinished frame).

---

### INSTRUCTIONS

**1.** Set aside glass and backing from frame. If using light-colored frame, cover work space and spray-paint frame. Let dry following manufacturer's recommendations.

**2.** Select twig portions between ¼" and ⅜" in diameter in 6"- to 8"-long straight sections. Discard remainder. Clip ends at 90-degree angle and snip off nubs and offshoots.

**3.** Lay frame face up. Lay one twig on frame border, positioning along one edge of picture opening so clipped end is even with perpendicular edge of opening and other end extends beyond frame. Rotate twig until as much surface area as possible touches frame. Mark branch ¼" beyond outer edge of frame.

**4.** Clip through branch at 90-degree angle on pencil mark. Double-check position and length. Apply glue along underside of twig. Press twig in place, ¼" extending beyond frame.

**5.** Proceeding clockwise, repeat steps 3 and 4 with three more twigs. Butt each new twig against the previously glued twig at a right angle (*see* illustration 1). Let glue set 20 minutes.

**6.** Repeat steps 3 and 4 to fill one flat section of frame with four or five additional twigs, working from picture opening out toward edge of frame (illustration 2). Repeat to fill remaining sections (illustration 3). Let glue dry 1 hour.

**7.** To cover sides of frame, grip frame between knees so frame front faces you and one side of frame faces up. Lay one twig on frame side, as close to frame front as possible and with clipped end even with left edge. Mark branch ¼" beyond right edge of frame and even with parallel branches on frame front. Repeat step 4 to clip and glue twig, then repeat with two to three additional twigs. Wrap tape around middle of frame to secure twigs until glue dries. Proceed clockwise around frame to cover remaining three sides. Let glue dry 1 hour, then remove tape.

**8.** Fit, clip, and glue four additional twigs to cover small gap at frame edges where front and sides of frame meet. ◆

---

# Brown Kraft Paper Giftwrap

*For versatility, availability, and low cost, brown kraft paper proves the giftwrap choice.*

🐦 BY MICHIO RYAN

I AM ALWAYS SEARCHING FOR AN alternative to commercial giftwrap, which tends to be expensive (between $4 and $6 for two sheets), or graphically unappealing. For this reason, I have experimented with making my own giftwrap.

I used to use white butcher paper trimmed only with black ribbon, but now it seems too stark and dated. I've also used leftover wallpaper, but since wallpaper is only about twenty inches wide, it rarely covers larger packages. Wallpaper also has a tendency to tear when pulled too vigorously over a box corner. Marbled, Japanese, and other handmade decorative papers from art or paper stores are elegant, yet better suited to smaller boxes, as they are predominantly only available in twenty-by-thirty-inch sheets.

I finally tried working with brown kraft paper and found it a perfect alternative. It is inexpensive (about $2 for thirty square feet), widely available in a variety of weights, and its generous thirty- to thirty-six-inch width covers even large boxes. With so many attributes, it deserved further experimentation.

After a series of experiments with different colors of paint, I found that its natural, warm tan color is a rich, yet neutral backdrop for gold, whether applied as gold leaf or paint, and its matte finish enhances the metal's luster.

## Wrinkled Paper

Begin with sheet three times the size of box. Crumple sheet into ball, squeezing tightly. Gently unfurl, smoothing out wrinkles. Repeat process. To preserve effect, don't wrap paper too tightly around box. To define shape, lightly crease along box edges. Tie with silk ribbon accented with gilded leaf (*see* "Gilded Autumn Leaves," page 21).

## Paint Droplets

Protect workspace with newspaper, then lay sheet of paper down on top. Stand above sheet with plastic bottle of gold, oil-based, stamp pad paint. Squeeze out droplets one by one so they "rain" down in random pattern. Let dry overnight. The oil will bleed, forming halos around each droplet.

## Gold Leaf Checkerboard

Protect workspace with newspaper. Wrap gift box with paper, then lightly pencil 1" to 2" grid on each side. Brush thin coat of rubber cement onto every other square, checkerboard style. (The cement will dry quickly, enabling you to do all six sides in sequence.) Wait 5 minutes and apply second coat. Let dry 15 minutes. Lay squares of gold leaf on each surface and tamp down with fingertips. Burnish squares with cotton ball. Tie package with metallized leather cord.

## Fortuny Pleats

Lay paper on flat surface. Fold into accordion pleats about ¾" wide. Squeeze stack of pleats in order to create wrinkles along pleated length. Gently unfurl. Wrap longer sides of box first to form pleated tube, tucking ends last. Tie bow of velvet ribbon and gold twisted cord, accented with two leaves.

## Gold Wash

Lay paper on flat work surface and tape down corners. Dilute acrylic gold paint with water to milky consistency. Apply wash to surface with flat, wide brush, "agitating" the bristles in order to create mottled texture. Repeat. Crisscross gold trim, and tie into a bow.

## Lemon Prints and Stars

Cut lemon in half. Apply thin coat of yellow acrylic paint to one cut side using sponge brush. Press on scrap paper to shed excess paint and juice. Press onto paper to make print, reloading paint as necessary. Let dry. Paste on gold stars. ◆

**Giftwraps above, left to right: wrinkled paper, paint droplets, gold leaf checkerboard, Fortuny pleats, gold wash, lemon prints and stars.**

# Testing Air-Dry and Heat-Set Clays

*Not sure whether to use a heat-set clay such as Fimo or an air-dry clay like Celluclay? Here's how to choose.*

🐌 BY MICHIO RYAN

YOU'VE PROBABLY SEEN THEM at craft shows, or maybe you have a friend or neighbor who makes them: jewelry items, small figurines, even Christmas ornaments sculpted from modeling compounds such as Fimo or Sculpey. In the last few decades, a new category of modeling clay has emerged that offers craftspeople a safe, easy to use, and relatively inexpensive solution for a wide range of crafting projects. A recent visit to my local art store presented a bewildering display of seventeen such candidates, and I set out to sort through their differences.

I excluded from my tests all casting clays because they usually require the addition of water or mixing mediums, which is too skill- and time-intensive. Also ruled out were solid clays used for mold making and bronze casting (such as Plastilena) since they never harden. Furthermore, I excluded products such as Friendly Plastic, a thermoplastic that softens when immersed in hot water and sets very hard when cooled. Because this product cools too quickly for real sculpting, I decided it didn't really fit into my desired range of modeling materials: those that are quickly mixed or packaged ready to use and that are additionally easy to form, safe to handle, and simple to harden and finish. In the end I found two general categories that satisfied my expectations: air-dry and heat-set clays.

Air-dry clays are usually composed of a particulate material, such as volcanic ash or talc, and/or cellulose fiber, such as shredded paper, that is held together with a water-based binder (glue). As the water evaporates and the glue dries, the clay mass hardens. Heat-set clays, conversely, are usually polymers (such as PVC, a type of plastic) dispersed in a softening agent. They come packaged ready to use in two- to eight-ounce quantities and are typically more expensive than air-dry clays (*see* charts, at left and page 28). Rather than drying out, they are hardened by heat, such as in a kitchen oven.

## Testing and Rating the Clays

The differences between air-dry and heat-set clays affect both the working qualities in their raw state and the characteristics of the finished product. For this article, I tested how each clay performed within a variety of categories: malleability; ease and quality of press molding as well as hand modeling; drying time; and durability, attractiveness, post-formability (i.e., filing, sanding), and paintability of the finished result. By forming a thin rod, a solid lump, and a thin-edged petal from each clay, I was able to compare how the clays withstood various stresses and processes. I also tested each clay using a press mold of a face to determine how well each reproduced the various details. (Watch for the Father Christmas project, calling for heat-set clay, coming up in the November/December issue.)

Choosing the best clay to use for a particular project depends

## Rating the Heat-Set Clays

### PERFORMANCE KEY

★★★ Excellent
★★ Very Good to Good
★ OK to Poor

Nine packages of heat-set clay were evaluated based on the following characteristics. Clays are listed in alphabetical order by type. Three stars indicates excellent performance, two stars indicates very good to good performance, and one star indicates OK to poor performance.

**Preparation:** How easy is it to get the clay ready for use; how much kneading is required; and, once ready, how malleable is the clay

**Press mold:** How clearly does the clay pick up the press mold image and how easy is it to remove the clay from the mold

**Hand building:** How easy is it to form the clay into a thin petal, a rod, and a solid shape, and how well does it hold each shape

**Finished durability:** How hard is the finished clay in terms of resilience, chip resistance, and waterproofness

| Brand of Clay | Suggested Retail Price/Quantity | Preparation | Press Mold | Hand Building | Finished Durability |
|---|---|---|---|---|---|
| 1. Cernit No.1 | $1.80/1.75 ounces | ★★★ | ★★★ | ★ | ★★★ |
| 2. Fimo | $1.91/58 grams | ★ | ★★★ | ★★★ | ★★★ |
| 3. Formello | $1.95/2 ounces | ★ | ★★ | ★★ | ★ |
| 4. Friendly Clay | $1.80/1.75 ounces | ★ | ★★ | ★ | ★★★ |
| 5. Promat | $2.80/4 ounces | ★★ | ★★ | ★ | ★★★ |
| 6. Sculpey | $6.20/32 ounces | ★★★ | ★★★ | ★★★ | ★★✦ |
| 7. Sculpey III | $1.16/2.02 ounces | ★★★ | ★★★ | ★★ | ★★★ |
| 8. Super Elasticlay | $6.30/8 ounces | ★ | ★★ | ★ | ★★ |
| 9. Super Sculpey | $6.40/16 ounces | ★★ | ★★ | ★★ | ★★ |

## Heat-Set Clays

on the working qualities and the finished result you're looking for. For molded doll faces, I recommend one of two heat-set clays: Fimo or Sculpey III. The latter was easier to form, but the former retained small imprinted details better. Sculpey (as opposed to Sculpey III), also a heat-set clay, is a good choice for molded items that require neither translucency nor tensile strength but for which imprinted designs need to be particularly detailed. Fimo and Cernit No. 1 were quite strong even in very thin or attenuated sections and are suitable for delicate, hand-modeled items.

In the air-dry category, I recommend Model Magic and Celluclay for larger items that must be extremely lightweight and do not require sharp detailing, such as Christmas ornaments or wreath decorations. Those that require finer detail can be made of Creative Paperclay, which, as a particulate/fiber blend, is both light and detailable. Della Robbia "Miracle" Clay and Air Dry Clay are best suited for solid, sculptural objects that must resemble fired ceramic or stone.

### Preparing the Clay for Sculpting

As a group, the air-dry clays were ready to use straight out of the package, and quite malleable without preparatory kneading. The single exception was Celluclay, a papiermâché, which is packaged in dry form and requires water. This disadvantage is offset by the fact that a one-pound package of dry Celluclay will yield about five pounds of clay once the water is added, making it an economical material for larger projects.

Heat-set clays, on the other hand, varied a great deal in malleability. They all needed to be kneaded, to make them pliable enough to shape; most were ready after a few minutes of gentle kneading. Fimo, Formello, and Friendly Clay not only started out rock hard and crumbled apart when first kneaded, but also took considerable working time to reach acceptable malleability: eight to nine minutes of kneading for Fimo and Formello and about fifteen minutes for Friendly Clay. I tried mashing the clay with a pestle, but this produced smaller crumbs and slivers, which had to be gathered up and kneaded back into one lump by hand. I also tried dunking one-inch-diameter lumps of each clay in

very hot tap water to presoften the clay, with poor results.

To my relief, several manufacturers provide mixing mediums, which are designed to increase kneadability. I found Fimo's "Mix Quick" quite effective, alleviating its inordinate hardness. The only difference in the final result was increased translucency and a slight lightening of the color. Friendly Clay's equivalent, called "Super Softener," performed similarly.

### Testing the Clays in the Press Molds

On the whole, the air-dry clays were smooth, heavy, and dense.

The particulate type of air-dry clay, including Standard Clay Mines' Air Dry Clay and Marblex, contains finely ground particles in a water-based carrier, similar to a moist pottery clay. The density and fine grain of these clays allow them to capture finely detailed impressions and hold their shape better. When pressed into a mold, for instance, most of them captured details quite accurately. Because the particles are so small, however, the clay did not always hold together well. As a result, when the clay was pulled from the mold, extremities such as the point of a nose could be left behind.

When I tested these clays in a plaster mold, all of them separated easily from the mold, as the moisture on the clay's surface was drawn out by the absorbent plaster. Many ready-made craft molds, however, are made of plastic (such as the face press mold I tested) or other nonporous materials to which wet clay will stick, leaving pieces of the clay in the mold.

This problem can be largely eliminated using various mold release agents, although I had mixed results. Traditional wet mold releases such as green soap, used for plaster casting, only exacerbated the problem by producing a suction effect in the extremities of the mold. Finely knit cloth, such as cheesecloth, imprinted unsightly weave marks into the clay although the clays lifted easily out of the mold. A

fine dusting of talcum powder, applied to the inside surface of the mold with a shaving or sabeline brush, worked quite well. If high detail is desirable, the particulate air-dry clays yield excellent results using talc.

The fibrous kind of air-dry clay possesses different characteristics. Celluclay, for example, is made with shredded paper, and the fiber strands rendered the clay very pulpy and mushy. It was hard to form it into small shapes, its coarse texture didn't allow it to pick up fine details in a mold, and its glue binder was so strong that pieces of the clay stuck to the mold. Although unsuitable for use with press molds, it was versatile as a

1. Cernit No.1

2. Fimo

3. Formello

4. Friendly Clay

5. Promat

6. Sculpey

7. Sculpey III

8. Super Elasticlay

9. Super Sculpey

hand-molding clay.

Some air-dry clays, such as Creative Paperclay, Darwi, and DAS pronto, contain both gritty materials and fibers. Although they are more chip-resistant, the surface is lumpier, meaning they are not as smooth as the denser air-dry clays. In addition, this category doesn't hold shapes as well given that the fibers render the clay body resistant to being pushed into the mold.

Model Magic is in a category of its own because it is neither gritty nor fibrous. This extremely light material feels like a marshmallow in consistency and is so rubbery that it won't hold a shape particularly well when hand-formed or press-molded. On the other hand, this elasticity prevents chipping or cracking.

Heat-set clays act quite differently from air-dry clays. After varying amounts of kneading, they become plastic, and since they contain little if any particulate material, they're all creamy smooth. These clays proved consistently good at rendering fine details from the press mold. There was, however, a great deal of variation in: 1) the softness of these clays, which affected their ability to extend into the mold's extremities to take an impression; 2) their elasticity, or ability to retain a shape; and 3) the stickiness of the clay surface, or an ability to separate easily from the mold without distorting the molded image. In general, the stiffer, less rubbery, and drier the clay, the better the rendering of the fine details of the impression.

Fimo, being stiff, firm, and dry, was outstanding, followed closely by Sculpey, Sculpey III, and Promat, which were moderately stickier and softer but still sufficiently stiff to take and retain crisp impressions. Cernit No. 1, and particularly Super Sculpey and Super Elasticlay, were softer, stickier, more elastic, and thus more difficult to pull away cleanly from the mold without distortion. Using talc as a mold release proved helpful for these clays. Interestingly, the stickiness that was a disadvantage for press molding enabled better adhesion of separate pieces of the same clay, a distinct advantage when assembling or hand building. In this area, Cernit No.1, Super Sculpey, and Super Elasticlay were particularly notable.

Heat-set clays, especially the softer ones, are easily dented and take fingerprints easily, so they should be handled with care after the imprint is made. An easy way to handle the molded face is to use a much bigger piece of clay than will fit into the mold cavity, which allows you to form a handle at the back of the mold.

## Hardening the Clays

Air-dry clays harden in the open air through evaporation of water and other vehicles. Depending on the density of the clay and the thickness of the pieces, drying times varied widely. Under normal conditions, quarter-sized medallions of each clay dried within two hours, but thicker, solid forms took much longer. The instructions on the package of Della Robbia "Miracle" Clay, for instance, stated that although small objects would dry in several days, larger, solid masses (for example, the size of a modeled head) could take two weeks.

I considered several ways of accelerating the drying process, but after testing, concluded that rushing the drying of any but the smallest objects is inadvisable. If the surface is forcefully dried (for example, by using a blow-dryer or oven) while the inside remains quite wet, the surface shrinks inordinately and can crack open.

Heat-set clays, on the other hand, can be placed in an oven immediately after forming, and most hardened well within the manufacturer's stated times using the recommended oven temperatures. Della Robbia "Miracle" Clay, which is not a polymer like most heat-set clays, must first be thoroughly dried like an air-dry clay (a process that took three days for a one-inch-thick piece) before being heat-cured.

All of the clays recommend ventilation during the curing process since they can release toxic fumes while setting. The final products, however, are labeled as nontoxic, except for

## Rating the Air-Dry Clays

### PERFORMANCE KEY

★ ★ ★ Excellent

★ ★ Very Good to Good

★ OK to Poor

Eight packages of air-dry clay were evaluated based on the following characteristics. Clays are listed in alphabetical order by type. Three stars indicates excellent performance, two stars indicates very good to good performance, and one star indicates OK to poor performance.

**Preparation:** How easy is it to get the clay ready for use; how much kneading is required; and, once ready, how malleable is the clay

**Press mold:** How clearly does the clay pickup the press mold image and how easy is it to remove the clay from the mold

**Hand building:** How easy is it to form the clay into a thin petal, a rod, and a solid shape, and how well does it hold each shape

**Finished durability:** How hard is the finished clay in terms of resilience, chip resistance, and waterproofness

| Brand of Clay | Suggested Retail Price/Quantity | Preparation | Press Mold | Hand Building | Finished Durability |
|---|---|---|---|---|---|
| 1. Air Dry Clay | $6.00/4 pounds | ★ ★ ★ | ★ ★ | ★ ★ | ★ |
| 2. Celluclay II | $5.57/1 pound | ★ ★ | ★ | ★ | ★ |
| 3. Creative Paperclay | $2.93/4 ounces | ★ ★ ★ | ★ | ★ ★ | ★ |
| 4. Darwi | $6.79/1 kilogram | ★ ★ ★ | ★ | ★ ★ | ★ ★ |
| 5. DAS pronto | $3.00/17.1 ounces | ★ ★ ★ | ★ ★ | ★ ★ | ★ |
| 6. Della Robbia "Miracle" Clay* | $5.00/3.5 pounds | ★ ★ ★ | ★ ★ ★ | ★ ★ | ★ ★ |
| 7. Marblex | $5.49/2 pounds | ★ ★ ★ | ★ ★ ★ | ★ ★ | ★ |
| 8. Model Magic | $3.80/4 ounces | ★ ★ ★ | ★ | ★ | ★ |

*air-dry/heat-set hybrid

# Air-Dry Clays

Formello and Cernit No. 1, which do not bear the Art and Craft Materials Institute's AP label. The products also caution against exceeding the manufacturer's recommended oven temperatures, which can cause the clays to break apart.

## Quality of Finished Product

All the air-dry clays lost their glossy surface when dry, and some became even a bit rough or granular. The darker colors lightened significantly, and the off-white clays became bright white. The dried version of Creative Paperclay appeared particularly chalky and rough in texture. Denser, water-logged clays such as Air Dry Clay and Marblex shrank noticeably, losing the sharper, more defined facial features along the way, especially in projections such as noses.

Significantly, the dense modeling clays such as Marblex had virtually no chip resistance and were still instantly resoluble in water, requiring painting to achieve permanence. (This disadvantage can be turned to good use, however, because any surface imperfections can be easily repaired by moistening the surface lightly and burnishing out the defect with a fingertip or sculpting tool.) Fibrous clays such as Darwi were somewhat more chip-resistant, although thin petals and attenuations were easily snapped off. As a result, I don't recommend these types of clays for fragile items.

The heat-set clays acquired an eggshell sheen after baking, which effectively simulated skin in the case of the pressed face mold. Cernit No.1 had a moderately higher sheen than the others, although not undesirably so. Shrinkage, distortion, and weight change were minimal (if even noticeable) for all the clays, and the color remained consistent.

The heat-set clays became quite stiff, with, nevertheless, a slight flexibility, which was detectable in thin sections. Super Elasticlay was the exception, hardening into a rubberlike block of very flexible material. Because of the moderate resilience of the heat-set clays, and because the material has fused into one solid piece, they are much more resistant to breakage than the brittle, air-dry clays.

Della Robbia "Miracle" Clay, the hybrid air-dry/heat-set clay, became very hard after drying but chipped as easily as the air-dry clays. When baked, however, it fused into a much harder material, almost resembling a low-fired, ceramic clay body. It still remained water-soluble, however, like the air-dry clays.

## Sanding and Painting the Hardened Clay

Filing or sanding the air-dry clays to refine the finished shape was not a problem, and the roughened surface was easily smoothed with a wet fingertip. The one exception was Model Magic, where the surface of the pressed face tore off in shreds, leaving an irregularly feathery texture.

All the heat-set clays except Super Elasticlay were easily filed, although fine-grade sandpapers under 400-grit had little effect. Emery boards, essentially sandpaper laminated onto a thin stick, are excellent for this purpose, as are needle files, which can be purchased in hobby shops. Any sanding will eliminate the sheen of the finished product, and since heat-set clays are not water-soluble, this effect is not easily fixed except by careful sanding with 400-grit paper to try to match the sheen of the untouched areas. The hardened clays could also be carved with an X-Acto knife although the rubbery Super Elasticlay was hard to shape because it gave way and distorted under pressure. Since the heat-set clays proved so easy to handle before baking, I found it much more expedient to put on the finishing touches and remove defects such as dents or fingerprints before baking.

The differences between the types of clays were also apparent in painting. Air-dry clays were generally porous and absorbent, requiring sealer before painting, or the application of two coats of paint before achieving a level surface. Celluclay, in particular, required three coats of paint, and even then the surface was so bumpy that a gloss-finish paint looked quite unappealing.

The heat-set clays, on the other hand, were nearly impervious, and one coat of spray enamel was sufficient to cover each of them. Both acrylic craft paints and alkyd hobby enamels also adhered well to the heat-set clays although it is advisable to use a soft brush to avoid streaks across the surface. The clays with more matte surfaces such as Sculpey took an even opaque coat particularly well while shinier ones such as Cernit No. 1 required a touch-up coat. ◆

**1. Air Dry Clay**

**2. Celluclay II**

**3. Creative Paperclay**

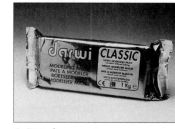
**4. Darwi**

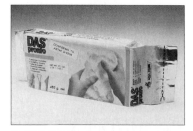
**5. DAS pronto**

**6. Della Robbia "Miracle" Clay**

**7. Marblex**

**8. Model Magic**

# Field Guide to Decorative Tassels and Tiebacks

*Tassels have a wide range of decorating uses. Hang them on curtains, or use them as key fobs, to dress up the corners of a tablecloth, or as Christmas ornaments.*

🐚 BY MICHIO RYAN

SAY "TASSEL" AND I THINK OF A stiff, formal curtain tieback or a decoration on a graduation cap. With the return of traditional decorating, however, tassels have enjoyed something of a comeback, and they can now be found in an ever wider variety, in styles ranging from traditional to very adventurous, and to suit almost any decor.

Tassels are universal in origin; essentially a fancy end binding to prevent raveled ends on cords and ropes, they are found in virtually every culture. In its simplest form, a tassel is made by tying off a part of a twisted cord and raveling the ends from that point on to form a loose fringe (*see* #7). Fringe may also be added to the end of a cord, or simply hung with a loop, eliminating the cord entirely. Very simple "Spanish" tassels, made of rayon, are shimmery, festive trims; mortarboard graduation caps are usually trimmed with this type (#12). Some Spanish tassels are even decorated with a Turk's head knot, which resembles a turban, making them look much more finished (#22). Others are made of cotton or blends, of floss rather than chainette; these are poufed instead of draping (#14). As a group these simple poufed tassels are inexpensive, ranging from one to several dollars, and usually fairly small in size, from about two to five inches.

From this basic construction springs a host of more involved designs, including a wide range of materials from which the tassels are made. Conventional passementerie (fabric-based) tassels range from plain folksy types to highly evolved confections (#1) designed for more serious traditional decor. Some tassels feature turned wooden cores covered with woven or spun cord (#9, among others) or sleeves of fabric such as velvet (#3) or even brocade (#10), with silk or metal-thread fringe attached below. The fringe may also be made of twisted cord as seen on conventional rope fringe. Some tassels may have knotted mesh or criss-crossed ribbon covering the heads (#1, #11), silk-covered beads, or rows of smaller tassels amidst the fringe for more elaborate effects (#11, #17).

At the top of the conventional passementerie category are the museum-quality reproductions of historic designs. These decorator-quality tassels, made with the finest workmanship and materials available, can cost hundreds of dollars each. Some tassels in this category, however, are less expensive and can be ordered by mail. For example, tassel #1, available in an assortment of colors, is priced at $85 for the pair. In the less expensive range, prices start at around $30.

There are also many less expensive tassels that are derived from the traditional passementerie styles (#6, #17). Theses tassels closely resemble the fancy handmade versions, but are actually composed of less expensive materials such as rayon, acetate, and cotton. When I look closely—and you can see the difference—they are not as elaborately detailed or finely crafted. The floss threads are not as silky nor the rope fringe as lustrous. Instead of carefully wound mesh or tape on the head, you are apt to find looped floss. In spite of these differences, this more affordable range of tassels still looks quite good; the styles resemble the fancier ones, capturing their essential silhouette and mix of textures. Because they are sold in larger quantities, the range of colors is quite wide and the prices are more reasonable, ranging from $5 to $50 for a very elaborate tassel.

Tassels made of natural fibers such as raffia and unbleached cotton (for example, Conso's King Cotton line, not shown) are a fresh, new take on the traditional tassel. While they retain the traditional silhouette of a tassel, their more casual look suits many off-white decorating schemes.

Beyond fiber, tassels can be made from a variety of materials, including gilded or carved wood, crystal beads, papier-maché, and even resin. Bullion, or woven metallic wire spun to the thickness of thread, is also used to make tassels. The metal's flexibility allows it to be wound and woven into elaborate designs such as beads (#2) or hoops (#15), and lustrous and flexible fringe is formed by winding the wire into tight spirals. Tinsel Trading in New York, for instance, sells new and vintage bullion tassels (#5) in brass or silver. The tarnished patina on such vintage tassels adds to their glamour, although some new bullion tassels are treated especially to forestall tarnishing (#8). As a group, bullion tassels tend to be rather expensive, ranging from $20 to $60 for smaller (up to five inches) sizes. Others are made of a metallized plastic such as lurex, whose sheen is brighter than bullion. The six-inch-long lurex tassel shown here (#13) is priced at $35.

Tassels can also become art. Patricia Fox, an artist and designer in New York, uses only antique and vintage trims in designing her tassels, layering tiers of hand-dyed silk floss with crystal and jet beads and decoupaged, antique, chromolithographic images on a leafed core (#21). Tassels such as Fox's are singular objets d'art, hardly needing the backdrop of a curtain to justify their presence. Small versions start at $10; a four-inch design with silk floss and a velvet rosebud (#19) is priced at $48. Larger tassels range from $150 to as high as $500.

Tassels almost always end up attached to something else, so their

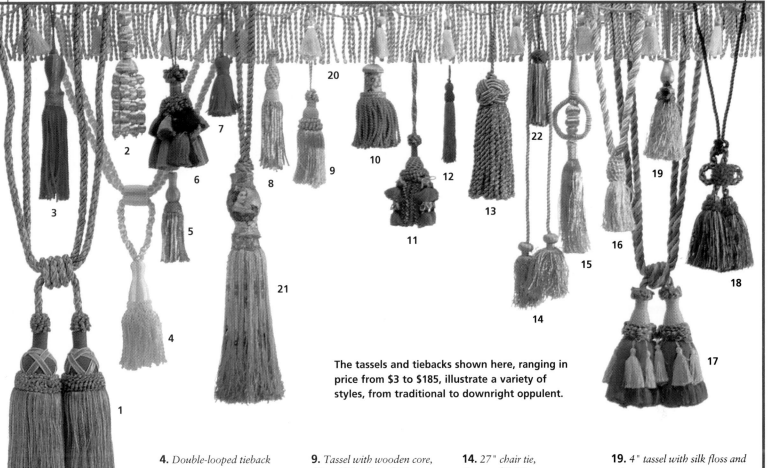

The tassels and tiebacks shown here, ranging in price from $3 to $185, illustrate a variety of styles, from traditional to downright oppulent.

*Tassel description*, source, suggested retail price:

**1.** *Traditional tassel*, M&J Trims, $85

**2.** *Metal bead tassel*, M&J Trims, $59.98

**3.** *Tassel with velvet sleeve*, Tinsel Trading, $15

**4.** *Double-looped tieback with adjustable glide*, Conso, $6.50

**5.** *Vintage bullion tassel*, Tinsel Trading, $35

**6.** *Traditional tassel*, Conso, $22.50

**7.** *Loose-fringed tassel*, Tinsel Trading, $5

**8.** *New bullion tassel*, Tinsel Trading, $45

**9.** *Tassel with wooden core*, Tinsel Trading, $10

**10.** *Tassel with brocade sleeve*, M&J Trims, $24.98

**11.** *Tassel with smaller tassels amongst fringe*, M&J Trims, $50

**12.** *"Spanish" tassel*, M&J Trims, $3.98

**13.** *Lurex tassel*, Tinsel Trading, $35

**14.** *27" chair tie*, Conso, $8.99

**15.** *Tassel with metal hoop*, M&J Trims, $22

**16.** *Looped-cord tieback*, Conso, $3

**17.** *Double-looped tieback with slip knot*, Conso, $36

**18.** *Tieback with double loop*, M&J Trims, $29.75

**19.** *4" tassel with silk floss and velvet rosebud*, Patricia Fox Passementerie, $48

**20.** *Tassel bullion*, Calico Corners, $13.99

**21.** *Tassel with decoupage*, Patricia Fox Passementerie, $185

**22.** *"Spanish" tassel with Turk's head knot*, M&J Trims, $10

loops or cords also take a variety of forms. The most basic tassel has a loop at the top end from which it can be hung or sewn. Other loops are designed for specific uses, such as the double-looped tieback with a slip knot (#17) or an adjustable glide (#4). Other tiebacks can be as simple as a loop of cord (#16), attached singly or in pairs (#18) to frogs or pinwheels so they can be sewn onto the end of a bolster pillow, or attached to fringe, which allows neatly spaced rows to be applied to the edges of a valance (#20).

Just as there are a wide variety of tassels available, so there are a wide variety of uses for them. I've seen them used on curtain tiebacks, or as key fobs hanging from a secretary or armoire. They also have a range of uses about the home: as napkin rings, either tied on by their silken cords or attached to a traditional ring as an accent; as dressy clip-on weights for the corners of tablecloths; as fancy hatbox pulls (use the ones with the frog backing); as lamp cord or shade pulls; as zipper pulls on purses or satchels; or as Christmas ornaments. Designer Fox hangs her creations from wall sconces as long pendants and winds them onto drawer knobs. She's also created a valance—casual in execution but dramatic in effect—with a simple piece of fabric running across the top of a window frame, bound up in the center with the tassel's cord looped loosely several times, allowing the tassel to hang in the arch created in the center. ◆

# Sources
## AND RESOURCES

Most of the materials needed for the projects in this issue are available at your local craft supply, hardware, or paint store, florist's, fabric shop, or bead and jewelry supply. Generic craft supplies, such as scissors, all-purpose white glue, paint, ribbon, and thread, can be ordered from such catalogs as Craft King Discount Craft Supply, Dick Blick, Newark Dressmaker Supply, Pearl Paint, or Sunshine Discount Crafts. The following are specific mail-order sources for particular items, arranged by article. The suggested retail prices listed here were current at press time. Contact the suppliers directly to confirm prices and availability of products.

**Notes from Readers**; *page 2*
*Tips on Faux-Finishing a Tabletop:* Acrylic glaze from $4.40 from Dick Blick. *Preparing Knotted Wood for Painting:* Clear shellac for $2.95 from Constantine's Woodworker's Catalog. *Adhering Fabric to a Blank Book:* Bone folders from $2.90 from The Bookbinder's Warehouse.

**Quick Tips**; *page 4*
*Downsizing Silk Flowers:* Variety of silk flowers from $1.50 from May Silk. *Nonslip Hangers:* Pearl shank buttons for $1.75 per dozen from Newark Dressmaker Supply. *Wiring a Pine Cone Invisibly:* Pine cones for $2.49 per pound from Craft King.

**Apple Tree Carved Pumpkin**; *page 6*
Votive candles for $13.50 per set of six from Pottery Barn. Pastry tubes for $12.95 per twelve-piece set from Kitchen Krafts.

**Bronze Stenciling with Acrylics**; *page 8*
Selection of acrylic paint from $2, latex paint from $5, and alkyd paint from $4.87, vellum sheet for 82¢, varnish from $2.50, self-healing mats from $5.82, stencil brushes from $1.69, Rustoleum Rust Reformer for $8.16 per 8 ounces, Rustoleum metal primer for $6.05 per can, 3M's Safest Stripper for $9.67 per quart, and denatured alcohol for $3.70 per quart, all from Pearl Paint. Variety of wood items from 25¢ from Craft

King. 3M steel wool for $3.95 and wood sealer from $6.95 per pint from The Woodworkers' Store.

**Quick Dried Hydrangea Wreath**; *page 11*
Selection of dried hydrangea from $2.50 from Floral Express. 16" wreath base for $5.99 from Best Buy Floral Supply.

**Lined Velvet Pouches**; *page 14*
Velvet fabric from $20 per yard from Calico Corners. Velvet press board for $31.65, acetate lining for $2.95 per yard, Olfa self-healing cutting mat for $12.55, and rotary cutter for $5.50 from Atlanta Thread & Supply.

**Folk Art Frame**; *page 16*
11" x 14" mirror for $14.99 from Caldor. 7½" x 9½" oval cutout mat for $1.54 and acrylic paint from $2 from Pearl Paint. Brass upholstery nails for $3.25 per hundred-pack, Titebond glue for $2.95 per 8 ounces, and selection of lumber priced according to size, all from The Woodworkers' Store.

**Fast and Easy Wood Grain Finish**; *page 20*
Variety of wood items in a variety of shapes and sizes from 39¢ and acrylic paint from 85¢ per 2 ounces from Sunshine Discount Crafts. Silicon carbide paper for 45¢ per sheet and satin polyurethane for $10.95 per quart from The Woodworkers' Store.

**Quick Gilded Autumn Leaves**; *page 21*
Composition leaf for $7.50 per twenty-five-sheet book, 23-karat gold leaf from $36.20, and gold size from $4.30, all from Dick Blick.

**Bittersweet Topiary**; *page 22*
Silk berry spray from $3.90 from May Silk. Plasterra pots

from $1.29 from Akro-Mils Specialty Products. Plaster of Paris for $2.90 per 4-pound carton, acrylic paint from $1.45 per 2-ounce tube, and fine-gauge wire from 80¢ from Dick Blick.

**Adirondack Twig Frame**; *page 24*
Twigs and branches from $3.50 per bunch from Floral Express. Selection of wood frames custom-designed and matte finish sprays from $5.99 from The Jerry's Catalog.

**Brown Kraft Paper Giftwrap**; *page 25*
Brown kraft paper from 89¢ per roll, gold leaf from $3.70 per 25 sheets, acrylic paint from $2, and gold, oil-based stamp pad from $1.80, all from Pearl Paint. Velvet ribbon for $3.20 per 25-yard spool, satin ribbon for $1.75 per 30-yard spool, leather cord from $1.33, and metallic craft cord from $2.15 per 27-yard skein, all from Craft King.

**Testing Air-Dry and Heat-Set Clays**; *page 26*
Clays available from Pearl Paint, Dick Blick, Earth Guild, and New York Central Art Supply.

**Field Guide to Decorative Tassels**; *page 30*
Tassels available from Calico Corners, Conso, M&J Trims, Patricia Fox Passementerie, and Tinsel Trading. Prices range from $3 to $185.

**Quick Projects**; *page 33*
*Basic Topiary:* Selection of Plasterra clay pots from $1.49 from Akro-Mils Specialty Products. Styrofoam balls from 12¢ from Craft Catalog. Plaster of Paris for $2.90 per 4-pound carton and acrylic paint from $1.45 per 2-ounce tube from Dick Blick. *Della Robbia Topiary:* Variety of artificial fruits and berries from $1.50 from Best Buy Floral Supply. Large plastic fruits from $2.40

and silk leaves from $1.90 per spray from May Silk. *Silk Rose Leaf Topiary:* Deluxe silk rose stems for $2.90 per stem from May Silk. Village Classic metallic gold spray paint for $3.10 from Craft King. *Golden Safflower with Purple Ribbon:* Safflower for $4.99 per 3 ounces from Best Buy Flower Supply. Village Classic metallic gold spray paint for $3.10 from Craft King. *Moss and Berry Topiary:* Berry spray from $3.90 from May Silk. *Magenta Cockscomb Topiary:* Cockscomb from $5.80 per bunch from Floral Express. *Tea Rose Topiary:* Selection of dried roses from $6.40 per bunch from Floral Express.

**Decorative Autumn Urn**;
*back cover*
Flowering cabbage in pink, red, or white for $2.75 per seed packet and English ivy plant from $9.95 from Burpee Gardens. White roses for $5 per stem and hydrangea heads for $5.50 from Village Flowers.

---

The following companies are mentioned in the listings provided above. Contact each individually for a price list or catalog.

**Akro-Mils Specialty Products,** P.O. Box 989, Akron, OH 44309; 800-253-2467
**Atlanta Thread & Supply,** 695 Red Oak Road, Stockbridge, GA 30281; 800-847-1001
**Best Buy Floral Supply,** P.O. Box 1982, Cedar Rapids, IA 52406; 800-553-8497
**The Bookbinder's Warehouse,** 31 Division Street, Keyport, NJ 07735; 908-264-0306
**Burpee Gardens,** 300 Park Avenue, Warminster, PA 18974; 800-888-1447
**Caldor, Inc.,** 20 Glover Avenue, Norwalk, CT 06856; 203-846-1641
**Calico Corners,** 203 Gale Lane, Kennett Square, PA 19348-1764; 800-777-9933
**Conso,** 513 N. Duncan

By-Pass, P.O. Box 326, Union, SC 29379; 800-845-2431
**Constantine's Woodworker's Catalog,** 2050 Eastchester Road, Bronx, NY 10461-2297; 800-223-8087
**Craft Catalog,** P.O. Box 1069, Reynoldsburg, OH 43068; 800-777-1442
**Craft King Discount Craft Supply,** P.O. Box 90637, Lakeland, FL 33804; 800-769-9494
**Dick Blick,** P.O. Box 1267, Galesburg, IL 61402-1267; 800-447-8192
**Earth Guild,** 33 Haywood Street, Asheville, NC 28801; 800-327-8448
**Floral Express,** 11 Armco Avenue, Caribou, ME 04736; 800-392-7417
**The Jerry's Catalog,** P.O. Box 1105, New Hyde Park, New York, NY 11040; 800-U-ARTIST
**Kitchen Krafts,** P.O. Box 805, Mt. Laurel, NJ 08054-0805; 800-776-0575
**M&J Trims,** 1014 Sixth Avenue, New York, NY 10018; 212-391-8731
**May Silk,** 16202 Distribution Way, Cerritos, CA 90703; 800-282-7455
**Newark Dressmaker Supply,** 6473 Ruch Road, P.O. Box 20730, Lehigh Valley, PA 18002-0730; 800-736-6783
**New York Central Art Supply,** 62 Third Avenue, New York, NY 10003; 800-950-6111
**Patricia Fox Passementerie,** 16 West Ninth Street, New York, NY 10011; 212-674-4110
**Pearl Paint,** 308 Canal Street, New York, NY 10013; 800-221-6845
**Pottery Barn,** P.O. Box 7044, San Francisco, CA 94120-7044; 800-922-5507
**Sunshine Discount Crafts,** P.O. Box 301, Largo, FL 34649-0301; 813-538-2878
**Tinsel Trading,** 47 West 38th Street, New York, NY 10018; 212-730-1030
**Village Flowers,** 297 Main Street, Huntington, NY 11743; 516-427-0996
**The Woodworkers' Store,** 21801 Industrial Boulevard, Rogers, MN 55374-9514; 800-279-4441

Photograph on page 11 from *Decorating with Wreaths, Garlands, Topiaries, and Bouquets* by Carol Endler Sterbenz (Rizzoli International, 1993). ◆

# Quick PROJECTS

The globe topiary is an elegant, easily constructed foundation for floral decoration. It's comprised of three parts—a common clay flower pot, a wooden dowel for the trunk, and a foam ball, which can be decorated with a variety of materials to suit different decorating schemes. A second foam ball within the clay pot provides support for the dowel.

Any size of material can be used as long as certain overall proportions are observed: The balls and the pot opening should be of equal diameter, and the dowel length should be two and a half times the pot height. Each of the six variations listed below are based on the globe topiary. The quantity of dried and artificial materials described in each entry is sufficient to cover a three-inch-diameter ball.

D.

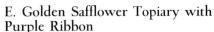

E.

F.

A.

## A. Basic Globe Topiary

Set green foam ball firmly in pot and slice off protruding excess even with pot rim. Remove half-sphere from pot, then cut second half-sphere into scraps and use them to line pot bottom and sides. Reposition first half-sphere to check fit. Remove and pour freshly mixed plaster of Paris into pot until half full. Reposition half-sphere, then push dowel straight down through center of half-sphere into plaster. Let plaster set 15 minutes. Push second green foam ball onto top of dowel to form topiary head. Tint dowel green by brushing on watercolor or diluted acrylic paint, and cut sheet moss to conceal foam at base.

## B. Moss and Berry Topiary

Cover foam ball with sheet moss and secure with floral pins. Trail long, leafy stem up dowel and around ball, and secure with floral pins. Attach several berry clusters to ball with floral pins.

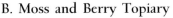

## C. Della Robbia Topiary

Cover ball with sheet moss, securing with floral pins. Insert wire stems of artificial cherries, strawberries, and red and yellow berries into ball at random to create an allover design. Use floral pins to attach a few larger fruits such as pears and plums. Fill in bare spots with silk leaves, nuts, acorns, and miniature pine cones, securing them with floral pins. Finish by attaching several stems of blueberries to top center so they cascade over sides.

B.

C.

## D. Tea Rose Topiary

This topiary, while expensive, is beautiful and everlasting. Cut stems of six dozen dried tea roses 2" below bloom, then insert stems into foam ball one by one until entire ball is covered. Hot-glue two rose leaves to dowel.

## E. Golden Safflower Topiary with Purple Ribbon

Cut forty dried safflower blooms and buds, leaving 2" stem on each. Insert stems into foam ball at random, then hot-glue extra leaves to fill in bare spots. Give entire topiary a light dusting with gold spray paint. Tie 25"-long, 1"-wide, purple, wire-edged ribbon in bow around dowel and notch streamer ends.

## F. Silk Rose Leaf Topiary

Clip or break off light green silk rose leaves from six to eight artificial sprays. Spray twenty of the leaves with gold metallic paint and let dry. Insert wire stem of each individual leaf into foam ball, striving for random all-over coverage and scattering of the gold leaves. Use hot-glue to further secure leaves if necessary.

## G. Magenta Cockscomb Topiary

Break off fifteen heads of dried magenta cockscomb and carefully divide each into three to four fan-shaped sections. Hot-glue sections to foam ball in radiating pattern, then go back and fill in bare spots with smaller pieces. ◆

G.

# Decorative Outdoor Urn

Select 17"-high urn with 34"-wide opening. Plug drainage hole with small stone, then spread 1" to 2" crushed stones or charcoal across bottom, followed by 1" potting soil. About 2" in from rim, at seven o'clock position, plant 6"-diameter ornamental cabbage. Plant second ornamental cabbage at twelve o'clock position, and two ivy plants at three o'clock position. Top off soil level in urn. Place seven white roses and three fresh hydrangea heads into water-filled florist tubes and insert among cabbages and ivy. Top off water level in tubes after 12 hours. When flowers have faded (about 3 days), remove and let ivy and cabbages fill in.

NUMBER TEN

DECEMBER 1995

# Handcraft
## ILLUSTRATED

SPECIAL
HOLIDAY
ISSUE

*Use everyday materials such as stickers, glitter, and paint to make fantastic Christmas ornaments.*

### The Fastest Holiday Ornaments
*Emboss, Decoupage, and Paint Elegant Tree Decorations*

### One Technique, Hundreds of Wreaths
*Our Binding Method Yields Designs of Any Size or Material*

### Make Your Own Wire-Edged Ribbon
*The Trick: Your Sewing Machine's Cording Foot*

### Testing Sewing Machines
*Read This Before You Upgrade*

### Secrets of Antique Velvet Roses
*Tint, Cut, and Glue Velvet Ribbon*

---

## ALSO
10-Minute Place Mat
Foolproof Greeting Cards
Cuffed Christmas Stockings
Quick Candied Flowers
Heirloom Father Christmas

---

$4.00 U.S./$4.95 CANADA

0 74470 83731 2

12 >

# Contents

Looking for quick and easy gift ideas? Consider making potpourri, hand-molded soap, ornaments, place mats, or rubber-stamped gift tags.

Hand-molded soap, page 20

Gift cards, page 22

Antique velvet roses, page 27

COVER PHOTOGRAPH:
**Carl Tremblay**

## FEATURE STORIES

### 6
**TRIO OF GLASS BALL ORNAMENTS**
Make elegant tree decorations using rubber bands, stickers, and a pour-in paint process.

### 8
**HOW TO MAKE AN INFINITE VARIETY OF WREATHS**
The secret: binding bouquets of fresh, silk, or dried flowers and foliage to a wreath base.

### 12
**HOW TO MAKE YOUR OWN WIRE-EDGED RIBBON**
A cording foot is the key to making your own ribbon in any color or width.

### 14
**CHRISTMAS POTPOURRI DEMYSTIFIED**
Designing your own potpourri or modifying an existing recipe is easy. The trick is understanding the role that each ingredient plays.

### 16
**THREE CUFFED DECORATOR CHRISTMAS STOCKINGS**
Sewing stockings from soft furnishing fabrics may create a variety of stitching problems. Here's how to solve them in time for the holidays.

### 20
**THE FASTEST WAY TO MAKE HAND-MOLDED SOAP**
Forget tallow, lye, or soap molds. All you need are a few bars of Ivory soap, a Mouli grater, and a microwave oven.

### 22
**SPECIAL INSERT: FOOLPROOF GREETING CARDS**
Start with store-bought stationery and a special image or photo, then add your own jacket using card stock. The result: professional-looking homemade cards.

### 27
**HOW TO MAKE ANTIQUE VELVET ROSES**
The trick: Use velvet ribbon instead of fabric, color the velvet yourself, and cut and glue the pieces separately.

### 30
**HEIRLOOM FATHER CHRISTMAS**
Use these simple solutions to create a proportional and lifelike doll: a wooden artist's manikin and a push mold.

### 33
**CANDIED VIOLET AND HOLLY HOLIDAY DECORATIONS**
The secret to making your own: gumdrops and a simple thumb-press method.

### 34
**THE BEST WAY TO TIE MULTILOOP BOWS**
Use our ripple technique to tie an infinite number of bows from wire-edged ribbon.

### 36
**TULLE-WRAPPED ORNAMENT**
Recycle a tired ornament by wrapping it in tulle decorated with glitter fabric paint.

### 37
**10-MINUTE TASSEL PLACE MAT**
Quick-sew a place mat that's roomy enough for holiday place settings.

### 38
**BUYER'S GUIDE TO RUBBER STAMPS**
Understanding the basics of how rubber stamps are made can help you predict the quality of the image before you stamp.

### 41
**TESTING SEWING MACHINES**
The Pfaff Hobby 382 and Brother XL 3030 top the list of ten machines in the $499 to $550 price range.

### 46
**PATTERNS FOR PROJECTS**
Patterns for the Father Christmas, Stockings, Place Mat, and Antique Velvet Rose articles.

IN EVERY ISSUE
NOTES FROM READERS ............... 2
QUICK TIPS ............................... 4
FIELD GUIDE ............................ 45
SOURCES AND RESOURCES ........ 48
QUICK PROJECTS ..................... 49
TANNEBAUM TOPIARY ... BACK COVER

# Handcraft
### ILLUSTRATED

EDITOR
**Carol Endler Sterbenz**

EXECUTIVE EDITOR
**Barbara Bourassa**

ART DIRECTOR
**Amy Klee**

SENIOR EDITOR
**Michio Ryan**

EDITORIAL PRODUCTION DIRECTOR
**Maura Lyons**

ASS'T MANAGING EDITOR
**Tricia O'Brien**

DIRECTIONS EDITOR
**Candie Frankel**

COPY EDITOR
**Gary Pfitzer**

PUBLISHER AND FOUNDER
**Christopher Kimball**

EDITORIAL CONSULTANT
**John Kelsey**

MARKETING DIRECTOR
**Adrienne Kimball**

CIRCULATION DIRECTOR
**Elaine Repucci**

ASS'T CIRCULATION MANAGER
**Jennifer L. Keene**

CIRCULATION COORDINATOR
**Jonathan Venier**

CIRCULATION ASSISTANT
**C. Maria Pannozzo**

PRODUCTION DIRECTOR
**James McCormack**

PROJECT COORDINATOR
**Sheila Datz**

PRODUCTION COORDINATOR
**Pamela Slattery**

ASSISTANT COMPUTER ADMINISTRATOR
**Matt Frigo**

PRODUCTION ARTIST
**Kevin Moeller**

VICE PRESIDENT
**Jeffrey Feingold**

CONTROLLER
**Lisa A. Carullo**

ACCOUNTING ASSISTANT
**Mandy Shito**

OFFICE MANAGER
**Tonya Estey**

*Handcraft Illustrated* (ISSN 1072-0529) is published bimonthly by Boston Common Press Limited Partners, 17 Station Street, P.O. Box 509, Brookline, MA 02147-0509. Copyright 1995 Boston Common Press Limited Partners. Second-class postage paid at Boston, MA, and additional mailing offices, USPS #012487. For list rental information, please contact Direct Media, 200 Pemberwick Road, Greenwich, CT 06830; (203) 532-1000. Editorial office: 17 Station Street, P.O. Box 509, Brookline, MA 02147-0509; (617) 232-1000, FAX (617) 232-1572, email: hndcftill@aol.com. Editorial contributions should be sent or emailed to: Editor, *Handcraft Illustrated.* We cannot assume responsibility for manuscripts submitted to us. Submissions will be returned only if accompanied by a large, self-addressed stamped envelope. Subscription rates: $24.95 for one year; $45 for two years; $65 for three years. (Canada: add $3 per year; all other countries add $12 per year.) Postmaster: Send all new orders, subscription inquiries, and change of address notices to *Handcraft Illustrated*, P.O. Box 7448, Red Oak, IA 51591-0448. Single copies: $4 in U.S., $4.95 in Canada and other countries. Back issues available for $5 each. PRINTED IN THE U.S.A.

Rather than put ™ in every occurrence of trademarked names, we state that we are using the names only and in an editorial fashion and to the benefit of the trademark owner, with no intention of infringement of the trademark.

**Note to Readers:** Every effort has been made to present the information in this publication in a clear, complete, and accurate manner. It is important that all instructions are followed carefully, as failure to do so could result in injury. Boston Common Press Limited Partners, the editors, and the authors disclaim any and all liability resulting therefrom.

## FROM THE EDITOR

CHRISTMAS IS FOR CHILDREN, OR SO IT IS said, and yet ask anyone about the Christmas of their childhood, and you will see their face become younger and more joyful. You'll see the little girl or little boy emerge from memories that are recounted in simple yet compelling detail, as if the experiences were lying there just waiting to be expressed. It's remarkable that childhood, which lasts a mere decade or so, has such a pervasive influence on everything we do thereafter. Nowhere do we see the child in ourselves more than in the way we talk about how we spent the holidays as children.

If you asked my mother what her Christmas was like as a child in Finland, she would describe the huge Christmas tree in the great room, lit with a thousand burning candles, enough to make the whole room glow, and how the children would dance around the tree after opening their gifts. She was careful to explain that the gifts she received were practical. Although one year she got a pair of skis made by her brother that would be used to get to school each day during the hard winter, most times her gifts were of more modest proportion, like knitted sweaters and socks and books. My mother carried her sense of Finnish practicality forged by lessons of a country at war, along with the Christmas traditions of her later childhood in New York, where she immigrated as a teenager, into her elder years.

If you had asked my father to recount his childhood Christmas, he would have presented a stream of stories, one trailing off and another beginning, all of them blending into one magical time. My father was a storyteller. He would start out in conspiratorial whispers and draw me and my sisters into that little barn in Denmark where he would place a bowl of porridge for the *nisse* (gnomes), hoping they might be persuaded to leave a gift instead of a chunk of coal. He would move quickly to other stories, including one about a sea voyage he had taken with his family two days before Christmas. With light snow falling, the ship had left port, forging stalwartly into the Baltic Sea. By the first nightfall, the snow had turned to pouring rain, which continued throughout the next day, Christmas Eve. Most of the passengers stayed in their cabins, waiting out the winter storm, including my father, who slept fitfully as the ship pitched and rolled. He awoke suddenly in a dark cabin that was strangely still. He left his room and walked down a dimly lit corridor, per-

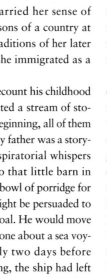

> Nowhere do we see the child in ourselves more than in the way we talk about how we spent the holidays as children.

plexed at the steadiness of his steps. When he arrived on deck, he saw a calm sea stretched before him and a night sky that was silent and clear, revealing a million stars. The once deserted deck now held passengers who gathered to sing Christmas carols with a large moon shining behind the ship's smokestack. When he finished that story, we begged for another, and we usually got our wish.

What stands out from my childhood were the Christmas trees. Although they were never fir trees cut from a nearby forest, they appeared just as majestic to me. And though they were less than six feet tall and so skinny you could easily count the branches, each one was the most perfectly symmetrical tree amongst the others leaning on a rope between two streetlamps. One Christmas, we went out to buy our tree during a snowstorm and were thrilled to find ourselves making snow angels in the middle of the busiest intersection in Queens, traffic lights swinging in the wind and not one car in sight.

When we finally found the perfect tree, we brought it home, where it was transformed by morning with tiny lights, tinsel, woven heart-shaped baskets filled with marzipan, and chocolate rings hanging from every branch. Underneath was a veritable mountain range of wrapped gifts; most were practical, but there was always some indulgence slipped into the pile.

Finally there were the fairy tales, a cornerstone of every Christmas Eve. I can still hear the sound of my father's voice reading "The Little Match Girl" by Hans Christian Andersen. I know now what enchanted me so back then: It was the fantastic dreams of the little girl, each dream held in the light of a single match. I carried forward the tradition of reading that story to my children at Christmas, but I always found myself holding back tears as I reached the end of the tale. Finally the kids begged me to find another story. I did, but it was one improvised from many; it was about a room with a thousand candles, and a night with a million stars. In the telling I became a child once again, with an unyielding faith in the rightness of the world, and in the hopes and dreams that were formed back then. Have a joyful holiday.

# Notes
## FROM READERS

### Working Neatly with Glitter

*Is there a trick to working neatly with glitter? Is there a way to prevent it from flaking off?*
MARTHA VILLARD
FLAGSTAFF, AZ

There are several products currently on the market that combine glitter with other media for easier application.

The best of the lot, according to our tests, is Elmer's GluGlitter, a thick, gel-like glue that includes pre-mixed glitter. The gel keeps the glitter suspended in the glue (both in the bottle and when dry) yet dries smoothly—without loose flakes. GluGlitter comes in three-bottle packs (each bottle holds one and one-quarter ounces) of red, gold, and blue, or green, purple, and silver. The pack retails for about $4.

We also tested Washable Glitter Glue and Glitter Finger Paint, both of which are made by Crayola. Glitter Glue comes in a penlike applicator, making it great for detail work but not as useful for covering surfaces. One pack contains three tubes and retails for $3.49. Glitter Finger Paint is more like paint than glitter, and we had trouble applying it evenly. The product is probably best suited for kids' applications. An eight-ounce package with three tubes retails for $2.30. All are available at art supply stores.

### Removing a Metallic Taste from Flatware

*I recently purchased a set of bone-handled knives and forks that have a metallic taste when used. What can I use to eliminate this? I have tried various stainless cleansers that resemble Ajax.*
SANDRA L. HORNE
ELIZABETHTOWN, PA

We gave a description of your flatware to Thome Silversmith, Inc., in New York and were told that you probably have a set of Victorian flatware made of a base metal that has been plated with tin, silver, or gold. Base metals such as iron, lead, nickel, and brass can impart a metallic taste, which is why they are plated with metals that do not. The plating on your flatware is wearing, or has worn, away.

Plating is the only way to neutralize the metallic taste produced by base metals. Vigorous cleaning will not help; in fact, you may be worsening the problem by using an abrasive cleanser, as it will scratch the metal. (Metals such as silver, pewter, copper, and brass, by the way, should all be carefully cleaned with products made specifically for them—and nothing else.)

We recommend taking your flatware to a local silversmith for an evaluation and estimate. Replating costs can vary tremendously; silver plating, for example, might range from $9 to $12 a piece while gold plating can run from $30 to $40.

### Locating an Electric Styrofoam Cutter

*Can you tell me where I can purchase an electric or battery-operated Styrofoam cutter?*
DOROTHY NELSEN
GARFIELD, AZ

Pearl Paint carries both electric and battery-operated Styrofoam cutters. The electric cutter comes with three interchangeable blades—two straight, one curved—and retails for $9. The battery-operated cutter has a wire blade, requires two D batteries, and sells for $6.88. You can find out more about the products by contacting Pearl Paint, 308 Canal Street, New York, NY 10013; 800-221-6845.

### Hard to Find Craft Supplies

*I would like to know where I can buy plastic and rubber molds to cast plaster as well as polyester resins to cast molds, either by the gallon or wholesale. I'm also wondering where I can buy gold size varnish, either quick- or slow-drying, by the gallon.*
LUZ D. O'LEARY
BRENHAM, TX

Ready-made molds for plaster casting are not widely manufactured items although most art supply stores carry all of the necessary materials to cast your own molds. For ready-made molds, start by consulting the yellow pages under "Molds," "Mold Makers," "Plaster—Ornamental," and "Ceramics." If the manufacturers listed there don't have exactly what you need, they may be able to refer you to another source.

Most art supply stores carry polyester resins as well, but if you have trouble locating these materials, check under "Plastic Products" in the telephone directory for a list of suppliers. If all else fails, Pearl Paint in New York (*see* address and phone number, left) carries polyester resins. Another good plastic source is Industrial Plastic Supply, 309 Canal Street, New York, NY 10013; 212-226-6010.

You can order gold size varnish by the gallon from Gold Leaf and Metallic Powders, which offers a free catalog and carries materials for mold making. You can contact the company at 74 Trinity Place, Suite 1200, New York, NY 10006; 800-322-0323.

### Integrating Flowers Whose Stems Have Broken

Judith H. Bridges of Naperville, Illinois, wrote us in response to a Notes from Readers tip in our March/April 1995 issue on integrating a fresh flower whose stem has snapped into an arrangement.

Rather than discarding the broken flower, Bridges suggests slipping the stem into an orchid tube, which simultaneously supports the broken flower head and gives it a water supply.

Orchid tubes come in clear and green, in a variety of sizes, including one type that fits on a skewer to provide extra length. This last device is not essential, though. Once you've inserted the stem into the vial, you can affix the tube to a wooden skewer with florist tape.

### Removing Wax from a Tablecloth

*What's the best way to remove wax from a tablecloth?*
SUZANNE BERGMAN
WASHINGTON, DC

We tested a handful of solutions to this age-old problem, and our winner is as follows. Start by rubbing the area with an ice cube in order to make the wax hard and brittle, then scrape off the wax with a butter knife. Place the tablecloth between two sheets of blotting paper and press it with a hot iron.

To remove persistent stains, wash the stain in warm, soapy water. If it is still there, dab it with a bit of turpentine and wash again. Repeat until clean.

### In Search of Unadorned Bobeches

*In the stores here, bobeches (candle collars that keep the wax from falling on the table) can be purchased already decorated with beads or large crystals. I'd like to purchase bobeches with the holes already drilled in but unadorned so that I can decorate them myself.*
DODY LANZ
PORTLAND, OR

We were unable to locate a source for bobeches with holes already drilled into them, but we can refer you to a source for a great variety of simple, unadorned bobeches you could either drill into or decorate by other means.

Yankee Candle Company carries many bobeches, including silver-plated, brass, and over twenty-five styles in glass. The bobeches will fit a standard taper (three-quarter-inch diameter) and are available in one-and-one-half- and two-inch widths. The company can be reached at Routes 5 and 10, South Deerfield, MA 01373; 800-243-1776.

Two other possibilities: Purchase a plastic bobeche, as we did for our March/April 1995 back cover project, and drill holes in it by heating one end of a straightened paper clip; or buy an already adorned bobeche, remove any hanging decoration, and refashion the piece yourself.

### Identifying Shagreen

*What is shagreen? I was admiring a desk set at an antiques fair recently and was told that it was made of this material, but the seller couldn't seem to tell me much about it.*
CAROL HASTINGS
BRATTLEBORO, VT

Shagreen is skin, usually that of sharks and rays, that has usually been dyed green. Along with ivory, horn, and tortoiseshell, shagreen was popular in the twenties and thirties for use on decorative objects and desk accessories.

## Selecting an All-Purpose Paintbrush Cleaner

*Can you recommend a good all-purpose paintbrush cleaner?*

STEVE GRIFFIN
STATE COLLEGE, PA

As far as cleaning paint, and just about everything else, off paintbrushes, we like Fastrip Brush Cleaner. A one-pint container costs only $3.99, and the solution can be reused time and time again—just pour it back into the container after use, and the paint and grime will settle to the bottom.

Fastrip removes paint, varnish, shellac, enamel, lacquer, and polyurethane. Soak dirty brushes in the solution, then remove and scrape the softened debris from the outside of the brush. Soak and repeat, then finish by rinsing the brushes thoroughly with water.

## Preventing Silver from Tarnishing

*Is there any way to prevent silver from tarnishing?*

LOIS HATHAWAY
CEDAR SPRINGS, MI

Silver tarnishes as a result of coming in contact with the naturally occurring sulfur and moisture in the atmosphere, so there really is no way to prevent it. You can, however, minimize tarnishing by making sure that your silver is completely dry before you put it away, and storing it properly. Special silver bags and lined silver chests are available for this purpose, but we found a cheaper solution: heavy-gauge, sealable plastic bags. Just take care to press out as much air as possible when closing the bag.

## Mail-Order Shaker Furniture

*Do you know where I can buy kits for making Shaker furniture? The designs are too difficult to hand build.*

MICHAEL RAPPAPORT
DOWNERS GROVE, IL

Shaker Workshops, of Concord, Massachusetts, offers a wide range of furniture kits, all of which are based on specific Shaker pieces featured in museums and private collections. The company also offers stains and gifts such as beeswax candles, oval boxes, and hand-carved toys. The company can be reached at P.O. Box 1028, Concord, MA 10742; 800-840-9121.

## Nontoxic Textile Markers

*Can you recommend a high-quality, nontoxic textile marker?*

JUDY BRYANT
SANTA FE, NM

We tested and recommend Zig Textile Markers, manufactured by EK Success. The nontoxic markers can be used on a wide range of textile surfaces from cotton T-shirts to needlepoint canvas and even wood. Available in over twenty colors (permanent and opaque), the markers retail for $3.10 each. The company can be reached at 611 Industrial Road, Carlstadt, NJ 07072; 800-524-1349.

## Cleaning Floral Containers

*What is the best way to clean floral containers? Dishwashing liquid doesn't seem to get everything off.*

KATHY HELLER
ABERDEEN, ID

We found that bleach, water, antibacterial soap, and a bottle brush are indispensable tools when it comes to cleaning floral containers. Usually, washing the container with an antibacterial soap such as Dial will do the trick. But for debris that is harder to remove, including dried-on petals, mold, or Oasis, combine one-quarter teaspoon of bleach with one gallon of water (or reduce amount appropriately) in the container and let it soak, using the bottle brush to remove any stubborn remains.

## Nonirritating Skin Cleansers

*Can you recommend a strong hand cleaner that won't irritate the skin? I'm having trouble finding one.*

JANINE STUART
CARTHAGE, MS

While there are many extra-strength hand cleaners on the market today, we like Gojo Orange Hand Cleaner. Gojo is fortified with lanolin, vitamin E, and aloe and should leave your hands soft after the cleaning. You can find it at most hardware stores; a twenty-eight-ounce container retails for $1.99.

## Storing Leftover Wrapping Paper

*Do you have any suggestions for storing leftover wrapping paper? I keep everything in a large paper shopping bag, and it's always a mess, particularly during the holidays!*

LISA CALDER
LEONIA, NJ

How about storing your materials in a cardboard storage box? Many discount department stores, as well as mail-order companies that feature organizers, such as Hold Everything (800-421-2264) and Lillian Vernon (800-285-5555), offer a variety of storage boxes, many of which are partitioned to keep belongings neat.

## Locating Materials for Snow Globes

*Where can I purchase materials for making my own snow globes?*

MIMI GRANT
SAN FRANCISCO, CA

Your local art supply store may be able to order the basic components—globes, bases, and flakes—for you. The National Artcraft Company (23456 Mercantile Road, Beachwood, OH 44122; 216-292-4944) carries a variety of these materials, and its catalog is free. You can purchase the silicone adhesive required to seal the dome to the base at most art supply or hardware stores.

More critical is finding the miniature figures to include in your snowscape. For ready-made miniatures, you might wish to consult a hobby shop or locate some dollhouse furnishings—although the dome can contain an array of free-floating memorabilia as well. If you're really intent upon creating an "environment," you may wish to acquire a comprehensive listing of miniatures manufacturers. The New York International Gift Fair Directory is a great source. Published by George Little Management, Inc., a company that organizes trade shows, the directory includes listings of many miniatures manufacturers as well as other crafts and gift suppliers (dried flowers, party goods, paperweights, picture frames, and more) nationwide. Send a check for $10 for the directory to George Little Management, Inc., 10 Bank Street, White Plains, NY 10606, or call 800-272-7649.

## Priming Terra-Cotta Flowerpots

*I'd like to paint some terra-cotta flowerpots. Do I have to prime the pots first?*

LEE SEYMOUR
DAYTONA BEACH, FL

If the flowerpot is already glazed, priming is not necessary. As clay is so porous, however, it's possible that unglazed clay would absorb too much paint, meaning you would probably need a coat of primer in this case. Be sure to use a water-based primer if you'll be using water-based paint and an oil-based primer for oil-based paint. (Oil-based paint is a better choice for outdoor pots.)

## Toll-Free Assistance with Sewing Problems

*In the recent past, I noticed that your magazine provided a telephone number that people could call with woodworking questions. I was wondering, does a service like this exist for sewing problems?*

AILEEN GODDU
LYME, NH

If you're having difficulty executing a particular technique described in a pattern, here are two possible solutions. You could take your work to the store where you purchased your fabric and/or pattern and ask the salespeople for assistance. This way, you'll be able to show your project to the person helping you. If that's not possible, most pattern companies, such as McCall's, Butterick, and Vogue, have 800 numbers that you can call for assistance. (The toll-free numbers are usually listed in small print on the pattern itself.) This way, you can speak with someone who is both an experienced sewer and is familiar with the company's patterns. Although most consumer service departments will answer general sewing questions, they prefer to answer questions related to their specific patterns. ◆

# Quick
## TIPS

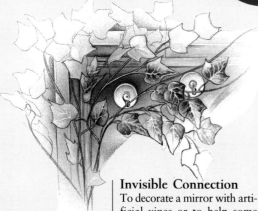

ILLUSTRATION:
**Harry Davis**

ONE-MINUTE WREATH ILLUSTRATION:
**Nenad Jakesevic**

## Invisible Connection

To decorate a mirror with artificial vines or to help some wandering ivy or philodendron wind its way around a window, try using clear plastic suction hooks. They are practically invisible underneath the greens, and the hooks won't harm your plants the way tape might do.

## Perking Up Limp Silk Flowers

When silk flowers start looking old and stale, you can give them a face-lift using blush.

**1** Brush pink blush on the petals, concentrating the color near the center of the flower.

**2** Clip any stray threads that appear along the petal edges for a cleaner, more realistic look.

## Stand Up Straight

To help long-stemmed flowers in a wide-mouthed vase stand tall without leaning, you can make a grid using clear strapping tape.

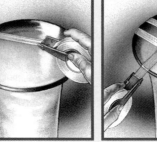

**1** Stretch the tape across the widest part of the vase from edge to edge.

**2** Add parallel strips ½" to 1" apart, then lay perpendicular strips until the entire opening is covered with the grid pattern.

**3** Insert individual stems into the grid openings. Fill in the arrangement with shorter-stemmed flowers and foliage to hide the tape.

## Reviving Limp Bows

Instead of spending money to make new wreath bows each year, Margaret Fite of Christiansburg, Virginia, uses a curling iron to "restyle" bows she takes out of annual storage. Preheated to a low setting, the iron quickly revives limp or crushed loops and streamers.

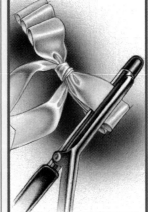

## Fancy 4-Watt Bulbs

You can turn ordinary 4-watt bulbs into one-of-a-kind novelties for nightlights, chandeliers, and candelabras by adding silicone gel designs.

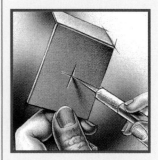

**1** Using an X-Acto knife, score and bend a small cardboard rectangle into an L-shaped holder. Cut a "plus" sign in the center.

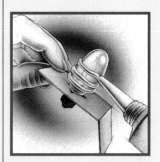

**2** Insert the bulb securely in the holder. To make the design, squeeze silicone gel directly from the tube and "write" on the glass bulb surface. When you are through, set the bulb down so that the holder keeps it upright as the gel dries.

**3** Design variations include dots, swirls, and spirals.

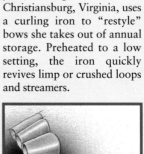

## Weaving Your Own Wreath

You can weave your own grapevine wreath using well-soaked, pliable vines and an ordinary bucket.

**1** Turn the bucket upside down, tapered end up. Choose a long vine and wind it around the bucket several times, interweaving the ends so they stay put.

**2** Intertwine additional vines around the bucket to build up the wreath base. Clamp springy vines with clothespins until you can weave in more vine.

**3** When the wreath is full, let it dry on the bucket for at least a week, then lift it off and remove the clothespins.

## Find the Center

Try this fast and easy way of finding the center of a wall or floor when you're stenciling or hanging pictures. Stretch two strings diagonally from corner to corner, taping the ends so the strings lie taut. Where they cross is the center.

## One-Minute Wreath

Any 3- to 4-foot-long silk foliage vine can be shaped into a lush wreath in about a minute.

**1** Uncoil the vine so none of the foliage is clinging to itself.

**2** Starting at one end, shape the vine once around in an 8" circle, then weave in the remaining length to secure the shape. Weave in a second vine if desired.

## Custom Borders

To give purchased wallpaper borders a custom look, or to shorten a border that is too deep for your space, cut a contoured edge to line up with the image, using a sharp X-Acto knife and a self-healing cutting mat.

## Easy Stripes

In order to beat the cost of expensive striped wallpapers, Crystal Kolke of Renton, Washington, uses two colors of latex paint and painter's tape. Here's a variation on her approach:

  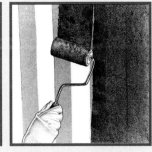 

**1** Paint the wall in the base coat color. When the paint is dry, lay down strips of tape side by side.

**2** Peel up every other strip.

**3** Paint the exposed wall surface between the remaining strips with the second color of paint.

**4** Let the second coat dry completely. Peel off the remaining tape to reveal the stripes.

# Trio of Glass Ball Ornaments

*Make your own elegant tree decorations using rubber bands, stickers, and a pour-in paint process.*

❧ BY CAROL ENDLER STERBENZ

Each of the ornaments pictured above was created using one of these three techniques. The gold stripe ball (front, left) uses the reverse-stenciling technique, while the gilded ball at right uses the sticker decoupage technique. The two balls toward the back use the pour-in painting technique.

IT'S THE HOLIDAY SEASON, AND there's little time to spare. What's the quickest way to customize an ordinary glass ornament? I discovered three shortcuts—using stickers and rubber bands to reverse stencil, a pour-in painting technique, and a no-glue decoupage method—each of which yield fast, easy, and beautiful Christmas tree decorations.

## Reverse Stenciling

To create a reverse-stenciled design, I needed to block out the desired shapes before applying glitter. The solution: Use self-stick stars and rubber bands. I used embossing powder instead of ordinary glitter because it created a crisp line around the masked area.

My original plan was to use the stars or rubber bands to mask those shapes, brush or spray on glue, and roll the ball in extrafine glitter. I tried spray-on glue and rubber cement, but both seeped under the foil stars, dissolving their adhesive. In contrast, ordinary white high-tack craft glue went on smoothly without affecting the adhesive.

To make narrow stripes, I tried masks of typist's correction tape, but it was difficult to keep it straight and parallel. Then I discovered rubber bands. Not only were they easy to apply and adjust, they also hugged the ball with no gaps.

Glitter comes in a brilliant gold color but also includes large granules. It covers the ball unevenly and clumps together. Embossing powder, however, which is used with rubber stamps, is finer than glitter. It covers the ball with a smooth, even coat. In addition, the powder's graphite-colored patina makes the ball appear antique gold.

### INSTRUCTIONS

**1.** Remove cap from one ball. Insert straw into opening, then tape around straw and neck of ball. Clean ball with glass cleaner. *Note:* To free both hands during work, insert straw "handle" into foam brick as needed.

**2.** *For star design:* Apply stars to ball surface at random. *For striped design:* Select rubber band slightly smaller than ball diameter. Stretch rubber band around equator of ball, then release band gently. Add two additional bands parallel to first band, adjusting spacing as necessary. Brush glue over entire surface of ball, covering stars or rubber bands (*see* illustration A).

**3.** To add glitter, pour embossing powder onto typing paper. Holding straw handle, roll ball in powder, manipulating paper to coat all surfaces (illustration B). Place handle in foam brick. Repeat steps 1 through 3 for second ball. Let balls dry 1 hour.

**4.** To remove stars, pry up point with straight pin, then remove with tweezers. Remove any remaining adhesive with cotton swab dipped in alcohol. Lift rubber bands with straight pin, clip with scissors, and pull off using tweezers (illustration C). Remove tape and straws. Replace ornament caps.

---

REVERSE STENCILING TECHNIQUE

**A.** Stretch the rubber bands around the ball, then brush glue over the entire surface.

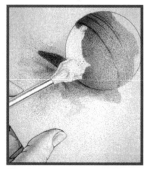

**B.** Roll the ball in the embossing powder, moving the paper to coat the entire surface.

**C.** Clip the rubber bands with scissors, then peel them off with tweezers.

## Pour-In Painting Method

For this set of ornaments, I needed to color the background of the balls in order to set off the polka dot and star stickers. My solution—painting the inside of the ball—introduced color while protecting the painted surface.

Originally I had applied the stars randomly, then painted between them using white acrylic paint. I liked the contrast between the shiny stars and the white background, but the paint was uneven, and it scratched off too easily. Then it occurred to me to paint the *inside* of the ball. To test this, I poured acrylic paint into the ornament, swirled it around, then drained it into a disposable cup. The result was an even background coat in addition to a smooth surface for adhering the stickers.

**D.** Pour acrylic paint into the ball through its opening.

**E.** Rotate the ball so the paint coats the inside surface.

**F.** Set the ball into the cup and let it drain 24 hours.

**G.** Apply the star stickers, then burnish them with a coffee stirrer.

### MATERIALS
**Poured Paint Ornaments**
*Yields 2 ornaments*

Two 2½"- to 3"-diameter glass ball ornaments
Adhesive ¾" foil stars and ½" circle labels
2-ounce container white acrylic paint

*You'll also need:*
two 3-ounce disposable cups; wooden coffee stirrer; paper towels; spray glass cleaner; and single-hole punch.

### INSTRUCTIONS

**1.** To prepare cups for drying process, punch holes around rims. Remove ornament cap from one ball. Pour half of acrylic paint into ball through opening (*see* illustration D).

**2.** To distribute paint, rotate ball so paint coats entire inside surface (illustration E), then pour excess paint back into original container.

**3.** To dry paint, set ball open end down into cup (illustration F). Punched holes will allow air to circulate freely. Repeat steps 1 through 3 to paint second ball. Let balls drain 24 hours or until inside of each is bone-dry.

**4.** Before proceeding, clean balls. Apply stars or circles to ball surfaces at random. Burnish each sticker with coffee stirrer, pressing gently from center out to edges (illustration G). Replace ornament caps.

### Sticker Decoupage

For this ornament, I devised a no-glue method of decoupage using stickers. Though stickers may still need some careful cutting, depending on their background, their adhesive replaces the need for glue.

My next challenge was how to fit a flat image on a rounded shape. The solution, however, is simple: Make tiny cuts around the image's edges, which overlap one another and help the sticker hug the ornament's globelike surface. As I positioned and smoothed the stickers on the ball, I pressed down the tabs one by one so that they overlapped. By making the cuts at a break or contour in the image, and by staining the cuts with brown magic marker, I was able to camouflage them.

I gilded between the images using gold leaf and Winsor & Newton's fast-drying japan size, which becomes tacky in just about ten minutes.

### INSTRUCTIONS

**1.** To prepare ornament for decoupage, remove ornament cap. Insert straw into opening, then wrap masking tape around straw and neck of ball. To free both hands during work, insert ornament's straw "handle" into foam brick as needed.

**2.** Prepare stickers by clipping into individual motifs. Make tiny clips (⅜" deep and about ⅜" apart) perpendicular to edge around perimeter of each cutout (*see* illustration H). If possible, position cuts along breaks or contours in image. If necessary, stain raw paper edges using magic marker.

**3.** Before proceeding, clean ball. Peel backing off sticker and position it on ball (illustration I). Use coffee stirrer to smooth cutout from center out, so clipped edges overlap as they conform to ball's curves. Repeat to affix second cutout to opposite side of ball.

**4.** Cover work surface with kraft paper. Using ¼" brush, apply size to glass ball around edges of each cutout (illustration J), then use ½" brush to apply size to rest of ball. Let dry 5 to 15 minutes; clean brushes. Open book of gold leaf. Slide two sheets of gold leaf onto work surface. Use fingers to tear both sheets into irregular 1" to 2" pieces.

**5.** Test tack by touching tip of coffee stirrer to surface; stirrer should stick and pull off as if touched to transparent tape. When size is tacky, touch fingertip to piece of leaf, lift and transfer to ball, and gently tap in place. Repeat, tearing additional leaf if necessary, until entire ball is covered (illustration K). Press dry ½" brush gently over entire surface. Let ball dry overnight, then burnish surface with cotton ball. Remove tape and straw and replace cap. ◆

### MATERIALS
**Sticker Decoupage Ornaments**
*Yields 1 ornament*

■ 3"- to 4"-diameter glass ball ornament
■ Two to three 5"-square sheets composition gold leaf
■ 75 milliliters (2.5 fluid ounces) Winsor & Newton japan gold size
■ Brown magic marker
■ Pair of adhesive 2½" x 4" cherub or floral stickers

*You'll also need:*
drinking straw; brown kraft paper; one ¼" and two ½" round soft-bristled paintbrushes; manicure scissors; table knife; florist foam brick; masking tape; ruler; wooden coffee stirrer; paper towels; spray glass cleaner; cotton ball; and mineral spirits or turpentine.

STICKER DECOUPAGE

**H.** To ready the sticker, make small cuts about ⅜" apart around the edges.

**I.** Overlap the clipped edges as you press the sticker to the ball.

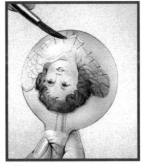

**J.** Apply size to the areas surrounding the sticker.

**K.** When the size is tacky (5 to 15 minutes), apply the gold leaf using your fingertip.

# How to Make an Infinite Variety of Wreaths

*The secret: binding bouquets of fresh, silk, or dried flowers and foliage to a wreath base.*

✍ BY CAROL ENDLER STERBENZ

TYPES OF
WREATH BASES

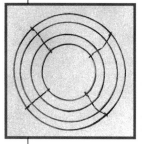

**Wire wreath base**

**Vine wreath base**

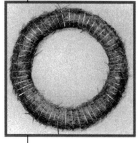

**Straw wreath base**

ILLUSTRATION:
**Nenad Jakesevic**

COLOR PHOTOGRAPHY:
**Steven Mays**

By binding bouquets of flowers, fruit, or foliage to a wreath base, you can create hundreds of different wreaths for every season of the year. This Della Robbia wreath, for example, uses plastic fruit bound to a wire wreath base.

MANY WAYS EXIST TO DECOrate a wreath, including hotgluing or pinning materials to a wreath base, but I've discovered that one of the simplest methods relies on binding. Binding, in which bouquets of decorative material are lashed to a base, will let you create an infinite variety of designs, dependent only on your choice of materials.

Binding requires three components: a wreath base, the decorative material, and a binding agent such as wire or string.

The wreath base can be made from any substance that will support the weight and volume of the decorative material—circles of interlacing vines, extruded foam, welded metal, or packed straw. Ready-made bases range in price from $2 to $12, depending on the material and diameter.

Match your specific choice of base to the volume, weight, and type of decorative material. If you choose boughs of pine, balsam, or fir, for instance, you'll need a base that can support their heavy weight and girth, such as a vine or straw base. By contrast, stems of dried roses and statice, which are very light, could be affixed to a foam base.

The weight of the wreath also determines how it should be displayed. Lightweight wreaths of dried flowers can be hung without worry whereas voluminous wreaths of fresh foliage, especially water-saturated evergreens, need to be hung on a sturdy hook or else displayed on a flat surface.

Decorative materials for wreath making include fresh, dried, and/or silk flowers and foliage. The type of material chosen determines the life of the finished wreath. Fresh material is perishable, dried material more enduring, and silk decoration everlasting. The choice of material also communicates a particular style and season. Dried roses and lavender in a slender circle create a Victorian feel whereas armloads of balsam and fir send a traditional wintry message.

## Using Fresh Material
Before you begin binding, you'll need to prepare your decorative material.

Fresh flowers and foliage need to be conditioned. Because fresh flowers are so perishable, they are not usually recommended for wreath making. You can extend their display life by a day or so if you encapsulate each stem in a plastic orchid vial, such as those sold by florists, but in general, cut flowers are an expensive choice.

For making fresh wreaths, green, leafy branches, evergreens, and other plants with woody stems are preferable to flowers. These types of plants hold their moisture well, though even the hardiest plants need water to stay fresh-looking.

I tested three different ways to counteract dehydration. The first involves letting the plant absorb water through immersion before it is placed on the wreath. Cut the stems of the plants diagonally one inch from the bottom, then immerse the stems in a mixture of water and floral food for several hours. Commercially prepared floral foods, such as Floralife, not only provide the plant with nutrients but also discourage the growth of bacteria that will eventually rot the plant.

The second way to counteract dehydration is by misting. Once you have bound the foliage into a wreath, lightly mist the leaves with water. Your third choice is to display the wreath outdoors, where the natural humidity can prolong the life of the foliage, or cold temperatures can slow the rate of dehydration. Whether it is displayed in summer or winter, avoid hanging the wreath in direct sunlight.

Unfortunately, every cut plant eventually dries out. However, some fresh-cut plants, including lemon leaves, caspia, salal, oak, and birch branches, look attractive even when dry.

## Using Dried and Silk Material
Dried material needs no conditioning with one exception: If the dried plants have broken or missing stems, they will need to be repaired. (*See* "Creating a False Stem," page 21, May/June 1995.) Though dried materials are easy to handle, some dried plants or flowers are more resilient

than others. This is due in part to the plant variety (roses, for instance, are notoriously fragile) and in part to the way the plant was dried.

Flowers and foliage can be dried in one of three ways: by air-drying, by submersion in a desiccant such as silica gel, or by placement in a commercial freeze-dryer. Freeze-drying preserves the original color and texture the best. Freeze-dried plants and those dried in desiccant are more resilient than air-dried material. The added sturdiness carries a price, however: These types of dried material are about 15 percent more expensive when they are purchased in a craft or specialty store.

The speed of air-drying depends partly on the plant and partly on the humidity. When I hung a sample of fresh roses and lemon leaves in a dry, dimly lit place, the roses took about four days to dry completely, while the lemon leaves required seven to ten days. I also discovered that I needed to thin the leaves around the stems where they would be bound onto the wreath to prevent the layers of leaves from rotting.

Silk flowers and foliage are the Rolls Royce of decorative material. They are resilient, available in a large number of varieties, and designed to last for years. Their cost, however, can be prohibitive: One silk rose costs around $3 while a single dried rose retails for about $1.50.

I satisfy my love of silk flowers by interspersing them with dried material or by designing a smaller wreath. Silk flowers rarely need preparation, although silk flower wreaths need to be dusted from time to time and kept out of direct sunlight to avoid fading.

### Attaching the Decorative Material to the Wreath

The last requirement for a bound wreath is a binder, or some form of string, waxed twine, or fine-gauge wire to bind the materials to the wreath base.

The choice of binder depends on the fragility, thickness, and weight of the dec-

orative material. Wire is the strongest binder and can withstand large amounts of tension from the decorative material before snapping; waxed twine has a non-slip surface and is strong enough for moderate tension; and string is the least strong of the three.

Fresh material with thick, woody stems and silk flowers and foliage with wire armatures can be bound using medium-gauge wire or waxed twine. Dried flowers and foliage can be bound with any of the three—wire, twine, or string—but the stems are fragile and may need to be wrapped in florist tape for protection.

It's best to gather any type of plant with small, slender, fragile stems together in small bouquets and wrap the stems in florist tape before binding. (See "How to Make Bouquets," below.) Using prepared bouquets, with a set number and type of plants per bouquet, will create a design with a uniform pattern. You can also block out bands of color by alternating between bouquets of different plants.

If the stems are thick and long, you can gather several together and bind them onto the base without worrying about breaking the material or having it slip out of the binding. This technique, called binding loose bunches, creates a more random look. All of the designs shown on pages 10 and 11, however, use the bou-

quet method of binding, since the wreath bases are generally small- to medium-sized and require shorter stems to get around the narrow arc.

### MASTER INSTRUCTIONS
### How to Make Bouquets

1. Assemble flowers, foliage, or fruit into bouquet, keeping back of bouquet flat (see illustration A).
2. Bind stems with wire, then conceal wire with florist tape (illustration B).
3. Clip off ends, leaving 2" stem (illustration C).

### How to Bind Bouquets

1. Tie wire in slipknot around wreath base. Lay one bouquet on base, flat side down and facing wreath center. Wind wire around stem and wreath base several times (see illustration D).
2. Hold wire steady. Lay second bouquet on base so it faces out and stems cross. Resume winding wire to secure stem of second bouquet (illustration E).
3. Add third bouquet, facing in, and bind to base (illustration F). Continue adding bouquets, alternating their direction, to fill front of wreath all around.
4. To add final bouquet, slip its stem under head of first bouquet and bind it securely. To end off, anchor wire to original slip knot and clip off excess (illustration G). ◆

HOW TO MAKE BOUQUETS

**A.** Assemble the flowers into a bouquet.

**B.** Bind the stems with wire, then conceal them with tape.

**C.** Clip off the ends, leaving a small stem.

**MATERIALS**
**Making Bouquets**

- Dried, silk, or fresh flowers and foliage, and, if desired, artificial fruit on stem
- 30-gauge florist wire
- Florist tape

*You'll also need:* pruning shears.

**MATERIALS**
**Binding Method**

- Assembled bouquets
- Wreath base (straw, vine, wire, etc.)
- 30-gauge florist wire

*You'll also need:* pruning shears.

HOW TO BIND BOUQUETS

**D.** Tie the wire to the base, then wind it around the stem.

**E.** Wind the wire to secure the stem of the second bouquet.

**F.** Bind a third bouquet to the base.

**G.** To end, anchor the wire to the base.

## 1. ENGLISH COUNTRY GARDEN

### MATERIALS
- 14 dried pink roses
- 14 stems dried pink globe amaranth
- 14 stems dried purple globe amaranth
- 14 stems dried pink everlasting
- 14 stems dried blue everlasting
- 42 sprigs dried yellow yarrow
- 1 large bunch white sea lavender
- 5" vine wreath base
- Sheet moss
- Spray mister

### INSTRUCTIONS
Following "How to Make Bouquets" (page 9), make fourteen bouquets, each containing one rose, one stem pink amaranth, one stem purple amaranth, one stem pink everlasting, one stem blue everlasting, three sprigs yarrow, and two to three sprigs lavender. To cover base with moss, start by tying wire in slipknot around base. Press misted moss around vine, covering short sections at a time, then wind wire around it. Continue adding and binding moss around base. To end off, anchor wire to original slipknot and clip off excess. Following "How to Bind Bouquets" (page 9), bind bouquets onto wreath base.

## 2. COCKSCOMB, YARROW, AND STATICE

### MATERIALS
- 36 sprigs red celosia cockscomb
- 30 sprigs purple statice
- 10 sprigs golden yarrow
- 8" vine wreath base
- Spanish moss

### INSTRUCTIONS
Following "How to Make Bouquets" (page 9), make six cockscomb bouquets, each containing six stems. Make five statice bouquets, each containing six stems. To cover base with moss, start by tying wire in slipknot around base. Press misted moss around vine, covering short sections at a time, then wind wire around it. Continue adding and binding moss around base. To end off, anchor wire to original slipknot and clip off excess. Following "How to Bind Bouquets" (page 9), bind bouquets and individual yarrow sprigs onto three-quarters of base, alternating colors to create bands.

## 3. SILK FLOWERS AND FRUIT

### MATERIALS
- Two 20" vines with wild roses (approximately 20 blooms and buds)
- Seven 9" stems white freesia (with blooms and buds)
- 7 berry clusters, assorted sizes
- 5 miniature apples with wired stems
- 20" branching stem with green foliage
- 8" wire wreath base

### INSTRUCTIONS
Cut rose vine and green foliage into separate stems. Following "How to Make Bouquets" (page 9), make seven bouquets, each containing one or two rose stems, one freesia stem, one berry cluster, and one or two foliage stems. Following "How to Bind Bouquets" (page 9), bind onto base. Fill in bare spaces by wiring apples to base.

## 4. DELLA ROBBIA

### MATERIALS
- 15 sprigs pea-sized plastic berries
- 5 sprigs olive-sized plastic berries
- 4 pinecones
- 3 cherries
- 3 miniature apples
- 2 miniature oranges
- 2 miniature pears
- 2 miniature pomegranates
- 2 strawberries
- 6-10 other fruits
- 10 small sprays assorted silk foliage
- 8" wire wreath base
- 18-gauge florist wire

### INSTRUCTIONS
Cut 6" lengths of wire as needed to wire pinecones and any fruit that does not have a stem. Following "How to Make Bouquets" (page 9), make ten bouquets, each containing one foliage spray, two sprigs of berries, and two fruits from list above. Following "How to Bind Bouquets" (page 9), bind bouquets to base, filling in bare spaces with single stems of fruits or foliage. Wire on pinecones as desired.

## 5. FRESH BOXWOOD AND EUONYMUS

**MATERIALS**
- Forty 6" sprigs fresh euonymus
- Thirty 6" sprigs fresh boxwood
- 8" straw wreath base

**INSTRUCTIONS**

Trim leaves from bottom 2" of each sprig. Following "How to Make Bouquets" (page 9), make ten bouquets, each containing four sprigs euonymus at back of bouquet and three sprigs boxwood in front. Following "How to Bind Bouquets" (page 9), bind onto base, directing all foliage away from wreath center.

## 6. EVERGREEN, ROSES, AND LIMES

**MATERIALS**
- Forty 7" sprigs fresh juniper
- Forty 7" sprigs fresh fir
- Forty 7" sprigs fresh euonymus
- Forty 7" sprigs fresh blue spruce
- Forty 7" sprigs privet hedge
- 6 cream roses with 7" stems
- 4 whole limes
- 6 orchid vials
- 10" straw wreath base
- Sharp kitchen knife

**INSTRUCTIONS**

Following "How to Make Bouquets" (page 9), make twenty evergreen bouquets, each containing two sprigs juniper, fir, euonymus, spruce, and privet hedge. Cut twenty slices lime, each ⅜" thick. Thread 10" length florist wire through each slice near rind and twist to secure. Insert rose stems into vials filled with water. Following "How to Bind Bouquets" (page 9), bind bouquets onto wreath base, then wire on lime slices and insert vials into straw.

## 7. CASPIA

**MATERIALS**
- 144 stems green caspia, fresh or dried, about 6" long
- 5" to 6" vine wreath base
- Sheet moss
- Spray mister

**INSTRUCTIONS**

Snip extraneous foliage from bottom 2" of each caspia stem. Following "How to Make Bouquets" (page 9), make twenty-four bouquets, each containing six stems caspia. To cover base with moss, start by tying wire in slipknot around base. Press misted moss around vine, covering short sections at a time, then wind wire around it. Continue adding and binding moss around base. To end off, anchor wire to original slipknot and clip off excess. Following "How to Bind Bouquets" (page 9), bind onto base.

## 8. LEMON LEAF

**MATERIALS**
- Thirty 9" stems lemon leaves (4 to 8 leaves per stem)
- Nine 9" stems eucalyptus
- Nine 9" sprigs fresh juniper
- Nine 9" sprigs fresh box-wood
- 10" straw wreath base
- Silver spray paint
- Newspaper

**INSTRUCTIONS**

Cover work surface with newspaper. Spray-paint half (15) of lemon leaf stems silver and let dry. Following "How to Make Bouquets" (page 9), make nine bouquets, each containing three or four plain and silver lemon leaf stems, one stem eucalyptus, one sprig juniper, and one sprig boxwood. Following "How to Bind Bouquets" (page 9), bind onto base.

# How to Make Your Own Wire-Edged Ribbon

*A humble cording foot is the key to making your own ribbon in any color or width.*

❧ BY CANDIE FRANKEL

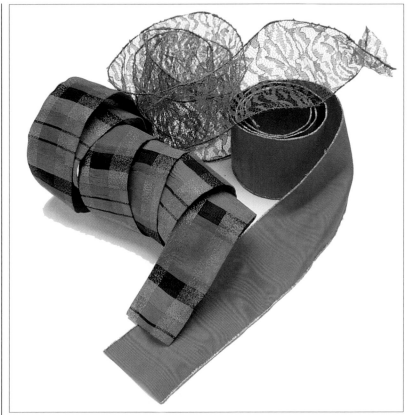

**By varying your fabric, you can create an assortment of wire-edged ribbon. The ribbon at the left uses a plaid taffeta, the center example uses lace, and the ribbon on the right uses a moiré.**

ILLUSTRATION:
**Harry Davis**

COLOR PHOTOGRAPHY:
**Richard Felber**

AROUND THE HOLIDAYS, WIRE-edged ribbon is invaluable for a wide variety of projects. While beautiful, however, high-quality ribbon is also expensive. With your sewing machine and one attachment—a cording foot—you can make your own ribbon, which lets you select the color and pattern, control the ribbon's width, and save money to boot.

Wire-edged ribbon became popular in the 1980s when it was first imported from France. It's made by capturing very strong, thin-gauge wire in the selvages (edges) as the ribbon is sewn. The machinery is sophisticated, finely calibrated, and expensive, so the final product costs $3 and up per yard.

Duplicating the French method of manufacture was obviously not an option for me—I would be starting with purchased fabric and investigating ways to trap a wire in the edges. By examining some of the wire-edged ribbons available on the market, I found two methods worth exploring: sewing and gluing. My preferred method is sewing, but when the stitching will detract from the appearance of a particular fabric, I use the invisible glue method instead.

## The Miraculous Cording Foot

Some of the wire-edged ribbons I examined captured the wire with machine overcasting along the edges. The overcasting threads included cottons, shiny rayons, and metallics that either matched or contrasted with the ribbon fabric. In some ribbon, the overcasting was bulky and unattractive, but in others it was quite delicate. I was especially drawn to the edges sewn with metallic thread because they appeared integral to the ribbon, as in the woven French mode, not tacked on.

I knew an overlock machine (serger) could accomplish this look: It cuts the fabric and hems the edge in one operation. But since I didn't own one, I was limited to whatever effects I could achieve on my sewing machine, a ten-year-old Riccar with a dozen assorted presser feet. I began by putting the cording foot to the test. Used conventionally, this foot decorates fabric by letting you sew narrow cording over the face of the fabric. A metal guide on the front of the foot feeds the cording in the path of the needle, which zigzags back and forth to secure it in place. By using wire instead of cording and tightening up the zigzag to the satin stitch setting, I was able to create wire edges on strips of fabric as easily as I sew a straight line. (If your machine doesn't come with a cording foot, you can order one from catalogs such as Sewing Emporium for about $10. *See* Sources and Resources, page 48.)

I found that using the cording foot was easy. To make the ribbon, I slipped 28- or 30-gauge steel wire into the slot on the foot and placed a fabric strip on the machine bed so that the raw edge extended slightly to the right of the needle. I set the machine for a medium zigzag width and chose a very short stitch length (close to zero on my stitch length dial gave me a satin stitch setting). As the needle toggled back and forth, I adjusted the fabric so that the needle came down just a hair beyond the fabric edge. This encased the raw edge almost perfectly, with just a few stray fibers to be snipped off later. Thin fabrics, such as sheers and lace, actually curled up within the stitching, producing an edge with a tidy rolled look. When I tested lace, I set the zigzag to its widest to bulk up the edge and maximize this effect (*see* photo, page 13).

### THE CORDING FOOT

This cording foot allows you to feed the cord (or wire) into the foot. Other designs include a foot with a large groove underneath to sit over the cord, or a foot that sews with twin needles on either side of the cord.

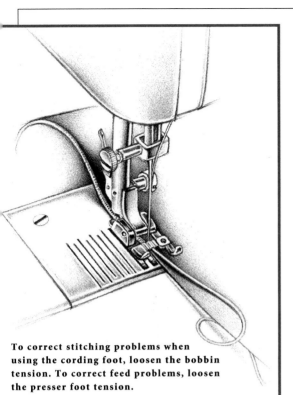

To correct stitching problems when using the cording foot, loosen the bobbin tension. To correct feed problems, loosen the presser foot tension.

## Controlling the Tension

My machine made crisp, neat edges. Sometimes the bulky satin stitch got caught on the foot edge just behind the needle, so I let up on the presser foot tension one notch at a time until the problem resolved itself. Since this adjustment caused the feed to miss a beat now and then, I gripped the fabric from behind the foot and gently escorted it out as I sewed. Thread tension problems were worst with metallic threads, which stretch more than mercerized cotton. Occasionally, the upper thread got lassoed onto the bobbin mechanism, but looser tension resolved the situation.

I tested a wide range of fabrics. Knits proved too limp and drapey to be effective, so I concentrated on woven fabrics. Open-weave damasks and crepes were a disappointment: The satin stitching never fully captured the longer surface fibers, and the flyaway threads were impossible to tame. The fabrics that worked best for me were full-bodied and firmly woven, many with a crisp texture: curtain-weight sheers, metallics, chintz, taffeta, moiré, velvet, and stiff lace. (*See* photographs, right, for samples of good and bad fabric choices.)

## Gluing:
## The No-Edge Edge

I don't like wire-edged stitching on print or plaid fabrics—it reminds me of the utilitarian overcasting used to finish seams inside a garment. To make wire-edged ribbon using these fabrics, I worked out a simple gluing method by folding the fabric edge over the wire. For a neat finish, I pressed wide folds that overlapped at the back of the ribbon. (My first samples had skimpy three-eighth-inch flaps that gave the ribbon an unfinished look.) For lightweight fabrics, I used a 28- to 30-gauge wire, but for medium-weight fabrics, I switched to heavier 24-gauge wire to carry the double fabric weight.

To hold the flaps (and wire) in place, I experimented with iron-on fusible tape, a liquid fusible requiring an iron, and fabric glue. I had no complaint with the hold from any of these products, but it was impossible to manage both a hot iron and a springy wire simultaneously. I could not always keep the wire in position, and once a section was fused, I couldn't go back and straighten out my mistakes. Thus, the fusibles lost out right away, and I moved on to glue, specifically, Aleene's Liquid Fusible Web. Despite the name, this product actually works like glue, with no ironing. It allowed me to position the wire and seal it within the fold without mishap.

### INSTRUCTIONS
### Sewn Edge Method

**1.** To cut strips of fabric, use rotary cutter along lengthwise or crosswise grain of fabric. Cut strips to desired width of ribbon. Set aside scraps for practice.

**2.** Start by attaching cording foot to machine. Adjust tension for straight stitch sewing, then reset machine for closely spaced zigzag stitch. Guide end of wire into cording foot, lower foot onto edge of practice fabric, and begin sewing. Adjust fabric position and stitch width to enclose wire and edge of fabric in stitch.

**3.** When machine is properly adjusted, sew wire along both edges of each cut strip. Use scissors or wire cutters to cut

wire ends. Snip off any stray threads from wired edges.

### Glued Edge Method

**1.** To cut strips of fabric, use rotary cutter along lengthwise or crosswise grain of fabric. Cut strips to two times desired width of ribbon plus ½".

**2.** Press long edges of each strip to wrong side, overlapping them by ½" at center of strip. Pink long edge of overlapping strip.

**3.** In preparation for gluing, open flaps. Brush very thin coat glue to wrong side of each flap. Let dry 5 to 10 minutes. Brush second coat on unpinked flap only. Working in short segments, position wire on inner edge of fold, then fold flap over wire and press firmly with fingers until glue adheres. Continue until wire is enclosed along entire fold. Use scissors or wire cutters to cut wire ends. Glue pinked flap over wire in same way. ◆

---

### MATERIALS
### Sewn Edge Method

- **Firmly woven fabric**
- **Matching or contrasting sewing thread**
- **28- or 30-gauge steel wire**

*You'll also need:* sewing machine with cording foot; rotary cutter; and old scissors or wire cutters.

---

### MATERIALS
### Glued Edge Method

- **Firmly woven fabric**
- **28- or 30-gauge steel wire (for lightweight fabric) or 24-gauge steel wire (for medium-weight fabric)**
- **Aleene's Liquid Fusible Web glue**

*You'll also need:* rotary cutter; iron; pinking shears; ½"- to 1"-wide flat, stiff natural bristle brush; and old scissors or wire cutters.

---

## GOOD FABRIC CHOICES

The edge at the left was sewn using mercerized cotton sewing thread that matches the color of the lace. The rolled hem look is achieved by allowing a small amount of the lace edge to get caught up in the stitching. The sheer, firmly woven fabric on the right was edged using Sulky metallic thread, which appears as a fine filament on the spool. Despite the delicacy of the stitching, there are virtually no loose threads escaping along the edge.

## BAD FABRIC CHOICES

No matter how close the edging stitches are set, loose weaves such as this crepe-backed metallic fabric (shown at left) tend to fray along the edges. The damask fabric shown at the right is another example of a loose weave that produces a ragged edge.

# Christmas Potpourri Demystified

*Designing your own potpourri or modifying an existing recipe is easy.*
*The trick is understanding the role that each ingredient plays.*

**Keep proportions in mind when selecting bowls and baskets for displaying pot-pourri. Mixtures with very large ingredients will look out of place in small bowls while potpourri with small, delicate materials will look lost in a large basket.**

ILLUSTRATION:
**Wendy Wray**

COLOR PHOTOGRAPHY:
**Carl Tremblay**

MAKING FRAGRANT POTPOURRI in time for Christmas is eas-ier than you think. All pot-pourri is composed of three kinds of ingredients: fragrant materials, fixative, and decorative accents. Once you learn the function of each ingredient, you can modify an existing recipe or design your own potpourri with ease.

We asked Kathleen Meskill, owner of The Ginger Tree, an herb shop in Opelika, Alabama, to concoct our pot-pourri recipe. We wanted only ingredi-ents that would be familiar and easy to find, and a fragrance that would remind us of the holidays: the aroma of baked spice cookies, cinnamon sticks in mulled wine, and seasonal evergreens.

Meskill offered us a recipe dating back about one hundred years, which she had simplified, but it still listed twenty-one ingredients. Guided by the three primary functions of potpourri ingredients—adding scent, adding volume while bind-ing the scent, or serving as decoration—we set out to reduce the number of ingre-dients without sacrificing the potpourri's spicy-woodsy scent.

Making the potpourri involves mixing the fixative and the balsam oil and letting it cure for forty-eight hours, then mixing those ingredients with the rest of the materials and letting the entire concoc-tion cure for two to three weeks. Once the potpourri is done, it can be displayed in an open bowl or basket in order to dis-sipate its scent.

## Fragrant Materials

The most essential ingredients in pot-pourri are those that provide scent. Spices and herbs offer fragrance while essential oils enhance and fortify the scent of the natural materials. Meskill's original recipe called for six spices (cinnamon bark, cin-namon sticks, allspice, cloves, star anise, and cardamom), three herbs (rosemary leaves, bay leaves, and juniper berries), and balsam oil.

Armed with this list, we headed to a local grocery store, where we found everything except cinnamon bark, juniper berries, and balsam oil.

We found the spices in both whole and ground form. We compared their value by putting two tablespoons of both types of allspice in separate open bowls. The ground allspice had a very strong scent when first dispensed, but the fragrance faded after only a few days; the whole all-spice was milder at first but was still emit-ting fragrance a week later. (We did press the whole allspice gently with the back of a soupspoon to release the scent before setting it out, and this may have con-tributed to its longevity.) While whole spices cost more because they require more careful selection and handling, they will keep the potpourri fragrant longer.

We ordered the cinammon bark by mail, then compared it to cinammon sticks. Other than differing textures, the cinammon sticks were just as fragrant, so we dropped the cinammon bark from the recipe.

We found juniper berries and balsam oil at a natural foods store. Meskill explained that the berries are used in making gin and recommended we substi-tute two teaspoons of gin. When we tried this in the potpourri, however, the juniper smell evaporated with the alco-hol. We decided to stick with the berries.

To keep the cost reasonable, many pot-pourri recipes replace essential oil, which offers the most potent fragrance, with fra-grance oil, a mixture of essential oil and a carrying agent. It is the purity of essential oils that makes them more expensive. Balsam oil, however, is an exception: Both types of this oil are priced anywhere from $2.50 to $5 for one-quarter ounce. Perfume, by the way, is not an effective substitute because it is more expensive than essential oil, and neither is cologne because the alcohol content causes the scent to evaporate too quickly.

### Fixatives

Fixatives are bulky materials that bind or "fix" the fragrance in the potpourri, keep the powdered spices and herbs from end-ing up on the bottom of the bowl, and give the mixture its volume.

Meskill's recipe called for oak moss and orrisroot, two unfamiliar ingredients that we had to order by mail. Oak moss is a light-scented, silver-colored lichen with tendrils shaped like antlers. We kept it in the recipe since it is reasonably priced ($3.90/pound), effective at holding the scent of the fragrant ingredients, and of decorative value. Orrisroot, or iris root, is dried and cut into chunks or crushed into powder. It is an effective fixative, but very expensive ($11.85/pound). A good substitute is cellulose fiber, which only costs $1.45/pound. We opted to skip both ingredients and use oak moss alone.

## Decorative Materials

Decorative materials, which give the potpourri color and texture, can be natural or synthetic. Meskill chose only those materials with naturally occurring color, such as red rosebuds and petals, pink rose hips, and brown birch cones. We found all three of these ingredients easily (although our cones were gilded) and added our own citrus spirals from lemon and orange rinds. We decided to omit globeflowers, cedar tips, angel wings, and sandalwood chips because we were happy with the colors presented by the roses and the cones.

## INSTRUCTIONS

**1.** Cut or tear oak moss into ½"- to ¾"-long pieces. Place thin layer in jar and dispense about 10 drops oil over top (*see* illustration A). Add new layer of moss

### MATERIALS
*Yields 5 to 6 cups*

**FRAGRANT MATERIALS**
**Spices**
- ¼ cup 1" cinnamon stick pieces
- 2 tablespoons whole allspice
- 2 tablespoons whole cloves
- 1 tablespoon star anise, whole and pieces
- ½ tablespoon green cardamom pods

**Herbs**
- 2 tablespoons dried rosemary leaves
- 15 to 20 bay leaves
- 2 tablespoons blue juniper berries

**Oil**
- 1/16 ounce (60 to 80 drops) balsam essential oil

**FIXATIVE**
- ¾ cup whole oak moss

**DECORATIVE MATERIALS**
- ¼ cup dried pink rose hips
- 1 cup dried red rosebuds and petals
- ½ cup gilded birch cones
- 1 lemon
- 1 orange

*You'll also need:* eyedropper; sharp knife; heavy glass bowl; soup-spoon; measuring cup; 2-quart glass jar with tight-fitting lid; 4-quart or larger glass or ceramic mixing bowl; 4-quart or larger plastic sweater box with lid; and wooden spoon (do not reuse with food).

and 10 more drops oil. Continue layering moss and oil until both are used up. Screw on lid, then shake jar to distribute oil. Set aside away from direct sunlight and let cure 2 days. Shake several times each day.

**2.** Score rind of lemon and orange as if

cutting wedges. Peel off rinds, then trim rinds from zest. Keeping zest from lemon and orange separate, cut it into narrow strips and let dry, away from direct sunlight, 1 to 2 days; rinds will curl as they dry.

**3.** Place allspice in heavy glass bowl and press back of soupspoon against them (illustration B). Repeat to gently bruise cloves, rosemary leaves, and cardamom pods in turn. Break or crumble several bay leaves.

**4.** Measure 2 tablespoons each of lemon peel spirals and orange peel spirals. Combine spirals with all ingredients except cured oak moss and birch cones in 4-quart mixing bowl. Toss gently with wooden spoon as you would salad (illustration C). When combined, toss in oak moss in same way.

**5.** To age potpourri, transfer mixture to plastic box (illustration D). Cover box with lid and set aside away from direct sunlight. Stir or shake gently each day for 2 to 3 weeks. The potpourri is ready to use when the strong, sharp scent has mellowed to a more delicate fragrance.

**6.** Add birch cones to potpourri (illustration E), then display in open bowl or basket. ◆

DESIGNER'S TIP
To dry your own rose petals, stretch cheese-cloth across an embroidery hoop and lay the petals in a single layer on top. The elevated cheesecloth bed will allow air to circulate on all sides. The petals will dry in one to three days.

---

MAKING THE CHRISTMAS POTPOURRI

**A.** Cut or tear the oak moss into ½"- to ¾"-long pieces. Place a thin layer in the jar and dispense about 10 drops of oil over the top. Add a new layer of moss and 10 more drops of oil. Continue layering the moss and oil until both are used up.

**B.** Gently bruise the allspice, cloves, rosemary leaves, and cardamom pods in turn.

**D.** Transfer the mixture to a plastic box, then set aside for 2 to 3 weeks.

**C.** Combine the spirals with all the ingredients except the oak moss and cones, then toss with a spoon.

**E.** Add the birch cones, then display in an open bowl.

# Three Cuffed Decorator Christmas Stockings

*Sewing stockings from soft furnishing fabrics may create a variety of stitching problems. Here's how to solve them.*

❧ BY CANDIE FRANKEL

One way to customize your holiday decorations is by lining a mantel with stockings sewn from decorator fabrics.

## MATERIALS
**Velvet Stocking**

- ½ yard 45"-wide velvet
- ⅛ yard 45"-wide velvet (for cuff)
- ½ yard 45"-wide acetate or satin
- 1¾ yards ¼"-diameter cord welting
- 4" piece narrow ribbon or cord
- Matching thread

*You'll also need:* stocking and cuff patterns (*see* page 46); sewing machine; iron; scissors; pins; hand-sewing needle; tracing paper; and pencil.

ILLUSTRATION:
**Mary Newell**

SILHOUETTE PHOTOGRAPHY:
**Steven Mays**

COLOR PHOTOGRAPHY:
**Carl Tremblay**

**W**HILE THE BASIC SHAPE OF your Christmas stocking may not change from year to year, one way to customize your holiday decorations is to select decorator or soft furnishing fabric. My choices of velvet, damask, and sheer fabrics raised a series of unexpected problems, but the remedies all involve simple sewing techniques.

My first velvet stocking was disappointingly limp, despite the lining I added, and my damask stocking had so little body that I was afraid it would stretch out of shape. While the sheer stocking held its shape, the cuff needed crisper points and the fabric was difficult to handle during sewing.

To shore up the drooping velvet, I first tested a variety of trims, including moss fringe and metallic rickrack, but finally settled on one-quarter-inch-diameter cord welting. By enclosing the welting in the stocking seams, I was able to firm up the edges all around while introducing some color and textural contrast.

For the damask fabric, my goal was similar except I didn't want to add any weight to aggravate the stretching problem. Here, I tested two invisible stabilizers: one-half-inch-wide seam binding, and bias tape, which I folded in half and stitched down as I sewed the seam. The seam binding won out—unlike bias tape, it didn't stretch. By folding it in half to a narrow one-quarter-inch width, I could ease it around the curved seam line (without creating pleats) to give the damask stocking some much-needed backbone.

The sheer fabric was difficult to sew. The fabric was so thin, it bunched up under the machine's feed dogs, especially during the starting stitches. In addition, my design called for two layers of fabric to be used together for each pattern piece, and the cut pieces, particularly the cuff points, were difficult to keep aligned. So, I tried doing the steps in reverse—sewing first, then cutting. I layered the fabric, pinned a tracing paper pattern on top, then stitched through all the layers along the pattern lines. When I was through stitching, I tore away the tracing paper and cut the fabric one-quarter inch beyond the stitching. Because I had a clear stitching line to follow and the fabric layers didn't shift during sewing, I could easily and quickly produce crisp, uniform points on the stocking's cuff.

## Velvet Stocking
### INSTRUCTIONS

Start by copying and enlarging cuff and stocking patterns on page 46. The stocking should measure 8" across at the topmost edge, and the cuff should measure 5¼" deep and 15" wide. Fold stocking velvet in half, wrong side out, and pin stocking pattern to rectangle. Cut along marked lines to yield two mirror-image velvet stockings. Repeat process to cut two linings from acetate or satin. Use cuff pattern in similar manner to cut two cuffs from cuff velvet. Use illustrations A through I as reference for these directions.

**1.** Right sides facing, stitch short edges of each cuff together to make tube. Press seam open. Using zipper foot, machine-baste 17" length of welting to raw edge of one cuff so "tails" hang over edge at

Bright colors such as turquoise, raspberry, moss green, and yellow add a festive touch to holiday decorations.

# Making the Velvet Stocking

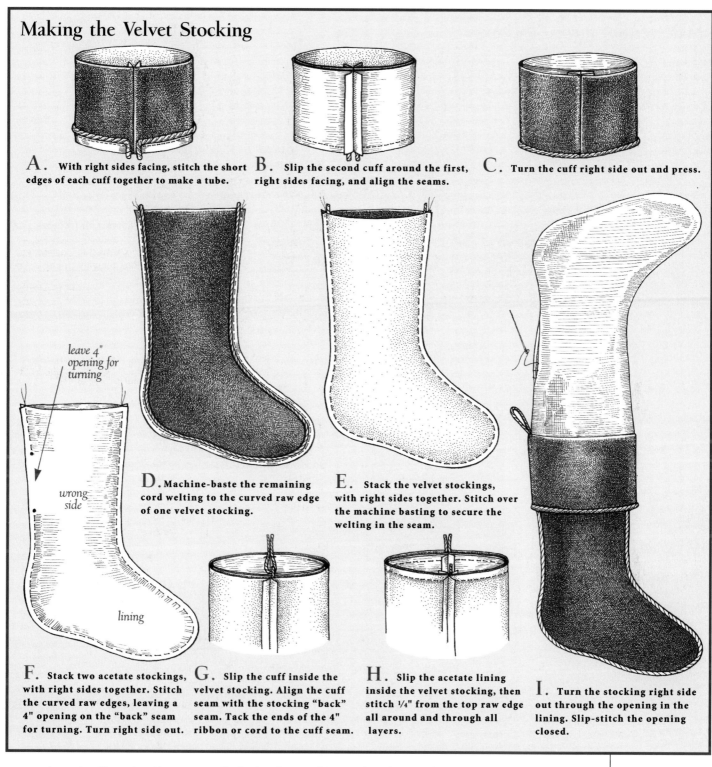

**A.** With right sides facing, stitch the short edges of each cuff together to make a tube.

**B.** Slip the second cuff around the first, right sides facing, and align the seams.

**C.** Turn the cuff right side out and press.

leave 4" opening for turning

wrong side

lining

**D.** Machine-baste the remaining cord welting to the curved raw edge of one velvet stocking.

**E.** Stack the velvet stockings, with right sides together. Stitch over the machine basting to secure the welting in the seam.

**F.** Stack two acetate stockings, with right sides together. Stitch the curved raw edges, leaving a 4" opening on the "back" seam for turning. Turn right side out.

**G.** Slip the cuff inside the velvet stocking. Align the cuff seam with the stocking "back" seam. Tack the ends of the 4" ribbon or cord to the cuff seam.

**H.** Slip the acetate lining inside the velvet stocking, then stitch ¼" from the top raw edge all around and through all layers.

**I.** Turn the stocking right side out through the opening in the lining. Slip-stitch the opening closed.

seam as shown (*see* illustration A).

**2.** Slip second cuff around first cuff, right sides together, and align seams. Stitch all around bottom edge, over machine basting, to secure welting in seam (illustration B).

**3.** Turn cuff right side out and press (illustration C).

**4.** Machine-baste remaining cord welting to curved raw edge of one velvet stocking (illustration D).

**5.** Stack velvet stockings, right sides together. Stitch over machine basting to secure welting in seam (illustration E). Clip curves. Do not turn.

**6.** Stack two acetate stockings, right sides together. Stitch curved raw edges, leaving 4" opening on "back" seam for turning (illustration F). Turn right side out.

**7.** Slip cuff inside velvet stocking. Align cuff seam with stocking "back" seam.

Tack ends of 4" ribbon or cord to cuff seam (illustration G).

**8.** Slip acetate lining inside velvet stocking, aligning seams and matching top raw edges. Stitch ¼" from top raw edge all around and through all layers (illustration H).

**9.** Turn stocking right side out through opening in lining, exposing hanging loop. Slip-stitch opening closed (illustration I).

# Making the Sheer Stocking

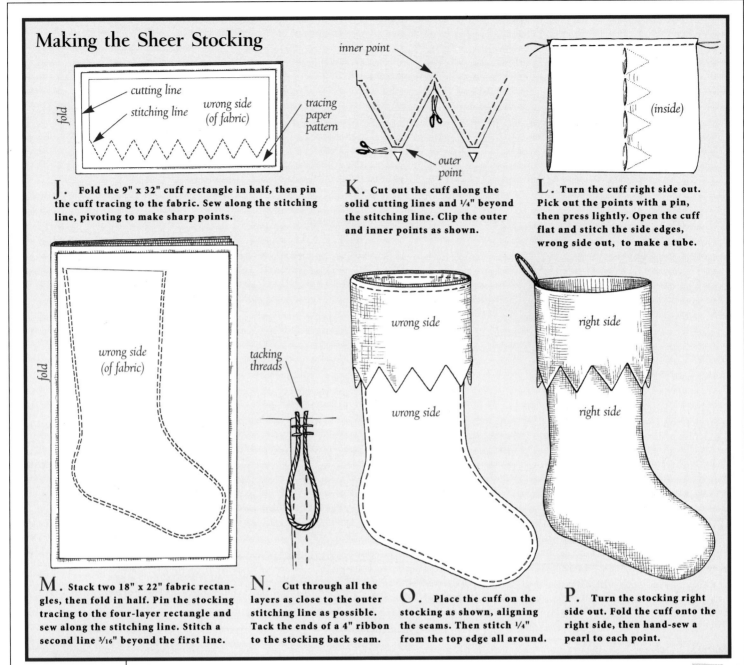

**J.** Fold the 9" x 32" cuff rectangle in half, then pin the cuff tracing to the fabric. Sew along the stitching line, pivoting to make sharp points.

inner point

outer point

**K.** Cut out the cuff along the solid cutting lines and ¼" beyond the stitching line. Clip the outer and inner points as shown.

(inside)

**L.** Turn the cuff right side out. Pick out the points with a pin, then press lightly. Open the cuff flat and stitch the side edges, wrong side out, to make a tube.

cutting line
stitching line
fold
wrong side (of fabric)
tracing paper pattern

fold
wrong side (of fabric)

tacking threads

wrong side

wrong side

right side

right side

**M.** Stack two 18" x 22" fabric rectangles, then fold in half. Pin the stocking tracing to the four-layer rectangle and sew along the stitching line. Stitch a second line ³⁄₁₆" beyond the first line.

**N.** Cut through all the layers as close to the outer stitching line as possible. Tack the ends of a 4" ribbon to the stocking back seam.

**O.** Place the cuff on the stocking as shown, aligning the seams. Then stitch ¼" from the top edge all around.

**P.** Turn the stocking right side out. Fold the cuff onto the right side, then hand-sew a pearl to each point.

## Sheer Stocking
### INSTRUCTIONS

Start by copying and enlarging pointed cuff and stocking patterns on page 46. Stocking should measure 8" across at topmost edge; cuff should measure 6¼" deep and 14½" wide. *Note:* For the stocking, you should trace the stitching line, *not* the outer cutting line. Cut one 9" x 32" rectangle from the cuff fabric and two 18" x 22" rectangles from the stocking fabric. Use illustrations J through P as reference for these directions.

**1.** Fold 9" x 32" cuff rectangle in half, wrong side out. Pin cuff tracing to fabric as shown (*see* illustration J). Sew along stitching line, pivoting to make sharp points.

**2.** Using scissors, cut out cuff along solid cutting lines and ¼" beyond stitching line. Tear off tracing pattern. Clip outer and inner points as shown (illustration K).

**3.** Turn cuff right side out. Pick out points with pin, finger-press, then press lightly with iron. Open cuff flat, then stitch side edges, wrong side out, to make tube (illustration L). Press seam to one side, then turn cuff right side out.

**4.** Stack two 18" x 22" fabric rectangles, right sides up, then fold them in half. Pin stocking tracing to four-layer rectangle. Sew along stitching line. Stitch second line ³⁄₁₆" beyond first line all around (illustration M).

**5.** Cut through all layers as close to outer stitching line as possible and straight across top. Tack ends of 4" rib-bon or cord to stocking "back" seam (illustration N).

**6.** Place cuff on stocking as shown, aligning cuff seam with stocking "back" seam. Stitch ¼" from top edge all around (illustration O).

**7.** Turn stocking right side out. Fold cuff onto right side, exposing hanging loop (illustration P). Hand-sew pearl to each point.

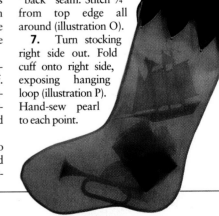

# Making the Damask Stocking

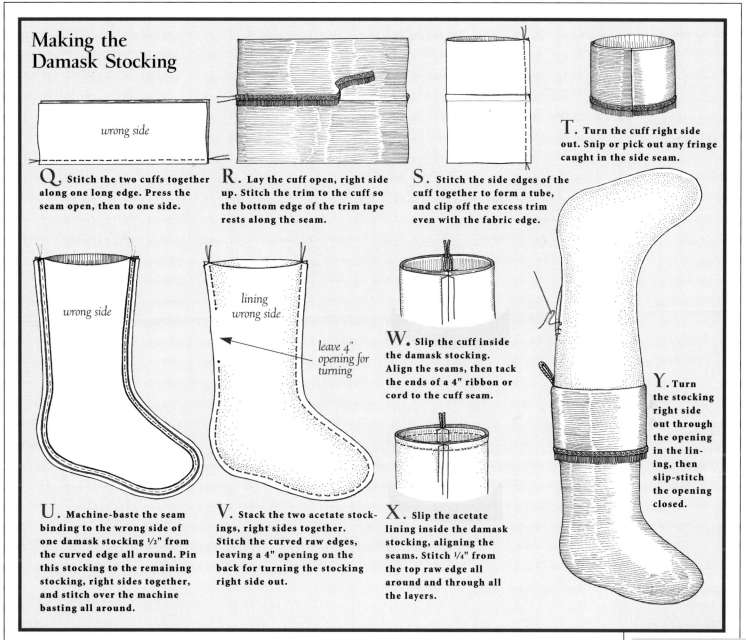

**Q.** Stitch the two cuffs together along one long edge. Press the seam open, then to one side.

**R.** Lay the cuff open, right side up. Stitch the trim to the cuff so the bottom edge of the trim tape rests along the seam.

**S.** Stitch the side edges of the cuff together to form a tube, and clip off the excess trim even with the fabric edge.

**T.** Turn the cuff right side out. Snip or pick out any fringe caught in the side seam.

*wrong side*

*wrong side*

*lining wrong side*

*leave 4" opening for turning*

**U.** Machine-baste the seam binding to the wrong side of one damask stocking ½" from the curved edge all around. Pin this stocking to the remaining stocking, right sides together, and stitch over the machine basting all around.

**V.** Stack the two acetate stockings, right sides together. Stitch the curved raw edges, leaving a 4" opening on the back for turning the stocking right side out.

**W.** Slip the cuff inside the damask stocking. Align the seams, then tack the ends of a 4" ribbon or cord to the cuff seam.

**X.** Slip the acetate lining inside the damask stocking, aligning the seams. Stitch ¼" from the top raw edge all around and through all the layers.

**Y.** Turn the stocking right side out through the opening in the lining, then slip-stitch the opening closed.

## Damask Stocking
### INSTRUCTIONS

Start by copying and enlarging cuff and stocking patterns on page 46. The stocking should measure 8" across at the topmost edge, and the cuff should measure 5¼" deep and 15" wide. Fold stocking damask in half, wrong side out, and pin stocking pattern to rectangle. Cut along marked lines to yield two mirror-image damask stockings. Repeat to cut two linings from acetate or satin, then repeat again using cuff pattern to cut two cuffs from cuff damask. Use illustrations Q through Y as reference for these directions.

**1.** Stitch two cuffs right sides together along one long edge (*see* illustration Q). Press seam open, then to one side.

**2.** Lay cuff open, right side up. Stitch trim to cuff so bottom edge of trim tape rests along seam and fringe extends below seam (illustration R).

**3.** Stitch side edges of cuff together, wrong side out, to form tube, and clip off excess trim even with fabric edge (illustration S). Steam-press seam open until flat.

**4.** Turn cuff right side out, then fold along seam with trim. Snip or pick out fringe caught in side seam until it hangs freely (illustration T).

**5.** Machine-baste seam binding, folding it in half lengthwise as you go, to wrong side of one damask stocking ½" from curved edge all around. Pin this stocking to remaining stocking, right sides together, and stitch over machine basting all around (illustration U). Clip curves. Do not turn.

**6.** Stack two acetate stockings, right sides together. Stitch curved raw edges, leaving 4" opening on seam for turning (illustration V). Turn right side out.

**7.** Slip cuff inside damask stocking. Align cuff seam with stocking "back" seam. Tack ends of 4" ribbon or cord to cuff seam (illustration W).

**8.** Slip acetate lining inside damask stocking, aligning seams and matching top raw edges. Stitch ¼" from top raw edge all around (illustration X).

**9.** Turn stocking right side out through opening in lining, exposing hanging loop. Slip-stitch opening closed (illustration Y). ◆

### MATERIALS
**Damask Stocking**
- ½ yard 45"-wide damask
- ⅛ yard 45"-wide damask (for cuff)
- ½ yard 45"-wide acetate or satin
- ½ yard braid trim
- 4" piece narrow ribbon or cord
- 1¼ yards ½"-wide seam binding
- Matching thread

*You'll also need:* stocking and cuff patterns (see page 46); sewing machine; iron; scissors; pins; hand-sewing needle; tracing paper; and pencil.

# The Fastest Way to Make Hand-Molded Soap

*Forget tallow, lye, or soap molds. All you need are a few bars of Ivory soap, a Mouli grater, and a microwave oven.*

 BY SALLY SEAMANS

ILLUSTRATION:
**Wendy Wray**

COLOR PHOTOGRAPHY:
**Carl Tremblay**

Using just three 4.5-ounce bars of Ivory soap, you can make twelve handmade soap balls for holiday gift giving. The soap pictured above feature the following ingredients (front to back): rosemary, lemon zest, oatmeal, and fragrance.

I MADE SOAP FROM SCRATCH ONCE, back in the 1960s. I remember rendering lard and mixing it with lye, the unpleasant odor as it cooked, and the two-week wait for the soap to "cure." This time, I decided to try and make new soap out of existing soap. After a variety of tests, I discovered all you need are a Mouli grater and a microwave oven.

My first step was researching how to make the soap. All the instructions I found, however, involved making soap from scratch—time-consuming and somewhat messy in that it involves cooking fat (i.e., tallow or lard) and an alkaline base (i.e., lye) together. After a long search, I found a single line of text in one reference that said old soap could be shredded, melted in a double boiler, and pressed into molds to form new soap.

I immediately gathered up a variety of household soaps and began experimenting. In order for the soap to melt evenly, the pieces needed to be of uniform size. I tried dicing the soap into smaller pieces using a kitchen knife, but the task was harder than it looked, and it proved difficult to get uniformly sized pieces. I tried chopping the soap using my mini food processor, but I never achieved a consistently fine chop. I pureed the soap with a little water in my blender, but the soap literally curdled. I tested both hard and glycerin soap, but the results were consistently lumpy or grainy.

I noted that the chopper called for some foods, such as chocolate and cheese, to be cold during chopping, but that didn't seem to help with soap. Then I tried a traditional up-and-down cheese grater (you hold the grater stationary and move the soap) and a handheld, cylinder-style Mouli grater. Although they both worked equally well, the Mouli grater proved the fastest.

To melt the grated soap, I tried boiling, steaming, simmering, stewing, baking, whisking, and whipping the soap, but it would not break down uniformly. I tried melting the soap directly in hot water and wringing it out, but all I got was soggy soap.

As a last resort, I decided to try my microwave oven. After cooking the soap shavings on high for about sixty seconds, the soap turned into a huge, foamy mass. Thinking I had another failure on my hands, I grabbed a fork and began scooping the mess back into the container. It was then that I realized that the soap had melted evenly. After a few moments, when it was cool enough to handle, I rolled the soap into a ball between the palms of my hands. Although the surface

of the resulting ball was slightly uneven, the soap itself was beautiful.

To smooth the soap a little further, I rolled it on a dinner plate, which reduced the unevenness and gave the soap ball a slight sheen.

I spent the rest of my time microwav-

MAKING NEW SOAP FROM OLD SOAP

A. If using a Mouli grater, first cut each bar of soap into 1" chunks.

B. Measure ½ cup of grated soap in a bowl and add herbs.

C. Microwave the soap on high until it foams as high as it will go.

D. Shape the microwaved soap into a rough ball.

E. Burnish the ball to its finished size by rolling it on a dinner plate.

ing soap. I tested several different types and found that plain white floating soap (such as Ivory) worked the best. Floating soap is made by mixing a warm soap solution with air. The microwave heats up the air, causing it to expand, which in turn causes the soap to foam. One 3.5-ounce bar of Ivory yields approximately one and one-half cups of grated soap, or enough for three balls; one 4.5-ounce bar yields approximately two cups of grated soap, or enough for four balls of soap.

Finally, I experimented with a variety of additives in order to change the color and/or the texture of the soap. I found that a few drops of food coloring added a lovely pastel hue while ten to twenty drops of essential oil gave the soap a nice scent and reduced the prevailing Ivory smell. (You may need to experiment, however.) I got the strongest scent by adding the oil onto the foam before I started molding the ball.

Chopped lemon zest and herbs gave the soap balls different textures, as did wheat germ and oatmeal. Soap that used "wet" additions such as minced herbs or lemon zest seemed to form better. With "dry" additions such as oatmeal or wheat germ, which absorb the moisture in the soap, the soap became a bit more crumbly. Adding less of these ingredients minimized this problem.

**INSTRUCTIONS**

1. If using Mouli grater, cut each bar of soap into 1" chunks. Grate soap into fine strings (*see* illustration A).

2. For each soap ball, measure ½ cup grated soap and place in bowl. If adding lemon zest, peel off lemon skin (yellow portion only) from a single lemon using vegetable peeler, then mince. If desired, add 2 to 5 drops food coloring and/or any one of the following: the zest, 1 tablespoon minced fresh herb (illustration B), 1 teaspoon wheat germ, 1 teaspoon quick

oats. Combine with fork.

3. Microwave on high 30 to 60 seconds, or until soap foams completely. Remove from oven (illustration C).

4. Turn foam upside down onto clean countertop. If scent is desired, apply 10 to 20 drops scented oil or perfume to surface at random. Working quickly, while foam is still warm, compress into rough ball shape. To prevent cracks, do not knead, crease, or fold foam but simply

compact it evenly from all sides between palms (illustration D).

5. Continue making ball more compact until it reaches golf ball size. Let set 2 to 5 minutes, then burnish against plate in order to smooth and shine surface (illustration E). ◆

*Sally Seamans is a freelance writer and craftsperson living in Beverly Farms, Massachusetts.*

## HOW SOAP WORKS

The cleaning process can be broken into three stages: wetting the soiled material, removing particles of dirt, and holding the dirt particles in water until they are rinsed away.

The cleaning agents in soap (called surfactants) lower the surface tension of water, letting it penetrate the soiled material. The surfactants also help remove dirt. One part of the surfactant holds on to and surrounds the dirt, while a second portion pulls the dirt away from the material, toward the water. Once the dirt particles are in the water, the thin layer of surfactant surrounding the dirt particles prevents them from settling on the washed material again. The dirt particles remain suspended in the water until they are rinsed away.

HISTORICAL TIDBIT
Although no one knows who first discovered the chemical reaction between fat and lye, some historians give the credit to the Romans. At Sapo, a hilly area near Rome, the Romans sacrificed burnt offerings to their gods. The fat and ash (a common substitute for lye among pioneer women) accumulated at the base of the altars and washed down the hillside. Washerwomen found this "Sapo clay," perhaps the earliest form of soap, conducive to laundering their soiled togas. Whether this story is true or not, today's term derives in part from "Sapo" in many languages: "soap" (English), "savon" (French), and "sapone" (Italian).

# Foolproof Greeting Cards

*Start with store-bought stationery and a special image, then add your own jacket using card stock. The result: professional-looking homemade cards.*

**BY FRANCOISE HARDY**

**1** To isolate area to appear on card, cover image with tracing paper. Trace around image at least 1/4" in from edges.

**2** Cut stock to match stationery using ruler and X-Acto knife. Then slice 1/4" off two adjacent edges of stationery.

**3** To test-fit, fold both sheets in half, slip stationery inside card stock, and slip both into envelope. If necessary, trim edge of jacket to fit.

**4** To mark position where image will show through jacket, open jacket flat on mat with front facing up. Tape tracing from step 1 to front. Using X-Acto knife and ruler, cut through tracing paper and jacket along traced lines. Remove tracing paper, tape, and cutout section.

**5** As preparation for attaching image, reinsert stationery inside jacket. Position image so it shows through window. Hold image down to prevent it from shifting, then carefully open jacket.

**6** To attach image, bend back top edge and apply thin bead glue to underside. Smooth with brush, then roll edge back into position and rub gently with clean fingertip. Let dry 1 minute. Clean brush with water.

**7** To finish, open jacket flat. Using scissors, cut ribbon or cord two times length of fold plus 5" to 10". Tie around jacket and stationery at fold.

**For variations on this greeting card design, use the images on the special insert, color photocopies of favorite images, or small photographs.**

## MATERIALS

- Small printed images (see special insert, pages 24 and 25) or photographs
- Single-fold sheets of stationery with matching envelopes
- Card stock or stiff decorative or textured paper
- 1/16" double-faced satin ribbon or thin decorative cord (see step 7 for how to determine length)
- Clear glue

*You'll also need:* self-healing cutting mat; metal-edged ruler; scissors; X-Acto knife; tracing paper; pencil; removeable tape; and 1/2"-wide stiff paintbrush.

ILLUSTRATION:
**Judy Love**
COLOR PHOTOGRAPHY:
**Carl Tremblay**

MAKING YOUR OWN GREETING cards can be a time-consuming and complicated endeavor. The secret to foolproof gift cards, however, starts with matching stationery and envelopes. To customize my cards, I make an inside folio by folding a sheet of stationery in half, then cut an outside jacket from card stock. Last, I cut a window out of the jacket to highlight a special image.

In the past, I folded a sheet of card stock in half, then glued on a pretty postcard and slipped it in a homemade envelope. Making my own envelopes took too much time, however, and using readymade envelopes meant the card never really matched the envelope.

Then I discovered matching sheets of stationery and envelopes made from handmade and commercially made papers. Since the stationery was already measured and cut to fit, the problem of making an envelope to fit the card (or vice versa) was solved.

The next step was finding a way to customize the card. I started looking into heavier weight papers, which reminded me of a book cover, so I made a jacket for the stationery. The jacket also gave me another idea: cutting a small window where an image could show through. I folded the stationery in half and slipped it into the jacket, giving me space for a personal message on the innermost section. Since the sheet of stationery already fit the envelope perfectly when folded in half, I only had to cut the outer jacket to the same size, then trim the inner paper slightly to tuck inside the folded jacket.

The final problem was how to hold together the two sheets of folded paper without using glue, which can be messy, or without hand-stitching a spine, which is too complicated. The solution: tying a ribbon around both folded sheets. ◆

*Francoise Hardy, of Boston, enjoys card making and crafts in her free time.*

The color images on this issue's insert
(see following pages) are designed for use with the
Foolproof Greeting Cards story on page 22.

A Merry Christmas to you

Christmas Chimes.

I hope you folks are happy and the Christmas chimes,
Your happiness will double at least one hundred times.

415B

# How to Make Antique Velvet Roses

*The trick: Use velvet ribbon instead of fabric, color the ribbon yourself, and cut and glue the pieces separately.*

❧ BY MICHIO RYAN

**Velvet roses make wonderful decorations for packages, hats, or pillows. To make this rose, we colored the outer one-third of a bone white velvet ribbon with sepia-colored watercolor paint.**

I 'VE LONG ADMIRED THE LOOK OF vintage velvet roses, but they're rare, fragile, and expensive. While trying to make my own, I discovered some expedient shortcuts to achieving the look of hand-stitched antique roses.

For starters, I discovered that velvet ribbon is easier to work with than upholstery and apparel velvets. Second, creating an antique effect is as simple as subtly shading wet ribbon using watercolors. I also compared several methods of constructing the roses and determined that cutting and gluing separate lengths of ribbon is the best method of achieving the look of hand-stitched flowers without any sewing.

## Choosing Your Ribbon
Among the wide variety of velvet available, I prefer ribbon for a number of reasons. While velvet fabric yields more cloth per yard than ribbon, and is more economical, it must be carefully cut into small pieces of equal size to make the petals, whereas ribbon comes in one consistent width and has finished edges. The pile on both upholstery and apparel velvets is thick, and the fabric itself is either stiff or slinky. The fabric used for velvet ribbon is more finely woven, and the pile thin enough to fold as needed.

I found cotton and rayon/cotton velvet ribbon worked the best; they are soft and pliable without being too limp, and take color quite well. Polyester ribbons did not fold, crease, or pick up color at all, while nylon velvet colored well but had an overly stiff quality. If you find a velvet

ribbon you like but can't determine the fiber content, buy a small piece and try coloring it before buying more.

One type of velvet ribbon should definitely be avoided: fused-edge velvet, which is designed for floral arrangements and crafts. This very stiff ribbon has flocking on one side, and the binder for the flocking dissolves when water-based dyes are applied. I also tested a silk velvet ribbon, which, while beautiful, was too fragile when wet.

Choose the width of your ribbon depending on the scale of the finished flower. For instance, one-and-one-half-inch-wide ribbon works well for roses about three to four inches in diameter while one-inch-wide ribbon is better suited for a rose roughly two to two and one-half inches in diameter. If you plan to make a particularly large tea rose, more than four inches in diameter, select a narrower width ribbon for the center cluster of petals and a wider ribbon for the outside petals. Each of the three-inch-diameter roses shown with this article requires about two feet of ribbon. If you're not sure what color of ribbon to buy, or if the color you want is not available, start with a white or off-white ribbon and dye it accordingly (*see* "Using Fabric Dyes," below). It's faster, however, to buy the ribbon in the color of rose you want.

## Coloring Your Ribbon
Adding subtle shading to the rose petals makes them more beautiful and is easy to accomplish.

I started out experimenting with cold-water fabric dyes such as Jacquard's Precion MX Dye, but most dyes such as

MATERIALS
- 1½"- to 2"-wide white or pastel velvet ribbon (¾ to ⅞ yard per rose, including leaves)
- Scraps of green firmly woven linen or cotton fabric (for calyx)
- 1" to 2" silk leaves (one or two per rose)
- Florist wire
- Florist tape
- Dr. Ph. Martin's ½-ounce concentrated watercolors in one or all of the following colors: rose, aubergine, mauve, yellow, pink, green, brown, etc.
- Calyx pattern (see page 46)

*You'll also need:* hot-glue gun; newspaper; access to a photocopier with enlarger; large plastic sheet (such as dry cleaner bag); brown kraft paper; 1- to 2-ounce squeeze bottles, one per color, or plastic watercolor palette; spray mister; several small jars water; ruler; scissors; tracing paper; pencil; and old towels.

## USING FABRIC DYES
If you need permanent color for your roses, you'll need to use fabric dye to color the velvet ribbon. Sennelier, Jacquard, and Tinfix, among others, make dyes designed for use on silk, rayon, and cotton, in a wide range of colors. Even standard grocery store dye brands such as Tintex will work although the range of colors is more limited.

You'll need a fixative (e.g., vinegar or salt) to render the colors permanent and a heat source (either by steaming or immersion in a hot dye bath) to fix the color. For the best results, follow the manufacturer's directions.

this require either a setting agent to fix the color or need to be heat-set. Although they produced excellent colors, and are appropriate when light and water permanence is needed for the finished product, I discovered it was much simpler and faster to use Dr. Ph. Martin's Synchromatic Transparent Watercolors. Priced at $2.95 for one-half fluid ounce at a local craft store, Dr. Martin's comes in a glass bottle equipped with an eyedropper, and can be diluted easily. Although it is not lightfast

ILLUSTRATION:
**Wendy Wray**

COLOR PHOTOGRAPHY:
**Carl Tremblay**

SILHOUETTE PHOTOGRAPHY:
**Furnald/Gray**

To color this rose, crimson watercolor was applied along the bottom two-thirds of a cream/yellow-colored ribbon. To create the leaf, ivory ribbon was colored with a combination of green, persimmon, and beige watercolors.

and will run, it is convenient to use, requires no premixing, and comes in a wide range of colors.

Using Dr. Martin's watercolors straight from the bottle produced colors that were too intense, so I diluted them with an equal amount of water. This dilution worked well to color medium- to light-toned ribbons, but for very pale effects, such as beige or sepia on an ivory ribbon, I increased the dilution even more, using as many as 4 parts water for every 1 part dye. Keep in mind that the color appears darker when first applied, and lightens as it dries.

## Applying the Color

I found the most convenient way to apply color was with a tiny one- to two-ounce plastic squeeze bottle (usually sold in the same aisle as fabric dyes). The tip can be snipped off to create a hole about the diameter of a pencil lead. When I needed

just a small amount of a color, instead, I diluted the watercolor in one of the small wells of a plastic watercolor paint palette and applied it directly with the Dr. Martin's dropper.

Over the course of my experimentation, I discovered several ways to achieve realistic effects. By tinting the outer one-third of the ribbon, I could simulate a tea rose whose edges are darker than its center. By coloring the inner two-thirds of the ribbon, on the other hand, I could create the appearance of a one-color rose with a more intense tint in the heart of the flower and outer edges that are lighter in color. It's also possible to layer several hues (e.g., pearl gray, lavender, brown) arranging them so they fade gradually from dark to light in a graduated *ombré* effect. It doesn't really matter if the color lines are uneven, since any wavering will create a natural look on the finished rose.

Before applying any color, I wet the ribbon. I found the moisture helped the color bleed, rather than forming hard edges the way it would on dry fabric. To get started, loosely bunch the ribbon in your hand, then hold it under cool running water or spray it with a mister. When the ribbon is properly saturated, you'll feel the springiness give way and the cloth will stiffen slightly. If it still feels springy, warm water and a bit of detergent will help remove any sizing and further reduce the water's surface tension to help wet the fibers; just be sure to rinse out the detergent thoroughly. Wetting the ribbons also gave the finished roses a more antique look by matting down the nap to resemble panné velvet. I was able to accentuate this matted effect by squeezing the wet ribbon into a ball as I wrung out the excess water.

To create a work surface for applying the color, I set a sheet of brown kraft paper on a bed of newspapers, and unfurled the ribbons on top, nap side up. As I worked, the layered papers absorbed the excess water and dye, and the kraft paper surface prevented the newspaper ink from transferring to the ribbon. By slipping a dinner plate under the section of ribbon I was coloring, I could pool any excess liquid and bathe the ribbon in it for subtle color gradations. If an area dried out and the color didn't diffuse well, I simply misted the ribbon to rewet it. I also found I could move the color around by pressing down on the velvet with my finger.

After applying the dyes, I let them set for thirty seconds, rinsed out the excess in cool water, then squeezed the ribbons and hung them to dry. This method worked well for cotton and rayon ribbons, but for nylon ribbons, the color ran off when hung, so I dried them flat on old towels instead.

When layering several colors on the same ribbon, it helps to do each color separately, rinsing thoroughly between colors, in order to better gauge the final effect. Experimentation is a must, since fibers accept dyes at varying intensities; once I got started, achieving interesting color blends and highlights accidentally became part of the fun. When I was concerned about a color becoming too saturated, I proceeded more cautiously, using a weak dye solution and applying it bit by bit until I achieved the level that I wanted. (If you don't like a color, just dunk the ribbon in a weak chlorine bleach solution and rinse it thoroughly. As long as you execute the bleaching process quickly, the ribbon's original color should remain intact.)

Even if you decide not to color the ribbon, you should follow the washing, bunching, and unfurling routine to give the velvet nap a panné, or crushed, effect. If you don't want to wait for the ribbon to air-dry, you can iron it dry from the wrong side, which will preserve the panné effect.

## Constructing the Rose

I've seen fabric flowers made with cut petals, with stiffened backings, cupped or molded shapes, wired edges, and with hard cores forming the center. I wanted my roses to be different—soft to the touch—and I wanted to avoid sewing because it requires dexterity as well as accuracy. Above all, I wanted to make the roses quickly with a minimum of work.

One folding technique I tried produced a convincing rose, but required double-sided ribbon, a type of ribbon that is rare at best. Rolling the ribbon produced a compact, cinnamon bun look, but I desired a full-blown tea rose with separate, discrete petals. After further experimentation, I found it fastest to cut the ribbon into individual pieces and assemble the final rose using a hot-glue gun. The result is a more realistic, three-dimensional flower.

To attach the petals to the center, I chose hot-melt glue because it sets up immediately, with little mess and no clamping. The glue adhered to the ribbon's nap very nicely, and the nap insulated my fingertips from burning so that the petals were easy to press into place as the glue was cooling and setting.

My finishing touch was a stem and leaves. Ready-made velvet leaves can be hard to find, so I made my own by using silk leaves as a base.

### INSTRUCTIONS

**1.** Protect work surface with plastic sheet topped with at least ten layers newspaper and one sheet kraft paper. Using eyedropper, measure and mix

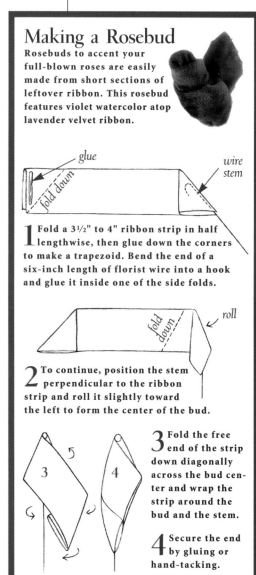

## Making a Rosebud

Rosebuds to accent your full-blown roses are easily made from short sections of leftover ribbon. This rosebud features violet watercolor atop lavender velvet ribbon.

*glue*

*wire stem*

*fold down*

**1** Fold a 3½" to 4" ribbon strip in half lengthwise, then glue down the corners to make a trapezoid. Bend the end of a six-inch length of florist wire into a hook and glue it inside one of the side folds.

*fold down*

*roll*

**2** To continue, position the stem perpendicular to the ribbon strip and roll it slightly toward the left to form the center of the bud.

**3** Fold the free end of the strip down diagonally across the bud center and wrap the strip around the bud and the stem.

**4** Secure the end by gluing or hand-tacking.

equal amounts of paint and water in plastic squeeze bottle or palette well for each color desired. Cut and set aside 3" length of ribbon per rose for leaves. Crumple remaining ribbon into loose wad and mist or hold under running tap until damp. Squeeze out excess. Lay moistened ribbon across work surface, setting plate underneath ribbon if desired. Apply diluted paint along one edge, covering one- to two-thirds of ribbon width (*see* illustration A). Slide ribbon along surface until entire length is colored. Reapply color to increase intensity as desired. Let stand 30 seconds, rinse well, and wring out excess moisture. If desired, apply second and third colors in same way and/or run wet brush along surface to bleed color(s). Moisten reserved ribbon, then tinge it with green and/or brown color for leaves. Dry all ribbons overnight by hanging or laying flat on towels.

**2.** Cut ribbon into seven 3½"- to 4"-long sections. Lay one section flat, wrong side up, with color along petal edges at top. Apply hot glue to each short end, then fold ends diagonally to make trapezoid (illustration B).

**3.** To make rose center, turn trapezoid right side up, then (a) roll pointed end at right toward middle, (b) fold back short top edge toward wrong side and apply bead of hot glue to lower edge, then (c) finish roll (illustrations C and D).

**4.** To build up rosebud, (a) apply hot glue to long velvet edge of new section, then (b) wrap it around rose center so its peak lines up with crossover edge (illustrations E and F).

**5.** Add remaining petals in same way. Position outer petals slightly lower on core so edges flare out. Compress base of rose with fingers (illustration G).

**6.** To add stem, bend one end of 6" length wire into loop. Apply spot of hot glue to base of rose and embed loop within ribbon folds (illustration H).

**7.** To add calyx, copy and enlarge pattern on page 46 so it measures 2⅞" across. Trace solid lines of pattern on page 46 and cut one calyx from green fabric. Fold and glue each sepal along dashed lines. Glue calyx to base of rose, inserting wire stem straight through center (illustration I).

**8.** To make leaves, glue silk leaves face down to wrong side of ribbon colored for leaves in step 1. Trim excess velvet even with leaf edge (illustration J).

**9.** Bind entire stem once with tape, then bind it again to attach leaf stems. Trim any loose threads from sepal tips. ◆

We created the slight pink tinge on the outer portion of this roses's petals by tinting a cream-colored ribbon with pink watercolor paint, then attached a store-bought leaf.

## Making Your Own Antique Velvet Roses

**A.** Apply paint along one edge of ribbon, let dry, and cut into seven 3½"- to 4"-long sections.

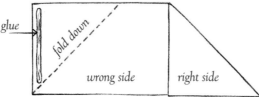

glue → fold down
wrong side     right side

**B.** Apply glue to each short end, then fold ends diagonally to make trapezoid.

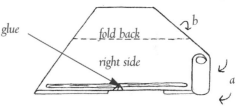

glue     fold back     b
right side     a

**C.** To make rose center, (a) roll pointed end at right toward middle, then (b) fold back top edge and apply glue to lower edge.

Position this crossover edge against velvet in step 4b

**D.** Finish rose center by rolling along lower edge (c).

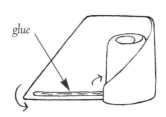

peak     glue

**E.** To build up rosebud, start by applying glue to long edge of new section.

glue

**F.** Then wrap long edge around rose center from step D.

**G.** Add remaining petals in same way.

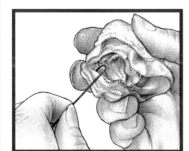

**H.** To add stem, apply glue to base and embed loop within folds.

**I.** Insert stem through center of calyx and glue calyx to rose base.

**J.** Glue leaves face down to wrong side of ribbon, then trim excess.

**K.** Bind entire stem with tape, then bind again to attach stems.

# Heirloom Father Christmas

*To create a proportional and lifelike doll, use these simple solutions: a wooden artist's manikin and a mold.*

☙ BY MAUREEN CARLSON

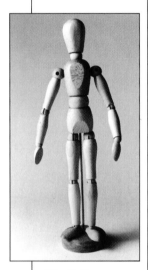

The Father Christmas doll is based on the jointed wooden artist's manikin pictured above.

DESIGNER'S TIP
If you find the Fimo clay difficult to knead, consider using Fimo's Mix Quick, a mixing medium that is designed to increase kneadability.

ILLUSTRATION:
Judy Love

COLOR PHOTOGRAPHY:
Carl Tremblay

FACE DETAIL:
Steven Mays

This version of the Father Christmas doll features a hand-sculpted face and glasslike eyes, which add to his sense of personality, but beginning doll makers should opt for making the face using a push mold.

LIKE MANY DOLL-MAKING PROJects, this Father Christmas doll presented two problems: how to produce a lifelike face easily and how to guarantee a proportional body. I created a realistic face by molding it out of modeling clay and using glasslike eyes, and solved the proportion issue by constructing the doll on a jointed wooden artist's manikin.

The face is easily the doll's most arresting feature. Its sense of character is due in part to the eyes and to the translucent quality of the skin tone, which is achieved with Fimo modeling clay. There are actually two techniques for making the doll's face: by sculpting, an art form that becomes easier and more controllable with practice, or by using a push mold. Experienced Fimo users may prefer to sculpt; although more challenging and time-consuming, this approach lets you develop a unique facial expression for the doll. The push mold, on the other hand, yields more consistent results in much less time and is better suited for beginning doll makers.

I chose a wooden manikin, available for about $12, as the armature because all the proportions are correct, and because the jointed arms and legs make the finished doll quite poseable. To give the doll's body shape and padding, I pulled a boy's white cotton tube sock over the doll form and stuffed it with fiberfill. This solution is much quicker than sewing a separate casing for the body, and the sock's natural give let me stuff it as full as I wanted.

The finishing touches include molding the doll's hands in a push mold and/or sewing mittens; gluing the hair and the beard of Tibetan lamb's wool; sewing and trimming the boots, mittens, gown, and coat; and dressing the finished doll. To speed the clothing construction, I sewed all the seams but glued the hems and trims with a fast-drying fabric glue. I found this last phase, during which I brought the face, body, and clothes together in a single figure, to be the most satisfying part of the entire project.

*Maureen Carlson, a clay artist, designer, and teacher, operates Wee Folk Creations in Prior Lake, Minnesota.*

## INSTRUCTIONS
### Preparing the Clay
*Note:* Wear lint-free clothing and work in a clean, dust-free environment when handling Fimo clay. Clean your hands with baby wipes before and during work as necessary. If the clay picks up small specks of dust or lint, pick them out with the tip of a knife blade.

**1.** Crumple 12" x 24" sheet foil around pencil to form head same size and shape as manikin head (*see* illustration A, below). Foil head can be slightly larger than manikin head but not smaller.

**2.** Lay sheet waxed paper on work surface. Cut clay into approximately twenty pieces. Warm pieces between palms, rolling and squeezing until they become pliable like putty. If crumbly texture persists, knead in small pieces of kneading medium, increasing volume by no more than 15 percent, until mix assumes uniform color. To make face and hands using push mold, proceed to next section. To hand-sculpt face, proceed to "Sculpting a Face," page 31.

FORMING THE HEAD

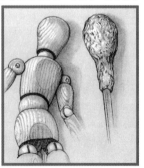

**A.** To form a head the same size and shape as the manikin's, crumple a sheet of aluminum foil around a pencil.

**B.** If sculpting the face, start by flattening a pancake and pressing it onto the foil head.

## Making a Push Mold Face and Hands

*Use illustrations K through N as a reference for these directions.*

**1.** Before filling mold, use #3 round brush to lightly dust interior of both molds with talc. Shape 1" ball of clay into Hershey's Kiss–shaped cone. Push cone tip into nose section of face mold, then compress remainder of clay to fill mold entirely without gaps.

**2.** To remove face from mold, immediately peel it from mold and hold in palm. Use blunt needle tool (or substitute) to open nostrils and deepen facial lines. Use sharp needle tool to push blue seed bead into each eye so bead hole forms pupil. Compress face in hand so eyelids droop around eyes. Set face on foil head and smooth edges against foil. Using filbert (or makeup) brush, apply pink chalk or matte blush to cheeks, lips, and nose, respectively.

**3.** To mold hands, shape two ⅞" balls of clay into two 2¼"-long sausages. Shape two-thirds of sausage into mitten to correspond to finger and thumb positions of mold. Press into mold, and remove any excess clay above mold surface. Peel hand from mold and shape wrist. Using blunt needle tool, smooth away mold marks around edges of fingers. Cut off forearm just above wrist, about 1½" from fingertips. Cut two straight 1½" lengths of hanger or wire and insert each into end of wrist so ¾" of hanger or wire protrudes.

**4.** To bake face, preheat oven to 235 degrees. Set molded head (attached to foil) and hands on baking sheet and bake 30 minutes. Turn off oven and let pieces cool in oven, about 2 hours.

## Sculpting a Face

**1.** To prepare base for face, flatten 1¼" ball of clay into pancake 2¼" in diameter and ¼" thick. Press onto foil head. (*see* illustration B, page 30).

**2.** To divide pancake into three equal sections, lightly etch two horizontal lines with blunt needle tool. To mark eye position, make two holes just below top line. To mark nose position, etch "U" above bottom line. Press handle of needle tool on each side of "U" to indent two eye sockets (illustration C).

**3** To divide lower third of face into three equal sections, lightly etch two horizontal lines. To mark mouth position, make crescent-shaped indentation on middle line. To begin nose, shape ⅜" ball of clay into narrow ¾"-tall pyramid. Place base of pyramid against "U," then press top between eye sockets to form bridge of nose (illustration D).

**4.** Blend edges of nose pyramid and eye sockets into face using blunt needle tool and/or fingertip. Shape lower half of nose. To begin lower lip, flatten ⅜" ball of clay into triangle ½" across at base. Keep base edge thick to form lip, but press rest of triangle flat. Repeat to form upper lip, starting with ¼" ball. Position both triangles over mouth opening so lips almost touch. Roll finger under bottom lip line to accentuate curve (illustration E). Blend outer edges into face.

**5.** To make cheeks, flatten two ½" balls of clay into two commas, concentrating bulk near centers and compressing ends until quite thin. Position commas on face as shown (illustration F) and blend in outer edges. Use blunt needle tool to deepen creases at each side of mouth.

**6.** To insert eyes, clip off wire extension at back of each eye. Press eyes into sockets with fingertip. To add forehead and brow, flatten ⅝" ball of clay into 1½" x ⅝" rectangle. Using handle of needle tool, press two indentations in one long side for eyes. Press forehead/brow onto face above eyes (illustration G) and blend in edges.

SCULPTING THE FACE

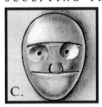

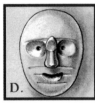

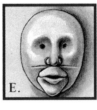

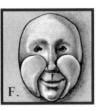

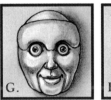

**Between sculpting steps, examine the face from all angles.**

### MATERIALS

- **12" wooden artist's manikin**
- **58-gram package flesh pink #43 Fimo modeling clay**
- **4" square Tibetan lambskin**
- **⅜ yard 45"-wide cranberry velvet**
- **⅜ yard 45"-wide green crushed velvet**
- **¾ yard 1½"-wide imitation white fur**
- **½ yard ½"-wide white flat braid trim**
- **½ yard ⅝"-wide gold metallic ribbon**
- **1¼ yards ⅛"-diameter white cord**
- **1⅓ yards narrow gold metallic cord**
- **½ yard narrow green cord**
- **4" x 6" piece off-white felt**
- **6" x 10" piece black felt**
- **1 boy's white cotton tube sock (shoe size 3 to 9)**
- **2-ounce containers acrylic paint, one each in brown and white**
- **Powdered pink chalk or matte blush makeup**
- **Fiberfill**
- **Friendly Plastic Arts & Crafts Goop glue**
- **Beacon FabriTac fabric glue**
- **Sewing thread to match fabrics and felt**
- **Patterns (see pages 46 and 47)**

*You'll also need:*
blunt and sharp needle tools or homemade substitutes (*see* "At-Home Tools," page 32); #2 filbert, #3 round, and #0 round paintbrushes; lid from plastic tub; waterless hand cleaner; disposable baby wipes; scissors; 2 pencils; ruler; aluminum foil; waxed paper; table knife; X-Acto knife; access to photocopier with enlarger; wire cutters; baking sheet; round toothpick; hand-sewing needle; pins; safety pin; and sewing machine.

*Other items, if necessary:*
What a Character push mold #10 Jolly Old Nick, What a Character push mold #11 Large Hands, 2 blue seed beads, Heavy Wire coat hanger or 16-gauge galvanized steel wire, *and* talcum powder (if molding face and/or hands using push mold); 1 pair 8mm acrylic eyes (if sculpting face); 180-gram package Fimo Mix Quick kneading medium (for softening Fimo clay); mirror (for spotting irregularities in sculpted face); tiny wrapped boxes and/or miniature toys (for stuffing bag).

USING THE PUSH MOLDS

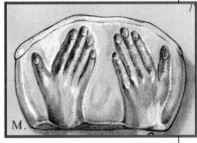

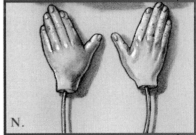

**Before using a mold, dust the inside with talcum powder. This will prevent the clay from leaving extremities behind.**

FILLING OUT THE DOLL'S BODY

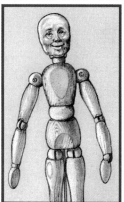

**O.** Test-fit the Father Christmas face on the manikin head, then use Goop glue to affix the face.

**P.** Cut the cuff up to the manikin's crotch in front and back, then hand-sew the cut edges together.

**Q.** To pad the doll's body around his belly, fill the sock with fiberfill.

**R.** Sew the sock closed at the shoulders, then use long stitches to anchor the fiberfill.

## DESIGNER'S TIP

**At-Home Tools**
Two of my favorite tools for hand-sculpting a doll's face are ones I make myself. Purchase a blunt tapestry needle and a sharp darning needle. Make handles for each from balls of Fimo clay that have been rolled into sausages. Insert the needles into one end of each handle. Smooth the other end until round. Bake the handles at 265 degrees for thirty minutes, then let them cool in the oven for two hours.—M.C.

---

**7.** To add eyelid folds, roll six ³⁄₁₆" balls of clay into six short sausages, then flatten. Place one "fold" under each eye, one above, and one angled across each outside corner connecting to forehead/brow (illustration H). Blend seams but leave crease between two folds above eye.

**8.** Study face from various angles to evaluate work. To spot irregularities, turn face upside down or view in mirror. Refine features by resmoothing edges as necessary. Use blunt needle tool to open up nostrils, build up chin and forehead, deepen circles under eyes, and part lips slightly. Once features are well defined, press sharp needle tool into face around eyes and mouth to create smile lines. To deepen smile lines around eyes, gently push up on cheeks. Using filbert (or makeup) brush, apply pink chalk or matte blush to cheeks, lips, and nose, respectively. Trim edges of face for clean finish (illustrations I and J).

**9.** To bake face, preheat oven to 235 degrees. Set sculpted head (attached to foil) on baking sheet and bake 30 minutes. Turn off oven and let cool in oven, about 2 hours.

### Assembling and Dressing the Manikin

**1.** Test-fit baked face on manikin head, using X-Acto knife to scrape off any clay that prevents snug fit. Affix face to head with Goop glue (illustration O). To attach hands, unscrew wooden hands from manikin and glue wire end of molded hands inside wrist sockets. Let glue dry overnight.

**2.** To create lashes, paint very thin brown line above and below eyes using #0 fine brush. For eyebrows, brush white paint in short upward strokes above each eye along edge of forehead. To shade eyebrows, mix small amount of white and brown paint on plastic lid.

**3.** To create body for stuffing, measure 10" from cuff end of tube sock and mark with pin. Cut straight across sock at pin; discard toe section. Place cut piece, cuff first, over manikin head and slide down to cover legs. Cut cuff up to manikin crotch in front and back (illustration P). Remove manikin from stand. Using white thread, hand-sew cut edges together to form sock around legs. Replace manikin on stand. Stuff fiberfill into sock to pad body (illustration Q), then sew sock closed at shoulders. Sew long basting stitches around crotch and through body to anchor fiberfill (illustration R).

**4.** Copy and enlarge robe/gown, hood, boot, and sole patterns on pages 46 and 47 to specified lengths. From red velvet, cut one coat back on fold, two coat fronts (reverse one), and one hood. From green velvet, cut one gown front and one gown back, both on fold, as well as one 9" x 13" rectangle for sack. From black felt, cut two boots on fold and two soles.

**5.** Copy and enlarge mitten pattern on page 47 to specified length, making two tracings of pattern. Cut white felt in half, stack pieces, and pin both tracings on top. Stitch along curved lines of each tracing; leave straight wrist edge open. Cut out mittens ⅛" beyond stitching and wrist line. Tear away tracing paper. Turn mittens right side out and place on molded hands. If not using molded hands, then stuff mittens with fiberfill. Slip mittens onto manikin hands.

**6.** To sew boots, fold each one in half, right side inwards, and stitch ⅛" from curved edge. Hand-sew sole into bottom opening, matching dots. Turn right side out. Stuff toes with fiberfill and slip boots onto manikin. Poke extra fiberfill around ankles until boots are firm.

**7.** To assemble gown, stack front and back, right sides together, and sew shoulder and side/underarm seams ¼" from edge. Turn hem ½" to wrong side and glue. Work short segments at a time, since FabriTac glue sets up quickly. Turn neck edge of gown ¼" to wrong side and hand-baste. Turn right side out. Slip gown over manikin, gather neckline around neck, and tie off. Cut one 20" length from white cord and two 24" lengths from gold cord. Braid together, then tie braided cord around gown waist.

**8.** To assemble coat, stack left and right coat fronts on coat back, right sides together, and sew side/underarm seams ¼" from edge. Turn lower hem and long raw edges of left and right fronts ½" to *right* side and glue. Cut gold ribbon and white braid trim into two 9" lengths. Glue ribbon, topped by braid, down each front to conceal lapped edge. Cut 18" strip white imitation fur and glue to lower hem to conceal lapped edge. Glue 18" strip from remaining white cord to coat just above fur hem. Refold coat, right side inward, and sew shoulder seams. Turn each wrist edge ½" to right side, and glue in place. Cut and glue remaining fur and white cord to wrists.

**9.** To assemble hood, fold long edge ¾" to wrong side and glue to form face edge. Fold hood in half, right side inwards, and stitch from A to B. Hand-baste neck edges of hood and coat and pull threads to gather. Pin both neck edges together, right sides facing, and hand-sew. Set coat aside.

**10.** To add hair and beard, examine lambskin from front to identify fullest area. Turn wool side down, and sketch face-sized oval on skin, with hair growth in "long" direction of oval. Sketch second concentric oval about ⅝" beyond first oval. Using X-Acto knife, cut on both oval lines through skin only (try not to cut long hairs). Test-fit "doughnut" around Santa face, then glue using FabriTac. To hide lambskin edge and create more natural appearance, cut locks of wool and glue to chin and forehead. To make mustache, cut two locks slightly longer than desired length, apply glue to cut ends, and let dry until stiff. Trim stiffened ends, then glue just below nose.

**11.** To make sack, fold green velvet rectangle in half, right sides together, to make 4½" by 13" rectangle, then stitch ¼" from edge along three edges. Fold raw edge ¾" to wrong side and sew ½" from fold all around to make casing. Turn sack right side out. Open up a few stitches in seam and thread green cord through casing using safety pin. Stuff sack three-quarters full with fiberfill and, if desired, top off with small wrapped packages and/or miniatures. Pull drawstring partially closed. Tie sack on doll arm. Trim drawstring and knot ends. ◆

# Secrets of Candied Violet and Holly Holiday Decorations

*Forget buying candied violets. The trick to making your own: gumdrops and a simple thumb-press method.*

BY CANDIE FRANKEL

**Add these quick and easy holly and violet decorations to your Christmas cookies, a flat white cake, or individual servings of dessert. For variation, try building roses from red gum drops, daisies from white or yellow gum drops (use a small piece of black gum drop for a pistil), or make up your own flowers using a variety of shapes and colors.**

CANDIED VIOLETS, USUALLY found in gourmet and specialty shops, are an expensive but beautiful decoration for holiday cakes. You can make your own cheaply and in just minutes, however, by flattening a gumdrop with your thumb and molding the petal shapes with your fingers.

I tested a variety of gumdrops, including Chuckles Spice Sticks & Drops, Chuckles Jelly Rings, Brach's Spicettes, and Sunkist Fruit Gems. All the brands offered a purple gumdrop (ideal for making violets) except for Sunkist and Chuckles Jelly Rings. Chuckles Spice Sticks & Drops offered the richest shade of purple; the color was slightly darker and definitely more appealing than the other brands.

I then focused on finding a way to flatten the gumdrop so I could shape the petals and leaves. First, I placed a single gumdrop between two sheets of waxed paper and rolled over it with a rolling pin. The flattened gumdrop, however, stuck to the waxed paper and ripped when I tried removing the paper. I added granulated sugar and rerolled the gumdrop, but the disk was uneven and lumpy. By chance, a second—and superior—flattening method emerged. I pressed down on the gumdrop with my thumb to flatten it before rolling it with the pin. As it turned out, the rolling pin was unnecessary—the thumb-press method worked fine alone.

Once the disk was flattened, I tried several methods of hand-molding the flower and leaf shapes. For the violets, I began by pinching the bottom of the disk and gathering the candy together at the bottom, which formed the disk into several soft folds at the top. To further define the petals, I cut down into the folds, but the single petals were uneven and a few fell off. So, I tried cutting the petal sections before gathering them into a flower shape, and found that approach allowed me to construct more uniform petals.

The leaves were easy because several could be formed separately from a single gumdrop rolled flat. To make a holly leaf, I flattened a green gumdrop with my thumb, then simply pulled away some candy at each side to create reverse scallops. I rolled holly berries with small pieces of red gumdrop.

### MATERIALS

- **Purple, green, red, and yellow gumdrops**
- **Granulated sugar**

*You'll also need:* waxed paper; teaspoon; and paring knife.

## INSTRUCTIONS

### Violets and Leaves

**1.** Drop heaping teaspoon granulated sugar on waxed paper. Set purple gumdrop on sugar mound. Press down on gumdrop with thumb (*see* illustration A, top right). Release thumb, sprinkle with sugar to prevent sticking, then repeat until disk forms. Flip disk over. Continue pressing, sugaring, and flipping until disk is approximately 1" in diameter and 3/16" in thickness.

**2.** Use tip of knife blade to make five 1/4"-long cuts in gumdrop. Space each cut evenly around edge of gumdrop disk (illustration B).

**3.** To form petal with slightly pointed tip, pinch each cut section between thumb and forefinger (illustration C).

**4.** To draw out and shape short stem on back of flower, cup five petals up toward center. Then squeeze and elongate stem from behind with fingers of other hand (illustration D).

**5.** To finish, gently manipulate petals so they overlap slightly. To make pistil, pinch off small piece from yellow gumdrop, roll into 3/16" ball, sugaring as needed, and place in center of violet (illustration E).

**6.** To make leaves, flatten green gumdrop (as in step 1) into disk 1 1/4" in diameter and 1/8" thick. Tear flattened gumdrop into four wedges. Pinch point of each wedge to form stem, then mold curved edge into heart shape.

**7.** To assemble flower, pinch violet stem and several leaf stems together until they adhere.

**DESIGNER'S TIP**
For a flower with larger dimension, construct single petals from one gum drop. Using this method, you can also mix gum drops to create a flower with different colored petals.

### Holly and Berries

**1.** Following step 1 of "Violets and Leaves," above, flatten green gumdrop into disk 1 1/8" in diameter and 1/4" thick.

**2.** Using fingertips, pull away small portions of leaf to form reverse scallops. Score vein down center of leaf.

**3.** To make berries, pinch off small bits from red gumdrop and roll into 3/16" balls, sugaring as needed, and place in small cluster at one end of leaf. ◆

**A.** Flatten the gumdrop.

**B.** Cut the edge five times.

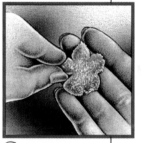

**C.** Pinch the cut sections.

**D.** Form the stem in back.

**E.** Roll a ball for the pistil.

ILLUSTRATION:
**Harry Davis**

COLOR PHOTOGRAPHY:
**Steven Mays**

# The Best Way to Tie Multiloop Bows

*Use our ripple technique to tie an infinite number of bows from homemade or store-bought wire-edged ribbon.*

❧ BY CANDIE FRANKEL

**Using our simple formula, you can tie bows of any size for use on packages, wreaths, or doors.**

TO MAKE A LARGE BOW FOR A wreath or gift package, I use wire-edged ribbon. Because it holds its shape, I can form large, full loops that give the finished bow volume and a sculptural quality not possible with ordinary ribbon. For the best way to tie bows from wire-edged ribbon, I recommend the continuous ripple technique.

I tested several different approaches to tying the bows. First, I tied two shoelace-style bows, one on top of the other. This method gave me four loops extending from a fist of knots. I next considered the notched bow method used by commercial stationers. A length of ribbon is wound lasso-style, then notched and tied in the center with a separate string. The multiple loops are next lifted out and separated in a pouf. I rejected this method since cutting into the wire-edged ribbon would fray it, therefore ruining it for future use.

The method I finally adopted was inspired by ribbon candy, which is made by folding a strip of candy back on itself in a continuous ripple. I applied the same basic principle when tying ribbon. I started with a length of ribbon two yards long. I stretched an eighteen-inch section across the tabletop, then doubled back twelve inches to form the first loop and one of two streamers. I continued forming loops in this way until I used up all the ribbon, then I tied the stack of multiple loops at the center with a separate length of ribbon. This separate ribbon tie gave me an additional two streamer ends.

I continued my experimentation with this ripple method of bow making, using increasingly longer lengths of ribbon, to make two-, four-, six-, and eight-loop bows. (An even number of loops is essential if you want the streamer ends to fall to the opposite sides of the bow.)

I then tested my technique with a variety of ribbon widths, from a little less than one inch wide to up to four inches wide, and each one yielded a new lesson in proportion. In general, the wider the ribbon, the greater the number and size of loops required for a beautiful presentation. Narrow ribbon needs small loops so they don't appear floppy or skimpy.

I've consolidated the proportions I prefer in chart form (*see* chart 1, below) to make your ribbon-tying projects less exploratory than mine were. Once you find a ribbon in a color and width you like, use chart 2, next page, to determine how much yardage to buy. The basic construction method is the same no matter what width ribbon you use or how many loops you make. The measurements shown in the illustrations on the next page are for two-and-one-half-inch-wide ribbon. If using ribbons of other widths, substitute the appropriate

## CHART 1: ASSEMBLY MEASUREMENTS

**Substitute the measurements in this chart for those in the illustrations to make bows from ribbons of varying widths.**

| RIBBON WIDTH | LENGTH FOR TIE (STEP 1) | FOLDOVER LENGTH (STEP 2) | STREAMER END/LOOP LENGTH |
|---|---|---|---|
| ⅞"-1½" | 12" | 9" | 3", 6" |
| 1½"- 2" | 16" | 12" | 4", 8" |
| 2"-2½" | 20" | 15" | 5", 10" |
| 2½"-4" | 24" | 18" | 6", 12" |

measurement from the chart above. To measure the ribbon as you work, lay a yardstick on the work surface and hold the ribbon alongside it.

*Note:* Be sure to select a double-faced ribbon, that is, viewable from both sides. If you choose a ribbon with a "right" and a "wrong" side, half of your loops will appear inside out.

One other caveat: To avoid fraying, don't notch the streamer ends until after the bow is complete. ◆

Use this chart to determine the length of ribbon needed for different size bows. For widths that fall in two ranges (1½", 2", and 2½"), I typically lean toward the longer yardage for 6- and 8-loop bows, but prefer the shorter yardage for 2- and 4-loop bows to keep the loops from appearing too spindly. Those marked with asterisks (***) are not recommended.

| RIBBON WIDTH | 2-LOOP BOW | 4-LOOP BOW | 6-LOOP BOW | 8-LOOP BOW |
|---|---|---|---|---|
| ⅞"-1½" | 1 yard | 1⅓ yards | 1⅔ yards | 2 yards |
| 1½"- 2" | 1⅓ yards | 1¾ yards | 2¼ yards | 2⅔ yards |
| 2"-2½" | *** | 2¼ yards | 2¾ yards | 3⅓ yards |
| 2½"-4" | *** | *** | 3⅓ yards | 4 yards |

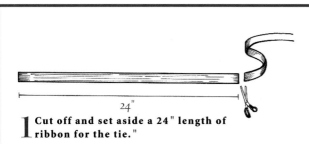

24"

**1** Cut off and set aside a 24" length of ribbon for the tie."

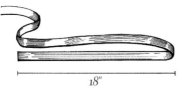

18"

**2** Measure an 18" length of the longer ribbon, then fold the ribbon back on itself in order to form loop 1.

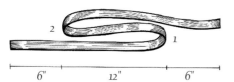

2

1

6"   12"   6"

TWO-LOOP BOW

**2a** Fold the ribbon back on itself 12" to form loop 2. Skip to step 3 to complete the two-loop bow, or proceed to the next step in order to make a four-, six-, or eight-loop bow.

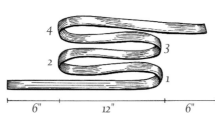

4

2

3

1

6"   12"   6"

FOUR-LOOP BOW

**2b** Fold the ribbon two more times, even with the two previous folds, to add loops 3 and 4. Skip to step 3 in order to complete the four-loop bow, or proceed to the next step.

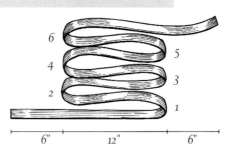

6

4

2

5

3

1

6"   12"   6"

SIX-LOOP BOW

**2c** Fold the ribbon two more times, even with the four previous folds, to add loops 5 and 6. Skip to step 3 in order to complete the six-loop bow, or proceed to the next step.

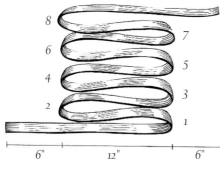

8

6

4

2

7

5

3

1

6"   12"   6"

EIGHT-LOOP BOW

**2d** Fold the ribbon two more times, even with the six previous folds, to add loops 7 and 8. Proceed to step 3 in order to complete the eight-loop bow.

**3** Tie the reserved streamer ribbon around the center of the loops to secure them, then turn the streamers so the knot falls at the back of the bow. Fluff and arrange the loops and streamers.

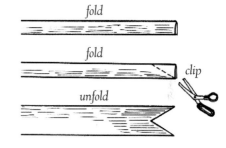

fold

fold

unfold

clip

**4** To notch the four streamer ends, fold each streamer lengthwise, then clip in diagonally towards the fold.

TWO-LOOP BOW          FOUR-LOOP BOW          SIX-LOOP BOW          EIGHT-LOOP BOW

# Tulle-Wrapped Ornament

*Recycle a tired ornament by wrapping it in tulle decorated with glitter fabric paint.*

🐚 BY CAROL ENDLER STERBENZ

**Use these tulle-wrapped ornaments to decorate a tree, a chandelier, a window, or a garland. Or make a set of three balls and box them for a quick and easy hostess or party gift.**

**DESIGNER'S TIP**
**For a variation on this design, consider wrapping your ornaments in squares or circles of lace, chiffon, organza, georgette, or other lightweight, drapey fabrics.**

ILLUSTRATION:
**Nenad Jakesevic**

COLOR PHOTOGRAPHY:
**Steven Mays**

ONE FAST AND EASY WAY TO recycle old ornaments is to wrap them in a square or circle of fabric, then tie off the fabric with a festive cord or ribbon. While ordinary fabric isn't really special enough for the holidays, I turned to tulle, a very fine nylon netting used in bridal wear, and decorated it with gold glitter fabric paint.

At first, I applied the decorations with a glitter pen. The glitter, however, seeped right through the tulle, leaving no design on the fabric at all. Next, I tried Tulip Glitter Fabric Paint, which, when applied, sat up and held onto the ultrathin netting.

Even with the use of Tulip Glitter, I still needed a backing that would help hold the glitter glue in the tulle (and protect my work surface) yet be flexible enough to pull off when the glue was dry. I tested both plastic wrap and waxed paper. Plastic wrap was too flexible and lightweight, and the paint stuck to it, making it difficult to remove the tulle without pulling off some of the glitter. Waxed paper, on the other

hand, helped the paint to cure, minimized sticking, and stabilized the tulle during the final cutting.

I made both square and round veils, using a ten-inch dinner plate as a template for the latter. For color variation, try drawing the designs using red, blue, silver, or green fabric paint, then wrapping the tulle around a ball of a contrasting color.

**INSTRUCTIONS**

**1.** Protect work surface with waxed paper. Cut tulle in fourths to yield four 18" squares. Lay squares on waxed paper without overlapping and tape down corners. Center plate face down on one square. Squeezing gently, apply glitter paint onto scrap paper to test flow, then use paint to draw circle or square design on each tulle square as follows.

**2.** *To create the circular design:* Using edge of plate as guide, draw wavy line ½" from edge of plate all around (*see illustration A*). Carefully remove plate. Add circle of dots just inside wavy line, touching down applicator tip to surface every ¼" to ½". Repeat to add one or two additional circles of dots.

**3.** *To create the square design:* Using outer edge of tulle square as reference, draw square on tulle ½" beyond edge of plate. Do not stop flow of glitter paint at corners, but make right angle turns and continue drawing until you reach starting point. Carefully remove plate, then fill interior of square with lines of dots radiating from center out to four corners and edges.

**4.** Let paint cure overnight. When dry to touch, cut all around outer cured edge of each circle or square through tulle and waxed paper (illustration B). Peel up tulle and discard paper.

**5.** Clean balls with glass cleaner. Wrap tulle veils around each ball (illustration C), drawing them together at neck of ball, and fasten with wire tie. If desired, wind ribbon around balls by dividing it into four equal segments and anchoring ends in wire tie after winding. To further decorate balls, accent them with small silver bells, clusters of silk flowers, crystal beads, or other small trinkets. ◆

MAKING THE TULLE-WRAPPED BALL

**A.** **Place the plate face down on the tulle. To create the circular design, draw a wavy line with glitter paint around the plate.**

**B.** **Let the glitter paint cure overnight, then cut all around the outer edge. Peel up the tulle and discard the waxed paper.**

**C.** **To complete the ornament, wrap the tulle veil around the ball, drawing it together at the neck.**

# 10-Minute Tassel Place Mat

*Quick-sew a place mat that's roomy enough for holiday place settings and elegant enough to replace a tablecloth.*

❧ BY MICHIO RYAN

**You can make a set of eight matching place mats from five and one-third yards of the same material or make each place mat from different fabric.**

THE PROBLEM WITH PLACE MATS is twofold: They're too casual for an elegant holiday table, and they're not large enough to accommodate the extra forks, spoons, and glasses used in holiday entertaining. I overcame both drawbacks by designing an oversized twenty-one-inch-by-twenty-two-inch place mat from more formal fabric.

To determine overall size, I gathered a full place setting of silver, china, and crystal. The breadth of the arrangement suggested a rectangle measuring twenty-one by twenty-two inches. My next task was to locate a wide fabric with a formal pattern. The final measurements of the place mat provided two options: apparel- or soft furnishing-weight fabric.

When designing the shape of the place mat, I considered its relationship to other place settings and the overall effect of laying several mats in a continuous line, aspects that would affect drama and formality. Since tablecloths traditionally drape over the side of the table, I decided to design the front of the place mat to drape over the table edge. To add interest, I cut the bottom section of the place mat into a point and accented it with a tassel. This embellishment made my table even more festive. ◆

---

**MATERIALS**
*Yields 2 place mats*

- 1⅓ yards 45"-wide apparel- or soft furnishing-weight fabric
- Two 2" tassels with loop
- Matching sewing thread

*You'll also need:*
place mat pattern (*see page 47*); access to photocopier with enlargement feature; sewing machine; iron; scissors and/or rotary cutter; pins; ruler; and hand-sewing needle.

---

## Making the Tassel Place Mat

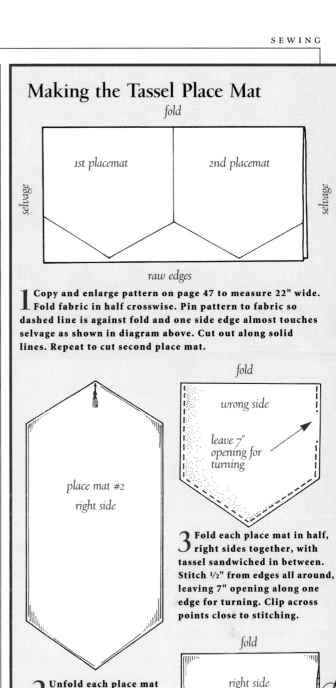

1. Copy and enlarge pattern on page 47 to measure 22" wide. Fold fabric in half crosswise. Pin pattern to fabric so dashed line is against fold and one side edge almost touches selvage as shown in diagram above. Cut out along solid lines. Repeat to cut second place mat.

2. Unfold each place mat and lay it right side up. Place tassel loop across one point and machine-baste loop in place. Repeat for second place mat.

3. Fold each place mat in half, right sides together, with tassel sandwiched in between. Stitch ½" from edges all around, leaving 7" opening along one edge for turning. Clip across points close to stitching.

4. To finish, turn place mat right side out. Pick out points with pin, and press. Slip-stitch opening closed.

---

**DESIGNER'S TIP**
Caring for place mats is similar to caring for any fine linen. Spot clean stains immediately, then have the place mats dry cleaned.

ILLUSTRATION:
**Mary Newell DePalma**

COLOR PHOTOGRAPHY:
**Steven Mays**

# Buyer's Guide to Rubber Stamps

*Understanding the basics of how rubber stamps are made can help you predict the quality of the image before you stamp.*

**❧ BY FRANCOISE HARDY**

## TIPS AND TECHNIQUES

- To simulate the blur of rapid movement, stamp your image and then slide it in the direction from which your image is coming without lifting the stamp.

- Make a fade-out image by stamping the image, then stamping again next to it without reinking to create a fainter image. Tilt the stamp to keep from overprinting.

- For other movement effects, ink a small makeup sponge or wedge and paint in a streak as the after-image, or simply use a pen or marker to make a few sketchy lines behind the object.

- Quotation marks can make the image appear to shake or wiggle.

You can create a wide variety of gift tags and cards for holiday gift giving using rubber stamps. For added interest, make a deckle edge for each tag with pinking shears or emboss your stamped images.

## HAVING A RUBBER STAMP MADE COMMERCIALLY

If you find an intricate design that would make a good rubber stamp, it's possible to have a stamp commercially made. Check your local yellow pages under "Rubber Stamps," or check with a local stationery store or printer. (See Sources and Resources for mail-order sources.) Prices typically range from $2.75 to $5 for rubber stamps made from stock images; custom images range from $5 to $21 or more depending on the size of the resulting stamp.

THE MARKET FOR RUBBER STAMPS has expanded very quickly over the past several years, bringing with it hundreds of new products and special techniques. The choices can be overwhelming, but a basic understanding of how rubber stamps are made and what types of inks and paper are available will help you predict the quality of the stamped image before you ever make your purchase.

For this article, we investigated only rubber stamps since they are readily available in a wide variety of designs and are reasonably priced (starting at around $3). Although other types of stamps are available (i.e., hardened plastic, magnet-backed, and clear Plexiglas), rubber stamps hold the shape of the image and stand up to frequent use better than other types.

A rubber stamp has three parts: an image set in relief on a slab of rubber (the die), a block of wood that serves as a handle, and an intervening layer of foam or rubber that elevates the die on the block. Though all stamps share this common construction, there are crucial differences among them that affect the quality of the stamped images.

### How Rubber Stamps Are Made

The process of creating a rubber stamp begins with the selection of a black and white illustration. The image's lines must be crisp; if they are smudged or uneven, or the detail is crowded into too small an area, they will not reproduce on a stamp. Once an illustration is chosen, it is photographed and made into a very high-contrast negative with strong black and white tones. This negative is used to create a contact print for the plate engraver.

The engraver then chemically transfers the image onto a plate, which is exposed to a very intense white light source, then rinsed and placed in a nitric acid bath. The nitric acid eats away the unexposed portions of the plate, leaving the positive image etched into the plate.

The thickness of the engraved plate is important because it determines the height of the die's relief. The deeper the etching, the higher the relief, and the better the stamped image.

The next step in the process requires a vulcanizer, a specialized machine that uses heat and hydraulics to impress the image from the engraved plate onto a plastic mold, imprinting a reverse version of the image.

The shallower the imprint on the mold, the lower the relief on the rubber stamp, and the greater the chance of printing halos (faint impressions from the areas around the die) and smudges. This is caused by the wood block hitting the ink pad and carrying ink to the paper. A low relief can also cause bottoming out, in which the areas in between the die's relief end up printing. (*See* samples, page 39.)

The mold is filled with gum rubber to create the unmounted rubber stamp. The red or gray gum rubber, which comes in eighteen-inch rolls, is forced into the mold and cured. The resulting sheet contains multiple dies, which are then carefully trimmed. The trimming process is important, as trimming too close to or just slightly under the die can weaken the support for the outline of the image, in turn creating a poor print.

Finally, the die is mounted on its handle. First, it is adhered with rubber cement to a foam cushion about one-sixteenth inch thick. After trimming of the cushion by hand, the die/cushion is glued onto a block of wood. The image is then recorded on the wood block in one of two ways: by stamping it directly on the varnished wood block or stamping it on a separate piece of plastic, which is then glued to the wood block. It is important that the stamped reference and stamp actually correspond; otherwise how would you know which way was up?

## Before You Buy

Before you buy a stamp, check for the following requirements:

**1.** The die on the stamp should be deep and even; if the relief is too low and/or close to the cushion, the floor of the stamp can bottom out. A low relief can also cause halos.

**2.** If the die has uneven spots, or bubbles are present on the stamp's floor, the stamped image will mirror these flaws.

**3.** Examine the height of the cushion. If it is too thin or untrimmed, it will print halos or smudges, or print unevenly.

**4.** The wooden block should be sealed with some kind of shellac or varnish and indexed with a clean representation of the stamped image.

**5.** The block should also fit the size of the image. In other words, the die should not hang over the edge or be lost in the middle. If there is too much block around the die, the stamp tends to rock, which can also cause halos or smudges.

## Selecting Your Ink and Paper

After you've chosen a rubber stamp, you'll need ink and paper. Keep in mind that a direct correlation exists between the quality of the stamped image and your choice of ink and paper. In general, the runnier the ink, the less porous or absorbent the paper should be. If you use a thin, runny ink on a highly absorbent paper, the color will bleed.

There are two primary types of ink. Dye-based inks are thin, are more likely to bleed, and leave a more transparent image. Pigment-based inks are denser and somewhat thicker than dye-based inks, don't bleed as easily, and leave a rich, opaque image.

Ink comes in a variety of containers, including bottles, pads, and pens, but pads are the best place to start. Dye-based inks come on a fabric-covered felt pad that has been soaked with ink while pigment-based inks come on felt or foam. Though pigment-based pads are more expensive than dye-based pads, they are available in a wider and more brilliant range of colors, including pastels and metallic tones.

A wide selection of paper is available for stamp projects. In order to determine which paper works best with which ink, I stamped a leaf image using both types of ink on fourteen different types of paper. With both types of ink, I found that the smoother the paper, the cleaner the stamped image. The more textured the paper, the more mottled the line. For the brightest and cleanest image, I recommend a bright white, smooth-surfaced paper in glossy or matte finish. ◆

*Francoise Hardy, of Boston, enjoys crafts and paper projects in her free time.*

## Common Stamping Problems

This stamp was created with Design-A-Stamp. Because the die is very close to the wood block, with no intervening foam cushion, it's possible for the wood block to pick up and print ink.

A halo, or a faint impression from the area around the die, can be caused by low relief on the die.

This image suffers from two problems. The stamp was overinked, which caused the leaf's veins to fill in. In addition, by pressing too hard on the stamp, we caused it to bottom out, meaning the area next to the die's relief picks up and prints ink.

## How to Emboss Images

One of the easiest ways to customize your rubber stamp projects is by embossing, a process that gives the image a raised, finished look.

For this process, you'll need embossing powder, which come in a range of finishes, from clear and opalescent to metallic, tinsel, and enamelware. Clear and opalescent powders take on the color of whatever ink was used to make the original image whereas colored opaque powders, like gold, silver, and copper, will hide the underlying color of ink. Sold in one-half- and one-ounce jars, prices range from $2.50 to $5.

**MATERIALS**
- Rubber stamp
- Pigment-based ink
- Paper
- Embossing powder

*You'll also need:* toaster or toaster oven; narrow brush; and scrap paper.

**1** Stamp image on bright white and smooth-surfaced paper.

**2** While ink is still wet, sprinkle powder over image. Tap off excess powder onto scrap paper and funnel into original container for future use. Dab off any stray particles with brush.

**3** Hold paper face up over hot toaster, or set paper face up in 350-degree toaster oven with door open. Melt powder 20 to 30 seconds, then remove paper and allow to cool.

Start by stamping the image using pigment-based ink (you *cannot* use regular dye-based ink), then sprinkle it with embossing powder. Heat the powdered image using any 300- to 400-degree heat source, such as a toaster oven or heated toaster. You can also use a heat gun, available in craft stores at a cost between $18 and $25. Don't overheat the image as this can cause the powder to soak into the paper, making the image appear flat or dull.

# How to Cut Your Own Rubber Stamp

### BY SYLVIA LACHTER

Although a wide variety of commercially produced rubber stamps are available, there are advantages to cutting your own. For starters, you're assured that no one else will have your image. Secondly, there's a certain satisfaction in making your own tools.

Don't expect the fine-lined, detailed stamps available at craft and rubber-stamp stores, however. The key in cutting your own is to select simple shapes that are easy to draw or trace and that can be cut out from an eraser or rubber slab using an X-Acto knife. (*See* accompanying story, "Testing Materials for Cutting Your Own Rubber Stamp," below.)

For the best results,

seek out designs that look good in solid chunks of color or shapes with simple silhouettes. If you're especially bold and creative, you can draw directly onto your eraser, but it helps to practice the design on paper. Sketch, copy freehand, or photocopy your image.

I've tested a number of ways to transfer designs to an eraser or rubber slab. My preferred method is to trace the image, fill in the "print" areas using a pencil, lay the tracing face down on the eraser, and rub a pencil

across the back, which will transfer the image to the eraser (*see* illustrations, below).

When carving the rubber, keep these points in mind. Whatever you cut away will end up being the color of your paper, and whatever you leave will become the inked image. In addition, your printed image will be a mirror image of the rubber stamp.

The #11 X-Acto blade is my favorite all-purpose tool, as it's good for everything from trimming the outline to cutting out fine details on the inside of your stamp.

## MATERIALS

- **Eberhard Faber Magic Rub eraser or substitute**

*You'll also need:* design source; X-Acto knife with #11 blade; #2 lead pencil; tracing paper; and self-healing cutting mat.

*Other items, if necessary:* X-Acto knife with #151 U-veiner blade (for cutting angled lines).

Remember to always cut away from the image. Using a straight edge or the X-Acto, first roughly chop down the

eraser close to the outer edges of your design. Save good-sized chunks for ministamps, tiny stars, bubbles, or exclamation points. Then start cutting at an angle away from the outline, and trim the whole design. Remember, it doesn't have to be perfect, and the circles don't have to be absolutely round.

---

*Sylvia Lachter, a freelance producer and stylist, now creates all her own stationery and cards. Special thanks to Marie Browning for consulting on this piece.*

## MAKING YOUR OWN RUBBER STAMP

**1** **Trace image from design source or draw your own. Fill in all "print" areas of image using pencil.**

**2** **Lay tracing face down on eraser. Rub pencil across back of tracing, then lift off to reveal image.**

**3** **Cut away all light areas of image from eraser. Cut details first, then outer edges.**

**4** **Press completed stamp on stamp pad to load ink and make prints.**

---

# Testing Materials for Making Your Own Rubber Stamp

### BY CANDIE FRANKEL

The most versatile performer, capable of handling curves, intricate cuts, and details such as veining, was Eberhard Faber's Magic Rub.

The familiar Pink Pearl eraser, also made by Eberhard Faber, proved denser and firmer than the Magic Rub, making it more difficult to cut accurately. Since I couldn't follow my drawn lines exactly with the X-Acto blade, the

stamps had a cruder woodcut quality, but they still printed sharp and clear.

Speedball's Speedy Cut Printing Block is designed for linoleum print–type projects in which a design is carved in relief on the surface of the block using special tools. When I tried cutting shapes from the block, the material tended to crumble and the cut edges produced granular particles that no amount of swabbing or wiping

would remove. While the prints were clear around the edges, the interior was grainy, not smooth and even.

Design-A-Stamp features two thin sheets of spongy material that can be cut with scissors into various shapes. An adhesive back lets you affix each cutout to a small block of wood for an easy-to-handle stamp. Stamps printed from this material had a spongy texture not nearly as dark and rich as my

eraser stamps, and the material was not really sturdy enough to etch details with an X-Acto knife with any predictability or accuracy. In addition, because the material is mounted directly on the wood block without an intervening layer of foam rubber, there is a greater chance that the wood block can pick up ink (*see* sample, page 39). The product was easy to use, however, and is a good alternative for children who are too young

to handle an X-Acto knife.

The third eraser I tested, the Design kneaded rubber eraser, was easy to cut into simple shapes but not capable of fine details. For simple, solid shapes, however, the print quality was superior, showing crisply defined edges and a dark, velvety interior. It was difficult to cut fine details, however, because the rubber gummed up the crevices as I was cutting them.

### PERFORMANCE KEY
★★★ Above average
★★ Average
★ Poor

| Type or Brand | Size | Quantity/Price | Cutting Ease | Print Quality | Overall Rating |
|---|---|---|---|---|---|
| 1. **Design kneaded rubber eraser** | 1¾" x 1¼" x ¼" | $1.59 each | ★ | ★★★ | ★★ |
| 2. **Eberhard Faber Magic Rub** | 2¼" x 1" x 7⁄16" | 3 for $1.75 | ★★★ | ★★★ | ★★★ |
| 3. **Eberhard Pink Pearl** | 13⁄16" x 2" x 3⁄8" | 3 for $1.49 | ★★ | ★★★ | ★★ |
| 4. **Speedball Speedy Cut Printing Block** | 3" x 4" x 3⁄8" | $1.59 each* | ★ | ★★ | ★ |
| 5. **Design-a-Stamp** | 8" x 9" x 1⁄16" | 2 for $5.95 | ★★★ | ★ | ★★ |

*other sizes and prices available

# Testing Sewing Machines

*The Pfaff Hobby 382 and Brother XL 3030 top the list of ten machines priced between $499 and $550.*

☙ BY LISA SHERRY

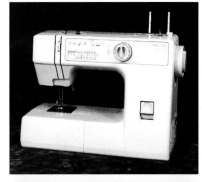

The top-rated Pfaff Hobby 382 (top) and Brother XL 3030 (bottom).

PHOTOGRAPHY:
**Peter Muller**

THE SEWING MACHINE MARKET includes a wide range of prices and features: from the $199 entry-level machine to a $3,500 model with the power and smarts of a personal computer. For this article, I tested ten zigzag, free-arm sewing machines with a suggested retail price between $499 and $550.

This focus on a specific price range, instead of a feature-by-feature comparison, means that my lineup includes some machines that are considered entry-level models by their manufacturers, and some that are clearly more intermediate machines. My goal was to show intermediate sewers most interested in home decorating (versus dressmaking or quilting) what $499 to $550 can buy in terms of performance, features, options, and stitches. (For a feature-by-feature comparison, *see* chart 2, page 43.)

I conducted three main tests on each machine. First, in order to gauge how intuitive the machine was to sew with, I set up and used each one without referring to its manual. Next, I read each manual thoroughly, evaluated its usefulness, and tried each stitch, foot, or technique described as per the instructions. Third, in order to evaluate the machine's performance and ease of use, I sewed a variety of stitches on an assortment of commonly used home-decorating fabrics, and performed a number of common tasks such as attaching welting, sewing a buttonhole, and inserting a zipper.

For each test, I ranked a top performer and then used those rankings to determine the two best machines. Most of the sewing machines were easy to use without the manual, but the clear winner was the Pfaff Hobby 382. The machine with the most thorough manual was the Brother XL 3030; it even included a diagram showing how to repack the machine in the original box. In terms of performance, I preferred the Pfaff due to the dependability with which it sewed all the fabrics, and its consistency of stitches, especially in reverse. Overall, I recommend either the Pfaff or the Brother machine. The Pfaff is easier to use and well suited for someone who doesn't like to have to refer to the manual or is put off by technology (e.g., it features a liquid crystal display that includes a trou-

bleshooting guide in a choice of languages). The Brother, on the other hand, is more suitable for someone who's not afraid of a more sophisticated machine and who's willing to refer to the manual when necessary.

## Using the Machines Without the Manual

My first test involved setting up and using each machine without referring to its manual. This phase entailed unpacking each machine and its accessories; plugging it in; winding and loading the bobbin; changing the needle; threading the machine; adjusting the thread tension,

## Rating the Sewing Machines

**PERFORMANCE KEY**

★ ★ ★ Excellent

★ ★ Very Good to Good

★ OK to Poor

Ten machines priced between $499 and $550 were evaluated based on the following characteristics. Machines are listed in alphabetical order. Three stars indicates excellent performance, two stars indicates very good to good performance, and one star indicates OK to poor performance.

**Use without manual:** How easy was it to set up and use each machine without referring to the manual.

**Rating the manual:** Evaluating each manual for usefulness and clarity of instructions.
**Performance:** How well the machine sewed straight and zig-zag stitches on a range of commonly used home decorating fabrics, and performed common tasks such as attaching welting, sewing a buttonhole, and inserting a zipper.
**Overall rating:** How the machine fared overall.

| Machine/Model | Suggested Retail Price | Using w/o Manual | Rating the Manual | Performance | Overall Rating |
|---|---|---|---|---|---|
| 1. Baby Lock BL 2600 Pro Quilt | $499.00 | ★★ | ★★★⌐ | ★★ | ★★ |
| 2. Bernina Bernette 705A | $499.00 | ★★ | ★★★⌐ | ★★★⌐ | ★★★⌐ |
| 3. Brother XL 3030 | $549.95 | ★★ | ★★★ | ★★★ | ★★★ |
| 4. Elna 2004 | $549.00 | ★★ | ★★★⌐ | ★★★ | ★★★⌐ |
| 5. JIC Jaguar 386 | $499.00 | ★★ | ★★★⌐ | ★★ | ★★ |
| 6. Necchi 525 | $529.00 | ★★ | ★ | ★ | ★ |
| 7. Pfaff Hobby 382 | $529.00 | ★★★ | ★★ | ★★★ | ★★★ |
| 8. Riccar R7610 | $499.95 | ★ | ★ | ★★★ | ★★⌐ |
| 9. Singer 9210 | $529.99 | ★★ | ★★★ | ★★★⌐ | ★★★⌐ |
| 10. White 1888 | $499.00 | ★★ | ★ | ★★ | ★★⌐ |

presser foot pressure (where possible), and stitch width and length; selecting stitches; changing the presser feet; and lowering or covering the feed dogs. I also sampled all the stitch variations in different lengths and widths, including straight stitching and zigzag stitching in reverse, on a double layer of cotton broadcloth.

For the most part, there weren't many differences in terms of design. Many of the exceptions weren't significant—it just took longer to figure them out without looking at the manual. The Bernina's bobbin winder and thread cutter, for instance, were located on the right side of the machine, instead of the top, where I found it on the other models.

The clear winner, however, was the Pfaff Hobby 382. Operating the machine was practically foolproof, as there's a small diagram identifying each presser foot right on the front of the machine. In addition, the stitch selection dial shows which foot, stitch width, and stitch length to use for each particular stitch, a feature unique to this machine.

The Brother XL 3030 was easier to thread than the Pfaff because it includes a complete threading diagram right above the presser foot, but overall it is a more complex machine, making it about even with the other eight machines except for the Riccar R7610. This machine was the toughest to use without the manual, as it threads left to right from the thread take-up lever (all the others thread right to left), and the buttonhole sequence is actually used in the reverse order of the way it appears on the front of the machine, something I couldn't have known without reading the instructions.

## Studying the Manuals

Next, I read each manual thoroughly and tried out each stitch, foot, or technique as described in the instructions. My conclusion: Not all manuals are created equal. A good manual is a godsend and can save you time and prevent you from making (sometimes costly) mistakes, but only if you use it. Overall, Brother had the best and most thorough manual, followed by Singer and Bernina. The toughest manuals to decipher were those from Riccar and Necchi, as the printing was difficult to read and the diagrams were hard to understand.

Some manuals were clearly translated from other languages. The Pfaff manual, for instance, refers to a seam ripper as a slitting knife while the Baby Lock and Jaguar manuals call it a buttonhole opener. These peculiarities of translation require a little bit of ingenuity on the part of the sewer.

Although the Pfaff manual had excellent illustrations, it was designed with three other languages (Dutch, French,

## THE CONTESTANTS

1. Baby Lock BL 2600 Pro Quilt

2. Bernina Bernette 705A

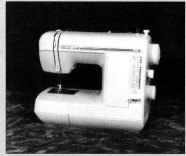
3. Brother XL 3030

4. Elna 2004

5. JIC Jaguar 386

6. Necchi 525

7. Pfaff Hobby 382

8. Riccar R7610

9. Singer 9210

10. White 1888

and German) besides English on each page, making it very hard to follow. The Bernina manual also offered additional languages besides English, but the English text was placed next to the illustrations, making it easier to follow.

## Evaluating the Machines

My education complete, I loaded each machine with a different color top and bobbin thread and began sewing.

I sewed straight runs and curves using straight and zigzag stitches in a variety of stitch lengths and widths. Each stitch was tested on a double layer of the following

and buttonholes and a blind hem stitch (a zigzag stitch that finishes the raw edge of a hem and secures it at the same time) on broadcloth. I also used the straight and zigzag stitches in reverse on broadcloth.

With each test, I took note of the machine's overall performance, its ability to sew a wide variety of fabrics with consistency, and whether the thread or bobbin tension or presser foot pressure needed adjustment. I also paid special attention to the way each machine stitched in reverse, as sometimes it is easier to sew a seam in reverse and let the fabric hang to the left of the machine

times, especially when using the zigzag stitch.

Sewing two layers of chenille was a challenge for the Baby Lock BL 2600 Pro Quilt and JIC Jaguar 386 machines, and I had to adjust the presser foot tension to keep the fabric moving. Although the Baby Lock, Jaguar, and Singer machines had trouble sewing four layers of chenille, with several adjustments, they managed. The Necchi machine, on the other hand, just couldn't move two layers of this fabric, and the chenille portion of the combination strip of fabric proved difficult (although not impossible) for the Baby

# Feature-by-Feature Comparison of Sewing Machines

All of the machines had the following features/accessories: **1)** snap-on presser feet, including a standard zig-zag foot and a zipper foot; **2)** one spool holder; **3)** foot pedal speed control; **4)** bobbin winder; **5)** thread cutter; **6)** stitch length adjustment; **7)** thread length adjustment; **8)** center needle position; **9)** ability to sew forward and in reverse; **10)** and the following stitches: straight stitch, zigzag (preset or adjustable), and blind hem stitch. The machines also included a few of the basics needed to use and maintain them, such as extra bobbins, needles, oil, screwdriver, spool pin, spool holder, lint brush and seam ripper.

| Machine/Model | Needle Position | Built-in Needle Threader | Storage in Free Arm | Location of Bobbin Load | No. of Spool Holders | Adjust. Foot Pressure | Handle, Case, or Cover | Light Switch Controls Power | No. of Zig-zag Width Settings | No. of Stitch Patterns |
|---|---|---|---|---|---|---|---|---|---|---|
| 1. Baby Lock BL 2600 Pro Quilt | left, center | yes | yes | front | 2 | yes | case | yes | 8 | 26 |
| 2. Bernina Bernette 705A | center | no | no | front | 2 | no | handle and soft cover | yes | 5 | 5 |
| 3. Brother XL 3030 | left, center | yes | yes | front | 2 | no | handle | yes | 3 | 19 |
| 4. Elna 2004 | left, center | no | yes | front | 2 | no | handle and soft cover | yes | adjustable | 17 |
| 5. JIC Jaguar 386 | left, center | yes | yes | front | 2 | yes | case | yes | 8 | 26 |
| 6. Necchi 525 | left, center | no | yes | front | 2 | yes | handle | no | 10 | 15 |
| 7. Pfaff Hobby 382 | left, center | no | yes | front | 2 | no | handle and hard cover | yes | 13 | 17 |
| 8. Riccar R7610 | left, center | no | yes | front | 2 | yes | handle | yes | 10 | 15 |
| 9. Singer 9210 | left, center, right | no | yes | top | 1 | no | handle | yes | adjustable | 13 |
| 10. White 1888 | center | no | yes | front | 2 | yes | handle | no | adjustable | 13 |

fabrics: 100 percent polyester voile, 100 percent cotton broadcloth, 100 percent cotton canvas, 100 percent woven cotton chenille, upholstery velvet, and tapestry. Then I tested the same stitches on a sandwich consisting of a single layer and a double layer strip of all the aforementioned fabrics. I also sewed a quilt sandwich (a bottom layer of broadcloth, a single and a double layer of batting, another layer of broadcloth, and a top layer of two pieces of broadcloth sewn together); four layers of woven cotton chenille; welting between two layers of tapestry; a button and a zipper on upholstery velvet;

than to try and fit the material into the open area between the needle and the right side of the machine. In this case, the reverse stitches should be identical to those sewn forward.

The Brother, Elna 2004, Pfaff, and Riccar machines needed little to no adjustments in thread or bobbin tension or presser foot pressure.

None of the machines had trouble sewing the broadcloth, velvet, canvas, or the quilt sandwich. Sewing on voile was a bit of a problem for the Necchi 525, Singer 9210, and White 1888 machines; I had to adjust the thread tension several

Lock, Jaguar, and Necchi machines.

The Baby Lock, Jaguar, Pfaff, and Riccar machines sewed the best in reverse as well as forward. The stitches were even and straight, and measured the same length in both directions with no changes in thread tension.

I looked carefully at the quality, balance (i.e., between stitches on the right and left sides), and consistency of the buttonholes made in broadcloth and determined that the Bernina Bernette 705A, Brother, Elna, and Singer machines did the best job. They were followed closely by Pfaff while the Baby Lock, Jaguar,

Necchi, Riccar, and White models all performed about the same.

For buttonholing, I liked the Brother machine the best because it offers a one-step buttonhole, which I found extremely easy to use. The buttonhole foot actually measures the size of the button and holds it in place to ensure that the buttonhole is the right size every time. (The Bernina also measures the button in the foot, but you must adjust a screw to keep the button in place.) Another nice feature of the Brother (and the Singer) machine was the ability to adjust the stitching on both sides of the buttonhole so it is balanced, meaning there are no differences between the stitches made going forward and those done in reverse. The one drawback to the Brother machine is that you must read the manual's instructions carefully before making a buttonhole, as the procedure is not entirely standard, and your buttonhole may not end up where you expected it to.

Most of the other machines feature a four-step buttonhole, which is more complex than a one-step buttonhole because you must manually change the stitch selection for each step. In addition, sometimes the stitches worked in reverse do not mirror those sewn going forward. The Bernina's and Elna's buttonholes, however, came out balanced every time.

All the machines except the Pfaff and Singer came with the same style zipper foot. The Singer zipper foot is much narrower than the other zipper feet, and this combined with the choice of right or left needle position allowed me to stitch much closer to the welting and zipper without the bulk of either getting in the way of the presser foot shank. The Pfaff model also has a unique zipper foot in that it allows a center position (all the others had right or left), which permits the teeth of the zipper to run under a guiding groove.

All the machines except the Brother and White came with a blind hem foot, although it's possible to make a blind hem without one. The Pfaff machine is the only machine without a buttonhole foot. The Baby Lock and Jaguar machines both came with five buttonhole guides that snap on to a standard zigzag foot; the guides worked fine, but it's easier to make a buttonhole with a dedicated foot. I like the clear plastic zigzag foot found on the Elna, Pfaff, and Singer machines because in addition to being transparent, it can substitute for a buttonhole foot or button sewing foot, which most of the machines did not come with. ◆

*Lisa Sherry, a freelance writer living in Sag Harbor, New York, has been sewing for more than ten years.*

# What to Look for When Testing Machines

■ **Are the stitches uniform and consistent as well as attractive? Examine the underside of the fabric samples as well and pay extra attention to the stitches you'll be using most. Features such as the ability to balance the stitches on both sides of the buttonholes are a plus.**

■ **Are the stitches easy to select? Are they adjustable, or do they come in preset stitch widths?**

■ **Does the machine perform well on the types of fabric and trim you sew most often? Does the machine "eat" any of the fabrics (especially when finishing edges)?**

■ **Are the presser feet easy to change? Is there a wide enough variety of feet? Are there other feet available? Does the presser foot rise** high enough for you to fit bulky fabric underneath?

■ **Does the thread tension or presser foot pressure need adjustment? If so, are the adjustments easy to make and the results satisfactory? Constant adjustments should not be necessary.**

■ **Is the machine ergonomically comfortable for you? Pay close attention to the location of the stitch controls, presser foot lever, reverse lever/button, bobbin winder, and thread guides, the size of the flat bed, the removal of the free arm, and so forth.**

■ **Is the machine easy to thread? Is the bobbin easy to wind and does it wind evenly? Is the bobbin easy to load? Is the bobbin case easily accessible (front-loading is more accessible** than drop-in) and easy to disassemble in case of a jam?

■ **Is the manual clearly written and printed? Are the diagrams understandable? Is the manual accurate and thorough?**

■ **If you have small children at home, check to see, when the machine is plugged in, if the power is turned off when the light is off. This check is important if you plan to leave the machine set up at all times.**

■ **Is the machine portable?**

■ **Is the dealer you're buying from reputable, and will he or she be able to service your machine and answer all your questions? Does the dealer or manufacturer offer courses, training, or videos? If so, what is the cost?**

## PREPARING A TEST KIT

**If you're serious about shopping for a sewing machine, I recommend assembling a test kit and taking it with you each time you try out a different machine.**

**You'll need the following: two spools of thread in two different colors, both made from the same material (e.g., cotton or polyester); a brand new needle for each machine in the correct size and type for the fabrics you'll be sewing, plus a few spares, just in case; a** notebook for jotting down observations or questions; a zipper, several buttons, a section of trim, and straight pins; and the fabric.

I recommend bringing several samples of the type of fabric you sew with most frequently, about one-half yard per machine. Be sure to use the exact same brand, style, and size of each item in your test kit so you're sure the differences are in the machines and not in the items.

Make sure you actually use the machine yourself; don't let somebody else demonstrate it for you. Thread it, wind a bobbin, adjust the tension (if you need to), and try all of the stitches on your fabric samples. (The dealer or retailer may have fabric, but if it's not what you usually sew on, you'll never know if the machine does just what you need it to.)

# Field Guide to Fresh Greens

*Here's how to select greens and make your arrangements last throughout the holidays.*

🐦 BY MARY SHAUGHNESSY

COLOR PHOTOGRAPHY:
**Steven Mays**

WHETHER YOU USE THEM in an arrangement, a wreath, or a centerpiece, everyone loves fresh greens for holiday decorating. The greens shown here are only a sample of the many varieties available, but all those pictured should be easy to find wherever you live.

Fresh greens can be purchased by the bundle or by the pound. When buying them, look for those with good color. If possible, find out how they were stored before you make your purchase. Prior refrigeration is ideal.

When caring for fresh greens, it's important to keep them moist and out of direct sunlight. Mist wreaths and other cut fresh greens without a water source to prolong their freshness.

In the cold winter months, a wreath made with fresh greens won't last much longer than two months, whether it is displayed indoors or outdoors. Certain situations will shorten the wreath's life, however. Avoid placing the wreath on the sunny side of your house, which will dry it out faster, or trapping it between a main door and a glass outer door, which will overheat and compress the foliage. ◆

*Mary Shaughnessy is an editorial intern with Handcraft Illustrated.*

1. **Rocky Mountain Douglas Fir**
2. **Eastern White Pine**
3. **Balsam Fir**
4. **False Cypress**
5. **Holly (blue hybrid)**
6. **English Ivy**
7. **Heti Juniper**
8. **Colorado Blue Spruce**
9. **Colorado Spruce**
10. **White Cedar**
11. **Fraser Fir**
12. **Red Pine or Norway Pine**
13. **Andromeda**
14. **Common Boxwood**
15. **Douglas Fir**
16. **White Spruce**
17. **Princess Pine**
18. **Euonymus Evergreen**
19. **Mountain Laurel**
20. **Norway Spruce**
21. **Canadian Hemlock**
22. **Eucalyptus**
23. **Winterberry**
24. **Blue Atlas Cedar**
25. **Red Cedar**
26. **White Spruce**

# Patterns for Projects in This Issue

## Father Christmas

*(see* article, page 30)

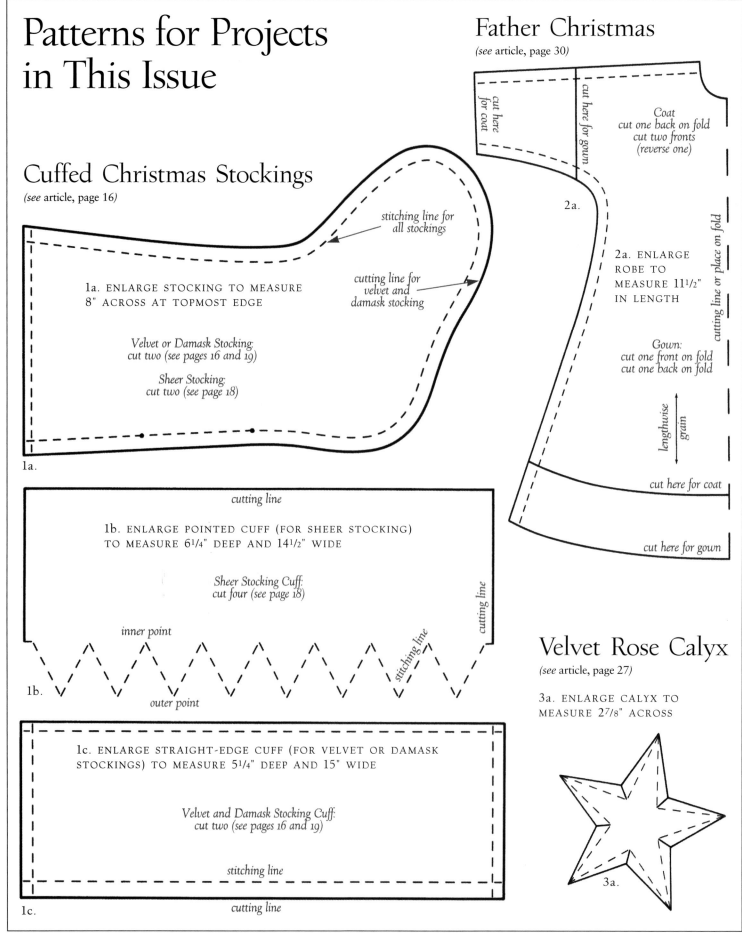

## Cuffed Christmas Stockings

*(see* article, page 16)

stitching line for
all stockings

cutting line for
velvet and
damask stocking

1a. ENLARGE STOCKING TO MEASURE
8" ACROSS AT TOPMOST EDGE

*Velvet or Damask Stocking:*
*cut two (see pages 16 and 19)*

*Sheer Stocking:*
*cut two (see page 18)*

1a.

cut here
for coat

cut here for gown

Coat
*cut one back on fold*
*cut two fronts*
*(reverse one)*

2a.

cutting line or place on fold

2a. ENLARGE
ROBE TO
MEASURE 11½"
IN LENGTH

*Gown:*
*cut one front on fold*
*cut one back on fold*

lengthwise
grain

cut here for coat

cut here for gown

cutting line

1b. ENLARGE POINTED CUFF (FOR SHEER STOCKING)
TO MEASURE 6¼" DEEP AND 14½" WIDE

*Sheer Stocking Cuff:*
*cut four (see page 18)*

inner point

stitching line

cutting line

1b.

outer point

## Velvet Rose Calyx

*(see* article, page 27)

3a. ENLARGE CALYX TO
MEASURE 2⅞" ACROSS

1c. ENLARGE STRAIGHT-EDGE CUFF (FOR VELVET OR DAMASK
STOCKINGS) TO MEASURE 5¼" DEEP AND 15" WIDE

*Velvet and Damask Stocking Cuff:*
*cut two (see pages 16 and 19)*

*stitching line*

1c.

cutting line

3a.

PATTERNS: **Roberta Frauwirth**

# 10-Minute Tassel Place Mat

*(see* article, page 37*)*

4a. ENLARGE PATTERN TO MEASURE 22" WIDE AND 23" DEEP

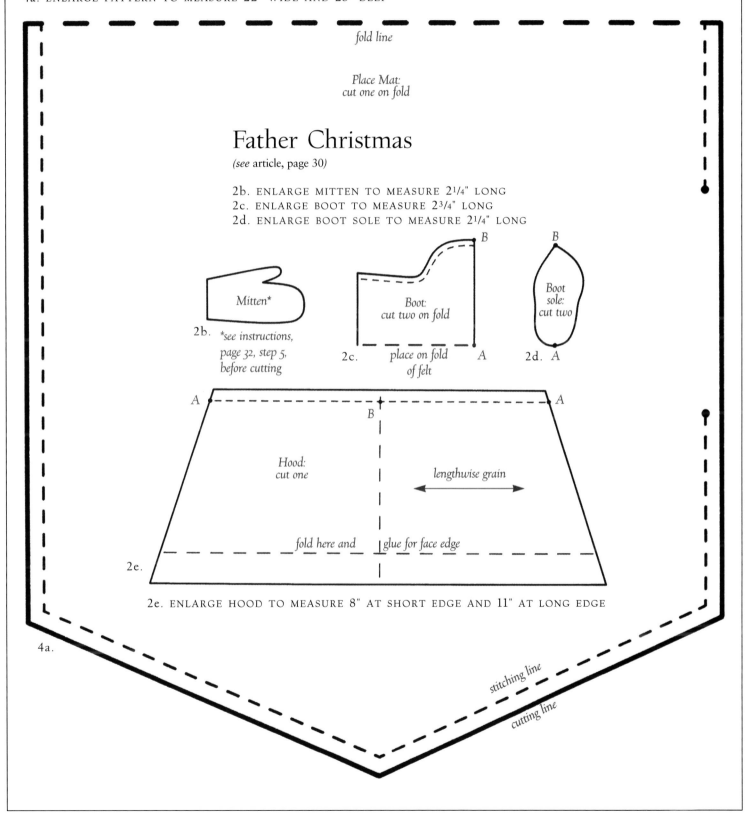

*fold line*

Place Mat:
*cut one on fold*

# Father Christmas

*(see* article, page 30*)*

2b. ENLARGE MITTEN TO MEASURE 2¼" LONG
2c. ENLARGE BOOT TO MEASURE 2¾" LONG
2d. ENLARGE BOOT SOLE TO MEASURE 2¼" LONG

B

B

*Mitten\**

Boot:
*cut two on fold*

*Boot
sole:
cut two*

2b. *\*see instructions,
page 32, step 5,
before cutting*

2c.    place on fold
of felt    A

2d.  A

A                                                A

B

*Hood:
cut one*

*lengthwise grain*

*fold here and*   *glue for face edge*

2e.

2e. ENLARGE HOOD TO MEASURE 8" AT SHORT EDGE AND 11" AT LONG EDGE

4a.

*stitching line*

*cutting line*

Most of the materials needed for the projects in this issue are available at your local craft supply, hardware, or paint store, florist's, fabric shop, or bead and jewelry supply. Generic craft supplies, such as scissors, all-purpose white glue, paint, ribbon, and thread, can be ordered from such catalogs as Craft King Discount Craft Supply, Dick Blick, Newark Dressmaker Supply, Pearl Paint, or Sunshine Discount Crafts. The following are specific or mail-order sources for particular items, arranged by article. The suggested retail prices listed here were current at press time. Contact the suppliers directly to confirm prices and availability of products.

# Sources
## AND RESOURCES

### Trio of Glass Ball Ornaments; *page 6*
Box of six glass ball ornaments from $10.95 from Eastern Art Glass. Victorian stickers, $3.95 for 83 designs, and Old-Fashioned Christmas stickers, $3.50 for 55 designs, from Dover Publications, Inc. Packet of gold embossing powder from Embossing Arts Company for $3.50. 1/2"foil stars (420 count) for $1.58 from Quill. One-half-inch circle labels (800 count) from $4.35 from Reliable Corporation. Gold leaf from $3.70 per twenty sheets, gold size from $5.37, and 75 milliliters (2.5 fluid ounces) of japan gold size for $4.73, all from Pearl Paint.

### How to Make an Infinite Variety of Wreaths; *page 8*
Assorted dried flowers from $2.50 per bunch from Opus Topiarium. Vine wreath bases from $1.09 from Sunshine Discount Crafts. Wire wreath bases from $1.59, pinecones from $2.09, miniature apples from $3.39, and individual and assorted fruit from $1.19, all from Creative Craft House. Straw wreaths from $1.49 from Craft King Discount Craft Supply. Assorted silk flowers, berry clusters, and branching stems from $1, all from May Silk.

### How to Make Your Own Wire-Edged Ribbon; *page 12*
Firmly woven fabric from $7.99 from Calico Corners. Singer slant-, short-, and high-shank cording feet for $9.95 each from Sewing Emporium.

### Christmas Potpourri Demystified; *page 14*
Spices, herbs, oil, moss, roses, birch cones, and berries from 71¢ from San Francisco Herb Co. (minimum order $30). Spices, herbs, oil, moss, roses, birch cones, and berries from 40¢ from The Ginger Tree.

### Three Cuffed Decorator Christmas Stockings; *page 16*
Velvet from $20 per yard, sheer fabric from $3.99, damask from $13.99, and braid trim with fringe from $1.99, all

from Calico Corners. Crepe-backed satin from $4.65 from Newark Dressmaker Supply.

### The Fastest Way to Make Hand-Molded Soap; *page 20*
Stainless steel Mouli grater for $20 from A Cook's Wares. Panasonic microwave oven for $189.99 from Chef's Catalog.

### Foolproof Greeting Cards; *page 22*
Small printed images or photos in Dover Pictorial Archive Books, priced from $3.95 from Earth Guild. Single-fold sheet of stationery with matching envelopes from $3.25 from Embossing Arts Company. Stiff decorative or textured paper from $1.50 per sheet from Rugg Road. Special scissors with scallops, waves, and so forth from $2.50 from Family Treasures.

### How to Make Antique Velvet Roses; *page 27*
1 1/2"-wide white or pastel velvet ribbon from $7.59 from Creative Craft House. Green firmly woven linen/cotton blend from $13.99 from Calico Corners. Silk leaves from $4.90 from May Silk. Dr. Ph. Martin's 1/2-ounce Synchromatic Transparent concentrated watercolors for $3.11 from New York Central Art Supply.

### Heirloom Father Christmas; *page 30*
Wooden artist's manikin for $15.90 from Dick Blick. Clays available from Pearl Paint, Dick Blick, Earth Guild, and New York Central Art Supply. Tibetan lambskin for $18 from The Fiber Studio. Imitation white fur from $4.65, 5 yards of gold metallic ribbon for $2.40, 10 yards of white cord for $1.90, 5 yards of narrow gold metallic cord for $1, and four pieces of black felt for $1.25, all from Newark Dressmaker Supply. Velvet from $20 per yard, flat braid trim from 59¢, and narrow green cord from $1.99, all from Calico Corners. 8mm acrylic eyes for $2.70 per pair from G. Schoepfer, Inc. "What a Character" push molds, #10 (face) and #11 (hands), for $4.99 each from Wee Folk Creations. Tiny wrapped gifts for $2.69 from Sunshine Discount Crafts. Miniature toys from 69¢ from Kirchen Bros. Crafts.

### The Best Way to Tie Multiloop Bows; *page 34*
Sheer wire-edged double-faced ribbon from $1.75 from Newark Dressmaker Supply.

### Tulle-Wrapped Ornament; *page 36*
Box of six glass ball ornaments from $10.95 from Eastern Art Glass. White tulle from $7.59 per 25-yard roll from Creative Craft House. Small bells from 49¢ from Sunshine Discount Crafts. Crystal beads from $3.09 from Maplewood Crafts. Decorative silk flowers from $1 from May Silk.

### 10-Minute Tassel Place Mat; *page 37*
Apparel- or soft furnishing-weight fabric from $7.99 per yard and two 2" tassels from $1.99, both from Calico Corners.

### Buyer's Guide to Rubber Stamps; *page 38*
Rubber Stamps from $2.50 from Stamp Francisco. Ink from $1.60 from Clearsnap, Inc. Ten sheets of paper for $1 from Paper Source. Embossing powder from $3.25 from Embossing Arts Company. Four erasers or rubber slabs for 75¢ from Jerry's Artarama. Mail-order custom rubber stamps from Rubber Stamps Inc., Klear Copy Rubber Stamps, or Long Island Stamp Corp.

### Testing Sewing Machines; *page 41*
Contact individual manufacturers for the closest retail location.

---

The following companies are mentioned in the listings provided above. Contact each individually for a price list, catalog, or the closest retail store.

A Cook's Wares, 211 37th Street, Beaver Falls, PA 15010-2103; 412-846-9490

Allyn International (Necchi sewing machines), 1075 Santa Fe Drive, Denver, CO 80204; 800-525-9987

Bernina of America, Inc., 3500 Thayer Court, Aurora, IL 60504; 800-350-1630

Brother International Corp., 200 Cottontail Lane, Somerset, NJ 08875; 800-42-BROTHER

Calico Corners, 203 Gale Lane, Kennett Square, PA 19348; 800-777-9933

Chef's Catalog, 3215 Commercial Avenue, Northbrook, IL 60062; 800-338-3232

Clearsnap, Inc., P.O. Box 98, Anacortes, WA 98221; 360-293-6634

Craft King Discount Craft Supply, P.O. Box 90637, Lakeland, FL 33804; 800-769-9494

Creative Craft House, P.O. Box 2567, Bullhead City, AZ 86430; 602-754-3300

Dick Blick, P.O. Box 1267, Galesburg, IL 61402-1267; 800-447-8192

Dover Publications, Inc., 31 East 2nd Street, Mineola, NY 11501. (telephone orders not accepted)

Earth Guild, 33 Haywood Street, Asheville, NC 28801; 800-327-8448

Eastern Art Glass, P.O. Box 341, Wyckoff, NJ 07481; 800-872-3458

Elna Inc., 7642 Washington Avenue South, Eden Prairie, MN 55344; 800-848-ELNA

Embossing Arts Company, P.O. Box 626, Sweet Home, OR 97386; 503-367-3279

Family Treasures, 16161 Nordhoff Street, Suite 116, North Hills, CA 91343; 818-891-3529

G. Schoepfer, Inc., 460 Cook Hill Road, Cheshire, CT 06410; 800-875-6939

Jerry's Artarama, P.O. Box 1105, New Hyde Park, NY 11040; 800-827-8478

JIC, Inc. (Jaguar sewing machines), 1013 South Boulevard, Oak Park, IL 60302; 800-959-5421

Kirchen Bros. Crafts, Box 1016, Skokie, IL 60076; 708-647-6747

Klear Copy Rubber Stamps, 55 7th Avenue South, New York, NY 10014; 212-243-0357

Long Island Stamp Corp., 54-31 Myrtle Avenue, Queens, NY 11385; 718-628-8550

Maplewood Crafts, Humboldt Industrial Park, P.O. Box 2010, Hazleton, PA 18201; 800-899-0134

May Silk, 16202 Distribution Way, Cerritos, CA 90703; 800-282-7455

Newark Dressmaker Supply, 6473 Ruch Road, P.O. Box 20730,

Lehigh Valley, PA 18002; 800-736-6783

New York Central Art Supply, 62 Third Avenue, New York, NY 10003; 800-950-6111

Opus Topiarium, 980 Pacific Gate, Unit 16, Mississauga, Ontario, Canada L5T 1Y1; 905-564-7960

Paper Source, 232 West Chicago Avenue, Chicago, IL 60610; 312-337-0798

Pearl Paint, 308 Canal Street, New York, NY 10013; 800-221-6845

Pfaff American Sales Corp., 610 Winters Avenue, Paramus, NJ 07653; 800-526-0273

Quill, P.O. Box 94080, Palatine, IL 60094; 800-789-1331

Reliable Corporation, P.O. Box 1502, Ottawa, IL 61350-9914; 800-421-1222

Rubber Stamps Inc., 30 West 24th Street, New York, NY 10010; 212-675-1180

Rugg Road, 105 Charles Street, Boston, MA 02114; 617-742-0002

San Francisco Herb Co., 250 14th Street, San Francisco, CA 94103; 800-227-4530

Sewing Emporium, 1079 3rd Avenue, Suite B, Chula Vista, CA 91911; 619-420-3490

Singer Sewing Company, P.O. Box 1909, Edison, NJ 08818; 800-877-7762

Stamp Francisco, 466 Eighth Street, San Francisco, CA 94103; 415-252-5975

Sunshine Discount Crafts, 12335 62nd Street North, Largo, FL 34643; 800-729-2878

Tacony Corporation (Baby Lock and Riccar sewing machines), 1760 Gilsinn Lane, Fenton, MO 63026; 800-422-2952

The Fiber Studio, P.O. Box 637, Henniker, NH 03242; 603-428-7830

The Ginger Tree, 245 Lee Road #122, Opelika, AL 36801; 334-745-4864

Wee Folk Creations, 18476 Natchez Avenue, Prior Lake, MN 55372; 612-447-3828

White Sewing Machine Company, 11760 Berea Road, Cleveland, OH 44111; 800-446-2333

---

## CORRECTIONS

In the September/October 1995 issue, the prices listed with the "Testing Air-Dry and Heat-Set Clays" article on page 26 were not suggested retail prices but prices from Pearl Paint.

The original folk art paintings in the September/October 1995 insert were painted by David Carter Brown. We apologize for the production error. ◆

# Quick
## PROJECTS

In Victorian times, the same cloth napkins were used at several meals before being washed. Napkin rings were essential accoutrements to table etiquette to ensure that each napkin would lie over the correct lap or be tucked under the right chin. Often made of silver, the napkin ring might have had the user's monogram etched into a surface medallion for identification. Nowadays, napkin rings serve a more aesthetic function by conveying the decorating themes of a season or expressing the personality of the guest by whose place the napkin ring is placed. They can be made from every conceivable material. Here are six ideas to inspire you.

### A. Silk Ribbon Bow
Cut a 40" length of 2"-wide, wire-edged silk ribbon in red, or any holiday color. Tie the ribbon around the "waist" of the napkin, then cut notches in the streamer ends with scissors.

### B. Velvet Bow
Cut a 2½" x 12" strip of cotton velvet. Lay it nap side up on a flat surface. Fold the ends over until they meet in the middle, and pin. Stitch ¼" in from the edge along each long edge through both layers. Turn the bow right side out. To make the tie, cut a 2" x 3½" strip. Press the long edges ½" to the wrong side. Pinch the bow in the center, wrap the tie snugly around the pinched section, and tack the ends in back. To finish, cut an 8" length of florist wire. Slip the wire through the tie at the back of the bow, then twist the wire ends together to make a loop. Conceal the twisted ends behind the tie, tacking to prevent slipping. Place the wire loop around the napkin.

### C. Fake Fur
Cut a 2½" x 9" strip from fake fur. Fold it in half lengthwise, right side out, and whipstitch the long edges together. Shape the piece into a ring, inserting one end inside the other for 1½". Adjust the ring so the whipped seam is centered on the inside, then hand-tack the lapped ends. Slip the ring over the napkin.

### D. Velvet Leaves and Berries
Twist together the stems of four sprigs of velvet leaves and one cluster of artificial berries, arranging the leaves in two sprays, one on each side of the berries. Wrap the stems with florist tape, then curl the single wrapped stem around the napkin.

### E. Sequin and Bead Medallion with Pearls
Cut a 27" strand of 5mm artificial pearls. Remove seven pearls from each end, then tie the exposed strings together to make a "necklace." Wind the necklace around a paper towel tube to make a "bracelet" four strands wide. Even up the strands, then hot-glue a 1½" sequin-and-bead medallion across all four strands. Slip the bracelet off the tube and around the folded napkin.

### F. Gilded Cherub
Using a narrow sponge brush, apply a thin coat of japan gold size to a 5" plastic cherub. Let the size dry 10 minutes, or until tacky. Tear a sheet of gold leaf into irregular pieces. Apply the pieces to the cherub one by one, tapping lightly with the eraser end of a pencil to fill in the crevices. Continue adding gold leaf until the entire cherub is covered. Let dry overnight, then burnish the surface with a cotton ball. Slip a napkin between the cherub's arms. ◆

# Tannenbaum Topiary

Hammer 1¹/₄" -brad halfway into end of 20"-long, ¹/₂"-diameter dowel. Stand other end upright in 6¹/₂" terra-cotta pot lined with florist foam. Mix approximately 3 cups liquid plaster of Paris, pour in up to pot rim, and let set 20 to 30 minutes. Conceal plaster surface with sheet moss. Heat brad in flame 10 seconds, then gently press base of 5"-long, 1¹/₄"-diameter white candle onto hot brad until candle touches dowel and let cool. Cut twelve to fifteen 8" sprays each of fern, coffee bean, and cedar foliage. Using 30-gauge florist wire and starting 5" above pot rim, bind sprays to dowel so foliage arcs out and down; wind wire in continuous tight upward spiral and vary the greens as you go. As you near candle, trim sprays to taper the tree top. Wire on twenty-four 1" plastic apples at random. When candle is lit, do not leave tree unattended.

COLOR PHOTOGRAPHY:
**Carl Tremblay**

TOPIARY DESIGN:
**Lauren Adams**